The NAUGHTIEST GIRL in the School

CW01676469

Have you read them all?

1. The Naughtiest Girl in the School
2. The Naughtiest Girl Again
3. The Naughtiest Girl is a Monitor
4. Here's the Naughtiest Girl
5. The Naughtiest Girl Keeps a Secret
6. The Naughtiest Girl Helps a Friend
7. The Naughtiest Girl Saves the Day
8. Well Done, the Naughtiest Girl
9. The Naughtiest Girl Wants to Win
10. The Naughtiest Girl Marches On

Enid Blyton®

The Naughtiest Girl in the School

HODDER

HODDER CHILDREN'S BOOKS

First published in Great Britain in 1940 by George Newnes
This edition published in 2021 by Hodder & Stoughton
For further information about the editorial history of this book, see enidblyton.co.uk/books

9 10 8

Enid Blyton® and Enid Blyton's signature
are registered trade marks of Hodder & Stoughton Limited
Text © 2021 Hodder & Stoughton Limited
Illustrations by Claire Powell © 2021 Hodder & Stoughton Limited

No trade mark or copyrighted material may be reproduced without the express written permission of the trade mark and copyright owner.

The moral right of the author has been asserted.

All characters and events in this publication, other than those clearly in the public domain, are fictitious and any resemblance to real persons, living or dead, is purely coincidental.

All rights reserved.
No part of this publication may be reproduced, stored in a retrieval system, or transmitted, in any form or by any means, without the prior permission in writing of the publisher, nor be otherwise circulated in any form of binding or cover other than that in which it is published and without a similar condition including this condition being imposed on the subsequent purchaser.

A CIP catalogue record for this book is available from the British Library.

ISBN 978 1 444 95860 7

Typeset in Caslon by Avon DataSet Ltd, Alcester, Warwickshire

Printed and bound in Great Britain by Clays Ltd, Elcograf S.p.A.

The paper and board used in this book are made from wood from responsible sources

FSC www.fsc.org MIX Paper | Supporting responsible forestry FSC® C104740

Hodder Children's Books
An imprint of
Hachette Children's Group
Part of Hodder & Stoughton
Carmelite House
50 Victoria Embankment
London EC4Y 0DZ

An Hachette UK Company.
www.hachette.co.uk
www.hachettechildrens.co.uk

CONTENTS

INTRODUCTION

by Cressida Cowell

bestselling author of the
How to Train Your Dragon series

Like so many, many children before and after me, Enid Blyton's books played a crucial role in turning my nine-year-old self into a passionate reader.

That is because Enid Blyton had an extraordinary knack for writing the kind of books that children actually *want* to read, rather than the kind of books that adults think they *should* read.

Enid Blyton could tap into children's dreams, children's desires, children's wishes, with pinpoint accuracy. She knew that every child, however good and well-behaved they might look on the outside, secretly longed to be Elizabeth Allen, the naughtiest kid in the school. I'm afraid I entirely cheered Elizabeth on, as she defied her parents, the headmistresses, her schoolmates, and the very serious School Meetings. If anything, I wanted her to be even naughtier.

But *The Naughtiest Girl* books were really my favourite of Enid Blyton's school stories because of Whyteleafe, a very different school from Malory Towers or St Clare's. What if there could be a school in which discipline was administered by the children rather than the adults? In which all money was given in at the start of the term and distributed among the children along socialist lines? Wouldn't this be the kind of school that children would actually *want* to go to, rather than the kind of school that children *have* to go to?

It was an interesting proposition to a nine-year-old, and it remains an interesting proposition.

I hope you enjoy this story as much as I did when *I* was nine years old.

Cressida Cowell

CHAPTER ONE

THE NAUGHTY, SPOILT GIRL

'YOU'LL HAVE to go to school, Elizabeth!' said Mrs Allen. 'I think your governess is quite right. You are spoilt and naughty, and although Daddy and I were going to leave you here with Miss Scott when we went away, I think it would be better for you to go to school.'

Elizabeth stared at her mother in dismay. What, leave her home? And her pony and her dog? Go and be with a lot of children she would hate? Oh, no, she wouldn't go!

'I'll be good with Miss Scott,' she said.

'You've said that before,' said her mother. 'Miss Scott says she can't stay with you any longer. Elizabeth, is it true that you put earwigs in her bed last night?'

Elizabeth giggled. 'Yes,' she said. 'Miss Scott is so frightened of them! It's silly to be afraid of earwigs, isn't it?'

'It is much sillier to put them into somebody's bed,' said Mrs Allen sternly. 'You have been spoilt, and you think you can do what you like! You are an only child, and we love you so much, Daddy and I, that I think we have given you too many lovely things, and allowed you too much freedom.'

'Mummy, if you send me to school, I shall be so naughty there that they'll send me back home again,' said Elizbeth, shaking her curls back. She was a pretty girl with laughing blue eyes and dark brown curls. All her life she had done as she liked. Six governesses had come and gone, but not one of them had been able to make Elizabeth obedient or good-mannered!

'You can be such a nice little girl!' they had all said to her, 'but all you think of is getting into mischief and being rude about it!'

And now, when she said that she would be so naughty at school that they would have to send her home her mother looked at her in despair. She loved Elizabeth very much, and wanted her to be happy – but how could she be happy if she did not learn to be as other children were?

'You have been alone too much, Elizabeth,' she said. 'You should have had other children to play with and to work with.'

'I don't like other children!' said Elizabeth sulkily.

It was quite true – she didn't like boys and girls at all! They were shocked at her mischief and rude ways, and when they said they wouldn't join in her naughtiness she laughed at them and said they were babies. Then they told her what they thought of her, and Elizabeth didn't like it.

So now the thought of going away to school and living with other boys and girls made Elizabeth feel dreadful!

'Please don't send me,' she begged. 'I really will be good at home.'

'No, Elizabeth,' said her mother. 'Daddy and I *must* go away for a whole year, and as Miss Scott won't stay, and we could not expect to find another governess quickly before we go, it is best you should go to school. You have a good brain and you should be able to do your work well and get to the top of the form. Then we shall be proud of you.'

'I shan't work at all,' said Elizabeth, pouting. 'I won't work a bit, and they'll think I'm so stupid they won't keep me!'

'Well, Elizabeth, if you want to make things difficult for yourself, you'll have to,' said Mother, getting up. 'We have written to Miss Belle and Miss Best, who run Whyteleafe School, and they are willing to take you next week, when the new term begins. Miss Scott will get all your things ready. Please help her all you can.'

Elizabeth was very angry and upset. She didn't want to go to school. She hated everybody, especially silly children! Miss Scott was horrid to say she wouldn't stay. Suddenly Elizabeth wondered if she *would* stay, if she asked her very, very nicely!

She ran to find her governess. Miss Scott was busy sewing Elizabeth's name on to a pile of brown stockings.

'Are these new stockings?' asked Elizabeth in surprise. 'I don't wear stockings! I wear socks!'

'You have to wear stockings at Whyteleafe School,' said Miss Scott. Elizabeth stared at the pile, and then she suddenly put her arms round Miss Scott's neck.

'Miss Scott!' she said. 'Stay with me! I know I'm sometimes naughty, but I don't want you to go.'

'What you *really* mean is that you don't want to go to school,' said Miss Scott. 'I suppose Mother's been telling you?'

'Yes, she has,' said Elizabeth. 'Miss Scott, I *won't* go to school!'

'Well, of course, if you're such a baby as to be afraid of doing what all other children do, then I've nothing more to say,' said Miss Scott, beginning to sew another name on a brown stocking.

Elizabeth stood up at once and stamped her foot. 'Afraid!' she shouted. '*I'm* not afraid! Was I afraid when

I fell off my pony? Was I afraid when our car crashed into the bank? Was I afraid when – when – when—'

'Don't shout at me, please, Elizabeth,' said Miss Scott. 'I think you are afraid to go to school and mix with obedient, well-mannered, hard-working children who are not spoilt as you are. You know quite well that you wouldn't get your own way, that you would have to share everything, instead of having things to yourself as you do now, and that you would have to be punctual, polite and obedient. And you are afraid to go!'

'I'm not, I'm not, I'm not!' shouted Elizabeth. 'I shall go! But I shall be so naughty and lazy that they won't keep me, and then I'll come back home! And you'll have to look after me again, so there!'

'My dear Elizabeth, I shan't be here,' said Miss Scott, taking another stocking. 'I am going to another family, where I shall have two little boys to teach. I am going the day you go to school. So you can't come back home because I shan't be here, your father and mother will be away, and the house will be shut up!'

Elizabeth burst into tears. She sobbed so loudly that Miss Scott, who was really fond of the spoilt, naughty girl, put her arms round her and comforted her.

'Now don't be silly,' she said. 'Most children simply *love* school. It's great fun. You play games, you go for walks, all together, you have the most lovely lessons, and you will make such a lot of friends. You have no friends now, and it is a dreadful thing not to have a single friend. You are very lucky.'

'I'm not,' wept Elizabeth. 'Nobody loves me. I'm very unhappy.'

'The trouble is that people have loved you too much,' said Miss Scott. 'You are pretty, and merry, and rich, so you have been spoilt. People like the way you look, the way you smile and your pretty clothes, so they fuss you, and pet you, and spoil you, instead of treating you like an ordinary child. But it isn't enough to have a pretty face and a merry smile – you must have a good heart too.'

Nobody had spoken to Elizabeth like this before, and the little girl was astonished. 'I *have* got a good heart,' she said, tossing her curls back again.

'Well, you don't show it much!' said Miss Scott. 'Now run away, please, because I've got to count all these stockings, and then mark your new vests and bodices.'

Elizabeth looked at the pile of stockings. She hated them. Nasty brown things! She wouldn't wear them! She'd take her socks to school and wear *those* if she wanted to! Miss Scott turned to a chest of drawers and began to take out some vests. Elizabeth picked up two brown stockings and pinned them toe to toe. Then she tiptoed to Miss Scott and neatly and quietly pinned them to her skirt!

She skipped out of the room, giggling. Miss Scott carried the vests to the table. She began to count the stockings. There should be six pairs.

'One – two – three – four – five,' she counted. 'Five. Dear me – where's the sixth?'

She looked on the floor. She looked on the chair. She was really vexed. She counted the pile again. Then she went to the door and looked for Elizabeth. The little girl was pulling something out of a cupboard on the landing.

'Elizabeth!' called Miss Scott sharply. 'Have you got a pair of brown stockings?'

'No, Miss Scott,' said Elizabeth, making her eyes look round and surprised. 'Why?'

'Because a pair is missing,' said Miss Scott. 'Did you take them out of this room?'

'No, really, Miss Scott,' said Elizabeth truthfully, trying not to laugh as she caught sight of the stockings swinging at Miss Scott's back. 'I'm sure all the stockings are in the room, Miss Scott, really!'

'Then perhaps your mother has a pair,' said Miss Scott. 'I'll go and ask her.'

Off marched the governess down the landing, the pinned brown stockings trailing behind her like a tail. Elizabeth put her head into the cupboard and squealed with laughter. Miss Scott went into her mother's room.

'Excuse me, Mrs Allen,' she said, 'but have you one of Elizabeth's new pairs of stockings? I've only five pairs.'

'No, I gave you them all,' said Mrs Allen, surprised. 'They must be together. Perhaps you have dropped them somewhere.'

Miss Scott turned to go, and Mrs Allen caught sight of the brown stockings following Miss Scott. She looked at them in astonishment.

'Wait, Miss Scott,' she said. 'What's this!' She went to Miss Scott, and unpinned the stockings. The governess looked at Mrs Allen.

'Elizabeth, of course!' she said.

'Yes, Elizabeth!' said Mrs Allen. 'Always in mischief. I really never knew such a child in my life. It is high time she went to school. Don't you agree, Miss Scott?'

'I do,' said Miss Scott heartily. 'You will see a different and much nicer child when you come back home again, Mrs Allen!'

Elizabeth was passing by, and heard what her mother and her governess were saying. She hit the door with the book she was carrying and shouted angrily.

'You won't see me any different, Mother, you won't, you won't! I'll be worse!'

'You couldn't be!' said Mrs Allen in despair. 'You really *couldn't* be worse!'

CHAPTER TWO

ELIZABETH GOES TO SCHOOL

FOR THE rest of her time at home Elizabeth was very naughty and also very good.

I'll try being very, very good and obedient and polite and sweet, and see if Mother changes her mind, she thought. So, to the surprise of everyone, she became thoughtful, sweet-tongued, good-mannered and most obedient. But it had quite the wrong effect, because, instead of saying that she would keep her at home now, her mother said something quite different!

'Well, Elizabeth, now that I know what a really nice girl you can be, I'm not so afraid of sending you to school as I was,' she said. 'I thought you would get into such trouble and be so unhappy – but, now that I see how well you really can behave, I am sure you will get on nicely at school. I am very pleased with your behaviour!'

And you can guess what happened after that. Elizabeth at once became naughtier than she had ever been before!

If being good makes Mother feel like that, I'll see what being naughty does! she thought.

So she emptied the ink bottle over the cushions in the drawing room. She tore a hole in one of the nicest curtains. She put three black beetles into poor Miss Scott's toothbrush mug, and she squeezed glue into the ends of both Miss Scott's brown shoes, so that her toes would stick there!

'Well, all this makes it quite certain that Elizabeth needs to go to school!' said Miss Scott angrily, as she tried to get her feet out of her sticky shoes. 'I'm glad to leave her! Naughty little girl! And yet she can be so sweet and nice when she likes.'

Elizabeth's things were packed and ready. She had a neat brown trunk, with E. ALLEN painted on it in black. She had a tuckbox too, with a big currant cake inside, a box of chocolates, a tin of toffee, a jam sandwich and a tin of shortbread.

'You will have to share these things with the others,' said Miss Scott, as she packed the food neatly inside.

'Well, I shan't then,' said Elizabeth.

'Very well, don't!' said Miss Scott. 'If you want

to show everyone what a selfish child you are, just take the chance!'

Elizabeth put on the outdoor uniform of Whyteleafe School. It was very neat, and she looked nice in it. But then Elizabeth looked nice in anything!

The outdoor uniform was a dark blue coat with a yellow edge to the collar and cuffs, a dark blue hat with a yellow ribbon round it, and the school badge at the front. Her stockings were long and brown, and her lace-up shoes were brown too.

'My goodness, you do look a real schoolgirl!' said her mother, quite proudly. Elizabeth wouldn't smile. She stood there, sulky and angry. 'I shan't stay at school long,' she said. 'They'll soon send me back!'

'Don't be silly, Elizabeth,' said her mother. She kissed the little girl goodbye and hugged her. 'I will come and see you at half-term,' she said.

'No, Mother, you won't,' said Elizabeth. 'I shall be home long before that!'

'Don't make me sad, Elizabeth!' said Mrs Allen. But Elizabeth wouldn't smile or say she was sorry. She got into the car that was to take her to the station, and sat there, very cross and straight. She had said goodbye to her pony. She had said goodbye to Timmy, her dog. She had said goodbye to her canary. And to each of them she had whispered the same thing.

'I'll soon be back! You'll see – they won't keep the naughtiest girl in the school for long!'

Miss Scott took her to the station and then up to London in the train. She went with Elizabeth to a big station where trains whistled and chuffed, and people ran about in a hurry.

'Now we must find the right platform,' said Miss Scott, hurrying too. 'We have to meet the teacher there, who is in charge of the girls going by this train.'

They came to the right platform and went through to where a big group of girls stood with a teacher. They were all dressed in dark blue coats and hats, with yellow hatbands like Elizabeth. The girls were of all ages, some big, some small, and most of them were chattering hard.

Two or three stood apart, looking shy. They were the new ones, like Elizabeth. The teacher spoke to them now and again, and they smiled gratefully at her.

Miss Scott bustled up to the teacher. 'Good morning,' she said. 'Is this Miss Thomas? This is Elizabeth Allen. I'm glad we are in good time!'

'Good morning,' said Miss Thomas, smiling. She held out her hand to Elizabeth. 'Well, dear,' she said, 'so you are going to join the happy crowd at Whyteleafe School!'

Elizabeth put her hand behind her back and would not shake hands with Miss Thomas. The teacher looked surprised. The other children stared. Miss Scott blushed red, and spoke sharply to Elizabeth.

'Elizabeth! Shake hands at once!'

Elizabeth turned her back and looked at a train puffing nearby. 'I'm *so* sorry she's behaving so rudely,' said Miss Scott, really upset. She spoke in a low voice to Miss Thomas. 'She's an only child – very, very spoilt, rich, pretty – and she doesn't want to come away to school. Just leave her alone for a bit and I expect she'll be all right.'

Miss Thomas nodded. She was a merry-looking young woman, and the girls liked her. She was just going to say something when a man came hurrying up with four boys.

'Good morning, Miss Thomas,' he said. 'Here is my batch! Sorry I can't stop, I've a train to catch! Goodbye, boys!'

'Goodbye, sir,' said the four boys.

'How many boys have you at Whyteleafe this term?' asked Miss Scott. 'As many as girls?'

'Not quite,' said Miss Thomas. 'There are some more boys over there, look, in the charge of Mr Johns.'

Miss Scott liked the look of the boys, all in dark blue overcoats and blue caps with a yellow badge in front. 'Such a good idea,' she said, 'to educate boys and girls together. For a child like Elizabeth, who has no brothers, and not even a sister, it is like joining a large family of brothers and sisters and cousins to go to a school like Whyteleafe!'

'Oh, they'll soon knock the corners off your Elizabeth,' smiled Miss Thomas. 'Look – here comes our train. We have our carriages reserved for us, so I must find them. The boys have two carriages and the girls have three. Come along, girls, here's our train!'

Elizabeth was swept along with the others. She was pushed into a carriage with a big label on it, RESERVED FOR WHYTELEAFE SCHOOL.

'Goodbye, Elizabeth; goodbye, dear!' cried Miss Scott. 'Do your best!'

'Goodbye,' said Elizabeth, suddenly feeling very small and lost. 'I'll soon be back!' she shouted.

'Gracious!' said a plump little girl next to her. 'A term's a long time, you know! Fancy saying you'll soon be back!'

'Well, I shall,' said Elizabeth. She was squashed in a heap by the plump little girl and another girl on the other side, who was rather bony. She didn't like it.

Elizabeth felt sure she would never, never learn who all the different girls were. She felt a little afraid of the big ones, and she was horrified to think there were boys at her school! Boys! Nasty, rough creatures – well, she'd show them that a girl could be rough too!

The little girl sat silently as the train rattled on and on. The others chattered and talked and offered sweets round the carriage. Elizabeth shook her head when the sweets were offered to her.

'Oh, come on, do have one!' said the plump little girl, whose sweets they were. 'A sweet would do you good – make you look a bit sweeter perhaps!'

Everybody laughed. Elizabeth went red and hated the plump little girl.

'Ruth! You do say some funny things!' said a big girl opposite. 'Don't tease the poor little thing. She's new.'

'Well, so is Belinda, next to you,' said Ruth, 'but she does at least say something when she's spoken to!'

'That will do, Ruth,' said Miss Thomas, seeing how red Elizabeth had gone. Ruth said no more, but the next time she offered her sweets round she did not offer them to Elizabeth.

It was a long journey. Elizabeth was tired when at last the train drew up in a country station and the girls poured out of the carriages. The boys came to join them, and the children talked eagerly of all they had done in the holidays.

'Come along now, quickly,' said Mr Johns, pushing them out of the station gate. 'The coach is waiting.'

There was an enormous coach outside the station, labelled WHYTELEAFE SCHOOL. The children took their places. Elizabeth found a seat as far away as possible from the plump little girl called Ruth. She didn't like her one bit. She didn't like Belinda either. She didn't like anyone! They all stared at her too much!

The coach set off with a loud clank and rumble. Round the corner it went, down a country lane, up a steep hill – and there was Whyteleafe School at the top! It was a beautiful building, like an old country house – which, indeed, it once had been. Its deep red walls, green with creeper, glowed in the April sun. It had a broad flight of steps leading from the green lawns up to the school terrace.

'Good old Whyteleafe!' said Ruth, pleased to see it. The coach swept round to the other side of the school, through a great archway and up to the front door. The children jumped down and ran up the steps, shouting and laughing.

Elizabeth found her hand taken by Miss Thomas. 'Welcome to Whyteleafe, Elizabeth!' said the teacher kindly, smiling down at the sulky face. 'I am sure you will do well here and be very happy with us all.'

'I shan't,' said naughty Elizabeth, and she pulled her hand away! It was certainly not a very good beginning.

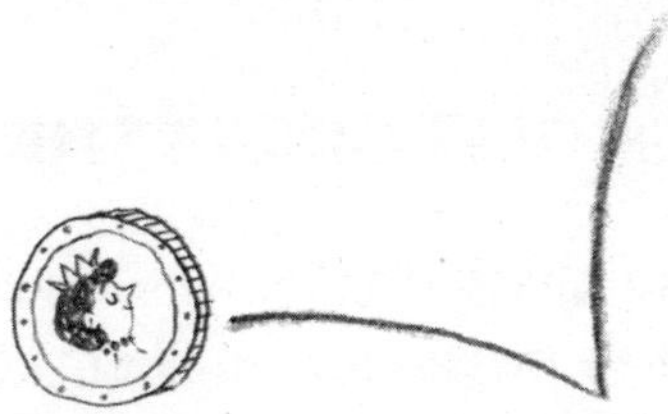

CHAPTER THREE

ELIZABETH MAKES A BAD BEGINNING

IT WAS half past one by the time the children arrived, and they were all hungry for their dinner. They were told to wash their hands quickly, and tidy themselves and then go to the dining hall for their meal.

'Eileen, please look after the three new girls,' said Miss Thomas. A big girl, with a kindly face and a mass of fair curls, came up to Belinda, Elizabeth and another girl called Helen. She gave them a push in the direction of the cloakrooms.

'Hurry!' she said. So they hurried, and Elizabeth soon found herself in a big cloakroom, tiled in gleaming white, with basins down one side, and mirrors here and there.

She washed quickly, feeling rather lost in such a crowd of chattering girls. Helen and Belinda had made friends, and Elizabeth wished they would say something to her instead of chattering to one another. But they said nothing to Elizabeth, thinking her rude and strange.

Then to the dining hall went all the girls and took their places. The boys clattered in too.

'Sit anywhere you like today,' said a tall mistress, whose name, Elizabeth found, was Miss Belle. So the children sat down and began to eat their dinner hungrily. There was hot soup first, then beef, carrots, dumplings, onions and potatoes, and then rice pudding and golden syrup. Elizabeth was so hungry that she ate everything put before her, though at home she would certainly have pushed away the rice pudding.

As it was the first day the children were allowed to talk as they pleased, and there was such a noise as they told one another what they had done in the holidays.

'I had a puppy for Easter,' said one girl with a laughing face. 'Do you know, my father bought a simply enormous Easter egg, and put the puppy inside, and tied up the egg with a red ribbon? Goodness, didn't I laugh when I undid it!'

Everybody else laughed too.

'I had a new bicycle for *my* Easter present,' said a round-faced boy. 'But it wasn't put into an egg!'

'What did *you* have for Easter?' said Eileen to Elizabeth in a kindly tone. She was sitting opposite, and felt sorry for the silent new girl. Belinda and Helen were sitting together, telling each other about the last school they had been to. Only Elizabeth had no one to talk to her.

'I had a guinea pig,' said Elizabeth in a clear voice, 'and it had a face just like Miss Thomas.'

There was a shocked silence. Somebody giggled. Miss Thomas looked rather surprised, but she said nothing.

'If you weren't a new girl, you'd be jolly well sat on for that!' said a girl nearby, glaring at Elizabeth. 'Rude creature!'

Elizabeth couldn't help going red. She had made up her mind to be naughty and rude, and she was going to be really bad, but it was rather dreadful to have somebody speaking like that to her, in front of everyone. She went on with her rice pudding. Soon the children began to talk to one another again, and Elizabeth was forgotten.

After dinner the boys went to unpack their things in their own bedrooms, and the girls went to theirs.

'Whose room are the new girls in, please, Miss Thomas?' asked Eileen. Miss Thomas looked at her list.

'Let me see,' she said. 'Yes – here we are, Elizabeth Allen, Belinda Green, Helen Marsden – they are all in Room Six, Eileen, and with them are Ruth James, Joan

Townsend and Nora O'Sullivan. Ask Nora to take the new girls there and show them what to do. She's head of that room.'

'Nora! Hie, Nora!' called Eileen, as a tall, dark-haired girl with deep blue eyes went by. 'Take these kids to Room Six, will you? They're yours! You're head of that room.'

'I know,' said Nora, looking at the three new girls. 'Hallo, is this the girl who was rude to Miss Thomas? You just mind what you say, whatever-your-name-is. I'm not having any cheek from *you*!'

'I shall say exactly what I like,' said Elizabeth boldly. '*You* can't stop me!'

'Oho, can't I?' said Nora, her blue Irish eyes glaring at Elizabeth. 'That's all *you* know! Get along to the bedroom now, and I'll show you all what to do.'

They all went up a winding oak staircase and came to a wide landing. All around it were doors marked with numbers. Nora opened the door of Number Six and went in.

The bedroom was long, high and airy. There were wide windows, all open to the school gardens outside. The sun poured in and made the room look very pleasant indeed.

The room was divided into six by blue curtains, which were now drawn back to the walls, so that six low white beds could be seen, each with a blue eiderdown. Beside each bed stood a wide chest of drawers, with a small mirror on top. The chests were painted white with blue wooden handles, and looked very pretty.

There were three washbasins in the room, with hot and cold water taps, to be shared by the six girls. There was also a tall white cupboard for each girl, and in these they hung their coats and dresses.

Each bed had a blue rug beside it on the polished brown boards. Elizabeth couldn't help thinking that it all looked rather exciting. She had only shared with Miss Scott before – now she was to share with five other girls!

'Your trunks and tuckboxes are beside your beds,' said Nora. 'You must each unpack now, and put your things away tidily. And when I say tidily I *mean* tidily. I shall look at your drawers once a week. On the top of the chest you are allowed to have six things, not more. Choose what you like – hairbrushes, or photographs, or ornaments – it doesn't matter.'

How silly! thought Elizabeth scornfully, thinking of her own untidy dressing table at home. *I shall put as many things out as I like!*

They all began unpacking. Elizabeth had never packed or unpacked anything in her life, and she found it rather exciting. She put her things neatly away in her chest of drawers – the piles of stockings, vests, bodices, blouses, everything she had brought with her. She hung up her school coat and her dresses.

The others were busy unpacking too. While they were doing this two more girls danced into the room.

'Hallo, Nora!' said one, a red-haired girl with freckles all over her face. 'I'm in your room this term. Good!'

'Hallo, Joan,' said Nora. 'Get on with your unpacking, there's a lamb. Hallo, Ruth – I've got you here again, have I? Well, just see you're a bit tidier than last term!'

Ruth laughed. She was the girl who had handed round her sweets in the train, and she was plump and clever. She ran to her trunk and started to undo it.

Nora began to tell the new girls a little about the school. They listened as they busily put away their things in their drawers.

'Whyteleafe School isn't a very large school,' said Nora, 'but it's a jolly fine one. The boys have their lessons with us, and we play tennis and cricket with them and we have our own teams of girls only too. Last year we beat the boys at tennis. We'll beat them this year too, if only we can get some good players. Any of you new girls play tennis?'

Belinda did but the others didn't. Nora went on talking, as she hung up her dresses.

'We all have the same amount of pocket money to spend,' she said. 'And it's plenty too. Two shillings a week.'

'I shall have a lot more than that,' said Belinda in surprise.

'Oh, no, you won't,' said Nora. 'All the money we have is put into a big box, and we each draw two shillings a week from it, unless we've been fined for something.'

'What do you mean – fined?' asked Helen. 'Who fines us? Miss Belle and Miss Best?'

'Oh, no,' said Nora. 'We hold a big Meeting once a week – more often, if necessary – and we hear complaints and grumbles, and if anyone has been behaving badly we fine them. Miss Belle or Miss Best come to the Meeting too, of course, but they don't decide anything much. They trust us to decide for ourselves.'

Elizabeth thought this was very strange. She had always thought that the teachers punished the children – but at Whyteleafe it seemed as if the children did it! She listened in astonishment to all that Nora was saying.

'If there's any money over, it is given to anyone who particularly wants to buy something that the Meeting approves of,' went on Nora. 'For instance, suppose you broke your tennis racket, Belinda, and needed a new one, the Meeting might allow you to take the money from the box to buy one – especially if they thought you were a very good player.'

'I see,' said Belinda. 'It sounds a good idea. Look, Nora – here are the things out of my tuckbox. What do I do with them? I want to share them with everybody.'

'Thanks,' said Nora. 'Well, we keep all our cakes and sweets and things in the playroom downstairs. There's a big cupboard there, and tins to put cakes into. I'll show you where. Elizabeth, are your tuckbox things ready? If so, bring them along, and we'll put them into the cupboard to share at teatime.'

'I'm not going to share,' said Elizabeth, remembering that she hadn't been naughty or horrid for some time. 'I shall eat them all myself.'

There was a horrified silence. The five girls stared at Elizabeth as if they couldn't believe their ears. Not share her cakes and sweets? What sort of a girl was this?

'Well,' said Nora, at last, her merry face suddenly very disgusted. 'You can do what you like, of course, with your own things. If they're as horrid as you seem to be, nobody would want to eat them!'

CHAPTER FOUR

ELIZABETH GETS INTO TROUBLE

AS NORA was about to lead the way down to the playroom, she glanced at the chests of drawers to see that they were tidy on the top. To her surprise she saw that Elizabeth had put about a dozen things on her chest!

Nora stopped and looked at them. There were two hairbrushes, a mirror, a comb, three photographs, a bottle of scent, two small vases and a clothes brush.

'Look here!' said Nora, to the others. 'This poor child can't count up to six! She's got eleven things on her chest. Poor Elizabeth! Fancy not being able to count to six.'

'I *can*,' said Elizabeth fiercely. 'One, two, three, four, five, six.'

Everybody squealed with laughter. 'She *can* count!' said Nora. 'Well, Elizabeth, count your things, and take five away – or can't you do taking-away? There are eleven things on your chest – take away five and it will leave six, which is the number I told you to have.'

'I'm not going to take any away,' said Elizabeth rudely.

'Aren't you?' said Nora in surprise. 'Well, if you won't – I will!'

The angry Irish girl picked up a hairbrush, the three photographs and the mirror. She went to a box under the window, took a key from her pocket and unlocked it. She put the five things inside and locked the box.

'That's what happens when people can't count,' she said. Elizabeth stared at her in a rage.

'Give me my things back,' she said. 'I want those photographs at once! They are of Mummy and Daddy and my pony too.'

'Sorry,' said Nora, putting the key into her pocket. 'You can have them back when you apologise, and tell me that you know how to count.'

'I shan't,' said Elizabeth.

'Just as you please,' said Nora. 'Now come on, everybody, and let's take the eatables down to the playroom.'

'I don't want to bring mine,' said Elizabeth. 'I want to leave them here.'

'Well, if you do, they'll go into that box along with the photographs,' said Nora firmly. 'The rule is that all eatables go downstairs.'

Elizabeth stood sulking, looking at her cake, her jam sandwich, her chocolates, toffees and shortbread. Then she picked up her tuckbox and followed the others. She did not want them to go into that box! She had seen enough of Nora to know that that young lady was very determined!

They clattered down the oak staircase. At one side of the hall was an open door, leading into a very large room lined with cupboards and bookcases. It was full of boys and girls.

Some were talking, some were playing games, some were putting away cakes into tins. They were all busy and happy, and called out greetings to Nora as she came into the room.

There was a gramophone going in one corner. Elizabeth stopped to listen to it, for she loved music. It was playing a tune that her mother played at home, and suddenly the little girl felt as if she wanted her mother badly.

But never mind! she thought to herself. *I shan't be here long! I don't expect they'll keep me more than a week if I go on being awfully naughty.*

'Here are some empty tins,' said Nora, handing them down from a shelf. 'Catch, Helen. Catch, Elizabeth. Here's a big one for you, Belinda, to take in that enormous cake!'

Soon they were all putting away their things. Nora took slips of paper from a pile and wrote their names on. 'Stick your name on your tin,' she said, licking hers and sticking it to the side of her tin.

'I'd like to see the classrooms,' said Belinda. Ruth said she would show her round the whole school, and off she went with Belinda and Helen. Elizabeth followed a little way behind, curious to see what a school was like, for she had never seen inside one before.

The dining hall she had already seen – a great high room, with big windows. Tables ran down the middle of it. It was only used for meals.

Then there were the classrooms, big, sunny rooms all over the place, with neat desks and chairs, and a bigger desk for the teacher. There were blackboards everywhere, just like the one that Miss Scott had used for Elizabeth.

'This is *our* classroom,' said Ruth to the new girls. 'I expect we'll all be in Miss Ranger's class. She's pretty strict, I can tell you! Nora's in a higher class, of course. She's older. She's a jolly good sort, don't you think so?'

'Yes,' agreed Helen and Belinda at once. But Elizabeth thought differently. She pursed up her mouth and said nothing.

'This is the gym,' said Ruth, and the three new girls looked in wonder at the great room, with its ropes and climbing ladders, and bars and poles. Elizabeth suddenly felt excited. She loved climbing and swinging and jumping. She hoped she could do some gym before she left.

There were many other bedrooms like her own, and then there was the part of the house put aside for Miss Belle and Miss Best and the other teachers.

'You'll each have to go and see the heads after tea,' said Ruth. 'They're good sorts.'

By the time the four girls had gone over the lovely grounds and had seen the cricket fields, the tennis courts and the flower-filled gardens, it was time for tea. A bell rang loudly, and the girls looked cheerful.

'Good! Tea!' said Ruth. 'Come on. Wash first, all of you, and do your hair. Yours looks awful, Elizabeth.'

Elizabeth did not like her dark curls being called 'awful'. She went up to her bedroom and did her hair neatly, and washed her hands. She was very hungry, and thought with pleasure of her currant cake and jam sandwich.

'I've got the most gorgeous chocolate cake you ever saw!' said Belinda to the others. 'It just melts in your mouth! You must all have a piece.'

'And I've got some homemade shrimp paste that's too delicious for words,' said Ruth. 'You wait till you taste it.'

Chocolate cake and homemade shrimp paste seemed

even more delicious to Elizabeth than currant cake and jam sandwich, which suddenly seemed rather ordinary. She ran downstairs, wondering if she would have *two* pieces of Belinda's gorgeous chocolate cake.

Tea was laid in the dining room. The long tables were spread with white cloths, and plates with big slices of brown bread and butter were set all the way down. There were some large plain cakes here and there, and some big pots of plum jam.

The children put their tuckboxes on a bare table, and placed on some empty plates there the cake or sandwich, jam or paste they meant to share at tea. These plates they took to their own table.

Once again they were allowed to sit where they liked. Elizabeth put out her sandwich and her currant cake and took her place too. Grace was said and then the boys and girls began to chatter quietly.

Suddenly Nora banged on the table. She was at the head of it. Everyone at her table stopped speaking.

'I nearly forgot to say something,' said Nora. 'Elizabeth Allen does not wish to share her things with anyone, so don't ask her for a piece of her cake, will you? She wants it all herself.'

'All right!' said the other children, and they stared at Elizabeth in surprise. Elizabeth went on eating her bread and butter. Next to her was Ruth, opening a large pot of shrimp paste that smelt simply delicious. She passed it round the table – but did not offer Elizabeth any.

Nobody offered her anything at all. Belinda counted how many there were at the table – eleven – and then cut her cake into *ten* big pieces. Ten was enough, because she missed Elizabeth out! Elizabeth watched the others munching the chocolate cake, which looked and smelt marvellous, and longed for a piece.

She cut her currant cake. It looked quite nice. She suddenly felt that she really couldn't eat it all by herself; she *must* offer it to the others too. She didn't mind being thought naughty, but being thought mean was different.

'Will you have a piece of my cake?' she asked Ruth.

Ruth stared at her in surprise. 'How you do change your mind!' she said. 'No thanks. I've had enough.'

Elizabeth offered her cake to Belinda. Belinda shook her head. 'No thank you,' she said. Elizabeth held out her plate to Helen, but Helen simply made a face at her and turned away.

Nobody would have any of Elizabeth's cake or of her sandwich either. Everyone else had either cut up half or all their cakes, and had finished up their pots of jam or paste. Only Elizabeth's cake and sandwich stood almost untouched on their plates.

A bell rang. Miss Thomas stood up and spoke to the

girls and boys. 'You may go out to play,' she said, 'but the new children must stay behind in the playroom, and see the headmistresses.'

So Helen, Elizabeth and Belinda went to the playroom, and also two boys named Kenneth and Ronald. They set the gramophone going. Belinda did a funny dance and made them all laugh.

Then someone poked her head in at the door and called to the children.

'Miss Belle and Miss Best are waiting to see you. Go and line up outside the drawing-room door – and mind you each say you're going to do your best for Whyteleafe School, and will work and play hard!'

The girl disappeared. The new children went to line up outside the drawing-room door. It opened and Miss Best appeared. 'Come in,' she said to Belinda, and in Belinda went. The door shut.

Well, I'm *not going to say I shall work hard and play hard*, said Elizabeth to herself. *I'm going just to warn them that I won't stay here and I'll be so bad they'll have to send me away. I* won't *stay at this horrid school!*

The door opened and Belinda came out, smiling. 'You're to go in next, Elizabeth,' she said. 'And for goodness' sake behave yourself!'

CHAPTER FIVE

ELIZABETH IS NAUGHTY

ELIZABETH PUSHED open the door and went into the big drawing room. It was a lovely room, with a few beautiful pictures on the walls, and glowing cushions on the chairs and the couches. The two mistresses were sitting on chairs near the window. They looked up as Elizabeth came in.

'Well, Elizabeth! We are very glad to see you at Whyteleafe School,' said Miss Belle. She was young and pretty, but Miss Best was older, and, except when she smiled, she had rather a stern face.

'Sit down, Elizabeth,' said Miss Best, smiling her lovely smile. 'I hope you have made a few friends already.'

'No, I haven't,' said Elizabeth. She sat down on a chair. Miss Best looked at her in surprise when she answered so shortly.

'Well, I expect you will soon make plenty,' said the headmistress. 'I hope you will be very happy with us, Elizabeth.'

'I shan't be,' said Elizabeth in a rude voice.

'What a funny little girl!' said Miss Belle, and she laughed. 'Cheer up, dear – you'll soon find things are very jolly here, and I am sure you will do your best to work hard, and make us proud of you.'

'I'm not going to,' said Elizabeth, turning red. 'I'm going to be as bad and naughty and horrid as I can possibly be, so there! I don't want to go to school. I hate Whyteleafe School! I'll be so bad that you'll send me home next week!'

The little girl glared at the two mistresses as she said all this, expecting them to jump up in anger. Instead they both threw back their heads and laughed and laughed!

'Oh, Elizabeth, what an extraordinary child you are!' said Miss Belle, wiping away the tears of laughter that had come into her eyes. 'You look such a good, pretty little girl too – no one would think you wanted to be so bad and naughty and horrid!'

'I don't care how you punish me,' said Elizabeth, tears coming into her own eyes, but tears of anger, not of laughter. 'You can do all you like – I just shan't care!'

'We never punish anyone, Elizabeth,' said Miss Best,

suddenly looking stern again. 'Didn't you know that?'

'No, I didn't,' said Elizabeth in astonishment. 'What do you do when people are naughty then?'

'Oh, we leave any naughty person to the rest of the children to deal with,' said Miss Best. 'Every week the school holds a Meeting, you know, and the children themselves decide what is to be done with boys and girls who don't behave themselves. It won't bother *us* if you are naughty – but you may perhaps find that you make the children angry.'

'That seems funny to me,' said Elizabeth. 'I thought it was always the teachers that did the punishing.'

'Not at Whyteleafe School,' said Miss Belle. 'Well, Elizabeth, my dear, perhaps you'd go now and tell the next child to come in, will you? Maybe one day Whyteleafe School will be proud of you, even though you are quite sure it won't!'

Elizabeth went out without another word. She couldn't help liking the two headmistresses, though she didn't want to at all. She wished she had been ruder to them. What a funny school this was!

She spoke to Helen outside the door. 'You're to go in now,' she said. 'The Beauty and the Beast are waiting for you!'

'Oh, you naughty girl!' said Helen, with a giggle. 'Miss Belle and Miss Best – the Beauty and the Beast!

That's rather clever of you to think of that, Elizabeth!'

Elizabeth had meant it to be very rude. She did not know enough of other children to know that they always loved nicknames for their masters and mistresses. She was surprised that Helen thought her clever – and secretly she was pleased.

But she stuck her nose in the air and marched off. *She* wasn't going to be pleased with anything or anybody at Whyteleafe School!

She wandered around by herself until the supper bell went at seven o'clock. She felt hungry and went into the dining hall. The children were once more opening their tins of cakes, and a lively chatter was going on. It all looked very jolly.

There were big mugs on the table and big jugs of steaming hot cocoa here and there. There were piles of bread again, butter, cheese and dishes of stewed fruit. The children sat down and helped themselves.

Nobody took any notice of Elizabeth at all, till suddenly Helen remembered what she had called Miss Belle and Miss Best. With a giggle she repeated it to her neighbour, and soon there was laughter all round the table.

'The Beauty and the Beast,' went the whisper, and chuckles echoed round. Elizabeth heard the whispers and went red. Nora O'Sullivan laughed loudly.

'It's a jolly good nickname!' she said. 'Belle means Beauty, and Best is very like Beast – and certainly Miss Belle is lovely, and Miss Best isn't! That was pretty smart of you, Elizabeth.'

Elizabeth smiled! She really couldn't help it. She didn't want to – she wanted to be as horrid as possible – but it was really very pleasant to have everyone laughing at her joke.

It's strange, though, she thought. *I meant to be horrid and rude, and the others just think it's funny. I guess Miss Belle and Miss Best wouldn't think it was funny, though!*

Nobody offered Elizabeth any of their goodies, and she did not like to offer hers, for she felt sure everyone would say no. The meal went on until half past seven, and then after grace was said the children all got up and went to the playroom.

'When's your bedtime?' said Nora to Elizabeth. 'I expect it's eight o'clock. You'd better see. The times are on the noticeboard over there. My bedtime is at half past eight, and when I come to bed I expect all the rest of you to be safe in bed.'

'I don't want to go to bed at eight o'clock,' said Elizabeth indignantly. 'I go to bed much later than that at home.'

'Well, you shouldn't then,' said Nora. 'No wonder you're such a crosspatch! My mother says that late hours make children stupid, bad-tempered and slow.'

Elizabeth went to see the times for going to bed. Hers was, as Nora had said, at eight o'clock. Well, she wouldn't go! She'd be naughty!

So she slipped out into the garden and went to where she had seen two or three big swings. She got on to a swing and began to push herself to and fro. It was lovely there in the evening sunshine. Elizabeth quite forgot that she was at school, and she sang a little song to herself.

A boy came into the place where the swings were, and stared at Elizabeth. 'What are you doing here?' he said. 'I bet it's your bedtime!'

'Mind your own business!' said Elizabeth at once.

'Well, what about you going off to bed, and minding *yours*!' said the boy. 'I'm a monitor, and it's my job to see that people do what they're told!'

'I don't know what a monitor is, and I don't care,' said Elizabeth rudely.

'Well, let *me* tell you what a monitor is,' said the boy, who was just about Elizabeth's size. 'It's somebody put in charge of other silly kids at Whyteleafe, to see they don't get *too* silly! If you don't behave yourself, I shall have to report you at the Meeting! Then you'll be punished.'

'Pooh!' said Elizabeth, and she swung herself very

hard indeed, put out her foot and kicked the boy so vigorously that he fell right over. Elizabeth squealed with laughter – but not for long! The boy jumped up, ran to the swing and shook Elizabeth off. He caught hold of her dark curls and pulled them so hard that the little girl yelled with pain.

The boy grinned at her and said, 'Serve you right! You be careful how you treat me next time, or I'll pull your nose as well as your hair! Now – are you going in or not?'

Elizabeth ran away from him and went indoors. She looked at the clock – quarter past eight! Perhaps she would have time to go to bed before that horrid Nora came up at half past.

So she ran up the stairs and went to Bedroom Number Six. Ruth, Joan, Belinda and Helen were already there, half undressed. Their curtains were pulled round their cubicles, but they were talking hard all the same. Elizabeth slipped into her own cubicle.

'You're late, Elizabeth,' said Ruth. 'You'll get into trouble if you're caught by a monitor.'

'I have been,' said Elizabeth. 'But *I* didn't care! I was on the swing and I put out my foot and kicked him over!'

'Well, you're very silly,' said Ruth. 'You will get into trouble at the Meeting if you don't look out. And that's not pleasant.'

'I don't care for any silly Meeting,' said Elizabeth, jumping into bed. She remembered that Nora had put her three photographs into the locked box, and she jumped out again. She went to the box and tried to open it – but it was still locked. Nora came in at that moment and saw Elizabeth there.

'Hallo, kid,' she said. 'Do you want your things back? Well, apologise and you can have them.'

But Elizabeth was not going to say she was sorry. She made a rude face at Nora, and flung herself into bed.

'Well, you *are* a sweet child, aren't you!' said Nora mockingly. 'I hope you get out at the right side of your bed tomorrow!'

Then there was a creak as Nora sat on her bed to take off her stockings. A clock struck half past eight downstairs. 'No more talking now,' said Nora. 'Sleep tight, all of you!'

CHAPTER SIX

ELIZABETH JOINS HER CLASS

ELIZABETH WONDERED where she was when she awoke the next morning, but she soon remembered. She was at that horrid school!

A bell rang. Nora sat up in her bed and spoke to the others. 'That's the bell for getting up,' she said. 'Stir yourselves! You've got half an hour.'

Elizabeth thought she wouldn't get up. She lay there warm in her bed, and looked up at the white ceiling. Nora's voice came sharply to her.

'Elizabeth Allen! Are you getting up or are you not?'

'Not,' said Elizabeth cheekily.

'Well, I'm in charge of you five, and it's my job to get you down to breakfast in good time,' said Nora, poking her nose round the curtain. 'Get up, you lazy creature!'

'Are you a monitor?' asked Elizabeth, remembering the boy of the evening before.

'I am,' said Nora. 'Come on, get up, Elizabeth, and don't make yourself such a nuisance.'

Elizabeth still lay there. Nora nodded to plump Ruth, and the two went beside Elizabeth's bed. Together they stripped all the clothes off the lazy girl, and then tipped up the mattress. Elizabeth gave a shriek and slid on to the floor. She was very angry.

She rushed at Nora – but Nora was big and strong, and caught hold of the angry girl's arms at once. 'Don't be silly now,' she said. 'Get dressed and hurry up or I'll give you what for! Monitors do that sometimes, you know!'

Elizabeth felt that she couldn't bear to test Nora's threat. She washed very sulkily, dressed, cleaned her teeth and did her hair. She was just going downstairs when Nora, who had gone into everyone's cubicle to see if they were tidy, called her back.

'Elizabeth! Come and put your chest of drawers tidy! Do you want me to put the rest of your things into the locked box?'

Elizabeth went back and tidied her things. It was quicker to do that than argue with Nora. She wondered if Nora would notice that she had put socks on instead of the long brown stockings!

But Nora didn't notice. She was in too big a hurry to get down to breakfast in time, and besides she didn't dream that anyone would wear socks instead of stockings at Whyteleafe School!

But a great many of the other children noticed Elizabeth's bare legs at once, and giggled. Miss Thomas noticed them too, and called to Elizabeth.

'You've put the wrong things on, Elizabeth. You must change your socks for stockings afterwards.'

But Elizabeth didn't! When she went up to make her bed afterwards, she didn't change at all. Nora saw that she hadn't and spoke to her.

'For goodness' sake put stockings on, Elizabeth. Really, I shouldn't have thought anyone could be quite so silly as you seem to be!'

'I'm not silly,' said Elizabeth. 'I prefer socks. Stockings make my legs too hot. And I'm going to keep my socks *on*.'

Ruth spoke to Nora. 'Nora, Elizabeth is really babyish,' she said. 'And the babies at Whyteleafe are allowed to wear socks, aren't they? I've seen them in the kindergarten, with their dear little bare legs. Well, why not let Elizabeth keep her socks, to show that she is really only a baby, though she's getting on for eleven? You can easily explain that to Miss Thomas.'

'That's a good idea,' said Nora, with a laugh. 'All right, Elizabeth – keep your socks on, and we'll explain to everyone that we're letting you because you're really not much more than a baby!'

The girls went out of the room, laughing. Elizabeth put on her bedspread and stood thinking. She didn't think she wanted to keep her socks on now! If only the younger children wore them, because they were the babies of the school, *she* didn't want to. The babies would laugh at her, and so would the others.

Elizabeth tore off her shoes, grabbed her socks and pulled them off in a temper. She took out her stockings and pulled them on. Bother, bother, bother! Now she would have to wear stockings after all!

She flew downstairs to the gym, where she had been told to go after making her bed and tidying her cubicle. All the others were there. Elizabeth had felt sure that they would all make remarks about her stockings being on after all – but nobody took any notice of her at all.

Hymns were sung and prayers said. Miss Best read part of a Bible chapter in her rather stern voice. Then she called the names of all the girls and boys to see that they were there.

Elizabeth had a good look around. The boys and girls were in separate rows. There were a great many masters and mistresses. The matron of the school, who looked after the children when they were ill, stood on the platform with some of the other mistresses, a jolly-looking person, dressed like a nurse, in apron and cap. The music master played the piano for the singing, and again when the children marched out.

He made up a fine marching tune, and Elizabeth liked it very much for she loved music. She wondered if she was supposed to learn music at Whyteleafe. Miss Scott had taught her at home, but Miss Scott was not musical and Elizabeth had not enjoyed her lessons at all.

Out marched the children to their classrooms. 'You are in Miss Ranger's class,' said Ruth, poking Elizabeth in the back. 'Come with me and I'll show you.'

Elizabeth followed Ruth. She came to a big, sunny classroom, and into it poured six boys and nine girls, all about Elizabeth's age.

'Bags I this desk,' squealed Ruth. 'I like to be by the window!'

She put her things into the desk. The other children chose their desks too, but the new ones were told to wait till Miss Ranger came. Ruth sprang to hold the door open as soon as she heard Miss Ranger's rather loud voice down the passage.

In came Miss Ranger. 'Good morning, children!'

'Good morning, Miss Ranger,' said everyone but Elizabeth.

'All the old children can sit, but the new ones must stand while I give them their places,' said Miss Ranger.

She gave Elizabeth a desk at the back. Elizabeth was glad. It would be a good place to be naughty in! She meant to be bad in class that very morning. The sooner that everyone knew how naughty she meant to be, the sooner she would be sent home.

Books were given out. 'We will take a reading lesson first,' said Miss Ranger, who wanted to make sure that the new children could read properly. 'Then dictation – then arithmetic!'

Elizabeth could read beautifully, spell well and she liked arithmetic. She couldn't help feeling that it was rather fun to do lessons with a lot of people instead of by herself! When her turn came she read very nicely indeed, though she had a great many difficult words in her page.

'Very good, Elizabeth,' said Miss Ranger. 'Next, please.'

Elizabeth got all her dictation right. She thought it was very easy. Miss Ranger took a red pencil and marked 'VERY GOOD' on Elizabeth's page. Elizabeth looked at it proudly – and then she suddenly remembered that she had meant to be naughty!

'This won't do!' she said to herself. 'I can't get Very Goods like this – they'll never send me home. I'd better be naughty.'

She wondered what to do. She looked at Ruth by the

window, and wondered if she could flip her rubber at her and hit her. She took her ruler, fitted her rubber against the end of it, bent it back and let it go. *Whizzzzzz!* The rubber flew across the schoolroom and hit Ruth on the left ear!

'Ooooh!' said Ruth in surprise. She looked round and saw Elizabeth's grinning face. Others began to giggle when they saw Ruth's angry look.

Elizabeth grew bolder. She folded up a bit of paper, and flipped it at Helen, who sat in front. But Helen moved her head, and the pellet of paper flew past her and landed on Miss Ranger's desk. She looked up.

'Playtime is for things like this,' she said. 'Not lesson time. Who did that?'

Elizabeth didn't answer. Miss Ranger looked up and down the rows. 'WHO DID THAT?' she said again. The boy next to Elizabeth poked her hard with his ruler.

'Own up!' he whispered. 'If you don't, we'll all be kept in.'

So Elizabeth owned up. 'I did it,' she said.

'Well, Elizabeth, perhaps you would like to know that I don't allow behaviour like that in *my* class,' said Miss Ranger. 'Don't do it again.'

'I shall if I want to,' said Elizabeth. Everybody looked at her in amazement. Miss Ranger was surprised.

'You must be very bored with these lessons to want to flip paper about,' she said. 'Go outside the room and stay there till you feel it would bore you less to come back than to stand outside. I don't mind how long you stand there, but I do mind anybody being bored in my class. Now, children, get out your paintboxes, please.'

There was a clatter as the desks were opened and paintboxes were taken out. Elizabeth loved painting and was very good at it. She wanted to stay. She sat on in her desk and didn't move.

'Elizabeth! Go outside, please,' said Miss Ranger. There was no help for it then – up Elizabeth got and went to the door.

'You may come back when you think you can really behave yourself, and not disturb my class,' said Miss Ranger.

It was very dull standing outside the door. Elizabeth wondered if she should wander away and have a swing. No, she might meet the Beauty and the Beast! Ha ha! She was being naughty all right!

But it *was* dull standing so long outside a door and hearing happy talking coming from inside, as the children painted blue and pink lupins that Miss Ranger had brought in. Elizabeth couldn't bear it any longer. She opened the door and went in.

'I can behave myself now,' she said in a low voice to Miss Ranger. Miss Ranger nodded, without a smile.

'Take your place,' she said. 'There's no time for you to do any painting – you can do a few more sums!'

Sums again! thought Elizabeth angrily. *Well – I'll just be bad as soon as ever I can think of something really naughty again!*

CHAPTER SEVEN

THE FIRST SCHOOL MEETING

THAT EVENING, after tea, the first Meeting was held. The whole school attended it, and Miss Belle, Miss Best and Mr Johns came too. They sat at the back and did not seem to be taking a great deal of notice of what was going on.

'But, all the same, they never miss a word!' said Ruth to Belinda, who was feeling just a little scared of this first important Meeting.

The two head children of the school, a grave-looking girl called Rita, and a merry-eyed boy called William, sat at a large table in the gym, where the Meeting was held. They were the Judges. Twelve other children, six boys and six girls, big and small, sat round a table just in front of the two Judges. They were called the Jury. All the others sat on forms around.

At first Elizabeth had thought she would not go to

the Meeting. Then she had felt rather curious about it, and decided to go just this one time. She had seen a notice on the noticeboard that said, PLEASE BRING ALL THE MONEY YOU HAVE, and she had brought hers in her purse – though she was quite determined not to give it up if she was asked to do so.

All the children stood up when the two Judges and the two mistresses and master came into the room – all but Elizabeth! However, she got up in a great hurry when she felt Ruth's hard fingers digging into her back to make her move! She glared round at Ruth, and was just going to speak angrily to her when there was the sound of a hammer being rapped on a table.

'Sit, please,' said one of the Judges. Everyone sat. Elizabeth saw that there was a wooden hammer or mallet on the table in front of the Judges, and also a large notebook and some sheets of paper. There was a large box as well, like a big moneybox. It all looked important and exciting.

'The twelve children round the smaller table are the monitors,' whispered Ruth to Elizabeth. 'They are chosen by us all every month.'

Elizabeth saw that Nora was at the Jury table, and so was the boy she had kicked the day before. She didn't know any of the others, except Eileen, the girl who had been kind to her yesterday.

The girl Judge rose in her seat and spoke clearly to the school. 'This is our first Meeting this term,' she said. 'We have very little to do today, because school only opened yesterday, but we must just make our rules clear to the new children, and we must also take in the money. We do not need to choose new monitors because we elected those at the last Meeting of the Easter term. You see them at the Jury table. They will remain monitors for one month unless any Meeting decides to choose others instead. As you know, monitors are chosen for their common sense, their loyalty to the school and its ideas, and their good character. They *must* be obeyed, because you yourselves have chosen them.'

The girl Judge stopped and looked down at a paper she held, on which she had written notes to remind her of what she wanted to say. She looked round at the listening children.

'We have very few rules,' she said. 'One rule is that we place all the money we get into this box, and we draw from it two shillings a week each. The rest of the money is used to buy anything that any of you especially want – but you have to state at the weekly Meeting what you need the money for, and the Jury will decide if you may have it.'

One or two of the children clinked their money as

if they would like to put it into the box at once. The Judges smiled. 'You'll be able to give your money in a minute,' said the girl Judge. 'Now, to go on with our rules. The second rule is that if we have any complaint at all, we must bring it to the Meeting and announce it there, so that everyone may hear it, and decide what is to be done with it.

'Any bullying, unkindness, untruthfulness or disobedience may be brought before the Meeting, and we will decide what punishment shall be given. Please be sure you understand the difference between a real complaint and telling tales, because telling tales is also punished. If you are not sure of the difference, ask your monitor before you bring your complaint to the Meeting.'

The girl Judge sat down. The boy Judge got up, and beamed round at the listening company. 'We will now take the money,' he said. 'After that we will hand out the two shillings to everyone, and then see if anybody wants extra this week. Thomas, take the box round, please.'

Elizabeth was quite sure she was *not* going to give up her money. She quickly pushed her purse under her and sat on it hard.

Thomas came round with the box. Money clinked into it – shillings and sixpences, half crowns and even a ten-shilling note or two went into the big box.

The box came to Elizabeth. She passed it on without putting her money into it. But Thomas the monitor noticed it at once. 'Haven't you any money at all?' he asked.

Elizabeth pretended not to hear. Thomas said no more, but went on taking the box round. Elizabeth was pleased. *I did what I wanted to them and they couldn't stop me!* she thought.

Thomas took the box up to the Judges. It was very heavy now. He put it on their table and said something to them in a low voice.

William, the boy Judge, rapped on his table with the hammer. Everyone stopped chattering.

'Elizabeth Allen did not put her money into the box,' he said. 'Elizabeth, have you no money?'

'Yes, I have,' answered Elizabeth defiantly. 'But I'm going to keep it.'

'Stand up when you speak to me,' ordered the Judge. Elizabeth felt Ruth's hard fingers poking her again and she stood up. Ruth saw the purse on the floor, and quickly picked it up.

'Why do you want to keep your money to yourself?' asked William. 'Are you so very selfish?'

'No,' said Elizabeth. 'But I think it's a silly idea.'

'Listen,' said William patiently. 'In this school we don't like to think that some of us have heaps of money to spend and others have hardly any. We all get the same, and if you want anything extra you can always have it if the Meeting agrees.'

'Well, I'm not going to stay at this school very long,' said Elizabeth in a rude, defiant voice. 'And I shall want some money to go home by train – so I'm not going to give it to *you*.'

There was a buzz of surprise and horror. The Judges and the Jury stared at Elizabeth as if she was something very strange indeed.

The two headmistresses and the master looked up with great interest, wondering what the Judges would say. William and Rita spoke together in low voices. Then they banged on the table with the hammer. Everyone was silent at once.

William spoke in a grave voice. 'We think Elizabeth is wrong and silly,' he said. 'Her parents are paying a lot of money to keep her in this fine school and, even if she goes home in a short while, her term's fees still have to be paid. Also we think she is very feeble not to try and see if she likes Whyteleafe.'

'If I'm not sent home, I'll *run* away,' said Elizabeth, angry at being spoken of like this.

'That can't be allowed,' said William at once. 'You would worry your parents and everyone here, just because you are a selfish, silly girl. Ruth, is that Elizabeth's money I see you waving at me? Bring it here.'

Elizabeth made a snatch at her money, but it was too late. Ruth took the bag to the table and emptied six shillings, two half crowns and five sixpences into the moneybox. Elizabeth blinked her eyes. She wanted to cry, but she wasn't going to.

'Elizabeth, we can't allow you to keep your money in case you are foolish enough to use it for running away,' said Rita in a kind but stern voice.

One of the Jury stood up. It was a tall boy called Maurice. 'I should like to say that the Jury think that Elizabeth Allen must not have any money at all to spend this week, because of her behaviour,' he said.

All the Jury put up their hands to show that they agreed.

'Very well,' said the Judge. 'Now, Elizabeth, we shan't say any more to you today, because you are a new girl, and must be given a chance to settle down. I hope you will have a good report at next week's Meeting. We shall be very pleased if you do.'

'Well, I shan't then,' said Elizabeth in a furious voice. 'You just wait and see what I'll do.'

'Sit down,' said William, losing his patience with the defiant little girl. 'We've had enough of you for one Meeting. Nora, give out the money to everyone, please.'

Nora gave two shillings to everybody, except

Elizabeth. The little girl sat sulking on her form, hating everybody. How dared they take her money? She would pay Ruth out for taking her purse like that!

When everyone had their money, the Judges knocked for silence again. 'Does anyone want extra money this week for anything?' asked William.

A small boy stood up. 'I should like sixpence extra,' he said.

'What for?' asked William.

'I've been told I must give some money to the School Club, to help towards a new gramophone,' he said.

'Well, take it out of your two shillings,' said William. 'Sit down. Sixpence extra not granted.'

The boy sat down. A girl got up. 'May I have one and ninepence extra to pay for an electric light bulb I broke by accident in the playroom?' she asked.

'Who's your monitor?' asked Rita. One of the Jury stood up, a girl called Winnie.

'Was it a proper accident, Winnie, or just fooling about?' asked Rita.

'It was a proper accident,' said Winnie. 'Elsie was trying to open a tin, and the opener flew out of her hand and broke the light bulb.'

'Give her one and ninepence out of the box then,' ordered Rita. Winnie took the money and gave it to the girl, who was very pleased.

'Any more requests?' asked William. Nobody said anything.

'Any complaints or grumbles?' asked Rita.

Elizabeth felt uncomfortable. Would Nora complain about her? Would that boy she had kicked, who was a monitor, complain too? Goodness, this Meeting was lasting much too long!

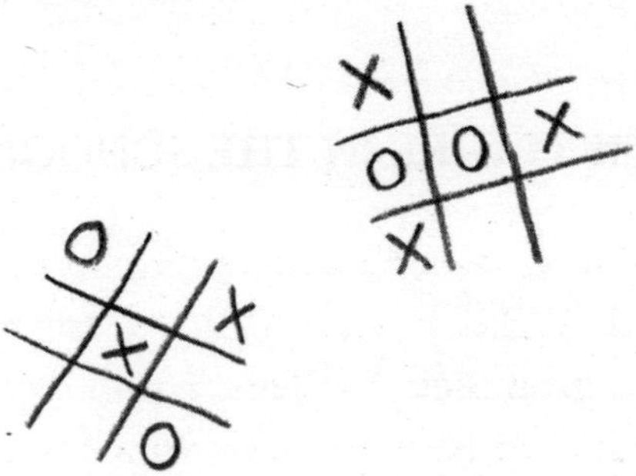

CHAPTER EIGHT

THE FIRST WEEK AT SCHOOL

NOBODY MADE any complaints at all. Elizabeth couldn't help feeling glad. *All the same, they'll have plenty of complaints to make about me next week!* she thought. *I'll just show them that I mean what I say!*

Somebody had a grumble. It was a small boy called Wilfred. He stood up, looking rather shy.

'I have a grumble,' he said.

'Go on then,' said William, the Judge.

'Please,' he said, 'I learn music, and one of the times put down for my practice is half of cricket time on Tuesday. Could I have it changed, because I do hate missing cricket?'

'Certainly,' said William. 'Mr Johns, do you think that could be changed?'

'I'll see to it,' said Mr Johns, from the back of the room. 'I'll speak to the music master and have it put right for Wilfred.'

'Thank you,' said William and Wilfred together. There were no more grumbles. William hammered on the table.

'The Meeting is over,' he said. 'The next will be held at the same time on the same day next week. Everyone must attend.'

The children jumped up, talking loudly, and went out to their various tasks. Some had lessons to prepare for the next day. Some had pets to feed. Some wanted to practise cricket or tennis. Everyone seemed to have something to do.

All except Elizabeth. She seemed to have no one to talk to, no one to walk with. She knew it was her own fault, but she didn't like it. She wandered off by herself and came to a little room where someone was playing the piano softly and beautifully.

Elizabeth loved music with all her heart. She crept into the little music room and sat down to listen. Mr Lewis, the music master, was there, playing to himself. When he finished, he turned round and saw Eizabeth.

'Hallo!' he said. 'Did you like that?'

'Yes, I loved it,' said Elizabeth. 'It sounded to me like the sea.'

'It was supposed to be the sea on a summmer's day,' said Mr Lewis. He was an old man, with gentle eyes and a small grey beard. 'It was written by a man who loved to put the sea into his music.'

'I wish I could learn to play it,' said Elizabeth. 'I really do wish I could. Am I supposed to be learning music at this school, do you know?'

'What's your name?' asked the music master, taking out a small notebook and opening it. 'Mine is Mr Lewis.'

'Mine is Elizabeth Allen,' said Elizabeth.

'Yes, here's your name,' said Mr Lewis. 'You *are* down for music lessons with me. That's fine. We shall get on well together, and perhaps by the end of the term you will be able to play this sea piece you like so much.'

'I'd like that,' said Elizabeth, 'but I shan't be here long. I hate school.'

'Dear me, what a pity,' said Mr Lewis. 'Most children simply love it – especially Whyteleafe School. Well, if you think you won't be here long, perhaps I had better cross your name off my list. It seems a waste of time to have any music lessons if you mean to go.'

'Well, I might as well have one or two lessons,' said Elizabeth. 'I suppose I couldn't have one now, could I?'

Mr Lewis looked at his watch. 'Yes,' he said. 'I've got twenty minutes. Fetch your music and we'll see what you can do.'

Elizabeth was happy for the first time when she sat

down at the piano with the music master by her side. She played one of her favourite pieces. Mr Lewis jerked his foot in time to the music and nodded his head when she had finished.

'Yes, Elizabeth,' he said, pleased. 'You will be one of my best pupils. I must ask you to change your mind about leaving us soon – it will be a pleasure for me to teach you that sea piece.'

Elizabeth felt pleased and proud. But she shook her head. 'I'm afraid I shan't stay,' she said. 'They've taken my money away so that I can't run away, but I'm going to be so horrid that they'll have to *send* me away!'

'What a pity!' said Mr Lewis. He looked at his watch again. 'Play me something else,' he said. 'I've a little more time.'

At the end of the lesson Mr Lewis showed Elizabeth the name of the sea piece he had played. 'There is a most beautiful recording of it,' he said. 'Why don't you ask for some money to buy it at the next Meeting? Everyone would love the record in the playroom, and I know they haven't got it.'

'I'd love to get it,' said Elizabeth. 'Then I could hear it whenever I wanted to. But I know the Meeting wouldn't give *me* any money! Why, they've even not let me have the two shillings everyone else has.'

'Dear, dear,' said Mr Lewis, smiling. 'You must really

be a *very* bad little girl – and yet you play my piano like an angel!'

'Do I really?' said Elizabeth in delight – but the music master had gone, leaving Elizabeth to put away her music and shut the piano.

Elizabeth soon found out that there were many pleasant things that the children of Whyteleafe were allowed to do. Every other day they were allowed to go down to the village in twos, to buy sweets, toys, books and anything they wanted. They were also allowed to go to the cinema once a week, provided that they paid for themselves.

They could go riding every day, and this Elizabeth simply adored, for there were rolling hills and commons around the school, on which it was perfectly lovely to gallop. Elizabeth rode very well indeed, for she had had her own pony for years.

Then, on two evenings a week, the music master gave a little concert to those children who really loved music. The concert was from half past seven to eight, after supper, and Mr Lewis gathered round him about twelve boys and girls who loved to hear the beautiful music he drew from his piano. Sometimes he played the violin too, and Elizabeth longed to learn to play it when she heard Mr Lewis drawing the bow across the strings of his fine violin.

On another evening there was a small dance, beginning at half past seven, for an hour. Elizabeth loved dancing too, and, when she saw the notice on the noticeboard, she was pleased.

No wonder the children were happy at Whyteleafe! There seemed always something lovely to look forward to, something exciting to do. Helen and Belinda, the other new girls, soon settled down well, made firm friends with one another and were very happy. The two new boys also made friends. Once Joan tried to make friends with Elizabeth, but the little girl made a rude face and turned away.

As the days went on, Elizabeth kept to her plan. She took every chance of being naughty and rude, till everyone was tired of her. She spent most of the mornings outside the door of the classroom because Miss Ranger could not have her in the room as she disturbed the class so much.

One morning she caught the school cat and put it inside Miss Ranger's desk before anyone entered the room. When Miss Ranger opened the lid, the cat jumped out, and Miss Ranger squealed in fright. Everyone giggled. They knew it was Elizabeth, of course.

Another time Elizabeth put the classroom clock ten minutes fast, and Miss Ranger stopped the lesson too soon. When Miss Ranger found out, she was angry.

'As you all have missed ten minutes of your arithmetic lesson,' she said, 'I am going to give you two extra sums to do for your preparation time this afternoon.'

The class was angry with Elizabeth. 'You wait till the next Meeting!' said Ruth. 'There'll be some fine complaints about you there!'

'I don't care,' said Elizabeth. And she didn't.

One afternoon after tea Elizabeth wanted to go and see the village of Whyteleafe. She went to Nora, her monitor, and asked her for permission to go and look at the shops in the village.

'Yes, you can go,' said Nora. 'But get someone to go with you. We are only allowed to go in twos.'

Elizabeth went to Ruth. 'Will you come with me to the village?' she asked. 'I want to look at the shops.'

'No thanks,' said Ruth. 'I don't want to go with anyone like *you*! I don't know how you might behave in the road. I might be ashamed of you.'

'I know how to behave in the road,' said Elizabeth crossly.

'Well, you don't know how to behave at school!' said Ruth, and walked away.

Elizabeth asked Belinda. But Belinda shook her head. 'I don't want to go,' she said.

Helen wouldn't go either, nor would Joan. Elizabeth didn't like to ask any of the boys, because they always laughed at her when they saw her coming.

'Here's the bold bad girl!' they said to one another. And soon poor Elizabeth began to be known as the Bold Bad Girl!

Elizabeth went back to Nora. 'Nobody will go with me,' she said.

'It serves you right,' said Nora. 'You can't go if nobody will go with you. We are not allowed to go alone.'

'Well, *I'm* going alone!' said Elizabeth to herself. And she slipped out of the school door, down the steps, round to the right and through the big archway! Down the hill she ran to see the village.

She had a lovely time looking in all the shops. She looked longingly into the sweetshop and wished she had some money to buy some toffee. She looked into a music shop and wondered if they had the record of the sea piece she loved. She looked into the toyshop and good gracious! Coming out of it was Rita, the head girl of Whyteleafe School!

Now what was naughty Elizabeth to do?

CHAPTER NINE

RITA HAS A JOB FOR ELIZABETH

ELIZABETH HAD no time to run away. Rita came out of the shop almost on top of her. She smiled at the little girl and then she saw that she was alone. Her smile faded, and she looked stern.

'Surely somebody is with you?' she asked.

'No,' said Elizabeth.

'But Elizabeth, you know by now that no one is allowed in the village by herself,' said Rita. 'You must always come with somebody. Why didn't you?'

'Because nobody would come with me,' said Elizabeth. 'I did ask a whole lot of them.'

'Well, you had better come with *me* now,' said Rita. 'I am alone, because the girls of the top class are allowed to shop by themselves. So walk along with me.'

Elizabeth was just going to say that she didn't want to when she saw what lovely kind eyes Rita had. Rita was looking at her, and Elizabeth thought she was the kindest-looking girl she had ever seen – even nicer than Eileen. So she walked along by Rita in silence.

'You know, Elizabeth, it is strange that no one would go with you,' said Rita. 'Doesn't anybody at all like you?'

'No,' said Elizabeth. 'Don't you remember, Rita, that I told you I was going to be as horrid as could be so that I could go home? Well, everybody thinks I *am* very horrid, so nobody wants to talk to me or walk with me.'

'And are you *really* horrid?' asked Rita.

Elizabeth looked up. She was surprised that Rita should talk to her kindly, after having found her out in disobedience. But Rita did not look angry, only very understanding and wise.

Elizabeth thought for a moment. *Was* she really horrid? She remembered all the governesses she had had. She remembered that Miss Scott wouldn't stay with her. Perhaps she really and truly *was* a horrid girl.

'I don't know,' she said at last. 'I believe I am horrid really, Rita. I make myself horrider than I truly am – but, all the same, I believe I can't be very nice.'

'Poor little Elizabeth!' said Rita. 'I wonder what has made you grow so horrid? You look such a nice little girl, and when you smile you are quite different. I do feel sorry for you.'

A lump suddenly came into Elizabeth's throat, and

tears into her eyes. She blinked the tears away angrily. Now Rita would think she was a baby!

'Don't feel sorry for me,' she said. 'I *want* to be horrid, so that I can go home.'

'Couldn't you try to be nice for a change, and just give yourself a chance?' asked Rita.

'No,' said Elizabeth. 'I shan't be sent home if I am nice. I simply must be as bad as I can be.'

'But you will make yourself very unhappy,' said Rita. 'And you will make other people unhappy too.'

'Shall I?' said Elizabeth in surprise. 'Well, I don't mind making myself unhappy, if I can get what I want in the end – but I don't want to make other people unhappy. I think I *am* a horrid girl, but Rita, I wish you'd believe me when I say that I really don't mean to make the others unhappy.'

'Well, listen, Elizabeth,' said Rita, walking all the time back towards the school, 'there is someone in your room who isn't very happy. Have you noticed it? You might at least do what you can to make things nicer for her.'

'Who is it?' asked Elizabeth in surprise.

'It is Joan,' said Rita. 'She hasn't a happy home, and she comes back to school very miserable each term. She worries about her father and mother all the time, because they don't seem to want her or to love her.

They never come to see her at half-term.'

'Oh,' said Elizabeth, remembering that Joan usually did look rather sad. 'I didn't know.'

'Nobody knows except me,' said Rita. 'I live near Joan at home, so I know. I am telling you this, Elizabeth, because if you really *do* mean what you say about not wanting to make other people unhappy, you can just try to make things better for Joan. She hasn't any friend, any more than you have, but for a different reason. She is afraid of making friends in case anyone asks her to stay with them for the holidays – and she knows her mother wouldn't bother to ask any friend back to stay with Joan. And Joan is very proud, and can't bear to take kindnesses she can't return. Now, there's a job for you to do! Can you do it?'

'Oh, yes, Rita,' said Elizabeth at once. Although she was spoilt, she had a tender heart and, when she saw that someone was in trouble, she would always go to help them. 'Thank you for telling me. I won't tell anyone else.'

'I know you won't,' said Rita. 'It *is* such a pity that you mean to be bad, Elizabeth, because I can see you would be splendid if you would give yourself a chance.'

Elizabeth frowned. 'It's no good,' she said. 'I'm going to do what I meant to do – get sent home as soon as ever I can. And I can't be sent home if I'm good.'

'Well, come and talk to me any time you think you would like to,' said Rita, as they walked in at the school gates. 'And I say, Elizabeth – don't go alone into the village again, will you? Can you promise that?'

Elizabeth was just going to say no, she wouldn't promise, when she thought of how kind and gentle Rita had been – and she felt she *must* promise.

'I promise, Rita,' she said, 'and – and thank you for being so nice. You make it rather difficult for me to be as horrid as I want to be.'

'*That's* a good thing!' said Rita, with a laugh, and the tall head girl walked away to her own room.

Nora met Elizabeth as she walked to the playroom. '*Did* you go to the village?' she asked.

'Yes, I did,' said Elizabeth.

'Who went with you?' asked Nora.

'Nobody,' answered Elizabeth defiantly.

'Then I shall report you at the next Meeting,' said Nora angrily.

'Report me all you like!' said Elizabeth in a don't-care tone. '*I* shan't mind!'

'You'll mind all right when the time comes, Miss Don't-Care,' said Nora.

Elizabeth went to the playroom and put a record on the gramophone. She looked through the pile of records to see if the sea piece was there that she loved. But it wasn't. She wondered how much it would cost. But what was the use of wondering that? She would never have any money now to buy anything! This horrid, horrid school!

Joan Townsend came into the playroom. People were used to her quiet ways, and nobody took much notice of her. They called her the Mouse, and often asked her where she kept her bit of cheese!

Elizabeth looked up and thought that Joan did indeed look very sad. 'Has the afternoon post come yet?' asked Joan.

'Yes,' said Helen. 'Long ago. Nothing for you, Joan.'

Perhaps she hoped to hear from her mother or father, thought Elizabeth. *I hear from Mummy often, and Miss Scott has written twice, but I don't remember Joan getting a single letter!*

She was just going to say something to Joan when the supper bell rang. The children all trooped into the dining hall. Elizabeth tried to sit next to Joan, but she couldn't. She noticed that Joan hardly ate anything.

After supper there was a concert in the music master's room. Elizabeth ran up to Joan and spoke to her. 'Joan! Come and hear Mr Lewis playing tonight. He's going to play a lovely thing to us – my mummy plays it at home, and I know it very well.'

'No thanks,' said Joan. 'I've got a letter to write.'

Elizabeth stared after her as Joan went to the playroom. Joan always seemed to be writing letters – but none ever came for her. Elizabeth ran to tell Mr Lewis she was coming to his little concert, and then she ran and peeped in at the playroom. Joan was there alone, but she was not writing letters.

She sat with her pen in her hand, and two big tears dropped on to the writing pad on the desk below. Elizabeth was horrified. She hated to see anyone crying. She stepped into the room – but Joan turned and saw her coming. She wiped her tears away at once and spoke fiercely to Elizabeth.

'What are you spying on me for, you horrid thing? Can't you leave anybody alone? You're always making a nuisance of yourself.'

'Joan, I only wanted to . . .'

'Yes, I know what you wanted!' said Joan, just as fiercely. 'You wanted to see me crying, and then laugh at me and tell all the others I'm a baby! You say you want to be as horrid and nasty as you can – but just you try telling the others you saw me crying!'

'Oh, please, Joan! I wouldn't do that, I really wouldn't!' said Elizabeth, full of dismay to think that Joan should think such a thing of her. 'Joan, please listen . . . I'm not quite as horrid as I make myself be. Oh, do please let me be friends with you.'

'No,' said Joan, who was almost as obstinate as Elizabeth when she was unhappy. 'Go away. Do you suppose I'd let the naughtiest girl in the school be my friend? I don't want *any* friend. Go away.'

Elizabeth went. She felt dreadful. How could she help Joan if Joan wouldn't believe that she was not quite as horrid as she pretended to be? She thought of Joan's unhappy, freckled face and, although the music master played really beautifully that evening, for once Elizabeth did not listen in delight – for once she was thinking of somebody else, and not herself!

If only Joan would let me help her, thought Elizabeth. *Rita wouldn't have told me if she hadn't thought I could do it. I wish I could have a chance of showing Rita I can really do something for somebody.*

Elizabeth's chance came that very night. When she and the other five girls in her room were in bed, and Elizabeth was almost asleep, she heard a sound from the end bed, where Joan slept. Joan was sobbing quietly under the bedclothes!

Elizabeth was out of bed at once, although she knew that the rule was that no one was to leave her own cubicle till morning. But Elizabeth didn't care for rules anyhow – and she meant to go to Joan, even if Joan pushed her away as fiercely as before!

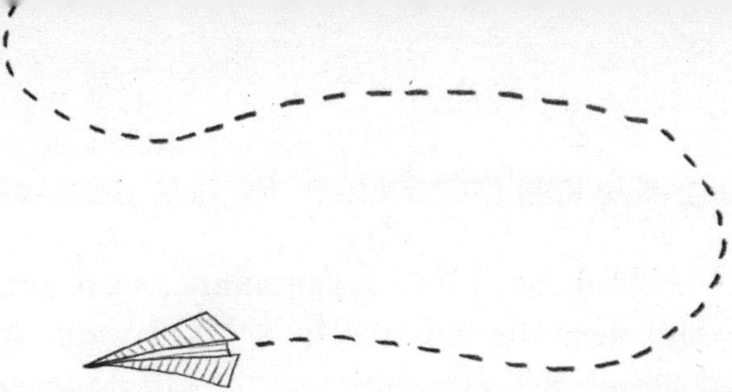

CHAPTER TEN

JOAN'S SECRET

ELIZABETH SLIPPED by Nora's bed, and by Belinda's. She came to Joan's, at the end beside the wall. She squeezed in between the curtains and went to sit on Joan's bed.

Joan stopped crying at once and lay quite stiff and still, wondering who it was on her bed. Elizabeth whispered to her.

'Joan! It's me, Elizabeth. What's the matter? Are you unhappy?'

'Go away,' said Joan in a fierce whisper.

'I shan't,' said Elizabeth. 'It makes me unhappy myself to hear you crying all alone. Are you homesick?'

'Go away,' said Joan, beginning to cry softly again.

'I tell you I *shan't*,' said Elizabeth. 'Listen, Joan. I'm unhappy too. I was so bad at home that no governesses would stay with me – so my mother had to send me away to school. But I love my mummy, and I can't bear to be sent away from home like this. I want my dog and my pony – and even my canary – so I do know how *you* feel if you are homesick.'

Joan listened in surprise. So that was why Elizabeth was so horrid – partly because she was unhappy too, and wanted to be at home.

'Now, Joan, tell me what's the matter with *you*,' begged Elizabeth. 'Please do. I won't laugh, you know that. I only want to help you.'

'There's nothing much the matter,' said Joan, wiping her eyes. 'It's only that I don't think my mother and father love me – and I do love them *so* much. You see they hardly ever write to me and they never come to see me at half-term – and it's my birthday this term, and everyone knows it – and I shan't get a present from them or a birthday cake or anything. I know I shan't. And it makes me feel so dreadful.'

'Oh, Joan!' said Elizabeth, and she took the girl's hand in hers and squeezed it. 'Oh, Joan. That's awful. When I think how my mummy spoilt me and gave me everything I wanted – and fussed me – and I was cross and impatient all the time! And here are you, just longing for a little tiny bit of everything I had. I feel rather ashamed of myself.'

'Well, so you ought to be,' said Joan, sitting up. 'You

don't know how lucky you are to be loved and fussed. Goodness! I should be really thrilled and frightfully happy if my mother wrote to me even once a fortnight and yours has sent you cards and letters almost every day. It makes me jealous.'

'Don't be jealous,' said Elizabeth, beginning to cry herself. 'I would share everything with you if I could, Joan; I really would.'

'Well, you can't be quite so horrid as everyone thinks you are then,' said Joan.

'I think I am rather horrid, but I do make myself much worse,' said Elizabeth. 'You see I mean to be sent back home as soon as possible.'

'That will make your mother very unhappy,' said Joan. 'It is a great disgrace to be expelled from school, sent away never to come back. You are very odd – you love your mother, and she loves you, and you want to go back to her – and yet you are willing to make her very unhappy. I don't understand you. I'd do anything in the world for my mother, and she doesn't love me at all. I try to make her proud of me. I do everything I can for her, but she doesn't seem to bother about me. *You're* as bad as you can be, and I expect your mother will love you all the same. It isn't fair.'

'No, it doesn't seem fair,' said Elizabeth, thinking hard. She was glad her mother wasn't like Joan's. She made up her mind to be very nice to her mother when she went back home, to make up for making her unhappy by her behaviour at school.

'You see, Elizabeth, the other girls see me waiting for letters every day, and they laugh at me behind my back, and think my parents must be very peculiar people,' said Joan. 'And I do hate that too. Last term I sent some letters to myself, just so that I should have some – but the others found out and teased me dreadfully.'

'It's a shame,' said Elizabeth. 'Joan, don't worry so. Perhaps things will come right. Couldn't we be friends, please? Just while I'm here. I don't mean to be here for long, but it would be nice to have somebody for a friend for a little while.'

'All right,' said Joan, and she took Elizabeth's hand. 'Thank you for coming to me tonight. I'm so glad you're not as horrid as I thought. I think you're *very* nice!'

Elizabeth slipped back to her own bed, her heart feeling warm and glad. It was good to have a friend. It was lovely to be thought very nice. No boy or girl had ever said that of Elizabeth before!

I won't let the others laugh at Joan! thought Elizabeth fiercely. *She's my friend now! I shall look after her – she's just a timid mouse.*

To the astonishment of everyone the two girls soon became fast friends. They went down to the village together. Joan spent some of her two shillings on sweets, which she shared with Elizabeth. Elizabeth helped Joan with her sums during preparation in the afternoon, for Joan was bad at arithmetic and Elizabeth was quick.

Joan asked Elizabeth many questions about her father and mother. She was never tired of hearing how wonderful they were, and the presents they gave Elizabeth, and the fuss they made of her.

'What are they like to look at?' asked Joan.

'I could show you their photographs, but Nora locked them up in her box, by the window,' said Elizabeth.

'Well, fancy letting them stay there when all you've got to do is to say you're sorry and that you know how to count,' said Joan, remembering what had happened. 'Goodness, I wouldn't let *my* mother's picture stay in that dirty old box!'

'I shan't apologise to Nora,' said Elizabeth sulkily. 'I don't like her – interfering creature.'

'She's not,' said Joan. 'She's a good sort. Sometimes I think you are an awful baby, Elizabeth. Only a baby would talk like that.'

'Oh! So you think I'm a baby, do you?' cried Elizabeth, flaring up in a rage, and tossing her curls over her shoulder. 'Well, I'll just show you!'

Nora was coming into the bedroom at that very moment. She was astonished to find Elizabeth flinging herself almost on top of her, shouting loudly, 'Nora! I'm sorry about those things you put in the box. I know how to count and I'll show you I can put six things on my chest of drawers.'

'Good gracious! Don't shout at me,' said Nora. 'All right – you can have them back.'

Nora unlocked the box, took out all Elizabeth's things and gave them to her.

'You're an awful goose, you know,' she said, half scolding, half kindly. She had been pleased to see that Elizabeth had really tried to make friends with someone at last.

Elizabeth proudly put her photographs on her chest and showed them to Joan. The bell went for tea and they had to go downstairs before Elizabeth had finished saying all she wanted to. As they passed the hall letter rack, Elizabeth glanced up to see if there were any letters for her.

'Goody! A letter from Mother and one from Daddy too – and this looks like one from Granny!' said Elizabeth. She took them down. Joan had no letters at all.

'Hallo, Joan! Still glooming over the letter rack as usual!' called Helen's voice. 'I'm sure I don't know what you'd do if ever you *did* find a letter there one day! Jump through the roof, I should think!'

Joan went red and turned away. Elizabeth saw that she was hurt, and she jumped round on Helen.

'I suppose you think you're funny!' she shouted. 'Well, perhaps you'd like to know that Joan had four letters and a card this morning, and she *didn't* jump through the roof. She's not quite such a cuckoo as you are!'

Helen was so astonished to hear Elizabeth sticking up for anyone that she couldn't say a word. Elizabeth made a rude face at her, tucked her arm through Joan's and walked off with her.

Joan turned to Elizabeth. 'What an awful story you told!' she said. 'I didn't have any letters today and you know I didn't.'

'Yes, I know,' said Elizabeth. 'It *was* a story, but I really couldn't help it, Joan. You looked like a timid mouse that's been clawed at by a cat, and I felt like a dog that wanted to bark something horrid at the cat!'

Joan threw back her head and laughed. 'You do say the funniest things, Elizabeth!' she said. 'I never know what you will say or do next.'

Nobody ever did know what Elizabeth would take into her head to do or say. The days were slipping by now, and another week had almost gone. Elizabeth enjoyed her work, for she had a good brain and things came easily to her. She enjoyed the riding lessons, the gym, the painting, the walks, the concerts and, above all, her music lessons. She liked cricket, and she was getting quite good at tennis.

She had to keep reminding herself that she mustn't enjoy these things. She must really be naughty, or she wouldn't be sent home in disgrace. So every now and again she was very naughty indeed.

One morning she did every single thing wrong in her class. She wrote badly and spelt every word wrong. She got all her sums quite wrong. She spilt ink over her neat geography map. She whistled and hummed till she drove Miss Ranger quite mad.

Miss Ranger had been told to be patient with naughty Elizabeth, and she tried to be. But even the children became angry with her, although at first they giggled and laughed and thought she was funny.

'I shall report you at the Meeting tomorrow,' said a boy at last. He was a monitor, and had the right to report anyone. 'I'm sick of you. You disturb everyone.'

'And *I* shall report you too!' said Nora that afternoon. 'Three times you've not gone to bed at the right time this week. Last night you even came up later than I did! And look at this – you've spilt ink over your blue bedside rug. That will have to be cleaned.'

'Well, *I'm* not going to clean it,' said Elizabeth rudely. 'I'll make it a bit worse, just for fun!' And the naughty little girl tipped up some more ink over another part of the rug.

Nora stared at her in disgust.

'You're too silly for words,' she said. 'Well, you'll be sorry at the Meeting tomorrow!'

'Pooh! That's all *you* know!' said Elizabeth.

CHAPTER ELEVEN

THE MEETING PUNISHES ELIZABETH

THE MEETING the next day was at the same time as before. All the children went, and once again the two Judges, Rita and William, sat at the big table, and the twelve monitors, the Jury, sat at the smaller table.

Other teachers were there too, this time, besides Miss Belle and Miss Best. They sometimes came to hear what was being done at the Meeting, although they never interfered.

Rita hammered on the table for quiet. Elizabeth sat, looking sulky. She knew quite well that she would be scolded and punished, and she kept telling herself that she didn't care. But one week at Whyteleafe School had made her see that it really was a splendid school and she couldn't help feeling rather ashamed of her behaviour.

Well, it can't be helped. They won't send me home unless I behave badly, she kept saying to herself.

'Has anyone any more money to put into the box?' asked William. He looked at a sheet of paper. 'Jill Kenton and Harry Wills have received money this week and have already put it in. Has anyone else any?'

Nobody had. 'Nora, give out the two shillings to everyone, please,' ordered William.

Nora began to give out the money. She even gave it to Elizabeth, who was most surprised. She had quite thought that, owing to her behaviour, she would get no money at all. She made up her mind to buy some peppermints and some toffee and share them with Joan. She whispered this to her friend, who was sitting beside her.

'Thank you,' whispered back Joan. 'I shall want most of my money to buy stamps this week, so I would love to share your sweets!'

'Does anyone want extra money?' asked William. George got up and spoke.

'We need a new cricket ball for a practice game,' he said. 'We lost ours in the shrubbery.'

'You must look for it again before you get the money,' said William. 'Come to me tomorrow.'

George sat down. Queenie got up. 'Could I have some money to buy a birthday present for somebody?' she asked. 'It's my old nurse's birthday this week, and

I'd like to send her something. Half a crown will do nicely.'

Half a crown was given to Queenie.

'I'd like a new garden spade,' said John Terry, standing up. 'I'm afraid it will cost rather a lot, though.'

Mr Warlow, the games master, got up and spoke for John.

'I should just like to say that in my opinion John deserves a new spade,' he said. 'He is the best gardener in the school, and I believe the peas we had for dinner today were due to his hard work.'

John's spade was passed at once. 'Give him the money,' said William. 'How much is it, John?'

'I'm afraid it is twelve shillings and sixpence,' said John. 'I've asked at three shops and the price is the same in each.'

Twelve shillings and sixpence was handed out. John sat down, blushing with pleasure.

Other things were asked for. Some were granted and some were refused. Then came the complaints and grumbles.

'Any reports or complaints?' asked Rita, knocking on the table for silence.

'I want to report Harry Dunn for cheating,' said a monitor firmly.

There was a buzz at once. Everyone knew Harry

Dunn, a sly-faced boy in the class above Elizabeth's. He sat on his form, looking red.

'Cheating is awful!' said William, shocked. 'We haven't had a proper case of that here for three terms.'

'Don't give him any money to spend for the rest of the term!' called someone.

'No. That's a silly punishment for cheating,' said William at once. 'It wouldn't stop him and would only make him angry.'

There was a loud discussion about Harry. Rita banged on the table with her hammer.

'Quiet!' she said. 'I want to ask Harry something. Harry, what lesson do you cheat in?'

'Arithmetic,' said Harry sulkily.

'Why?' asked William.

'Well, I missed five weeks last term, and I got behind in my arithmetic,' said Harry. 'My father doesn't like me to be bad at arithmetic, and I knew I'd be almost bottom if I didn't cheat. So I thought I'd better cheat, and copy Humphrey's sums. That's all.'

'Yes, he did miss five weeks last term,' said a monitor. 'He had mumps, I remember.'

'And his father does get wild if he isn't near the top in arithmetic,' said another monitor.

'Well, it seems to me that we'd better ask Mr Johns if he'd be good enough to give Harry extra help in arithmetic this term, so that he can catch up what he missed,' said William. 'Then he won't need to cheat. Mr Johns, I can see you at the back this evening – do you think it would help Harry if you gave him extra time?'

'Rather!' said Mr Johns. 'I've already suggested it to Harry – and now that this has happened I think he'll be glad of extra help in arithmetic, won't you, Harry?'

'Yes, thank you, sir,' said Harry.

But William hadn't finished with Harry.

'We can't let you sit with the others in your class until we know you won't cheat again,' he said. 'You had better put your desk apart from the others until you have caught up with the arithmetic you've missed – and then you can go back, if you will come and tell me that you won't cheat again.'

'All right, William,' said Harry. He hated the idea of being set apart because he was a cheat and he made up his mind he would soon know as much as anyone else – and then he'd beat them with his own brains, and never cheat again.

'Cheating is only done by stupid or lazy people,' said William. 'Now – any more complaints?'

Then it was Elizabeth's turn to go red and look sulky! Up got Nora at once.

'I have a serious complaint to make,' she said. 'It is about Elizabeth Allen again. I am the monitor in her bedroom, and I can't make her go to bed at the right time. Not only that – she is awfully rude and horrid. I don't think she cares how she behaves at all.'

'Anything else?' asked Rita, staring in disgust at Elizabeth.

'Yes, she has poured ink twice over her bedside rug, and refused to clean it,' said Nora.

'Well, we will send it to the cleaner's and Elizabeth can pay for it,' said Rita. 'It costs two shillings to get those rugs cleaned – so I am afraid you will have to give up your two shillings, Elizabeth.'

Elizabeth really didn't like to be rude to Rita. So she meekly took out her two shillings and passed them back to Nora, who put them into the moneybox.

'About the going late to bed,' said William, 'that's easily dealt with. In future Elizabeth's bedtime will be altered, and she will go at half past seven, instead of eight.'

'But I shall miss the concerts and the dancing,' said Elizabeth in dismay.

'That's your own fault,' said Rita sternly. 'If you are sensible, we will alter your bedtime next week – but *only* if you are sensible.'

'And now about the rudeness and horridness,' said William. 'I'm not sure we can blame Elizabeth for that. You know, we've usually found that rude children are caused by silly parents, who spoil them and let them say and do what they like. I should think Elizabeth's *parents* are to blame for her present rude behaviour. They haven't taught her good manners.'

Elizabeth leapt up at once, her face full of anger. 'Mummy and Daddy *have* taught me good manners!' she said. 'They've beautiful manners themselves, and Mummy is never rude to anyone.'

'Well, we shall only believe that when we see that you are following their example!' said William. 'Whenever you are rude this week we shall each say to ourselves, "Poor Elizabeth! She can't help it! She wasn't brought up properly!"'

'I'll show you I've got good manners!' shouted Elizabeth. 'I'll just show you, you horrid boy!'

Everyone began to laugh at the angry little girl. William banged on the table with his hammer. 'Silence! Elizabeth wants to show us that she has good manners. Go on, Elizabeth, shout a little more and call us names. Then we shall see exactly what your good manners are.'

Elizabeth sat down, boiling. So they thought her mother and father didn't know how to bring children up with good manners, did they? Well, nobody would be more polite than she would be next week! They would have to say they were wrong!

Kenneth, the monitor in Elizabeth's class, got up

next. 'Please, William and Rita,' he said, '*could* you do something about Elizabeth's behaviour in class? It is simply impossible. She spoils all our lessons, and we are getting very tired of it. I guess Miss Ranger is too.'

'This is really dreadful,' said Rita. 'I had no idea Elizabeth was so bad. I am very disappointed. Has *nobody* a good word to say for her?'

No one spoke. No one said a word. And then everyone got a surprise, for up got Joan Townsend, the Mouse! She was blushing red, for she hated to speak in public.

'I – I – I should like to speak for Elizabeth,' she said. 'She can be very kind. She isn't really as horrid as she pretends to be.'

Joan sat down with a bump, as red as fire. Elizabeth looked at her gratefully. It was good to have a friend!

'Well, it's something to hear *that*!' said William. 'But it isn't enough. What are Elizabeth's favourite lessons?'

'Music, painting and riding!' shouted Elizabeth's class.

'Well, Elizabeth, until you can behave in the lessons you don't *seem* to like, you must miss those you *do* like,' said William, after consulting with Rita for a while. 'You will miss riding, music and painting this week, and you will not go down to the village at all. We hope there will be better reports next week, so that we can give you back the things you love. We simply can't let you spoil lessons for the rest of your class.'

Elizabeth could not stand the Meeting for one moment more. She stood up, pushed a chair aside and rushed out. 'Let her go,' she heard Rita say in a sorry sort of voice. 'She's being awfully silly, but she's really not as bad as she makes out!'

Poor Elizabeth! No money to spend and an early bedtime – no concerts, no dancing, no riding, painting or music! Thc little girl sat on her bed and wept. She knew it was all her own fault, but it didn't make things any better. Oh, when, when would she be able to leave this horrid school?

CHAPTER TWELVE

ELIZABETH HAS A BAD TIME

JOAN WENT to find Elizabeth as soon as the Meeting was over. She guessed she would be in their bedroom. Elizabeth dried her eyes as soon as she heard Joan coming. She wasn't going to let anyone see her crying!

'Hallo!' said Joan. 'Come down to the playroom. It's raining or we could go and have a game of tennis.'

'Joan, it was decent of you to speak up for me,' said Elizabeth. 'Thanks awfully. But don't do it again, because, you see, I want *everyone* to think I'm too bad for this school, so that I'll be sent home.'

'Oh, Elizabeth, do get that silly idea out of your head!' said Joan. 'I'm quite sure that the school won't send you home, and you'll only go on getting yourself into more and more trouble. Do be sensible.'

'Do you really think they won't send me home, *however* badly I behave?' said Elizabeth in dismay. 'But surely no school would want to keep a really bad child?'

'Whyteleafe School has never expelled anyone yet,' said Joan. 'So I don't expect they'll start on *you*. You'll just have a perfectly horrid time, instead of having a lovely one. You'd have much more chance of going home if you went to Rita and said you'd be good if only she would do her best to get you home because you were so unhappy here.'

'Really?' said Elizabeth, astonished. 'Well, I didn't think of that. Perhaps I'll go to Rita. I'll see. I am really getting a bit tired of remembering to be bad. There are so many nice things to do here that I can't help enjoying myself sometimes.'

'I think you're a silly goose,' said Joan. 'Come on down. It will soon be seven o'clock, and you know you've got to go to bed directly after supper for a whole week, instead of at eight o'clock.'

Elizabeth frowned. 'I've a good mind to go at eight o'clock, just to spite them!' she said.

'Oh, don't be foolish,' said Joan. 'Do you suppose the Meeting cares if you go to bed at seven or eight? You'll only be hurting yourself, not anyone else, if you're silly.'

'Oh,' said Elizabeth, seeing for the first time that she was spoiling things for herself far more than she was spoiling them for other people. She sat and thought for a minute.

'Listen, Joan,' she said, 'I'll do as I'm told this week. See? I'll obey the orders of the Meeting, and go to bed early, and miss all the things I love – and at the end I'll go to Rita and tell her I'm so unhappy that I simply *must* go home, and I'll see what she says. I'm sure she could tell Miss Belle and Miss Best and they could write to Mummy for me.'

'Well, you do that,' said Joan, getting a bit tired of Elizabeth's curious ideas. 'Now do come on – bother, there's the supper bell, and we've wasted all this time!'

They had supper – and then poor Elizabeth had to go straight upstairs to bed. Nora popped in to see that she had obeyed the orders of the Meeting and felt quite surprised to see Elizabeth under the sheets.

'Good gracious!' she said. 'You are learning to be sensible at last! Now just you listen to me, Elizabeth – the Meeting hates punishing anyone as much as they have punished you this week so be good and sensible and obedient, and you'll find that everything will be all right at the next Meeting. By the way, I'll take up your bedside rug – the cleaner comes tomorrow, and I'll see that it's put ready for him to take.'

'Thank you, Nora,' said Elizabeth in a very good voice.

The week that followed was not a pleasant one for

Elizabeth. She had to see the others go out riding without her. She had to sit indoors and copy out sums instead of going out sketching with the painting class. Worst of all she had to tell Mr Lewis that she couldn't have her music lessons that week.

Mr Lewis was disappointed. 'Well, aren't you a little silly?' he said, patting her on the shoulder. 'What a pity! And we were going to do something rather exciting this week too – I've got Richard Watson to learn a duet, and I thought you and he could play it together. Duets are fun.'

'Oh dear,' said Elizabeth in dismay. 'I've never played a duet, and I've always thought it would be fun. Could you wait till next week, do you think, Mr Lewis? I might get all my punishments taken off by that time.'

'I should hope you *would*!' said the music master. 'Now, Elizabeth, although you are going to miss your lessons with me this week, there is no need for you to miss your practice. Take this duet and try to learn your part by yourself – and next week I'll have Richard alone too, and we'll all have a go at it. Practise your other pieces too, and don't forget your scales.'

'I won't forget,' promised Elizabeth, and she ran off. Richard Watson was a big boy, and Elizabeth couldn't help feeling rather proud to think that Mr Lewis had chosen her to play a duet with him. She knew that Richard Watson played the piano and the violin beautifully.

Elizabeth turned over a new leaf that week. Nobody could have worked harder in class than she did. She only got one sum wrong the whole of the week. She didn't get a single mistake in dictation. Even the French mistress, Mam'zelle, was pleased with her because she learnt a French song so quickly.

'Ah, but you are a clever little girl!' she said to Elizabeth. 'Will you not help this poor little Joan to learn her piece? Always she makes mistakes, and is at the bottom of my class.'

'Yes, I'll help Joan,' said Elizabeth eagerly. 'I can easily teach her the song.'

'You have a good heart,' said Mam'zelle. Elizabeth went red with pleasure. The other children stared at her. They couldn't understand this strange girl who was so bad and horrid one week, and so good and helpful the next!

Elizabeth helped Joan to learn the song. She and Joan went off to a corner of the garden and Elizabeth sang each line of the song in her clear voice, and made Joan sing it after her. It wasn't long before Joan knew it perfectly.

'You are very decent to me, Elizabeth,' said Joan gratefully. 'I wish I was going to have a birthday cake on my birthday – I'd give you the biggest piece of all!'

'When is your birthday?' asked Elizabeth.

'It's in two weeks' time,' said Joan. 'And I do hate it so, because I know I shan't get a single card, and my parents are certain not to remember it. Everyone else seems to have a big cake, and presents and cards.'

'I think it's a shame,' said Elizabeth warmly. '*I* shall give you a present anyhow – that is if only the Meeting will give me my two shillings! I shan't pour ink on my rug again anyway – that was an awful waste of two shillings. I could have bought toffees with that. I haven't had a sweet for ages!'

'I'll buy some this afternoon and share them with you,' said Joan. 'I want most of my money for stamps, but I shall have a few pence over for sweets. It's a pity you can't go down to the village with me and choose the sweets. It would be fun to go together.'

'It would,' agreed Elizabeth. 'But I'm not going down till I'm allowed to. For one thing I promised Rita I wouldn't go alone – and for another thing I'm jolly well not going to have the Meeting taking away my good times any more!'

They went indoors. On the way they met three of the boys, going out to practise bowling.

'Hallo, Bold Bad Girl!' said one of them. Elizabeth

went red, and tried to rush at them. But Joan held her arm firmly.

'Don't take any notice,' she said. 'They only want to see you get angry – and, after all, you do deserve the name, you know!'

The boys went off to the cricket field, grinning. Elizabeth felt very angry. She still had not got used to the good-natured teasing that went on all around her. She wished she could tease back, or laugh, as the other children did.

Miss Ranger was delighted with Elizabeth that week. The little girl really had a fine brain, and was fond of a joke. She could say clever things that made Miss Ranger and the class laugh heartily. She had only to look at a page once or twice and she knew it by heart! She liked her work and did everything well.

'Elizabeth, you are a lucky little girl,' said Miss Ranger. 'Lessons come easily to you, and you should be able to do something fine in the world when you grow up. Whyteleafe School and your parents will be proud of you one day.'

'Whyteleafe School won't,' said Elizabeth firmly. 'I shan't be here long enough. Half a term is as long as I shall stay, and I may go home before that.'

'Well, we'll see,' said Miss Ranger. 'Anyway, it is a pleasant change to see the other side of you this week, and not the unpleasant rudeness of last week.'

Elizabeth practised hard at the piano all the week. She wanted to show Mr Lewis that she could play that duet with Richard! Over and over she played the pages of the music, trying to get the right time, and to play softly and loudly at the proper moments.

One morning she got a letter from her mother enclosing some stamps. 'Now that you have to buy your own stamps I thought perhaps it would help you if I sent you some,' wrote her mother. 'Then you can spend all your money on the things you like.'

Elizabeth counted the stamps. There were twelve penny ones and twelve ha'penny ones. She divided them in half and went to find Joan.

'Joan! Here are some stamps for you! Now you needn't spend all your money on them,' said Elizabeth.

'Oh, thanks,' said Joan, delighted. 'What a bit of luck! Your mother must be a darling to think of things like that. I'll go straight down and buy some toffee.'

She did – and the two girls sucked it happily after tea that day, as they wandered round the school garden. They came across John Terry busy gardening with his new spade. He showed it to the girls, and they admired it. Elizabeth told John about the garden she had at home.

'You sound as if you know a lot about gardening,' said John. 'Not many girls do. I suppose you wouldn't like to come and help me sometime, would you, Elizabeth? There's a lot to do, and in the summertime not many people come and help.'

'I'd love to,' said Elizabeth proudly. Fancy clever John Terry asking her to help him! 'I'll come whenever I can.'

'You do look happy, Elizabeth,' said Joan, staring at her friend's bright eyes. 'I don't believe you want to leave Whyteleafe at all.'

'Well, I do then,' said Elizabeth, quite fiercely. 'I don't change my mind as quickly as all that! You'll soon see. I'll ask Rita to get me sent back home before half-term!'

CHAPTER THIRTEEN

THE THIRD MEETING

THE THIRD Meeting came. Everyone went to the gym as before, and took their places. Some of the teachers sat at the back as usual. Rita and William came in last of all and the children rose and stood until their two Judges sat down.

Joan was sitting next to Elizabeth. She was hoping very much that Elizabeth would not say anything silly, and so spoil her week's good work and behaviour. Elizabeth wished the Meeting was over. She was not used to having her behaviour discussed and dealt with, and she didn't like it at all. But she knew that everyone was treated the same, and she saw that it was quite fair.

Money was put into the box. One girl, Eileen, had had a whole pound sent to her by her grandmother, and she put it into the box very proudly. She was glad to feel that she could add so much to the spending money of the school.

The two shillings were given out to everyone. Elizabeth took hers gladly – now she would be able to buy some sweets for Joan.

'Does anyone want anything extra this week?' asked William, rattling the moneybox.

Eileen wanted a shilling to get her watch mended, and it was granted at once. Nobody else said anything.

'Nothing else?' asked Rita, looking round.

Elizabeth suddenly found herself standing up. 'I don't expect you will let me have it,' she said, 'but I would very much like something – it isn't only for myself, but it would be nice for everyone else too.'

'What is it you want?' asked Rita.

'Well, there's a lovely sea piece that Mr Lewis plays,' said Elizabeth eagerly. 'He says there is a beautiful recording of it, and I *would* so much like it. I'm sure everybody would love it too. I know I could buy it with my two shillings, but I owe Joan Townsend a lot of sweets, and I'd like to buy her some this week.'

William and Rita looked at the twelve monitors below them at the small table. 'What do you think about it?' Rita asked them. 'You might discuss it for a moment.'

The Jury discussed it for a few minutes. Then Nora stood up.

'We think the money might be granted to Elizabeth,' said Nora. 'We have heard her practising like anything every morning this week before breakfast, and we think she deserves a reward.'

'An extra two shillings is granted then,' said William. 'Give the money to Elizabeth, Nora.'

Elizabeth was given another two shillings. She was really delighted. She thought the monitors were very decent to have granted her wish. She forgot that she had hated them all last week!

The Meeting passed on to complaints and reports. One boy, Peter, was reported for scribbling over one of the cloakroom walls.

'A disgusting habit!' said William severely. 'You will spend your next two playtimes cleaning off the scribble with soap and hot water, and then you will buy some yellow distemper from the school stores out of your two shillings, and repaint that bit of wall yourself. I shall come to see it at the end of the week.'

Peter sat down, very red. Never again in his life would he scribble on walls. He was not angry at his punishment for he knew that it was just – he must remove the mess he had made, and make the wall good.

'We *all* see the walls,' said William, 'and we certainly don't want to see your silly scribbles on them.'

Then there was a report on Harry, who had cheated

the week before. Mr Johns had sent in a written note to William about him. William read it to the Meeting.

'I have to report that Harry is rapidly catching up with the rest of his class in arithmetic,' wrote Mr Johns. 'After another week he will be as good as the rest. As he will then have no reason to cheat, I propose that at the next Meeting Harry is told he may sit with the others again, and not apart.'

'What about letting Harry sit with the rest of his class *this* week?' asked one of the monitors. 'He's had a week of sitting apart, and it's not very nice.'

'No,' said William firmly. 'He cheated before because he didn't know as much as the others – and, if we let him go back too soon, he'll be tempted to cheat again. We don't want it to become a habit. Harry, next week we hope to put you back in your old seat with the others.'

'Yes, William,' said Harry. He made up his mind to work so hard at his arithmetic that he would be top of the class before the end of the term – then the Meeting and Mr Johns would know he had no reason to cheat at all!

'And now for the Bold Bad Girl, Elizabeth Allen,' said William. Everyone laughed. Elizabeth laughed too. It sounded funny, not horrid, when William called her by those names. 'Nora, what report have you to give?'

Nora stood up. 'An excellent report,' she said. 'Elizabeth has obeyed all the orders of last week's Meeting, and as far as I know has obeyed them cheerfully and well.'

'Thank you,' said Rita. Nora sat down. Rita opened a note. It was written by Miss Ranger.

'Here is a report to me from Miss Ranger,' said Rita. 'This is what she says: "It has been a pleasure to have a girl like Elizabeth in my class this week. She has worked well, could easily be top of her class, and has been very helpful to others who cannot work as quickly as she can. She has been as good this week as she was bad last week!"' Rita looked up. She smiled her lovely smile at Elizabeth, and William smiled too.

'This is very good, Elizabeth,' said Rita. 'I too have noticed a great difference in you this week.'

'Have you?' asked Elizabeth, pleased to think that Rita had taken any notice of her. 'Rita, did you notice that my manners were better? Because I'd like you to think that my mother and father *have* taught me good manners and brought me up properly. I don't like people to think they haven't.'

'Well, we take back what we said about your parents being at fault,' said Rita. 'But you really must see, Elizabeth, that if a boy or girl is rude or horrid, it often means that their parents are to blame for not having taught them any better.'

'I do see that,' said Elizabeth. 'Well, you'll see my father and mother at half-term, and then you'll know that they couldn't possibly be nicer.'

'Oh, so you have made up your mind to stay with us then?' asked Rita, with a sudden smile of amusement. She couldn't help liking Elizabeth, for the little girl said such funny things, and was so serious about everything.

'Oh, no, I haven't,' said Elizabeth at once. 'But I see now that you wouldn't let me go home if I behave too badly – you'll only be angry with me and *make* me stay just to show me I can't get my own way. But Rita, if I do try hard to be good, and do everything I ought to, will you please ask Miss Belle and Miss Best to let me go home? They can ask my parents at half-term to take me away. My mother wouldn't want me to stay anywhere where I was unhappy.'

William and Rita looked at Elizabeth in surprise, very puzzled to know what to do with such a strange little girl.

Rita spoke to William, and the Jury discussed things together too. But nobody could decide anything at all. Rita hammered on the table and everyone was quiet.

'Well, Elizabeth,' said Rita, 'we simply don't know what to say to you. We've never been asked such a thing before. We think we'd better ask Miss Belle and Miss Best to help us. Please, Miss Belle and Miss Best, could you advise us what to do best for Elizabeth?'

The two headmistresses came up to the platform, and Rita got them chairs. Mr Johns came too, and sat with them. It was not often that the masters and mistresses came on to the platform at the weekly Meetings, and it seemed to make things much more important and serious.

'Well, first,' said Miss Belle, 'I think we should all discuss this thing together – and as it is not very pleasant to discuss a person when she is present, and Elizabeth may find it a little awkward to hear us, I suggest that she shall be given the chance to leave the room until we have finished. What do you think about it, Elizabeth?'

'I'd rather go out of the gym and wait till you say what's decided,' said Elizabeth. 'But please, Miss Belle, I shall be awfully naughty again if . . .'

'Don't say anything more, Elizabeth, my dear,' said Miss Best hurriedly. She didn't want the children to feel annoyed with Elizabeth. She knew it was very difficult to be fair if people were feeling angry.

Elizabeth went out of the gym. She went to a music room nearby and began to practise her part of the duet. She hoped that she would be able to have her music lessons the next week, then she could play the piano with Richard.

The Meeting began to discuss Elizabeth and what to do with her. Everyone had a say, and everyone was listened to.

'We don't want her, she's a nuisance,' said one girl. 'Why not let her go?'

'We *do* want her,' said Miss Belle. 'I think we can help her a great deal.'

'She's been spoilt,' said William. 'It's always difficult for spoilt children to fit in anywhere. They think the world's made for them and them alone.'

'But you can't think how *kind* Elizabeth is really,' said Joan eagerly. 'I'm her only friend, and I know more about her than anyone. She really has a good heart. Mam'zelle said she had too.'

'That is quite true,' came Mam'zelle's voice from the back of the gym. 'This little Elizabeth is a good child at heart, and a clever one. But she is *so-o-o-o-o* obstinate.'

Everyone laughed at Mam'zelle's long '*so-o-o-o-o*'.

'It's so silly to think that Elizabeth *can* be simply splendid, but means to be awful if we don't give her what she wants,' said William. 'Fancy *wanting* to leave Whyteleafe School! I've never, never known anyone want to do *that* before.'

The discussion went on. Nobody could imagine how

Elizabeth could want to leave such a fine school as Whyteleafe, where the children were so happy, and where they ruled themselves. Miss Belle, Miss Best and Mr Johns smiled at one another when they heard the excited children blaming Elizabeth for wanting to leave Whyteleafe.

'I think I can see the answer to your problem,' said Miss Belle, at last. 'Shall we say this to Elizabeth – that she may certainly leave us after half-term if she is really unhappy, and can say so honestly to the Meeting? She does not need to be rude or naughty or disobedient any more, but may be good, hard-working and enjoy herself all she likes – because we are *quite* willing to let her go, if she really wants to, in a few weeks' time!'

'Oh, I see,' said Rita, her eyes shining. 'You mean that Elizabeth can't possibly come and say she is unhappy, after enjoying herself at Whyteleafe till half-term! So she won't want to go after all – but we're offering her what she wants, so she needn't be bad any more?'

'That's right,' said Miss Belle. 'If Whyteleafe School is all you say it is, and I am very proud to hear it, then I think we can safely say that you children and the school will be able to keep Elizabeth here of her own free will. *We* shall see Elizabeth at her best – and we can all help her to be good and happy.'

Everyone stamped their feet and agreed. It seemed

comical to them – they were going to tell Elizabeth she could leave when she wanted to, but when the time came they were sure she wouldn't want to! What a good idea! They all made up their minds to be as nice as possible to Elizabeth so that she simply *couldn't* say she was unhappy when half-term came!

'Call Elizabeth in,' said Miss Best. 'We'll tell her.'

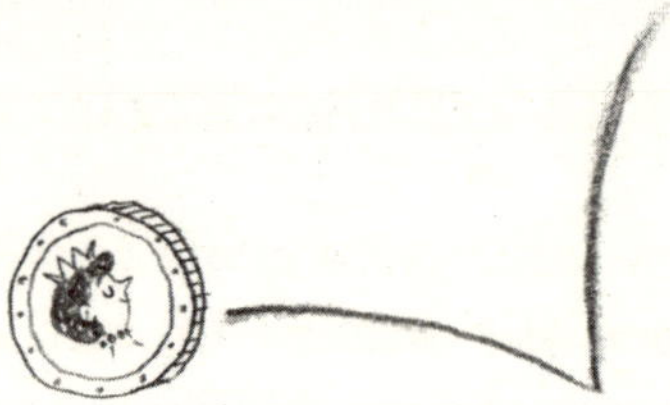

CHAPTER FOURTEEN
A LOVELY WEEK

ELIZABETH WAS called back to the Meeting by Nora. She stopped playing the piano and went back to her place in the gym.

She wondered what the Judges were going to say. They looked serious, but not angry. Rita knocked on the table.

'Quiet,' she ordered. 'Elizabeth, we have all discussed what you want us to do. And we have decided that if you come to us at the Meeting after half-term, and tell us honestly that you are unhappy here, and want to go home, Miss Belle and Miss Best will advise your parents to take you away.'

'Really!' said Elizabeth in delight. 'Oh, thank you, Rita. I *am* pleased. Now I don't need to be horrid and rude any more. I can wait till half-term, but I warn you that at the very first Meeting after that I shall ask to go home. I hate being at school.'

Elizabeth wondered why everyone roared with laughter when she said that. She looked round in surprise. Even Joan was laughing.

'Well, Elizabeth, that's settled then,' said Rita. 'Please be as nice as you know very well how to be until half-term – and then, if you wish, you can certainly go home, if your parents will take you away.'

'I know they will, if I'm unhappy,' said Elizabeth. 'Thank you, Rita. I promise to be really good now.'

'Very well,' said William. 'All your punishments are lifted from now on. Your bedtime will be as before, at eight o'clock. You can take riding and painting and all your favourite lessons.'

'Good!' said Elizabeth, beaming. She felt very pleased with herself. She had got what she wanted! She could go home at half-term!

I'm glad it's not before then, thought the little girl. *I do want to learn that duet with Richard. And I want to give Joan a present for her birthday. And I want to do some more riding – oh, yes, and buy that record too! How everyone will love to hear it when I first put it on*.

Elizabeth was very happy. She beamed round at everyone, not listening to anything else that was said at the Meeting. There was very little else to discuss, anyway, and very soon the gym was empty, and the children ran off to their various tasks or hobbies.

'Well, Elizabeth, I've got you till half-term at least!' said Joan, tucking her arm into Elizabeth's. 'That's something.'

'Well, make the most of me!' said Elizabeth with a laugh. 'For you won't have me afterwards. I jolly well mean to go back home to my pony and my dog. I mean to show my parents that I just *won't* be sent away to school!'

A lovely week began for Elizabeth then. After supper that night there was a little dance, and the boys and girls had great fun. When eight o'clock struck Elizabeth and the others of her age went upstairs to bed, leaving the older ones to go on dancing.

The next day she and Joan went down to the village to buy sweets, and the gramophone record that Elizabeth wanted. The music shop didn't have it, but they said they would send for it to the town over the hill, and get it for Elizabeth. They would send it up to the school for her.

Joan bought some chocolate and a book. Elizabeth bought some toffee, and two packets of lettuce seeds. She hadn't forgotten that she was going to help John Terry with his gardening! Dear me, what a lot of things there were to do!

'You can have the first lettuce that grows from these seeds,' she promised Joan.

'Well, you'll have to stay till the end of the term then,' laughed Joan. 'Lettuces don't grow quite so quickly as you think, Elizabeth.'

'Oh,' said Elizabeth, disappointed. 'Well, *you'll* have to cut the first lettuce then, after I'm gone. Have a toffee?'

It was fun to eat toffees and talk to a friend. It was fun to feel the lettuce seeds rattling in their packets. It was lovely to think of going riding that afternoon and having a music lesson after tea. Perhaps Richard would be there, and they could play their duet.

The riding lesson was glorious. Twelve boys and girls were taken out on the hills by the riding master. Elizabeth had been used to her pony and she rode well, enjoying the jog-jog-jog, and sniffing the fresh early-summer breezes. This was much better fun than cantering along on her old pony at home.

That afternoon the postman brought a parcel for Elizabeth. She undid it – and inside she found a large chocolate cake, sent to her by her granny!

'Oh, I say! Look at this!' cried Elizabeth. 'We can all share it at teatime!'

'My word, Elizabeth, you're rather different from when you first came!' said Nora, staring at the excited girl as she put the cake into her tin in the playroom. 'You wouldn't share a *thing* then!'

Elizabeth blushed. 'Don't remind me of that, Nora,' she begged. 'I'm ashamed of it now. All I hope is that you won't all say no when I offer you some of this cake!'

Well, nobody did say no! Elizabeth counted the number of people at her table – eleven. She cut the cake into twelve pieces. They were very large. Elizabeth offered the plate round and soon there were only two pieces left.

'Thanks, Elizabeth! Thanks, Elizabeth!' said everyone, taking a piece. They were delighted to have it, because by now everyone's tuckbox was empty, and no more goodies had come yet from their homes, for no one had had a birthday.

'Your granny must be jolly generous!' said Nora. 'This is the finest cake I've ever tasted.'

Elizabeth was proud and pleased. She took the plate to Miss Ranger and offered her one of the two pieces that remained on it. Miss Ranger took it and nodded.

'Thank you, Elizabeth,' she said. Then Elizabeth helped herself to the last piece and settled down happily to eat it. This was better than keeping everything to herself! It was lovely to share. She looked round at all the contented faces, and liked to see the girls and boys eating *her* cake.

Miss Scott would be surprised at me, thought Elizabeth

suddenly. *She wouldn't know me! What a horrid girl I must have seemed to her.*

After tea Elizabeth got her music and raced off to Mr Lewis. Richard was there too, a big, serious boy with long, clever fingers. He meant to be a musician when he grew up. He looked at Elizabeth and didn't smile.

I suppose he doesn't think girls can play at all, thought Elizabeth. She was right. Richard was disgusted to find that he was expected to play a duet with a girl – and Elizabeth too, that Bold Bad Girl! What would *she* know of music?

They began. Elizabeth had practised so hard that she knew her part wonderfully well. She took the lower part, the bass, and Richard had the more difficult part, the treble, where the higher notes were.

'I shall count the first few bars,' said Mr Lewis. 'Now *one* two three four, *one* two three four, *one* two three four . . .'

He soon stopped, for the two children found their own time, and the duet went with a swing. Mr Lewis let them play it all the way through and then he smiled.

'Very good,' he said. 'You have a feeling for each other's playing. Now, Richard, wasn't I right when I said I had found someone you need not be afraid of playing with?'

But Richard was as obstinate in his way as Elizabeth

was in hers. He looked at the little girl's flushed face and did not answer. Elizabeth was disappointed.

Mr Lewis laughed. 'Thank you, Richard,' he said. 'You may go, but come back in half an hour's time, and I will give you your lesson then. I am going to give Elizabeth hers now. Can you manage to practise together sometimes?'

'I suppose so,' said Richard ungraciously.

'Well, don't if you don't want to!' said Elizabeth, flaring up. 'I play my part just as well as you play yours. You made two mistakes.'

'And you made three!' said Richard.

'Now this won't do,' said Mr Lewis, patting Richard on the back. 'You can choose which you would rather do, Richard – play the duet with Harry, or with Elizabeth. I can find someone else for her, you know – but she's the best, after you.'

'Well, I'll have Elizabeth,' said Richard. 'Harry plays the piano as if his fingers were a bunch of bananas.'

Elizabeth went off into a peal of laughter. It tickled her to think of a bunch of bananas playing the piano. Richard laughed too.

'I'll practise with Elizabeth, sir,' he said to Mr Lewis. 'She's really jolly good.'

Elizabeth glowed with pride, because Richard was one of the bigger boys. She settled down to her music lesson happily. Mr Lewis made her play over the duet with him, and pointed out places where she went wrong. Elizabeth used to get cross when Miss Scott pointed out her mistakes, but with Mr Lewis it was different. She thought he was very clever indeed, and she could listen all day long to his playing!

'I've ordered that gramophone record, Mr Lewis,' she said. 'The shop is getting it for me.'

'I'll come and hear it when it arrives,' promised Mr Lewis. 'Now let's get on with tackling the sea piece on *our* piano, Elizabeth. You want to learn it, don't you? But it won't be easy. Perhaps you could play it for me at the school concert at the end of the term, if you're good enough.'

'Oh, I'd love to,' said Elizabeth, pleased, and then she stopped and looked disappointed. 'Oh, but I can't. I forgot. I shall be going home at half-term.'

'Really?' said Mr Lewis, who knew all about it. 'Still being the Bold Bad Girl? Dear, dear, what a pity!'

'Isn't there a concert at half-term?' asked Elizabeth, her voice trembling.

'Afraid not,' said Mr Lewis. 'Come along – get on with your scales now. Don't worry about not being able to play that sea piece. I can easily get someone else to learn it for me.'

'Let me learn it anyhow,' said Elizabeth. 'Even if I

can't play it for you at a concert, I can still learn it for myself, because I love it.'

'Good,' said Mr Lewis. 'All right. I'll play it for you now, and you must listen hard.'

So Elizabeth listened and was happy. She was happy all the day, and she couldn't help being surprised at herself.

It is *a nuisance!* thought funny Elizabeth. *I really can't go about being happy like this – whatever shall I say to the Meeting at half-term?*

CHAPTER FIFTEEN

TWO TRICKS – AND A QUARREL

THE WEEK slipped by quickly. Elizabeth practised her pieces, and loved her music lessons. She and Richard practised their duet together, and had such fun that they asked Mr Lewis for an even harder piece.

'I'm glad you chose me to play with you instead of Harry,' said Elizabeth to Richard. 'I do love the way you play, Richard. You are as good as Mr Lewis.'

'No, I'm not,' said Richard. 'But some day I shall be far, far better, Elizabeth. Some day you will come to London to hear me play at a great big concert! And some day you will hear the music *I* make up, played all over the world!'

It didn't seem like boasting when Richard spoke like this. Elizabeth didn't mock at him or laugh at him. She believed him, and although he was sometimes very moody and bad-tempered she grew to like him very much.

I always hated boys before, thought Elizabeth, surprised at herself. *I do seem to be changing. I'd better be careful, or I* will *be different when I leave here, just as Miss Scott said!*

So, to show that she really did still hate boys, she played a trick on Harry. She knew that he would have to go to the music room to fetch some music he had left behind. Elizabeth took a sponge, filled it so full of water that it dripped and then, climbing on a chair, she balanced the wet sponge on the top of the door.

She arranged the sponge so that anyone who opened the door would move the sponge, which would at once drop down on to the surprised person's head!

Then Elizabeth hid in a cupboard in the passage outside, and waited for Harry. He soon came along, rushing to fetch his forgotten music before the bell rang. He pushed open the door – and down fell the sponge on top of his head, squelch, squash!

'Oooh!' said Harry in the greatest astonishment. 'Whatever is it?'

He soon found out! He took the sponge off his neck and threw it down on the floor in a rage. '*Now* I've got to go and change my coat!' he said. 'Who did that?'

Nobody answered, of course. But, as Harry knew quite well that people who set traps for others usually like to hide somewhere near to see what happens, he guessed that the joker was in the passage cupboard!

He stole up to the cupboard, and flung the door open. Inside was Elizabeth, trying her best not to laugh loudly. Her handkerchief was stuffed into her mouth and tears of laughter were trickling down her cheeks.

'Oh, it's *you*, is it?' said Harry, hauling her out. 'It's the Bold Bad Girl! Well, I'll just stuff this wet sponge down your neck, see!'

But he didn't have time to, because the bell rang and he had to run. 'I'll pay you out for that!' he yelled. But Elizabeth only laughed mockingly.

'I hate boys!' she shouted. 'They're silly! Ha ha! I tricked you properly, Harry!'

But Harry soon paid Elizabeth back for her trick. He waited until the painting class, and then, when Elizabeth was quite lost in her work, bending over her painting, he stole up behind her. In his hand was a large sheet of paper.

He neatly pinned it to Elizabeth's back. The little girl felt something and shook herself – but the paper was safely on, and she didn't know it. She went on with her painting.

Harry went back to his place, giggling. The class was nearly over, and if Miss Chester, the art mistress, did not notice what he had done, there was a good chance of Elizabeth going about with the paper on her back.

Everyone saw the paper and giggled. On it was printed in big letters: I'M THE BOLD BAD GIRL! BEWARE! I BARK! I BITE! I HATE EVERYBODY!

Joan was not in that painting class or she would have told Elizabeth what Harry had done. All the others thought it was very funny, especially as Elizabeth was known as the Bold Bad Girl.

The bell rang. Everyone cleared up their things. Miss Chester began to prepare for the next class, and did not notice Elizabeth's paper. The children went out of the art room and off to their own classrooms.

Once in her classroom all the others there saw the paper; they nudged one another and giggled. Joan was holding the door for Miss Ranger to come in, and did not see what everyone was laughing at. Soon Elizabeth noticed that the class was giggling at her, and she grew red.

'What are you all laughing at?' she demanded angrily. 'Is my hair untidy? Have I a smudge on my nose?'

'No, Elizabeth,' answered everyone in a chorus.

Then Miss Ranger came in, and the class settled down to work. They worked hard until break, when the school had fifteen minutes play out-of-doors, and could have biscuits and milk if they wished.

Harry looked to see if the paper was still on Elizabeth's back. It was! He ran round to all his friends, pointing it out. All the boys kept behind Elizabeth, reading the paper and giggling.

'She's the Bold Bad Girl,' they whispered. 'Look at the notice!'

Every time that poor Elizabeth turned round she found somebody behind her, giggling. She grew so furious that she called out she would slap anyone who giggled behind her again.

Joan came out at that moment, and Elizabeth called to her. 'Joan! What's the matter with everyone today? They keep going behind my back and giggling. I hate it!'

Joan knew more of the ways of children than Elizabeth did. She guessed at once that someone had pinned a notice to Elizabeth's back.

'Turn round,' she said. Elizabeth turned round, and Joan saw the notice: I'M THE BOLD BAD GIRL! BEWARE! I BARK! I BITE! I HATE EVERYBODY!

Joan couldn't help giggling herself. 'Oh, Elizabeth!' she said. 'Do look what you've been going around with all morning! It's too funny! No wonder everyone laughed.'

She unpinned the paper and showed it to Elizabeth. The little girl, who was not used to being teased, went red with rage. She tore the paper in half and faced the laughing children.

'Who pinned that on me?' she asked.

'I didn't, Bold Bad Girl!' shouted someone.

Everybody laughed. Elizabeth stamped her foot.

'Look out!' cried John. 'She barks! She bites! She'll show her teeth next!'

'I suppose the person who pinned that on me doesn't *dare* to own up!' shouted Elizabeth.

'Oh, yes, I dare!' grinned Harry nearby. 'I pinned it on you, my dear girl – in return for the wet sponge!'

'*Don't* call me your dear girl!' cried Elizabeth in a rage. 'You're a hateful boy, and a cheat, cheat, cheat! How *dare* you pin a notice on me like that! Take that!'

The furious little girl slapped Harry in the face. The boy stepped back in surprise.

'Stop that,' commanded Nora, coming up at that minute. 'Elizabeth! That sort of behaviour won't do. Apologise to Harry. He's too much of a gentleman to slap you back, as you deserve.'

'I won't apologise,' cried Elizabeth. 'Nora, I want you to report Harry at the next Meeting – and if you don't I *shall*!'

'Come with me,' said Nora to Elizabeth. She saw that Elizabeth was really upset, and needed to be quietened. 'You can tell me about it in the playroom. There's nobody there.'

Holding the torn bits of paper in her hand Elizabeth followed Nora, trembling with anger. Nora made her sit down and tell her what had happened.

Elizabeth pieced the bits of paper together and Nora read what Harry had written. She stopped herself smiling, but she really thought it was very funny.

'And why did Harry play this trick on you?' asked Nora.

'Just because I played a trick on him!' said Elizabeth. 'I put a wet sponge on the music-room door and it fell down on his head!'

'And why shouldn't Harry play a trick on you then, if you play tricks on him?' asked Nora. 'You know, you wet his coat, and he was late for his class because he had to change it. If you weren't quite so silly, Elizabeth, you would see that the joke he played on you was quite as funny as the one you played on him. After all, you *know* that we call you the Bold Bad Girl!'

'You're not to,' said Elizabeth.

'Well, we certainly shall if you go on behaving so fiercely,' said Nora.

'Will you report Harry at the Meeting?' said Elizabeth.

'Certainly not,' said Nora. 'We don't report jokes!'

'Then *I* shall report him!' said Elizabeth.

'Elizabeth, that would be telling tales, not reporting,' said Nora firmly. 'You mustn't do that. Don't spoil this good week of yours by being silly. And, you know, I really *should* report *you*!'

'Why?' asked Elizabeth defiantly.

'Because I heard you call Harry a cheat, and you slapped him,' said Nora. 'It is very mean to call him a cheat when you know he isn't now. We try to help one another at Whyteleafe, and it was hateful of you to remind Harry and everyone else of something he's ashamed of.'

Elizabeth went red. 'Yes,' she said. 'That *was* hateful of me. I wish I hadn't. And I wish I hadn't slapped Harry now. I knew he wouldn't slap me back. Oh, Nora, I really have tried to behave decently, and now I've spoilt it all!'

'No, you haven't,' said Nora, getting up, pleased that Elizabeth's temper had gone. 'Little things like this can always be put right. Harry is a good-tempered boy. Go and say you're sorry and he won't think any more about it.'

'I don't like saying I'm sorry,' said Elizabeth.

'Nobody does,' said Nora. 'But it's a little thing that makes a big difference. Go and try it, and see if I'm not right!'

CHAPTER SIXTEEN

AN APOLOGY – AND ANOTHER MEETING

ELIZABETH WENT to find Harry. She noticed that everyone turned away as she came, and she was sad.

They were all so friendly to me, she thought. *And now I've been silly again, and they don't like me any more. I do wish I didn't lose my temper.*

She didn't want to say she was sorry. She felt sure Harry would say something horrid, or would laugh at her. All the same, Elizabeth was truly sorry that she had called Harry a cheat. It was most unfair when the boy was doing his best to make up for his cheating. And Elizabeth was just a little girl, although she did such funny things when she was in a rage.

Harry was playing with about eight other boys and girls in a corner of the garden. Elizabeth stopped and looked at them. They turned their backs on her. It was horrid.

'Harry!' she called.

'I don't want to speak to you,' said Harry.

'But Harry, I want to say something to you in private,' said Elizabeth, almost in tears.

'Say it in public then, in front of everyone,' said Harry. 'It can't be anything important.'

'All right then,' said Elizabeth, going up to the group of children. 'I've come to say I'm sorry for calling you a cheat, when I know you're not now – and – and I'm sorry for slapping you, Harry. Nora has explained things to me, and I feel different now.'

The children stared at her. They all knew how hard it was to apologise, especially in front of others, and they admired the little girl.

Harry went up to her. 'That's decent of you,' he said warmly. 'You've got an awful temper, Elizabeth, but you're a good sort all the same.'

Everybody smiled. Everybody was friendly again. What a difference a little apology made! Elizabeth could hardly believe it. She suddenly felt that everything was perfectly all right, and she wanted to skip for joy.

'Come and see my rabbits,' said Harry, slipping his arm through Elizabeth's. 'I've got two, called Bubble and Squeak, and they've got three babies. Would you like one?'

Elizabeth had always longed for a rabbit. She stared

at Harry in delight. 'Oh, *yes*!' she said. 'Let me buy one from you.'

'No, I'll *give* you one,' said Harry, who was a very generous boy, and was eager to make Elizabeth forget all about the quarrel. 'I've got a little old hutch you can have for it. It will be ready to leave its mother about half-term.'

'Oh!' said Elizabeth, disappointed. 'I shan't be here after that. I shall be going home, you know. I can't have the rabbit!'

The bell rang for school again, so she couldn't see the baby rabbit. She didn't want to now either, because she wouldn't be able to have it. What a pity she couldn't have it now, and give it back to Harry at half-term!

She asked Harry and Richard to come and listen to the new gramophone record that evening. It had come, and was, as Mr Lewis said, very lovely. The three children sat and listened to it. They played it five times. They were all fond of music, and Harry played quite well although his fingers were, as Richard had said, rather like a bunch of bananas! But he couldn't help that!

'You know, Elizabeth, we have a marvellous concert at the end of the term,' said Harry, putting the record on for the sixth time, and letting the sea piece flood the room again. 'It's a pity you won't be here for it. You could have played at it, and your parents would have been jolly proud of you.'

Elizabeth had a quick picture in her mind of herself playing the lovely grand piano at the concert, and her mother and father sitting proudly to listen to her. For the first time she really wished she was staying on at Whyteleafe School.

'But it's no good,' she said to herself quickly. 'I've made up my mind, and that's that! I shan't stay a minute longer than half-term.'

After supper that night Mr Lewis gave one of his little concerts. About nine children were in the music room listening, all music-lovers. Mr Lewis had asked Elizabeth to bring her new record for them all to hear, and the little girl proudly put it on Mr Lewis's fine gramophone.

It was such fun to sit around, listening. When two of the children thanked Elizabeth for getting two shillings to buy such a fine record, Elizabeth nearly burst with pride and pleasure.

It really is fun to share things, she thought. *I simply loved all the others listening to* my *record. How could I ever have thought it was horrid to share things? I didn't know much!*

Joan was not such a music-lover as Elizabeth was, but she came to the concerts to be with Elizabeth.

Joan was much happier now that she had a friend – though, as she said, it was rather like being friends with a thunderstorm! You never quite knew what Elizabeth was going to do next.

Elizabeth looked forward to the next School Meeting. She knew now that it was the most important thing of the whole school week. She was beginning to see that each child was one of a big gathering, and that, because its behaviour brought good or ill to the school as a whole, each child must learn to do its best so that the whole school might run smoothly and happily.

This was a difficult thing for a spoilt only child to learn – but Elizabeth was not stupid, and she soon saw what a fine thing it was for the children to rule themselves and help each other. But she also saw that they would not be able to do this as well as they did, if they had not had excellent teachers, able to teach and guide the classes in the best way.

'I see why everyone is so proud of Whyteleafe School now,' said Elizabeth to herself. 'I'm beginning to feel proud of it myself!'

Elizabeth enjoyed the next Meeting very much. Nora had said that she had nothing bad to report of her, and so Elizabeth had nothing to fear. She sat listening to the reports, complaints and grumbles, and beamed with delight when she heard that Harry had been second in his class in arithmetic, and was now to be allowed to sit with the others again.

'Thank you,' said Harry to William. 'I shall never in my life cheat again, William.'

'Good,' said William. Everyone knew that Harry meant what he said and they were as pleased about it as Harry himself. The boy was different to look at now too – his sly face had gone, and his eyes looked straight at everyone. He and everyone else had seen and known his fault, and he and the whole school had conquered it – there was nothing to be ashamed of now!

There was a report that Peter had carefully cleaned and newly distempered the wall that he had spoilt by scribbling.

'See that you don't have to waste your two shillings on buying distemper again,' said William to Peter.

'I certainly won't,' said Peter heartily. He had had to go without his weekly visit to the cinema, and had missed all his sweets for a week. He wasn't going to let *that* happen again!

There was a complaint about a small girl called Doris. The monitor who complained of her was very angry.

She stood up and made her report. 'Doris has two guinea pigs,' she said. 'And on two days last week she forgot to feed them. I think they ought to be taken away from her.'

'Oh, no, please don't,' begged Doris, almost crying. 'I do love them, really I do. I can't think how I came to forget, Rita. I've never forgotten before.'

'*Has* she ever forgotten before?' asked William.

'I don't think so,' answered the monitor who had reported Doris.

'Then it was probably quite a mistake, which will never happen again,' said William. 'Doris, pets trust us completely for their food and water, and it is a terrible thing to forget about them. You must write out a card and pin it over your chest of drawers to remind you. Print on it: "Feed my guinea pigs". Take it down after three weeks, and see that you remember without being reminded. If you forget again your guinea-pigs will be taken away and given to someone who will remember them.'

'I'll never forget again,' said small Doris, who was very much ashamed that everyone should know she had forgotten her beloved guinea pigs.

Nora reported that Elizabeth was behaving well, and said no more. Another monitor complained that somebody had been picking and eating the peas out of the school garden.

But John Terry immediately got up and said that the boy who had taken the peas had gone to him, and had apologised and paid him a shilling for the peas he had eaten.

'Then we'll say no more about that,' said William.

When the Meeting was over, Elizabeth went out to the garden to see Harry's rabbits. Harry was not there and the little girl looked at the furry babies running round the big hutch.

As she was standing there looking, she suddenly remembered something. She had meant to ask for extra money at the Meeting – and she had forgotten!

And what was the extra money for? It was to buy Joan a nice birthday present! Now Elizabeth would have to save her two shillings and buy it with that. She was cross with herself, for she had meant to ask for half a crown to buy Joan a little red handbag she had seen in the draper's shop.

Joan had said nothing to anyone but Elizabeth about her coming birthday. She hoped no one would notice it, because she knew she would have no cake to share with her friends, and no presents or cards to show. She became a timid mouse once more, as her birthday came near, ashamed because nobody ever remembered her.

But a surprise was coming to Joan! And, of course, it was that Bold Bad Girl, Elizabeth, who planned it!

CHAPTER SEVENTEEN

ELIZABETH HAS A SECRET

DURING THE next week, a registered letter came for Elizabeth from her Uncle Rupert. She opened it – and stared in delight. There was a pound note inside!

'Twenty shillings!' said Elizabeth in surprise. 'Two hundred and forty pence! Ooooh! How kind of Uncle Rupert!'

She read her uncle's letter. He said that he had just heard that she had gone to school, and had sent her some money to buy some nice things to eat.

'A whole pound!' said Elizabeth, hardly believing her eyes. 'I can buy heaps of things with that! I can buy Joan a *lovely* present!'

She went off to her bedroom to put the money into her purse. Plans began to form in her mind – wonderful plans!

'Oh!' said Elizabeth, sitting on her bed, as she thought

of the plans. 'What fun! I shall go down to the village and order a fine birthday cake for Joan! She will think it comes from her mother, and she will be so pleased!'

Elizabeth went on thinking. 'And I shall order the new book that Joan wants, and send that through the post too – and I'll put a card in "With love from Mother!" Then Joan won't be unhappy any more.'

The little girl thought these were marvellous plans. She didn't stop to think that Joan would find out sooner or later that the cake and the book were *not* from her mother. She just longed to give her friend a fine surprise.

She couldn't ask Joan to come down to the village with her, in case Joan found out what she was doing. So she asked Belinda.

'All right,' said Belinda. 'I want to buy some stamps, so I'll go after tea with you. Don't spend your two shillings all at once, Elizabeth!'

All that day Elizabeth thought about the cake and the presents for Joan. She thought about them so much in the French class that Mam'zelle got cross with her.

'Elizabeth! Three times I have asked you a question, and you sit there and smile and say nothing!' cried the French mistress, who was very short-tempered.

Elizabeth jumped. She hadn't heard the questions at all. 'What was it you asked me, Mam'zelle?' she asked.

'This girl! She thinks she will make me repeat myself a hundred times!' cried Mam'zelle, wagging her hands about in the funny way she had. 'You will listen to me properly for the rest of the lesson, Elizabeth, or else you will come to me for an extra half-hour after tea.'

Gracious! thought Elizabeth, remembering that she wanted to go shopping after tea. *I'd better stop dreaming and think of the French lesson.*

So for the rest of the lesson she did her best, and Mam'zelle smiled graciously at her. She liked Elizabeth, and found her very amusing, though she sometimes wanted to shake her when she said, 'Well, you see, Mam'zelle, you needn't bother about whether I shall be top or bottom in exams, because I'm not staying after half-term.'

'You are the most obstinate child I have ever seen,' Mam'zelle would say, and rap loudly on her desk, half angry and half smiling.

After tea Elizabeth went to get her money and to find Belinda. Helen said she would come too, so the three of them set off.

'What are you going to buy, Elizabeth?' asked Helen curiously.

'It's a secret,' said Elizabeth at once. 'I don't want you to come into the shops with me, if you don't mind, because I really have got some secrets today. It's to do with somebody else, that's why I can't tell you.'

'All right,' said Helen. 'Well, we are going to have strawberry ice creams in the sweetshop. You can join us there when you have finished your shopping. Don't be too long.'

Helen and Belinda went off to the sweetshop, and sat down at a little marble-topped table there to enjoy their ice creams. Elizabeth disappeared into the baker's shop.

The baker's wife came to see what she wanted. 'Please, do you make birthday cakes?' asked Elizabeth.

'Yes, miss,' said the woman. 'They are two shillings and sixpence, five shillings, or, for a very big one with candles on and the name, ten shillings.'

'Would the ten-shilling one be big enough for heaps of children?' asked Elizabeth, feeling certain that Joan would like to share the cake with everyone.

'It would be big enough for the whole school!' answered the woman, smiling. 'It's the size people often order for Whyteleafe School.'

'Oh, good,' said Elizabeth. 'Well, will you make a cake like that for Friday? Put eleven candles on it, all different colours – and put "A happy birthday for my darling Joan" on it. Will there be enough room for all that, do you think?'

'Oh, yes,' said the woman. 'I'll decorate it with sugar

flowers, and make it really beautiful, and it shall have two layers of thick cream inside.'

'I'll pay now,' said Elizabeth. 'Oh, and will you please send it to Miss Joan Townsend, Whyteleafe School, on Friday morning, early?'

'Any message inside, miss?' asked the baker's wife, writing down the name and address.

'No,' said Elizabeth. She took the pound note out of her purse, and was just giving it to the shop woman when Nora came into the shop. She smiled at Elizabeth. Then she looked round the shop. 'Are you alone?' she asked. 'Surely you didn't come down to the village by yourself?'

'Oh, no, Nora,' said Elizabeth. 'I came with Helen and Belinda. They're waiting for me at the ice-cream shop.'

The little girl paid for the cake, and received ten shillings change. Nora stared at the money, and looked puzzled. Elizabeth waved goodbye and went out.

She went to the bookshop and ordered the book she knew Joan wanted. It was a book all about birds and cost five shillings. Elizabeth asked the shopman to send it by post, and to put inside a little card that she gave him. On the card she had written: 'With love, from Mother'.

Now Joan will think her mother has sent her a fine cake

and *a present!* thought Elizabeth, pleased to think of Joan's surprise. *I'll buy some birthday cards now.*

She bought three nice ones. In one she wrote 'With love, from Daddy', in the second she wrote 'With love, from Mother' and in the last she wrote 'With love, from Elizabeth', and added a row of kisses. She bought stamps for them, and put them safely in her pocket, ready to post on Thursday.

Then she went to buy the handbag she had seen in the draper's shop. She had four shillings left by that time, so she bought the red bag, paid for a red comb and a red handkerchief to put inside, and put the change into the little purse belonging to the bag! There was sixpence change, and Elizabeth thought it would be fun to put that in too.

Then she went to the ice-cream shop. Helen and Belinda were there, tired of waiting for her.

'You *have* been a time, Elizabeth,' said Helen. 'Whatever have you been doing? You can't possibly be so long spending only two shillings!'

And then, for the first time, Elizabeth remembered that all money had to be put into the school moneybox, and asked for! And she had spent a whole pound that afternoon, and hadn't even put a penny into the box.

She frowned. Goodness, now what was she to do? How *could* she have forgotten?

Well, perhaps it's a good thing I did *forget*, said Elizabeth to herself. *If I'd put the money into the big moneybox, and asked for a pound to spend on somebody's birthday, I'm sure Rita and William wouldn't have given me so much. It* is *an awful lot to spend all at once – but I did so want to give Joan a fine birthday!*

All the same, Elizabeth was rather worried about it. She had broken a rule – but she couldn't mend the broken rule because she had spent all the money! It was no use saying anything about it. The thing was done. And anyway Joan would have the finest surprise of her life!

But Elizabeth had a very nasty surprise on her way back to school with Helen and Belinda. Nora ran up to them and said, 'Elizabeth! I want to speak to you for a minute. Helen, you and Belinda can go on by yourselves. Elizabeth will catch you up.'

'What is it, Nora?' asked Elizabeth in surprise.

'Elizabeth, where did you get that money from that I saw you spending in the baker's shop?' asked Nora.

'My uncle sent it to me,' said Elizabeth, her heart sinking when she knew that Nora had seen the money.

'Well, you knew the rule,' said Nora. 'Why didn't you put it into the moneybox? You knew you could have out what you wanted, if you really needed it for something.'

'I know, Nora,' said Elizabeth in a small voice. 'But I forgot all about that till I'd spent the money. Really I did.'

'Spent *all* the money!' cried Nora in horror. 'What! A whole pound! Twenty shillings! Whatever did you spend it on?'

Elizabeth didn't answer. Nora grew angry. 'Elizabeth! You *must* tell me! Whatever could you have spent a whole pound on in such a little time? It's a real waste of money.'

'It wasn't,' said Elizabeth sulkily. 'Please don't ask me any more, Nora. I can't tell you what I spent the money on. It's a secret.'

'You're a very naughty girl,' said Nora. 'You break a rule – and spend all that money – and then won't tell me what you spent it on. Well, you can tell the next Meeting, if you won't tell *me*!'

'I shan't tell them,' said Elizabeth. 'It's a secret – and a secret I can't possibly tell. Oh dear! I always seem to be getting into trouble, and this time I really didn't mean to.'

Nora would not listen to any more. She sent Elizabeth to catch up Helen and Belinda. Poor Elizabeth! She simply did not know what to do. She couldn't tell her secret, because then she would have to own up that she was buying things for Joan, and pretending that they came from Joan's mother. And the Meeting would be angry with her just when she was being good and enjoying herself!

'Well, never mind – Joan will have a good birthday anyhow,' said Elizabeth, thinking of the cake and the book. '*How* surprised she will be!'

CHAPTER EIGHTEEN

JOAN'S WONDERFUL BIRTHDAY

'JOAN, YOU will soon be eleven!' Elizabeth said at breakfast the next day, as she chopped the top off her boiled egg. 'Gracious! You *are* getting old.'

Joan went red and said nothing. She hated anyone to talk about her birthday, because she knew there would be no cards or presents or cake for her. She was such a timid little mouse that she had no friends at all, except Elizabeth – and Joan was always feeling astonished that the bold Elizabeth should be *her* friend!

'I wonder if you'll have a cake?' went on Elizabeth, knowing perfectly well that Joan was going to, because she herself had ordered it! 'I wonder what it will be like?'

Joan scowled at Elizabeth. She really felt angry with her. *How silly Elizabeth is, talking about my birthday, and if I'm going to have a cake, when she knows quite well that I don't want anything at all said about it*, thought Joan.

She frowned at Elizabeth and signed to her to stop, but Elizabeth happily went on talking.

'Let me see – it's Friday that's your birthday, isn't it, Joan? I wonder how many cards you'll have?'

'Joan didn't have a single one last year, and she didn't have a cake either,' said Kenneth. 'I don't believe she's got a father and mother.'

'Well, I have,' said Joan, feeling quite desperate.

'Funny they never come and see you, not even at half-term then,' said Hilda, who liked to see Joan getting red.

'You be quiet,' said Elizabeth suddenly, seeing that things were going too far. 'What *I'm* surprised at is that *your* parents bother to come and see a girl like *you*, Hilda! If I had a daughter like you, I'd go to the end of the world and stay there.'

'That's enough, Elizabeth,' said Nora, who pounced on Elizabeth very often since the little girl had refused to tell her her secret. Elizabeth said no more. She longed to say quite a lot, but she was learning to control her tongue now. Miss Scott would indeed not have known her!

Nothing more was said about Joan's birthday just then, and after breakfast, as the girls were making their beds, Joan went up to Elizabeth.

'Please, Elizabeth,' she said, 'for goodness' sake don't

say any more about my birthday. You make things much worse if you do – think how I shall feel when everyone watches to see what cards and presents come for me by the post, and I haven't any! You are lucky – you have two grannies, and two grandpas, and uncles and aunts – but I haven't a single uncle, aunt, or granny! So it's no wonder I don't get many treats.'

'You *are* unlucky, Joan,' said Elizabeth in surprise. 'Really you are. Well, I won't say any more about your birthday to the others, if you don't like it.'

But she longed to, all the same, for she kept hugging her delicious secret – Joan would have a wonderful cake, with eleven candles on, and cards, *and* presents too!

Nora was not kind to Elizabeth that week. She did not say any more to Elizabeth about her secret, but she had quite made up her mind to report her at the next Meeting. She thought Elizabeth was very deceitful and mean not to give up her money as everyone else did, and not to tell her what she had spent it on.

'After all, we gave her a fine chance to be as decent as possible, at the last Meeting,' said Nora to herself. 'We really did – and the funny thing is, *I* felt sure that Elizabeth would be worth that chance, and would do her best to keep our rules, and help the school, as we all try to do. But I was wrong. I don't feel as if I like Elizabeth a bit now.'

When Thursday came Elizabeth posted the three birthday cards she had bought. She could hardly go to sleep that night for thinking of Joan's pleasure in the morning! It really was lovely to give a surprise to someone.

Friday came. Elizabeth leapt out of bed, ran to Joan's bed, hugged her and cried, 'Many happy returns of the day, Joan! I hope you'll have a lovely birthday! Here's a little present for you from me!'

Joan took the parcel and undid it. When she saw the red handbag inside, she was delighted – and she was even more thrilled when she found the comb, the handkerchief and the sixpence. She flung her arms round Elizabeth and squeezed her so hard that Elizabeth almost choked!

'Oh, thank you, Elizabeth!' she cried. 'It's perfectly lovely. I did so badly want a handbag. I only had that little old purse. Oh, how I shall love using it! It's the nicest present I have ever had.'

There was another surprise for Joan before she went down to breakfast. Hilda slipped into the bedroom with a lace-edged handkerchief for Joan. She had felt rather ashamed of herself for teasing Joan the day before, and had taken one of her best hankies to give for a present.

Joan was thrilled – in fact, she was *so* thrilled that a

bright idea came into Elizabeth's head. She flew down to the playroom to see if Harry was there. He wasn't – but she could hear him practising in the music room.

'Harry! Harry!' cried Elizabeth, rushing up to him, and startling him so much that his music fell to the floor. 'Will you do something for me?'

'Depends what it is,' said Harry, picking up his music.

'Harry, it's Joan Townsend's birthday,' said Elizabeth. 'You know you said you'd give me one of your rabbits, don't you, and I said it wasn't any good, because I was going at half-term? Well, would you *please* give it to Joan instead, because you can't *think* how pleased she is to have presents!'

'Well—' said Harry, not quite sure about it.

'Go on, Harry, do say yes – be a sport!' begged Elizabeth, her blue eyes shining like stars. It was very difficult to refuse Elizabeth anything when she looked like that. Harry nodded.

'All right,' he said. 'What shall I do – bring the baby rabbit in at breakfast time?'

'Oooh!' said Elizabeth, with a squeak of delight. 'Yes! Do! Say, "Shut your eyes, Joan, and feel what I've brought you!" and then put it into her arms. What a surprise for her!'

'Well, I'll go and get it now,' said Harry, putting his

music away. 'But she'll have to look after it herself, Elizabeth. It will be her rabbit.'

'I'll look after it for her,' said Elizabeth, feeling delighted at the thought of mothering a baby rabbit each day. 'Hurry, Harry!'

Elizabeth went back to the bedroom. The breakfast bell rang as she was tidying her chest of drawers. She slipped her arm through Joan's, and they went downstairs together. They stopped at the letter rack. There was one card for Elizabeth from Mrs Allen – and in Joan's place were three envelopes, in which were the cards that Elizabeth had bought!

Joan took them down, going red with surprise. She opened them. She took out the first card and read it: 'With love, from Mother'. She turned to Elizabeth, her eyes shining.

'She's remembered my birthday!' she said to Elizabeth, and her voice was very happy. She was even more surprised when she found a card marked 'With love, from Daddy', and she was delighted with Elizabeth's card.

'Fancy! Three cards!' said Joan, so happy that she didn't notice that the writing on the envelopes was the same for all three. She went into breakfast, quite delighted.

And on her chair was an enormous cardboard box from the baker, and a small, neat parcel from the bookshop; Joan gave a cry of astonishment. 'More presents! Who from, I wonder?'

She opened the little parcel first, and when she saw the book about birds, and read the little card, her eyes filled suddenly with tears. She turned away to hide them. 'Look,' she whispered to Elizabeth, 'it's from my mother. Isn't it lovely of her to remember my birthday! I didn't think she would!'

Joan was so happy to have the book, which she thought came from her mother, that she almost forgot to undo the box in which was the enormous birthday cake.

'Undo this box, quickly,' begged Elizabeth.

Joan cut the string. She took off the lid, and everyone crowded round to see what was inside. When they saw the beautiful cake, they shouted in delight.

'Joan! What a fine cake! Oooh! You *are* lucky!'

Joan was too astonished to say a word. She lifted the cake out of the box, on its silver board, and stood it on the breakfast table. She stared at it as if it was a dream cake. She couldn't believe it was really true.

'I say!' said Nora. 'What a cake! Look at the candles – and the sugar roses! And look at the message on it – "A happy birthday for my darling Joan!" Your mother has been jolly generous, Joan – it's the biggest birthday cake I've seen.'

Joan stared at the message on the cake. She could

hardly believe it. She felt so happy that she thought she would really have to burst. It was all so unexpected and so surprising.

Elizabeth was even happier – she looked at her friend's delighted face, and hugged herself for joy. She was glad she had spent all Uncle Rupert's pound on Joan. This was better than having a birthday herself – much, much better. Something that Miss Scott had often said to her flashed into her head.

'It is more blessed to give than to receive,' Miss Scott had said, when she had tried to make Elizabeth give some of her toys to the poor children at Christmas-time.

And Miss Scott was quite right! thought Elizabeth, in surprise. *I'm getting more fun out of giving these things, than if I was receiving them myself!*

'Everybody in the school must share my birthday cake,' said Joan in a happy, important voice, and she lifted her head proudly, and smiled around.

'Thanks, Joan! Many happy returns of the day!' shouted everybody.

And then Harry came in and cried, 'Joan! Shut your eyes and feel what I've got for you!'

In amazement Joan shut her eyes – and the next moment the baby rabbit was in her arms. She gave a scream and opened her eyes again. She was so surprised that she didn't hold the rabbit tightly enough – and it leapt from her arms and scampered to the door, through which the teachers were just coming to breakfast.

The rabbit ran all round them, and the masters and mistresses stopped in astonishment.

'Is this a rabbit I see?' cried Mam'zelle, who was afraid of all small animals. 'Oh, these children! What will they bring to breakfast next?'

'I'm so sorry,' said Harry, catching the rabbit. 'You see, it's Joan's birthday, and I was giving her one of my rabbits.'

'I see,' said Miss Best. 'Well, take it out to the hutches now, Harry, and Joan can have it again after breakfast.'

'Oh, Elizabeth! I'm *so* happy!' whispered Joan, as they sat down to their eggs and bacon. 'I can't *tell* you how happy I am!'

'You needn't tell me,' said Elizabeth, laughing. 'I can see how happy you are – and I'm glad!'

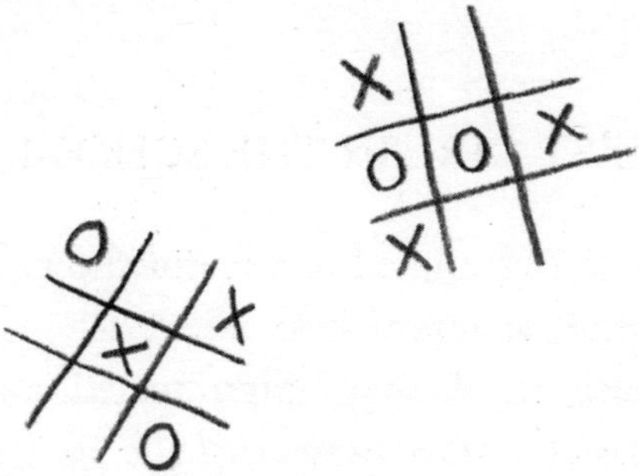

CHAPTER NINETEEN

JOAN GETS A SHOCK

JOAN HAD a wonderful birthday. She laughed and chattered in a way that no one had ever seen before. The little girl become quite pretty with happiness, and when she cut her birthday cake, and gave a piece to everyone in the school, her face was a picture!

Nobody could possibly look happier, thought Elizabeth, eating the delicious cake. *Goodness! That baker certainly did make Joan's cake well. It's gorgeous!*

That evening, after supper, Elizabeth asked Joan to come and help her plant the lettuce seeds she had bought, but Joan shook her head.

'I can't,' she said. 'I'd love to, Elizabeth, but I've got something important to do.'

'What is it?' asked Elizabeth, rattling the seeds in her packets.

'Well, I've got to write and thank my mother and

father for their cards, and the lovely cake and the book,' said Joan. 'I *must* do that tonight.'

'Oh,' said Elizabeth in dismay. She turned away, biting her lip and frowning. *Good gracious!* she thought. *I didn't think of Joan writing to say thank you. Whatever will her mother think when she gets Joan's letter, thanking her for things she hasn't sent? Will she write and tell Joan she doesn't know anything about them – and what will poor Joan do then?*

Elizabeth went out to the garden, thinking hard. Now she *had* made a muddle! Why hadn't she thought of Joan writing to her mother? It was silly of her. Joan was going to be very unhappy – and perhaps angry – when she found out the truth.

'Perhaps it wasn't such a good idea after all,' said Elizabeth to herself. 'Bother! Why do I do things without thinking first? I wonder if Joan's mother will be angry with me for pretending those cards and the book and the cake were from Joan's parents. I don't feel happy about it any more. I feel dreadful.'

She went to give John Terry the seeds. He was delighted.

'Good!' he said. 'Just what I wanted. I plant a new row of lettuce every week, Elizabeth, and then we have new lettuces growing in different sizes, so that each week I have a fresh row to pull. Did you like the lettuces we had for tea yesterday? Those were out of the frames. I was rather proud of them.'

'They were simply lovely, John,' said Elizabeth, still busy thinking about Joan. She simply couldn't imagine what would happen and she felt worried.

She helped to plant the lettuce seeds, but John scolded her because she sowed them so thickly. 'I thought you knew something about gardening!' he said. 'Do you want the lettuces to come up like a forest?'

'Sorry, John,' said Elizabeth. 'I was thinking about something else.'

'You haven't been naughty, I hope?' asked John, who liked Elizabeth, and was always pleased when she came to help him in his garden. 'I hope you won't get ticked off at the Meeting again. You've had enough of that!'

'I'm afraid I *shall* be!' said Elizabeth, sighing. She was worried about that too – she was sure Nora would report her for spending a whole pound – and whatever would she say about it? She wasn't going to give away her secret, and let everyone know that it was she, and not Joan's parents, who had sent the cake and the book. Things were suddenly getting very difficult.

Joan was very happy for two days – and then she got a letter from her mother that took away all her happiness.

Elizabeth was with Joan when she found the letter at tea time in the letter rack. 'Oh! Mother has written very quickly to answer my letter,' said Joan happily, and she took the letter down. She tore it open and stood reading it.

Then she turned very pale and looked with wide, miserable eyes at Elizabeth.

'Mother says – Mother says she didn't send me a card – she forgot,' said Joan in a trembling voice. 'And – and she says she didn't send me a cake – or that book – and she can't understand why I'm writing to thank her. Oh, Elizabeth!'

Elizabeth didn't know what to do or say. She put her arm round Joan and took her to the playroom. No one was there, for everyone had gone in to have tea. Joan sat down, still very white, and stared at Elizabeth.

'I don't understand it,' said poor Joan. 'Oh, Elizabeth, I was so very happy – and now I feel dreadful! Who could have sent those things if it wasn't my mother?'

Still Elizabeth couldn't say a word. How could she say *she* had done it? Her kindness now seemed like a cruel trick. Poor Joan!

'Come in and have some tea,' said Elizabeth at last, finding her voice. 'You look so pale, Joan. Come and have some tea – it will do you good.'

But Joan shook her head. 'I'm not hungry. I couldn't eat *anything*,' she said. 'Let me alone. You go in to tea without me. I want to be alone – *please*, Elizabeth.

You are kind and sweet to me, but I don't want anybody just now. I'm going out for a walk. I'll be better when I come back.'

Joan slipped out of the playroom. Elizabeth stared after her, unhappy and worried. Joan had gone out alone – without anyone, which wasn't allowed. Elizabeth simply didn't know *what* to do. So she went in to tea, very late, and was scolded by Nora.

'You're late, Elizabeth,' snapped Nora. 'You'll have to go without cake today.'

Elizabeth slipped into her place and said nothing. As she ate her tea, she noticed that the room was getting very dark indeed.

'There's a good old storm blowing up,' said Harry. 'My goodness – look at that rain!'

'Splendid!' said John. 'I badly need it for my broad beans and peas!'

But Elizabeth did not think it was splendid. She was thinking of poor Joan, out for a walk all alone in the storm. A roll of thunder sounded, and lightning flashed across the window.

'Joan hadn't even got a hat on,' said Elizabeth to herself. 'She'll be soaked! If only I knew which way she had gone I'd go and meet her with a mackintosh. Oh dear, everything's going wrong!'

She could hardly eat any tea. When the meal was

over, she ran to the playroom and then to the bedroom to see if Joan was back. She wasn't. Elizabeth looked out of the window. She felt very ashamed and guilty.

I meant to be so kind – and all I've done is to give Joan a dreadful shock, make her very unhappy, and now she's out in this dreadful thunderstorm! thought Elizabeth.

For a whole hour Elizabeth watched for Joan to come back. The thunder gradually rolled itself away and the lightning stopped. But the heavy rain went on and on, lashing down on the new leaves of the trees, and making a noise like the waves breaking at sea.

At last Joan came back. Elizabeth saw a small dripping figure coming in through the garden door. She rushed to Joan at once.

'Joan! You're simply soaked through! Come and change at once.'

Water dripped off Joan's dress, for the rain had been tremendous. The little girl was soaked through to the skin. She was shivering with cold.

'Oh, poor Joan,' said Elizabeth, dragging her friend upstairs. 'You'll catch a dreadful cold. Come on, you must change into dry things straight away.'

On the way up, the two girls met the matron of the school, who looked after them when they were ill, and who bandaged their arms and legs when they hurt themselves. She was a jolly woman, and everyone liked her, though she could be very strict when she liked. She stopped when she saw Joan.

'Good gracious!' she said. 'Wherever have you been to get into that state, you silly child?'

'She's been out in the rain,' said Elizabeth. 'She's awfully cold, Matron. She's going to put on dry things.'

'I've got some of Joan's things airing in my hot cupboard,' said Matron. 'She'd better come along with me. Gracious, child, what a sight you look!'

Joan went with Matron. She was hurriedly stripped of her soaking clothes, and Matron rubbed her down well, with a rough towel. Joan said nothing at all, but stood looking so sad and miserable that Matron was worried.

'I think I'd better take your temperature,' she said. 'You don't look right to me. Put this warm dressing gown round you for a minute. I'll get the thermometer.'

She sent Elizabeth away. The little girl went off to the music room to practise, feeling very upset. She practised her scales steadily, and somehow it comforted her. She went to look for Joan at suppertime, but she was nowhere to be seen.

'Haven't you heard?' said Belinda. 'Joan's ill! She'd got a high temperature, and she's in bed in the san.'

The san, or sanatorium, was where any boy or girl was put when they were ill. It was a cheerful, sunny room, built apart from the school. So Joan was there, ill!

Elizabeth's heart sank. She felt that it was all her fault.

'Cheer up! She'll be all right tomorrow, I expect,' said Belinda, seeing Elizabeth's dismayed face.

But Joan wasn't all right. She was worse! The doctor came and went with a grave face. It was dreadful.

I know what would make Joan better, thought Elizabeth in despair. *If only her mother could come and see her, and love her a bit – Joan would be quite all right! Her chill would go, and she'd be happy again.*

Elizabeth sat and wondered what she could do. Then an idea came into her head. She would write to Joan's mother! She would tell her of the presents she had given to Joan, pretending that they were from Joan's mother. She would tell her how much Joan loved her mother, and wanted her to think of her and remember her – and she would beg her to come and see Joan because she was ill!

Elizabeth jumped up. She ran to Joan's writing paper, which she kept on a shelf in the playroom. In it she found the letter from Joan's mother, and Elizabeth copied the address for herself. Then she slipped the letter back.

'Now I'll write to Mrs Townsend,' said the little girl. 'It will be the most difficult letter I've ever written – but it's got to be done. Oh dear – what an awful lot of trouble I'm going to get into!'

CHAPTER TWENTY

MORE TROUBLE!

ELIZABETH SAT down to write to Joan's mother. She bit the end of her pen. She began twice and tore the paper up. It was very, very difficult.

It took her a long time to write the letter, but at last it was done, and put in the box to be posted. This is what Elizabeth had written:

Dear Mrs Townsend,

I am Elizabeth Allen, Joan's friend. I am very fond of Joan, but I have made her unhappy, and now she is ill. I will tell you what I did.

You see, Joan told me a lot about you, and how she loved you, and she said she didn't think you loved her very much because you hardly ever wrote to her, and you didn't remember her birthdays.

It is awful not to have your birthday remembered at school, because most people have cards and a cake. Well, I had a pound from my Uncle Rupert, and I thought of a good idea. At least, I *thought* it was a good idea, but it wasn't. I ordered a big birthday cake for Joan, with a loving message on it – and I got cards and wrote in them "With love, from Mother", and "With love, from Daddy", and sent them. And I got a book and pretended that was from you too.

Well, Joan was awfully happy on her birthday because she thought you had remembered her. You can't think how happy she was. Then she wrote to thank *you* for the things. I quite forgot she would do that – and of course you wrote back to tell her that you hadn't sent them. Joan got a dreadful shock, and she went out for a walk by herself and a thunderstorm came. She was soaked through, and now she is very ill.

I am very unhappy about it, because I know it is all my fault. But I did really mean to make Joan happy. What I am writing for is to ask you if you could come and see Joan, and make a fuss of her, because then I think she would be so glad that she would soon get better. I know you will be very angry with me, and I am very sorry.

Elizabeth Allen

That was Elizabeth's letter, written with many smudges because she had to stop and think what she wanted to say, and each time she stopped she smudged her letter. She licked the envelope, stamped it and left it to be posted. What would Joan's mother say? If only she would come and see Joan and put things right for her; it would be lovely – but goodness, she would be very, very angry with Elizabeth!

Elizabeth missed Joan very much. The next day she went to ask Matron if she might see Joan, but Matron shook her head.

'No,' she said. 'The doctor says no one must see her. She is really ill.'

Elizabeth went to find John. He was putting sticks in for his peas to climb up. Every spare moment he spent in the school garden. That was the nice part of Whyteleafe School – if you had a love for something, you could make it your hobby and everything was done to help you.

'John,' said Elizabeth, 'Joan is ill. Do you think you could spare me some flowers for her?'

'Yes,' said John, standing up straight. 'You can pick some of those pink tulips if you like.'

'Oh, but they are your best ones, John,' said Elizabeth. 'Aren't you keeping them for something special?'

'Well, Joan's being ill is something special,' said

John. 'Pick them with nice long stalks. Slit the stalks at the end before you put them into water – the tulips will last a long time then.'

Elizabeth just had time to pick the tulips, find a vase and run to Matron with it before the school bell went. Matron promised to give the flowers to Joan. Elizabeth shot back to the classroom, and was only just in time.

'Don't forget it's the School Meeting tonight,' Belinda said to Elizabeth at the end of school that morning.

'Bother!' said Elizabeth in dismay. She had forgotten all about it. 'I don't think I'll come. I know I'm going to get into trouble.'

'You *must* come!' said Belinda, shocked. 'Are you afraid to?'

'No,' said Elizabeth fiercely. 'I'm *not* afraid to! I'll be there!'

And she was, sitting angrily on a form beside Harry and Helen, knowing perfectly well that Nora was going to report her as soon as possible.

Well, if she does, I shan't give Joan's secret away, thought Elizabeth. *They can punish me all they like – but if they do I'll start being naughty again! Worse than ever!*

Of course Nora reported Elizabeth almost at once. She stood up and spoke gravely to Rita and William, the two Judges.

'I have a serious report to make,' said Nora. 'It is about Elizabeth. Although we gave her every chance to be good and helpful last week, I am sorry to say that she has been mean and deceitful. She went down to the village this week, and took with her a pound note to spend, instead of putting it into the moneybox to share out. She spent the whole pound and would not tell me anything about it.'

Everyone stared at Elizabeth in surprise.

'A *pound*!' said Rita. 'Twenty shillings – spent in one afternoon. Elizabeth, is this true?'

'Quite true,' said Elizabeth sulkily.

'Then it's too bad!' cried Eileen. 'We all put our money into the box and share it out – and we gave Elizabeth extra money for a record – but she puts *her* money into her own purse, the mean thing!'

Everybody thought the same. The children began to talk angrily. Elizabeth sat silent, looking red and sulky.

Rita hammered on the table. 'Quiet!' she said. Everyone was silent. Rita turned to Elizabeth. 'Stand up, Elizabeth,' she said. 'Please tell me what you spent the pound on – you can at least let us judge whether or not you spent the money well.'

'I can't tell you what I spent it on,' said Elizabeth, looking pleadingly at Rita. 'Don't ask me, Rita. It's a secret – and not my own secret really. As a matter of fact, I quite forgot that I ought to put my money into the box, and then ask for what I wanted. I really *did* forget.'

'Do you think we would have allowed you to spend the money on what you bought?' asked Rita.

'I don't know,' said Elizabeth, rather miserably. 'All I know is that I wish I hadn't spent it on what I did! I was quite wrong.'

Rita felt sorry for Elizabeth. 'Well,' she said, 'you used the money wrongly and you know it – if you had only kept our rule, we should have known whether or not to let you have the money to spend as you did. Don't you see what a good idea our moneybox is, Elizabeth?'

'Yes, I really do, Rita,' said Elizabeth, glad that Rita was speaking kindly to her.

'Well, now listen, Elizabeth,' said Rita, after talking with William for a while, 'we will be as fair as we can be to you about this, but you must trust us and tell us what you wanted the money for first. If we think it was for a very good purpose, we shall say no more about it, but ask you to remember the rule another time.'

'That's very fair of you, Rita,' said Elizabeth, almost in tears. 'But I can't tell you. I know now that I did something wrong with the money – but there's somebody else mixed up in the secret, and I simply can't say any more.'

'Who is the other person in the secret?' asked Rita.

'I can't tell you that either,' said poor Elizabeth, who had no wish to bring Joan in. After all, it wasn't Joan's fault at all that this had happened.

'Have you told anybody about this secret?' asked Rita.

'Yes, one person,' said Elizabeth. 'It's a grown-up, Rita.'

'What did the grown-up say when you told her?' asked William.

'She hasn't said anything yet,' said Elizabeth. 'I told her the secret in a letter, and she hasn't answered my letter yet. I only wrote it yesterday.'

William, Rita and the monitors spoke together for a little while. Everyone was puzzled to know what to do. It was a very serious matter, and somehow it had to be dealt with.

'The Beauty and the Beast aren't here tonight,' said Nora, looking towards the back of the room. 'They are worried about Joan Townsend being ill. Only Miss Ranger and Mr Johns are here. If the others were here, we could ask them for advice again – but somehow I feel I'd like to settle it without asking Miss Ranger or Mr Johns.'

'I think I know what we'll do,' said William at last. 'We'll leave the matter until Elizabeth has had an answer to her letter.'

'Good,' said Rita. She hammered on the table. 'Elizabeth,' she said, 'we are going to leave the matter until you have had an answer to your letter. Will you please come to me and tell me when you have?'

'Yes, Rita,' said Elizabeth gratefully. 'I think the person I wrote to will be very, very angry with me, and I wish I could tell you all about it, but I can't.'

'Well, it seems to me as if Elizabeth is being punished quite enough without us saying anything more,' said William. 'We'll leave it for a day or two. Then please go to Rita, Elizabeth, and tell her what answer you have received.'

Elizabeth sat down, glad that things were not worse. She thought the children were very fair and just. She hadn't even been punished!

When the two shillings were given out to everyone, Elizabeth put hers back into the box.

'I won't have it this week,' she said. 'I'll do without it.'

'Good girl,' said William. There was a nicer feeling in the room at once. Everyone felt that Elizabeth had tried to make up a bit for her mistake.

After the Meeting Elizabeth went to ask how Joan was. Matron came to the door of the san and shook her head.

'She's not any better,' she said. 'She's worrying about something, the doctor says – and she even says she doesn't want to see her mother, though we have asked her if she would like us to send for her!'

'Oh,' said Elizabeth, and ran away in dismay. Now Joan didn't want to see her mother – and Elizabeth had written to ask her to come!

'I always seem to do the wrong thing!' said Elizabeth to herself. 'I wish I could go and tell Rita everything – then perhaps she could help me – but I can't do that without giving Joan away. She would hate to think that anyone knew her cake didn't come from her mother after all! Oh dear! Whatever *is* going to happen? I wish Mrs Townsend would hurry up and write to me.'

CHAPTER TWENTY-ONE

JOAN'S MOTHER ARRIVES

TWO DAYS later Joan was seriously ill, and Matron and doctor were very worried indeed.

'We must send for her mother,' said Miss Belle at once.

'The child begs us not to send for her,' said Matron in a puzzled voice. 'It is very strange. I hardly know whether it would be good for Joan to see her – she seems so much against having her mother sent for.'

'Well,' said Miss Best, 'the mother ought to come, for her own sake, if not for Joan's. She would be very angry if we did not send for her. We can tell her that Joan is behaving rather strangely about her. It may be her illness that is making her think funny thoughts.'

But Mrs Townsend arrived before she was sent for! She had received Elizabeth's odd letter, and had packed a bag, and taken a train to Whyteleafe the same day.

Elizabeth saw the taxi coming up through the archway of the school wall, but she did not know that Mrs Townsend was inside it. She did not see her get out, pay the man and ring the bell.

Mrs Townsend was shown into the headmistresses' drawing room at once. Miss Belle and Miss Best were most astonished to see her.

'I've come about Joan,' said Mrs Townsend. She was a small, sad-looking woman, beautifully dressed, and with large eyes just like Joan's. 'How is she?'

'Not any better, I'm afraid,' answered Miss Belle. 'But how did you know she was ill?' she asked in surprise.

'I had a letter from a girl called Elizabeth Allen,' said Mrs Townsend. 'A very strange letter – about Joan's birthday. Did she tell you anything about it?'

'No,' said Miss Belle, even more surprised. 'I know nothing about it. May we see the letter?'

Mrs Townsend gave the two mistresses Elizabeth's smudgy letter. They read it in silence.

'So that is what Elizabeth wanted the money for!' said Miss Best, her lovely smile showing for a moment. 'Well! Children are always surprising, but Elizabeth is the most astonishing child we have ever had – so naughty and yet so good – so defiant, and yet so kind-hearted and just!'

'I understand now why Joan keeps saying that she doesn't want you to be sent for, Mrs Townsend,' said Miss Belle. 'She is ashamed, poor child, because she thought you had sent her those presents – and now she finds you didn't – and she is bewildered and hurt.'

'I think perhaps I ought to explain a few things to you,' said Mrs Townsend. 'I must explain them to Joan too.'

'Yes, please tell us anything that will help us with Joan,' said Miss Best.

'Well,' said Joan's mother, 'Joan had a twin, a boy called Michael. He was the finest, loveliest boy you ever saw, Miss Best. His father and I couldn't help loving him more than we loved Joan, because we both wanted a boy, and we didn't care much for girls. He was brave and bonny and always laughing – but Joan was always rather a coward, and beside Michael she seemed sulky and selfish.'

'Don't you think that might have been because you made such a fuss of the boy, and perhaps rather left Joan out?' asked Miss Belle. 'She may have been jealous, and that does strange things to a child.'

'Yes, you may be right,' said Mrs Townsend. 'Well, when they were three, both children fell ill – and Michael died. And, because we loved him so much, we both wished that – that . . .'

'That Joan had been taken and Michael had been left to you?' said Miss Best gently. 'Yes, I understand, Mrs Townsend – but you did a great wrong to poor Joan. You have never forgiven her for being the only child left. Does Joan know she had a twin?'

'She soon forgot,' said Mrs Townsend, 'and we didn't tell her as she grew older. I don't think she knows even now that she ever had a brother.'

'Well, Mrs Townsend, I think you should tell Joan this,' said Miss Best firmly. 'She loves you very much and is miserable because she can't understand why you don't seem to love her.'

'I *do* love her,' said Mrs Townsend. 'But somehow it is difficult to show it to Joan. When I got this strange little letter, telling me how somebody tried to buy Joan presents, pretending to be me, I felt dreadful. I felt I must come and see my poor little Joan at once.'

'Come and see her now,' said Miss Belle. 'Tell her what you have told us. Joan will understand and, once she is sure of your love, she will not mind how little you show it! But it shouldn't be difficult to love a child like Joan – she is so gentle and kind.'

'And what about Elizabeth?' asked Mrs Townsend. 'I must speak to her. I think she must be a very kind child, to try to make Joan happy.'

'Go and see Joan first,' said Miss Best. So Mrs

Townsend was taken to the san. She opened the door and Matron beckoned her in, seeing at once that she was Joan's mother.

'She is asleep,' she whispered. 'Come over here and sit by the bed till she wakes.'

Mrs Townsend sat beside the bed. She looked at Joan. The little girl was thin and pale, and her sleeping face was so unhappy that her mother couldn't bear it. She leant over Joan and kissed her gently on the cheek.

Joan awoke and stared up. Her large eyes grew larger as she saw her mother. She looked at her for a moment and then spoke. 'Are you really here? Was it you who kissed me?'

'Of course,' said Mrs Townsend, with tears in her eyes. 'Poor little Joan! I was so very sorry to hear you were ill.'

Joan's mother put her arms round her little girl and hugged her. Joan flung her arms round her mother's neck in delight.

'Oh, Mother! I didn't want you to come! But now I'm so happy!'

'I'm sorry I didn't remember your birthday, darling,' said Mrs Townsend. 'I think we've got a few things to say to one another. Why didn't you want me to come?'

'Because – because – oh, because I didn't think

you would be pleased that somebody pretended to be you and sent me things,' said Joan. 'I was afraid of seeing you.'

'Now listen, Joan; I want to tell you something,' said Mrs Townsend, sitting on the bed and cuddling Joan beside her. And she began to tell the little girl of her lost brother. 'You see, I grieved so much for him that I almost forgot I had a little daughter to make up for him,' said Mrs Townsend in a trembling voice. 'You have always been so quiet and timid too, Joan – you never asked for things, never pushed yourself forward. So I never knew that you minded so much. You didn't say a word.'

'I couldn't,' said Joan. 'But I'm very happy now, Mother. This is the biggest surprise of my life. I understand things now! I do wish you had told me before. But it doesn't matter. Nothing matters now that I've got you close beside me, and I know you really do love me, and won't forget me again.'

'I will never forget you,' said Mrs Townsend. 'I didn't think you minded at all – but, now that I know what you have been thinking, I shall be the kind of mother you want. But you must hurry up and get better, mustn't you?'

'Oh, I feel much, much better already,' said Joan. And indeed she looked quite different. When

Matron came in, she was surprised to see such a happy-looking child.

'I shall want lots of dinner today!' said Joan. 'Because Mother is going to have it with me, Matron, and she wants to see how much I can eat!'

As they were eating their dinner together, they talked about Elizabeth. 'I guessed that it was Elizabeth who sent those things when you said it wasn't you,' said Joan. 'It was just the sort of mad, kind thing she *would* do! You know, Mother, she's the first real friend I've had, and *I* think she's splendid, though the first weeks she was here she was really the naughtiest, rudest girl in the school. The sad thing is she's made up her mind to go at half-term, so I shan't have her very much longer.'

'I want to see Elizabeth,' said Mrs Townsend. 'She wrote me such a funny, sad letter. If it hadn't been for her letter, and what she did for your birthday, we shouldn't have come to understand one another as we now do, Joan! And, although she thinks she did a very wrong thing, somehow or other it has come right, because she really did mean to be kind.'

'Matron! Do you think Elizabeth might come and see me while my mother is here?' asked Joan, when Matron came in to take her temperature.

'We'll see what your temperature is doing,' said Matron, pleased to see the empty plates. She slipped the thermometer into Joan's mouth. She waited a minute and then took it out again.

'Good gracious! Just below normal!' she said. 'You *are* getting better quickly! Yes, I think Elizabeth might come. I'll send for her.'

Elizabeth was practising her duet with Richard when the message came. One of the school maids brought it.

'Mrs Townsend is in the san with Joan and says she would like to see you,' said the maid. 'Matron says you can go for twenty minutes.'

Elizabeth's heart sank. So Mrs Townsend had come to the school! She had got her letter – and now she was here, and wanted to see Elizabeth!

'I don't want to go to the san,' said Elizabeth. 'Oh dear – isn't there any excuse I can make?'

'But I thought Joan was your friend?' said Richard in surprise.

'She is,' said Elizabeth, 'but you see – oh dear, I can't possibly explain. Things have just gone wrong, that's all.'

The little girl put her music away, looking glum. 'Cheer up!' said Richard. 'Things aren't so bad when you go and face them properly!'

'Well, I'll face them all right,' said Elizabeth, throwing her curls back. 'I wonder what's going to happen to me *now*?'

CHAPTER TWENTY-TWO

RITA TALKS TO ELIZABETH

ELIZABETH WENT to the san. Matron was just coming out, smiling.

'How is Joan now?' asked Elizabeth.

'*Much* better!' said Matron. 'We shall soon have her out and about again now.'

'Oh good,' said Elizabeth. 'Can I go in?'

'Yes,' said Matron. 'You can stay for twenty minutes, till afternoon school. Talk quietly, and don't excite Joan at all.'

Elizabeth went in. She shut the door quietly behind her. Joan was lying in a white bed under a big, sunny window, and Mrs Townsend was sitting beside her.

'And is this Elizabeth?' asked Mrs Townsend with a welcoming smile. Elizabeth went forward and shook hands, thinking that Mrs Townsend didn't look very angry after all. She bent over and kissed her friend.

'I'm so glad you're better, Joan,' she said. 'I do miss you.'

'Do you really?' said Joan, pleased. 'I've missed you too.'

'Come here, Elizabeth,' said Mrs Townsend, drawing Elizabeth to her. 'I want to thank you for your letter. I was so surprised to get it – and I know it must have been hard to write.'

'Yes, it was,' said Elizabeth. 'I was awfully afraid you would be angry with me when you got it, Mrs Townsend. I meant to make Joan so happy on her birthday – and I didn't think she'd find out it wasn't you who sent the things! I know it was a silly thing to do now.'

'Never mind,' said Joan's mother. 'It has made things come right in the end!'

'Have they come right?' asked Elizabeth in surprise, looking from Joan to her mother.

'Very right,' said Mrs Townsend, smiling. 'Joan will tell you all we have said, one day, and you will understand how they went wrong. But now I want to tell you that I am very, very glad Joan has such a kind little friend. I know she will be much happier at Whyteleafe now that she has you. It is so horrid to have no friends at all.'

'Oh, Elizabeth, I *do* so wish you were staying on at

Whyteleafe,' sighed Joan, taking her friend's hand. 'Couldn't you possibly, possibly stay?'

'Don't ask me to, Joan,' said Elizabeth. 'You know I've made up my mind to go, and it's feeble to change your mind once you've made it up! I've said I shall go, and, if the Meeting says I can, I shall go back with my parents when they come to see me at half-term.'

'Do you think *you* will be able to come and see me at half-term?' asked Joan, turning to her mother.

'Yes, I will,' answered Mrs Townsend. 'I hope by then that you will be up and about, and we will go to the next town, and spend the day there, Joan.'

'Oh good,' said Joan happily. It was the first time her mother had ever come to take her out at half-term, and the little girl was delighted. 'I shall get better quickly now, so that I shall be ready for you at half-term!'

A bell rang in the school. Elizabeth got up quickly. 'That's my bell,' she said. 'I must go. Goodbye, Mrs Townsend, and thank you for being so nice about my letter. Goodbye, Joan. I'm so glad you're happy. I'll come and see you again if Matron will let me.'

She ran off. Mrs Townsend turned to Joan. 'She's a very nice child,' she said. 'How funny that she should have been so naughty at first – and what a pity she wants to leave! She's just the sort of girl that Whyteleafe School would be proud of.'

Elizabeth thought of Rita as she sat in class that afternoon, doing her painting. *I told Rita I would go to her as soon as I had an answer to my letter*, she thought. *Well, I haven't* exactly *had an answer – and yet I* do *know the answer, because Mrs Townsend came herself and told me!*

She wondered if she should go to Rita after tea. What should she tell her? She didn't know!

She need not have worried herself. Miss Belle and Miss Best had sent for Rita that day, and had told her about Elizabeth, and her odd letter to Joan's mother.

'She spent the money her uncle gave her on buying that big birthday cake for Joan, and other presents and cards,' said Miss Belle. 'That is where the money went, Rita!'

'But why didn't Elizabeth say so?' asked Rita, puzzled.

'Because, if she explained that, the school would know Joan's unhappiness at being forgotten by her mother,' said Miss Best. 'If Elizabeth had been longer at Whyteleafe School, she would have gone to you, Rita, or to one of the monitors she trusted, and would have asked their advice, but she has been here such a short time, and is such a headstrong, independent child, that she takes matters into her own hands – and gets into trouble!'

'All the same, she has the makings of a very fine girl in her,' said Miss Belle. 'She is fearless and brave, kind and clever and, although she has been the naughtiest, rudest girl we have ever had, that only lasted for a little while.'

'Yes,' said Rita. 'I liked her almost from the beginning, although she has been very difficult. But she really is the sort of girl we want at Whyteleafe. I'm afraid now, though, that she will go home, for we have promised that she shall, if she wants to.'

'You must send for her and have a talk with her, Rita,' said Miss Best. 'She was supposed to come and tell you when she had an answer to her letter to Mrs Townsend, wasn't she? Well, we know the answer now – and it is not an answer that can be explained fully to a School Meeting. Have a talk with Elizabeth, and then decide what to do. I think you will feel that although Elizabeth did wrong, the kindness that was at the bottom of it more than makes up for the upset she caused!'

'Yes, I think so too,' agreed Rita, who had been very interested in all that Miss Belle and Miss Best had told her. She was glad to know that Elizabeth had spent the pound on somebody else, glad that it was only kindness that had caused such a disturbance! She went out to look for Elizabeth.

It was after tea. Elizabeth was running to see if Matron would let her sit with Joan again. She bumped into Rita round a corner.

'Good gracious! What a hurricane you are!' said Rita, her breath knocked out of her. 'You're just the person I want to see. Come to my study.'

Rita had a little room of her own, a study all to herself, because she was head girl. She was very proud of it, and had made it as nice as she could. Elizabeth had never been in it before, and she looked around in pleasure.

'What a dear little room!' she said. 'I like the blue carpet – and the blue tablecloth – and the pictures and flowers. Is this your very own room?'

'Yes,' said Rita. 'William has one too. His is just as nice as mine. He is coming here in a minute. Have a sweet, Elizabeth?'

Rita took down a tin from her small cupboard and offered it to Elizabeth, who at once took a toffee. Elizabeth wondered what Rita and William were going to say to her. There was a knock at the door, and William strolled in.

'Hallo,' he said, smiling at Elizabeth. 'How's the Bold Bad Girl?'

Elizabeth laughed. She liked William calling her that, though she had hated the name not so very long ago.

'Elizabeth, William and I know now what you spent that pound on, and why you did it,' said Rita. 'And we want to say that we quite see that you couldn't tell the Meeting.'

'And *we* shan't tell the Meeting either,' said William, sitting down in Rita's cosy armchair.

'But won't you have to?' asked Elizabeth in surprise.

'No,' said William. 'Rita and I are the judges of what the Meeting can be told, and what need not be explained, if we think best. We shall simply say that we have had a satisfactory answer and explanation, and that the matter is now finished.'

'Oh, thank you,' said Elizabeth. 'It wasn't really myself I was thinking of, you know, it was Joan.'

'We know that now,' said Rita. 'You tried to do a right thing in a wrong way, Elizabeth! If you had been at Whyteleafe a little longer, you would have done things differently – but you haven't been here long enough.'

'No, I haven't,' said Elizabeth. 'I do see that I have learnt a lot already, but I haven't learnt enough. I wish I was wise like you and William.'

'Well, why not stay and learn to be?' said William with a laugh. 'You are *just* the sort of girl we want, Elizabeth. You would make a fine monitor, later on.'

'Me! A monitor!' cried Elizabeth, most astonished. 'Oh, I'd never, never be a monitor! Good gracious!'

'It may sound funny to you now, Elizabeth,' said William. 'But in a term or two you would be quite responsible and sensible enough to be made one.'

'I'd simply *love* to be a monitor, and sit in the Jury!' said Elizabeth. 'Whatever would Mummy say – and Miss Scott, my old governess, would never, never believe it. She said I was so spoilt I would never do anything worthwhile!'

'You *are* spoilt!' said Rita, smiling. 'But you would soon get over that. What about staying on, Elizabeth, and seeing what you can do?'

'I'm beginning to feel it would be nice,' said Elizabeth. 'But I can't change my mind. I said I meant to go home at half-term, and I'm going to. It's only feeble people that change their minds, and say first one thing and then another. I'm not going to be like that.'

'I wonder where you got that idea from?' said William. 'I mean, the idea that it's feeble to change your mind once it's made up? That's a wrong idea, you know.'

'Wrong?' said Elizabeth in surprise.

'Of course,' said William. 'Make up your mind about things, by all means – but *if* something happens to show that you are wrong, then it is *feeble* not to change your mind, Elizabeth. Only the strongest people have the pluck to change their minds, and say so, if they see they have been wrong in their ideas.'

'I didn't think of that,' said Elizabeth, feeling puzzled.

'Well, don't puzzle your head too much about things,' said William, getting up. 'I must go. Think about what we have said, Elizabeth. The next Meeting will be your last one, if you are leaving us – and we shall keep our word to you and let you go if you want to. You can tell your parents when they come to see you at half-term, and Miss Belle and Miss Best will explain everything to them. But we shall be sorry to lose the naughtiest girl in the school!'

Elizabeth left the study, her head in a whirl. She did like William and Rita so much. But she couldn't change her mind – she would be so ashamed to climb down and say she had been wrong.

CHAPTER TWENTY-THREE

ELIZABETH FIGHTS WITH HERSELF

THE NEXT day or two were very pleasant. Elizabeth was allowed to see Joan whenever she liked, and she took her some more flowers from John. She also took her a jigsaw puzzle from Helen, and a book from Nora.

Joan was looking very pretty and very happy. Her mother had gone, leaving behind her a big box of velvety peaches, a tin of barley sugar and some books. But best of all she had left Joan a promise that never, never would she let Joan think she was forgotten again!

'It's all because of *you*, Elizabeth,' said Joan, offering her friend a barley sugar to suck. 'Oh, Elizabeth – do please stay on at Whyteleafe. Don't make me unhappy by leaving, just as I've got to know you!'

'There are plenty of other people for you to make friends with,' said Elizabeth, sucking the barley sugar.

'I don't want them,' said Joan. 'They would seem

feeble after you, Elizabeth. I say – have you been looking after my rabbit for me?'

'Of course,' said Elizabeth. 'Oh, Joan, it's the dearest little thing you ever saw! Really it is. Do you know, it knows me now when I go to feed it, and it presses its tiny woffly nose against the wire to welcome me! And yesterday it nuzzled itself into the crook of my arm and stayed there quite still till the school bell rang and I had to go.'

'Harry came to see me this morning and he said he wishes you were not leaving, because he wants to give us two more baby rabbits, to live with my tiny one,' said Joan. 'He said they could be between the two of us.'

'Oh,' said Elizabeth, longing for the two rabbits. 'Really, if I'd known what a nice place Whyteleafe School was, I'd never have made up my mind to leave it!'

She had to go then, because it was time for her music lesson. She rushed to get her music. Richard was in the music room, waiting for her with Mr Lewis.

The two were getting on well with their duets. Richard was pleased with Elizabeth now, for he knew that she really loved music, as he did, and was willing to work hard at it. They played two duets very well indeed for Mr Lewis.

'Splendid!' he said. 'Elizabeth, I'm pleased with you. You've practised well since your last lesson, and got that difficult part perfect now. Now – play Richard your sea piece that you love so much.'

Elizabeth was proud to play to Richard, for she thought him a wonderful player. She played her best. Mr Lewis and Richard listened without a word or a movement till she had finished.

'She ought to play that at the school concert at the end of the term,' said Richard, when the piece was ended. 'It's fine!'

Elizabeth glowed with pleasure. She liked praise from Richard even more than praise from the music master.

'That's what *I* suggested to her,' said Mr Lewis, sitting down at the piano and playing some beautiful chords. 'But she doesn't want to.'

'I *do* want to!' cried Elizabeth indignantly. 'It's only that I'm leaving soon.'

'Oh, that silly old story again,' said Richard in disgust. 'I thought better of you, Elizabeth. You can stay here if you want to, but you're just too jolly obstinate for words. Your music may be good – but I don't think much of your common sense.'

He stalked off without another word, his music rolled under his arm. Elizabeth felt half angry, half tearful. She hated being spoken to like that by Richard.

'I expect Richard is disappointed with you because I know he hoped that you and he would play the duets in the concert this term,' explained Mr Lewis. 'He'll have to play them with Harry now – and, though Harry likes music, he's not a good player.'

Elizabeth finished her music lesson without saying very much. She was thinking hard. She was in a muddle. She wanted to stay – and she wanted to go, because her pride told her to keep her word to herself and leave.

She went out to do some gardening when her lesson was over. She and John had become very friendly indeed over the garden. Elizabeth did not mind working hard with John, and he was pleased.

'So many of the others like to pick the flowers, and trim the hedges when they feel like it,' he said, 'but hardly anybody really works *hard*. When the tiny plants have to be bedded out, or the kitchen garden has to be hoed, who is there that offers to do it? Nobody!'

'Well, aren't I somebody?' demanded Elizabeth. 'Don't I come?'

'Oh, yes – but what's the use of *you*?' said John. 'You're leaving soon, aren't you? You can't take a real interest in a garden that you won't ever see again. If you were going to stay, I would make all my plans with you – I believe Mr Johns would let you take part-charge of the garden with me. It really would be fun.'

'Yes – it would,' said Elizabeth, looking round the garden. 'Are you the head of the garden, John?'

'Yes – under Mr Johns,' said John. 'Nobody needs to garden unless they like, you know – but if it's anyone's hobby, as it is mine, they are allowed to spend most of their spare time here. I've had charge of the garden for two years now, and it's pretty good, don't you think so?'

'Oh, yes, I do,' said Elizabeth, looking round it. 'It's lovely. I could think of lovely things for it too, John. Don't you think a row of double pink hollyhocks would be nice, looking over that wall?'

'Fine!' said John, standing up from his hoeing. 'Fine! We could get the seeds now and plant them – and we could set out the new little plants this autumn, ready to flower next summer. Let's ask for money for the seeds at the next Meeting, shall we?'

'Well, you can, if you like,' said Elizabeth. 'I'm afraid it will be my last Meeting, John.'

'Your last Meeting!' said John scornfully, and he dug his hoe into the hard ground as if he was digging it into a Meeting. 'What a feeble goose you are, Elizabeth.'

'Feeble!' cried Elizabeth angrily. 'I like *that*! Just because I'm keeping my word and sticking to what I said, you call me feeble.'

'Well, it *is* feeble to give up everything you like so much here – your gardening, your riding, your friend and your music – just because you're too proud to climb down and change your mind,' said John. 'I'm disappointed in you.'

Elizabeth stamped off in a rage. She hated to be called feeble. It was the one thing she had always thought that she wasn't.

She went to the swings. There was no one else there. Elizabeth sat on the highest swing and began to sway to and fro. She thought very hard.

'Now let's get things clear in my own mind,' said Elizabeth to herself. 'First of all – I didn't want to come here, and I vowed to myself, to Mummy and Miss Scott that I'd get sent home as soon as possible. Well, I got the Meeting to say I *could* leave at half-term, and I was jolly pleased. I'd got what I wanted!'

Elizabeth swung high, and the swing creaked as it went to and fro.

'Yes, I'd got what I wanted,' said Elizabeth. 'I needn't even stay a term at this horrid, hateful school. That was what I called it.

'And now I find it isn't horrid or hateful. I can't help being happy here. The others seem to like me now that I've given up being so awful. I have a friend who is longing for me to stay and will be unhappy when I go. I've disappointed Richard, who wants to play with me at the concert. I've disappointed Mr Lewis. John is angry with me because I don't like his garden enough to stay – though really I do like it awfully. And Harry wants to give me those lovely rabbits.'

She swung even higher as her thoughts sped along.

'And why am I going? Now I'll just be really honest with myself. I'm *not* going because I'm unhappy. I'm very happy now. I'm going simply because I can't bear to change my mind and say I'm wrong. I'm too proud to say I'll stay, when I've said I'll go. I'm not strong enough to change my mind, and own up I'm wrong!'

Elizabeth slowed down the swing and put her feet on the ground. She frowned and looked at the grass. She had never thought so hard in her life. She spoke to herself sternly.

'Elizabeth Allen, you're feeble! Richard is right and Harry is right. You're feeble! You're a coward! You don't dare to stand up at the next Meeting and say you're too happy to leave! You aren't strong enough to change your mind! You're proud and silly! Elizabeth Allen, I'm ashamed of you!'

Elizabeth spoke these words to herself more sternly than anyone had ever spoken to her. She stopped for a moment, thinking deeply.

'But *am* I really so silly? *Am* I really so feeble? Can I really spoil my happiness here, and Joan's too, by being so stupid and proud? No, I can't! I'm stronger than I thought. I *can* change my mind! I will change my mind!

What did William say? He said that only the strongest people could change their minds when they saw they were wrong – it was the feeble ones who *couldn't*!'

She began to swing again. 'Well, I'm strong!' she sang, as she swung. 'I can change my mind! I can say I'm wrong! Elizabeth Allen, you're not such a poor thing as I thought! Just wait till the next Meeting – and I'll give them the biggest surprise they've ever had!'

The little girl laughed as she swung. She felt very happy. She was no longer obstinate and proud. She was strong enough to change her mind.

'I wish the next Meeting would come soon!' she said to herself. 'What a shock I shall give them!'

CHAPTER TWENTY-FOUR

A SURPRISE FOR THE SCHOOL

THE LAST Meeting before half-term met at the same time as usual in the gym. Everyone was there except Joan, who was in the san, rapidly getting better.

Elizabeth sat on her usual form, between Harry and Belinda, feeling rather excited. What a surprise she was going to give everyone!

The ordinary business of the Meeting went through as usual. Money was taken from the box, but none was put in. Most of the children were expecting money from their parents when they saw them at half-term, and the next week the box would be very full again!

A few complaints were made, and one or two reports. Doris, who owned the guinea pigs, beamed when her monitor reported that she had not forgotten her pets once.

'And,' said the monitor, 'they look the finest guinea

pigs I've ever seen now.'

'Good,' said Rita. 'See that they keep like that, Doris!'

Then Elizabeth's turn came, at the end of the reports. Rita knocked on the table with the mallet, and everyone was silent.

'I haven't much to say about Elizabeth Allen this week,' said Rita. 'But I must just say this – both William and I know now why Elizabeth spent so much money and what she spent it on. We are quite satisfied about it, and we hope that the Jury and the rest of you will accept our word when we say that we can only say that we are satisfied, and not tell you any more. Elizabeth was wrong to do what she did, but she was right not to tell us about it. Now the matter has come right, and we have no more to say.'

'Wait, Rita,' said William. 'We *have* more to say! This is the Meeting at which we were to ask Elizabeth if she wanted to leave us – it is our half-term Meeting. Well, we are keeping our word to you, Elizabeth. If you want to go, and you have made up your mind to do so, we give you our permission. Miss Belle and Miss Best will tell your parents and, if they agree, you may go back with them when they see you tomorrow.'

Elizabeth stood up. Her cheeks were flaming red, and her voice was not quite the same as usual.

'I've got something to say,' she said. 'It's not very easy – and I don't quite know how to say it. But anyway, it's this – I'm not going!'

'Not going!' cried everyone in surprise, turning to look at Elizabeth.

'But why not?' asked Rita. 'You said you had made up your mind to go, and that you never changed your mind.'

'Well, William said that only feeble people never change their mind if they know they are wrong,' said Elizabeth. 'And I know I was wrong now. I only made up my mind to be as naughty as possible because I was angry at being sent to school when I didn't want to go, and I vowed I'd go back home as soon as possible, just to show I'd have my own way. Well, I like Whyteleafe. It's a lovely school. And I want to stay. So I've changed my mind, and though you've said I can have what I want, and it's very nice of you, I don't want it now! I want to stay – that is, if you'll let me after all I've done!'

Everyone began to talk at once. Harry thumped Elizabeth on the back. He was very pleased. John nodded at her in delight. Now she could help him with the garden! Richard actually left his place and came to whisper to her.

'You're a good sort,' he said. 'You can play the game as well as you play the piano.'

William banged with the mallet. 'Richard, go back to your place!'

Richard went back, grinning. Belinda and Helen smiled at Elizabeth, trying to catch her eye. Everyone seemed as pleased as could be.

'Elizabeth!' said William. 'We are very pleased with you. You've made a lot of silly mistakes, but you have made up for them all – and we admire you for being able to change your mind, admit you were wrong and say so to us all! You are the sort of person we want at this school. We hope you will stay for years, and do your very best.'

'I will,' said Elizabeth, and she meant it. She sat down, looking happy and excited. It was lovely that everyone was pleased. She wasn't the Bold Bad Girl any more – she was Elizabeth Allen, the sort of person that Whyteleafe School wanted. She was proud and happy.

The Meeting ended soon after that – and Elizabeth sped off to the san to find Joan. Joan was sitting up in a chair, reading.

'Hallo!' she said. 'What happened at the Meeting? Anything exciting?'

'Well, the Meeting said I could go home with my parents tomorrow,' said Elizabeth. 'So I got my own way, you see.'

'Oh, Elizabeth – I *shall* miss you so!' said Joan.

'You won't!' said Elizabeth. 'Because, you see, I'm not going! I'm staying on! I've changed my mind, Joan. I love Whyteleafe, and I won't leave it for years and years and years! Oh, what fun we'll have together! We'll be monitors one day – think of that! Shan't we be grand?'

'Good gracious!' said Joan, so delighted that she hopped out of her chair, and flung her arms round her friend. 'I can't believe it! Oh, I do feel so glad.'

Matron came into the room and looked horrified to see Joan out of her chair.

'What are you doing?' she said sternly. 'I shan't let Elizabeth come in here if that's the way you behave, Joan!'

'But Matron, I was so pleased because Elizabeth is staying on instead of leaving,' said Joan, sinking back into her chair.

'Dear me! Fancy being pleased because a bad girl like this is staying with us!' said Matron, with a twinkle in her eye.

The girls laughed. They liked Matron – she was cheerful and friendly, though strict. She gave Joan some medicine, and went out.

'We shall have a lovely half-term now,' said Joan. 'My mother's coming to take me out. Is yours coming too?'

'Yes, I had a letter this morning,' said Elizabeth. 'Oh,

Joan – let's ask our mothers to take us out together! That would be much more fun than going alone.'

'Yes, we will,' said Joan happily. 'I am sure I shall be well enough tomorrow to get up properly. Now you'll have to go, Elizabeth. That's the supper bell.'

'Well, I'll see you tomorrow,' said Elizabeth. 'What fun we'll have! Oh, I *am* glad I'm not going home with my mother tomorrow. I wonder what she'll say when she hears that I want to stay on. Every letter I've written to her I've told her that I want to leave!'

Mrs Allen was very much astonished when she saw Elizabeth the next day. The little girl looked so bright and happy – her mouth was no longer sulky, and there was no sign of a frown at all! Elizabeth flung herself into her mother's arms and hugged her.

'It's lovely to see you, Mummy,' she said. 'Do come and see everything – the playroom, and my classroom, and our bedroom – it's Number Six – and the garden and everything!'

Her mother followed Elizabeth around, marvelling at the change in her little girl. *Could* this really be Elizabeth – this good-mannered, polite, happy child? Everyone seemed to like her. She had lots of friends, especially the gentle Joan, who seemed to be Elizabeth's special friend.

'Well, Elizabeth, you're quite a different child!' said

her mother at last. 'Oh look – there is Miss Best. I must just have a word with her.'

'Good morning, Miss Best,' said Mrs Allen. 'Elizabeth has just been showing me around – and really, she does seem so happy and jolly. What a change you have made in her! I feel quite proud of her!'

'She has made a change in herself,' said Miss Best, smiling her lovely smile. 'You know, Mrs Allen, she was the naughtiest girl in the school – yes, she really was! It was difficult to know what to do with her – but she knew what to do with herself. One of these days she will be the best girl in the school, and how proud you will be of her then!'

'Then you want to stay on, Elizabeth?' said her mother in astonishment. 'Well, I *am* glad! What a surprise!'

Mrs Townsend arrived to see Joan at that minute, and Elizabeth ran to see if Joan was ready. She had been kept in bed to breakfast, but was to get up afterwards and allowed to go in her mother's car. She was tremendously excited.

'It's the first time I've ever had a half-term treat like this!' she chattered excitedly, as Elizabeth helped her to dress quickly. 'And it's all because of *you*, Elizabeth!'

'Oh rubbish!' said Elizabeth. 'Hurry up, Joan. What a time you take with your stockings. We're going to have lunch at a hotel – fancy that! I hope there will be strawberry ice creams, don't you?'

Joan was ready at last, and the two girls went to find their mothers, who had already made friends. Then they settled down in Mrs Townsend's car, for she said she would drive them all.

'Now we're off for our treat!' said Elizabeth happily, as the car sped through the archway. She looked back at the beautiful building.

'Goodbye for a little while!' she said. 'I'm coming back to you, and I'm glad it's not goodbye for ever!'

We must say goodbye too, though maybe we will see Elizabeth again, and follow her exciting adventures at Whyteleafe School. Goodbye, Elizabeth – naughtiest girl in the school!

BONUS BLYTON

Enid Blyton has been one of the world's best-loved storytellers for over seventy-five years. Her interest in writing began as a child, and before she loved receiving letters from the children who read her books, she enjoyed working with them as a teacher. *The Naughtiest Girl* stories are inspired by real schools and experiences. Turn the page to learn more about Enid as a child and as a teacher. Afterwards you might like to write about your school and teachers and the people in *your* class!

THE LIFE AND TIMES OF ENID BLYTON

11 August 1897	Enid Blyton was born in East Dulwich, London. Two brothers are born after her – Hanly (b. 1899) and Carey (b. 1902).
1911	Enid enters a children's poetry competition and is praised for her writing. She's on the path to becoming a bestselling author . . .
1916	Enid begins to train as a teacher in Ipswich. By the time she is 21, she is a fully qualified Froebel teacher, and starts work at a school in Kent.
1917	Enid's first 'grown-up' publication – three poems in *Nash's Magazine*.
June 1922	Enid's first book is published. It's called *Child Whispers*.
1926	Enid begins editing – and writes – the phenomenal *Sunny Stories for Little Folks* magazine. (She continues in this role for 26 years!)

1927	So vast is Enid's output that she has to learn to type. (But she still writes to children by hand.)
1931	Having married Hugh Pollock in 1924, the couple's first child, Gillian, is born. Imogen, their second daughter, was born in 1935.
1942	The Famous Five is launched with *Five on a Treasure Island.*
1949	The first appearance of *The Secret Seven* and of *Noddy* mark this year as special.
1953	Enid moves away from *Sunny Stories* to launch *Enid Blyton's Magazine.* She is now renowned throughout the world – she even established her own company, called Darrell Waters Limited (the surname of her second husband).
1962	Enid Blyton becomes one of the first and most important children's authors to be published in paperback. Now, she reaches even more readers than ever before.
28 November 1968	Enid dies in her sleep, in a nursing home in Hampstead.

Enid's death wasn't the end of her remarkable legacy. In the 1970s the Famous Five became TV stars (*Noddy* having already hit our screens in 1955). In 1996 the Enid Blyton Society was formed so that fans across the world could share their enthusiasm for Enid's work (www.enidblytonsociety.co.uk) In 2012 the Famous Five celebrated seventy years of continuous publishing, with special editions featuring covers by top illustrators, led by Quentin Blake. New book, film and merchandising deals are being struck all the time. Enid's work is definitely here to stay!

YOUNG ENID

Enid, aged seven, 1904

Ipswich High School, where Enid studied, 1917

Bickley Park School, where Enid taught, 1919

Photos of Enid Blyton courtesy of Tony Summerfield, the Enid Blyton Society.

ENID AS A CHILD: ON THE PATH TO BECOMING A WRITER – PART ONE

Enid claimed that she was an ordinary child – except for *one thing*, which marked her out as a future writer. As soon as she lay awake at night, her imagination would fire up and stories would unfold in her head. She once said, 'They came out nowhere – out of my imagination.' The stories weren't quite like dreams, which are often muddled and confusing. Enid's stories had their own threads, and . . . a beginning, a middle and an end.

Enid kept a diary, and wrote in it every single day. She also wrote lots of letters to people. Both of these things were excellent training for becoming a writer. Later on in life, her advice to children wanting to write was, 'Fill your mind with all kinds of interesting things – the more you have in it, the more will come out of it.'

Enid also created a magazine called *DAB* – named after the last names of the three girls who contributed to it (Mirable Davis, Mary Attenborough and Enid Blyton, of course). Enid wrote stories, Mirabel wrote poems and Mary provided the illustrations. If you and your friends had a magazine, and named it after your initials, what would the title be?

The three friends sent each other postcards when they were away on holiday – but they were written in code, so the postman couldn't read them!

Quotations from The Story of My Life *by Enid Blyton*
© Hodder & Stoughton Limited, 1952.

WHAT THEY DID AT MISS BROWN'S SCHOOL

In 1920 Enid Blyton became a governess to the four Thompson children, whose ages ranged from four to ten. The family lived in Surbiton, in Surrey, in a house called 'Southernhay'. Enid had a small room which overlooked the garden, and it was there that she wrote many of her stories. Enid's tiny class often had lessons outdoors in the summer months.

Enid was very popular with her students, because her lessons were both practical and creative. She worked with them to put on performances for which they made props, costumes and invitations – and even sold tickets.

In 1941, she published a long story called 'What They Did at Miss Brown's School', which was divided into monthly episodes. It's been hard to find for many years, but you can read extracts in these new editions of the Naughtiest Girl books. The character of Miss Brown and her tiny class is very much based on Enid Blyton and her school at the Thompsons' . . .

Here's the first episode . . .

1. January. Out in the Snowy Fields

THERE WERE only four children at Miss Brown's school!

Wasn't it a tiny school? The children were Mary, John, Peter and Susan, and their ages were ten, nine, eight and seven. So there were four classes, one for Mary, aged ten, one for John, aged nine, one for Peter, aged eight, and one for Susan, who was the baby, because she was only seven.

They all worked together in the little classroom at Miss Brown's. It was a room just like yours, with a cupboard for the handwork things, a big windowsill for flowers, and desks, shelves and a nice big blackboard.

The children all met in January for the beginning of the Easter term – but they looked rather gloomy.

'We shan't have any fun at this school,' said Mary. 'It's so small!'

'I'm sure Miss Brown won't think it's worthwhile doing all the things that a big school does,' said John.

'It will be as dull as can be,' said Peter.

'I wish we didn't need to come,' said Susan, feeling quite sad when she saw the others' discontented faces.

Just then Miss Brown came into the room and was surprised to see such gloomy looks.

'Dear me!' she said. 'Anyone would think you didn't want to come to school – and there are such a lot of lovely things to do together!'

'Well, that's just it,' said Mary, at once. 'We're such a small school that we shall miss doing all the nice things that big schools do. We shall be dull.'

'Rubbish!' said Miss Brown, putting her books inside her desk. 'I promise you we'll have more fun this year than you've ever had before, when you were at a larger school. We'll make things and find things and have more excitement than you think!'

'Oh good!' said Susan. 'But what excitement can we have this month, Miss Brown? Look at the snow! It is thick on the ground. We can't even go for a nature walk.'

'What nonsense!' said Miss Brown. 'You've walked to school, haven't you? Well, why can't we have a nature ramble this afternoon?'

'We shouldn't find much!' said John. 'But I'd love to go!'

'Well, work well this morning at your reading, writing and arithmetic, and we'll go,' said Miss Brown. So Mary, John, Peter and Susan did their very best. In fact, Susan tried so hard at her writing that her little red tongue came out of her mouth nearly all the time, and Miss Brown wanted to know if she would like to write with her tongue!

That afternoon they all set off. 'You know, it's rather fun going for a nature ramble in the snow, but we shan't see anything but snow and frost!' said Mary to John. 'There won't be much nature!'

Miss Brown took them out of the gate and down the lane. They followed her to the farm gate and went into the snowy field, where the little stream still ran through the rushes and reeds.

'Look at our footprints in the snow!' cried Susan, dancing along. 'We've made five rows of them. Mine are the smallest – look! John's are the biggest – bigger than Miss Brown's even! She has pointed toes – look, you can easily tell which are *her* prints.'

Everyone looked down. Peter gave a shout. 'I say! We aren't the only folk that have been in this field – look at all these prints round about. Whatever are they, Miss Brown?'

'Well, perhaps somebody can tell *me*,' said Miss Brown.

'This is the print of Farmer Straws' cow,' said Mary. 'Look – she walked down to the stream to drink. You can see the print of her hoofs, each one cut in two, quite plainly.'

'Well, what's this smaller very neat set of marks, each footprint cut into two as well?' asked Susan. 'I know! It's a sheep's set of footprints! Oh, look – there are heaps over here in the snow, all muddled up. And here is quite a different set – those don't belong to sheep, *I* know!'

Everybody bent down to look. The snow was in an excellent condition for showing prints, and the children could see what looked like the mark of small claws at the top edge of each of the footprints they were examining.

'A cat!' said Peter. 'There's the mark of its claws!'

'Wrong!' said Miss Brown, at once. 'A cat always draws its claws in when it walks, for it likes to keep them sharp. What animal cannot draw its claws in and has coarse, blunt ones, not much good for scratching?'

'The dog!' cried Mary. 'It's the farmer's dog that has been here, rounding up the sheep for the farmer. Look, there are his prints all round the sheep – he ran here – he stopped for a moment there – and then he jumped, because the prints are very deep just there.'

'Very good, Mary,' said Miss Brown. 'And now look here, by the hedge. What do you think this neat set of footprints is? A little like the dog's, but smaller and much neater – each little pad showing clearly, but with no claws.'

'Your cat, Whiskers!' said John. 'And look, there he is, the other side of the hedge! Whiskers, Whiskers! Come here and let's see what kind of footprints you make!'

Whiskers most obligingly came, with a mew. The children watched him stepping neatly and delicately over the snow, leaving the same tracks as those they had just been looking at.

'Yes – it *was* your track,' said John. 'I shall always know a cat's print now. I say! This is rather fun! Let's wander about and see how many other footprints we can find. I feel rather like a detective, reading footmarks like this!'

'There are a lot of footprints, all exactly the same, over here!' called Mary, who had wandered off. 'They are rather funny ones – in fours, but two of the prints are very small and round, and the others are longer.'

Everyone looked. 'I should think they are rabbits' footprints,' said Peter. 'Those tiny marks are the paws of the front legs – and these longer marks are the strong hindlegs. I've seen a rabbit running. He puts his powerful hindlegs right in front of his front legs – doesn't he, Miss Brown?'

'He does,' said Miss Brown. 'So does the hare. But we shan't find the hare's footprints all mixed up with many others, for he lives alone, not in a crowd, as the rabbits do. If we found his, we should see that they were rather like the rabbit's, but bigger and further apart, for he is a larger animal.'

'Miss Brown! Look at this funny little chain of round footprints,' said John. 'And, oh – there are bits of rabbit fur here, and I'm afraid a little rabbit must have been caught by the animal who made those neat marks.'

'You are quite right, John,' said Miss Brown. 'A stoat came along while the rabbits were here – he ran up to them – do you see his neat chain of footprints – he puts his hindfeet almost exactly where he puts his front feet, so the marks are on top of one another. And then, just here, he pounced, and killed the little rabbit! And look over there – he walked off with the rabbit, or part of it, for you can see how his footprints have opened out, and you can see that he dragged something beside him, for the snow is furrowed and still marked with red. Yes, we can read a whole sad story out of *those* snowmarks!'

'Let's go away from here,' said Susan, who was very tender-hearted. 'Let's look at these funny little three-toed prints all over the place.'

'Birds, of course!' said Peter. 'Look, Miss Brown – this must be the print of a sparrow or a finch, I should think.'

'Why must it?' asked Miss Brown.

'Because the prints are placed close together in pairs,'

said Peter. 'They are the marks made by a bird that hops and puts its feet side by side always – isn't that right, Miss Brown?'

'Quite right,' said Miss Brown, pleased. 'And now look, here is a very big bird footprint – the bird went right down to the water. Who knows what bird it is? It walks, as you see – and it places each foot almost exactly in front of the other, so that the prints are in a long, straight line.'

'Miss Brown, it's a moorhen!' cried Mary. 'It has big feet, and it walks and runs; it doesn't hop. And I've seen how it puts one foot exactly in front of the other. But I don't know why it does that.'

'Well, *I* do!' said Peter. 'It is because it has to make its way through rushes and long grass, and it can get along more easily if it walks like that. And look – there it is on the stream, Miss Brown!'

So it was, chugging along by itself, its little black head bobbing to and fro like clockwork. As the children watched, they heard a loud quacking noise and from the stream two big white ducks climbed, and then waddled over the snow to sit in the December sun.

'Thank you, ducks, thank you for showing us *your* prints so nicely!' cried John in delight. 'Come and look, everybody!'

They all looked and saw the big, webbed prints of the

ducks, their feet turning very much inwards. They were easy to tell.

'Well, my dears,' said Miss Brown, 'I'm afraid it's time to go back. I hope you haven't had a dull afternoon!'

'It's been lovely! Please let's go and find some more prints another day!' cried John.

'What other prints are there?' asked Susan, as they went back to the schoolroom to draw the prints they had seen.

'Mice!' said John.

'Rats!' said Mary.

'Hedgehogs! And lots more birds,' said Peter. 'And we might see a squirrel's on a fine day. Mightn't we, Miss Brown?'

'We certainly might,' said Miss Brown, smiling. 'Well, January won't be so dull after all, will it, if we can do a little detective work in the snow!'

'What about February?' asked Peter. 'The snow will be gone by then. What fun shall we have in February, Miss Brown?'

'You wait and see!' said Miss Brown. 'I promise you I'll think of something!'

More classic stories from the world of

Enid Blyton

The Naughtiest Girl Again

The naughtiest girl is back. And this term she's trying to be *good*. But someone wants to spoil things for her – and they're not going to let her forget how she got her nickname!

A sparkling new edition of this classic story, with an introduction by Cressida Cowell (author of the *How To Train Your Dragon* books), behind-the-scenes facts and stories and new illustrations by Claire Powell.

And remember, there are ten books in the series to enjoy!

Join the Adventure

THE FAMOUS FIVE

Have you read them all?

Enid Blyton

THE SECRET SEVEN

SOLVE THE MYSTERY!

HAVE YOU READ THEM ALL?

Enid Blyton®

THE SECRET SEVEN

SOLVE THE MYSTERY!

Don't miss…

Two action-packed Secret Seven stories from prizewinning author **PAMELA BUTCHART**!

THE MYSTERY SERIES

Read all 15 classic stories!

ENIDBLYTON.CO.UK

IS FOR PARENTS, CHILDREN AND TEACHERS!

Sign up to the newsletter on the homepage for a monthly round-up of news from the world of

Enid Blyton®

Illustration by Laura Ellen Anderson.

JOIN US ON SOCIAL MEDIA

EnidBlytonOfficial BlytonOfficial

Enid Blyton®

is one of the most popular children's authors of all time. Her books have sold over 500 million copies and have been translated into other languages more often than any other children's author.

Enid Blyton adored writing for children. She wrote over 700 books and about 2,000 short stories. *The Famous Five* books, now 80 years old, are her most popular. She is also the author of other favourites including *The Secret Seven*, *The Magic Faraway Tree* and *Malory Towers*.

Born in London in 1897, Enid lived much of her life in Buckinghamshire and loved dogs, gardening and the countryside. She was very knowledgeable about trees, flowers, birds and animals. Dorset – where some of the Famous Five's adventures are set – was a favourite place of hers too.

Enid Blyton's stories are read and loved by millions of children (and grown-ups) all over the world. Visit enidblyton.co.uk to discover more.

Illustration by Laura Ellen Anderson.

The NAUGHTIEST GIRL Marches On

Have you read them all?

1. The Naughtiest Girl in the School
2. The Naughtiest Girl Again
3. The Naughtiest Girl is a Monitor
4. Here's the Naughtiest Girl
5. The Naughtiest Girl Keeps a Secret
6. The Naughtiest Girl Helps a Friend
7. The Naughtiest Girl Saves the Day
8. Well Done, the Naughtiest Girl
9. The Naughtiest Girl Wants to Win
10. The Naughtiest Girl Marches On

Enid Blyton®

The Naughtiest Girl Marches On

HODDER

HODDER CHILDREN'S BOOKS

First published in Great Britain in 1999 by Hodder & Stoughton
This edition published in 2021
For further information about the editorial history of this book,
see enidblyton.co.uk/books

5 7 9 10 8 6 4

Enid Blyton® and Enid Blyton's signature are registered
trade marks of Hodder & Stoughton Limited
Text © 2021 Hodder & Stoughton Limited
Illustrations by Claire Powell © 2021 Hodder & Stoughton Limited

No trade mark or copyrighted material may be reproduced without the
express written permission of the trademark and copyright owner.

The moral right of the author has been asserted.

All characters and events in this publication, other than those clearly in the public domain, are fictitious and any resemblance to real persons, living or dead, is purely coincidental.

All rights reserved.
No part of this publication may be reproduced, stored in a retrieval system, or transmitted, in any form or by any means, without the prior permission in writing of the publisher, nor be otherwise circulated in any form of binding or cover other than that in which it is published and without a similar condition including this condition being imposed on the subsequent purchaser.

A CIP catalogue record for this book is available from the British Library.

ISBN 978 1 444 95869 0

Printed and bound in Great Britain by Clays Ltd, Elcograf S.p.A.

Typeset in Caslon by Avon DataSet Ltd, Arden Court, Alcester, Warwickshire

The paper and board used in this book are made from wood
from responsible sources.

MIX
Paper | Supporting responsible forestry
FSC® C104740

Hodder Children's Books
An imprint of Hachette Children's Group
Part of Hodder & Stoughton
Carmelite House
50 Victoria Embankment
London EC4Y 0DZ

An Hachette UK Company
www.hachette.co.uk
www.hachettechildrens.co.uk

CONTENTS

INTRODUCTION

by Cressida Cowell

bestselling author of the
How to Train Your Dragon series

Like so many, many children before and after me, Enid Blyton's books played a crucial role in turning my nine-year-old self into a passionate reader.

That is because Enid Blyton had an extraordinary knack for writing the kind of books that children actually *want* to read, rather than the kind of books that adults think they *should* read.

Enid Blyton could tap into children's dreams, children's desires, children's wishes, with pinpoint accuracy. She knew that every child, however good and well-behaved they might look on the outside, secretly longed to be Elizabeth Allen, the naughtiest kid in the school. I'm afraid I entirely cheered Elizabeth on, as she defied her parents, the headmistresses, her schoolmates, and the very serious School Meetings. If anything, I wanted her to be even naughtier.

But *The Naughtiest Girl* books were really my favourite of Enid Blyton's school stories because of Whyteleafe, a very different school from Malory Towers or St Clare's. What if there could be a school in which discipline was administered by the children rather than the adults? In which all money was given in at the start of the term and distributed among the children along socialist lines? Wouldn't this be the kind of school that children would actually *want* to go to, rather than the kind of school that children *have* to go to?

It was an interesting proposition to a nine-year-old, and it remains an interesting proposition.

I hope you enjoy this story as much as I did when *I* was nine years old.

Cressida Cowell

CHAPTER ONE

JAKE IS GRUMPY

ELIZABETH ALLEN was enjoying life in the second form at Whyteleafe School. By early October, she could barely remember what it had felt like to be a first-former. How young the new first-formers looked now, how small for their age! Surely, she would say in amazement to her best friend Joan, *they'd* never been that small when they were first-formers? Joan would smile gently and assure her that a year ago they must have looked every bit as small.

Being a second-form monitor with Joan this term made Elizabeth feel all the more grown-up. She was delighted to be a monitor again and refused to let her friend Julian put her off her stride.

'How long will the naughtiest girl last this time?' he asked her, an amused light in his green eyes. 'One week? Two weeks? Or till half-term perhaps?'

'Wait and see, Julian Holland. You might get a surprise. It's exciting being a monitor. Thomas and Emma have got really good ideas. I've not the slightest intention of blotting my copybook!'

It was a long time since Elizabeth really *had* been the school's naughtiest girl, but the nickname had stuck. And how Julian loved to tease her about it!

Privately Elizabeth now considered Whyteleafe the best school in the world. She liked the way the pupils made most of the rules themselves, through the weekly Meeting, which was a kind of school parliament. And she loved the monitors' get-togethers that Thomas and Emma, the new head boy and girl, had introduced. All twelve monitors now met Thomas and Emma once a week for tea and biscuits in their study. They helped to plan the main Meeting and were encouraged to put forward ideas. It was known simply as the Monitors' Meeting, or MM for short.

'Don't forget we've got an MM before tea, Elizabeth!' Joan reminded her friend one day.

They were still outside, after games. Elizabeth was loitering near the main hockey pitch, where members of the school's first eleven were having a team practice. There were some important matches coming up soon.

'I know, Joan,' replied Elizabeth. 'I'm looking forward to it. Wasn't it good last week?'

There had been three MMs so far and Elizabeth had enjoyed each one. She wanted to play her full part in the smooth running of the school. She was determined to be a dynamic and successful monitor. She took her responsibilities to heart.

'But we haven't got time just to stand around,' Joan said softly. 'We've got to wash and change and smarten up . . .'

'I'm not just standing around, Joan!' Elizabeth pointed out patiently. 'I'm looking at Jake and his poor ankle, that's all. I'm worried about him, aren't you? We *are* his monitors after all. I think the least we can do is go over and have a few words with him. He looks so grumpy! Come on, let's try and cheer him up.'

Only then did Joan realise that her friend was gazing not at the team practice but at a forlorn figure sitting on the grass, with his ankle heavily strapped. Joan knew Jake well. He had been in the second form even longer than she had. He was a big, strapping boy for his age. He was a brilliant hockey player and at the end of last season had been selected for the school's first hockey team. He was the youngest pupil ever to have made it into the first eleven. He had played superbly.

'Poor Jake!' she agreed. 'All right then. But we'd better not talk to him for too long.'

Elizabeth was already striding ahead.

It was sad to see the big boy sitting there, staring miserably into space, while his teammates practised running and passing and shooting goals. He had returned to school from the summer holidays a different boy, thought Joan. It seemed he had fallen badly on the last day of the holidays and injured his ankle. It had been strapped up for nearly a month now and he was still limping heavily. The injury seemed to have affected his confidence too. He was much quieter this term than Joan had ever known him.

'Cheer up, Jake!' Elizabeth was telling him, with her bright, friendly smile. 'We just want you to know how proud we are to have a second-former who's already in the first hockey team. And already a star! It's such an honour for us. It won't be long now before that ankle of yours is better and it won't be a moment too soon! Mr Warlow says there are some very important matches coming up and the team's not the same without you. We can't wait to see you in action again, I can tell you. The whole second form will be cheering you on from the sidelines!'

Even at the best of times, Jake was the strong, silent sort of boy. He seemed taken aback by such effusiveness. His cheeks turned red.

'Oh, leave off, Elizabeth,' he said grumpily.

'Don't be embarrassed, Jake!' said Joan tactfully. 'We

just want you to know that our thoughts are with you. It's such a shame for you, not being able to play games. We do hope the ankle will be better soon.'

'Thanks, Joan,' mumbled the big boy.

'It's got to be!' declared Elizabeth in her boisterous way. 'I am going to wish and wish and *wish* your ankle to get better, Jake! Just you wait and see!'

The boy shrugged and made no response.

'Come on, Elizabeth. We must dash now!' Joan tugged at Elizabeth's arm. 'We mustn't be late for the MM!'

As they went indoors, Elizabeth sighed. She'd hoped to cheer Jake up, but instead she seemed to have made him grumpier than ever!

'He seemed surprised at my coming over and talking to him,' she frowned. 'I got the impression that he'd quite forgotten I'm one of his monitors this term.'

'He probably had,' laughed Joan.

'Do you think it would be a good idea if all monitors had a special armband?' continued Elizabeth. 'Shall we bring it up at the MM and see what Thomas and Emma say?'

'Don't be hasty, Elizabeth,' replied Joan. 'We can't bring ideas up just to please ourselves. We go to the MM as representatives of form two. We'd need to find out what lots of other people in the form think about it first – and there isn't time.'

'Here come Kathleen and Jenny!' exclaimed Elizabeth. 'We can ask them what they think while we're getting ready.'

The four girls shared Dormitory Fourteen, a big, sunny room on the first floor. As Elizabeth and Joan prepared to go to the Monitors' Meeting, they talked to the other two about the armband idea.

'Do you think we really need monitors to have an armband?' said Kathleen, her cheeks rosier than ever after an hour on the games field. 'Everybody knows who they are.'

'I'm not sure they always do,' pouted Elizabeth.

'It's a good idea in some ways,' reflected Jenny. 'But it would mean the school having to spend money to get them made. The Beauty and the Beast might think it's a waste of money!'

Miss Belle and Miss Best were the joint headmistresses. They weren't greatly in favour of unnecessary fripperies and frills.

'We could make our own,' suggested Elizabeth.

By the time she had finished chattering and brushing her hair and (at Joan's suggestion) sponging a jam mark off her school skirt, it was getting late. The two friends hurried off along the corridor to go to the meeting – and bumped straight into Julian.

He had come looking for Elizabeth. He was still wearing his tracksuit after games and was disappointed to see her looking so smartly dressed.

'Oh, why have you changed, Elizabeth? We were planning to go for a pony ride before tea!'

Elizabeth's hand flew to her mouth.

'Oh, Julian, sorry! How awful of me. I forgot I had an MM today. Can we go for a ride tomorrow instead? But listen, there's an idea I want to tell you about. I need to know your opinion . . .'

At that moment two other second-form boys appeared.

'Harry . . . Martin . . . I need your opinions as well.'

Elizabeth stood there in the corridor and declaimed her idea about the special armbands for school monitors. Joan looked anxiously at her watch.

'Well, Julian, what do you think?' ended Elizabeth.

Her friend threw back his head and roared with laughter.

'What a horrible idea, Elizabeth! Do you want to be mistaken for a member of the secret police or something?'

Harry and Martin started tittering. Elizabeth . . . armband . . . secret police. What a joke!

'All right, all right. I was only asking!' protested Elizabeth.

She suddenly went off the idea herself. It had fallen flat. All the fizz had gone out of it. Although she hated being teased by Julian, she always valued his opinion. By the time the two girls had reached the door of Thomas and Emma's big study her mind was made up.

'I don't think we'd better say anything about the armband idea, Joan,' whispered Elizabeth. 'It doesn't seem to have a lot of support.'

Joan murmured her agreement.

Privately, she was thinking about Jake. It might have slipped the big boy's mind that Elizabeth was one of his monitors, but how could he have escaped the fact? Elizabeth was so keen! She was so determined to be a successful and dynamic monitor. There was really no need for her to think about wearing an armband!

It was much more likely, reasoned Joan, that the boy was upset at being reminded about his injury, by a monitor or anybody else, no matter how kindly meant. It only made him grumpier. Elizabeth had better go easy in that quarter, she thought.

Out loud, she simply said, 'I expect there will be a lot of other things to talk about.'

'Yes!' replied Elizabeth eagerly. 'I wonder what Thomas and Emma have got in store for us to discuss this week? I expect it will be something interesting!'

CHAPTER TWO

THOMAS AND EMMA AIR A NEW IDEA

'HELLO, ELIZABETH! Hello, Joan!' The head girl ushered them in with a smile. 'You'd better grab your tea and biscuits before you sit down. We're all crammed together like sardines as usual.'

'Sorry we're a bit late, Emma!' apologised Elizabeth.

The study was packed. The two friends had to squeeze past all the other boys and girls to get to the table where their mugs of tea awaited them. The mugs stood next to a plate of biscuits. Elizabeth chose her biscuits with care – a shortbread and a chocolate digestive.

'If you can *find* anywhere to sit down!' laughed Thomas. The tall fair-haired boy was standing by the window, waiting to start. 'Last to arrive had better sit on the floor if they can't find anywhere else!'

Joan managed to find a perch on the arm of a chintz-covered armchair normally reserved for visitors.

Then Donald stood up and insisted on giving Elizabeth his place on a wooden bench that had been brought in.

'I'll sit on the floor next to Peter,' smiled the older boy. 'I don't mind at all. Budge up a bit, Peter.'

Peter was the youngest there. He had gone up from the junior class to the first form this term and had been made a monitor.

Elizabeth sandwiched herself on to the bench between Eileen and Richard, who were also monitors now. What fun these get-togethers were, she decided. She sipped her tea slowly and gazed round the room. All twelve monitors had turned up, as in previous weeks.

Whereas the main Meeting in the school hall each week was a formal affair, these little MMs were just the reverse, everybody squashed into a small space, the atmosphere relaxed and jolly.

'Thank you all for coming!' began Thomas. 'I see we've got a full house as usual. And that's good because Emma and I want to give something an airing. It's a completely new idea. We need to know whether you like it yourselves – and whether you think your classmates would approve. Emma, you explain the thinking behind it.'

Emma finished her tea, placed the cup down and swung round in her chair to face them all.

'Tom and I were talking the other day about how

we all like to win honours. It's part of human nature. If we're good at games, we try to get into the teams. And, if we're good at lessons, we try to come top in class. However, some boys and girls are not especially good at games or brainy either, but they may have other fine qualities. We thought, is there a way *they* can be given recognition at Whyteleafe too? Some honour they can compete for on equal terms? What do you think?'

The monitors received the idea with enthusiasm.

'You mean, people who do something unselfish?' asked young Peter.

'A noble deed?' exclaimed Elizabeth eagerly.

'An act of bravery?' suggested Donald.

'Exactly!' said Emma, pleased to see how quickly the monitors were warming to the idea. 'All of those things. Hands up all of you who think such a prize would be popular with the boys and girls in your form.'

At once every hand in the room shot up. Thomas smiled as he looked round at the forest of hands.

'Good!' he said. 'In that case Emma and I would like to announce the plan at this week's Meeting. Let's work out the details. How often should we give out the honour? Perhaps once a term, do you think?'

'Yes! And keep it separate, so award it at half-term!' suggested Eileen.

'But what will the honour be called, Thomas?' asked Donald.

'Now there's a good question,' smiled Thomas. 'Let's put our thinking caps on.'

After that the discussion raged for several minutes. Elizabeth was aglow. She liked the head boy and girl's idea. Now they were all being asked to think of the name for the new honour. It was so exciting to be in at the very beginning of things like this. A new tradition at Whyteleafe School . . .

Suggested names for the honour came thick and fast.

'The Bravery Award!'

'The Gold Star for Good Conduct!'

'No – the Gold Star for Courage . . .'

'What about the Good Deed Award?'

In the end it was one of the fourth-form monitors, Eric, who came up with the best name. He was a thoughtful, learned-looking boy. He got to his feet, adjusted his glasses and cleared his throat.

'May I say something? I'll never forget some of the things that William and Rita told us about courage at camp last term. They knew the true meaning of courage, didn't they? And they explained it so well. I'm sure the whole school would wish to remember them.'

'They were the finest head boy and girl that any school could hope for,' said Thomas humbly. 'Emma and I are going to have to work hard to live up to their example.'

Emma nodded, her eyes misting over.

'And so, Eric?' she asked.

Before Eric could reply, Elizabeth suddenly guessed what he was going to say. A thrill ran through her and she clapped her hands. She couldn't stop herself shouting it out loud.

'The William and Rita Award!' she cried. 'That's what you're going to say, isn't it, Eric?'

'Yes! That's it exactly. You've taken the words right out of my mouth, Elizabeth!'

There were surprised gasps all around and then everyone began to cheer. The William and Rita Award. Excellent!

Thomas and Emma looked at each other in delight.

'That's a lovely name for the honour, Eric,' smiled Emma. 'Quite brilliant.'

'Perfect!' exclaimed Thomas.

And the whole room agreed.

It turned into a long session after that. There was so much to discuss! But it was all very fruitful. By the end of the session, not only had the name of the award been decided, but so had all the details of how the winner would be selected. These would be announced in full at the School Meeting.

'Until then this is all hush-hush,' Emma reminded them. She placed a finger to her lips. 'Not a word to anyone. We don't want this leaking out in dribs and drabs. It must be announced in the proper way when the whole school is assembled.'

Elizabeth and Joan were used to this. Things that the monitors discussed at MMs often had to remain confidential, until the head boy and girl were ready to make them public.

'It's so lucky that we're friends, Joan!' remarked Elizabeth, as they went into the dining hall for tea. 'We can talk to each other as much as we like about things that are said at the MMs. I'd die if I couldn't talk to somebody about them! I wonder who'll get the first William and Rita Award? I wonder if it will be anyone in our form? Wouldn't that be an honour!'

She was still bubbling over with it all when she sat down for tea. Julian had saved her a place by the window, at one of the second-form tables.

'Hello, Elizabeth!' Julian wore his usual grin. 'How did the meeting of the secret police go then? What are you looking so excited about? Did you decide anything interesting?'

'As a matter of fact, we did,' Elizabeth blurted out.

'What then?'

'It'll be announced at the School Meeting,' said

Elizabeth. 'But my lips are sealed till then. Oh, sorry, Julian. I shouldn't have said anything, should I?'

A look of annoyance had crossed her friend's face.

'It's not *my* fault,' she added. 'It's a rule!'

'Since when has the naughtiest girl worried her head about rules?' asked Julian waspishly. 'If this monitor business is going to turn you into the school goody-goody, I will feel very badly let down, Elizabeth Allen.'

'Sorry, Julian,' Elizabeth repeated.

Then he gave her hair a friendly tweak and smiled.

'Only joking,' he said airily. 'No leaks allowed from the Cabinet Office, eh? Has to be announced at the full sitting of Parliament? Fair enough.'

Daniel Carter, sitting opposite, was looking solemn.

'Julian, Elizabeth would love to tell you what happened. You can see that just by looking at her face! I'm sure she *would* if she could. Gosh, I can't wait for the Meeting, to hear what it is. I wish I'd been at the MM, Elizabeth. They *do* sound fun.'

The wistful expression on Daniel's face gave Elizabeth a sudden pang.

For the first few days of term Daniel had been appointed as a form monitor in Elizabeth's place, while she had been in disgrace about something. But, as soon as Elizabeth had been vindicated, the boy had, of course, stood down to enable her to have her monitorship back. Poor Daniel!

But, before Elizabeth could brood about it, another boy called down the table to her. It was Julian's cousin, Patrick. The two cousins liked to keep their distance as they did not get on particularly well.

'Please stop gabbing, Elizabeth, and pass the bread rolls up this end! I'm starving! I've been practising my ping-pong for the last hour!'

Elizabeth smiled and passed the bread basket along the table. Patrick smiled back.

'Don't forget it's squad practice tomorrow,' he reminded her. 'I'm going to beat you for a change!'

They were both in the school table-tennis squad, but Patrick was only the team's first reserve. He was a very competitive boy and was striving with all his might to become a full team member, like Elizabeth.

'You *wish*, Patrick!' Elizabeth called back cheerfully.

After that she tucked into her tea with gusto.

She gave no further thought to Daniel's comments, nor Julian's. It would be some days before she would have good reason to recall them.

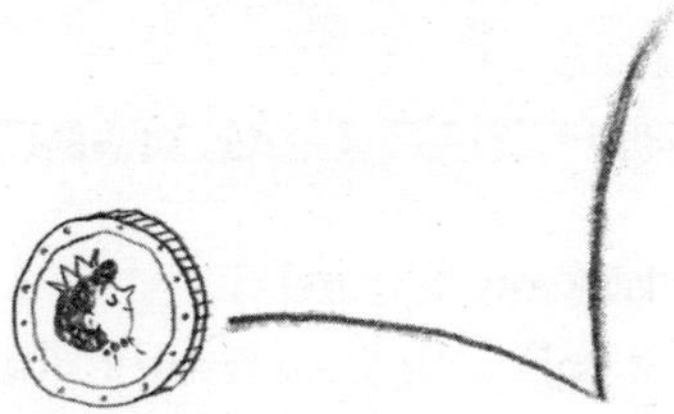

CHAPTER THREE

ELIZABETH HEARS ABOUT A BRAVE DEED

THE TABLE-TENNIS practice, the one that Patrick had mentioned, took place after lessons the following day. Mr Warlow, the sports master, had asked all team members and team reserves to attend. He and Emma, who was table-tennis captain, wanted to check that everyone was in good form for a match on Saturday. It would be an away match against Hickling Green School, their old rivals, to take place alongside a hockey fixture. Hickling Green had a very strong hockey eleven. Mr Warlow feared that Whyteleafe might do badly in the hockey match, especially with Jake out of the team. But he had high hopes of his table-tennis squad! It was a good one this term.

Elizabeth would not have been allowed to miss the practice, even if she'd wanted to. And, of course, she would not have dreamt of missing it. She was looking forward to the trip on Saturday. Miss Belle and Miss Best had hired a full-size coach to accommodate both teams and their supporters. It would be so exciting if they could beat their old rivals, thought Elizabeth, and they would be sure to get a lovely tea afterwards.

However, it was a great disappointment to have to put off going riding with Julian for the second day running.

'Don't worry, Elizabeth. It's not your fault,' he said good-humouredly. 'It's just a pity we're not allowed to go riding after tea this term, with the evenings drawing in. I'll fix up a ride with Robert instead.'

'Let's go and feed the ponies after tea. At least we're allowed to do that!' suggested Elizabeth. 'I haven't seen them for days and I'm missing them.'

'Good!' said Julian. 'I like that idea. Off you go to your ping-pong then. Don't wear yourself out. See you at tea!'

It was a busy practice session. Emma and Mr Warlow spent most of the time coaching the boys and girls. They were shown how to improve their footwork, as well as their batting technique. They were then split up to play a proper practice game, paired according to ability. Elizabeth was asked to play against Patrick. The two were evenly matched although Elizabeth was considered to have the edge.

She usually beat Patrick. But today he was determined to reverse that situation. He had been working on his game furiously, for days.

And he knew that both Emma and the teacher were keeping a watchful eye on all three tables, checking everybody's current form. It made him very focused.

But Elizabeth was equally aware that they were being kept an eye on. And she was very focused too.

They both played exceptionally well.

Patrick served first and took the lead, 3–2. Then Elizabeth served and lost only one of her service points to lead 6–4. After that the lead passed from one to the other, backwards and forwards, the scores tending to go with service. The rallies were long, fast and furious.

The score reached 20–20!

Now they had to change service on every point. The first to lead by two clear points would win the game. In the tension of the moment Patrick's service faltered. It twice missed the table and he lost the point: 21–20 to Elizabeth. Then Elizabeth did a safe, medium-paced service, nothing fancy. Patrick returned to her backhand. She gave back a spinning lob that just caught the edge of the table. Patrick had to swoop low and only just managed to return it.

It was a weak, loopy return. It bounced high on Elizabeth's side of the table. She changed to forehand grip, swung her arm back and then—

Whooosh!

A beautiful forehand smash to the far corner! Patrick dived . . . too late. He missed.

'Twenty-two–Twenty!' Elizabeth cried in delight. 'I've won! I've won!'

The ping-pong ball hit the far wall and came rolling slowly back towards Patrick's foot. In his fury and frustration, and in the heat of the moment, he stamped on it.

Crunch! The ping-pong ball was flattened.

The sudden sound made Emma glance round.

'Oh, Patrick, you clumsy boy! You've trodden on the ball!'

Already regretting his temper, Patrick stared at Elizabeth imploringly. He was silently begging her not to give him away! She was the only person who had seen him deliberately stamp on the ball.

Emma was scooping the poor ball up from the floor, examining it.

'It's past repair, I'm afraid,' she said.

'Oh, what a shame,' said Elizabeth innocently.

'I'll replace it, Emma,' Patrick said quickly. 'I'll go to the village and buy a new one with my own money. I'll go straight away if you like. Has the session ended now?'

'Oh, Patrick, you are a good sport,' said Emma. 'Will you really? As a matter of fact, we're getting rather low on balls at the moment. Would you like to go with him, please, Elizabeth? You've both got some time before tea.'

At Whyteleafe School pupils were allowed to go down to the village. But it was a strict rule that they went out in pairs and not on their own.

'The sun's coming out!' said Elizabeth cheerfully. 'I'll be glad of a walk to the village.'

As the boy and girl strolled out through the school gates and along the quiet road to the village, Patrick looked sullen and shamefaced.

'Thanks for not giving me away, Elizabeth,' he said.

Elizabeth felt slightly sorry for him.

'Cheer up,' she said. 'I've got an awfully hot temper myself, so I know just what it's like to lose it!'

Patrick did not reply. The fact was that, in spite of their occasional clashes, he could not help liking and admiring Elizabeth. He often wished that she would like and admire *him*. It was annoying the way she seemed so much to prefer his cousin Julian. And now he felt angry with himself for losing his temper like that. It had been childish.

'It's all right for you to lose your temper, Elizabeth,' he said. 'You're only a girl.'

Elizabeth couldn't help smiling to herself. It was a typical Patrick remark – and just one of the reasons why she much preferred his cousin Julian!

Patrick did not speak again until they reached the shop.

'The truth is, Elizabeth,' he confessed, as they stared in the shop window, 'that I really thought I might beat you today. You've been so busy with this monitor business. You haven't been practising so much lately. I was so hoping that they'd notice me. How well I was playing . . . Then maybe I'd get a chance to play in a match soon.'

'You *were* playing well, Patrick,' said Elizabeth truthfully. 'And the game could easily have gone the other way. And I'm sure they did notice you and that you'll be given a chance sooner or later.'

A little bell on the shop door tinkled softly as they pushed it open and went inside. It was a lovely, old-fashioned shop with a warm, musky smell. The table-tennis balls were in a cardboard box, jammed between the shuttlecocks and the birthday cards.

Patrick picked out a shiny new white ping-pong ball, took it to the counter and paid for it. Elizabeth followed him out of the shop.

They stood outside on the pavement, wondering whether there was time to go across to the sweet shop, on the opposite side of the road. They decided there was not.

Then suddenly a car squealed to a halt in front of them and a mother burst out of the car, with a small red-headed child. They seemed to be in a great state of excitement. They were looking this way.

Something strange was going on.

The little girl was pointing at Patrick! She was whispering to her mother. Her eyes were very big and round. Her cheeks had gone very pink.

'Are you *sure*, Sandra?' the woman kept asking. 'Are you really sure it was him?'

'Yes, Mummy. It was, it was, it was!'

'Look at his face. You are quite sure?'

'Sure as sure can be, Mummy!' squeaked the child, getting more excited by the minute. 'Cross my heart. It was him!'

Then an extraordinary thing happened. To Elizabeth's amazement, the woman ran up to Patrick and embraced him! There were tears of emotion in her eyes.

'Thank you!' she exclaimed. 'Thank you for saving my little Sandra's life! Every day when we come to the shops, I tell Sandra to look out for you, in case she should see you again. We so wanted to be able to thank you!'

Patrick stood there, blushing. And then the woman

picked the child up and thrust her at Patrick.

'Give the young man a kiss, Sandra. Tell him you're sorry for being such a silly girl and giving us all a fright. Say thank you nicely.'

Patrick's blushing increased tenfold as the little girl planted a kiss on his cheek and lisped her thank-yous.

The woman then set the child down on the pavement and turned to speak to Elizabeth.

'I don't suppose your friend's ever told you he's a hero?'

'No!' exclaimed Elizabeth. 'Whatever happened?'

'My Sandra ran out of this shop last week when my back was turned!' the woman explained. 'She ran across the road to go to the sweet shop. That's what happened! And your friend here—' The woman patted Patrick's arm, overcome with emotion. 'There was this car, you see,' she gulped. 'It came speeding round the bend. It didn't see my Sandra. And your friend – he was so brave. He ran into the road and pushed her out of the way, just in time! And he could have been killed himself. And he didn't even stop to let anybody thank him. He just ran off.'

'Patrick!' gasped Elizabeth.

Politely, Patrick bowed to both the mother and child. Then he backed away. 'I'm afraid we're in a bit of a hurry!' he said. 'Come on, Elizabeth.'

He took her arm and marched her swiftly away. Elizabeth could sense the boy's embarrassment. He would never have dreamt, she thought, that his brave deed might come out in this unexpected way. He was walking so fast, he was almost running!

'Thank you again,' the woman called out. 'I just had to stop the car when Sandra saw you. I didn't mean to embarrass you! You're a real hero, young man. I'll never forget you as long as I live!'

Worried that the woman would take Patrick's discomfiture for rudeness, Elizabeth looked back and gave mother and daughter a friendly wave. Elizabeth's face was flushed with excitement. Her eyes were shining.

'Think nothing of it!' she called. 'It was a pleasure.'

And, as soon as she and Patrick had gone a safe distance, she jerked at his arm and made him halt.

'Patrick! I am absolutely amazed!' she said, gazing at him. 'What a wonderful surprise! I know it's a horrid thing to say, but I had no idea that you could be such a brave person. I'm really ashamed of myself now. What a fine thing to do! And to think that when it happened you didn't even wait to be thanked!'

She gazed at him, wide-eyed. She was seeing him in a completely new light. 'Oh, Patrick. I do admire you for this.'

He lowered his gaze, crimson with pleasure.

'Lot of fuss about nothing,' he muttered.

They walked on in silence, each wrapped in their own thoughts. Patrick glanced at Elizabeth from time to time, as they wandered along. Her lips were parted and there was still that thrilled expression on her face.

She was thinking about the William and Rita Award! Surely, now, no other candidate could possibly match Patrick's claim to it? It was almost as though the very award itself had been designed with Patrick's deed in mind. What an honour for the second form if the very first William and Rita Award came their way!

'What are you thinking about, Elizabeth?' asked Patrick at length. 'Why are you so quiet?'

They were turning in through the school gates. They could hear a distant bell ringing for tea.

'I'm still thinking about your brave deed, of course. And Patrick, I can't explain yet – but there's a reason why the whole school is going to need to know about it soon!'

'WHAT?' exclaimed Patrick. He pulled her to a stop and gripped her arm.

'Don't you dare, Elizabeth! Nobody's to know about this. No one, you understand? You're to promise me at once that you will never say a word to anyone!'

Elizabeth looked at him in dismay. She pouted. 'Why not, Patrick? Whyever not? Quite apart from this

– er – special thing, it's right that people should know! I'd like *everybody* to know what you're really like. What a good, brave person you are. And how you've never once showed off about what you did.'

Patrick flushed, basking in Elizabeth's praise.

'Why must I keep it secret, Patrick?' Elizabeth repeated.

The boy thought long and hard, staring at the ground. When he replied, the words were carefully chosen.

'Look at it this way,' he said. 'If a boy in a Whyteleafe uniform was down in the village one day, and performed a brave action, why would nobody know about it? At least one other person should know about it, shouldn't they? I'm not admitting anything and certainly not to a monitor, but isn't there a rule at Whyteleafe School? Isn't there a very strict rule that must never be broken?'

'Oh!' gasped Elizabeth. 'Of course! You went down to the village on your own, Patrick! That's it, isn't it? You didn't pair up with somebody else, the way you're supposed to.'

Patrick did not reply. Instead he let go of Elizabeth's arm and strode on up the school drive.

He looked back over his shoulder. 'Come on, Elizabeth. You're going to be late for tea.'

She hurried after him. She was thinking things over

carefully. She caught up with him, outside the doors of the dining hall.

'Patrick, I can see you're in an awkward situation. But believe me, I'm sure this boy would be forgiven, just this once, for breaking an important school rule. Once everybody knew what a hero he'd been.'

'He's not interested in being a hero, Elizabeth, and that's final. A hero to you, if you like. I don't mind that. But nobody else. So now please shut up about it.'

Swallowing her deep disappointment, Elizabeth went in to tea. Julian and Joan were wondering where she'd got to. Julian's eyebrows rose high upon seeing her enter the dining hall with Patrick.

They explained how they'd gone down to the shops to buy the new ping-pong ball. Patrick whistled cheerfully and bounced it on the table a few times. Elizabeth watched admiringly.

Later, when they went to feed the ponies, Julian joked about Patrick.

'Poor Elizabeth. That's what comes of being a monitor. Bad luck!'

Elizabeth would normally have got the point at once and giggled. But today she looked at Julian in surprise.

'Bad luck? What do you mean exactly, Julian?'

'Having to partner Patrick down to the village shop,

of course,' he replied patiently. 'No wonder you looked cross when you got back for tea. Was he a pain as usual?'

'No, of course not. Patrick's not a pain!'

Julian looked at her in surprise.

'Oh, I know he is sometimes,' Elizabeth added hastily. She drew a deep breath. She must be careful. But she must also come to Patrick's defence. 'Your cousin's quite decent really. He's got hidden depths, you know.'

'Hidden depths?' Julian laughed out loud. 'So well hidden you'd never find them in a million years. Have you gone potty, Elizabeth? Or is this a bad attack of the goody-goody-monitor-itis disease?'

'Of course it isn't, Julian,' retorted Elizabeth indignantly.

'I think I prefer you when you're being the naughtiest girl,' he grinned.

Drat Patrick, thought Elizabeth, not letting her tell anybody about his brave deed! She was longing to tell Julian, but her lips had been sealed.

Patrick was pretending it was because he wanted nobody to find out that he'd been breaking a school rule. But Elizabeth was not convinced about that.

The real reason, she believed, was that, as with any true hero, Patrick was determined that his heroism should go unsung. And, although it made her cross, it also made her admire him all the more for it.

She decided she would try to express her admiration secretly. Somehow she'd find a way to be especially nice to him!

CHAPTER FOUR

AN UNEXPECTED DISCOVERY

WITH THE whole school assembled in the big hall Thomas and Emma announced the new award. They left it to the very end of Friday's Meeting. Every pupil listened attentively, from the junior children sitting cross-legged on the floor at the front, to the seniors on benches at the back. No boys and girls were allowed to miss the weekly 'parliament'. The joint headmistresses, with Mr Johns, the senior master, sat at the very back of the hall. They were there as observers. They never took part in the Meetings unless, for very difficult matters, their advice was needed.

Elizabeth and Joan sat in chairs on the platform with the other monitors, either side of the head boy and girl. Thomas and Emma sat at a special table, from where they conducted the Meeting.

There had been all the usual business to get through.

Money was collected from pupils who'd received some this week, then given out again to every member of the school in the form of the two shillings weekly allowance. At Whyteleafe School all money had to be fairly shared. Then special requests for extra money were listened to. They were discussed and then either granted or refused. There were no complaints or grumbles to be heard this week, but there were several sports announcements. Elizabeth was proud to hear her name read out as a member of the table-tennis team for tomorrow's match against Hickling Green.

Jake's name was again missing from the hockey team list. From her vantage point on the platform Elizabeth had watched him arrive for the Meeting. His limp, if anything, seemed more pronounced than ever. His ankle was still supported by a thick crepe bandage.

'We are all sorry that Jake will not be able to play for us at Hickling Green tomorrow,' announced Thomas, 'and we take this opportunity to wish him well and hope that his injury is better in time for our next hockey fixture, which will be against Milford Grange.'

Then Emma took over. 'Finally, we have some exciting news to tell you,' she said.

Elizabeth and Joan glanced at each other. At last! They had been waiting eagerly for the moment when the William and Rita Award would be announced. It had been a strain having to keep it secret since the MM. Now the whole school would hear about it. How would it be received? Had the monitors been correct when they'd all voted for it, so sure that their classmates would approve?

They need not have worried. The news was greeted with cheers and applause. It was very well received indeed! Soon a buzz of chatter ran up and down the rows.

A new honour, to be called the William and Rita Award!

To be given not for being brainy or good at games or anything like that, but for Outstanding Conduct, such as bravery or unselfishness . . . or exceptional kindness. It would be handed out each half-term. What a fantastic idea!

'What are you so quiet for, Patrick?' asked their classmate, Arabella Buckley. 'Don't you like the idea?'

'Just thinking, that's all,' muttered Patrick. He had been listening attentively to the announcement. He appeared to be scowling.

'I think it's an excellent idea,' continued Arabella primly. She was already trying to work out how she might get to win the new honour. 'The brainy people get paid too much attention around here.'

'What do you think, Julian?' asked Arabella's friend,

Rosemary. 'I like the way it's called after William and Rita, don't you?'

'It's a good idea,' conceded Julian. 'And yes, it's a good name too. I'm sure they'd approve!'

Julian glanced up towards the platform, at Elizabeth's glowing face. So this was what the secret had been the other day. He was pleased to be privy to it at last. It was difficult, in some ways, the naughtiest girl being a monitor.

As the noise level in the hall grew, Thomas had to bring the Meeting to order. He banged the gavel sharply on the small table.

'Silence! We're pleased you all like the idea! But, if you've any questions or suggestions to make, please address them to the whole Meeting and not just to each other!'

Arabella was the first to put her hand up. She rose to her feet.

'Please, Thomas, Emma says we're allowed to put forward names for the award. But when should we do it exactly?'

'At any time, Arabella. At any time you see someone in your own form behaving in a way that deserves a nomination. The school office has a supply of special forms, called citation forms. You simply collect a form, fill in the person's name and your reason for naming them, then hand it to your monitor.'

'What happens to the forms then?' asked Arabella eagerly.

'Any monitor who has been given a citation form will read it out, at the next Monitors' Meeting. Each one will be heard in the privacy of that meeting. The best will go on a shortlist. Just before half-term, Emma and I will go through the shortlist with Miss Belle and Miss Best. They will help us to decide who has won the first William and Rita Award. But the award will be presented once every term. It will, we hope, become a regular feature of school life and something that all can strive for.'

'Thank you, Thomas,' nodded Arabella. She sat down, her dainty face a little pinker than usual.

There were a few more questions. After that the Meeting was declared closed.

Patrick waited for Elizabeth as she came out of the hall and pulled her to one side. He seemed agitated.

'I couldn't bear it, Elizabeth. You do understand, don't you? You do promise?'

'Of course I promise, Patrick.'

She patted his arm soothingly and smiled. She was feeling in a very good mood. How well the announcement had gone. The whole school approved of it! Thomas and Emma were absolutely right: courage and kindness and unselfishness were the most important qualities in the world. It was right that they should be recognised.

'You are much too modest, Patrick,' she said. 'But your secret is safe with me. I can't help wishing you would change your mind, though! You were so brave!'

At that moment Julian came out of the hall, looking for Elizabeth. He was confronted by the sight of her with Patrick. The pair of them were whispering together, smiling and looking at each other in a silly way.

'Come on, Elizabeth,' he said sharply. 'Let's go and have tea.'

'Just coming, Julian!'

As they made their way to the dining hall together, a feeling of exasperation swept over Julian.

'You seem to be getting very thick with my horrible cousin,' he commented.

'Oh, please don't be silly, Julian,' replied Elizabeth.

She was thinking hard. The glimmering of an idea was forming in her mind. She had thought of a way in which she could recognise Patrick's modesty and courage with a small noble deed of her own. It was no more than he deserved and it would be a gesture that she would find deeply satisfying.

Unfortunately, it was going to annoy Julian even more.

'Drat! I've got a horrid headache,' announced

Elizabeth the next day. 'I don't think I'm going to be well enough to play in my match today!'

Julian stared at his friend in surprise.

It was Saturday dinnertime. Elizabeth had been laughing and talking cheerfully during the meal and had eaten heartily. The boys and girls had been out blackberrying during the week. From the bags full of succulent fruit brought to the school kitchens Cook had concocted a whole shelf-full of summer puddings. They had been served today, with a choice of cream or custard. Elizabeth had eaten three helpings. Delicious!

'You must have eaten too much,' observed Julian.

'Oh, poor Elizabeth,' said Joan anxiously. 'But you mustn't miss the match! The coach leaves in twenty minutes . . . You'd better go and see Matron for some aspirin straight away!'

Further along the table, Patrick's ears had pricked up.

'It's no good, Joan!' Elizabeth ran her hand across her brow for dramatic effect. 'I just know I won't be able to play my best today. Patrick will have to play in my place. He's first reserve and he is very good, you know.'

For a moment Patrick had felt upset that Elizabeth was feeling unwell. But now, unable to help himself, a look of incredulous joy crossed his face. The naughtiest girl felt very pleased with herself as she noted his expression.

'Oh, Elizabeth, I'll be glad to take your place if you're not feeling up to it. Shall we go and see Emma right away and talk to her about it?'

'Yes, Patrick. Let's!'

They rushed off to see Emma, who was just leaving the seniors' table. It was almost time to go and get ready. As team captain, she agreed at once that Patrick should take Elizabeth's place. A jolting coach journey to Hickling Green School would make the headache much worse for Elizabeth, she reasoned.

As Patrick and Elizabeth walked back to their own table, Julian strained his ears to hear what was being said. Elizabeth was gazing at Patrick with that silly expression on her face again. Patrick was talking to her as though they were very dear friends.

'Oh, Elizabeth, I've been waiting for this chance for so long. I won't let you down, I promise. I'll play the best table tennis of my life.'

'I know you will, Patrick.'

'And I'll do it specially for you, Elizabeth! I'm going to win my match today, as a present for you.'

'Thank you, Patrick.'

'I don't think I've got time to finish my pudding. I'd better dash straight off and get changed and find my lucky table-tennis bat.'

He rushed away, brimming over with excitement.

Elizabeth slipped back into her seat between Julian and Joan, a satisfied little smile on her face.

'Poor Elizabeth,' repeated Joan, who was just getting up from the table. 'What a shame. Promise me you'll have a quiet lie-down this afternoon.'

'We'll want to go and wave the coach off first, won't we, Joan?' replied Elizabeth eagerly. 'We can wave to them and wish them good luck!'

Secretly, the naughtiest girl wanted to see Patrick's face again as he climbed on to the coach in his smart tracksuit. That happy look on his face made it all so worthwhile.

'I can't, Elizabeth,' Joan apologised. 'I've promised to go on an outing with Susan this afternoon. Look, she's waiting for me now.'

Sure enough, Joan's friend Susan, who had gone up into the third form this term, was signalling to her. Miss Thomas was taking a group to the indoor swimming pool in the town and Susan was a very keen swimmer. Thinking that Elizabeth would be away at her match, Joan had arranged to go too.

As she hurried off, Elizabeth turned to Julian.

He was bent over his pudding, a puzzled gleam in his green eyes. He was a very clever, bright boy. He was not easily tricked. He was convinced that Elizabeth was play-acting and did not have a headache at all.

She was trying to give Patrick a chance in the table-tennis team, that was all!

He was used to never knowing what went on inside her head. At other times it was one of the things he liked best about her! But not today. Why was Elizabeth being so nice to his worthless cousin? It didn't make sense. And Julian found it intensely irritating.

'You'll come with me to see Patrick off on the coach, won't you, Julian?' smiled Elizabeth. 'And it's a lovely afternoon. We could go out on the ponies after that. We could have a good long outing.'

'Certainly not,' said Julian. 'Why would I want to see Patrick off on the coach? As for going for a ride, I thought you had a headache.'

'Well, yes, but . . .' Elizabeth thought quickly. 'I'm sure the fresh air will do it good!'

'I'm sorry, Elizabeth. I've fixed up to go riding with Harry and Robert. As you're not well enough to play in your match, I suggest you go and have a good lie-down, as Joan suggested.'

'Yes, of course,' sighed Elizabeth.

Soon after that she left the dining hall and went outside into the school grounds for a walk. She wanted to collect her thoughts. Julian was annoyed with her! He couldn't understand why she was being so friendly towards Patrick. If only she could explain to him what a fine person Patrick really was and that he *deserved* some reward. But she couldn't. She'd promised!

The coach was waiting on the back drive.

Shortly before it was due to leave, she went across there and hid in the shrubbery. She could see all the boys and girls climbing aboard, the hockey team as well. They were all laughing and talking together. Patrick was already in his seat, on the far side of the coach, so she couldn't see his expression after all. Unable to wave the coach off with her friends, she knew she would feel a bit silly doing it on her own. So she decided to watch it leave, from here, without being seen.

The warm glow that she'd felt a few minutes earlier had faded. As she watched the last passengers climb aboard and the coach doors shut, she felt very wistful. They were all off to Hickling Green without her. She was going to miss all the excitement! And what was she going to do with herself? The afternoon stretched ahead, bleak and empty . . .

As the coach moved away and trundled off down the drive, a figure standing behind it was suddenly revealed. He was waving, rather forlornly.

It was Jake, seeing the coach off. But, as soon as the vehicle disappeared, Jake's arm dropped to his side and he did an extraordinary thing.

Never dreaming that Elizabeth was watching him

from her hiding place, Jake shook his fist at the sky then ran furiously down the drive after the coach and took a flying kick at some loose gravel, to relieve his feelings. He then ran off down a side path and disappeared from view.

He was running! realised Elizabeth. *He didn't have a limp at all! He must have been pretending all this time. There's nothing wrong with his ankle whatsoever!*

It was a very surprising discovery.

CHAPTER FIVE

ELIZABETH GIVES JAKE AWAY

ELIZABETH FOLLOWED in Jake's tracks.

He's limping again, now that people can see him! she realised, as she reached the other end of the path where it emerged from the bushes. Here some junior boys and girls were playing on the back lawn.

Jake limped slowly past them, heading for the school buildings. For a moment she wondered if she could have just dreamt it. But only for a moment.

No. I definitely saw what I saw. So why is Jake play-acting like this? thought Elizabeth hot-temperedly. *It's so mean of him! How can he bear to let our form down in this way, as well as the hockey team and the whole of Whyteleafe School!*

She very nearly dashed after him there and then. But, even with her temper up, she did not quite dare to confront him. Besides, he was surrounded by some junior boys now. Jake was one of their heroes.

What should she do?

Julian will know the best thing to do! Elizabeth decided. *I'll ask his advice. I'd better run all the way, if I want to catch him before he goes off!*

She raced across the grounds to the school stables. But the boys had just left.

'They went that way, Elizabeth,' Mr Tucker, the stableman told her, pointing up the bridle path.

'Thanks!' gasped Elizabeth.

She veered off through the trees. She could hear voices some distance ahead and the clip-clop of the ponies' hooves. Then, through a gap, she glimpsed them turning off at right angles, where the path divided. They were riding in single file, Robert, then Harry, Julian bringing up the rear. She scrambled over a bank and through tangled undergrowth, to cut off a corner. It brought her within hailing distance. She cupped her hands to her mouth.

'JULIAN!' she shouted, with all her might.

Startled, Julian reined in his pony. He wheeled the animal round and spotted Elizabeth frantically waving her arms. He told Harry and Robert to wait for him.

He trotted back to meet her. 'Whatever's wrong, Elizabeth?'

Gulping to get her breath back, she told Julian what

she had just discovered. She was bristling with indignation. He listened carefully.

Then, to her surprise, he gave a dry laugh.

'So that's two of you trying to get out of playing in school matches, is it?' he commented. 'You're a fine one to be cross, Elizabeth. How's the headache by the way?'

Elizabeth fell silent. Julian spoke more gently then.

'I think you must have imagined it about Jake, you know.'

'I did not, Julian. I certainly did not! I was hoping to hear your ideas – about the best thing to do.'

'Well, I know that *you* have a reason for getting out of *your* match, Elizabeth. Even if it is a totally potty one! So *Jake* may have a reason too. You will have to go and speak to him and ask him to explain. After all . . .'

Down the bridle path Harry and Robert were signalling impatiently. They were cross to have been held up like this. Julian wheeled his pony round. He was suddenly feeling rather cross himself.

'. . . *you* are the monitor, Elizabeth, not me. Good luck!'

Julian rode off then, without a backward glance. He was annoyed to have been reminded like this of Elizabeth making sacrifices on behalf of his worthless cousin, Patrick. Just when he had managed to put it out of his mind!

Elizabeth walked slowly back to school, feeling very subdued.

Her temper had evaporated now. Julian's words had rather shamed her. He had guessed that she had made it up about the headache. He had also guessed the reason why! She longed to explain to him about Patrick's brave deed, but she was not allowed to. And, of course, Julian was right. She was a fine one to feel indignant about Jake!

But she also knew that Julian's advice was correct. As Jake's monitor, she should go and speak to him and give him a chance to explain the reason for his strange behaviour. She should then persuade Jake to go and own up to the teachers. However, Elizabeth remembered the last time that she had spoken to the big boy as his monitor. How grumpy he had been with her – and with good reason, with so much to hide.

How much grumpier he would be if she dared to confront him now! And he would probably think that she had been spying on him. He would be furious!

All that afternoon Elizabeth tried to screw up courage to go and speak to the older boy. But her courage failed her. She decided that perhaps she would speak to Joan about it, at teatime. If Joan agreed, they would go and see Jake together this evening.

It was only when Joan did not turn up at teatime that

Elizabeth remembered that the swimming group had been excused tea today. They were having tea in town.

Julian turned up late, glowing from his ride, and did not even bother to ask Elizabeth if she had spoken to Jake yet. Elizabeth was relieved about that.

After that she did her piano practice and then decided to go and wait for the return of the school coach. She longed to know how the table-tennis team had got on at Hickling Green. What fun Patrick would have been having today, so much more fun than her. She'd never known such a dreary time. How she would have loved to play in the match!

The first person off the coach was Mr Warlow.

'Hello, Elizabeth. Feeling better? You'll be pleased to know that we won the table tennis. Patrick played very well.'

Elizabeth felt some relief at those words. She had done the school no harm then, by not playing in the match! But she had never seen the sports master look so careworn.

'Is there anything wrong, Mr Warlow?' she asked.

'I'm afraid the hockey match was a disaster. We were beaten six–nil. We had our chances to score, but we didn't take them. We needed our star shooter and that's a fact. It would have made such a difference if Jake had played. That wretched ankle of his. I have never known a simple sprain take so long to get better!'

The young sports master looked so unhappy, Elizabeth longed to cheer him up! She smiled impetuously and, before she could stop them, the words flew out of her mouth, unbidden.

'It's better now, Mr Warlow! It's just got better!'

'Elizabeth, is this true?' asked the teacher, looking excited. 'Have you spoken to Jake then?'

Elizabeth gulped. What had she said? What had she *done*? There was no going back now.

'I – I haven't actually spoken to him. But I saw him outside and the ankle's suddenly looking . . . well, really fine. I'm sure it's going to be all right for the match against Milford Grange, Mr Warlow! I'm sure if you get Jake to have a check-up . . .'

'I'll drive him to the doctor myself!' exclaimed Mr Warlow in delight. 'I'll go and find him straight away! If we hurry, we'll just make surgery before it closes.'

He strode briskly away.

'This is very good news, Elizabeth!' he called back over his shoulder. 'Thank you so much for telling me! What a good monitor you are!'

'Hello, Elizabeth! What's this about good news? I've got some good news myself!'

Patrick had appeared at her side. Some members of the Whyteleafe first hockey team were beginning to trudge past, heads bowed, eyes downcast. But Patrick was beaming with pride.

'I won both my games, Elizabeth!' he was saying. 'I told you I would, didn't I?'

Elizabeth was watching Mr Warlow, as he disappeared into the school building. He was determined to find Jake at once. He wanted to take him to the doctor's! What a shock the big boy was going to get. Elizabeth could not help feeling a little trembly. She had let her tongue run away with her.

With an effort she turned her attention to Patrick.

'Congratulations!' she said, looking pale. 'I'm so pleased for you. Was it a good outing then?'

'A marvellous outing! We had the most splendid tea!' Patrick was looking elated. 'But you haven't heard the half of it, Elizabeth! Donald didn't play at all well today. If it hadn't been for me, we'd have lost. My last game decided it. From something Emma said to me I think I'm going to be chosen instead of Donald next time.'

They started to walk over to the school together.

'Oh, Patrick, I'm so glad I gave you your chance!' Elizabeth blurted out. 'It's no more than you deserve.'

'Gave me my chance?' asked Patrick, looking puzzled.

Elizabeth took a deep breath. She had been stung by Julian's words earlier. It would make her feel better if Patrick, at least, knew the truth . . .

'I didn't really have a headache,' she confessed. 'I was just desperate to make sure that you got some reward at least for your brave deed.'

'Elizabeth!' exclaimed Patrick. He looked horrified. 'You shouldn't have done that.'

'I had to,' she replied. 'You are such a fine person, Patrick. I don't know how I'm going to hold my tongue at the next MM, I really don't . . . You do deserve the William and Rita Award, you really do!'

'No!' The boy paled. 'You promised!'

'It's all right, it's all right,' she said soothingly. Seeing how upset he was, she slipped her arm through his as they walked towards the school steps together. 'Only joking, Patrick! I am sure a lot of fine deeds will be coming up at the MMs. I expect Thomas and Emma will have far too many to choose from when the time comes! I must say I'm looking forward to hearing some of them.'

Patrick nodded, visibly relieved. He liked having Elizabeth on his arm like this. Somebody was coming down the steps, and would be passing right by them in a moment . . .

'Hello, Julian!' he said cheerfully. 'I won my games today! Nice evening, isn't it?'

'Is it?' asked Julian curtly. 'Joan's back, Elizabeth. She was looking for you.' And he passed on his way.

Elizabeth took her leave of Patrick almost immediately.

She found Joan resting on the bed upstairs.

'Oh, Elizabeth, I have had such a wonderful time! But I am quite exhausted now!'

Gentle Joan had never shone at sports. But today she had made an exciting discovery. It seemed that Miss Thomas believed that she had the talents of a born swimmer. The teacher was hoping to get up a Whyteleafe swimming team some time. She had told Joan that, with the right training, she could well be a member of it.

'Miss Thomas is going to give Susan and me and some others regular fitness training in the gym,' Joan explained. 'Oh, Elizabeth, I never thought I'd ever be good at sports, but I really think I might enjoy swimming.'

'Joan, this is the most thrilling news!' exclaimed Elizabeth, pleased to see her friend so happy.

For once Joan was too full of her own news to question her friend about the headache, or how she'd spent the afternoon. That came as a relief to Elizabeth.

She was beginning to feel very ashamed that, instead of having the courage to go and speak to Jake, she had ended up blurting out his secret to a teacher. She could not bring herself to confess what she had done, even to her best friend.

But what would happen now?

CHAPTER SIX

A HORRID MESSAGE APPEARS

ON SUNDAY morning Jake was seen running up and down the hockey pitch with Mr Warlow, practising his stick work. The teacher wanted to see his star player back on top form as quickly as possible. He would be needed for the Milford Grange match, needed very badly!

Several second-form boys turned out to watch him. Martin, Kenneth, Harry and John McTavish were all fans of his. He was such a marvellous player for a boy of his age; Kenneth was already a friend of his in the second form. The others had admired him even when they were only in the first form.

It was great news, the boys all agreed, that the sprained ankle had now made a complete recovery. Mr Warlow had got the doctor to check it over last night. There had been no sign of bruising or swelling there. Jake was pronounced fit to play hockey again.

'What a shame it wasn't in time to play against Hickling Green yesterday!' observed Harry.

'But he'll be able to play against Milford Grange!' smiled Martin. 'It's a home match so we'll all be able to watch!'

'We'll thrash them!' said John jubilantly. 'Jake will see to that.'

They were all very pleased.

'Did you speak to Jake then, Elizabeth?' asked Julian, with interest, at one point during the day.

'Not exactly,' she mumbled in embarrassment, and hurried off.

For the only person who was not pleased was Jake.

Secretly, he was very upset. He did not want to play hockey against Milford Grange. He did not want to play hockey at all. When he passed Elizabeth in the dining hall at breakfast time, he had given her such a fierce look. Mr Warlow might think that Elizabeth was a good monitor, to have spotted that Jake's ankle had suddenly made a recovery, but Jake did not share that opinion! He was very taken aback by it all and became convinced that Elizabeth must have been spying on him in secret. How long had she been doing so? he wondered.

She had also got him into trouble. For the doctor had informed Mr Warlow that from all appearances any injury to the ankle must have repaired itself some time ago. The teacher was baffled that Jake had made out the injury to be far worse than it really was. He had accused him of laziness and of letting down the school.

Jake was such a big, silent, powerful character. The fierce look he had given Elizabeth had made her flinch! She spent the rest of the day avoiding him. She was very puzzled by his strange behaviour. At the same time she was truly ashamed that his secret had come out in the way that it had. She wanted to find some way of showing him that she was sorry.

By the evening, when she felt hopeful that Jake would have cooled down somewhat, she took her chance. He was standing, drinking cocoa in the second-form common room, surrounded by the gang of boys who admired him.

'Have my chocolate biscuit, Jake,' she said, walking up to him. 'It will build you up for the match against Milford Grange! May I come and cheer you on, please?'

'Don't bother,' replied Jake curtly, ignoring the plate. 'I can manage without you.'

Elizabeth had a hot temper. It immediately flared up.

'How rude!' she gasped, gazing up at the boy as he towered above her. 'You're not to talk to a monitor like that!'

That immediately inflamed Jake.

'I'm tired of girl monitors,' he stated. 'Girl monitors would do a lot better to mind their own business.'

'Hear, hear!' agreed Martin. He had no idea what Jake was talking about but he could see that the big boy was very angry.

Elizabeth's own anger easily matched Jake's.

She wanted to blurt out that it was not just her business but everybody else's if a person pretended they had something wrong with them when they hadn't and deliberately let a school team down! But then, to her horror, she remembered that she'd just done the same thing herself. Even if, by good fortune, Patrick had won his games and prevented the table-tennis team from being defeated.

She bit back her words, turned on her heel and marched out of the common room. She slammed the door loudly behind her.

'What's up between you and her, Jake?' asked his friend Kenneth.

'She told tales, that's all,' replied Jake, looking morose. 'She exceeded her authority. She shouldn't poke her nose in my private business. I'm fed up with bossy girl monitors thinking they know what's best for us boys.'

'Joan doesn't do that,' Harry pointed out fairly.

'No,' agreed Martin. 'And she's been one for ages.

Elizabeth's new, which makes it worse.'

'I expect it's gone right to her curly head,' sighed Jake wearily.

He clammed up then. He became his usual strong, silent self and refused to answer any more questions. But after he'd left the common room the other boys were all agog.

They liked the naughtiest girl. But they all knew how she'd got her nickname! And there was no doubt that she could still be headstrong and impulsive and do crazy things sometimes. They admired Jake and they trusted him. If he was angry with Elizabeth, then she must have seriously overstepped the mark in some way.

'She wanted to wear a monitor's armband, didn't she, Harry?' remembered Martin. 'And Julian teased her and said it would make her look like a member of the secret police!'

'And it sounds as though she's been behaving like one!' commented John McTavish. 'What a nerve, telling tales on someone like Jake. Thinking she knows what's best for him.'

'I wonder what it was all about?' pondered Harry.

The news of the quarrel spread around the boys' dormitories that night, and grew in the telling. The joke about the armband, and the secret police, was also passed around.

Julian felt rather badly when he heard his joke being repeated. He was going to say something in Elizabeth's defence, but then Patrick stepped in.

'Elizabeth is a very good sort!' he declared. 'Shut up, all of you.'

So Julian shrugged his shoulders and said nothing.

Elizabeth slept badly that night. There were tears of frustration in her eyes. She so much wanted to be a successful monitor, but things were starting to go wrong.

At breakfast time, on Monday morning, she could tell that some of the boys had started to turn against her.

'Where's your armband, Elizabeth?' Martin teased her. 'We won't know to do what we're told if you don't wear an armband.'

Arabella tittered loudly.

'It's not that funny, Arabella,' said Julian airily. 'It's rather an old joke by now. Can't you think of a new one, Martin?'

Elizabeth was glad to escape from the dining hall.

She went up to Room Fourteen to clean her shoes and brush her hair and get ready for lessons. Joan, Kathleen and Jenny, who had all been sitting at the other table today, drifted in. Elizabeth enjoyed chatting about other things with her roommates and began to feel a bit better.

Drat boys! she thought. It was fun just being with

girls sometimes! She began to look forward to her first lesson, which was French, with Mam'zelle.

'Let's get down to the form room nice and early,' suggested Joan.

'Yes!' nodded Elizabeth. 'My desk needs a bit of a tidy-up.'

The form room was empty when they arrived. The two friends had adjoining desks. Elizabeth boisterously flung up her desk lid.

'Oh!' She quickly closed it again, her cheeks pale.

'What was that?' asked Joan quickly. 'What was that piece of paper taped to the inside of your desk lid?'

'It – it seems to be some kind of horrid message,' said Elizabeth.

Gently, Joan opened the desk lid again. Together, the two friends gazed in silence at the anonymous message, carefully written in block capitals.

> WHY HAS THE SECOND FORM GOT TWO GIRL MONITORS? NOT FAIR! GIVE DANIEL HIS CHANCE BACK, ELIZABETH. GIVE THE BOYS A MONITOR OF THEIR OWN!

At that moment Mr Leslie, their form master, came into the classroom to put some things away. Joan carefully removed the message, folded it and placed it in her pocket. They would have to discuss it later.

CHAPTER SEVEN

THINGS GO FROM BAD TO WORSE

'WHAT'S ALL this about, Elizabeth?' asked Joan, at morning break. 'Have you any idea who could have written it?'

'I believe I know exactly who has written it!' replied Elizabeth.

The two friends were sitting on the school steps in the pale October sunshine. Joan had taken the piece of paper from her pocket and unfolded it. Why had somebody turned against Elizabeth? It was all very upsetting.

'Who?' asked Joan in surprise.

'Jake, of course!' Elizabeth blurted out. 'How mean of him not to sign it. What an underhand thing to do!'

'*Jake?*' asked Joan. She liked the gentle giant of a boy and felt she knew him quite well. He had joined the second form even earlier than she had. 'Whyever should

Jake be feeling cross with you, Elizabeth? Especially as I'm sure he must be in a very good mood at the moment with his poor ankle better.'

'That's just it, Joan! He's not in a good mood at all about his ankle! He should be, but he isn't. And he's simply furious with me!'

Joan's eyes widened. She spoke gently.

'What's been going on, Elizabeth? What have you been keeping from me?'

Shamefaced, Elizabeth told Joan everything that had happened concerning Jake the previous day. It was a relief to do so at last.

But Joan, as Elizabeth feared she would be, was very disapproving.

'It was very wrong of you to speak to Mr Warlow before you had spoken to Jake himself, Elizabeth!' she scolded. 'You know that's not the way we do things at Whyteleafe. Jake must have had some very private reason of his own for wanting to get out of hockey, something that he was determined to keep secret. As his monitor, you should have asked him to talk it through with you and then tried to persuade him to go and own up to Mr Warlow. No wonder he is cross with you!'

'I was too scared to,' Elizabeth confessed. 'I was sure Jake didn't respect me as a monitor and the note proves I was right. He thinks the other monitor should be a boy! And, because I've upset Jake, some more of the boys are turning against me! What should I do, Joan? Do you think I should resign?'

'Of course not, Elizabeth!' her friend replied firmly. She folded the note up and replaced it in her pocket. 'You can't give in to this sort of thing. It's not always easy being a monitor and we all make mistakes. Just try to tread carefully for a while, Elizabeth. Everybody likes you very much and wanted you to be a monitor this term. I'm sure this will all blow over in a few days.'

'Oh, do you really think so, Joan?'

Elizabeth felt very cheered. But her cheerfulness did not last long.

Far from blowing over, the trouble with the boys got worse.

Elizabeth was still being teased. And the feeling that it was unfair not to have a boy monitor seemed to be spreading. Jake continued to be unfriendly towards her and Elizabeth strongly suspected that, as well as writing the note, he was encouraging the other boys in some kind of campaign to get rid of her. Had she made a powerful enemy?

In Martin's dormitory they were starting to have pillow fights at night. These were forbidden, of course, but apparently great fun!

Martin openly bragged that, as girls were not allowed

to enter the boys' quarters, they could do what they liked as they only had girl monitors in the second form. No monitors could come and stop their fun!

Julian gave Elizabeth a friendly word of warning.

'I shouldn't report them, if I were you, Elizabeth,' he said. 'Not if you know what's good for you!'

Elizabeth had never actually admitted to Julian that she'd given Jake's secret away because she and Julian were far less close than usual. She was sad, but there was nothing she could do about it, without explaining to him the story of Patrick's bravery. However, on the Jake front, Julian had very quickly worked things out for himself. Like Elizabeth, he was mystified as to why the big boy had pretended about the injury in the first place.

'Don't worry, Julian,' she sighed. 'I know I'm in enough trouble already. I haven't the slightest intention of reporting them.'

She would love to have had a proper chat with him about everything. But he was already strolling away, whistling.

Patrick was a real nuisance! she thought.

She thought so again, the following day.

The next Monitors' Meeting was due. In Elizabeth's class only one written nomination had been handed in. Quivering with importance, Rosemary had handed the special form over to Joan. But Joan was not able to attend this week's MM. Miss Thomas had arranged the first fitness session for the would-be swimming team. It would clash directly with the MM, but it was the teacher's only free time. Joan dared not miss her very first workout.

'I'm afraid that you are going to have to read this out at the MM, Elizabeth,' she said later, with a wry smile, passing across Rosemary's form. 'What a lovely job for you!'

'Oh, no!' groaned Elizabeth, reading what was written there. 'This is going to be so embarrassing. Must I really? Ugh!'

They both laughed.

Nevertheless, after lessons that day, Elizabeth set off eagerly for the MM. This was going to be very interesting. What kind of citations would the other monitors be reading out from their classmates? Surely they'd be more exciting than Rosemary's? She certainly hoped so!

She arrived on time this week and collected her mug of tea. There were chocolate digestive biscuits again. Good!

'It's all right, Elizabeth, there are plenty. You may take two!' smiled Emma.

She settled down on the floor, next to Peter, letting

Donald have the place on the bench. It was quite comfortable on the floor this week as Thomas had managed to find some cushions.

'Hello, Peter,' she said to the young first-form monitor. 'Have you been given any citations yet for the William and Rita Award?'

Peter shook his head. He seemed to have something else on his mind.

'Not yet, Elizabeth. I keep asking for them, though.'

Soon all the monitors had crammed into the cosy study. Elizabeth was disappointed to see that not many had brought citations with them. She gave Joan's apologies. Then various minor school matters were discussed. Peter put his hand up.

'Please, Thomas and Emma, can you all give me some advice? Some of the boys in my class were squirting water pistols indoors. They wouldn't stop when I asked, so I confiscated them. When d'you think I should give them back?'

They all discussed Peter's problem.

'There we are then! We're all agreed,' Thomas concluded. 'You can keep them for a week. A week seems quite a long time when you're in the first form! Then, as long as they promise only to play with them out-of-doors in future, you can hand them back!'

At last it was time for the citations to be read out.

'You first, Elizabeth,' said Emma. 'I can see you've got one in your hand.'

'It's only just the one so far, I'm afraid,' apologised Elizabeth. 'It's been submitted by Rosemary Wing.'

She tried her best to hide her embarrassment as she read out loud the second form's only citation.

> 'Yesterday my hamster looked very droopy and I was worried about him. Then Arabella Buckley performed a very unselfish act. Arabella is very fond of chocolate herself, but she sacrificed all the chocolate she had left for the whole week and fed it to Hammy, so as to cheer him up. I would therefore like to nominate Arabella Buckley for the William and Rita Award.'

Some of the monitors snorted and sniggered.

'I expect poor Hammy was sick on the spot!' whispered Donald.

Elizabeth's cheeks burnt. She felt so ashamed of her classmates. It was obvious that Arabella had put Rosemary up to this! Surely, between them, they could at least have invented something better? She'd tried her best to read it nicely and put the correct expression in her voice. But it had still sounded completely silly.

'Thank you, Elizabeth,' said Emma sympathetically. 'That was very nicely read.'

'And those of you who are giggling, I'm ashamed of you,' added Thomas. 'All citations are to be listened to in silence, please. I think we are all agreed that this one's not suitable for the shortlist, so let us pass on.'

Elizabeth at once felt better. Now that the second-form citation had been dealt with, she could settle down and look forward to hearing the other forms' contributions.

But there were, indeed, only a few. And, although they were all much more genuine than Rosemary's effort, they were not very inspiring.

After hearing out the last one, read by Eric, the head boy and girl shook their heads.

'I don't think anything we have heard today is quite suitable for the shortlist, do you?' asked Emma ruefully. 'The William and Rita Award must be given for an act of real courage or unselfishness, not everyday acts of kindness, pleasing though it is to hear about them.'

'We seem to have got off to a slow start, I'm afraid,' agreed Thomas. 'Luckily there's plenty of time yet. We must look forward to something really splendid coming in over the next couple of weeks.'

But Elizabeth could tell that they were both very disappointed.

It was so frustrating! How she longed to tell them that a member of the second form had performed an act of real courage.

As she left the MM, she decided that she must go and find Patrick at once. He had just finished a game of table tennis with Daniel.

'Listen, Patrick, I've been thinking,' she said, as she took him outside. There was a pleading note in her voice. 'You know, about your brave deed. I know you don't want it talked about and I know you must be worried that you broke a school rule that day, being down in the village on your own. But supposing, when I go to the next MM, I just talk about this certain boy, without giving his name away? Supposing I just talk about this certain boy being worried about breaking this strict rule and see if they think that matters . . . ? And then . . .'

'Elizabeth! Stop being so tiresome!' exclaimed Patrick impatiently. 'I am not in the least bit worried about being punished for breaking a school rule. That has nothing to do with it really!'

'But . . .'

'I just don't want to be held up as some kind of hero, Elizabeth!' He stared at her, looking baffled and angry. 'Why are you bringing all this up again?'

'I'm sorry, Patrick. I just wondered if perhaps –

well, all us monitors want the first William and Rita Award to be something really special! Can't you see that? And I thought, if it was just the school rule you were worried about . . .'

'Well, it's not!' Patrick almost shouted the words. 'Please forget the whole thing. You promised.'

'I – I'll try.'

'Drop it, Elizabeth! Please don't mention this again!'

Elizabeth walked away after that. She was still filled with admiration for Patrick. How could she not be? But it was very annoying of him all the same. The William and Rita Award was such a lovely idea. But supposing nobody came forward with anything worthwhile by half-term? Thomas and Emma would not be able to give the award after all. What a bad start that would be.

Nothing seemed to be going right at the moment. In fact, things went from bad to worse.

When she went along to collect some homework from her desk, after tea, there was another anonymous message stuck inside the lid. Once again it was written in block capitals:

SOME OF US ARE FED UP. THERE ARE PILLOW FIGHTS NOW – KEEPING US AWAKE AT NIGHT. THE SECOND FORM NEEDS A BOY MONITOR TO KEEP

THE NAUGHTIEST GIRL MARCHES ON

ORDER. WHY NOT RESIGN, PLEASE, ELIZABETH?

Paling slightly, she hurried outside to find Joan.

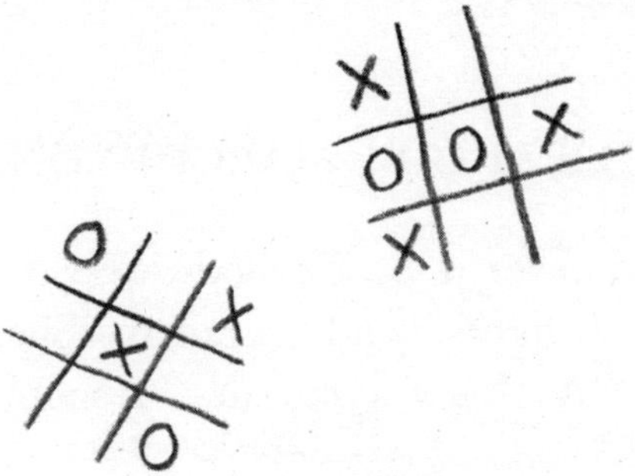

CHAPTER EIGHT

THE NAUGHTIEST GIRL VERSUS THE BOYS

'MY SO-CALLED secret enemy has struck again, Joan!' she said crossly, showing Joan the message. 'Not all that secret in fact. I'm quite convinced that it's Jake who's writing these notes. I know I'm a coward, Joan, but shall we go and see him together and tell him to stop it? He might take some notice of you.'

'We can't do that, Elizabeth,' replied Joan, biting her lip as she read the note carefully. 'We can't be sure it's Jake. Is this really Jake's sort of thing? And we certainly can't walk up to him and accuse him without any proof!'

'I suppose not,' sighed Elizabeth. She read the note through carefully, once again. 'To be fair, it must be very annoying for Jake if these pillow fights are keeping him awake.'

'If it is Jake,' Joan reminded her gently.

'Well, Jake or whoever it is. Anybody who doesn't specially enjoy pillow fights,' said Elizabeth. She was looking thoughtful. 'As I *am* a monitor, I should be thinking what to do.'

'I shouldn't worry, Elizabeth!' said Joan hastily, noting the light in her eye. 'We can't take any notice of anonymous messages. If anyone comes forward with a proper complaint about losing a lot of sleep, then that would be serious and you'd have to report it to the teachers.'

'What, tell tales?' asked Elizabeth, aghast, remembering Julian's advice to her. 'But that would make my position even worse, Joan.'

'This would be quite different, Elizabeth. You couldn't possibly deal with a whole crowd of boys on your own. But, of course, someone would have to make a formal complaint first, not just write a silly note like this. And I don't suppose anybody will.'

Elizabeth did not follow Joan's logic. In any case she was hardly listening.

She'd suddenly remembered young Peter's water pistols and an excited gleam came into her eye. She knew exactly how to handle this problem! She certainly didn't want anybody making a formal complaint to either Joan or herself and then having to go to the teachers. She didn't agree with Joan at all about that.

The boys would never forgive them.

She must act quickly, before there was any danger of it happening.

Later, a cheerful sparkle in her eye, Elizabeth slipped off to talk to some of the other girls. They were good sports, all of them. Then she went to find Peter.

I'm not going to involve Joan in this, she thought. *But I'll jolly well show those boys who's the monitor around here!*

Even as Elizabeth was borrowing the water pistols from Peter, an even younger boy was seeking out Joan, for the junior class did not have a monitor of its own. The small boy was in pyjamas and dressing gown but was not looking forward to going to bed. For two nights running he'd been woken up by bumpings and crashings in the second-form dormitory and had been unable to get to sleep again. His bed was right against the dividing wall. There were dark rings under his eyes.

'Go straight to bed now, Rupert,' Joan told him, after hearing him out. 'I'll see this is sorted out. I'll see to it myself, I promise.'

And I won't involve Elizabeth, she thought. *It's true what she says. She is in enough trouble already.*

After that, Joan decided, she would go to bed herself. The fitness training in the gym had been very enjoyable, but had left her tired out and aching in every muscle.

'Sh, Kathleen! Sh, Jenny!' whispered Elizabeth. 'We mustn't wake Joan!'

'No danger of that, Elizabeth. She's dead to the world!' Kathleen whispered back.

'Miss Thomas really puts them through it, I gather!' commented Jenny.

'Such luck!' giggled Kathleen.

'Sh!' repeated Elizabeth.

It was after lights out, and the three girls had slipped out of bed and were putting on their dressing gowns and slippers. They had waited until they were sure that Joan was in a very deep sleep. On no account, Elizabeth explained, did she want to involve Joan in her plan.

'I shall take full responsibility for this,' she had told her roommates earlier. 'I don't want to have to report those boys to the teachers and I don't want Joan to either. They think it's so clever having pillow fights, but we'll soon cool them down!'

Belinda and Tessa were waiting for them in the corridor.

'Got the water pistols, Elizabeth?' whispered Belinda eagerly.

'I've hidden them in the bathroom!' the naughtiest girl whispered back.

The five girls tiptoed along the corridor to the big bathroom. They were all trying hard not to giggle.

This was going to be such an adventure! Elizabeth took the five water pistols out from their hiding place in the big linen box. She handed her friends one each.

'Right,' she said. 'Now let's load them. As full as full can be.'

With Elizabeth their commander-in-chief leading the way the girls crept along the dimly lit corridors until they reached the boys' quarters. Their pistols were at the ready, loaded with water up to the hilt.

'Martin's dormitory,' she whispered crisply. 'Number Seventeen. Just at the bottom of these stairs. Come on now. Party – advance!'

'I think I can hear them now,' whispered Kathleen excitedly, as they crept down the short flight of stairs. 'Voices!'

The door was ajar. There seemed to be torches flashing around inside. It was after lights out, but there were figures moving about and some whispering going on. The nightly pillow fight must be just about to commence!

Eyes sparkling with anticipation, Elizabeth waved her water pistol above her head in a signal to the other four.

'Ready, steady – *charge!*' she hissed.

With their monitor at their head the girls hurled themselves down the last few stairs and burst into Room Seventeen.

'FIRE!' cried Elizabeth and they squeezed the triggers, spraying fine jets of water at the figures that moved in the dark.

'Break it up, boys!'

'Cool down!'

'Pillow fights not allowed!'

As they shouted their war cries, the girls were laughing with glee.

'Bull's-eye!' cried Elizabeth, as she squirted her best jet of water towards the back of somebody's neck.

'Got you!' she added triumphantly. 'Now perhaps *that* will cool you down just a little bit . . .'

At that very moment the figure turned, receiving it full in the face.

'ELIZABETH ALLEN!' roared the person, shining his torch on her. 'What on earth do you think you are doing?'

Elizabeth and her friends recoiled in dismay. It was a man's voice. They knew it well. Elizabeth shone her own torch, while behind her somebody switched on a light.

Elizabeth found herself face to face with Mr Leslie, their form master. He had three senior boys with him, including Thomas, the head boy. These were the only figures who'd been moving around! They were holding torches. All of them had water dripping down their shirts. Martin and the others, from all appearances, were asleep in bed. Only now were tousled heads raising themselves from various pillows.

'Hey!'

'What's going on?'

'Who's put that light on?'

came the innocent-sounding cries.

Elizabeth stared at her teacher in horror. 'I'm t-t-terribly sorry, sir,' she stammered.

Mr Leslie looked very cross.

'And so you should be, Elizabeth. We were told there might be some horseplay tonight, but we expected to find *boys* misbehaving not girls. Please return to your own quarters this instant, all of you.'

The five girls dived out of the door in relief. They couldn't wait to escape! From the stairs they heard Thomas's voice.

'It's all right, boys. Sorry you've been disturbed. You can go back to sleep now.'

The girls returned to their quarters in silence. What a disaster, thought Jenny and the others. Somehow the boys had got wind of Elizabeth's plan and neatly turned the tables. When the girl monitor and her troops had turned up to put a stop to the boys' pillow fights, they'd run straight into their teacher and his inspection party, with the second-form boys pretending to be fast asleep!

The boys had won. The girls were going to get into trouble and Elizabeth, as ringleader, would get into the biggest trouble of all!

But all Elizabeth could think about, as she tried to get back to sleep that night, was her enemy. *Somebody* had reported her plan to Mr Leslie. And she was sure she knew who. What a mean thing to do!

But the next morning she got a shock.

'Of course it wasn't Jake!' exclaimed Joan in horror, as she listened to Elizabeth's tale of woe. 'Oh, Elizabeth, what a dreadful mix-up. What a dreadful thing to happen! It was me!'

'You, Joan?' squealed Elizabeth in surprise.

Her loud squeal brought Jenny and Kathleen running over.

In distress Joan explained to her roommates about little Rupert.

'The child was desperate about it. He turned to me for help, as a monitor. It left me with no choice but to go and report to Mr Leslie that Room Seventeen was being noisy at nights, though I didn't say anything about the pillow fights. I'm sorry I didn't tell you, Elizabeth. I didn't want to involve you.'

'I'm sorry I didn't tell you about *my* plan,' said Elizabeth, very shamefaced. 'Oh, what a muddle!'

'Thank goodness it wasn't one of the boys anyway,'

said Kathleen, with a sigh of relief.

'Yes, that makes us feel a bit better about it,' agreed Elizabeth. She frowned. 'But Joan, how did Martin and the others know to be well behaved last night? That's what I can't understand.'

Joan thought about it carefully. 'John McTavish walked past last night, when Rupert was talking to me in the corridor. I didn't think he had heard anything. But obviously he must have done.'

'Ah!' said Elizabeth.

So that too was explained.

When Mr Leslie came into class to take the register that morning, the boys owned up about the pillow fights. That, at least, came as a great relief to Elizabeth, Joan and the others. They were a nice crowd really.

'Humph, yes, well, I'm not stupid, Martin,' said Mr Leslie. 'I did realise that something must have been going on. That the fault would not be all on one side. As your high jinks have been depriving some of the other boys of their sleep, Thomas is going to raise the matter at this week's Meeting.'

'Is he going to raise the matter of Elizabeth as well?' asked Jake, with interest. 'Our *monitor*.'

Some of the boys laughed. Elizabeth flushed deeply at Jake's intervention.

'I understand that Elizabeth will be dealt with at the

next Monitors' Meeting,' replied Mr Leslie curtly. 'Now, will everybody please get their pencils and paper ready. Miss Ranger will be here very shortly and today's the day you have your spelling tests.'

After that Julian made some sympathetic 'hen clucking' noises to try to cheer Elizabeth up. He had heard all about the episode in Room Seventeen and had found it highly diverting. Would the naughtiest girl even last till half-term as a monitor? he wondered.

But Elizabeth was not amused. She concentrated hard on the weekly spelling test. After that, for the rest of the English lesson, she kept her head bent over her work. She felt a sense of despair. She had so much wanted to be a successful and popular monitor this term, one who enjoyed the respect of the whole form, like Joan. But she could see that Jake was not going to allow that to happen.

Of course, the water pistols had not been such a good idea. She had been silly and hot-headed and she could not blame Jake for that. But it was getting those horrid notes that had stirred her up and made her behave foolishly. Now some of the boys were laughing at her.

She smouldered as she thought of the notes and she came to a decision.

'I have decided to tackle Jake about those mean notes,' she whispered to Joan, towards the end of the lesson. 'I know you don't want to, so I've decided to speak to him on my own. I shall tell him what I think of him!'

Joan just looked helpless and shook her head.

At that moment Miss Ranger called the two monitors out.

'Elizabeth and Joan, would you please give everybody their spellings back? I have marked them now.'

As the two friends shared out the bundle between them, the English teacher spoke pleasantly to the class.

'Elizabeth and Joan will bring your spellings round. Julian has come top today with twenty out of twenty. Jake, you would have had full marks, but once again you forgot your silent g's. You always forget them! You spelt both *sign* and *resign* without the *g*! When you think of *sign*, think of *signature* and that will help you remember. And when you spell *resign*, think of *resignation*. It's a shame you have such a blank spot about this, or you would have come equal top . . .'

'Yes, Miss Ranger.'

As the English teacher chatted on, Elizabeth was staring at Jake's spellings which were on top of the batch in her hand. Twenty words were written down. Eighteen had red ticks by them and two had been marked with a red cross.

'. . . I'm afraid, Jake,' the teacher was saying, with a

humorous smile, 'that *sign* and *resign* become two completely different words when you leave the *g*'s out. *resin* is something produced from sap. And *sin* is something you commit when you forget your silent *g*'s!'

Everyone laughed. But Elizabeth's scalp prickled as she gazed at Jake's spellings – at that word *resin*, with its cross beside it. Briefly, she shut her eyes, then opened them again.

And I've made a mistake, too, she realised. *Jake didn't write those notes. He couldn't have done.*

For on yesterday's message she was quite sure the word *resign* had been spelt correctly.

CHAPTER NINE

ELIZABETH LEARNS JAKE'S SECRET

'HOW CLEVER of you to remember, Elizabeth,' said Joan when they discussed it together at dinner time. 'I'd never have thought of it. Thank goodness you remembered the wording of this message and worked out that it couldn't be Jake. Only just in time. You were planning to rush off and accuse him!'

'You're the really wise one, Joan,' said Elizabeth humbly. 'You warned me I was being hot-headed! I was too stubborn to listen.'

They were both staring at the second anonymous message, which she had collected from upstairs. WHY NOT RESIGN, PLEASE, ELIZABETH? it ended and it was all spelt correctly. The message was written *before* today's spelling test. If Jake had looked up the spelling to write the message, he would hardly have forgotten it for an important test.

'Jake's always struggled with English,' mused Joan. 'That's why he's still in the second form. I couldn't quite imagine him putting pen to paper to write messages. Jake's style is just to say things straight out!'

'Yes,' nodded Elizabeth. She looked rueful. 'And he's certainly done that as far as I'm concerned. But it was wrong of me to leap to conclusions.'

It was a warm day. The girls were sitting beneath the weeping ash tree, in the school grounds. All the leaves had changed colour in the past week. They were starting to float down now, carpeting the grass around them. Elizabeth caught a fluttering leaf in her hands and examined it. She was thinking hard. She so loved it here at Whyteleafe School, but it was horrid having an enemy. Who *did* write those messages?

'If Jake isn't the enemy, then I want to know who is, Joan!' she said angrily.

The two girls discussed the mystery all dinner hour. They badly wanted to solve it. They went through possible suspects, as real detectives would.

'We can be sure it's a boy, and we can be sure he's in the second form,' said Joan softly. 'So that narrows it down.'

'Not very much, though,' replied Elizabeth ruefully. 'The first thing is to think of the motive. It's got to be somebody who hates the idea of there being two girl monitors, who thinks it's unfair. Somebody other than Jake.'

'What about Daniel?' suggested Joan tentatively.

'Oh, surely not Daniel!' exclaimed Elizabeth in dismay. He was a gentle, sensitive boy. 'I like Daniel! And I'm sure he likes me! Except . . .'

She broke off, remembering the wistful expression on Daniel's face last week, when she'd come from an MM. *They do sound fun*, he'd said. Under his gentle exterior, could Daniel secretly be regretting that he'd stood down after his few days as a monitor, to give Elizabeth her place back?

'I don't want to think it's Daniel, Joan!' she stated. 'Let's think of somebody else. In books it's always the last person you suspect . . .' she laughed. 'Say Julian, for instance . . .'

Even as Elizabeth spoke her friend's name out loud, her laughter faded on her lips and her heart gave a jolt.

'Julian!' she whispered. 'Is it possible? He has been quite cutting lately about my being a monitor!'

'Oh, that's just his usual teasing, Elizabeth! The reason he's so cool is because you're being nice to Patrick. You know how those two cousins hate each other!'

'But you don't understand, Joan. He thinks I'm being nice to Patrick only because I am a monitor!'

Is this a bad attack of the goody-goody-monitor-itis disease? he'd asked her.

'I see,' said Joan. Then she looked at her friend in surprise. What did Elizabeth mean by 'only'? What other reason could she have for being especially nice to Patrick? 'Perhaps you've been overdoing it, Elizabeth. I do believe Julian's a little jealous.'

Elizabeth rapidly changed the subject. It was more than she could bear to think of Julian being her enemy; far worse, even, than it being Daniel.

'We're being silly, Joan,' she declared. 'It couldn't possibly be Julian! Or Daniel, come to that. Let's think of some other people.'

After a while the two girls came to the most obvious conclusion. The message writer was probably one of the gang of boys who admired Jake. Martin, or Kenneth, or John McTavish . . .

'They're probably all in it together,' decided Joan.

But Elizabeth didn't find that any comfort either.

In the distance the bell went for afternoon lessons. As the two girls got to their feet and walked slowly back to school, Elizabeth looked thoughtful.

'Perhaps it doesn't matter who's writing the messages, Joan,' she sighed. 'The fact is I've made a mess of being a monitor. I shouldn't have told tales on Jake. And I shouldn't have allowed myself to get wound up and tried to stop the boys' pillow fights in the way I did. I'm no use as a monitor, if half the boys in the class don't respect me. Perhaps I'd *better* do as the note suggests. Offer to resign.'

'You can't do that, Elizabeth,' said Joan, giving her a sidelong glance. 'You can't give in to anonymous messages.'

'I'm in disgrace anyway,' the naughtiest girl pointed out. 'Don't forget that Thomas is going to deal with me at the next MM! That's what Mr Leslie said. I may have no choice in the matter. I may be asked to resign anyway!'

It was a horrid thought.

'We will just have to see about that, Elizabeth,' replied Joan kindly. 'Won't we?'

In spite of her own troubles Elizabeth began to feel very worried over the next few days about a member of her class.

She had a growing sense of there being something seriously wrong with Jake.

Nobody else noticed much, but Elizabeth found herself keeping a watchful eye on him. She was sure it was connected with the forthcoming hockey match against Milford Grange. She believed he might be dreading it with a sickening fear.

At first she thought it was her imagination, her own

guilty conscience at work. But as each day passed, and the match drew inexorably nearer, she was sure that the big boy was becoming more and more desperate.

'Why don't you want to talk about the big match, Jake?' she heard his friend Kenneth ask him peevishly. 'Why aren't you bothering to practise?'

'My hockey stick will have to do the talking,' Jake had snapped in reply. 'When it needs to!'

He seemed to be avoiding the other boys and they tactfully left him alone.

'He seems a bit tense about the match,' Martin commented. 'I suppose it's because he hasn't played since last season.'

'Jake? Tense about a hockey match?' scoffed John. 'It's schoolwork getting him down, I expect!'

On Friday evening, at the school Meeting, Elizabeth watched Jake from her vantage point on the platform. She thought how glum he looked, wrapped up in his own thoughts. He seemed to take no interest at all when the head boy and girl dealt with the matter of the pillow fights in Room Seventeen.

'As the culprits have owned up, we've decided to let them off lightly,' announced Thomas, while Emma wrote it all down in the school's big Book. 'They must sleep without pillows for a whole week. That will help them to remember that it is thoughtless to keep other boys awake at night! After next week their pillows will be returned to them.'

Even as Elizabeth sat there, wondering what her own punishment was going to be at next week's MM, she noticed that Jake had suddenly gone very pale.

'Finally, we hope you will all turn out and cheer the school hockey team tomorrow morning,' Thomas was saying. 'Milford Grange will be here at eleven o'clock and they are bringing two coachloads of supporters. I am sure you will all be very pleased to know that Jake is fully fit again and is now back in the Whyteleafe team. We are sure he plans to shoot plenty of goals for us tomorrow! Right, everyone. You are dismissed.'

There was laughter and cheers and the sound of benches scraping back. The Meeting was over! The boys and girls were all looking forward to the weekend.

Watching closely, Elizabeth saw Jake rise to his feet and sway slightly. She thought for a moment that he was going to faint. Then he hurried from the hall.

Jake is terrified of tomorrow's match! she realised. *I'm positive now. The very thought of it seems to be making him ill. And it's all my fault! I'm the person who's put him in this position. I think I may have done a dreadful thing!*

Elizabeth hurried down off the platform. Her heart was beating fast. She could not begin to understand what was wrong with Jake, nor why he had been going to such extraordinary lengths to get out of playing hockey for Whyteleafe. But she was racked with guilt to see his suffering.

I've got to catch up with him and tell him how sorry I am! she decided. *I don't care how rude he is to me, I've got to tell him I'm sorry and ask him to forgive me. Oh, what is wrong with him? I do wish there was some way I could make him feel better!*

She raced outside on to the lawn, just in time to see Jake disappearing in the direction of the school gardens. She hurried in pursuit.

When she got there, she saw him sitting quite alone on the wooden bench by the big greenhouse.

The gardens were silent and very still, with no breath of wind today. The rows of runner beans stood like withered green wigwams, their crop near its end. A blackbird rustled in the nearby yew hedge.

Elizabeth's warm heart ached with pity to see the big boy sitting on the bench, doubled up as though in pain. She tiptoed towards him. He was making little moaning sounds.

'Jake!' she whispered.

He raised his head. His eyes looked red.

'Elizabeth!' he gasped in surprise. 'What are you doing here? Please go away. I have such terrible stomach cramps. I can't bear anyone to see me like this.

Please go away – and don't tell anybody you've seen me in such a state!'

'I will *not* go away, Jake!' Elizabeth came and sat beside him and placed an arm round his big shoulders. 'I have come to ask your forgiveness. I know I have done something terrible, giving you away. And now you are scared to play in the match tomorrow. *I* can't bear it to see how scared you are.'

'You've guessed?' asked Jake in alarm.

He buried his face in his hands. Elizabeth patted his heaving back, trying to soothe him.

'I can't bear it that a girl should see me like this,' he moaned.

Elizabeth continued to pat his back gently.

'Please tell me what's wrong, Jake,' she begged. 'I promise on my honour that I'll keep your secret. But I'm so worried about you. I will cry *myself* if you don't tell me what's wrong!'

'I am so very, very scared, Elizabeth,' the boy blurted out. 'I am so frightened that the same thing could happen again.'

'What, Jake?' she prompted him gently, almost in tears herself.

He raised his head and gazed at her. He saw the anguished expression on her face and knew that, in this moment, she was living through his anguish with him. What a fine girl she was, he realised. He suddenly felt sure that he could trust her.

'A month ago, Elizabeth, I nearly blinded somebody,' he stated. 'The person I admire most in all the world. My coach, Henry Hill. Since my father died, he has been like a dad to me! He used to play hockey for England and he's coached me since I was a little boy. But I nearly blinded him. It was touch and go! He's only just come out of hospital.'

'What a terrible thing to happen!' gasped Elizabeth. 'Jake, please tell me the whole story. It will make you feel a little better to talk about it, even if it's only to me.'

At last Jake's strange behaviour began to make sense as he explained that, on the last day of the summer holidays, he'd played in a match for his hometown hockey club. The club's non-playing captain was Henry Hill, a former England international, the man whom Jake so loved and admired. He had coached Jake for years, convinced that the boy would himself play for his country one day. His own playing days were over but, because the team was one short that day, Henry had stepped in at short notice to fill the gap.

It had been a dramatic and closely fought contest, but then had come disaster. A hard-struck ball by Jake had flown off at an angle and the ball had caught Henry in the eye with great force. An ambulance had been called and he'd been rushed to hospital. Only an emergency operation had saved the sight in his left eye.

'It was the most terrible day of my life,' Jake confessed. 'I will never be able to forget it. Henry's cries of pain . . . the ambulance wailing . . . then waiting all afternoon for some news from the hospital . . . I still have bad dreams about it. I really *did* hurt my ankle that day. It was just a slight sprain and my mother bandaged it up for me. Then, when I got back to school, it gave me an idea. I desperately wanted to give myself time! To try to get over what had happened . . .'

'And you didn't want to explain things to Mr Warlow then?' ventured Elizabeth.

'No! He would have told me to put this behind me! He would have tried to rush me. And now I *have* been rushed and the terrible thing is that I *can't* put this behind me, Elizabeth. I will never put it behind me! It is cowardly of me, but I have completely lost my nerve. It could happen again, at any time! It could be something worse next time. Please don't tell anybody about this, Elizabeth. You are the only person who need ever know what a coward I am. I will have to find some new excuse, but . . .'

He buried his face in his hands again. 'I can't play in tomorrow's match. I just can't.'

Elizabeth touched his arm.

'You *must*, Jake,' she whispered. 'You really must, you know. There's somebody you haven't been thinking about in all this.'

He looked at her in surprise. 'Who?'

'Henry, of course. You say he has coached you all this time and believes you will play for your country one day. The accident was a terrible thing, but a younger person would have been able to react more quickly and dodge that flying ball. Henry shouldn't have been playing! But now, having given him one kind of pain, you are planning to make it much worse. You have been his life's work and now you are going to destroy all his dreams for you.'

Jake fell silent. 'I hadn't looked at it like that,' he said at last.

Elizabeth remembered the time that she had fallen badly from her pony. Her governess had forced her instantly to remount. *The longer you leave it, Elizabeth, the more frightened you will be*, she had told the little girl.

'You must play tomorrow, Jake,' she pleaded. 'For Henry's sake you must try to overcome your fears as quickly as possible and get back to playing a hard match once again. Please promise that you will try to overcome your terror.'

'I can't promise, Elizabeth,' Jake said in despair. 'I am so very, very scared about it. Let me just sit here on my own for a while and think things over.'

'Yes, Jake.' Elizabeth rose to her feet. 'And your secret is safe with me. But will you at least promise me something else?'

'What's that, Elizabeth?'

'Ask if you can use the school telephone this evening! Telephone your coach – he'd be pleased to hear from you. And ask his opinion about what he thinks you should do.'

Leaving Jake deep in thought, she tiptoed away.

And the following morning Jake did, indeed, turn out for the match against Milford Grange. His jaw was clenched and his face pale as he ran out on to the pitch with the rest of the Whyteleafe first eleven.

Two people cheered him even louder than the rest. One of them was Elizabeth. The other was a man on the opposite side of the field who had just arrived with his wife. He had a large dressing over one eye, held securely in place by special bandages.

'That's my boy, Jake!' he called out loudly, raising both fists high.

After last night's telephone call Henry Hill had asked his wife to drive him the thirty miles from their home town, so that he could watch Jake's match.

Jake made a nervous, even tentative start, but as the pace hotted up he began to get into his stride. He ran here, there and everywhere, tackling fiercely, soon caught up in the excitement of the hard-fought game. By the end of the match, Whyteleafe had won 6–4 and Jake had scored five of the six goals!

As he walked off the pitch, Henry Hill came striding across to shake his hand.

'That was marvellous, Jake.' His face was shining and so was Jake's. 'I'm very proud of you, my boy. Keep it up. What a tonic for a poor, sick invalid!'

'I've got to drag Henry away, Jake,' apologised Mrs Hill, tugging at her husband's arm. 'We're due at the hospital. The bandages come off today. Isn't that good news? I'm hoping the dear man has seen sense at last. I've told him to face the fact that his glory days are behind him. I hope that's going to be his last game!'

'It is. It is. But Jake's got all his glory days ahead of him. I'm so proud of you, my boy!' the man repeated, as he pumped Jake's hand and slapped him on the back. 'Good luck! See you at half-term!'

Jake watched his coach walk away. He was overcome with emotion.

Some of his classmates came racing over then and tried to close in on him. Martin, Kenneth, John . . . they were all very excited.

'Was that your famous coach, Jake?'

'Was that Henry Hill?'

But Jake strode away from them.

'Where's Elizabeth?' he demanded. 'Where's our famous monitor? That's who I want to see right now.'

To everybody's surprise, when he found Elizabeth, he lifted her clean off the ground and swung her up on to his shoulders.

'Thank you, Elizabeth! You're the best monitor in the school! If anybody says any different, tell them to come and see me!'

The second-form boys all looked at one another in amazement.

'What's Elizabeth done then?' asked Kenneth.

'Given me my nerve back, that's what she's done!' Jake informed them. He was not ashamed to admit it to anyone now. 'I'll tell you the whole story later!'

Julian and Joan were surprised to see Jake parading round the hockey pitch with Elizabeth perched up high on his shoulders. He wanted her to share in his glory. She was laughing and waving to everybody. Some of the boys were cheering her!

'What's the naughtiest girl been up to now?' wondered Julian.

The story of how Elizabeth had helped Jake soon spread round the school. There were no more anonymous messages after that.

But the Monitors' Meeting still lay ahead.

CHAPTER TEN

A MYSTERY STILL UNSOLVED

'IT WAS a reckless thing to do, Elizabeth. You had no business charging into the boys' quarters at night and encouraging some of your friends to join you! You must have known you were breaking a strict school rule,' said Thomas. 'That is hardly a sensible way for a monitor to deal with others who are breaking rules. By breaking one herself!'

The next MM was taking place. Silent and ashamed, Elizabeth sat next to Joan on the bench in the cosy little study. The moment of reckoning had come at last, the moment she had been dreading.

'You will never live down your naughtiest girl nickname if you do things like this, Elizabeth,' Emma pointed out. 'Because you are a monitor, we have spared you the shame of discussing this at the weekly Meeting. But it cannot go unpunished.'

'We understand that you were provoked,' went on Thomas, as the rest of the monitors listened with interest. 'Joan has told us that you were being teased and receiving anonymous messages from boys who appeared to think it unfair that your class has two girl monitors. They should have thought of that before, when they held the election! So Emma and I have decided on quite a modest punishment. You and your four friends must all go to bed one hour earlier for the next seven days. Do the other monitors think that sounds fair?'

There were murmurs of agreement from everyone. They all liked the naughtiest girl. She did crazy things sometimes, but she had a very warm heart. They had all heard the story about Jake by now.

How marvellous that Joan had been and spoken up for her, thought Elizabeth. She felt herself going weak at the knees. She had got off lightly! What a relief! And what a relief it would be to give the good news to Jenny, Kathleen, Belinda and Tessa. She had felt guilty about leading them into trouble. She was sure they would not mind having to go to bed early for a few nights, any more than she did.

But, just as her heart began to lighten, Emma spoke again.

'However, this whole situation has raised an

important issue. Tom and I have had a long talk about it and we've talked it over with Joan, too. There are a lot of boys in Form Two. We feel that perhaps a mistake was made in appointing two girl monitors. What do you think, Elizabeth?'

'I – I—'

Elizabeth's spirits plunged. So she was going to be asked to resign after all!

'If the form had had a boy monitor in office, some problems might have been avoided,' Thomas observed. 'For example, Jake is a big boy who prides himself on his physical strength. It was extremely difficult for him to confess to a girl how very frightened he felt. He might have found it easier to talk to another boy. It's just possible.'

'Yes,' agreed Elizabeth. She steeled herself. 'If you want me to stand down, then I will quite understand . . .'

'Oh, Elizabeth, of course not!' exclaimed Joan. 'Not you – me!'

'Yes, cheer up, Elizabeth!' smiled Emma. 'Joan has already offered us her resignation. She feels that she has had a very long stint as monitor, whereas you have only just started. Even more important, she is finding that being a monitor is starting to clash with her swimming commitments. She has assured me that she will be perfectly happy to make way for a boy and she believes this is necessary.'

'Joan!' whispered Elizabeth in surprise. 'Is this true? And is it true that you are going to be quite happy about it?'

'Perfectly true!' replied her friend. 'And perfectly happy!'

After further discussion it was agreed that Joan would stand down as monitor at the end of the next School Meeting. And after that the second-form boys could elect a monitor from among their number in time for the last Meeting before half-term.

Towards the end of the MM, the head boy and girl asked anxiously if any more citations had been handed in for the William and Rita Award.

There were three this week.

They all agreed that one of them was outstanding and should go on the shortlist. Elizabeth was very pleased about that. For it was one that Elizabeth herself had written out on the special form. Joan had read it beautifully.

'Won't it be lovely if our citation wins the award, Joan?' she said, as they walked into tea together. 'What an honour for the second form!'

'What's that?' asked Patrick in alarm, for he was just behind them.

'Don't worry, Patrick!' Elizabeth turned round and

smiled at him. 'You shouldn't eavesdrop. But you can relax now. Something else has come up, so you're quite safe!'

'Whatever was that about?' asked Joan, looking puzzled as she watched Patrick stroll on past them, whistling softly.

'Oh, nothing, Joan,' Elizabeth replied quickly.

She smiled to herself. Dear Patrick. He could sleep easily in his bed at nights. Perhaps one day she would be able to persuade him to be nominated, in time for a future award. But there was no hurry now.

She was so pleased that she was going to be able to continue as a monitor. Joan really did not want to be one any more. But she was going to miss her. It had been so wonderful having a best friend as the other monitor, somebody to talk over the MMs with, to their heart's content. Who would the new monitor be? she wondered. Who would the boys elect? She would find out soon enough. She hoped it would be somebody she liked.

The one small irritation was the matter of those anonymous messages. The person who'd written them had in part got his way! Although he'd not succeeded in getting rid of Elizabeth as a monitor, there *was* going to be a boy monitor, which would no doubt please him. It was annoying to think of her enemy being pleased.

A MYSTERY STILL UNSOLVED

Who had written the notes? Would she ever find out?

It was a mystery still unsolved.

CHAPTER ELEVEN

JULIAN SPRINGS A HUGE SURPRISE

TRUTH WILL always out and the truth about the enemy came out in an amazing way. It was the last person that Elizabeth suspected. It came out at the next Meeting.

All the usual weekly business had been conducted. And then Emma announced that Joan would be resigning as a monitor.

'There are a lot of boys in the second form this year. It has been decided by all concerned that it would be better to have one boy and one girl monitor. We shall be asking the second-form boys to elect their representative at next week's Meeting, ready for the second half of term. In the meantime could we all give Joan a round of applause, please, for her long and distinguished service to the second form.'

There was prolonged applause for Joan. Some of the boys and girls cheered and stamped their feet as well.

Sitting proudly next to her on the platform, Elizabeth glanced at her friend affectionately. How she was going to miss the great adventure of their being monitors together! But Joan had set her heart on getting strong and fit enough to be a member of Miss Thomas's swimming team and her time was going to be rationed now.

As the applause died away, the children all started chattering. They thought that the Meeting was over. But Thomas rapped the table sharply with the little gavel.

'Silence, please. There is one more matter to attend to. I'll let Emma do the talking.'

The head girl stood up.

'Somewhere in this hall there is a boy who broke a school rule and went to the village on his own, two or three weeks ago,' she stated. 'It was very wrong of him for the rule is a very strict one. But just this once he will not be punished. I can see you are all wondering why,' she added, for a great hush had fallen over the hall. 'Well, I can tell you why. A woman has been to see us today. She brought this with her.'

Lying on the table, next to the school Book, was a large cardboard box. Emma took something out of the box. With a dramatic flourish she held it up for the whole school to see.

It was a giant box of chocolates.

All the children gasped with excitement. What was coming next? Elizabeth stiffened. She stared down into the hall to the second-form benches. Patrick was sitting there, a slow pallor creeping up his cheeks.

'With no thought of danger to himself this boy rushed into the road and saved the woman's child from being run over. The child was walking straight into the path of an oncoming car and would no doubt have been injured – or worse – without this boy's intervention. However, he hurried away without waiting to be thanked.'

Emma paused for breath.

'After that, the woman saw the boy on a more recent occasion. The child recognised him at once. On this occasion the mother managed quickly to thank him, but once again he hurried off. She feels he deserves some proper reward and she has asked that he be presented with this box of chocolates in front of the whole school. So Thomas and I would now like our shy hero to stand up and make himself known. Who is he, please?'

The pupils were enthralled. They started whispering and nudging one another, gazing all round the hall. Who would stand up?

Elizabeth was staring at Patrick in deep fascination. What was going to happen now? In spite of all his efforts to keep his heroism a secret it was going to be impossible for him to hide it now!

Patrick seemed to be frozen to the bench. His eyes were darting this way and that. Once or twice he craned his neck to look round at the benches behind him.

He's still trying to keep it secret, even now! thought Elizabeth. *He's looking around, like everybody else. Pretending that he's waiting to see who's going to stand up.*

Emma stood there, holding the chocolates. The seconds ticked by. And Patrick still sat there, gazing all around. Two or three places along on the bench, Julian scratched his head and looked puzzled. Other children were talking in low voices. It was beginning to get embarrassing.

'Would the boy please stand up?' repeated Emma, colouring a little.

Still no one did so. Then Thomas lost patience. He banged the gavel hard on the table.

'Would the boy in question stand up at once, please?' he said. 'That's an order.'

Elizabeth managed to catch Patrick's eye. And then slowly, very slowly, Patrick rose to his feet, his face drained of colour. But then Elizabeth gave a little gasp. For something very strange was happening. At exactly the same moment Julian was slowly rising too! Languidly, his hands in his pockets.

Both boys were standing up together!

'Was this child a girl and did she have red hair by any chance?' enquired Julian.

'Yes, she was a girl. And her mother certainly has red hair,' replied Thomas. 'Why, do you know something about it? Please take your hands out of your pockets, Julian.'

With Patrick now standing frozen in horror, a little further along the same bench, Julian took his hands out of his pockets and grinned.

'I think it must have been me then. I'm afraid I'd forgotten all about it. What perplexed me was Emma saying the boy was seen in the village a second time. You see I haven't been down again since the other week when that kid ran in the road! But now I realise –' he turned and smiled at Patrick with a scornful gleam in his eye – 'that she could have confused me with somebody else.'

Patrick looked as though he wished the ground would swallow him up. Slowly, he subsided back down on to the bench.

Elizabeth gazed from one cousin to the other in shock. She was reminded how alike they looked, with their matted black hair and brilliant green eyes! How easy it would have been for the child to make her mistake!

It was not Patrick who'd performed the brave deed at all. It was Julian! And now Julian was strolling up to the platform and being presented with the chocolates! And the whole school was clapping and cheering him! Meanwhile, down below, Patrick sat miserably hunched on the bench.

And, when all the excitement had died down, Thomas held his hand up for silence one last time. He asked Patrick to get to his feet.

'Don't ever try to do that again,' he told him, shaming him in front of the whole school. 'Of all the kinds of stealing there are, to try to steal another person's glory is the most despicable.'

The head boy was angry enough, but Elizabeth's own anger put even his in the shade. She could hardly wait to vent her feelings.

'You complete and absolute worm!' she told Patrick afterwards, dragging him outside on to the terrace. 'No wonder you didn't want me to name you for the William and Rita Award! If I'd done that, the person who had really performed the brave deed would soon have had something to say about it, wouldn't they? How could you bear to let me think you were a hero all this time? You have made an absolute fool of me. I hate you!'

'Please don't hate me, Elizabeth,' begged Patrick.

'You never gave me the chance to explain that the little girl had made a mistake. You really didn't! I had no idea who'd really saved her. I hadn't a clue. But it was just so thrilling to have you looking up to me and liking me for a change! I would have explained straight away, but you never gave me the chance, Elizabeth! And after that I thought, what harm could it possibly do anyone else, the child making a silly mistake and you thinking it was me?'

Elizabeth's anger began to subside as she saw how distressed the boy was. She also realised that he was telling the truth. She'd given him almost no chance at all to explain there'd been a mistake! She'd made such a fuss of him at the time. It must have been awkward for him.

'It all seemed so simple at first,' Patrick confessed. 'It was so nice that you liked me. And the woman seemed really pleased to have someone to thank! I thought nothing more would come of it. But then it was dreadful when this business of the award came up and you wanted to put my name forward! I longed to make a clean breast of things but, when you told me that you'd given up your place in the table-tennis team, I was finished! That was the worst thing of all, Elizabeth. After that I became desperate that the truth should never, ever come out. I even wrote those silly notes—'

'*You* wrote the notes, Patrick?' gasped Elizabeth. '*You* were the enemy? I thought of everyone else, but I never thought of you!'

'I'm not an enemy, Elizabeth. But I knew that as long as you kept on going to those MMs of yours, sooner or later you'd have blurted something out about my so-called brave deed. I know what you're like! So I was hoping, with some of the boys making trouble for you anyway, that you might get fed up with being a monitor.'

'I see.'

Elizabeth frowned. She didn't know whether to be angry or amused. For she was relieved to discover that she did not have a real enemy.

'Patrick, I think you are pathetic!' she added.

'Well, I really *did* think it was unfair having two girl monitors,' Patrick objected. 'I've always said that.'

Elizabeth thought back over all the time she'd known Patrick.

It was true! He had often said it. In fact, he didn't really approve of the school having girls in it at all! How silly of her not to have remembered that.

'Well, there's going to be a boy monitor anyway,' she pointed out.

'Yes,' replied Patrick smugly. 'Thomas and Emma seem to agree with me on that.'

Elizabeth turned on her heel. Julian had appeared on the terrace, looking for her. She called back to Patrick, over her shoulder.

'I only hope it's not you, Patrick!'

Julian grinned. 'Hello, Elizabeth. Been giving my cousin a telling-off about something? Here, have a chocolate. They're delicious.'

It was the last Meeting before half-term. A gleaming little silver trophy stood on the head boy and girl's table. The very first William and Rita Award was about to be announced.

'We ended up with four citations on the shortlist,' Thomas was telling the assembled school, 'of which two were quite outstanding. Miss Belle and Miss Best and Emma and I had a very difficult job deciding between them. One was for Julian Holland, signed by several boys in his class, for his brave action in saving the little girl from being run over. The other was for Jake Johnson, signed by Elizabeth Allen, for his courage in overcoming a personal crisis.'

While the whole school hung on to his words Thomas paused for maximum effect.

'Which one were we to choose? Which boy had shown the greater courage? As we talked it over, we came to realise that Julian's fearless deed had come as second nature to him. It was truly fearless for he had felt no fear. He saw the child in danger and instantly took action. We are very proud of him for that. But his brave deed meant so little to him that he had some difficulty in remembering it afterwards.

'Jake, on the other hand, and I know he does not mind us telling you this now, felt absolute terror at the thought of playing hockey again after inflicting a grave injury on someone he loved and admired. Yet somehow he faced that fear and fought it and, in the end, he overcame it.

'Fearlessness and courage are not the same thing. A high form of courage is to know real fear – and then to overcome it. The school therefore takes great pride in giving the very first William and Rita Award to – Jake Johnson.'

The school clapped and cheered as the gentle giant of a boy shambled up on the platform and took the little silver trophy from Emma's outstretched hand. He clutched it proudly and shot Elizabeth an embarrassed smile. She was sitting behind Emma on the platform, clapping so hard that her palms stung.

As the Meeting broke up, she turned to the boy sitting next to her.

'A lot of the boys wanted you to have the award, Julian, but I think the Beauty and the Beast and Thomas and Emma have all made the right decision, don't you?'

'Most definitely,' agreed Julian.

'And at least the boys elected you as monitor!' she said, with a happy sigh.

It was nice to have Julian sitting next to her on the platform.

She would still have a friend as her fellow monitor after all. A truly marvellous friend. Poor Patrick! But what fun it was going to be from now on, she and Julian being monitors together!

'Yes, I'm a monitor,' replied Julian, with a cheerful grin. 'I still can't believe it and, as a matter of fact, Elizabeth, I don't know how I'm going to manage it. But for your sake I suppose I'd better try.'

'You suppose right, Julian,' she laughed.

BONUS BLYTON

Enid Blyton has been one of the world's best-loved storytellers for over seventy years. Her interest in writing began as a child and before she loved receiving letters from the children who read her books, she enjoyed working with them as a teacher. The Naughtiest Girl stories are inspired by real schools and experiences. Turn the page to learn more about Enid as a child and as a teacher. Afterwards you might like to write about your school and teachers and the people in *your* class!

THE LIFE AND TIMES OF ENID BLYTON

11 August 1897	Enid Blyton was born in East Dulwich, London. Two brothers are born after her – Hanly (b. 1899) and Carey (b. 1902).
1911	Enid enters a children's poetry competition and is praised for her writing. She's on the path to becoming a bestselling author . . .
1916	Enid begins to train as a teacher in Ipswich. By the time she is 21, she is a fully qualified Froebel teacher, and starts work at a school in Kent.
1917	Enid's first 'grown-up' publication – three poems in *Nash's Magazine*.
June 1922	Enid's first book is published. It's called *Child Whispers*.
1926	Enid begins editing – and writes – the phenomenal *Sunny Stories for Little Folks* magazine. (She continues in this role for 26 years!)

1927	So vast is Enid's output that she has to learn to type. (But she still writes to children by hand.)
1931	Having married Hugh Pollock in 1924, the couple's first child, Gillian, is born. Imogen, their second daughter, was born in 1935.
1942	The Famous Five is launched with *Five on a Treasure Island.*
1949	The first appearance of *The Secret Seven* and of *Noddy* mark this year as special.
1953	Enid moves away from *Sunny Stories* to launch *Enid Blyton's Magazine*. She is now renowned throughout the world – she even established her own company, called Darrell Waters Limited (the surname of her second husband).
1962	Enid Blyton becomes one of the first and most important children's authors to be published in paperback. Now she reaches even more readers than ever before.
28 November 1968	Enid dies in her sleep, in a nursing home in Hampstead.

SCHOOL RULES

Elizabeth is used to getting her own way, so it's a challenge to adapt to life at Whyteleafe where the students make their own rules. That said, the student council don't have many rules at all. Here are the ones explained to the new children in *The Naughtiest Girl in the School* . . .

'We place all the money we get into this box, and we draw from it two shillings a week each. The rest of the money is used to buy anything that any of you especially want – but you have to state at the weekly Meeting what you need the money for, and the Jury will decide if you may have it.

'The second rule is that if we have any complaint at all, we must bring it to the Meeting and announce it there, so that everyone may hear it, and decide what is to be done with it. Please be sure you understand the difference between a real complaint and telling tales, because telling tales is also punished.'

In that first book in the series we learn that 'monitors are chosen for their common sense, their loyalty to the school and its ideas, and their good character. They must be obeyed, because you yourselves have chosen them'.

MY HAPPIEST TIMES

During her lifetime, Enid Blyton received many hundreds of letters from the thousands of children – all over the world – who enjoyed reading her books. She took great pleasure in replying to them. She also loved meeting children and it is said that the suggestion for an autobiography came from a young fan who presented Enid with a list of questions. He thought he might write a book about his favourite author, called *Enid Blyton – The Story of Her Life*, but his mother suggested that Enid might write it herself. And so she did. *The Story of My Life* was published in 1952. Enid wrote about her family, where she lived, the inspiration for her books and her writing process. She also talked about her childhood. Have you ever imagined what your favourite writers were like as children – and what important events may have shaped their future lives? Here is an extract from *The Story of My Life*, which takes us back to Enid's younger days . . .

* * *

My happiest childhood times were when I was reading and dreaming, when I was playing games with other children, and when I was out in the country or by the sea. Very much like your happiest times, I expect!

The games I played were Burglars and Police Officers, Making a House somewhere – behind a bush, or up a tree, or under a table. We had tops and hoops and marbles as the seasons came round.

We played a great many card games, because we all loved cards. So do my own girls. We played Snap and Happy Families, Old Maid and Beggar-My-Neighbour.

We also played board games such as Snakes and Ladders (and sometimes Ladders and Snakes – going up the snakes and down the ladders, instead of the other way round!). When I was six, my father taught me to play draughts and a little later he taught me to play chess. That was just before I was seven. He thought that all young children should learn to play chess. I enjoyed the games immensely.

I think my father was more of a naturalist than anything else. I didn't even know what a naturalist was at that time – all I knew was that my father loved the countryside, loved flowers and birds and wild animals, and knew more about them than anyone I had ever met. And what was more he was willing to take me with him on his expeditions, and share his love and his knowledge with me!

In those days it was considered quite ordinary to collect birds' eggs. Nowadays we teach children not to, because it distresses the birds and it might lead to many kinds gradually becoming extinct.

My father collected birds' eggs, and he had a cabinet of little drawers full of beautiful eggs, neatly arranged and labelled. One of the things I had to do to help him was to insert my hand into holes in trees to see if any nests were there, and to feel for eggs.

I never did like taking the eggs. I did so hope the bird wouldn't mind. Fortunately my father never wanted more than one egg. He never knew how scared I was of putting my hand down into those small holes. Once I heard a hissing noise down a hole, and I was sure it was an adder hiding there. I was afraid of being bitten, but I didn't like to say so.

Weekend after weekend I went out with my father. Looking back, it seems as if those days were always warm, always sunny, and that the sky was always as deeply blue as the cornflowers in my garden, or as faintly blue as the harebells on the common.

We were lucky to have woods and commons, ponds and lanes so near. We explored everywhere and everything – watching the lizards play on the sunny banks, listening to the willow warblers singing, poking down a hole that my father said badgers had been in, looking for the white violets we knew always blossomed in a certain dell.

All my childhood was steeped in the sunshine of the woods and commons and lanes, and what I didn't find out from nature herself I read about in books, and then searched for it again. I was perfectly happy, even when I wandered about alone, finding flowers to look up in our reference books, trying to discover what bird was singing, learning the difference between a thrush's nest and a blackbird's, and a hundred other things.

'One day I'll put all these things into a book,' I said, though I didn't tell anyone that, of course.

WHAT THEY DID AT MISS BROWN'S SCHOOL

In 1920 Enid Blyton became a governess to the four Thompson children, whose ages ranged from four to ten. The family lived in Surbiton, in Surrey, in a house called 'Southernhay'. Enid had a small room which overlooked the garden, and it was there that she wrote many of her stories. Enid's tiny class often had lessons outdoors in the summer months.

Enid was very popular with her students, because her lessons were both practical and creative. She worked with them to put on performances for which they made props, costumes and invitations – and even sold tickets.

In 1941 she published a long story called 'What They Did at Miss Brown's School', which was divided into monthly episodes. It's been hard to find for many years, but you can read extracts in these new editions of *The Naughtiest Girl* books. The character of Miss Brown and her tiny class is very much based on Enid Blyton and her school at the Thompsons' . . .

Here's the eleventh extract . . .

11. November. Getting to Know the Birds

THERE WAS no doubt at all what the 'special thing' was to be for November! It was to be a bird table, of course, and all the children meant to bring something for it every day.

John made the table, and he made it very well. He brought an old post to school and dug a hole for it not far from the classroom. He set the post in the hole, filled in the earth and got everyone to stamp it down firmly. Then he brought a broad, flat piece of wood, on to which he had nailed an upright edge or rim around three sides.

'Why haven't you put a rim to the front edge, John?' asked Peter.

'So that we can clean the dirt easily off the table,' said John. 'I've put the rim on to keep our food from blowing off – but from one side we shall want to scrape off the old food and dirt.'

'You have made it nicely, John,' Susan cried, hopping

round it on one foot.

'Susan thinks she's a bird hopping about for food already!' laughed Mary. John hammered the tabletop on to the post. Soon it was fixed and the bird table was ready. It really was a very simple thing to make.

'And now we must each of us bring scraps and crumbs every day for the table,' said Mary. 'Can we take it in turns to clean the table and put out fresh water, Miss Brown?'

'Yes. Take a week each,' said Miss Brown. 'John can begin, as he is the eldest.'

Well, it *was* fun, having the bird table! All day long the birds were on it, either eating the food or waiting for it, or drinking the water or bathing in it! The children saw their little feathered friends every time they looked up from their books.

Each morning all kinds of scraps were put on the table. The children packed them into old ice-cream tubs or cartons, and brought them along.

'I've got rice-pudding scrapings!' cried Susan.

'And I've got soaked dog biscuits from my dog's dish!' said John.

'And I've got potato, a bone and breadcrumbs!' said Mary.

'And I've got some bacon rind!' said Peter.

'What a feast for the birds!' said Miss Brown, giving

John the crumbs from her table. 'No wonder they come all day long! We must make a bird chart, I think.'

So they made a bird chart, and put on it each bird that came to their bird table, and the things that every bird ate.

Sparrows, chaffinches, starlings, tits, hedge sparrows, blackbirds, thrushes, robins, wrens and wagtails visited the table. Each child looked for pictures of these birds in papers or magazines, and cut them out when they found them. Then the pictures were coloured correctly and pasted on the chart. The children put down the names of the birds and what kinds of things they ate. It was great fun.

They put a sunflower head on the table and that day they had a new visitor – a greenfinch with a pretty gold bar on its wing! It did love the sunflower seeds.

'Another bird for our chart!' said John in glee.

Then Peter brought a coconut and said he wanted to give it to the tits. So Miss Brown knocked a hole in each end and hung it up on a piece of string just outside the classroom window. The tits were on it all day long.

'Now we can easily learn the difference between the three tits!' said Mary, pleased. 'Great tit is the biggest and brightest, with its black head and green and yellow dress. Blue tit is the prettiest, with its blue cap and small body – and coal tit is the tiniest, with his black head, dull colouring and white streak down the back of its head!'

'Very good, Mary!' said Miss Brown, pleased. 'You are using your eyes well!'

The children became most interested in their birds, and longed to do more for them. So Miss Brown took them shopping one day, and they brought a bag of hemp seed, which the birds love, some brazil nuts and some peanuts.

'The hemp seed is a favourite of the seed-eating birds such as the sparrows and finches,' said Miss Brown. 'The peanuts and the brazil nuts will be enjoyed by the tits. They love all nuts.'

Miss Brown cracked the brazil nuts and tied each one on to a separate bit of string. Then she hung the nuts from nails round the bird table on their strings.

The tits soon found them – and how the children laughed to see them hauling up the brazil nuts 'hand over hand like a sailor' as Susan said. They held them firmly in their little feet and pecked away hard.

The children scattered a little hemp seed each day on the table and the hard-billed birds enjoyed it immensely. Sometimes there were as many as twenty or more birds on the table, and there really didn't seem room.

'Let's nail a few twigs to the back of the table, Miss Brown,' said John. 'Then those birds that come last can perch on the twigs and wait for their turn.'

So little branching twigs were nailed to the back of the table, and the birds always perched on these before flying on to the table itself. It was pretty to see them there.

'Now we mustn't forget our peanuts,' said Miss Brown. 'I have bought you a peanut feeder to hang up by the window, children – it will be such fun to watch it!'

She showed them the peanut feeder. It was quite a simple thing – just a cylinder of tin between two wooden pieces, top and bottom. The cylinder of tin had a slit down the middle each side, and through these slits the tits pecked away at the peanuts.

'We must shell the peanuts first, before we slip them into the feeder,' said Miss Brown. So they all shelled hard, and at last the feeder was full. Miss Brown corked up the hole at the bottom, through which she had slipped the nuts, and hung up the feeder just by the window.

In two minutes there were four tits on it – a great tit, two blue tits and a coal tit! How pleased and excited they were! So were the children. They could hardly do their arithmetic because they wanted to watch the tits.

'Miss Brown, I saw a funny wooden sort of bell thing in the seedshop today,' said Mary that afternoon. 'It was called a tit bell. Was it for the tits – and what has to be done to it? It wasn't very much money. I could buy it if you think it would be fun to have.'

'Oh, *yes*, Mary, it would be lovely to have a tit bell,' said Miss Brown. 'If you can afford to buy it, do get it and bring it tomorrow. I will show you how to use it.'

So the next day Mary came along, proudly carrying her tit bell. It was just like a wooden bell, with no clapper inside, of course, but just a tiny perch across the wide end.

'Now we fill this little bell with fat,' said Miss Brown. 'I've got some on my kitchen stove, ready for the bell. Mary, get a cup, and put the bell upside down in it, so that I can easily pour the fat inside.'

Mary stood the bell in a cup and Miss Brown came back with the melted fat. She poured it carefully into the tit bell.

'There!' she said. 'Now, as soon as the fat has set hard, we will hang the bell up by the peanut feeder – what fun! The tits will soon find it and will creep into the bell, hang upside down, and peck out the fat! No other bird can get the fat – though I expect the robin will try to – because, you see, the only birds that are true little acrobats are the tits!'

The fat soon set, and the bell was hung up outside. It wasn't long before a crowd of tits were all trying to get into the bell and peck the fat. They shouted at one another and the blue tits lifted up their little crests and cried '*Chururururr!*' very angrily indeed.

'I *do* wish I had a tit bell in my garden at home,' sighed Susan. 'I would like to see the tits coming to it all day long.'

'Well, Susan, ask your mother to save you a nice mutton bone,' said Miss Brown. 'Hang it to a branch by a string and the tits will come and peck away at the fat. It will be as good as a tit bell for you!'

'Oh, that's a lovely idea!' said Susan, pleased.

When the children went for their nature walks, they hunted for all kinds of berries and seeds to bring back for their bird table – and what a lot they found! Hips and haws, elderberries, privet berries, yew berries, spindleberries – and so many different kinds of seeds that the birds must have been really astonished at all they had.

Susan brought back some thistles, with downy heads still full of seeds. She asked John to tie them to the twigs at the back of the table for her.

'Who do you think is going to eat thistle seeds?' asked John.

'My mummy says that goldfinches are fond of thistle seeds,' said Susan seriously. 'And we haven't had goldfinches yet, have we? Well, I want them – so I've got these thistles!'

Well, Susan's mother was quite right – the goldfinches *did* love thistledown for the very next day there came not *one* goldfinch, but seven. They alighted on the twigs like a flock of fairy birds, brightly coloured, with plenty of shining yellow gold about them.

The children were too delighted for words. They left their writing and went to the window to watch. Miss Brown came too.

'We call a flock of goldfinches a *charm* of goldfinches,' she said. 'Don't you think it is a good name for such enchanting little birds!'

'*I* am going to put the goldfinches on our bird chart,' said Susan. 'Because it was *my* thistles that brought them here!'

And she found a beautiful coloured picture of a goldfinch and proudly pasted it on the chart. She wrote below the picture: 'This is a goldfinch. For its food it eats my thistledown.'

That made everyone laugh – but Susan didn't care. She was so pleased to have brought the prettiest of the birds to the bird table!

'I'm going to get my daddy to make me a bird table of my own,' she said.

'I've got one already,' said John.

'So have I,' said Mary.

'Well, I shall have one too, like Susan,' said Peter.

'It really is a lovely thing to have, and it's such fun to make friends with the birds like this.'

'I hoped you would all have tables of your own before the year was out!' said Miss Brown, smiling. 'I made up my mind not to suggest it at all, but to see if our own table would give you enough pleasure to make you each want one too. And sure enough it has!'

So after that there were five tables to see to, instead of one, and you will be glad to know that every table was spread with food and fresh water without being once forgotten. Good children, weren't they?

ENIDBLYTON.CO.UK

IS FOR PARENTS, CHILDREN AND TEACHERS!

Sign up to the newsletter on the homepage for a monthly round-up of news from the world of

Enid Blyton®

JOIN US ON SOCIAL MEDIA

EnidBlytonOfficial BlytonOfficial

Illustration by Laura Ellen Anderson.

Enid Blyton

is one of the most popular children's authors of all time. Her books have sold over 500 million copies and have been translated into other languages more often than any other children's author.

Enid Blyton adored writing for children. She wrote over 700 books and about 2,000 short stories. *The Famous Five* books, now 80 years old, are her most popular. She is also the author of other favourites including *The Secret Seven*, *The Magic Faraway Tree* and *Malory Towers*.

Born in London in 1897, Enid lived much of her life in Buckinghamshire and loved dogs, gardening and the countryside. She was very knowledgeable about trees, flowers, birds and animals. Dorset – where some of the Famous Five's adventures are set – was a favourite place of hers too.

Enid Blyton's stories are read and loved by millions of children (and grown-ups) all over the world. Visit enidblyton.co.uk to discover more.

Illustration by Laura Ellen Anderson.

The NAUGHTIEST GIRL Wants to Win

Have you read them all?

1. The Naughtiest Girl in the School
2. The Naughtiest Girl Again
3. The Naughtiest Girl is a Monitor
4. Here's the Naughtiest Girl!
5. The Naughtiest Girl Keeps a Secret
6. The Naughtiest Girl Helps a Friend
7. The Naughtiest Girl Saves the Day
8. Well Done, the Naughtiest Girl
9. The Naughtiest Girl Wants to Win
10. The Naughtiest Girl Marches On

Enid Blyton®

The Naughtiest Girl

Wants to Win

WRITTEN BY
ANNE DIGBY

HODDER

HODDER CHILDREN'S BOOKS

First published in Great Britain in 1999 by Hodder & Stoughton
This edition published in 2021
For further information about the editorial history of this book,
see enidblyton.co.uk/books

5 7 9 10 8 6 4

Enid Blyton® and Enid Blyton's signature are registered
trade marks of Hodder & Stoughton Limited
Text © 2021 Hodder & Stoughton Limited
Illustrations by Claire Powell © 2021 Hodder & Stoughton Limited

No trade mark or copyrighted material may be reproduced without the
express written permission of the trademark and copyright owner.

The moral right of the author has been asserted.

All characters and events in this publication, other than those clearly in the public domain, are fictitious and any resemblance to real persons, living or dead, is purely coincidental.

All rights reserved.
No part of this publication may be reproduced, stored in a retrieval system, or transmitted, in any form or by any means, without the prior permission in writing of the publisher, nor be otherwise circulated in any form of binding or cover other than that in which it is published and without a similar condition including this condition being imposed on the subsequent purchaser.

A CIP catalogue record for this book is available from the British Library.

ISBN 978 1 444 95868 3

Printed and bound in Great Britain by Clays Ltd, Elcograf S.p.A.

Typeset in Caslon by Avon DataSet Ltd, Arden Court, Alcester, Warwickshire

The paper and board used in this book are made from wood
from responsible sources.

FSC www.fsc.org MIX Paper | Supporting responsible forestry FSC® C104740

Hodder Children's Books
An imprint of Hachette Children's Group
Part of Hodder & Stoughton
Carmelite House
50 Victoria Embankment
London EC4Y 0DZ

An Hachette UK Company
www.hachette.co.uk
www.hachettechildrens.co.uk

CONTENTS

INTRODUCTION

by Cressida Cowell

bestselling author of the
How to Train Your Dragon series

Like so many, many children before and after me, Enid Blyton's books played a crucial role in turning my nine-year-old self into a passionate reader.

That is because Enid Blyton had an extraordinary knack for writing the kind of books that children actually *want* to read, rather than the kind of books that adults think they *should* read.

Enid Blyton could tap into children's dreams, children's desires, children's wishes, with pinpoint accuracy. She knew that every child, however good and well-behaved they might look on the outside, secretly longed to be Elizabeth Allen, the naughtiest kid in the school. I'm afraid I entirely cheered Elizabeth on, as she defied her parents, the headmistresses, her schoolmates, and the very serious School Meetings. If anything, I wanted her to be even naughtier.

But *The Naughtiest Girl* books were really my favourite of Enid Blyton's school stories because of Whyteleafe, a very different school from Malory Towers or St Clare's. What if there could be a school in which discipline was administered by the children rather than the adults? In which all money was given in at the start of the term and distributed among the children along socialist lines? Wouldn't this be the kind of school that children would actually *want* to go to, rather than the kind of school that children *have* to go to?

It was an interesting proposition to a nine-year-old, and it remains an interesting proposition.

I hope you enjoy this story as much as I did when *I* was nine years old.

Cressida Cowell

CHAPTER ONE

THE REAL KERRY DANE

'STOP A minute, Daddy!' cried Elizabeth Allen, flinging herself in front of the luggage trolley. 'Please, I need to get something out of my trunk.'

The long summer holidays were over. Elizabeth and her father were at the big London rail terminal where she would catch her train back to boarding school. Mr Allen had business to do in London today, so had driven her up to the station by car.

They'd arrived more than half an hour early, but, to Elizabeth's delight, her friends Julian and Joan were already at the station and keeping a lookout for her. She had rushed off to speak to them at once.

Now the three children caught up with Mr Allen as he laboured along with the laden luggage trolley, looking for Platform Fourteen.

'You'll never guess what Julian and Joan have

just told me!' exclaimed Elizabeth, as her father braked. 'Kerry Dane's due at any moment. The real Kerry Dane herself!'

'And who might she be?' asked Mr Allen.

'Oh, *Daddy*!' Elizabeth was already clearing her tuckbox and sports things off the top of her school trunk. It was a smart brown trunk with E. ALLEN painted on it in black letters. 'You know – *Zara's Journey*! That wonderful film Mummy took me to in the holidays. Joan's seen it too. Everybody has!'

'Ah. The one that you and your mother went to see twice? Starring the young girl that nobody's ever heard of?'

'Yes, Kerry Dane! She was an ordinary London schoolgirl until the film people found her, but now *everybody's* heard of her. Everybody except you, Daddy! And she's really marvellous.' Elizabeth dropped to her knees beside the trolley and managed to get her trunk open. She flung back the lid. 'I really admire her. She's exactly the sort of person that I would like to be.'

Elizabeth was hunting feverishly through her trunk, scattering its contents as she went. Books, garments and photo frames were starting to spill out. But she couldn't find what she was looking for. Where was it? Oh, surely she hadn't forgotten to bring it this term?

'You say she's due here? At the station?' asked

Mr Allen in surprise. 'Well, even if she is, Elizabeth, this is hardly the time or the place to start unpacking your trunk!'

'Not the station, sir,' explained Julian, his green eyes glinting with amusement at the sight of Elizabeth down on her knees, passers-by having to step round her. 'The big cinema next door. The film's playing to packed houses and we gather she'll be stopping by at ten o'clock to chat to all the fans in the queue.'

'She'll get wet then,' observed Mr Allen. 'It's raining.'

'There's a notice outside the cinema,' Joan rushed on. 'Julian spotted it coming in!' In her own quiet way Joan was as excited as Elizabeth. 'We're hoping we'll have time to get her autograph.'

'Hooray!' cried Elizabeth, waving something in triumph. 'My autograph book. I was *sure* I'd packed it. It was right at the bottom. Isn't that typical? Sorry, Daddy.'

While the others quickly stuffed everything back into the trunk and closed the lid, Elizabeth stroked the white leather binding of her prized autograph book. She peeped inside. Some of the leavers had written messages in it at the end of last term. And there were two very special entries from William and Rita, who had been the head boy and head girl. What a fine thing it would be to get Kerry Dane's autograph as well! It would be another treasured signature to add to her collection.

'We won't be long, Daddy,' she said quickly, as she helped her father stack the rest of her belongings back on the trolley.

'Now, just a minute,' her father protested. 'I can't have you missing the train, you know. I'm not sure I can allow—'

'Oh, *please*, Daddy!' she begged. 'I'll never, ever get a chance like this again. We won't miss the train, I promise. We've got half an hour!' She turned and appealed to her friends for support. 'We wouldn't dream of missing the train, would we?'

'Certainly not,' agreed Joan.

'I absolutely couldn't *bear* to miss it!' vowed Elizabeth.

It was the simple truth. She had been looking forward for days to the train journey back to Whyteleafe School. There would be lots of people she knew on board and some new pupils as well. It was always very exciting. And she was going up a form. She was going into the second form! There would be an election for a new head boy and head girl as soon as they got back to school and second-formers were allowed to vote in it!

'I'll make sure we're all back in good time. Platform Fourteen, isn't it, sir?' said Julian, sounding his most grown-up. 'The cinema's just through the archway over there. Bang next door to the station!'

'And Joan's a monitor, so she'll make sure too,' pleaded Elizabeth. She noticed that the other two had sensibly retained their raincoats when getting their luggage put on the train. 'I'll even wear my mac if you like, Daddy, so my school uniform doesn't get wet.'

'Very well,' relented her father. He knew how much Elizabeth hated wearing her old mac. He fished it out of a carrier bag and handed it to her. 'I'll get your luggage put on the train and meet you by the ticket barrier in fifteen minutes then.'

'Oh, thank you, Daddy!'

The three friends raced out of the station and over to the cinema. Although it was early in the day, queues had already formed. The cinema illuminations shone down on the rainy pavements. ZARA'S JOURNEY, they signalled brightly, STARRING KERRY DANE. And there was the notice that Julian had spotted earlier:

Announcement

We are pleased to announce a surprise visit from Miss Kerry Dane. She will be here to speak to the queues and sign autographs between 10 a.m. and 10.15 a.m. today.

The notice stood at the cinema's main entrance in front of the big glass doors. A policeman and a commissionaire in a bright red uniform were keeping the entrance clear.

'If you wish to see Miss Dane, please take your places in the cinema queue. Otherwise, pass along,' the doorman was saying. 'Miss Dane's car will be arriving at any moment.'

Excitedly, Elizabeth linked arms with her two friends. Her autograph book was safely stowed in her raincoat pocket.

'You didn't imagine it then, Julian!' she said. 'Isn't it sporting of her to want to come and speak to the queues on a horrid wet morning like this?'

'She pops up at cinemas a lot,' ventured Joan. 'I've read about it in the papers. She says she really likes to meet her fans.'

'It's all good publicity, I suppose,' grinned Julian. 'It's clever not to announce it in advance, so she doesn't have to cope with a big crowd each time. I can't wait to see my cousin Patrick's face when I pull out Kerry Dane's autograph. I shall sell it to him for a tidy sum. He's been raving about her film all holidays!'

'Where should we stand and wait?' said Joan anxiously. 'We're not allowed to hang around outside. We'll get moved on.'

'In the queue, of course!' replied Julian. 'We'll pretend we're waiting to go into the film like everybody else.'

The shortest queue was the one for the most expensive seats. It was sheltered from the rain by an awning. With Julian whistling nonchalantly the three friends tagged on the back of it.

'I feel a bit guilty!' whispered Joan.

'It's only for a few moments,' Elizabeth pointed out. 'It must be nearly ten o'clock now.'

'As a matter of fact,' said Julian, glancing at his watch and then at the road, 'it's five past! And no sign of her car yet. If she's only staying till quarter past, she'd better buck up!'

But Elizabeth wasn't listening. 'Look, Joan!' she was exclaiming. 'Do you remember this bit?'

The two girls had turned to gaze at the slim showcase fixed to the wall behind them. It contained, behind glass, a selection of film stills that portrayed dramatic moments from the story. The clip that Elizabeth was pointing to showed Kerry Dane, her golden hair matted and her face streaked with tears, stumbling down a mountainside with a small child in her arms.

'Yes!' agreed Joan, gazing at the still. 'My heart was in my mouth. I was convinced that little Stefan was going to die. After everything that Zara had done to get the younger children out of the war zone, to get them to safety. And they were so nearly home . . .'

Deeply engrossed, the two friends started to discuss

the film. Together they relived the story of how the brave refugee girl, Zara, played by Kerry Dane, had led a group of village children out of a war zone, narrowly escaping landmines and enemy fire. Then had endured a terrible journey over the mountains, through storms and blizzards, with little food and no warm clothes, trying to reach the safety of her uncle's farm, in the next valley. Zara had given all her rations to the younger children and towards the end only kept herself alive by eating snow. And then Stefan, the smallest of the children, had fallen desperately ill . . .

'I liked the bit when Zara made a raft and rowed the children across the river, one by one,' sighed Elizabeth. 'You remember – when they found that the bridge had been blown up? Oh, wasn't she brave? A born leader. I'm sure Kerry Dane must be a brilliant person in real life. It all seemed so *true* . . .'

'But where's she got to today?' came Julian's voice, sounding cross.

'Oh!' Elizabeth spun round to face Julian. He had been watching out for the car all this time. 'Is it getting late then?'

'It's nearly quarter past.' He shrugged. 'I'm afraid our train goes in fifteen minutes.'

'Then we must get back to the station,' said Joan, looking crestfallen.

'Surely we can wait another five minutes?' protested Elizabeth.

And suddenly a cheer went up. A car had arrived, its brakes squealing loudly, its tyres spraying water.

A radiant figure jumped out of the back of the small blue car. The mane of golden hair was unmistakable. So were the huge brown eyes and sweetly smiling mouth.

'It's her!' everyone cried.

'It's Kerry Dane!'

It was a thrilling moment for Elizabeth and Joan. The real-life Kerry Dane – at last. And she looked as pretty off the screen as on it!

But then came a disappointment. She ran through the rain, straight past the queues and up the cinema steps. The doorman was standing at the ready, waiting to open one of the big glass doors.

Pressing forward, Elizabeth could see the cinema manager and his staff inside. They were lined up in the foyer, waiting to present a bouquet of flowers.

The urgent hand signal that the car driver gave to the young actress, as she turned to face the waiting crowd, told Elizabeth the worst. Kerry wasn't staying! The car was already moving off at speed, round to the back of the cinema, preparing for her to leave from a rear exit.

From the top step the teenage actress gave a short address. It was charming and very spontaneous.

'It's wonderful to see you all here. I hope you will enjoy watching *Zara's Journey* every bit as much as I enjoyed acting in it. If you like the film, do please remember to tell all your friends about it! I so badly wanted to meet some of you this morning and stay and chat. But what can I say . . . ?

'Well, I know one thing I can say! It's a lot easier coming over mountains and through blizzards and storms than it ever is trying to get through the London traffic!'

There was appreciative laughter from the crowd.

'So now I'm in big trouble!' she told them. 'I'm due somewhere else later, way outside London. My driver, who is also my father, says I shouldn't be here at all, but I couldn't bear to let you down. Now all I can do is say bless you all. And run inside and give my thanks to the manager and his staff. Then on my way!'

It was such a friendly little speech that everyone swallowed their disappointment and applauded. Smiling and waving goodbye, Kerry Dane was ushered into the foyer. Most people pushed forward to witness her shaking hands with the cinema staff. What a beautiful bouquet!

But not Elizabeth. Elizabeth was hanging back. She had taken her autograph book out, gripped with a sudden excitement.

'Let's race round to the back of the cinema!' she whispered. 'She's going to leave by the back way, it's obvious!'

Joan looked worried.

'Don't be silly, Elizabeth!' Julian smiled. 'We've only got ten minutes!'

'That's long enough! She'll be out in a minute! I want to get her autograph even if you two don't!' she exclaimed hot-headedly. 'I'm not going to give up now!'

Elizabeth shot away. She rushed round the side of the building, following the route that the blue car had taken. The rain was getting heavier. She was splashing through puddles, but she didn't care.

Kerry Dane seems nice, she thought eagerly. *I'm sure she won't mind! I just hope I'm in time. You can tell she's in a tearing hurry!*

It had hardly been the moment to stop and have a debate with Julian!

She could hear his voice somewhere behind her and the sound of running footsteps. He and Joan were chasing after her, trying to fetch her back! But for once, the naughtiest girl decided, she didn't care if she *was* living up to her nickname. She was not going to allow herself to be thwarted – she must get that autograph!

She had been running fast and was now somewhere at the back of the big cinema building. Blindly, she rushed into the first turning she came to, but it led to a dead end. She merely found herself staring at a fence and a row of black bins.

Drat, it must be the next turning! she realised, as she heard Julian and Joan go racing past, still calling her name.

Then, to her dismay, there came the sound of an engine starting up. She turned.

A blue car nosed into view across the top of her turning, coming from the next one along.

She's leaving. I've missed her! thought Elizabeth.

But, with a squeal of brakes, the car suddenly stopped.

Elizabeth stared, open-mouthed. Kerry Dane was leaping out of the back, still holding her big bouquet of flowers. She was running into the little cul-de-sac. She was heading straight for Elizabeth!

How could this be? For a moment Elizabeth wondered if her friends had somehow explained . . .

No! She was racing straight past Elizabeth without so much as a glance. Golden hair flying, she reached the nearest bin and flung back the lid.

The car horn was honking.

'Shut up, Daddy!' she cried out. 'I won't be a sec. I can't take these stupid things with me. I've got to get rid of them!'

Julian and Joan reappeared, just in time to see Kerry

Dane drop the bouquet in the dustbin and slam down the lid!

Elizabeth was stunned, but nevertheless, as the actress turned and came racing back, she rushed to meet her, her autograph book outstretched.

'Please, Miss Dane, will you sign this for me?' she gasped.

The girl turned on her in contempt. The transformation from her screen persona was now complete. Gone was the pretty smile and warm manner. The eyes glittered; the expression was hard.

'Of course I won't, you little pest!' She brushed Elizabeth's book away. 'Can't you see I'm in a hurry?'

The autograph book went flying out of Elizabeth's hand and landed in a puddle.

'My book!' cried Elizabeth furiously, as she dived to rescue it. 'You've made it all wet and messy!'

'Just like you then!' Kerry Dane called back over her shoulder, as she ran the last few steps to the waiting car. She scrambled inside and the car zoomed away.

Elizabeth stood there for a moment or two, clutching her book, speechless at the girl's rudeness.

'How mean!' said Joan, taking the book and gently wiping it with a tissue.

'Did you see what she did with those beautiful flowers?' asked Elizabeth, finding her voice. 'Lovely fresh flowers too – wasn't that a cruel thing to do?'

'We thought she would be such a nice person,' said Joan, every bit as shocked as Elizabeth. 'But she isn't. She isn't nice at all.'

'She's absolutely horrible!' stated Elizabeth.

Julian had not been under the spell of Kerry Dane's film, having never seen it.

'You told your father we were going to meet the real Kerry Dane,' he pointed out. He gave a wry smile. 'And now we have.'

'Daddy!' realised Elizabeth in horror. 'The train! Now we're going to miss the train!'

'No, we're not,' said Julian, glancing at his watch. 'Not if we run!'

'I'll give Daddy the flowers to take back for Mummy!' exclaimed Elizabeth, darting back to the dustbin. 'That will cheer him up!'

Five minutes later Elizabeth had cheered up considerably herself. She had said goodbye to her father and now they were safely aboard the train.

'You see, Julian! I told you we had plenty of time!'

It had been an embarrassing episode. It had been humiliating. Kerry Dane had turned out to be a complctely different person in real life. A hateful person! But Elizabeth had no intention of talking about it to anybody. She could forget all about her now.

She was going back to Whyteleafe, the best school in the world.

The train moved off, then immediately juddered to a halt. Somewhere, right at the back, a late arrival climbed aboard the First Class section, laden down with luggage.

Then came the sound of banging doors and another blast from the guard's whistle . . . and at last they were on their way.

CHAPTER TWO

BELINDA SURPRISES ELIZABETH

'I'VE ALREADY decided who I'm going to vote for!' announced Elizabeth some time later, as the train rattled merrily along.

The rain had stopped and the sun was trying to come out. Her raincoat was stowed on the luggage rack and her damp curls were almost dry again in the warm railway carriage. Her father had been too surprised by those lovely fresh flowers to be cross with her. Elizabeth felt at peace with the world again.

Some of her classmates were on the train. They had caught up with their holiday news and then discussed going into the second form. Mr Leslie would be their new form teacher. Julian was pleased about that. Mr Leslie was the science master and a great favourite with the boys. But the girls had grown to like him too.

'He's quite strict about schoolwork, though,' Joan

had told the others. Being older than Elizabeth, Joan was already in the next class and was now a second-form monitor. 'He expects quite a lot from us and is always saying that we're not first-formers any more!'

'And neither are we!' Elizabeth had said proudly.

And her thoughts had turned to the forthcoming election for a new head boy and girl. As second-formers, they were allowed to vote, unlike the first-formers and the babies in the junior class!

'I've been thinking about it all holidays,' she said excitedly. 'You know, the election for the new heads.'

'I can't imagine anyone but William and Rita running the School Meetings,' confessed Jenny. 'They were both so marvellous, weren't they? They were always so fair and came to the right decisions. And we could all look up to them!'

'Yes, the new ones will have to be people the whole school can look up to!' agreed Martin.

'So who are you going to vote for, Elizabeth?' asked Belinda.

'For head boy I think Thomas,' she replied firmly.

Everybody at once murmured agreement.

'Yes, he'd be excellent,' nodded Julian. 'He's got real leadership qualities. And who's your head girl then, Elizabeth?'

Elizabeth hesitated. She didn't want to rush what

she was going to say. It was important to her.

'I've thought about it a lot,' she said. 'At first I couldn't think of *anyone* who'd be able to step into Rita's shoes! And then gradually it dawned on me – Emma!'

Elizabeth's suggestion created an instant buzz of interest.

'Emma?' said Belinda.

'Isn't she a bit quiet?' mused Jenny.

But Joan was nodding her head. She had gone into the next carriage earlier, to talk to her friend Susan. And she'd noticed Emma sitting with some new junior pupils who'd looked rather scared and homesick. Joan had admired the way that the senior girl was finding time to chat to them and was getting them to smile.

'I think I agree with you, Elizabeth,' she said eagerly. 'I do believe Emma would be just right. In her own special way, that is.'

'Yes. Excellent,' said Julian, after thinking about it. But Martin looked doubtful.

'She seems sort of shy to me,' he said. 'Especially as she'd have to speak up in front of the whole school all the time. And make sure to hold everyone's attention! Emma's nice, but she's sort of soft-spoken . . .'

'Strong underneath, though!' decided Julian. 'There's no softness there, if you ask me. I think Emma's got authority, but it's the best sort. It's quiet authority . . .'

'Rita wasn't exactly loud, Martin!' Elizabeth pointed out, rather impatiently. 'I bet Rita was very like Emma before she was elected head girl. Was she, Joan? You must have been at Whyteleafe then.'

Joan had been at Whyteleafe longer than the others. She frowned now, deep in thought.

'Why, Elizabeth, I do believe you're right! I remember overhearing some of the teachers say that Rita was a bit too young and as quiet as a mouse and might not be able to keep order! But they were proved wrong. Rita was nervous at the first Meeting or two. But after that she was such a success she stayed on as head girl for two years running.'

'There, Martin!' said Elizabeth.

'Lucky the teachers don't have any say in it then, isn't it?' laughed Julian. 'I think all schools should be run by the pupils, the way ours is.'

'What about Nora?' asked Jenny suddenly. 'She wouldn't be nervous of going on the platform.'

'She'd be good in some ways,' said Belinda, her mind now made up, 'but I don't think she'd be as good as Emma . . .'

They discussed it further. By the end, Elizabeth felt well satisfied. Everyone seemed to agree that Thomas was the right choice for head boy. And apart from Martin, who didn't know who he wanted, and Jenny, who still favoured Nora, everyone seemed to agree with her about Emma.

Because of the way that Whyteleafe School was run, in Elizabeth's opinion it was extremely important to get the right head boy and head girl. And she'd set her heart on Thomas and Emma. She felt that this discussion was a promising start.

Then suddenly, near the end of the train journey, Belinda raised something which made Elizabeth's scalp prickle with excitement.

'We haven't even talked about our *own* election! For a monitor to replace Susan. Now she's going up into the third form, we'll need someone new. We've got Joan, of course, but the second form always has two.'

She was looking straight at Elizabeth!

'We all think you should be the other monitor, Elizabeth,' explained Jenny. 'We talked among ourselves at the end of last term and everyone agreed. Would you be willing to stand?'

'I – I—'

Elizabeth was quite lost for words. Speechless with pleasure! She had already been a monitor once and William had assured her that her chance to be a monitor would surely come again. But she'd never expected it to come so soon!

'You see, Elizabeth,' Joan said gently, having been

in on the secret, 'everyone thinks it was very fine the way you stood down in favour of Susan last term. And that it's only fair you should take her place now she's going up.'

'Not to mention all the things you've done for the school. Even if we *do* always think of you as the naughtiest girl!' laughed Kathleen. 'We were really proud of you last term, Elizabeth. We were proud that you were in our form!'

'So *would* you be willing to stand?' repeated Jenny.

'Oh, yes, please!' exclaimed Elizabeth, glancing across at Joan in delight. Their classmates wanted her to be a monitor again, with her best friend Joan! The two of them would be second-form monitors together. 'There's nothing I'd like better!' she added.

What a wonderful surprise. What a marvellous term this was going to be!

They all piled off at the station and watched their luggage being loaded on to the school coach. Julian gave Elizabeth's back a pat. There was an amused gleam in his eyes.

'Well, well. It looks as though the naughtiest girl is going to be made a monitor again. At the first Meeting. When will that be? This Friday? Can she last that long without misbehaving?'

'Of course I can, Julian,' replied Elizabeth, refusing

to be amused. 'I'm going to jolly well make certain of that!'

That, at least, was her intention.

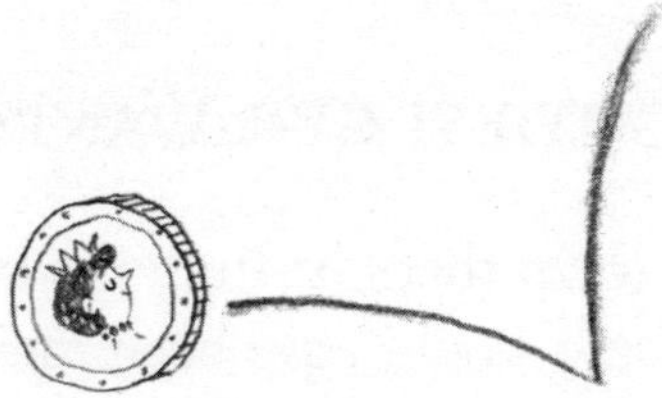

CHAPTER THREE

A GRAND ENTRANCE

ON THE coach they joined all the other boys and girls who'd been on the train. There were plenty of new first-formers and junior-class pupils. They were losing their shyness now and chattering away, excited to think that they'd be seeing their new school very soon. Mr Johns and Miss Thomas, who had both accompanied the train from London, checked names off on a list. Elizabeth and Joan looked around eagerly, wondering if there were any new pupils for their own class.

'Good. All aboard. Off we go!' said Mr Johns.

Soon the coach had left the town far behind and was labouring up the steep hill towards the school. A white station taxi overtook them on the hill. There were two large suitcases on its roof rack. Julian, always alert, watched it turn in through the gates of Whyteleafe School, ahead of them.

'I wonder who's in that taxi from the station?' he said to Elizabeth. 'There would have been room for them on the coach.'

'Perhaps it's a new teacher,' responded Elizabeth absently. She hadn't even noticed the taxi overtake them.

She was thinking instead about the coming Friday. She was imagining the scene at the first School Meeting of the year. The results of the election for head boy and head girl would be announced. Thomas and Emma would take their rightful places at the special table on the platform. As a monitor, Joan would be seated on the platform already. Then any new monitors required would be chosen by their respective classmates. Elizabeth would proudly leave the second-form benches and take her place up on the platform with Joan and the rest.

Together with the other monitors they would be helping their fine new head girl and head boy to govern the school . . .

The coach pulled up.

'We're here now, everyone.'

That was Emma's voice. The senior girl was standing at the exit, helping the teachers. Some of the new pupils were clambering about, peering out of the windows, trying to get a good look at their new school.

'No kneeling on seats, please,' she said quietly but

firmly. 'All the new children are to leave the coach first. Before you do so, please show me your hand baggage. Nothing is to be left on the bus! The girls will then please line up outside with Miss Thomas and the boys with Mr Johns. You will be shown to your dormitories and have a wash before dinner. Your main luggage will be sent upstairs later.'

Obediently, the new pupils queued up to leave the coach, showing Emma their hand baggage as they went. They were longing to get inside the building now, to see their new living quarters.

So too was Elizabeth. She waited impatiently for the last of the younger children to be ushered off the coach. She knew that she and Joan were to be in the same dormitory this year. But who would they be sharing with? And which room?

Just as their turn came to get off the coach, a small fair-haired boy reappeared and clambered back on board. He looked rather scared.

'Please, miss,' he said to Emma, blinking, 'I think I've left my teddy bear behind. I was sure it was in my carrier bag.'

'Don't look so frightened, Rupert!' replied the senior girl. 'We must try to find it quickly. We can't keep Mr Johns waiting.'

Elizabeth glanced round the empty seats at the front.

Suddenly she spotted a furry paw sticking out from under one of the seats.

'I can see it!' she laughed, diving forward to pick it up. 'It's fallen on the floor!'

She handed it to the grateful boy. What a dear little face he had, she thought. He looked a rather dreamy child.

'There you are, Rupert,' smiled Emma. 'Say thank you to Elizabeth. And my name's Emma, by the way.'

'Yes, miss.'

As the bewildered child ran to join the other new juniors, Emma turned to Elizabeth with a gentle laugh. How pretty she looked when she laughed! thought Elizabeth. And how clever of her to have memorized the boy's name already. There were so many new ones this term.

'Well spotted, Elizabeth,' she said. 'I think we're all going to have to keep a motherly eye on Rupert. He's rather young for his age.'

'He thinks you're a teacher, Emma!'

'He'll soon find out that I'm just an ordinary pupil, like him,' laughed the senior girl.

Elizabeth gave Joan a meaningful glance as they disembarked.

'I very much hope that Emma won't be an ordinary pupil for much longer!' she said. 'Don't you, Joan?'

'Yes, she's certainly got my vote!' agreed Joan.

'I can't understand why Jenny thinks Nora might be better!' complained Elizabeth.

To their delight, the two friends found that they had been put in Room Fourteen on the first floor. And they were sharing with Jenny and Kathleen.

'What a lovely sunny room!' exclaimed Elizabeth. She ran to the window. 'And look at the view! We can see right across the grounds. Does anybody want this bed in the corner, or can I have it?'

'I like this one by the door,' said Kathleen.

'And I'm happy with this one by the window,' said Jenny good-naturedly.

The four girls went off to the bathrooms to wash and tidy up before dinner. When they got back to Room Fourteen, they found their luggage waiting for them. It had been brought up from the coach.

'What's in your tuckbox, Elizabeth?' asked Kathleen hungrily. 'Let's see!'

Elizabeth showed them the big chocolate cake that she'd brought from home, to be shared out at teatime.

'I know I'll be starving again by then!' she said happily. 'I'm going to practise my table tennis this afternoon, after we've unpacked. If I can find someone to practise with!'

Second-formers were eligible to play table tennis and

to be chosen for school teams. Elizabeth had always loved the game and she knew she was good at it. She was pleased that she was old enough now to play it at Whyteleafe. She was longing to make one of the teams and play matches against other schools.

As they all looked in each other's tuckboxes, the four girls got hungrier and hungrier.

'That strawberry cake, Joan!' sighed Elizabeth. 'It's almost unbearable to look at it.'

'Mummy and I made it together,' said Joan proudly.

Luckily, before they could be tempted further, the dinner bell went.

'Hooray!'

In fact, it was the second dinner bell. They had somehow missed hearing the first one.

The girls raced downstairs to the dining hall, quickly realising that everybody else was already inside. Dinner was always served late on the first day of term, to allow time for all the pupils to get back. This made the boys and girls very hungry indeed. They knew there would be an extra-special meal today, with plenty of delicious meat and gravy and fresh vegetables from the school gardens. No wonder all the other pupils had got there early.

'What kept you?' frowned Julian. There was a strange look on his face.

He had saved Elizabeth and Joan places at a big table by the window.

'What's the matter with you, Julian?' laughed Elizabeth. 'We didn't hear the first bell, that's all.'

But she quickly realised that there was something unusual afoot. All their classmates were in a huddle round the table, talking in low voices. Julian's cousin Patrick kept looking around, as though expecting something.

It wasn't just happening at their table either. An air of expectancy hung over the dining hall.

'Whatever's going on, Julian?' she asked.

'I've had a horrible shock, Elizabeth.' There was still that funny expression on Julian's face. 'You and Joan are going to get one too. You'll never guess in a thousand years!'

'Sh!' said Patrick, rather bossily. 'Keep your voices down! You know we've been told not to make a fuss. Mr Leslie says we are all to behave perfectly normally.'

'Just because somebody's famous, they don't want to be stared and gawped at,' said Arabella primly. In fact, her hands were shaking slightly as she folded her napkin. She seemed hardly able to control her excitement. 'Mr Leslie's just been over to our table and had a word with us about it.'

'Famous?' asked Elizabeth. She settled down in her

seat between Julian and Joan. 'What's being famous got to do with anything, Julian?'

'Look for yourself, Elizabeth,' he muttered, as the doors swung open. 'Look who's here!'

The three friends were facing the swing doors. They had a perfect view as an elegant figure swept into the dining hall, her golden hair brushed to a gleaming halo, her smile radiant. It was a grand entrance. Miss Belle and Miss Best, the joint headmistresses, bustled the girl quickly across to the senior pupils' table. A boy called Paul was already on his feet, pulling out a chair for her.

All round the dining hall, conversation ceased. The clatter of knives and forks was stilled.

'What's *she* doing here?' whispered Elizabeth indignantly. 'And whatever does she think she's doing wearing our school uniform? I don't understand!'

It was Kerry Dane.

CHAPTER FOUR

ELIZABETH SHOWS RESTRAINT

'ELIZABETH, CAN'T you guess?' asked Julian. He tried not to laugh. The expression on Elizabeth's face was really comical!

The chatter in the dining hall had suddenly resumed, on a rather forced note, as the children remembered that they were supposed to take no notice of the new arrival and on no account to be rude and stare! It was a tall order, but they were managing it well, even the younger ones. Two exceptions, at the second-form table, were Patrick and Arabella. In spite of their fine words they had actually swivelled round to get a better look. Patrick's eyes were almost out on stalks.

Elizabeth lowered her gaze and busily piled vegetables on to her plate. She was trying to collect her thoughts. What an astonishing turn of events! For a moment, in her bewilderment, she'd wondered if a scene for some new film was being shot at Whyteleafe School. But a quick glance towards the seniors' table showed no sign of cameras, or camera operators, or special lighting . . . It was every bit a real-life happening.

Kerry Dane, golden-haired, elegant in a brand-new Whyteleafe uniform, was sitting with the other seniors, chatting, smiling, making friends . . .

'She's a new senior pupil, Elizabeth, that's what!' Julian was whispering. 'I'm very much afraid she's come to Whyteleafe! She must have been in that taxi that passed us. She must have been somewhere on our train.'

'So *that's* why she was in such a rush this morning!' realised Joan, with a slight gasp. She, like Elizabeth, could hardly believe her eyes. The vision from the silver screen, the girl they had queued up to meet in London that morning, who had turned out to be such a disappointment, was sitting in this very dining hall. She was now a member of their school. 'She had to catch the train. The same train as us!'

Elizabeth glowered. 'Just look at her now!' She tossed her curls in the direction of the senior table. Kerry was talking animatedly to her new friends. 'If only they knew what she's really like!'

Julian grinned. He hissed from behind his hand, 'She'd have a surprise if she knew where those flowers were now!'

'Not as big a surprise as Mummy must have had when Daddy brought them home! Mummy does love flowers so!' replied Elizabeth, cheering up.

The three friends started to laugh.

'Hey, pass the roast potatoes, please, Elizabeth.' That was Harry's voice. 'What are you three laughing and whispering about?'

'Oh, nothing!' Elizabeth said quickly.

'Isn't it wonderful that she's decided to come here?' Belinda was exclaiming. 'Of all the boarding schools her parents could have chosen, they chose Whyteleafe. I feel so proud.'

'It's going to be good for the school,' chimed in Kathleen, her rosy cheeks dimpling. 'And she's so nice. Wasn't she good in that film? Did you see it, Elizabeth?'

'Yes,' replied Elizabeth, at the same time giving both Julian and Joan a warning nudge.

Her feelings were still very raw. So far, the three friends had kept quiet about their adventure. And Elizabeth wanted to keep it that way. She wasn't going to tell her classmates about the humiliating episode in London. It had been such a horrible experience, asking Kerry Dane for an autograph!

But there was something else too.

She knew that if she didn't guard her tongue carefully she would soon be rude about Kerry Dane. And they would think her very catty. At the moment everybody believed that Kerry must be like Zara in the film. Elizabeth had believed that herself. They would find out soon enough, but this, reasoned Elizabeth, was hardly a good time to start upsetting her classmates. They were planning to elect her as a monitor at the end of the week!

'So what did you think, Elizabeth?' pressed Kathleen.

'She's a very good actress,' replied Elizabeth. 'Brilliant, I'd say.'

Julian was amused. It was not often that the naughtiest girl showed such restraint. She really *was* on her best behaviour. She must want to be a second-form monitor very badly!

After dinner, as soon as the three friends came out of the hall, Elizabeth gave full vent to her feelings.

'I don't feel in the least bit proud that she's come to Whyteleafe!' she declared. 'I wish she hadn't bothered! Why didn't she want to stay on at her London school? After all, she must be in the middle of studying for her certificate. It's a funny time to change schools.'

'Why go back to school at all, after you've been in a film and become famous?' wondered Joan. 'You'd think she'd want to leave school now and try to be a full-time actress.'

'Perhaps she's not quite old enough to leave school,'

Elizabeth pointed out. 'Or perhaps her parents think she should take her exams first.'

'But why Whyteleafe?' mused Julian, pushing his untidy black fringe back. He was puzzled. 'Why not some big famous school somewhere, with its own theatre and all that sort of thing? Somewhere really posh. We're only a small school buried away in the countryside!'

Elizabeth thought this over carefully. As far as she was concerned, Whyteleafe was the best school in the whole world. But it was a fair point.

'You're right, Julian. Somehow Kerry Dane and Whyteleafe School just don't go together.'

'Perhaps she wants to be a big fish in a small pond?' suggested Joan gently.

'She certainly wants to be noticed,' said Julian shrewdly. 'That warning from Mr Leslie about how she wants to be treated like any other pupil and not made a fuss of . . . Really! So why didn't she just slip quietly into the dining hall at the same time as the other seniors?'

'Yes! Why didn't she? Instead of making a grand entrance!' Elizabeth could feel a temper coming on. 'She wants to be the centre of attention all right. She doesn't belong here. I'm longing for everyone to find out how horrible she is and then perhaps she'll go away again!'

'But we must let them find out for themselves,

Elizabeth,' said Joan quietly. 'You've decided that, haven't you? At the moment I don't think anyone would believe us if we told them what she's really like.'

'Don't worry, Joan.' Elizabeth linked arms with her friend. She had instantly calmed down. 'I know I mustn't lose my temper or say anything silly. But I've just thought of something – you don't think she might recognise me, do you? That would be a bit awkward!'

'She won't recognise *any* of us,' declared Julian, who had been thinking about it. 'We were wearing raincoats over our school uniform. There was nothing to connect us with Whyteleafe at all. And she certainly wouldn't recognise *you*, Elizabeth. Your hair was all plastered down by the rain. As a matter of fact, you looked a sight! Anyway, she didn't even bother to look at you.'

'Thank you, Julian,' said Elizabeth. What a mean, horrid person the girl was. Oh, her lovely autograph book! All spoiled now.

But she felt relieved all the same. She had to make sure that she continued to keep her temper. It would make life very much simpler if Kerry Dane did not recognise her.

'I still find it odd, her coming to Whyteleafe, though,' mused Julian. 'You put it exactly, Elizabeth. She doesn't belong. Whyteleafe and Kerry Dane just don't mix. But now,' he continued airily, 'let's forget all about her, shall we? There's Harry looking for me. Isn't it time we all went and unpacked?'

'It certainly is,' agreed Joan. 'Come on, Elizabeth.'

Elizabeth needed no second bidding. Kerry Dane or no Kerry Dane, she was going to get on with her life! She was a second-former now. She had a lovely new room. She was longing to get her things out of her trunk and arrange them just how she wanted. After that she would go and practise her table tennis and work up an appetite for tea.

Her mouth watered at the thought of the delicious chocolate cake in her tuckbox.

And Kathleen had some excellent news for them.

It was to do with the choosing of the new heads of school.

CHAPTER FIVE

JULIAN IS PUZZLED ABOUT SOMETHING ELSE

'YOU'LL BE pleased when you hear my news, Elizabeth,' said Kathleen, as she came into Room Fourteen. 'I've been talking to some of the seniors and looking at the noticeboard.'

Joan smiled gently. 'I don't want to sound too monitorish, Kathleen, but you should have been up here unpacking. You know it's all got to be done by three o'clock.'

'Sorry, Joan!'

Jenny had unpacked her trunk already and left the room. Elizabeth and Joan had almost finished. Elizabeth was standing back and admiring the way she had arranged her ornaments and photograph frames. It was very satisfying to have been given a much larger chest of drawers this year and to be allowed to put extra things on top. How glad she was to be a second-former now.

'What news, Kathleen?' she asked.

'It looks as though your wish is going to come true, Elizabeth,' smiled the rosy-cheeked girl. 'You know, what we were discussing on the train. It looks very likely that Thomas and Emma will be the new head boy and head girl.'

'How do you know?' Elizabeth asked eagerly.

She and Joan exchanged delighted looks.

'There's a notice up about it!' explained Kathleen. 'And their names have been written up there. Some of the seniors are backing them. And there are no other names up at all!'

Elizabeth clapped her hands with pleasure.

They'd all been sure that Thomas would be made head boy. But – how pleasing – some of the top class agreed with her about Emma!

'Great minds think alike!' she said gleefully. 'Oh, I think Emma's going to make a very fine head girl.'

'So we may not even need an election then!' said Joan happily. 'If no more names are put up, Thomas and Emma will just be appointed the new head boy and girl on Friday and take the first Meeting.'

Now that William and Rita had left, Joan could think of no two nicer heads. As a monitor, she was looking forward to working with them and helping them in the running of the school.

And so was Elizabeth. Hoping that she was going to be chosen as a monitor at the Meeting, she could hardly wait for Friday to arrive.

She hummed happily to herself as she looked for her table-tennis bat. She would go and take a look at that notice herself sometime!

'And there are no other names up, Kathleen?' she asked. 'You're sure?'

'Quite sure!' laughed Kathleen.

Elizabeth spent the afternoon practising her table tennis. She had three quite even games with Patrick and then a long session with Harry. She found that she was able to beat Harry easily!

By the end, he was quite out of breath. A few people had gathered to watch them.

'I'm going off to have a shower now!' he told Elizabeth, as he left. 'You're a great player, though. I'm really impressed.'

'I'm impressed too,' said a quiet voice.

A senior girl had stepped forward. Elizabeth spun round to see who had spoken. It was Emma, captain of the table-tennis team.

'I think you might be school-team material, Elizabeth,' she said. 'I'm running some coaching sessions this term. Would you like to put your name down?'

'Oh, I'd love to!' replied Elizabeth eagerly, hardly

able to believe her ears. 'Thank you, Emma.'

'If you come with me, I'll show you the list.'

The senior girl led Elizabeth along to the main school noticeboard. Proudly she signed up for the table-tennis coaching sessions.

'Oh good. The first one's tomorrow!' she exclaimed.

But she realised that Emma was staring rather dreamily at the notice next to it. She followed Emma's gaze.

There it was, just as Kathleen had said:

Appointment of Head Boy
and Head Girl

Pupils in the second form and above may propose names. Please write the candidate's name in block capitals, with the name of the proposer in brackets. *Do not put anyone's name forward unless you have first obtained their permission.* If more than one name is put forward for either post, an election will take place on Friday in time for the first meeting of term.

The notice was signed by Miss Belle and Miss Best, the joint headmistresses of Whyteleafe School. There were only two names entered:

THE NAUGHTIEST GIRL WANTS TO WIN

EMMA GLOVER (John Terry)
THOMAS HILL (Philippa Dearing)

Elizabeth smiled. 'Some of us were really hoping you might be made head girl!' she blurted out. 'With Thomas as head boy! It's really good that it seems to be all decided!'

'Oh, I wouldn't say that, Elizabeth,' replied Emma lightly, a flush coming to her cheeks. She was feeling very excited, but was trying her best to hide it. 'I was very honoured when John and some of the others asked me if I would allow my name to go forward. But there's plenty of time for other names yet. There may have to be an election.'

'I'm sure there won't be!' said Elizabeth confidently. 'Everybody in the school respects John and Philippa's opinions. I shouldn't think anyone would want to go against them. I know I certainly shan't.'

'Thank you, Elizabeth,' said Emma. 'And I'll see you tomorrow then? I think I can help you a bit with that service.'

Feeling extremely pleased with life, Elizabeth went off to find John Terry. He was one of her favourite people at Whyteleafe. He was in charge of the school gardens and she knew that was where she would find him.

'Hello, Elizabeth!' he greeted her. He straightened up, trowel in hand. 'Look at what all the weeds have been doing while we've been away! Happy to be back then?'

'Very!' said Elizabeth. 'And even happier that you've persuaded Emma to stand as head girl. Won't she make a fine one?'

'Some of us think so,' he said.

'Only some of you?' asked Elizabeth.

'Well, there are those that are worried that she's not forceful enough. I don't agree with them.'

'Nor do I!' said Elizabeth.

'But a few of them *are* worried.'

'Like Jenny then,' laughed Elizabeth. 'She says the same thing. But it's silly, isn't it?'

John nodded wisely, and returned to his weeding.

At teatime Elizabeth was told that Jenny had gone along to see Nora. She had gone to ask her permission to put her name forward as head girl.

'What did she say?' asked Elizabeth when Jenny appeared.

'She refused,' said Jenny, with a sigh. 'She said she doesn't feel she can stand in Emma's way. Isn't that noble of her? Now I don't suppose there will be an election at all. It might have been fun. I was looking forward to it!'

'Well, never mind, Jenny,' said Elizabeth. 'She would

have lost anyway. Want a piece of chocolate cake? Doesn't it look scrumptious?'

Teatime on the first day back was always very enjoyable. The children were permitted to bring their tuckboxes to the dining hall and share some of the good things that they'd brought from home. They were allowed to go and chat to people at other tables. There was quite an informal atmosphere on the first day of term.

'Kerry Dane was with Nora when I went to see her,' Jenny confided, watching hungrily as Elizabeth divided up the cake. 'They seem to be quite friendly. She's really nice, you know. She's *just* like Zara in the film. She asked me all about myself.'

'Yes, everybody's saying how nice she is!' agreed Belinda.

'Hurry up with that cake, Elizabeth!' said Julian. He had been out all afternoon, helping Robert with the school ponies. 'It looks very good.'

'Wait a minute, Julian!' scolded Elizabeth. She had counted the number of children at the table. She wanted them each to have a piece. 'I'm trying to get the slices all exactly the same size.'

While completing this task, Elizabeth became aware of a sudden buzz of excitement around the table. She looked up quickly.

Kerry Dane had just strolled into the dining hall, arm in arm with Nora. They were heading this way! Kerry was giving Jenny a friendly little wave.

'Hello, Jenny!' she said, as she reached the table. 'You promised to introduce me to some of the second-formers. So here I am!'

There was a moment's awestruck silence. The radiant, golden-haired 'Zara' was in their midst! For a split second Elizabeth herself was affected by it. Even without make-up, and wearing just an ordinary Whyteleafe uniform, Kerry Dane had a mesmerising presence. She really did have star quality.

'What a lovely spread!' she said, as she gazed round at the open tuckboxes. 'Nobody told me that we could bring things in. I haven't got a tuckbox!' she added, screwing up her eyes and pretending to sob. 'Why didn't anybody tell me?'

The children laughed. The young star certainly knew how to put them at their ease! Soon they were all talking at once, introducing themselves. Jenny, flushed with pride at the unexpected visit, offered Kerry some shortbread.

'Do you like popcorn?' Patrick was asking eagerly.

But now Kerry had turned and walked over to Elizabeth.

Elizabeth froze, her head lowered as she pretended

to divide up the cake, though in fact the task was complete. She drew in a sharp breath.

The moment had come. Would Kerry Dane recognise her?

'Hello!' Kerry was saying. 'Nora tells me you're Elizabeth, otherwise known as the naughtiest girl in the school.' She gave a friendly little laugh. 'But that you're really one of our best pupils. A completely reformed character!'

Steeling herself, Elizabeth looked up and met Kerry's gaze full on. But she need not have worried. Julian's surmise had been correct.

There was not a flicker of recognition. Kerry had no idea that the two of them had met that morning, in such very different circumstances! Already her gaze was falling from Elizabeth's face to her real interest – the lovely big chocolate cake. And her mouth was watering.

'How do you do,' said Elizabeth politely.

'I would do very well with a piece of that gorgeous cake. I'm afraid chocolate is my great weakness!' replied the star sweetly. 'Can you spare a piece?'

She was looking full into Elizabeth's eyes again, willing her to agree. In the electric silence between them Elizabeth could feel the invisible force of that will. Kerry Dane wanted a piece of the chocolate cake. And whatever Kerry Dane wanted must be given to her.

'I'm sorry,' Elizabeth replied, meeting that fierce gaze, 'I'm afraid it's all spoken for.'

For a fraction of a second a cold hardness crossed Kerry's face, the exact look that Elizabeth had seen before. For that brief moment the mask slipped and the real Kerry Dane showed through.

'Oh, Elizabeth, how mean!' Arabella was exclaiming. 'You can have my piece, Kerry—'

'No, have mine,' Patrick added.

'No, mine!' said Martin.

As some of the boys and girls clamoured for the privilege of giving up their slice of chocolate cake, Kerry turned and faced them, at her most charming once again.

'I wouldn't dream of letting any of you give me your cake!' she smiled. 'How silly of me to ask! Really greedy of me. Nora will take me over to our own table and we'll see what's on offer there! But before we go—'

She looked directly at Jenny.

'There's something Nora wants to say to you, Jenny. I think you're going to be pleased.'

Elizabeth, Joan and Julian exchanged surprised looks. For the first time they realised that Nora, usually a calm, sensible person, had a rather silly, overexcited expression on her face.

'If you really think I would make a good head girl,

Jenny,' said Nora, her cheeks flushed, 'then I will let my name go forward after all. I might as well.'

'Oh good!' exclaimed Jenny, although she was rather taken aback. Less than ten minutes earlier, Nora had been so definite about not standing. 'I'm so pleased, Nora. I'll go and put your name up after tea. Oh, what fun! We'll be able to have a proper election now.'

'Always the fairest way,' smiled Kerry Dane. 'I do think Nora's made the right decision. She's told me how important the post is. The more candidates the better! May the best girl win!' she added lightly.

Elizabeth ground her teeth.

'I hate her!' she said to Julian and Joan later. 'What does she know about our school? It's not a bit fair of her to flatter poor Nora like that.'

'Yes,' agreed Joan. 'I think you're right and that's what's happened. She must have talked Nora into standing. Against her better judgement.'

'And she's bound to get beaten,' nodded Elizabeth. 'If any of the seniors really wanted Nora, they would have put her name up themselves. It's obvious they've decided they want Emma.'

'But it's not just the seniors who vote,' Julian pointed out. 'I think we should run an election campaign for Emma, don't you? Just to help her on her way!'

'Oh, Julian, what an excellent idea!' exclaimed

Elizabeth. 'We can make a banner. And we can get Belinda to do some posters. She's good at art!'

'I think your idea's a very good one, Julian,' said Joan, after due thought. 'The whole school is so taken in by Kerry Dane, the very fact that she approves of there being an election will tend to bring Nora a few votes. We must do all we can to help Emma.'

'The whole school won't be taken in much longer!' declared Elizabeth confidently. She was feeling cheerful again. 'Kerry Dane won't be able to keep up her act of being like Zara in the film forever! Did you see the way the mask slipped when I wouldn't give her any chocolate cake? Greedy pig! Did you see the look she gave me?'

'Well, no, she had her back to the rest of us,' said Julian, looking amused. 'I can imagine it, though! But I was right about her not recognising you, wasn't I, Elizabeth?'

'Yes, Julian!' laughed Elizabeth. 'You were right as usual!'

The three friends set off for the craft room, eager to start the preparations for Emma's election campaign.

As they walked along, Julian dug his hands in his pockets, deep in thought. He was frowning slightly.

'There's something that puzzles me about Kerry Dane.'

'You mean, why she's come to a little school like ours?' asked Elizabeth. 'Yes, it is puzzling.'

'Well, that, of course. But something else. Why should she work on Nora and get her to stand for head girl?'

'Well, she's probably jealous of Emma for being so nice,' volunteered Joan.

'But if you ask me,' said Julian darkly, 'what she'd *really* like is to be head girl herself.'

The two girls looked at Julian in surprise.

'She's new. She can't be!' exclaimed Elizabeth. 'Oh, Julian, what a ridiculous idea!'

CHAPTER SIX

THE NAUGHTIEST GIRL WANTS TO WIN

'GOOD MORNING, children,' said Mr Leslie, the next day, 'and welcome to the second form all of you who have come up this term. Please find yourselves a desk and get settled down. Then I'll give out the new timetable.'

Elizabeth stared round her new form room with pleasure. It was large and airy with windows on two sides. Those pupils already in the second form, like Joan and Jake and Howard, were seated back at their old desks. The rest of them, from the first form, had to find their own.

'Can we really sit anywhere we like, Joan?' whispered Elizabeth, making straight for the empty desk next to her friend's. 'When I first arrived in the first form, we had to remain standing until Miss Ranger told us where to go.'

'You're a second-former now, Elizabeth!' laughed Joan.

Elizabeth felt very pleased as she settled down next to Joan. Carefully she stacked her books in her desk. It was true. She really *was* in the second form at last. And very soon now – after this week's Meeting – she would hopefully be a second-form monitor!

She was going to enjoy having Mr Leslie as her class teacher, although she would miss Miss Ranger, of course. She was also going to enjoy having a new timetable and learning new things. But most of all she was going to enjoy the Meetings and being a monitor with Joan. They would sit on the platform each week, as second-form representatives, with all the other monitors. They would sit in a row, just behind the new head boy and girl.

Whyteleafe was a very unusual school. It was largely governed by the children themselves. The weekly Meetings were like a school parliament, where problems were discussed and grievances aired. When any cases of wrongdoing were reported to the Meeting, it then became more like a court, with the monitors as the Jury and the head boy and girl as the Judges. Miss Belle and Miss Best, the joint headmistresses, sat in on the Meetings, together with Mr Johns, the senior master, but they were mere observers. It was left to the pupils themselves to decide how things should be dealt with.

And Thomas was going to make an excellent head boy, Elizabeth felt. He could be relied upon to be totally fair, as William had been. Emma would be just the same, as head girl; she was truly worthy to step into Rita's shoes. Oh, they must make absolutely certain that it was Emma who became head girl, now there was to be an election!

'You are not to lose your new timetables,' said Mr Leslie, as Joan handed them round the class. 'There's just one each and none left over!'

Elizabeth stuck hers down inside the front cover of her rough book. She studied it carefully. They were going to have more science lessons this year, with Mr Leslie, and more French with Mam'zelle. There were to be more games lessons too. And they would still have Miss Ranger for English. Good! Elizabeth would be able to choose between various outdoor sports this term. And on rainy days they'd be allowed, during games lessons, to play either chess or table tennis.

Table tennis. Hurray! thought Elizabeth. *I do hope I get in a team!*

After school today Emma would be holding the first coaching session. Elizabeth was looking forward to it eagerly. But, before that, there was something else to look forward to.

The three friends had been very busy in the craft room last night. They had made a beautiful banner. Julian had fixed it to a light wooden frame, so that someone could hold it aloft and march along with it.

At dinnertime, the election campaign could begin in earnest. And so it did.

'Roll up, roll up!' shouted Julian, his hands cupped to his mouth. 'Join on the end if you support us. Roll up! Roll up!'

Julian stood by the open doors as boys and girls emerged from dinner. He was shouting encouragement.

It was a merry sight, as the naughtiest girl came marching on to the scene. Elizabeth was striding his way, holding aloft a bright banner. It said:

VOTE FOR EMMA
EMMA FOR HEAD GIRL!

With Harry banging a toy drum beside her, and Joan just behind, they began to parade round the big, sunny lawn. From the second form, Belinda and Kathleen quickly joined on. Then a gaggle of excited juniors, who all adored Emma, tagged on behind. They started singing at the tops of their voices, 'Roll up! Roll up for Emma . . . !'

Each time Elizabeth circled the lawn, the procession

grew longer. Soon there were more than twenty pupils in the parade, while others stood around, applauding. Some of them were seniors, like John Terry and Philippa Dearing. It was beneath their dignity to join the parade, but they were happy to clap and cheer.

'Well done, Elizabeth!' John Terry called out, each time she marched past him.

When the bell went for afternoon lessons, Elizabeth and Julian returned the banner to a cupboard in the craft room.

'Wasn't that good, Julian!' said Elizabeth, her face flushed with excitement.

'Very!' His eyes glinted with amusement. 'Pity some of them aren't old enough to vote. But we've made a grand start!'

'We must do it every day until the election,' vowed Elizabeth. 'I'll ask Sophie to play the flute tomorrow! We'll remind people every day who they should vote for! And Belinda's promised to make posters later today.'

After school Elizabeth collected her table-tennis bat and hurried to the coaching session. She was the first to arrive.

'I saw your parade at dinnertime,' confessed Emma. She looked very pleased, if slightly embarrassed. 'Elizabeth, I was very touched.'

'Nora hasn't got a chance!' replied Elizabeth in her usual forthright way. 'We respect her, but most of us think she's a bit too bossy to be head girl!'

Emma quickly turned to hide a smile. And, just at that moment, several other children arrived – including Julian's cousin, Patrick.

'Hello, Elizabeth,' he said in surprise. 'I didn't know you'd put your name down for coaching.'

'Emma suggested it,' replied Elizabeth sweetly.

Patrick frowned. He couldn't help liking Elizabeth, but he was very competitive. It would be rather annoying if a girl – and especially the naughtiest girl – managed to bag a place in the table-tennis team ahead of him. Emma clapped her hands.

'Right, everyone. First of all, I'm going to go through Elizabeth's service action with her. She needs some help with it. I want you all to gather round the table and watch, in case there are some tips for the rest of you.'

By the end of the session, Elizabeth's service action had already improved. In spite of the fact that Emma had helped him with his forehand smash Patrick was annoyed when Elizabeth managed to beat him 21–18 in a practice game.

'No wonder you want Emma to be head girl,' he said, as they went off to tea.

'Patrick! How dare you? She helped us all equally!'

'Sorry! Sorry!' he said quickly, seeing the tempestuous look in Elizabeth's eye. 'Only joking.'

'I should think so,' replied Elizabeth. 'But honestly, Patrick, who else *could* be head girl? Aren't you going to vote for her yourself?'

'I don't know yet. I'm not sure that she's got enough presence. But then I don't think Nora's quite right either.'

'She's quite wrong!' replied Elizabeth witheringly.

After tea Elizabeth helped Belinda put up her little posters round the school. She thought they were very effective. Written in large letters, in brightly coloured crayons, were some simple slogans.

VOTE ON SATURDAY
EMMA

DON'T FORGET
EMMA

EMMA FOR HEAD
USE YOUR VOTE

'They're really eye-catching, Belinda,' said Elizabeth admiringly, as they fixed one to the door of the third-form common room. 'Everybody's going to notice them!' She gave a little sigh. 'But I do wish Jenny hadn't put Nora's name forward. It's unsettling somehow, though she can't possibly win.'

'I agree,' replied Belinda. She surveyed her handiwork, feeling quite pleased with it. 'None of the boys wants to stand against Thomas. It's just taken for granted that he's going to be head boy. But, now Nora's standing against Emma, it's sort of raised doubts in people's minds. It's started lots of discussion and made them worry whether Emma will be forceful enough, even though they don't think Nora's right.'

'Yes,' said Elizabeth, 'it would have been better if Emma could have been elected unopposed. But, as Jenny told me last night, nobody's got an exclusive right to be head girl and they shouldn't be frightened of an election. It's a fair point. We've just got to make sure that Emma gets a huge vote on Friday. On her merits! I'm sure she will! As a matter of fact, Belinda, I'm quite enjoying this election campaign.'

'Yes, it's fun!'

Going upstairs, at bedtime, Elizabeth smiled as she saw some tiny notices on doors. They were written in Jenny's handwriting. They said simply: VOTE FOR NORA. She thought they looked rather feeble, compared with Belinda's efforts.

And, when she got to Room Fourteen, she found Jenny in a chastened mood.

'I'm not getting a lot of support for Nora,' she confessed, as the girls sipped their bedtime cocoa. 'I'm sure Kerry will vote for her and one or two other seniors. But I think she may only get about twenty votes altogether.'

'Serves you right, Jenny!' laughed Elizabeth.

Joan was gentler about it. 'Poor Jenny,' she said to Elizabeth when they went with Kathleen to clean their teeth.

'And poor Nora!' added Kathleen.

'Yes,' agreed Elizabeth. *And it's all Kerry Dane's fault for interfering. What does she know about Whyteleafe School?*

Elizabeth was longing for Kerry's mask to crack, for the rest of the school to see the young actress in her true colours. Only then could she tell her classmates about the adventure that she, Joan and Julian had had in London. And how the three of them had known all along that she was not nearly as nice as she seemed. That she was, in fact, perfectly horrid.

But three whole days passed by. And, by Thursday evening, Elizabeth was getting impatient.

'I don't know how Kerry Dane's managing to keep it up!' she complained to Julian, as they came indoors together after a ride on the ponies. 'She's so nice to everybody all the time, especially the older forms. Everybody thinks they're getting to know her properly. They keep saying she's even nicer than the part she played in the film. Really!'

'Yes. I hear she's offered to do something for the Earthquake Bazaar!' observed Julian. 'You know, the sale that the seniors are going to hold, to raise money for the earthquake victims. She's running the sweet stall, or something. Arabella's been making some fudge for it.'

'I know,' said Elizabeth, grinding her teeth. '*And* she's offered to get someone important from the film world to come and open it. Everybody thinks she's marvellous! How *does* she keep it up? It must be a terrible strain for her. I simply can't think why she bothers.'

'Hallo!' said Julian suddenly, as he looked down the corridor. 'What's going on? There's quite a crowd round the noticeboard.'

Elizabeth and Julian hurried over and pressed forward to get a good look. There was a buzz of excited chatter all around them. Everybody was gazing at the election list for head boy and girl.

Miss Belle and Miss Best would be taking the notice down tonight. But another name had been added, at the last moment!

A third nomination for head girl had been added to the list. The name was written clearly, in a senior boy's bold handwriting:

KERRY DANE (Paul Kirk)

Elizabeth backed away from the noticeboard, laughing out loud in shock.

Julian whistled to himself.

'There's your answer, Elizabeth,' he said. 'All is explained.'

CHAPTER SEVEN

A VERY CLOSE RESULT

ELIZABETH LISTENED to the babble of voices all around her. Everyone seemed to be talking at once. There were many conflicting opinions.

'Paul persuaded her! She shouldn't have listened to him!'

'She didn't really want to stand. She says she's too new.'

'And she is. Much too new! If she'd been here a while, and been a monitor, I'd definitely vote for her. She'd make a marvellous head girl. But—'

'But why not? Paul says the important thing is just to get the very best person. If people were so sure about Emma, why would Nora bother to stand?'

'Yes! And seeing there's going to be an election *anyway* . . .'

'I say, wouldn't Hickling Green be envious if we

had Kerry Dane for head girl! They're such a lot of stuck-up snobs! And, you know, I can just see her on the platform, taking the Meetings with Thomas. She's got such presence!'

'Yes, she has. But it wouldn't be right – it's got to be a real Whyteleafean. It's got to be Emma or Nora.'

'I agree with you, Candida!'

'Yes! I'll be voting for one of the old stagers.'

'Me too. Emma in fact . . .'

'But Kerry *would* have made a marvellous head girl.'

Elizabeth and Julian walked away.

'*A marvellous head girl?*' exploded Elizabeth. 'She'd be a disaster! Oh, Julian, do you think she's been planning this?'

'I'm sure she has,' frowned Julian. 'From the moment she saw the chance to provoke an election and unsettle things. What a schemer!'

'Julian, you don't think . . .' The idea filled Elizabeth with horror. 'You don't think there are enough people who'd be *silly* enough . . . to get sort of carried away and vote for her on the spur of the moment? So that she ends up being elected?'

It was like looking into the abyss.

'There'll be some,' said Julian thoughtfully. 'But not a majority, I'm quite sure. You heard what everyone was saying. Most people feel strongly that she's much too new. They may be dazzled by her, but they are going to vote for Emma or Nora.'

'Good! Then we've got to make sure it's Emma!' said Elizabeth fervently. 'Let's have one last parade tomorrow, Julian. The best parade yet! Straight after breakfast. Just before the election!'

Voting was at ten the next morning. The School Meeting would follow at eleven.

At bedtime Jenny looked unhappy.

'I am surprised,' she said, 'that Kerry's allowed her own name to go forward! She came to talk to me about it. She said she didn't want it to happen, but other people were insisting. And, after what she'd said to me about Nora standing, she couldn't really refuse, could she? But she told me not to worry. She's promised to vote for Nora herself, and she's going to tell everyone she meets to vote for Nora as well! Isn't that sweet of her?'

Elizabeth didn't believe a word of it. But out loud she said, 'So what's the matter then?'

'Oh, nothing!' Jenny replied quickly.

Jenny was too proud to admit to Elizabeth that Kerry Dane had forgotten her name already. She'd kept calling her Jane! It had left Jenny feeling rather uneasy. There was something odd about the whole thing, but she couldn't quite put her finger on what it was.

Friday morning dawned bright and sunny. The

election campaign for Emma reached its climax. Elizabeth organised the final parade with great flair. Sophie came with her flute and all the juniors brought tambourines. And Richard agreed to strum his guitar! For the last hour before the voting began Elizabeth marched her band round and round the outside of the school buildings, holding the banner aloft.

Each time they passed below dormitory windows, Harry banged the drum and Julian shouted, 'Wake up! Wake up! Don't forget to come and vote!'

And the juniors chorused, 'VOTE FOR EMMA! VOTE FOR EMMA! ROLL UP, ROLL UP AND VOTE FOR EMMA!'

Cheerful faces appeared at windows. There were smiles and waves.

Elizabeth found the whole thing very exhilarating. Afterwards she said, 'I'm sure Emma's going to win, Joan. I just feel it in my bones!'

'Let's hope so,' replied Joan gently. 'At least there should be a good turnout now! Come on, Elizabeth. We mustn't forget to cast our *own* votes. It's nearly ten o'clock.'

Miss Belle and Miss Best were in charge of the election, which took place in the dining hall.

As Elizabeth joined the queue of people waiting to cast their vote, her confidence grew. What an excellent turnout! If most of these people were voting for Emma, then Kerry Dane was in for a big disappointment.

When she reached the head of the queue, Miss Belle ticked her name off a list and Miss Best handed her a voting paper. Elizabeth then walked through to a special table, picked up one of the pencils there and firmly marked a cross against Emma's name. As she carefully folded her ballot paper, she squinted along the table and saw that a third-former was marking his cross in the same place. Good!

Under the watchful eye of the joint headmistresses, Elizabeth posted her voting slip into the big ballot box. It was a very satisfying feeling, to have cast her vote. The Beauty and the Beast, as the children called the heads, both smiled at her warmly.

I wonder if they know I'm going to be made a monitor today? wondered Elizabeth. *I seem to be in their good books.*

She met up with Joan and Julian outside the hall and the three friends wandered along to their common room together. Some fourth-formers, walking along the corridor ahead of them, were talking loudly.

'I was going to vote for Kerry,' one of them was saying, 'but I changed my mind this morning. Kerry persuaded me to vote for Nora. She's just so positive she'd be best!'

'Oh, how funny. She said something to me too. She's very persuasive, isn't she! I really had to fight with myself to stick to my guns and vote for Emma.'

'Isn't it decent of her not to expect people to vote for her, but to ask them to vote for Nora instead?'

The three friends heard this in some surprise.

'So it's true then!' said Elizabeth. 'Jenny told me that Kerry had promised to campaign for Nora. I didn't believe she really would.'

'How very odd,' said Joan.

Julian said nothing. He looked worried.

'Well, at least Kerry Dane can't possibly win herself now!' declared Elizabeth.

While the votes were being counted in the hall, all the boys and girls had a break. Then they went to their rooms to get spruced up for the Meeting. Elizabeth was in a state of high excitement by now.

Kathleen came and brushed some fluff off the collar of her blazer for her. She was smiling and rosy-cheeked as usual.

'Well, the suspense will soon be over!' she said. 'I'm sure Emma will have won. And we know Thomas has, because nobody stood against him. And then we'll be able to get on with all the proper business of the Meeting. You're still quite happy about being put forward as a monitor again, Elizabeth?'

'Kathleen, need you ask!' exclaimed Elizabeth, with a happy laugh.

The Meeting had arrived at last. She was looking forward to it.

They filed into the school hall, which doubled as a gym, and took up their new places on the second-form benches. Elizabeth sat next to Julian. Joan left them and took her place up on the platform, with the other monitors. The hall was filling up very quickly. Elizabeth glanced across to the senior benches. Emma was sitting there, next to John and Philippa. Kerry Dane was sitting beside Paul, her hair brushed to a beautiful golden sheen.

At the back of the hall sat Mr Johns and the Beauty and the Beast, as always, although they would take no part in the Meeting unless asked.

When everybody was seated, Thomas walked into the hall.

A cheer went up as the tall fair-haired boy mounted the platform and stood behind the special head boy and girl's table. He held up his hand for silence. In his other hand he held a piece of paper.

The election results!

A hush descended over the hall as Thomas started to speak. Elizabeth realised that she was clenching her hands into tight little fists and that her heart was beating faster than usual.

'I am very proud to be the new head boy of Whyteleafe School,' he told them in his clear, pleasant voice. There was a deadpan expression on his face. It gave nothing away. 'And now, without further ado, I am going to read out the results of the election for our new head girl. She will then be able to take her place on the platform beside me and the business of the Meeting can commence.'

He opened up the piece of paper. Elizabeth held her breath.

'The number of votes cast for each candidate was as follows: Nora – twenty-nine votes. Emma – thirty-four votes. Kerry – thirty-five votes.'

Elizabeth gasped. Was she having a bad dream?

Thomas was giving a signal to someone on the senior benches.

'I declare Kerry Dane the new head girl. Would you come up on to the platform, please, Kerry? And would everybody give Kerry a round of applause, please.'

The school buzzed with surprise and then began clapping.

What a close result! It could hardly have been closer. But, as Kerry ran lightly up to the platform, many of the first-formers and juniors looked crestfallen. They had never seen Kerry Dane's film. She was such a remote figure to them – not like Emma.

Elizabeth turned and looked at Julian in disbelief.

'It isn't possible,' she whispered in horror.

Julian was busily doing some calculations on his fingers.

'I'm afraid it is, Elizabeth,' he whispered back. 'How very clever of her. Very cunning indeed.'

Elizabeth tossed her head. She wasn't listening. She was glancing across at Emma. The senior girl was trying to smile, but was fighting back the tears. It would have been such a privilege, such an honour, to serve Whyteleafe School as its head girl. She had so longed to be chosen. John Terry placed an arm round her shoulders to comfort her. There was an angry expression on his face.

Suddenly Elizabeth was incandescent with rage. Her temper boiled over. She got to her feet.

'It's not fair! I don't know what's happened, but it's not fair!' she hissed at Julian. 'I'm going!'

She marched off towards the exit.

Julian didn't hesitate. He jumped up and followed her. 'Me too, Elizabeth,' he said, catching her up.

Trembling and upset, Joan scraped her chair back and left the platform with quiet dignity.

With Elizabeth leading the way the three friends walked out of the Meeting.

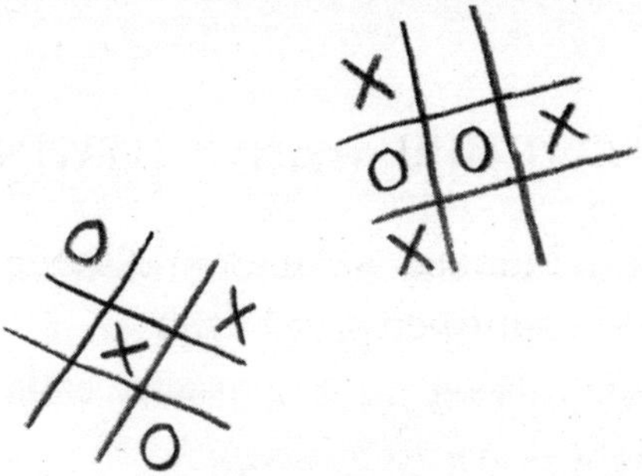

CHAPTER EIGHT

NEW MONITORS HAVE TO BE FOUND

'SILENCE, PLEASE, everyone,' said Thomas, banging loudly on the table with the gavel that William and Rita had always used. 'Will you settle down at once and pay attention?'

It was Thomas's first big test as head boy. The hall was in something of an uproar. The naughtiest girl had marched out of the Meeting, with two of her friends! What a surprise.

Thomas could have turned to the Beauty and the Beast for advice, but he had no intention of doing so. He must handle this himself. He thought hard about what William or Rita would have done. They would have handled it with a light touch. He must follow suit.

'That's better,' he smiled, as the Meeting came to order. 'I'm afraid that elections can make people very emotional sometimes, especially when the result is extremely narrow. Let us take no notice of what has happened. Elizabeth and her friends will soon calm down and come back to join us. But now I want the Meeting to get straight down to business . . .'

However, Kerry Dane had other ideas. She was not going to be deprived of her moment of glory by those three people walking out, or by Thomas wanting to get on with the silly Meeting. She had a speech all prepared!

'First of all, I'd like to say a few words, if I may, Thomas.'

She walked forward to the very front of the platform. She felt exultant, as she stood before the assembled school, her beautiful hair making a halo of golden light around her head. It felt so right somehow that she, Kerry Dane, should be up here, with all those faces gazing at her. Now she was mistress of all she surveyed. This was what she was used to, ever since becoming famous. This was how it should be!

'I want to tell you all how humble I feel,' she began. 'I never, ever dreamt of being elected. I never expected an honour like this. You had two such fine candidates for the position of head girl. I am merely a new girl. I am so proud that, in spite of this, I am the person who has been elected – and I promise to serve Whyteleafe School to the very best of my ability. Thank you.'

The children listened, mesmerised. She made an

impressive sight and it was an impressive little speech.

There was applause. Patrick, Arabella and Martin exchanged smug looks. They had all voted for Kerry, and some of their classmates had criticised them. How wrong they were. Even the first-formers and juniors began to feel more cheerful. Kerry seemed a nice person. They would just have to get used to not having Emma as head girl . . .

Kerry stood there, acknowledging the applause. She was in a happy state, wanting it to go on and on.

The applause was dying away now with only the die-hards like Arabella continuing to clap. But still Kerry stood there.

'Ahem,' said Thomas politely. 'Time to start, Kerry.'

She seemed not to hear.

Looking a little cross, Thomas had to bang the gavel again to bring the Meeting to order. Only then did the newly elected head girl come and take her seat beside him. She had almost forgotten where she was.

'Right, first things first,' Thomas told the Meeting. 'Will you all give your money in, please? Richard will come round with the school box.'

Kerry Dane watched in surprise as the wooden box was passed along the rows. Into the box went all the money that the children had brought back from home after the summer holidays.

'At Whyteleafe School,' Thomas explained to the new pupils below, 'it is not thought fair for some children to have more money than others. You will find that, at every Meeting, any money you've been sent will be collected up. After that each child in the school receives two shillings pocket money for the week. You are then allowed to make special requests if you need extra money for something important. Every request is listened to carefully and then the Meeting decides.'

While the box was going round, Kerry pulled out her wallet and counted the banknotes inside. She saw Thomas glance at them.

'Obviously, Thomas,' said Kerry sweetly, 'this rule doesn't apply to us? Not to the head girl and head boy of the school?'

'I'm afraid it does, Kerry,' he said tersely. 'Seniors do have more calls on their purse than the younger children, so you will find that no reasonable request is ever turned down. But in the meantime –' he looked at the banknotes hard – 'all of those must go in the box.'

Kerry managed to conceal her shock. What a ridiculous system! She would have to find some way of getting round it.

In the meantime, when the box came to the platform, she had no choice but to place all her money inside under Thomas's watchful gaze.

Soon the week's pocket money had been handed out to every pupil in the school and it was time to hear special requests for extra funds.

Julian's cousin was one of the first on his feet.

'I think Patrick *should* be allowed the money for a new table-tennis bat, Thomas,' Kerry decided. 'He tells me he's a very keen player.'

She was beginning to enjoy herself again. It was lovely to have so much power over the other children. Some of them would find their requests refused, if she didn't like the look of their faces!

Thomas did not agree at all that Patrick needed a new table-tennis bat, but he had to let it pass. Kerry obviously did not understand the rules about special requests. It would all have to be explained to her. Now Patrick had been given an unfair advantage over other children who were also hoping to get into Emma's table-tennis squad.

But it would not be right to have an argument with Kerry in front of the entire school. It would undermine her authority.

As more special requests came and went, Thomas was keeping an eye on the doors at the back. Surely the naughtiest girl would have cooled down by now? He very much hoped so.

She and her two friends should really come back to

the Meeting quickly. He expected to see them slip quietly back into their seats and show that they had now accepted the verdict of the ballot box. However regrettable, thought Thomas, that verdict had turned out to be.

Elizabeth had raced off to the school vegetable gardens. When Julian and Joan caught her up, she was marching up and down one of the little paths.

She walked up and down like that for some minutes, in order to work off her temper. When at last she grew tired, the three of them sat on a sunny bench, just in front of the greenhouses.

'Let's have an apple,' said Joan in her gentlest voice.

She picked three rosy apples from one of the little trees nearby. They each took a bite. As Elizabeth tasted the sweet, sharp tang of the fruit, she gazed around sorrowfully. These dear gardens, how she loved them. How she loved helping John Terry with the weeding and planting and hoeing.

Dear Whyteleafe School, the best school in the entire world. What happy times she had had here. But now, surely, it could never be the same again?

'It's the worst thing that's ever been,' she said miserably. 'And how did it happen? I just don't understand. Emma seemed to have so much support. You were wrong for once, Julian! You were so sure that most of the school wouldn't vote for Kerry, however much they admired her.'

'I wasn't wrong at all,' replied Julian patiently. 'You obviously haven't done your sums, Elizabeth. Most of the school did not vote for Kerry Dane. She only collected about one-third of the vote. She always knew that would be the best she could hope for. That was why she got Nora to stand. And *that* was why she went around persuading people to vote for Nora.'

'You mean . . . ?' Elizabeth frowned, trying to work it out.

'Julian means that Kerry guessed that a majority would never vote to elect a new girl,' explained Joan. 'But, if she could split that majority in two, as evenly as possible—'

'She could squeeze through the middle and maybe win!' finished Julian. 'And that's exactly what happened. It was a masterstroke, begging people to vote for Nora. It made some of them worry about voting for Emma and change their minds. And it made some of them, who may have been thinking of voting for Emma, but who didn't have strong principles about not electing a new girl, think, "I don't want to vote for Nora, but what a fine person Kerry is. I shall give her my vote." So she picked up some extra votes for herself as she went along. That's what made all the difference!'

'She would never have had a chance, if she'd just stood against Emma,' sighed Joan. 'She would have been very soundly beaten. But, as it turned out, she was able to split the vote three ways. What an impossible schemer! I realised what she had done as soon as Thomas read the result out. I felt such contempt for her that I just had to leave the platform, even though a monitor should never do a thing like that. I just had to.'

'It's not fair,' exclaimed Elizabeth. 'It's horrific!'

Julian threw his apple core so it landed on John Terry's compost heap. Then he glanced at his watch.

'Should you two be sitting here?' he asked. 'The Meeting must be racing along. They'll be getting to the bit about the second-form monitors soon.'

Joan and Elizabeth looked at one another.

'I'm not going back in there,' said Joan bravely.

'Nor me,' stated Elizabeth.

Her face crumpled and tears of anger came to her eyes.

'I don't want to be a monitor any more. Not with her as head girl! I couldn't bear, as a matter of fact, ever to sit on the same platform as her!'

'Those are my feelings exactly, Elizabeth,' declared Joan.

'Now,' said Thomas, gazing round the hall, 'we come to the last business of the day.'

NEW MONITORS HAVE TO BE FOUND

Complaints and grumbles had been dealt with. There had only been two.

'We have to sort out the second-form monitors,' he continued. 'As you know, you are allowed two. Joan is still in the second form and can remain as a monitor, if you so wish. Or you may elect a new person, if you prefer. Susan has gone up into the third form this term. So a new monitor will have to be chosen to take Susan's place. Do you want to choose one new monitor, or two? What have you decided, second-formers?'

Belinda rose to her feet. It had been agreed that she would be the spokesperson for the form. It had also been agreed what she should say. The words were written on a piece of paper.

Her cheeks hot with embarrassment, Belinda glanced round to see if there was any sign of Elizabeth and Joan coming back. For the past few minutes she had been looking out for them constantly. But they had not returned to the Meeting.

'Well, Belinda?' prompted Thomas.

Feeling awkward, Belinda read out the prepared statement.

'We, in the second form, have agreed unanimously that we would like Joan to continue as a monitor for another term. For our other monitor we are all of the same opinion. We would like to appoint Elizabeth.'

As she sat down, a buzz of conversation ran round the hall. The second form wanted Joan and Elizabeth as monitors. But both girls had walked out of the Meeting! This was going to be an unusual situation. What would happen now?

'Please!' said Arabella, putting her hand up.

'You wish to say something?' asked Kerry Dane eagerly, from the platform.

Arabella stood up. She was feeling outraged at the way that Elizabeth, Joan and Julian had walked out of the Meeting earlier. Just because their favourite hadn't won! The election had been fought fair and square and Kerry had won. She was going to make such a fine head girl. Perhaps she would be able to get Arabella a part in a film one day. She had almost hinted as much! It was extremely horrid and rude of Elizabeth and the others to walk out like that.

'When we've chosen monitors before, they've always had to stand up at the Meeting and agree,' she pointed out. 'But how can we elect Elizabeth and Joan if they're not here?'

'Shut up and sit down, Arabella!' hissed Daniel crossly.

'You know they've agreed,' whispered Belinda, looking anxious. 'You know Joan's agreed to stay on and Elizabeth wants to be the new one.'

'What do the rules say about it, Thomas?' Kerry asked

sweetly. 'Is there anything written about it in the Book?'

The Book was a large volume that stood on the table between them. It contained a record of everything important that had happened at Meetings and the many rules that had been agreed upon over the passage of time. Together, Kerry and Thomas pored over the Book together and soon found what they needed. They discussed it briefly with the monitors behind them and then Thomas turned to face the school. He looked upset.

'It appears to be an established rule that people must be here to be elected. The Meeting also feels that Elizabeth and Joan have ruled themselves out by such bad behaviour. So we've decided that the second form must now choose two new monitors. First find out if your choices are willing to stand, then write both names on a piece of paper.' He handed Kerry some slips of paper to take down to the second formers. 'We shall then count the votes and have a result very quickly.'

When Elizabeth and Joan went into dinner later, they learnt that Belinda and Daniel had been elected in their place.

They accepted the news bravely. Both girls were determined never to sit on the same platform as Kerry Dane, or recognise her as head girl in other ways.

'I expect next week's Meeting will have to decide on some sort of punishment for us,' Joan sighed to her friends, after dinner. 'It's a very serious offence to miss a whole Meeting.'

'See if I care!' pouted Elizabeth.

'I don't expect the Meeting will punish you two,' said Julian airily. 'They'll decide that you've been punished enough by losing your monitorships. They'll have to find some punishment for me, of course.'

Julian dug his hands in his pockets. His green eyes glinted.

'Whatever it is, it'll be worth it! It was good to make a stand. I really enjoyed it.'

'Yes,' nodded Elizabeth. 'I didn't mean to lose my temper. But it was good to show her what we think of her.'

Julian smiled to himself, in spite of everything. Life was never dull with the naughtiest girl around.

At bedtime that night Elizabeth discovered that Jenny was very upset.

'I feel it's all my fault, Elizabeth. I should never have asked Nora to stand! It's worked out all wrong. Much as I admire Kerry, I never expected her to be elected as head girl. She just doesn't seem right for it.'

'She doesn't seem right for anything!' said Elizabeth coldly. She had no need to keep her feelings to herself any longer. 'She's really hateful. I'll tell you all about it some time. But I expect you'll find out soon enough.'

'Really?' Jenny looked intrigued. She frowned. 'In a way, I suppose, she doesn't seem right here at Whyteleafe at all.'

Elizabeth felt tired after all the strains of the day. She climbed into bed. But it was nice that Jenny was beginning to see sense. She had already forgiven her.

'Kerry's completely wrong for Whyteleafe,' she said sleepily. 'What Julian and Joan and I can't understand is what she's doing here at all!'

CHAPTER NINE

EMMA SPEAKS TO ELIZABETH

IT WAS wet on Saturday. Elizabeth spent much of the day practising her table tennis. She hung around the green tables downstairs, getting as many games as she could. Soon she had perfected the new service that Emma had taught her. She then went on to improve her forehand smash. Patrick was practising hard too.

They'd both discovered there was to be a match next Saturday, a friendly against St Faith's. It would be the first fixture of the new school year. And Emma and Mr Warlow would be choosing the squad after this week's coaching session. Elizabeth was determined to get in the team!

She found the forehand smash particularly satisfying. She was still feeling angry and upset. She had left Joan sitting in the common room, hard at work with some knitting. Joan had decided to make a child's scarf for the

Earthquake Bazaar that the seniors planned for next Sunday. It would be a comfort to try to help the earthquake victims in some small way.

'It will take my mind off things, Elizabeth,' Joan had said, an expression of quiet fortitude on her face.

It upset Elizabeth that she was not to be a monitor after all. But it upset her even more that Joan had been stripped of the post.

'Kerry Dane's been too clever for us so far, Joan, but we're not going to let her win!' Elizabeth muttered darkly. 'We'll find some way – *some* way – of showing her up for what she is!'

By Saturday afternoon, Elizabeth was hitting the table-tennis ball with great venom and accuracy. It was an excellent way to relieve her feelings.

'Phew!' said Harry, as Elizabeth won their game with a beautiful smash.

'Your return just sat up and begged for a forehand smash, Harry!' laughed Elizabeth. 'You should try to spin it and keep it low – that's what Emma says. You ought to come to the coaching sessions; they're fun!'

'I'm not good enough,' said Harry. 'But you're getting brilliant. I'm sure you'll get into the team, Elizabeth.'

Most of her classmates were being very nice to her this weekend. She had worked so hard to get Emma elected. They felt sorry that she'd lost control of her temper and with it her chance of being monitor. It was sad about Joan too. Belinda and Daniel, the new monitors, felt especially unhappy.

At that moment one of the seniors appeared.

'Ah, found you, Elizabeth,' Philippa smiled. 'A treat for you! A telephone call from your mother. Would you like to run and take it?'

Philippa felt sorry for the naughtiest girl too and the trouble that her emotions had got her into the previous day. It was nice that her mother had rung!

I wonder what Mummy wants? Elizabeth thought, as she hurried along to the little room called the Telephone Room. It was just a tiny box room with a comfortable chair and a low table. On the table was a coin-in-the-slot payphone.

Boys and girls from the second form upwards were allowed to receive calls from their family on a Saturday, and even to make outgoing calls if they were important. It was an exciting privilege. But Elizabeth had not expected to receive a telephone call so soon! The receiver lay on the table, waiting to be picked up.

'Hello, Mummy!'

'Hello, Elizabeth dear.'

Mrs Allen had rung about the flowers.

'Thank you! It was such a lovely surprise when Daddy brought them home. They're still as fresh as ever, even now. I've arranged them in the big vase on the hall table. I wish you could see them!'

'I can just imagine them, Mummy,' said Elizabeth, closing her eyes and doing so. Mrs Allen loved flowers so and made wonderful arrangements. 'I'm glad you're pleased with them.'

'It must have been very interesting for you to meet Kerry Dane like that!' her mother was saying. 'I was so surprised that she didn't want to keep the flowers herself—'

'I think she had too much to carry, Mummy,' Elizabeth said hastily. The naughtiest girl had not, of course, told her father that the bouquet had been rescued from a dustbin. There'd hardly been time to explain all that! It was simpler just to say that the actress hadn't needed them. 'I expect she gets lots of flowers,' she added.

'It was still extremely kind of her to make us a gift of them,' continued Mrs Allen. 'I thought you would like to know how pleased I am. And, of course, I hope to find an address to write to. I would like to drop a thank-you note to Miss Dane. I expect she has an agent in London . . .'

'Oh, Mummy, I shouldn't bother to do that! I'm sure she would just find it embarrassing. Please don't bother to write a note!'

But her mother had become distracted.

'Oh, there's the doorbell!' said Mrs Allen. 'I have some friends coming to tea. They will be very impressed when they hear about the flowers. Thank you again, Elizabeth. How lovely to speak to you on the telephone.'

Elizabeth replaced the receiver and left the telephone room. It was a nice surprise to get a telephone call from her mother, but how she would hate it if Mrs Allen found out the agent's address and sent him a note for Kerry Dane!

If only her mother knew where Kerry was! One day, when this was all over, she would tell her mother the whole story.

'Where's my table-tennis bat?' she asked John McTavish when she returned. He was having a knockabout with Daniel, now that the table had come free.

'I expect you took it with you to the Telephone Room, Elizabeth!' laughed John. 'We haven't got it!'

'Yes, so I did! And I've left it there too. How silly of me!'

Elizabeth retraced her footsteps. She would pick up her bat and then go to have a shower before tea.

The door of the telephone room was ajar. Somebody else was already in there she could hear them speaking. The telephone was in use again!

Elizabeth hovered outside the door, wondering if the person would mind her just creeping in to get the bat. Then, as she recognised the voice, she stiffened. It was Kerry Dane. She was gloating. Elizabeth could hear every word.

'Mummy, it was brilliant of you and Daddy to find Whyteleafe School for me. I didn't believe you when you said you'd found a school like this where the pupils are in charge! No stupid teachers will ever boss me around again . . .'

Then a few moments' silence. Followed by laughter.

'Yes, of course it was cheeky of them at Horton High! Trying to behave as if I was still an ordinary schoolgirl. Trying to act as if I wasn't famous. It's different at this place. You said it would be. We can do what we like. And you'll never guess – I've been made head girl! Instead of being bossed around by grown-ups, I'm in charge of the other pupils, with a boy called Thomas. It's going to be such fun telling everybody what to do! There are one or two silly little rules, that's all. I'll tell you why I've rung, Mummy. Can you get some cash to me . . .'

More silence. And then the voice became sulky. 'Oh, don't be silly, Mummy. I can't be bothered to explain about the other cash. Why's it difficult? Can't you send banknotes by registered post?' Kerry was becoming increasingly petulant. 'I need to be able to buy myself treats when I want to, Mummy!'

Elizabeth tiptoed away. She had heard enough! Her table-tennis bat could wait! She raced off to find Joan and Julian.

Breathlessly, she told them everything she'd overheard.

'So *that's* why she's come to Whyteleafe School!' whistled Julian.

'Yes, she thinks there's no discipline here. That this is a soft school where she can do exactly what she likes!' said Elizabeth, outraged. 'But that's not how things work at Whyteleafe. A person like that can't be allowed to be head girl! It's an insult! Surely we can do something—'

'There's nothing we *can* do, Elizabeth,' said Joan calmly, 'except be very, very patient. It will only be a matter of time now before her true nature reveals itself.'

'I'm not sure I can just sit around and wait for "time"!' exclaimed Elizabeth furiously.

Julian ruffled her hair and grinned.

'Always the bold, bad Elizabeth!' he observed. 'I'm afraid we haven't any choice, whether we like it or not.'

There was strawberry ice cream for tea that day, but Elizabeth hardly tasted it as she spooned it down, silent and inwardly smouldering.

Looking across from the seniors' table, Emma saw how unhappy she seemed.

The senior girl came and sought her out later. Emma was still very unhappy herself, but she was determined not to let it show.

'Cheer up, Elizabeth!' she said lightly. 'I know how disappointed you must be feeling about the election result. But we must put a brave face on things, you know!' She smiled. 'We can't have people thinking we are bad losers, can we?'

'It's nothing to do with being a bad loser!' Elizabeth blurted out. 'It's just that Kerry Dane doesn't go with Whyteleafe School and she's certainly not a worthy person to be its head girl!'

'Sh, Elizabeth!' said Emma unhappily. 'You really mustn't go around saying things like that. I forbid it. The election is behind us now and we have the result. Kerry is our new head girl and I want you to tell me that you accept it.'

'I don't accept it, Emma,' replied Elizabeth firmly. 'I'll *never* accept it. I can't even bring myself to go to the next School Meeting. Not if she's still head girl!'

Emma's eyes widened.

'Stop it, Elizabeth! Of course Kerry will still be head girl at the next Meeting! And of *course* you must go! If you miss another Meeting over this, you will show a complete lack of self-discipline. You will be setting a bad example to the younger pupils in the school.'

Elizabeth tried to turn her eyes away.

'Look at me, Elizabeth,' said Emma gently. Elizabeth met her gaze. 'I want you to make me a promise. Even if privately you can't accept Kerry as head girl, you are to *promise* not to miss another Meeting. Do you give me your promise?'

Elizabeth could see that she was making Emma unhappy. She swallowed.

'All right,' she mumbled. 'I promise.'

That night she took out her autograph book and gazed at its spoilt white leather cover, with tears in her eyes. Then she opened it. She found the words that Rita had written at the end of last term, a beautiful line of poetry.

Kerry Dane isn't good enough to step into Rita's shoes, thought Elizabeth. *She never was and she never will be. Only Emma will do! It's an outrage!*

But, if the three friends tried to explain that to people, they'd only think, as Emma had gently tried to point out, that it was a case of Elizabeth and her friends being bad losers.

Julian and Joan were right. They would have to bide their time.

I only hope my patience can last out, thought Elizabeth

restlessly, as she tossed and turned and tried to get to sleep. *I only hope nothing unexpected takes place, to push me over the edge.*

But that was exactly what happened.

It was after school, the following Friday.

It had turned out to be a very good week for Elizabeth, in other respects. She was enjoying her new lessons in the second form. And, although it was horrid not being a monitor after all, Belinda and Daniel were both very kind about it. They kept saying that they weren't really cut out to be monitors and Elizabeth and Joan would have been so much better. She was also pleased that Miss Ranger had made her top in English this week.

But the best thing of all about the week was that she had got into the table-tennis squad! After the second coaching session Mr Warlow's list had gone up on the noticeboard – and there was her name! Patrick was only first reserve, in spite of his excellent new bat.

Tomorrow, Saturday, they'd travel by minibus to St Faith's and play their first match. How exciting that was going to be!

Before that, however, Elizabeth was trying to steel herself for the weekly Meeting. It was taking place on Friday as usual. That morning, a dark cloud had descended over her head. When lessons were over, she went for a walk around the school grounds, trying to calm herself.

'I just dread going into the hall today!' she muttered to herself. 'Even though I promised Emma I would. It will be too unbearable to sit there in silence and watch Kerry Dane being a drama queen. Acting the part of being a fine head girl! Everybody looking up to her! I really cannot bear it . . .'

Suddenly Elizabeth stopped. She had heard a funny little sound. She looked all around. There it was again! It seemed to be coming from the shrubbery.

It was the sound of someone sobbing.

CHAPTER TEN

ELIZABETH IS DEFIANT

'WHAT'S WRONG, Rupert?' asked Elizabeth, diving in among the bushes. 'Why are you hiding? Has somebody been bullying you?'

The small new boy gazed up at Elizabeth, his cheeks stained with tears. He had hidden so that nobody would think that he was a cry baby. Slowly he brought his sobs under control. Elizabeth gently dried his eyes with her clean white handkerchief.

'Well, have they?'

Rupert shook his head.

'Then why have you been crying?' coaxed Elizabeth. 'What's the matter?'

'Mustn't talk about it,' he muttered. 'Mustn't let people know I'm greedy.'

His lip trembled and he started sobbing again.

'I'm not greedy!' he wailed. 'I was going to share

them with all my friends!'

'Share *what*, Rupert?' asked Elizabeth. 'You are allowed to tell me about it. And it will make you feel better. Share *what* exactly?'

The words came tumbling out.

'My chocolate soldiers Grandfather sent me for my birthday! I was going to share them out at teatime. But she wouldn't listen to me. She took them away from me! She took them away!'

'Who did, Rupert?'

'Kerry did!'

Elizabeth stared at him in disbelief. 'The head girl?'

Rupert nodded solemnly.

'When?'

'This afternoon. She needs them for the earthquake.'

The earthquake? Elizabeth frowned. Of course. The Earthquake Bazaar next weekend. Kerry Dane was in charge of the sweet stall. But what a mean, horrid way to behave! She had no right to force the little boy to give up his birthday present for it!

Rupert looked scared and put a hand to his mouth.

'I promised not to tell anybody. Or else she'll tell everybody in the whole school I'm a very greedy little boy!'

Elizabeth bent down and gently placed an arm round his shoulders.

'You're not greedy, Rupert. Now listen to me. You're to go and wash your face and hands. It will soon be time for the Meeting. You're to stop worrying about this. It's just a – a horrid little mistake. Remember how I found your teddy bear for you, on the bus? Well, I'll make sure you get your chocolate soldiers back too! Off you go!'

The fair-haired boy looked pleased and grateful. 'Oh, thank you!'

Elizabeth stood and watched him walk back to the school buildings. He turned and waved. Calmly she waved back, but her cheeks were flushed with anger. What a despicable way for a head girl to behave. What an abuse of power!

The real Kerry Dane, Elizabeth thought. *The mask has started to crack at last!*

She reached a decision. She had promised Emma to attend the Meeting. Well, she would keep her promise!

And I know exactly what I'll do when I get there, thought Elizabeth, with a cheerful gleam in her eye.

'Silence!' shouted Thomas, banging the gavel loudly. 'I am trying to start the Meeting!'

The head boy was angry. The children were refusing to settle down. They all kept chattering and turning round to look at Elizabeth Allen.

It was such an amazing sight.

The naughtiest girl was seated on the second-form

benches, but she was facing the wrong way! She was sitting with her back to the platform.

What does Elizabeth think she's doing? wondered Emma in dismay.

Elizabeth sat stiffly on her bench. Instead of facing the head boy and girl and the monitors, she had turned her back on them and sat facing the other way. Her arms were folded stubbornly, in silent protest.

'Quiet, everybody!' cried Thomas.

The children forced themselves to stop looking at Elizabeth. The chatter died to a whisper and then to complete silence.

'Thank you,' said Thomas. 'We have a lot of business to get through today. But, before we begin, would Elizabeth please be kind enough to stand up and face the right way. I wish to speak to her.'

Elizabeth did so.

'What is the meaning of this tomfoolery, Elizabeth?' he asked.

'I do not wish to face the platform,' announced Elizabeth in clear, ringing tones. 'I do not accept Kerry Dane as head girl. She has proved herself an unfit person and I think she should resign.'

The school listened in astonishment. Julian and Joan exchanged troubled glances. What had provoked this? They had all agreed they would have to be patient.

Did Elizabeth know what she was doing? Was she not being very hot-headed?

Next to Thomas on the platform, Kerry Dane cast her eyes down. Her heart was bumping with anger. Who was this dreadful girl they called the naughtiest girl? What was this all about?

'I see,' replied Thomas calmly. 'That is a very dramatic statement, Elizabeth. Perhaps you would be good enough to explain to the Meeting your reasons for making it.'

'I will be very pleased to, Thomas.'

Elizabeth pointed accusingly at Kerry Dane.

'Kerry thinks that this is a school where she can do whatever she likes. She has behaved today no better than a common bully. Little Rupert was sent some chocolate soldiers for his birthday, by his grandfather. This afternoon Kerry Dane forced him to hand them over to her for her stall at the Earthquake Bazaar.'

A shocked gasp ran round the hall.

Kerry Dane leapt to her feet at once, a pained expression on her face.

'Elizabeth, how could you say such a thing?' she asked sorrowfully. 'How could you even *think* such a thing? I am very, very hurt.'

She then looked down at the juniors, sitting cross-legged on the floor at the front of the hall. Her eyes lighted on the smallest one, with very fair hair.

'Stand up, please, Rupert,' she said in a kindly voice. 'I think we need to sort this out together, don't you?'

The small boy rose. But he was left standing there, nervously blinking, as the young actress came to the edge of the platform and looked straight past him. With arms outflung she began to address the school, a radiant expression on her face, her lips sweetly smiling.

'First of all, this is exactly the right moment to say thank you! Thank you all for the wonderful response you've made so far! All the lovely things you've been bringing me for the sweet stall. Every day you come and see me and bring your goodies, knowing the money raised will help the earthquake victims. I find your generosity very touching. And I found Rupert's gift today perhaps the most touching of all . . .'

She then looked down and fixed her eyes on the small boy, who was now beginning to feel frightened and overwhelmed.

'Look at me, please, Rupert.'

The small child gazed up at the figure towering over him.

'Now, Rupert, where did Elizabeth get this funny idea from? Have you been making up naughty stories? Did you regret it afterwards, giving your chocolate soldiers away? Was it something you did on the spur of the moment because you felt sorry for the earthquake victims? But you were so insistent at the time, Rupert! Don't you remember? You told me you thought it would be a very greedy thing to keep them. Didn't you?'

Rupert gazed up into those mesmerising brown eyes. He was blinking non-stop, overcome with confusion. He was like a frightened rabbit in the thrall of a stoat.

'Now, think hard, Rupert. Don't you remember?' repeated Kerry.

She was daring him to contradict her. His sense of confusion increased.

'I – I can't remember exactly. I s'pose I must have done. I don't know. Elizabeth asked me why I was crying and I s'pose . . .'

Arabella whispered to Patrick behind her hand.

'Elizabeth making up naughty stories more like it!'

Kerry was finishing Rupert's sentence for him.

'You knew you'd given me your soldiers, but then you wished you hadn't and it made you cry. But you didn't dare tell Elizabeth how silly you'd been, so you made up a naughty little story instead! Now, please don't start crying again! There's no need to get upset about it. We all make mistakes.'

'You may sit down now, Rupert,' intervened Thomas, feeling sorry for the child. 'Nobody's going to punish you. Think carefully in future before you give things away. Make quite sure that you really want to do so.

Only babies give things to people and then want to have them back! You're a big boy now, remember.'

'Yes, Thomas.'

The child hastily sat down, feeling tearful and totally confused.

Elizabeth had listened to the whole exchange in stunned silence. What a brilliant actress Kerry Dane was. What an Oscar-winning performance!

Thomas now spoke to the naughtiest girl while the whole school listened with avid interest. Julian and Joan were feeling only total dismay.

'We already know, Elizabeth, that you have found it very difficult to accept the results of last week's election. And that you have lost your chance to be a monitor because of it. But you must know that the way you just spoke to our new head girl is not something that can be tolerated. She has been properly elected and she must be shown respect. You will please make a public apology to Kerry.'

'I certainly shall not,' said Elizabeth defiantly.

Thomas bit his lip. He felt worried and upset, but he dared not show it.

'Then you must leave the Meeting at once.'

Elizabeth barely heard him. She was already striding out of the hall. Her eyes were misted with anger and there was only one thought on her mind.

CHAPTER ELEVEN

THE NAUGHTIEST GIRL WINS THROUGH

I DON'T believe Kerry Dane for one instant! she thought. *I'm going to get Rupert's chocolates back for him!*

Elizabeth raced upstairs to the seniors' common room. She knew that she was strictly forbidden to enter without permission, but she didn't care. There was nobody to stop her. The entire school was seated safely at the Meeting.

I know where they keep everything for the Bazaar! thought Elizabeth. *It's going to be quite easy to get Rupert's soldiers! I promised him!*

Elizabeth was quite positive that Rupert had been telling her the truth. It was Kerry Dane who'd been telling the naughty little stories, as she called them! But how could the school know how awful she was? That she had actually taken a junior's birthday present away from him? Even for a good cause, it was such an unbelievable thing to do!

But that, Elizabeth felt quite sure, was exactly what had happened.

Goodness only knows why, thought Elizabeth, as she slipped into the big common room and headed for the cupboard in the corner. *But I'll see that Rupert gets his birthday present back if it's the last thing I ever do at Whyteleafe!*

At her boldest and most reckless Elizabeth found the key to the cupboard. She knew where it was because she'd been here with Daniel when he'd handed in some pottery for Philippa's craft stall. She turned the key in the lock.

The cupboard door creaked open.

The shelves were neatly labelled: CRAFT STALL . . . WHITE ELEPHANT . . . SWEET STALL . . .

The shelf set aside for the sweet stall was already nearly full. There were sweets of every description, some of them shop sweets, many of them homemade. There were jars of homemade peppermints, toffees and coconut ice. There were at least three sugar mice. There was Arabella's fudge too. Elizabeth recognized the box. How busy all the children had been, eager to please the young film star.

She frowned, beginning to feel uneasy.

It's true what she said then. The children have *been*

giving her stacks of things for the sweet stall. The shelf's almost full and there's still a whole week to go before the Bazaar! So there's hardly any danger of her stall not being a success then . . .

It made her mean behaviour seem more unbelievable than ever.

I know! Elizabeth said to herself. *Perhaps there isn't very much chocolate. Everybody's giving her sweets, but she wants to have some chocolate things to go with them.*

Elizabeth then checked each item on the shelf very carefully. And then she realised something. It wasn't that there was not *very much* chocolate. There was no chocolate at all!

Even Rupert's chocolate soldiers aren't here, she realised in surprise. She relocked the cupboard and carefully replaced the key in its hiding place, puzzled. *What* can *she have done with them?*

Elizabeth came out of the seniors' common room and closed the door. She looked up and down the corridor.

It must be that she simply hasn't bothered to put them in the cupboard yet, Elizabeth decided. *Yes, that will be it! They must still be somewhere in her room.*

Slowly, hesitantly, she walked along the corridor until she came to a door. It said HEAD GIRL, PRIVATE. She hesitated for many seconds. Much as she hated Kerry Dane, it seemed a very wrong thing to do.

But then she thought of Rupert, and his tears, and the terrible injustice he had suffered.

She turned the handle and eased open the door of Kerry Dane's private quarters.

The Meeting was in full swing. On the platform the head boy and girl had just been in a huddle with the monitors and come to a decision. Kerry and Thomas returned to their special table. It was Kerry's turn to pick up the gavel and bang for silence.

'Quiet, please, everybody!' she smiled. What a satisfying sound that gavel made. How quickly it brought the Meeting to order! She was beginning to enjoy herself again. 'The Meeting has now decided on the matter of punishment for the three pupils who walked out of last week's Meeting,' she announced. 'We have listened to the representations made by Belinda and Daniel on behalf of the two girls. And the Meeting has agreed that the losing of the monitorships is sufficient punishment for last week's behaviour. As far as Elizabeth's behaviour today is concerned, the Meeting has decided that she is not a fit person to represent the school at table tennis.'

Kerry had to fight hard to conceal her glee. This was all such fun!

Julian and Joan looked at one another in dismay. They had been sitting there, discussing Elizabeth's latest walkout in growing alarm. They had hoped all week that Elizabeth would not lose patience and do something reckless. But she had! She had tried to catch Kerry Dane out on quite the wrong thing! The story that Rupert had told Elizabeth was really rather preposterous. And, even if there had been a grain of truth in it, Kerry Dane had been much too clever to be caught out!

'Poor Elizabeth,' whispered Joan. 'We warned her to be patient.'

'The naughtiest girl doesn't know the meaning of the word,' Julian whispered back. 'Something like this was bound to happen.'

'Now we come to the matter of the boy,' the head girl continued. 'Would you stand up, please, er—'

Julian got lazily to his feet, a mocking expression in his eyes.

'My name's Julian,' he said. 'Julian Holland.'

'Yes, well – er – Julian. The Meeting has decided that you must apologise in front of the whole school and—'

'No!' shouted a voice from the back.

Elizabeth came running into the hall, panting for breath. She was holding something aloft. She halted and everyone turned round to look at her.

'You're the one who must apologise in front of the whole school, Kerry Dane,' she cried out. 'You must apologise to Rupert for your despicable behaviour.

For stealing his chocolates and pretending you wanted them for the Bazaar. When all the time . . .'

Slowly, deliberately, Elizabeth began to walk towards the platform. There was a high colour in her cheeks and a scornful expression on her face. She was holding aloft a floral patterned wastepaper basket. It had come from Kerry Dane's room.

'. . . you wanted to eat them yourself.'

The head girl turned white as she recognised the wastepaper basket.

What happened next was very un-head-girl-like.

With a cry of fury she leapt down from the platform and raced towards Elizabeth, her golden mane flying out behind her. Her face was contorted with rage.

'How dare you go into my private room!' she screamed. 'How dare you go poking around in my wastepaper basket—!'

She took a wild swing at Elizabeth. It knocked the wastepaper basket out of her hands and sent it flying to the ground.

Glittering tinfoil wrappings scattered in all directions. There were loud gasps throughout the hall.

Julian nipped across and picked one up. Quickly, he straightened it out. A soldier's face appeared and then the body, dressed in bright red tinfoil uniform. Silently, Julian held it up and displayed it to the shocked, silent children all around him. At the back of the hall Miss Belle and Miss Best and Mr Johns had gone very pale.

'The wrapping from a chocolate soldier, I presume,' he said drily.

'It's mine!' cried Rupert, his little voice piping up from the front of the hall. 'It's all eaten! I didn't give them to her. I didn't, I didn't. She took all my soldiers!'

'And this stupid school has taken all my money!' blazed Kerry Dane. 'I need to be able to buy chocolate when I crave some, don't I? As soon as some more money comes through, I'll replace your silly little soldiers. They weren't even all that chocolatey!'

Gradually, she began to regain her composure. The whole school watched, open-mouthed, as she turned on her heel. Slowly, majestically, she walked back to the platform. Her chin was thrust forward, her head held high.

'I would like to remind you all of something. I *am* the head girl of this school, you know.'

She remounted the platform and took her place beside Thomas. She did not even notice the horrified expression on the head boy's face, or on the faces of the monitors either side of him.

'Now, to more important matters,' she began. 'The question of Julian Holland—'

Suddenly a strange sound filled the hall. It was a

sound that had never before been heard at a School Meeting. It was started by some of the fourth-formers.

It was the sound of booing.

Within moments the whole school joined in the booing and hissing, drowning out the sound of Kerry Dane's voice.

'Resign!' cried the children.

'Resign! Resign!'

Elizabeth, Joan and Julian exchanged joyful looks.

'We want Emma!' cried the naughtiest girl. 'Emma for head girl!'

The booing stopped. Everybody clapped and cheered and stamped their feet, taking up Elizabeth's cry.

'We want Emma!'

'We want Emma!'

Kerry Dane gazed at the sea of faces in disbelief. She had suffered the disapproval of many teachers at her last school and it had annoyed her. But this was something very much worse. The disapproval of other pupils, of her schoolmates, was really horrid. It was humiliating.

She sank down in her chair, deeply shocked.

Thomas picked up the gavel and brought the Meeting to order. He knew that even William and Rita would, at a moment like this, have needed help from the joint headmistresses and the senior master. He looked to the back of the hall.

'Please, can you give the Meeting your advice?' he asked them. 'What should we do?'

Miss Best rose to her feet.

'The Meeting must follow its own advice, Thomas. It could hardly be clearer! Might we suggest that you now declare the Meeting closed? Next week, when Kerry has resigned and been replaced by her runner-up in the election, the slate can be wiped clean and a fresh start made.'

'Thank you, Miss Best,' replied Thomas, looking pleased.

He smiled across at Emma and his smile was returned.

Shortly after, Kerry Dane came down from the platform for the last time. She knew that she had no hope of ever returning to it.

CHAPTER TWELVE

A LOVELY MEETING

IT HAD been a chastening experience for the young film star. But the days that followed were worse. The seniors tried to be friendly towards her, but they found it very hard after what had taken place. Even kindly Emma found it difficult, although she tried her best.

The rest of the school, with few exceptions, shunned her.

To the many children who had seen *Zara's Journey* in the school holidays, and admired her as Zara, the shock of discovering her true nature had been very severe; just as it had been, that day in London, for Elizabeth and Joan. Kerry was left to her own devices a great deal. She had plenty of time on her hands to think and to contemplate. She was not used to this. She began to feel unhappy and to think about her real self and whether she liked what she found.

In the days before the next School Meeting Elizabeth by contrast was in very sunny spirits. She was allowed to play in the table-tennis match after all, and did well. Belinda and Daniel insisted on standing down as second-form monitors. Mr Leslie agreed that Joan and Elizabeth should take their places and be monitors after all.

Thomas, with Emma as the new head girl, called in all the monitors early in the week, to decide how much money the children should be allowed at the next Meeting. They would need a lot more than usual, for the Earthquake Bazaar.

Elizabeth was proud to have her opinion asked and to be part of the running of the school. She knew that she was going to enjoy every moment as a second-form monitor with her best friend Joan.

But she was beginning to notice how much time Kerry Dane spent on her own. For the very first time she began to feel slightly sorry for her.

One day, after school, when Elizabeth and Julian came back from a pony ride, they found her on her own as usual, by the stables. She was stroking one of the ponies.

'Hello, Kerry.'

The three of them stood and talked for a while. Elizabeth was as forthright as ever. She knew no other way.

'I was shunned when I first came to Whyteleafe, Kerry, so I know just what you're going through!' she said cheerfully. 'I was very spoilt, like you, and I made it my business to be as horrid as I could.'

'Did you?' asked Kerry in surprise.

'She wanted to be sent home, that's why,' explained Julian, glancing at Elizabeth in amusement. He never knew what his friend was going to say next. He always had to expect the unexpected. 'That's how she got her nickname, the naughtiest girl in the school. She didn't want to be at boarding school! She's not really horrid by the way.'

'You mean, she isn't like me?' commented Kerry drily.

'No, I wasn't anything like you!' Elizabeth declared truthfully. 'But I *did* behave badly. And I definitely remember that nobody liked me.'

'So what happened then?' asked Kerry.

'Oh, it doesn't last,' replied Elizabeth airily. 'Not if you mend your ways.'

Kerry patted the horse once more and then walked slowly back to school.

'I don't think she's a person who can *ever* mend her ways,' smiled Julian, as they rubbed down the ponies. 'She's too far gone for that.'

'Perhaps she'll make a tiny little start some time,' said Elizabeth hopefully. 'You never know.'

And at the Meeting the next day that was exactly what Kerry did.

She sat, pale and silent, on the senior benches while Thomas and Emma moved smoothly through complaints and grumbles. When, finally, they reached Any Other Business, she raised her hand.

'Yes, Kerry?' asked Emma encouragingly.

Kerry rose. She was trembling slightly. She was suffering from stage fright, something she'd never experienced before. But she was determined to go through with this. She held aloft a large box of chocolate soldiers. She had borrowed two weeks' allowance to be able to buy them. It had been hard work finding them too.

Her words came out in a rush.

'I'd like to present Rupert with this box of chocolate soldiers. And I'd like to apologise to him in front of the whole school for what I did.'

At a nod from the platform the little boy came running over and took the box. His face was shining.

'I'm sorry they're not exactly the same as the other ones, Rupert,' said Kerry.

'They're bigger! They're better!' Rupert beamed, his faith in Whyteleafe School restored. 'I will share them, I promise!'

There were approving murmurs around the hall.

Some people clapped. From her monitor's chair up on the platform Elizabeth saw the look on Julian's face and laughed. It was satisfying to think he could sometimes be wrong.

It had turned out to be a lovely Meeting.

Soon after that, Kerry Dane had a birthday. It was no longer a legal requirement for her to remain at school. She had received a batch of letters from her agent in London and among them was another film offer. In consultation with her parents it was decided that she should forego her certificate exams and leave school. She could now become a full-time actress.

From the joint headmistresses' window, on the day she left Whyteleafe School, the Beauty and the Beast watched her walk towards her father's small blue car. Her hair was as golden as corn in the sunshine as she stood waiting for her luggage to be loaded aboard.

'All that glisters is not gold,' sighed Miss Best, looking at that halo.

'She certainly glistered, though, didn't she?' observed Miss Belle. 'If, alas, not gold.'

'She was not with us very long,' continued Miss Best, 'but I would like to feel that she leaves Whyteleafe a better person than when she came.'

'Elizabeth Allen saw to that!' smiled Miss Belle. 'I will never understand how it was that Elizabeth and her friends divined her true nature long before the rest of us.'

'Nor me,' agreed Miss Best.

But it was no mystery to Kerry Dane. Not any longer.

Among the batch of letters that her agent had forwarded from his London office, had been a very odd little note:

Dear Miss Dane,

Thank you so much for the beautiful flowers you gave to my daughter Elizabeth last week. She was about to catch her train to boarding school and so passed them to her father to bring safely home. They are very much appreciated and still as fresh as ever.

Yours sincerely,

Audrey Allen

Slowly, the truth had dawned.

Cringing in embarrassment at the memory of their encounter, Kerry had gone to find Elizabeth and to apologise. She was playing chess with Julian.

'It's all right, Kerry,' Elizabeth had replied. 'But it just shows you should always be nice to everybody you meet. You never know where you might meet them again.'

'Yes, I can see that,' had been Kerry's humble reply.

'I suppose it's cruel and silly to be horrid to someone for no good reason.'

Especially when it's the naughtiest girl, thought Julian, with a smile.

BONUS BLYTON

Enid Blyton has been one of the world's best-loved storytellers for over seventy years. Her interest in writing began as a child and, before she loved receiving letters from the children who read her books, she enjoyed working with them as a teacher. The Naughtiest Girl stories are inspired by real schools and experiences. Turn the page to learn more about Enid as a child and as a teacher. Afterwards you might like to write about your school and teachers and the people in *your* class!

THE LIFE AND TIMES OF ENID BLYTON

11 August 1897	Enid Blyton was born in East Dulwich, London. Two brothers are born after her – Hanly (b. 1899) and Carey (b. 1902).
1911	Enid enters a children's poetry competition and is praised for her writing. She's on the path to becoming a bestselling author . . .
1916	Enid begins to train as a teacher in Ipswich. By the time she is 21, she is a fully qualified Froebel teacher, and starts work at a school in Kent.
1917	Enid's first 'grown-up' publication – three poems in *Nash's Magazine*.
June 1922	Enid's first book is published. It's called *Child Whispers*.
1926	Enid begins editing – and writes – the phenomenal *Sunny Stories for Little Folks* magazine. (She continues in this role for 26 years!)

1927	So vast is Enid's output that she has to learn to type. (But she still writes to children by hand.)
1931	Having married Hugh Pollock in 1924, the couple's first child, Gillian, is born. Imogen, their second daughter, was born in 1935.
1942	The Famous Five is launched with *Five on a Treasure Island.*
1949	The first appearance of *The Secret Seven* and of *Noddy* mark this year as special.
1953	Enid moves away from *Sunny Stories* to launch *Enid Blyton's Magazine*. She is now renowned throughout the world – she even established her own company, called Darrell Waters Limited (the surname of her second husband).
1962	Enid Blyton becomes one of the first and most important children's authors to be published in paperback. Now, she reaches even more readers than ever before.
28 November 1968	Enid dies in her sleep, in a nursing home in Hampstead.

THE NAUGHTIEST GIRL QUIZ

Can you answer the questions below on Elizabeth's adventure in *The Naughtiest Girl Wants to Win*?

1. What film have Elizabeth and her friends seen Kerry Dane in?
   a) *Zoe's Journey*
   b) *Zara's Quest*
   c) *Zara's Journey*
   d) *Zoe's Quest*

2. What possession of Elizabeth's does Kerry Dane damage by throwing it into a muddy puddle?
   a) Pencil case
   b) Maths book
   c) School blazer
   d) Autograph book

3. What is the name of the boy who loses his teddy on the school coach?
a) Robert
b) Rupert
c) Robin
d) Toby

4. Who does Kerry persuade to stand as head girl in order to take votes away from the favourite nominee?
a) Nora
b) Belinda
c) Emma
d) Arabella

5. How many votes does Kerry Dane get to be head girl?
a) 34
b) 35
c) 36
d) 37

6. Elizabeth makes it on to a school sports team this term! Which one?
a) Hockey
b) Lacrosse
c) Tennis
d) Table tennis

7. Where does Elizabeth find incriminating evidence against Kerry Dane?

a) The cupboard where things for the sweet stall are being kept

b) The senior common room

c) The head girl's wastepaper basket

d) The head girl's bedroom

8. Where does Elizabeth run into Kerry Dane and tell her about being the naughtiest girl?

a) Table-tennis practice

b) The dining hall

c) The stables

d) The senior common room

ANSWERS

1.c); 2. d); 3. b); 4. a); 5. b); 6. d); 7. c); 8. c)

THE NAUGHTIEST GIRL THROUGH THE YEARS . . .

1940

1962

1967

1971

1973

1979

1986

1999

2007

WHAT THEY DID AT MISS BROWN'S SCHOOL

In 1920 Enid Blyton became a governess to the four Thompson children, whose ages ranged from four to ten. The family lived in Surbiton, in Surrey, in a house called 'Southernhay'. Enid had a small room which overlooked the garden, and it was there that she wrote many of her stories. Enid's tiny class often had lessons outdoors in the summer months.

Enid was very popular with her students, because her lessons were both practical and creative. She worked with them to put on performances for which they made props, costumes and invitations – and even sold tickets.

In 1941 she published a long story called 'What They Did at Miss Brown's School', which was divided into monthly episodes. It's been hard to find for many years, but you can read extracts in these new editions of *The Naughtiest Girl* books. The character of Miss Brown and her tiny class is very much based on Enid Blyton and her school at the Thompsons' . . .

Here's the tenth episode . . .

10. October. Making the Wormeries

'MISS BROWN, it's the first of October!' said Susan, as she rushed in at the school door. 'I said, "Rabbits, rabbits!" this morning, to bring me luck.'

'And so did I!' said Miss Brown.

'What are we going to do this month for our special thing?' asked Peter. 'It's too early to put up a bird table, isn't it? And our school garden isn't ready to dig up and all our silkworms have laid their eggs – and . . .'

'Well, we shall think of something, don't worry!' said Miss Brown. 'What about making some wormeries?'

'Good gracious! What's a wormery?' asked Mary in surprise.

'I guess it's a home for worms!' said John. 'That's easy, Miss Brown. There are such a lot of worms about now – I see the wormcasts everywhere in the garden, and at night, if I shine my torch on the grass, I can see dozens of worms having a nice evening walk! They go back to their holes with a hissing noise when I come near.'

'Worms are most interesting creatures,' said Miss Brown. 'It would be fun to study them this month.'

'But aren't they very, very stupid?' asked Peter.

'Well, we'll see,' said Miss Brown. 'Now, tomorrow we will make our first wormery. I will bring in one of my large glass jars. Will you each bring two large worms, children?'

'I'm a bit afraid of worms,' said Susan.

'*Susan!*' cried the others. 'What a silly you are!'

'I suppose you think they'll sting you or bite you!' said Mary, with a giggle.

'No, but I don't like the feel of them,' said Susan.

'Oh, you feel like that because you've seen or heard somebody saying it,' said Miss Brown. 'But you can wrap a leaf round any worm you find, then you won't feel it, if you really can't bear to.'

Well, the next day all the children had brought worms, even Susan. One of hers was enormous and she was very proud of it. She picked it up to show the others.

'Susan! I thought you couldn't bear to pick up a worm!' cried Mary in surprise.

'Well, I found I could after all,' said Susan. 'I just thought I'd try – and it was quite all right after the first minute. I think I was rather silly.'

'You are a very sensible little girl, Susan,' said

Miss Brown. 'People who can do a thing like that at seven years old are going to do something remarkably fine later on!'

Susan was pleased and proud. She looked at all the worms. There were nine, because John had brought three instead of two. Miss Brown sent him to fetch a pail of earth from the garden, and he soon came back with it.

'Fill this large glass jar for me,' said Miss Brown, 'and we will put the worms into it. Then in a few days we shall see the tunnels they have made in it, for they will probably make them against the glass sides of the jar – and we shall see too how they cast up the little hillocks of earth on the top.'

The worms were put on the top of the jar of earth. One by one they disappeared downwards. By the end of the morning, not one was to be seen.

Two mornings later Susan went to look at the wormery, and she called to the others. 'Look! There are two tunnels made in the earth just against the glass! We can see them beautifully!'

The others came to see. Sure enough, there were two long, curving tunnels made round the jar. They were smooth with the passage of the worms' bodies, and looked very neat and well made.

'How nicely they have made them!' said Mary. 'And

see, Miss Brown, they have cast up little mounds of earth at the top of the jar – coils of earth rather than the shape of their bodies. How do the worms put the earth like that – in such neat wormcasts?'

'Well, as they tunnel, they eat the earth,' said Miss Brown. 'It goes right through their bodies and is cast up outside the wormhole.'

'Do they really *eat* the earth!' cried John in surprise. 'Good gracious! I should hate that!'

'I would like you to rub a wormcast between your fingers,' said Miss Brown. 'Feel how fine and powdery it is.'

The children picked up the earth of the wormcasts and crumbled it up. It was very fine indeed.

'Now, imagine millions of worms eating our soil and making it fine and powdery like that,' said Miss Brown. 'It keeps it in excellent condition. And not only that, but the worms are able to mix up the soil they tunnel in, and that does good too.'

'But can tiny things like worms really mix up the soil?' said John. 'I should have thought they just tunnelled and that was all.'

'Well, would you like to see how they mix up layers of soil?' asked Miss Brown. 'We'll use these nine worms to show us – but we shall need another jar of different materials, so that we may see the mixing. Get that big jar from the shelf over there, John. We will make a second wormery.'

John got the jar. Then Miss Brown filled it with an odd selection of material. First, she put a layer of gravel. Then she put a layer of ordinary earth. Then she put a layer of chalk. Then a fourth layer, of clay. Then she put in a layer of red sand, then a layer of coconut fibre and on top she put a layer of silver sand.

'Seven different layers!' said Susan, counting them. 'Will the worms really mix them, Miss Brown? Oh, I wish they'd do it today!'

'My dear Susan, they won't work quite as quickly as that!' said Miss Brown. 'You are always in such a hurry! My goodness, if you decided when things were to be done, seeds would come up and flower the same day, birds would lay eggs and hatch them out at once, and the world would be a very different place!'

'Well, worms, don't be too long!' said Susan, talking to the wormery. The others laughed.

Miss Brown put the worms on the top of the jar, and then, as it was time to go home, she sent the children off, though they badly wanted to see the worms disappear into their new wormery.

The next day was Saturday and there was no school. On Monday the first thing the children did was rush to their wormery to see if anything had happened.

There were no worms to be seen on the top. They had all gone. But two of the layers were already a little crooked!

'The worms are beginning to make the layers go funny!' cried Susan. 'Hurry up, worms!'

The worms didn't hurry, of course, but each day the layers went a little more crooked, and a little more crooked. The silver sand and the red sand touched at one place, and some of the coconut fibre seemed to be going down into the clay. No longer did the wormery look neat and trim.

As the time went on, the worms mixed up the layers so much that at last not one single layer could be seen in its proper place. The whole jar was simply a higgledy-piggledy mixture of clay, gravel, sand, coconut fibre, soil and chalk.

'Well, really, isn't it strange!' said Mary, looking at the muddle. 'The worms have mixed up the whole jar so that nobody could possibly tell what we put into it, or how we arranged our layers to begin with.'

'And so, Mary,' said Miss Brown, 'you can see very well what the worms do to our own earth in the gardens and fields! They mix up the layers, bring the old sour earth to the top, mix clay with sand and do an enormous amount of good. They are the farmer's friends, for they turn over his soil for him just as his plough does, but much more slowly and thoroughly.'

'I'd no idea they worked like this,' said Susan, looking at the wormery. 'I like worms now. I shall call them tiny ploughmen!'

'Miss Brown, do they do anything else?' asked Mary. 'Is there another sort of wormery we could make?'

'Well, Mary, they do something rather clever,' said Miss Brown. 'You know, when the frosty nights come, the cold gets down their holes to their little underground chambers at the end, and the worms hate that. So they crawl up to the surface and find something to stuff up their holes! They take a dead leaf perhaps, or a feather, or bits of straw – and these they use to close up their entrances to keep out the frost.'

'Well, I think that's really clever,' said Mary. 'Could we make a third wormery, and see them stuff up their holes, Miss Brown?'

So another wormery was made, just like the first one, filled with ordinary earth. But on the top of the soil the children put one or two dead leaves, a few bits of straw, some grass and three feathers from John's hen run.

'We must put the wormery into the garden tonight,' said Miss Brown, 'or the worms may not feel cold enough to stuff up their holes. It is going to be a very cold, frosty night, and there is an east wind. We will put the wormery where the wind will catch it – then the worms will hurry to stuff up their holes!'

So out into a cold part of the garden went the wormery – and, in the morning, what do you think! The worms had cleverly stuffed up three holes. One was stuffed with grass and a feather. The second was stuffed with bits of straw, and the third was stuffed with two feathers and two leaves! It was really most surprising!

'Well, Miss Brown, I'm quite sure people don't know how clever and hard-working worms are!' said Susan. 'Why, anybody would believe they really *think*!'

'I'd like you to see for yourselves if the worms think or not,' said Miss Brown. 'Look, do you see this bit of grass here, with many wormholes in it – and do you see that most of them are stuffed up, because it was a cold night? Well, watch what I am going to do!'

Miss Brown took away from the wormholes every scrap of stuffing. Then she took her broom and firmly swept the grass for some way around so that not a leaf, not a bit of straw could be seen.

'Now, John,' she said, 'fetch me a handful of those old dry pine needles that lie on the ground under the pine tree over there.'

John brought them. Miss Brown showed the children that each pair of long, thin leaves was joined together at one end. 'Now,' she said, 'if the worms use these to stuff up their holes, they will have to pull the pine needles in by the *joined end*, won't they? Otherwise the pine needles won't go in properly. We will see whether they are sensible or not tomorrow morning! They will need to close their holes tonight for it is cold – and they will find nothing on the lawn but our pine needles, so they must use those!'

Well, the worms *did* use them! And, to the children's great pleasure and surprise, every worm was sensible enough to draw in the pine needle by the *joined end*! What do you think of that? There were all the wormholes neatly stuffed with pine needles, the free ends sticking out of the holes.

'I didn't know what I was saying when I said that worms were very, very stupid!' said Peter. 'I shan't say things like *that* again!'

'Now we'll put our nine worms into the garden bed!' said Miss Brown. 'They have shown us a lot of things and been very good indeed – they deserve a holiday!'

She emptied the wormery on to the bed – and off wriggled the nine worms to have a well-deserved holiday.

Enid Blyton®

THE FAMOUS FIVE

Join the Adventure!

Have you read them all?

Enid Blyton

THE SECRET SEVEN

SOLVE THE MYSTERY!

HAVE YOU READ THEM ALL?

Enid Blyton

THE

SECRET SEVEN

SOLVE THE MYSTERY!

Don't miss…

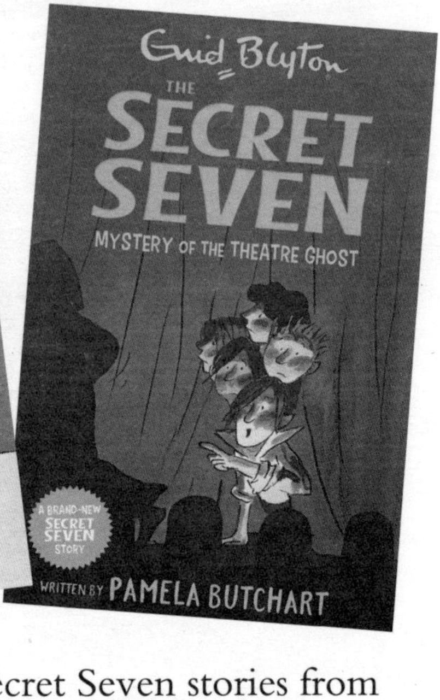

Two action-packed Secret Seven stories from prizewinning author **PAMELA BUTCHART**!

Enid Blyton®

THE SECRET SEVEN

SOLVE THE MYSTERY!

Solve every puzzle, just like the Secret Seven, in this fun book of 100 tricky codes, puzzles, sudokus, crosswords and more!

THE MYSTERY SERIES

Read all 15 classic stories!

ENIDBLYTON.CO.UK

IS FOR PARENTS, CHILDREN AND TEACHERS!

Sign up to the newsletter on the homepage for a monthly round-up of news from the world of

Enid Blyton®

Illustration by Laura Ellen Anderson.

JOIN US ON SOCIAL MEDIA

EnidBlytonOfficial BlytonOfficial

Enid Blyton®

is one of the most popular children's authors of all time. Her books have sold over 500 million copies and have been translated into other languages more often than any other children's author.

Enid Blyton adored writing for children. She wrote over 700 books and about 2,000 short stories. *The Famous Five* books, now 80 years old, are her most popular. She is also the author of other favourites including *The Secret Seven*, *The Magic Faraway Tree* and *Malory Towers*.

Born in London in 1897, Enid lived much of her life in Buckinghamshire and loved dogs, gardening and the countryside. She was very knowledgeable about trees, flowers, birds and animals. Dorset – where some of the Famous Five's adventures are set – was a favourite place of hers too.

Enid Blyton's stories are read and loved by millions of children (and grown-ups) all over the world. Visit enidblyton.co.uk to discover more.

Illustration by
Laura Ellen Anderson.

Well Done, The NAUGHTIEST GIRL

Have you read them all?

1. The Naughtiest Girl in the School
2. The Naughtiest Girl Again
3. The Naughtiest Girl is a Monitor
4. Here's the Naughtiest Girl
5. The Naughtiest Girl Keeps a Secret
6. The Naughtiest Girl Helps a Friend
7. The Naughtiest Girl Saves the Day
8. Well Done, the Naughtiest Girl
9. The Naughtiest Girl Wants to Win
10. The Naughtiest Girl Marches On

Enid Blyton®

Well Done, The Naughtiest Girl

WRITTEN BY
ANNE DIGBY

HODDER

HODDER CHILDREN'S BOOKS

First published in Great Britain in 1999 by Hodder & Stoughton
This edition published in 2021
For further information about the editorial history of this book,
see enidblyton.co.uk/books

5 7 9 10 8 6 4

Enid Blyton® and Enid Blyton's signature are registered
trade marks of Hodder & Stoughton Limited
Text © 2021 Hodder & Stoughton Limited
Illustrations by Claire Powell © 2021 Hodder & Stoughton Limited

No trade mark or copyrighted material may be reproduced without the
express written permission of the trademark and copyright owner.

The moral right of the author has been asserted.

All characters and events in this publication, other than those clearly in the public domain, are fictitious and any resemblance to real persons, living or dead, is purely coincidental.

All rights reserved.
No part of this publication may be reproduced, stored in a retrieval system, or transmitted, in any form or by any means, without the prior permission in writing of the publisher, nor be otherwise circulated in any form of binding or cover other than that in which it is published and without a similar condition including this condition being imposed on the subsequent purchaser.

A CIP catalogue record for this book is available from the British Library.

ISBN 978 1 444 95867 6

Printed and bound in Great Britain by Clays Ltd, Elcograf S.p.A.

Typeset in Caslon by Avon DataSet Ltd, Arden Court, Alcester, Warwickshire

The paper and board used in this book are made from wood
from responsible sources.

FSC
www.fsc.org
MIX
Paper | Supporting
responsible forestry
FSC® C104740

Hodder Children's Books
An imprint of Hachette Children's Group
Part of Hodder & Stoughton
Carmelite House
50 Victoria Embankment
London EC4Y 0DZ

An Hachette UK Company
www.hachette.co.uk
www.hachettechildrens.co.uk

CONTENTS

INTRODUCTION

by Cressida Cowell

bestselling author of the
How to Train Your Dragon series

Like so many, many children before and after me, Enid Blyton's books played a crucial role in turning my nine-year-old self into a passionate reader.

That is because Enid Blyton had an extraordinary knack for writing the kind of books that children actually *want* to read, rather than the kind of books that adults think they *should* read.

Enid Blyton could tap into children's dreams, children's desires, children's wishes, with pinpoint accuracy. She knew that every child, however good and well-behaved they might look on the outside, secretly longed to be Elizabeth Allen, the naughtiest kid in the school. I'm afraid I entirely cheered Elizabeth on, as she defied her parents, the headmistresses, her schoolmates, and the very serious School Meetings. If anything, I wanted her to be even naughtier.

But *The Naughtiest Girl* books were really my favourite of Enid Blyton's school stories because of Whyteleafe, a very different school from Malory Towers or St Clare's. What if there could be a school in which discipline was administered by the children rather than the adults? In which all money was given in at the start of the term and distributed among the children along socialist lines? Wouldn't this be the kind of school that children would actually *want* to go to, rather than the kind of school that children *have* to go to?

It was an interesting proposition to a nine-year-old, and it remains an interesting proposition.

I hope you enjoy this story as much as I did when *I* was nine years old.

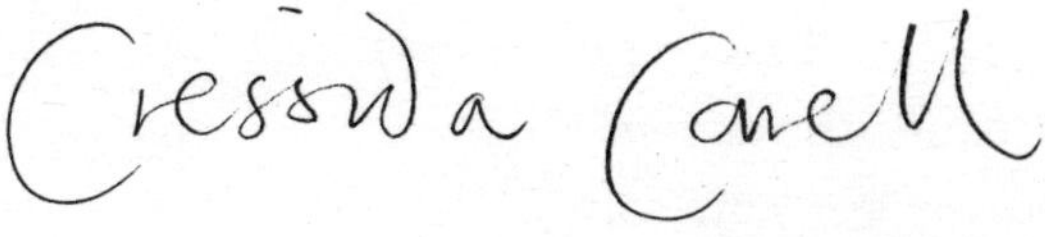

CHAPTER ONE

A NASTY SURPRISE FOR ELIZABETH

'THE LEAVERS' Concert is going to be something very special this year, Elizabeth,' said the music master. 'Very special indeed.'

Mr Lewis was in charge of music at Whyteleafe School and also taught piano, violin and flute. Elizabeth took piano lessons with him, but had been excused them for the past few weeks as she had been very busy with the summer play. The play had been performed now, so she was free to resume them, but she had almost forgotten her first lesson back. She had had to run all the way to the music room.

'Even more special than last year?' asked the naughtiest girl, puffing as she recovered her breath. 'I thought it was such a lovely concert last summer. I really enjoyed myself.'

She undid the straps of her regulation brown leather

music case. Then she scrabbled inside to find her sheet music. Which piece had they been working on? She couldn't recall.

'Yes, Elizabeth, I seem to remember you were excellent,' replied Mr Lewis. The elderly music master fingered his beard and looked thoughtful. 'You worked very hard for it.'

Elizabeth felt pleased. She was still basking in the warm afterglow of the first-form play. Her interest quickened. How exciting it would be to take centre stage again so soon. The school concert – of course! It was held right at the end of the summer term and parents were invited. Her mother and father would be coming, just as they had last year. Her one tiny regret about the play was that Mummy and Daddy had not been there to see her!

How well she remembered last year's concert, at the end of her very first term at Whyteleafe School. She had started the term as the naughtiest girl in the school, hating the idea of boarding school and doing everything bad she could think of – with the intention of getting herself sent home. But she had ended the term as a proud member of the school, playing two duets on the platform with a brilliant boy called Richard, as well as a little sea piece on her own. She remembered the applause ringing in her ears and the happy looks on her parents' faces . . .

'Why will this year's concert be so special, Mr Lewis?' she asked, as she found a piece of music and sat down at the piano.

'Because we have some very special leavers this time,' he reminded her. 'Last year only two or three boys and girls were old enough to leave Whyteleafe, but this year there's a whole batch. And what a fine batch they have been. Not just Roger, who's won his scholarship, but Charles and Colin and Lynette and – most important of all – our head boy and head girl. They have been the finest heads we have had at Whyteleafe for a long time.'

'William and Rita!' exclaimed Elizabeth. 'Of course. Oh dear. I just can't imagine Whyteleafe without them. I *do* wish I could make time stand still.'

'But then you would have to stay in the first form forever, Elizabeth,' chided Mr Lewis. 'And you wouldn't like that, would you?'

She shook her head so hard that her brown curls flew back and forth across her face.

'No, I would *not*!' she exclaimed.

If there was one thing she was looking forward to with all her heart, it was the prospect of moving up in September. It would be brilliant to go up into the second form with Julian and Kathleen and Belinda and all the other boys and girls in the first form who were old enough and clever enough to do so. How grown-up they would feel then! Her friend Julian would have to stop playing so many jokes in class and start behaving like a responsible second-former. And it would be lovely to be reunited with her best friend, Joan, who was already in the second form and a monitor. It was all going to be such fun! And, if losing William and Rita was the price that had to be paid for time not standing still, then Elizabeth had to be willing to accept it!

'I expect excellent replacements will be found for William and Rita when the time comes to elect a new head boy and girl,' Mr Lewis was pointing out. 'But, in the meantime, it's been decided to give them a very special send-off. To make the Leavers' Concert one of the best we've ever had. Something for them to remember forever.'

'How wonderful!' exclaimed Elizabeth. She suddenly felt very excited. What a privilege it would be to play at William and Rita's Leavers' Concert! She thought back to the duets she had taken part in last year. To play some beautiful duets with Richard again, to be part of William and Rita's last memories of Whyteleafe . . . How thrilling that would be.

'Richard won't be one of the Leavers, will he?' she asked suddenly.

'No! We've got Richard for another year or two yet,' replied Mr Lewis, 'I'm pleased to say. But even Richard won't be the star performer this year. You see, to make the concert extra special, Miss Belle and Miss Best have invited Courtney Wood, the well known concert pianist, to come and play. And he has accepted!' The music master could barely conceal his pleasure. 'Isn't that exciting news, Elizabeth?'

'Oh,' said Elizabeth dully. 'Won't any of the boys and girls be playing at the concert then?'

'Of course, of course,' replied Mr Lewis, a trifle impatiently. He was glancing at his watch now and turning over the sheet of music that Elizabeth had propped up in front of her. It was time for the lesson to begin. 'But we won't be able to have half as many children as usual. Just one musician from each form. That's all we'll be able to fit into the programme. There won't be any duets this year. The very best child from each form will play, that's all. Richard will represent his, of course . . .'

Elizabeth's hopes immediately rose again. So she still had a chance of being picked then. And as a solo performer!

She thought about it. In the first form Harry was keen, but not very good – his hands were like a bunch of bananas, Richard often said. Arabella had been learning the piano for a long time, but it was well known that she was always in trouble with Mr Lewis for never doing her piano practice. Belinda and Edward were both learning the violin, but they had only started last term . . .

'Tut-tut!' exclaimed Mr Lewis, breaking into her calculations. He was removing the sheet of music from the piano. 'This won't do, Elizabeth. You've put the music on its stand upside down! And . . . what's this?' He turned the sheet the right way up. 'We finished "Serenade" before half-term. We're on that difficult arrangement of "Greensleeves" now, don't you remember?'

Flustered, Elizabeth groped in her brown music case and found the correct sheet. It was right at the bottom.

'What's it doing buried down there?' scolded Mr Lewis, as he opened it up at the first page and placed it on the stand for her. 'Now let's see if you've been doing your piano practice.'

It was soon very obvious that she had not.

'Really, Elizabeth,' winced the music master, as she got all tangled up on the opening bars, 'what's happened to you? You were playing that opening beautifully not long ago. And look at the little finger of your right hand, all scrunched up! You'll never reach the high notes like that. Stretch it out wide, S-T-R-E-T-C-H.'

The lesson went badly.

'Elizabeth, you are a very naughty girl,' Mr Lewis said to her afterwards. 'I don't believe you've done any piano practice at all lately. I don't believe you once went near the piano while you were mixed up in that play of yours. Am I right?'

'Yes, you *are* right,' confessed Elizabeth, looking upset. 'I'm sorry.'

The little girl was too proud to make excuses. She was too proud to explain that going to all the rehearsals for the play, and learning such a big part until she was word perfect in every line, had been a difficult task. There had been other things to worry about too, which had taken up all her spare time and energy. Though they were all now sorted out, they had loomed large at the time.

In the meantime not only Elizabeth's piano practice but a lot of her school work too, had been pushed to one side. She would not have dreamt of explaining this to anyone, for fear of looking feeble.

In any case Mr Lewis was smiling at her now. He had spoken more in sorrow than in anger.

'Cheer up,' he said. 'I can see you really are sorry and will turn over a new leaf. If you do your practice every day, you will soon make up your lost ground. Practice makes perfect. That's what I'm always saying to Arabella.' He chuckled. 'Yes, that's what I've been telling her for a long, long time.'

Elizabeth mildly wondered what there was to chuckle

about as far as Arabella was concerned. But she was so relieved that Mr Lewis was not being cross any more, she cared not.

'I *will* do my practice every day, I promise!' she said happily, as she packed her music case and prepared to leave. 'When I come for my lesson next week, you will see such a difference!'

'I shall look forward to that, Elizabeth.'

She longed to ask more questions about the Leavers' Concert. In particular she longed to hear Mr Lewis say that she stood a good chance of being picked to represent the first form. But her good sense told her that this was hardly the right moment. She would ask him next week when she had had a chance to catch up on her piano practice. He would see how well she was progressing with the difficult new piece. Then, surely, she would be chosen to play it at the concert? It would be such an honour to play it for William and Rita and the other leavers, in front of the whole school, in front of all the parents! In front of her *own* parents. It was a thrilling thought.

'You're looking cheerful, Elizabeth,' said Julian Holland, as she came into the common room. 'Where've you been?'

The boy with the dark, untidy hair and humorous green eyes pushed his chessboard to one side. He had been working out a few interesting chess moves. But nothing was ever more interesting than talking to the bold, bad Elizabeth. They were great friends.

'Piano lesson,' she replied. 'Here, Julian, have a chocolate biscuit. As a matter of fact, I *am* feeling cheerful.'

'Must have been a good lesson,' grinned Julian.

'Not especially,' replied Elizabeth airily. She was not going to admit, even to Julian, that she had been unable to cope with her piano practice recently and how disappointed Mr Lewis had been in her. 'It's just that Mr Lewis had some interesting news.'

She told him all about Courtney Wood coming to play at the end of term. And then, even though the common room was empty, she dropped her voice low and confided in Julian her secret hopes.

'I do believe you're getting quite stage-struck, Elizabeth Allen!' teased Julian. 'Not content with being the star of the summer play, you've now decided you'd like to appear on the same platform as Courtney Wood!'

There had been a time when the naughtiest girl would have flared up at that. But now she just took the joke against herself in good part.

'It's not that, and you know it,' she smiled. 'I'll tell you what it is – it's because of William and Rita. Oh, Julian, I can hardly bear to think that this is their last term at Whyteleafe. I want to practise and practise until I can play my piece really *beautifully*. It's just the right music somehow and says everything I'm feeling and how sad I am at saying goodbye. They've given me so much and helped me to be a better person and . . .'

Julian gazed at his friend in admiration. He could see how sincere she was being. She was struggling to find the right words. He finished the sentence for her.

'. . . so this would be your way of saying thank you? Of giving them something back?'

'Yes, that's it exactly,' said Elizabeth gratefully.

'Well, I expect you'll be chosen,' said Julian airily. 'Nobody else in the first form is much good except you, Elizabeth. At least, that's what I've always heard. Blow it, I think I'd like to give William and Rita something myself. I think I'll carve them a little wooden animal each. A Mother Bear and a Father Bear. How about that, Elizabeth?'

'Oh, Julian, that's a brilliant idea.'

'I must start looking out for just the right bits of wood. I say, we *are* going to miss them, aren't we, Elizabeth?'

The two friends fell silent for a few moments.

Elizabeth swallowed hard. 'But it's got to be, hasn't it?' she said at last. 'Mr Lewis reminded me of what would happen if you made time stand still. If William and Rita were just to stay as head boy and head girl for ever and ever and never move on—'

'What?' asked Julian.

'We'd all have to stay in the first form for ever and ever too,' said Elizabeth wryly. 'We wouldn't be able to go up to the second form in September!'

'What a nightmare!' said Julian. He laughed. 'Oh, we couldn't stand for that. I don't know about you, Elizabeth, but I can't wait!'

'Me neither!' agreed the naughtiest girl.

It was such a happy thought that they both felt cheerful again.

But Elizabeth's happiness was to be very short-lived.

The next morning Miss Ranger, their form teacher, told the class the result of this month's tests. She read out the new positions in class.

Julian had come top as usual. His cousin, Patrick, had worked hard and come second. Elizabeth, who usually came very high, waited in vain to hear her name read out.

She was in for a nasty surprise. She had come third from bottom. Even Arabella, the oldest in the class but usually near the bottom, was two whole places above her. Since half-term she had been working frantically hard and had made her very best effort.

'You will have to do better than this in the end-of-term exams, Elizabeth,' said Miss Ranger. 'Or we may have to keep you in the first form a little longer.'

Elizabeth could hardly take it in. She had been beaten in class by Arabella!

However, the sight of Arabella's gloating face made her determined not to show her true feelings.

She spoke airily, almost defiantly. She repeated what Mr Lewis had said to her the previous day, the first words to come into her head.

'I shall soon make up any lost ground, I dare say, Miss Ranger.'

But inwardly Elizabeth was shaking. She had been given a dreadful fright.

CHAPTER TWO

TWO LITTLE PUZZLES

AFTER THAT Elizabeth decided that she must start revising very hard indeed for the exams. But she didn't want any of her classmates to know what a fright she had been given, not even Julian. She lost no time in finding herself a secret den, somewhere that she could study in peace.

She found the perfect place high up in an oak tree. She was there now.

Above her head came little rustling sounds as two doves moved along a branch. A pair of collared turtle doves, with black half-collars round the back of their pale, dusty brown necks – they were permanent residents of the old oak, along with all manner of other creatures. The doves were getting quite used to Elizabeth's presence. This was the third day running that she'd been here.

As she began to recite her French verbs, they began to croon, as though to keep her company.

'Je suis . . .

'Tu es . . .'

Coo-cooo, coo

'Il est . . .

'Nous sommes . . .'

Coo-coooo!

Elizabeth's little 'tree house' had been a wonderful find. She was delighted with it.

I'm quite near the school buildings, she thought with a smile, *yet nobody knows I'm here. Nobody can see me or hear me up here. It's my own secret place. Nobody can make fun of me now!*

The way that Arabella had gloated over her plunge down the form order had been almost too much to bear. The two girls disliked each other intensely. Elizabeth hated Arabella's pretty little face and perfect manners, her high opinion of herself and the airs and graces she put on. Arabella despised Elizabeth for her untidiness, her noisy, boisterous ways and the fact that she seemed to get away with things just because people liked her! It puzzled Arabella why they should.

Nor had Elizabeth taken kindly to the teasing from her classmates, even from Julian. The truth was that, unlike Elizabeth, none of them took Miss Ranger's words seriously, about her being kept down in the first form. And Elizabeth had taken such care to hide her true feelings they had no idea how scared she was feeling.

'What would you like for your next birthday, naughtiest girl?' Julian had joked. 'Remind me to buy you a rattle.'

Elizabeth had pretended to laugh. But it was soon after *that* that she noticed the oak tree and decided to explore it.

From the school grounds only the upper part of the tree was visible, for it stood on the other side of the school wall, somewhere in the outside world. But its heavy boughs brushed the top of the wall in places and some of the branches overhung the grounds.

Elizabeth had peered up into the dense green foliage. How mysterious and cool and inviting it looked up in that oak tree. Its boughs seemed to reach down like great arms, inviting her to come up into the tree's embrace. With a feeling of excitement she realised that, if she climbed to the top of the school wall, it would be extremely easy to crawl along the nearest bough and into the heart of the tree.

As soon as she did so, she knew that she had found the perfect hideaway. Where the boughs met the trunk in the midst of the tree, it was possible to sit, or even lie down, in comfort. Enclosed in a lattice work of foliage, it was like being in a secret little house – her own tree house. Wonderful!

On her first proper visit she took her maths book and learnt her eleven times table off by heart.

The next day she took her spelling book and carefully copied out several difficult words until she was sure that she knew how to spell them correctly.

Today Julian had asked her to help him look for pieces of wood, as he wanted to start on his bear carvings. But Elizabeth had made an excuse and headed straight for her hideout again, this time bringing her French verb book with her.

'*Vous êtes . . .*'

She cheated and peeked into the book.

'*Ils sont!*'

She put the book back in her pocket. Then, straddling a bough, her back pressed comfortably into the curve of the tree trunk, she closed her eyes and recited the verb 'to be' all the way through, slowly and carefully. Then again, but faster. By the third time she was able to rattle through it without stopping.

There! I know it now! she thought, with deep satisfaction.

It was so grand to be able to recite things out loud, as many times as she wanted to, with nobody to overhear.

It was so peaceful here, with only the natural world for company.

'Hello, robin,' she said, as she opened her eyes. The bird had hopped along the bough to within a yard. It was full grown, but had not yet got its red breast, so Elizabeth knew it must be very young. 'Aren't you the lucky one, then? You don't have to learn your verbs yet, do you?'

The young robin cocked its head to one side and gave her an enquiring look, followed by a friendly chirp.

I love it here, thought Elizabeth. *There's a whole busy life going on in this oak tree and, it's funny, I'm beginning to feel part of it. I'm even beginning to like the big brown moths that live here. And I think the creatures are starting to get used to me.*

She stared up into some higher branches where a family of squirrels had their drey. On her first visit they had chattered shrilly in great alarm and refused to come out. On the second day they had made their way up and down the tree very secretively, by a back route, hoping not to be seen. But today they had twice scampered down the tree quite close to her, taking no notice of her at all.

She settled further back and rested for a while, gazing up at the chinks of blue sky through the tree's top canopy. From the road below, to her left, came the drone of an occasional car. The mighty oak stood on a grass verge beside a narrow road that led to the village.

And across the school grounds to her right, from the school buildings, came the sound of a piano being played in one of the practice rooms.

Oh, that's a nice piece! thought Elizabeth. *All ripply and sweet like a journey through the English countryside. That must be Richard playing.*

Piano practice! She had forgotten to do it today!

Elizabeth roused herself and began to edge backwards along the bough, towards the top of the school wall.

As she did so, looking down, she spotted a knobbly little chunk of oak that the tree had shed. It was lying in the grass, close to its roots, not far from the road.

That's just the sort of wood Julian likes when he's carving things, she thought. *It's got an interesting shape. I wonder if I dare get it for him?*

She could see that it was an easy climb down to the ground. The trunk had several low, stubby branches sticking out. They would make perfect footholds and handholds. But, of course, it was strictly against school rules for children to venture outside the grounds on their own.

Only, I'm not really going anywhere, am I? Elizabeth told herself. *Just straight down the tree to pick up the wood for Julian, then straight back up again.*

It took Elizabeth less than a minute to climb down the tree and land on the grass verge on the other side of the school wall. She scooped up the piece of wood triumphantly. She examined it carefully. Yes, it was a really good piece. Julian should be pleased.

As she turned back towards the tree, she stared in surprise at its trunk.

How stupid! she thought.

On its handsome pale brown and mossy green bark someone had painted an ugly white cross.

At that moment, from beyond the bend in the road, she heard the distant sound of a car approaching. Supposing it was one of her teachers? Help!

Elizabeth shinned back up the oak tree at speed, dived into its leafy branches, bumped along the bough atop the school wall, then down into the grounds of Whyteleafe. Phew! That was risky. She must not do *that* again.

But as she wandered back towards the school buildings, past the end of the cricket pitch, her thoughts returned to the strange marking on the oak tree's trunk. She wondered why it made her feel uncomfortable. Then she remembered that they had once been told in a history lesson about the time of the Great Plague. How homes were similarly marked with a cross if the disease had struck.

Could the oak tree have some sort of disease? she wondered, in dismay. *Oh, surely not. It looks hale and hearty to* me.

She wondered if she could ask one of the teachers about it. In a roundabout way perhaps. It would be difficult, though, without giving away where she had seen it . . . Oh, surely somebody had just been fooling about . . . ?

'Elizabeth! Whoops! Look where you're going!'

She had almost crashed into someone! He was a tall boy carrying a cricket bat.

'Richard! Oh, I'm sorry. I was in such a dream.' She looked at the bat under his arm. 'Going off to play cricket?'

'No! Just coming *back*!' said the senior boy, smiling at her. 'I've had an hour's practice in the nets and that's long enough for me. I must get back to my piano.'

'Oh, I thought I heard you playing a few minutes ago,' said Elizabeth in surprise. 'A lovely ripply piece. Perhaps it was Mr Lewis then?'

'Not him. He's gone to town to buy the piece I shall be playing at the Leavers' Concert. And it doesn't ripple, Elizabeth, I can assure you.'

Elizabeth continued on her way, frowning slightly. Who had been playing that piece so well then, if it had not been Richard, or Mr Lewis himself?

With something new to puzzle about she forgot all about the white cross on the oak tree.

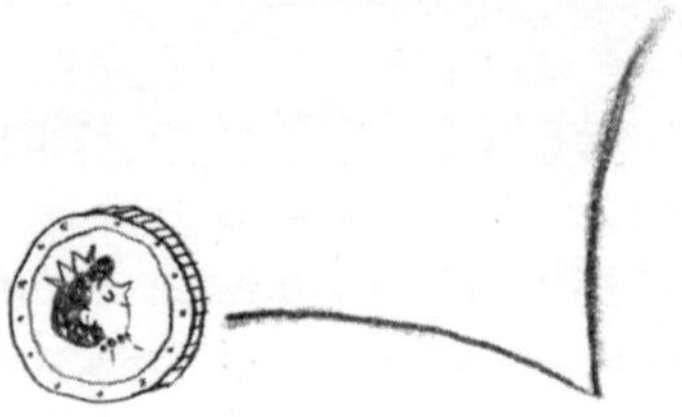

CHAPTER THREE

ELIZABETH HEARS THE MUSIC AGAIN

'WHAT AN excellent piece of wood, Elizabeth!' exclaimed Julian, with pleasure. 'Why, it's the very thing.' He rolled it between his palms. 'A solid little lump of oak. I shall cut it in half and make two. Those knobbly bits at each end already look rather like bears' heads, don't they?'

'That's just what I thought, Julian,' said Elizabeth eagerly. 'And one end's fatter than the other – that can be Father Bear.'

'And the other end can be Mother Bear. Excellent! I'm going to enjoy my wood carving! Oak's good to work with, you know.'

After a good wash and tidy-up Elizabeth had rushed through some piano practice and then come looking for Julian. She had found him in the common room. He was not bothering to revise for exams. He was reading a book about famous medical discoveries.

She had presented him with the piece of wood.

'Wherever did you find it?' he asked now.

'Oh, just lying on the ground,' replied Elizabeth truthfully.

'You've been gone for ages!' said Julian. 'I wondered where you were.'

'Well, for one thing, I've been doing my piano practice,' smiled Elizabeth.

'Ah, yes.' Julian gave a quick nod.

Some of the other boys and girls were coming into the first-form common room.

Julian quickly stuffed the piece of wood into his trouser pocket. He wanted to be quite sure that his bear carvings were successful before letting anyone know about them!

Belinda came and threw herself into a chair.

'If I have to revise another single French verb, I shall die!' she exclaimed.

'Only two weeks to go till the exams now,' said Julian cheerfully.

Jenny came and joined them. She was holding a tin. 'Have some of my birthday cake!' she said.

She cut them each a fat slice. It was a gooey chocolate cream sponge with thick chocolate icing on the top.

'It's delicious, Jenny!' exclaimed Elizabeth, as the cake melted in her mouth.

'I was trying to find you after tea, Elizabeth. Where do you keep disappearing off to?'

'I can't bear to be indoors at this time of year,' replied Elizabeth truthfully. 'I've been getting lots of fresh air.'

'I expect she's been helping John over in the vegetable garden,' put in Kathleen. 'That's where she usually disappears to!'

Elizabeth had no need to reply for Belinda at once jumped in with a teasing remark.

'I'm sure I'd be revising for exams if I'd come third from bottom! But, then again, I'm not Elizabeth. I'm not the naughtiest girl!'

'Blow the silly old exams,' said Elizabeth, keeping up her brave front.

But it was very satisfying in the maths lesson next day. Miss Ranger gave them some mental arithmetic problems. Twice Elizabeth was the first to call out the correct answer.

'Eleven boys have to share out eighty-eight sweets equally. What does each of them get—?'

'Eight, Miss Ranger!' cried Elizabeth.

'Tummy ache!' cried Julian.

Everybody laughed.

'That will do, Julian. Well done, Elizabeth. And, if twelve rabbits have to share out one hundred and thirty-two lettuce leaves equally, what do they get—?'

'Into a fight!' exclaimed Patrick Holland, determined not to be outdone by his smart cousin, Julian.

The laughter was more subdued this time, as Miss Ranger was beginning to look cross.

'Please, Miss Ranger, eleven lettuce leaves,' said Elizabeth, putting her hand up.

'Yes. Good.'

Belinda sighed to herself. Elizabeth was so lucky. Without appearing to do any work she was getting back into top form again. It was all right for some!

However, it was Arabella, not Elizabeth, who got the next question right.

'Twelve men walk twelve miles each, how many miles do they walk altogether?'

'One hundred and forty-four!' exclaimed Arabella eagerly.

'Very *good*, Arabella,' said Miss Ranger. 'My, that was quick.'

Then Patrick, as usual, had to overdo things and show off, spoiling what had been a fun session.

'Perhaps they didn't walk all together but in single file, Miss Ranger. In that case the answer should be none!'

After that they were all made to do sums in their books and had to remain silent for the rest of the lesson.

However, as she pored over her sums, Elizabeth felt well pleased. The hard swotting sessions in her secret hideout were already bearing fruit. Of course, it was annoying to find out that Arabella was ahead of her. Arabella had revised her *twelve* times table! Elizabeth resolved to make that her very next task.

But not today. It was the day of the weekly Meeting and no pupil at Whyteleafe was allowed to miss them. Not that Elizabeth minded. On the whole she very much enjoyed Meetings.

After tea the whole school trooped into the big hall, which doubled as a gym. There were the twelve school monitors, up on the platform, with the head boy and girl seated at their own special table.

Elizabeth thought how grown-up and dignified William and Rita looked, as she took her own place on the first-form benches. They had a large book in front of them, known simply as the Book, in which anything important that happened at Meetings was always written down. Elizabeth had read the Book once. It contained many fascinating case histories of pupils who had misbehaved, and showed the reasons for it and how their bad behaviour had been cured. She featured in the Book herself, from the days when she had been the naughtiest girl in the school!

For the remarkable thing about Whyteleafe School was that the children governed themselves in many respects. The Meeting was like a school parliament, where problems were discussed and solutions found. But it was also a kind of court, with William and Rita the Judges and the monitors their Jury. Pupils who behaved badly were forced to face up to their wrongdoing in front of the whole school and the Meeting would work out how best the problem could be dealt with and cured. And cured it invariably was, for no child was ever considered worthless, or beyond reform. No one was ever abandoned by Whyteleafe School.

The joint heads, Miss Belle and Miss Best, whom the children nicknamed the Beauty and the Beast, attended the Meetings. So did Mr Johns, the senior master. They were there simply as observers and never took part unless, in very difficult cases, their advice was sought.

Today's Meeting was not an eventful one.

All children who had received money during the week had to give it in. A monitor always brought round the school box. This week it was Joan's turn. As Elizabeth placed some money that her grandmother had sent her into the box, she exchanged smiles with her best friend. She was so proud that Joan, who had not been in the second form very long, was already a monitor.

Elizabeth had herself had a stint as a first-form monitor. She had enjoyed being a leader. She looked forward to the day when she might be elected as a monitor again, as William and Rita had once hinted might happen. For the moment, though, she was thinking only of her more modest ambition – to be allowed to go up into the second form!

She would die with shame if she was made to stay down. She would never be able to look Joan in the eye again!

Once the money had been collected up each pupil in the school was issued with two shillings for the week's spending money. 'Share and share alike' was the school motto.

Then, one by one, special requests for extra money were considered and judged on their merits.

'No, Chloe, we cannot give you extra money for your mother's birthday present. You should have saved up for it, out of your weekly allowance, as all the other children do,' said Rita.

The junior-form pupil looked disappointed and sat down cross-legged on the floor again, with the rest of her form.

John, the head of the school garden, was granted some extra money for a trowel, as one had broken. Harriet was given extra stamp money because her large family was in Australia for a year. It was expensive sending all her little brothers and sisters birthday cards and airmail letters.

Colin asked for money for a new tennis racket, as had been granted to Eileen on a previous occasion.

'That's a difficult one,' said William. 'Rita and I will have to confer with the monitors.'

It took them a while to come to a decision.

William banged his gavel on the table for silence.

'We hope you don't think it unfair, Colin, because we know you have played tennis for the school a few times. But Eileen is a regular member of the team and truly wore her racket out because she practises so hard every day. She has some years to go here and I'm sure will be playing for us much more. You will be leaving Whyteleafe in less than three weeks, as will we. When we go to our upper schools, there will be a different system. For the first time you'll be allowed to keep any money your parents send you, Colin. If you need a new racket badly by then, we're sure they will help you out!'

'Fair enough,' agreed Colin.

There were no complaints or grumbles this week and the two head pupils began to wind up the Meeting.

Elizabeth's mind was already moving on to other things. Talk of Colin and William and Rita leaving so soon had given her a fresh jolt! It reminded her that there was very little time left before the Leavers' Concert. She longed with all her heart to be a part of that concert, to pay her special tribute to William and Rita from the concert platform. The sweet, sad piece she was learning expressed her emotions far better than words.

But swotting for exams every day had not left her all the time she needed for her piano! And Mr Lewis would be expecting to see a big improvement at the next lesson. She had promised him! And, besides, her hopes depended on it.

It's too late to go to my secret den and do my times tables today!' Elizabeth decided. *I'll do extra piano practice instead. I'll do a whole hour!*

She collected her music case after the Meeting and set off for her usual practice room. But Sophie had got there ahead of her. She was practising the flute. Elizabeth reflected that Sophie would surely be chosen to represent the junior class at the Leavers' Concert. She was a remarkable little player.

'I think I'll be here till bedtime now, Elizabeth,' the younger girl said wryly. 'This is a Grade Five piece and I'm only on Grade Four, but Mr Lewis says he thinks I can master it.'

'Don't worry, Sophie! I'll go upstairs.'

There was a piano on the top floor, right at the end of a long corridor. It was rather out of the way. Nobody bothered to use that one much.

But, when Elizabeth reached the top landing and

walked down the corridor, she heard the distant rippling of the piano being played.

It's that lovely piece again! she realised. *The one I heard yesterday. It must be the same person. Now I can find out who it is.*

The piano was tucked away in an alcove, around a corner at the far end of the corridor. Anxious not to disturb the player, who was in the middle of a delicate diminuendo, she tiptoed the last distance. Then she peeped round the corner . . .

She stared in amazement.

It was Arabella! The fair-haired girl was seated at the piano, playing with the deepest concentration. Her friend, Rosemary, stood alongside her and was turning over the pages for her.

Elizabeth hurriedly drew back. Her heart was pounding. That Arabella should be playing like that!

Her mind could hardly take it in. The conceited Arabella was always showing off. If ever she had something to boast about, she liked the whole world to know.

Why had she never let anyone know she could play the piano so well? Why was she keeping it secret?

Elizabeth stood there quietly, her body pressed to the wall. And very soon there came the answer to her question.

CHAPTER FOUR

JOAN STATES HER OPINION

THE MUSIC stopped. Arabella had come to the end of her piece. Then Elizabeth heard Rosemary speak.

'It's perfect now, Arabella. It really is! Shall we go down to our dormy now and I'll test you on your spelling? You know Miss Ranger's said everybody has to pass the English exam before they can go into the second form—'

Out of sight, Elizabeth held her breath in alarm and shrank back harder against the wall. She would creep away quickly. She didn't want the pair to see her. It would look like spying!

About to turn and tiptoe back down the corridor, she heard Arabella's voice next . . .

'We're not going anywhere, Rosemary. We're staying right here! *You* may think the piece is perfect, but I do not. It *is* improving, though. Oh, yes, it's definitely getting better all the time!'

She sounded strangely elated. Gleeful. Elizabeth's attention was riveted.

'But what about the exams?' asked Rosemary timidly. 'You know I'll die if we can't go up into the second form together.'

'One thing at a time, please. Do stop bleating about the exams, Rosemary,' said Arabella impatiently. 'Do you really think I've been wearing my fingers to the bone for nothing? Just to throw it all away? Elizabeth's started practising again! I've heard her. Now the play's over, I expect she's decided to be in the school concert! Well, she's got such a surprise coming!'

'I bet Mr Lewis can't get over how much practice you've done,' giggled Rosemary. 'All the months you've complained to him about it being boring. He must be amazed.'

'I'm his pet now,' said Arabella conceitedly. 'Silly old man. He thinks I'm doing all this to please *him*.'

Rosemary knew the real reason.

'It's going to teach Elizabeth a lesson if you're chosen this year instead of her!' She was rather a weak character. She always said what her friend wanted to hear. 'Oh, won't that be fun, Arabella?'

'It's about time she was cut down to size,' said the other girl fiercely. 'After that I won't do a stroke of this boring old stuff again, I can tell you. Now, come on, let me play this through again. Then I shall do my scales . . .'

Elizabeth crept away down the corridor. She had heard enough. All kinds of thoughts and emotions were tumbling through her.

Envy. That Arabella could play the piano so beautifully when she really tried. She must have a real gift. How could someone so horrid create such a lovely, delicate sound?

Realisation. Now she knew why Mr Lewis had chuckled to himself about Arabella. He had been chuckling with pleasure. He would have recognised Arabella's gifts as soon as she arrived at Whyteleafe School. For months he had nagged at her to do her piano practice, to no avail. And suddenly she had turned over a new leaf! She seemed to want to please him after all. How delighted the elderly music master must be at her dramatic improvement. He lived for his pupils and loved to nurture their gifts.

Scorn. How could Arabella be so unkind about Mr Lewis? A silly old man, she had called him. What a horrid thing to say. How mean that she was not really trying to please him! Nor was she working hard for the love of music, or for the honour of playing at the Leavers' Concert. It was all being done simply to spite Elizabeth.

Elizabeth could feel a temper coming on. What a sneaky person Arabella was. While she had been busy with the school play, Arabella had been swotting away to beat her in class and plotting to steal her piano place as well. Just to get her own back on Elizabeth for being in the play!

It didn't occur to the naughtiest girl that Arabella's desire for secrecy was to be expected. She was learning from past mistakes. Encouraged by the feeble Rosemary, she had been cocksure about being chosen for the play. When Elizabeth had been chosen in her place, she had been made to look a fool. She had decided to be much more careful this time.

None of this crossed Elizabeth's mind as, feeling surprised and angry, she walked downstairs, her unopened music case bumping by her side. She didn't feel like doing her piano practice now. She didn't feel like doing anything!

She would go and find Joan. Joan would understand how she was feeling!

She met her best friend coming out of the second-form common room with Susan. Gentle Joan could see at once that something was wrong. Making an excuse to Susan, she linked arms with Elizabeth.

'Let's go and sit outside,' she said. 'It's a lovely evening.'

They sat on the school terrace. Elizabeth blurted out her secret ambition to Joan. Then she told her everything that she had overheard upstairs.

'What a trial Arabella is!' said Joan sympathetically.

'I don't know what to do now,' confessed Elizabeth. 'The worst thing is that I think she's playing better than I do. I don't know whether I should go on trying.'

Joan frowned and thought about it.

'I don't think it would be very nice if Arabella *was* chosen,' she ventured. 'I wouldn't feel happy knowing that someone was playing at the Leavers' Concert in such a mean spirit. They should want to do it for the honour! And to give the people who are going a happy last memory of Whyteleafe.'

'That's exactly how I feel,' said Elizabeth eagerly. 'Do you think I should go on trying then?'

'Of course,' smiled Joan, wanting to make her friend happy again. 'Arabella may be talented, but so are you, Elizabeth. She has got a head start at the moment, because you've been so busy since half-term. Given that you're both talented, it's all about who can get the most practice! You must practise and practise, Elizabeth, every spare minute of the day. You must at least give it your best!'

'I will!' promised Elizabeth, her eyes shining. 'I'll practise till my fingers are worn out, Joan. You just see!'

In stating her opinion Joan knew nothing of the fright Elizabeth had been given about dropping behind with her schoolwork. She never dreamt that her friend had a secret fear of the coming exams.

As with Julian and all Elizabeth's younger friends, Joan Townsend never imagined that the naughtiest girl could have any serious worries about her studies. And Elizabeth was certainly not going to tell her. Her pride wouldn't let her.

'Oh, Elizabeth, I *am* looking forward to your being in the second form,' were her friend's last words to her that evening.

'Yes. It's going to be really good!' replied Elizabeth stoutly.

That weekend, however, she blanked all thought of schoolwork out of her mind. It was easier that way. She did not once return to her secret hideout in the oak tree.

Her next piano lesson was looming and the weekend was her last chance of making it a different story from the last one.

She practised non-stop on Saturday and again on Sunday, only taking breaks for meals and other essential activities.

She went back to basics, with Grade I piano scales. Then she worked her way up through the grades, playing the more difficult scales and finger exercises over and over again. Only then would she tackle her latest piece, the difficult arrangement of 'Greensleeves'. She knew that she must achieve technical mastery before she could make it truly expressive.

Julian did not mind at that stage. He was pleased to see that the Bold Bad Girl had got the bit between her teeth! He was very busy with hobbies himself and also spent a lot of time in the craft room on his wood carvings.

Nor did Kathleen or Jenny or Belinda mind. They were busy too, revising for the exams, and only felt envious that Elizabeth could afford to be so casual about them.

The only person who minded was Arabella. She quickly noticed what a huge effort Elizabeth was making.

Arabella had planned to revise for exams this weekend. She was going to try to learn her French verbs and read her English set book. There would be questions about the book in the English exam!

But, as soon as she realised what Elizabeth was up to, she abandoned her studies and returned to the piano herself.

'She must have found out! Have you said something to her, Rosemary?' asked Arabella, pouting sulkily. '*Have* you?'

'No, of course I haven't!' said Rosemary indignantly.

'People must have noticed you coming up here to practise! You can hear it outside when this window's open. Elizabeth must have noticed. You can't expect to keep it secret forever.'

The new week dawned. All too soon, in Elizabeth's opinion, it was time for her next piano lesson.

'Hello, Elizabeth!' said Mr Lewis, as she appeared in the doorway, music case in hand. He gave her a warm smile. He had noticed how much practice the first-former had been putting in! 'Come and sit down. Let's see how we get on this week, shall we?'

The naughtiest girl sat down at the piano. Her fingers trembled slightly as she undid the case and found her music.

This was a lesson in which she must do her very best. She knew she had made great progress since last week, but would it be enough? She was longing to ask Mr Lewis about the Leavers' Concert.

'A marked improvement, Elizabeth,' the music master told her when the lesson was over. 'I can see you have worked very hard this week, to make up for lost time. I'm very pleased with you.'

Elizabeth rose from the piano. As she packed her music away, her throat had suddenly gone dry. This, surely, was the right moment to find out what she wanted to know?

'Please, Mr Lewis—' she began nervously.

'Yes, Elizabeth?'

'I just wondered if . . . if you'd decided yet . . . about the Leavers' Concert. I mean, who's going to play for the first form? It's not very long now, is it—'

'It certainly isn't!' he chuckled.

He stroked his beard thoughtfully before replying.

Elizabeth held her breath.

CHAPTER FIVE

THE RIVALS

'I CAN quite see that you would like to know, Elizabeth,' the music master said kindly. 'But the fact is I seem to have a difficult decision on my hands this year. I expect young Arabella has told you that she would like to be picked for the concert too?'

Of course, Arabella had told her no such thing. Fearing that her expression might give her feelings away, Elizabeth just mumbled and stared at the floor. She waited to hear what Mr Lewis would say next.

'I want to leave it as long as possible before I make up my mind, Elizabeth,' he went on. 'Apart from anything else, it seems only fair to give you more time to make up lost ground . . .'

Elizabeth's hopes rose. Only to be partly dashed again.

'I must warn you, though, that I can't make any

promises. Arabella has made remarkable progress lately. Quite remarkable. Our lessons together are becoming a real pleasure. One of the great satisfactions of teaching, Elizabeth, is when a pupil at last starts to respond. I must say I am very much looking forward to taking Arabella forward from here . . .' He quickly cleared his throat, suddenly aware that he had been speaking his innermost thoughts out loud. 'As well as you yourself, Elizabeth, of course. And all the other boys and girls I teach.'

In spite of the pain she was suffering herself Elizabeth's warm heart went out to the music master. Poor Mr Lewis! After this term Arabella would lose all interest in the piano as suddenly as she had found it! It would be so sad for him.

'So what I am proposing to do is to leave it until the last moment,' he explained. 'I shall have both of you in together, some time towards the end of next week. By then, you will both have had your final piano lessons of the term. You will each play your new piece and then we will decide. We can't leave it any later than that!' He chuckled. 'The programmes will need to be run off that weekend, so I will have to make my mind up, won't I?'

Elizabeth nodded eagerly. Her hopes were rising again.

Mr Lewis walked across, opened the door and

showed her out. His next pupil was waiting patiently in the corridor.

'I'll see you for your final lesson next week then. Keep it up, Elizabeth!'

'I shall, Mr Lewis,' she responded firmly.

Elizabeth went on her way, her heart pattering.

All was not lost. Time was on her side. Arabella had been so cocksure, so certain that she was teacher's pet and that she had everything in the bag. But it wasn't like that at all. Mr Lewis was very fair. He obviously thought that they were evenly matched. He said it was going to be a difficult decision. He was leaving the decision as long as he possibly could – until the week before the concert in fact. Until just one week before the last day of term!

In the meantime she had been given another week and a half to improve her playing of 'Greensleeves'. In today's lesson Mr Lewis had helped her to iron out some problems with the tricky part in the middle. There would be one more lesson, next week, to sort out any last-minute difficulties. To add the finishing touches. After that Arabella had better watch out!

The following day Arabella had her own weekly lesson. Mr Lewis explained the position to her. After the lesson, she came straight into tea. Elizabeth noticed she looked distinctly bad-tempered. This made her feel cheerful. She remembered the fable of the tortoise and the hare. Well, Arabella had hared ahead of her, but now she, the tortoise, had every chance to overtake her.

And that she was determined to do.

In the days that followed Arabella's hopes of keeping her ambition a secret were quickly dashed. Some of the first form soon began to notice that both Arabella and Elizabeth vanished away to play the piano in every spare moment. Patrick heard them on the upstairs landing one evening, fighting over the piano. He spread the news round the common room.

'The stupid way girls behave!' he said. 'I knew I shouldn't have come to a school with girls in it.'

Privately he was very put out that he had twice asked Elizabeth to give him a game of tennis. Twice she had made up some feeble excuse.

'If you *must* know,' said Rosemary, unable to hold her tongue any longer, 'it's all because Elizabeth knows that Arabella's going to be picked for the Leavers' Concert this year and she's jealous.'

'You *wish*,' said Julian sarcastically.

Before long, the whole class knew that the two girls were engaged in bitter rivalry for the place on the concert platform. They seemed to have swept all else aside!

It was true that the teachers were no longer giving out prep. But they were leaving it to the children's good sense to revise for the summer exams. These always took place in the last week of term. And neither Arabella nor Elizabeth were ever seen doing private study. They just seemed to be in the grips of their 'piano craze', as Belinda called it.

'It's all right for Elizabeth,' she said to Jenny one day. 'But Arabella's going to come badly unstuck at this rate. You know how hard she has to work, just to stand still!'

'And she's already the oldest in the form as it is,' agreed Jenny. 'She should have gone into the second form ages ago. What would happen if she didn't pass her exams? Would they have to keep her down again?'

'Miss Ranger says there's no point in anyone going into the second form if they can't do the work when they get there,' replied Belinda.

'They're both going crazy, if you ask me,' said Jenny. 'Even Elizabeth. I don't think she liked us teasing her about slipping down the form order, but it could be a bit more serious if she doesn't watch out!'

In Elizabeth's own mind, of course, it was already serious. Over the next ten days she woke up each morning, fully intending to find time to go to her secret hideout in the oak tree. *I must do some work for the exams today*, she would tell herself.

But, apart from a session on the Sunday afternoon, she never *did* find time.

The end of summer term was always hectic. There was compulsory strawberry picking to do in the school gardens. There were the knockout tennis tournaments, with all children expected to play in their different age groups. Of course, Elizabeth loved these activities. She loved it when she got to the semi-final of the first-form tournament. But it only left time for her vital piano practice and nothing else.

'I'm sorry I haven't been to see you lately,' she told the friendly little robin on the Sunday. 'You'll see more of me next weekend when I've got this piano business out of the way. You will see me then, *I* can tell you!'

In her heart Elizabeth knew that by then it might be much too late. The exams began on the Monday! But she could no longer bear to think about them. Lately, she had begun to console herself with a new thought.

I can't possibly be made to stay down in the first form, like a baby, if I'm chosen to play at the Leavers' Concert. It's going to be such a grown-up occasion this year, with a real concert pianist coming. Even if I don't do very well in the exams, surely Miss Ranger won't mind?

So, even on the Sunday, it only needed the distant notes of Arabella's piece starting up to bring Elizabeth scooting down from the oak tree and back indoors to the piano.

By the time both girls had taken their last piano

lessons of term with Mr Lewis, interest in the first form had reached fever pitch.

'How did you get on in your lesson, Elizabeth?' asked Daniel Carter, who had been helping her to practise by turning the pages. Unfortunately Julian had refused. He claimed not to be able to read music. He felt she was now overdoing things.

'Fine,' she replied confidently. 'I've sorted out that end bit now.'

Martin asked Arabella the same question the next day. He had been taking it in turns with Rosemary to be Arabella's page-turner.

'Mr Lewis seemed very pleased with me,' replied Arabella.

Julian started a sweepstake on the result of the contest, with the children putting in sweets for money.

'Five sweets for four if Arabella Buckley wins,' he announced. 'Three sweets for two if the naughtiest girl does.'

Their classmates were all finding it very exciting. But, when the summons from Mr Lewis finally came, the two girls themselves were pale with tension.

It was after tea on the Wednesday.

'Put your music case on the table there, Elizabeth, next to Arabella's,' he said, as she came into the music room. 'I must decide which order you will play in.'

He let both girls run through a few scales, to loosen up. Then he looked at his watch.

'Would you like to play in alphabetical order?' he asked, with a smile. 'You first, Elizabeth.' He meant alphabetically by surname, of course. Allen first, then Buckley.

With Mr Lewis turning the pages for her and Arabella seated quietly near the door Elizabeth solemnly played her piece.

She made no mistakes and put fine expression into it.

'Well done,' nodded Mr Lewis. 'Now you, Arabella, please.'

Looking neat and tidy as usual, her fair hair brushed and gleaming, Elizabeth's rival took over at the piano. Mr Lewis straightened her music for her.

Now it was the naughtiest girl's turn to sit very still and listen.

During the past two weeks, she had heard snatches of Arabella's piece a great many times. She had heard some of the more difficult passages being played over and over again. She knew it was a lovely melody, but only now, as she heard it through from beginning to end, did she realise just *how* lovely. It was a pastoral piece, longer and more difficult than Elizabeth's own, and played with deep expression.

For a brief time, listening to the music, Elizabeth quite forgot it was Arabella playing and their intense rivalry. She found herself, instead, feeling dreamy, with visions of fields and hedgerows and little wooded hills floating through her mind . . .

Even so, it was still a crushing disappointment when the decision came—

With a brief 'Well done' to Arabella Mr Lewis walked straight over to Elizabeth and placed a gentle hand on her shoulder. In that moment she knew that she had lost the contest.

'You played beautifully, Elizabeth. But I have made up my mind now. I think we should give Arabella the chance to perform that in public. It distresses me that we cannot have more than one person from each form this year. You deserve to be in the concert after all your hard work. But there it is.'

Arabella was still seated at the piano. She seemed transfixed, radiant. She had surpassed herself. Her own performance had surprised even her.

Elizabeth at once walked across and shook her hand.

'Congratulations,' she said. To hide her disappointment, she gave a wobbly little smile.

For once Arabella did not gloat. She seemed to be in a happy daze.

'Thank you,' she said politely.

'Thank you, Elizabeth,' echoed Mr Lewis. 'You may leave now if you wish.'

As the music master started to discuss with the other girl the arrangements for the concert, Elizabeth turned her face away and hurried to the door.

She wanted to flee now!

She grabbed the nearer of the two brown leather music cases, not realising that it was Arabella's. Then she scooped up her music and, without even pausing to put it in the case, she shot out into the corridor.

She ran all the way upstairs to Dormitory Six. Angrily, she hurled both the music and the leather case under her bed. Then she flung herself on top of the bed in despair.

Lying there, she could see the pile of schoolbooks on her white-painted chest of drawers. Standing there accusingly. It was all her revision, still waiting to be done.

She was not going to be in the concert after all.

And now she was going to fail her exams!

CHAPTER SIX

JULIAN LEARNS THE TRUTH

'CHEER UP, Elizabeth! Have some sweets!' said Julian, as soon as she came down stairs. He produced handfuls of barley sugars and toffees and liquorice allsorts from his bulging trouser pockets. 'Just look what I made on my sweepstake!'

Elizabeth smiled weakly. Everybody had been very kind.

Joan had been first into the dormitory to comfort her. 'You gave it your very best, Elizabeth. Nobody can do more than that. I'm proud of you. Now all we can do is accept the result.'

Other girls had come into the dormitory and said lots of nice things. Then her friends had dragged her outside and hustled her downstairs.

'Julian's looking for you, Elizabeth!'

'He made lots of sweets out of the sweepstake. Now

he wants to share them out with everybody.'

'Come on, Elizabeth, you mustn't brood! Julian wants you to have first pick!'

Elizabeth plucked a favourite stripey allsort from Julian's hand. She popped it in her mouth. Then she chose two black ones and put them in her pocket. Everybody cheered. Then, grabbing sweets themselves, they all hurried off to their evening activities, laughing and chatting happily. The contest between Elizabeth and Arabella was over. It had been very exciting while it lasted!

Elizabeth and Julian were left alone.

From another pocket he produced two extra-special, expensive-looking chocolates, in crinkly gold foil wrappings. He was determined to cheer Elizabeth up.

'Come on. Have one of these. You've worked too hard. Need to get your strength back, Elizabeth!'

'Who put these in the kitty?' she asked. She unwrapped the chocolate and popped it in her mouth. 'Mmm. Delicious.'

'Arabella! She backed you to win. A sort of insurance policy, I suppose. She's lost them now.'

'Oh well. That's some consolation,' sighed Elizabeth. She looked at her friend in mild curiosity. 'However did you end up with so many sweets, Julian? How did you work it all out?'

'Simple,' he shrugged. 'Nobody much likes Arabella, but everybody likes you. So I made your odds more tempting than hers and guessed everybody would want to back the bold, bad Elizabeth!'

'But you didn't think I would actually *win*?' realised Elizabeth, her face falling.

She had never seen Julian blush before.

'I had a little listen, a couple of times,' he confessed. 'It was a great surprise, but I thought Arabella just had the edge on you.'

'She did,' admitted Elizabeth. 'You were right.'

She looked sad as she spoke. Julian at once tugged her by the hand.

'Come and see what I've got to show you. I've been keeping them a surprise. I want to know what you think. I've been busy too, you know!'

He led her along to the craft room. Two or three boys and girls were working on their hobbies, completely engrossed. Otherwise it was empty. Julian led the way to his drawer, in the corner. He took something out, wrapped in tissue paper.

'Look!' he said, lowering his voice. 'Do you like them?'

It was Mother Bear and Father Bear.

They were completed. Julian had sawn the piece of weathered oak in two and stripped off the remaining bark. From the natural shapes of the two pieces he had wrought a pair of carved animals. Father Bear was thick-bodied and heavy jowled, with a stern but wise expression. The name WILLIAM was carved at the base. Mother Bear had a gentle face, full of kindness and understanding. Her name had been carved, too: RITA.

The wood had been sanded with great care, then polished until it gleamed. The carvings had taken Julian many hours to complete.

Elizabeth stared at them in silence. Julian was so clever. They were beautiful.

But as she looked at those two names, *William* and *Rita*, her own misery resurfaced. It gnawed at her.

William and Rita were leaving next week. Julian had used his time wisely. Now he had a beautiful memento to give them. The beautiful memento that *she* had been planning to give them, her music at the Leavers' Concert, had come to nothing.

She had not used her own time wisely. She had used it stupidly. Now she had nothing to give William and Rita. Instead she might well fail the exams next week and be kept down in the first form like a baby.

'What's the matter?' asked Julian, glancing at her scowling face. He felt very hurt. 'Don't you like them? Don't you think they're any good?'

'It's not that, Julian!'

'Why are you sulking then?'

Elizabeth could not bear Julian to think she was sulking, or jealous in any way.

'The carvings are lovely, Julian. I think you are very clever. It's just that – oh, I've been so stupid—'

Suddenly tears sprang to Elizabeth's eyes and without warning she found herself blurting out her secret fears to Julian.

He looked at her in amazement.

'I am sure Miss Ranger did not mean it about keeping you down!' he exclaimed. 'She was just trying to make you work hard and catch up—'

'But I haven't worked hard and I haven't caught up!' said Elizabeth in despair. 'And now there's no time left and it's hopeless . . .'

'Of course it's not hopeless, you goose.' He took hold of Elizabeth's arm and led her out of the craft room and into the corridor. He had a feeling that people could hear them in there! 'Look, if you're really taking this work business seriously, you'd better dash off and do some right now. At least that will make you feel better!' he added, with a grin.

He was humouring her. Privately, he thought her fears were silly.

'I will! I will!' exclaimed Elizabeth. It had been such

a relief to tell someone the truth at last. Julian was so calm about things. She began to feel slightly better. They were quite alone in the corridor now. 'I'll go and do my French verbs. I'm going right now. I've got a secret place, you see. Oh, Julian,' she begged. '*Please* don't tell anyone about this. Promise!'

'I promise. Off you go then!'

Julian watched as Elizabeth hurried off with a little skip. He shook his head and smiled to himself. The naughtiest girl was always full of surprises. You never knew what was going on in her head. That was one of the things he liked about her.

Whistling softly to himself, he went back into the craft room and replaced the wood carvings in his drawer. He was just leaving the room again when someone spoke.

Daniel had caught snatches of what Elizabeth had been saying earlier. Now he raised his head from his clay model and spoke to Julian.

'Poor Elizabeth!' Daniel was a sensitive boy. 'She's in a terrible stew about the exams, isn't she? I've never seen her in a state about schoolwork before. It's silly of her not to have done any swotting.'

'Oh, she'll cope all right,' said Julian airily. 'And don't you go noising this about either. It's Elizabeth's private business and you're a nosy parker!'

'Sorry, Julian.'

Unfortunately, the very next day Daniel gave Elizabeth's secret clean away.

CHAPTER SEVEN

ELIZABETH HAS A NEW WORRY

DANIEL DID not mean to blurt out Elizabeth's private fears. But next morning, after first lesson, he heard some of the others criticising her.

'Have you ever seen the naughtiest girl so gloomy in class?'

'She looks like the cat that's had the cream taken away!'

'It must be because Arabella won. She's in a sulk!'

'No, she's not!' butted in Daniel, unable to stop himself. 'She's worried about the exams, that's all. She's fearfully worried!'

'What? Elizabeth? We don't believe you!'

'It's true I tell you!' Daniel was determined to defend Elizabeth's good name. 'I heard her telling Julian. She doesn't want anybody to know, but she's convinced she's going to fail!'

This titbit of news passed round the class in the course of the morning. They observed Elizabeth's behaviour with interest. She certainly seemed very absorbed in lessons today, taking copious notes all the time. When Julian made a paper dart and sent it skidding across her desk, in the middle of French, she barely noticed. Nor did she raise her head at Mam'zelle's cry.

'*Zut alors, Julian!*'

The rumours must be true then. Elizabeth was really worried.

She was. But her worries were as nothing compared to Arabella's. After her great triumph of the previous day she had woken up this morning in a state of panic. When Miss Ranger asked her some simple questions on the English set book, the oldest person in the form got every single question wrong. That was the moment when terror struck at her heart.

However, Arabella struggling in class was so commonplace that nobody even noticed. For Elizabeth to be having problems was far more noteworthy.

But by teatime Elizabeth was in a much more positive frame of mind. Last night, in her secret den, she had revised all her French verbs. She had concentrated hard in lessons today and made lots of notes.

Straight after tea she would return to the oak tree for a good long session with her English set book. She could study it there, in peace. Miss Ranger had said they must be able to quote from it. She would spend at least an hour there and take extra cheese and biscuits with her, she thought, scooping some up and putting them in her pocket.

She hurried up to the dormitory to collect her English book. She noticed the sheet music flapping about under the bed, where she had hurled it the previous evening. There was to be a dormitory inspection tonight.

I'd better put it away, she thought shamefacedly. *I've no time for piano practice any more.*

As soon as she hauled the music case from under the bed and opened it, she realised that she had picked up Arabella's by mistake! The cases were almost identical but, inside the flap, Arabella had written her name. And there were some chocolate marks as well.

When she hid those peppermint chocolates in it! Elizabeth thought disapprovingly. *So she must have* my *case. I'd better go and get it.*

Arabella was still at tea. Her dormitory was empty.

Elizabeth quickly found her own music case. It was standing tucked between Arabella's chest of drawers and her bed. Elizabeth swopped the two cases over. Arabella's current music was lying loose on top of the chest of drawers. Like Elizabeth, she had not bothered to put it away yet.

So she's not even realised we've got our cases mixed up! thought Elizabeth. *Well, as she's never noticed, I won't bother to say anything.*

She hurried back to her own dormitory with her proper case.

I'll put 'Greensleeves' away later. When I tidy up my cubicle for the dormy inspection! Elizabeth decided, dumping the case on her bed. *I really must rush now. This is wasting time!*

Soon she was ensconced in her tree house once more. It was all very soothing. The leaves whispered and rustled around her. The big bough was as comfortable as any chair. It had protruding branches on which she could rest her feet, as she lay back against the warm, rough bark of the massive tree trunk.

She knew some of the set book quite well and now she must study the remainder. She worked hard for the next hour. She broke off once or twice to feed the robin some biscuit crumbs. She memorised two passages from the book that Miss Ranger had told them were important. She smiled as she saw a squirrel scuttle past.

'Yes, you've got me back!' she told it.

She closed her eyes for a few moments. The doves were cooing again. Oh, she did love this special tree. It was so full of life! Perhaps she would share her secret with Joan one day, and Julian . . .

Her eyes opened wide. She could hear the murmur of voices, somewhere down below.

Elizabeth peered down through the leaves. There were two men standing by the country road. They were looking at the tree and talking about it. Then they came and walked round its trunk, immediately beneath her.

They spoke again. This time she could hear exactly what they were saying. She frowned, puzzled by their words.

They were walking away now, in the direction of the village. They glanced back at the tree as they went, still deep in conversation. Elizabeth could no longer hear what they were saying, but she remained deeply puzzled.

What did they mean about a big 'un*? And something about some ropes?* she wondered. *I don't understand* . . .

She remembered the strange white cross that was painted down below and began to feel a sense of foreboding. Elizabeth had a new worry now.

Then suddenly, from the direction of the school grounds, she heard her name being called.

It was Julian's voice.

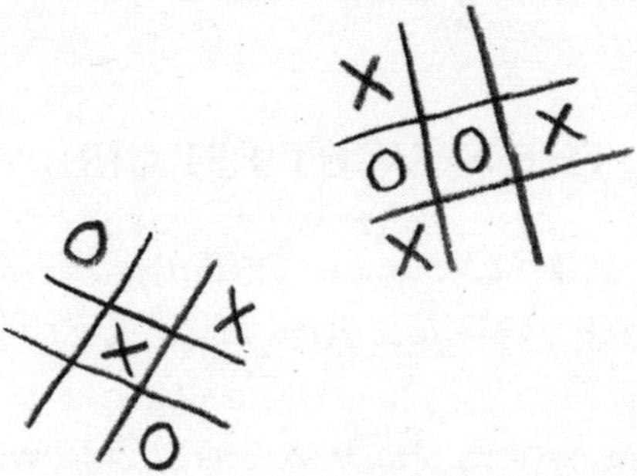

CHAPTER EIGHT

AN EXAM PAPER IS LOST – AND FOUND

'ELIZABETH! YOO-HOO! Where are you?' called Julian, hands cupped to his mouth.

Harry joined in as well.

'EE . . . LIZZZZZ . . . ABETH! Come on, wherever you are!'

'Special Meeting!' Julian shouted, to the empty air. 'We've all got to go inside! William and Rita's orders! Special Meeting of the first form!'

Elizabeth peered through the foliage. She could see the boys over by the school field. Now Harry was grabbing Julian's arm.

'Come on, it's no good, Julian,' he was saying. 'William and Rita told us to come straight back if we couldn't find her.'

The naughtiest girl watched the two boys run back to the school building. She felt ill at ease.

Drat! she thought. *Whatever are William and Rita having a special Meeting of the first form for? I don't want to go back inside yet.*

She wanted to stay where she was for a little while longer. She hated the idea of leaving her tree on its own this evening. Was it something to do with what those men had said? Perhaps. If she stayed for a while, they might come wandering back. They might start talking again. She would listen carefully and try to make sense of what they were saying . . .

But she dare not stay longer. Not when William and Rita had called a special Meeting. Why was it only for the first form? That was very unusual. She had better hurry!

Poor Elizabeth then found herself stuck up the tree in any case – for ten whole minutes! The grounds were very busy at this time of evening. The juniors were coming in from play to have their cocoa. The older pupils were strolling back and forth with cricket bats and tennis rackets. Every time she tried to edge along the bough to climb down the wall and get back into the grounds, she would hear fresh voices!

At last the coast was clear. She raced over to school, brown curls flying, and made straight for the hall. The doors were open. She slowed down to recover her breath, panting and dishevelled. A figure stepped forward.

'Stop! Elizabeth!'

It was Miss Ranger! She had been standing by the doors, observing the Meeting.

She took hold of Elizabeth's arm and surveyed her.

'There's no point in your going in now, Elizabeth. The Meeting's just ended! Wherever have you been? You know you should wash your face and brush your hair before you come to a Meeting! What *have* you been up to?'

'I – I was just out-of-doors, Miss Ranger,' Elizabeth said lamely.

She peered into the hall. She could hear benches being scraped back and the low buzz of conversation. William and Rita were leaving the platform. There were no monitors with them.

What a short Meeting! Miss Ranger was right. It had just ended.

'Why isn't the whole school here?' she asked, puzzled.

'Because something very unpleasant has happened, which concerns only the first form. William and Rita are hoping it can be sorted out quickly. They would rather not have to bring it up at the big weekly Meeting.'

Miss Ranger hurried off then, looking very upset.

'Where did you get to, Elizabeth?' asked her classmates, as they came out of the hall.

One or two of them were looking at her with

considerable curiosity.

'Why didn't you want to come to the Meeting?'

'Are you all right?'

'Of course I'm all right!' replied Elizabeth impatiently.

She pushed past them and found Julian, who was still in the hall. He was with Kathleen.

'We wondered what had happened to you, Elizabeth,' he said calmly. 'You've missed all the excitement.'

'What excitement? What was the Meeting about?'

'Something terrible's happened,' said Kathleen, her face pale. 'Somebody's stolen one of the first-form exam papers.'

Elizabeth was shocked. 'How could somebody do that?'

'It seems they've been printed ready for next week and are in a drawer in the school office,' explained Julian. 'But the Beauty and the Beast counted them this evening and there's one missing. It's a copy of the paper we were all going to get for our English exam. Somebody got hold of their paper in advance!'

'What a cheat!' said Elizabeth indignantly.

'Well, they haven't got away with it,' shrugged Julian. 'All the questions will have to be changed now. The joint heads must be furious! Shall we do a bit of detective work? That would be interesting.'

'I can't, Julian,' said Kathleen. 'I'm right in the middle

of tidying up my cubicle for dormy inspection. This Meeting's been a real nuisance.'

'Elizabeth?' queried Julian.

Elizabeth was also shaking her head.

Of course, it was terrible that someone had stolen the English paper. And it must be someone in their class! Who could it be? Normally, she would have been fascinated to do some detective work with Julian. They often solved things together.

But this evening she had something else on her mind. Something that was worrying her very much. A matter that she felt was of supreme importance. She had quite a different mystery to investigate.

'I'm sorry,' she said. 'I want to go and talk to somebody about something. In fact, I'm off there right now.'

Kathleen looked puzzled as the naughtiest girl rushed away.

'Don't forget, Elizabeth! We've got dormy inspection tonight. Don't go and disappear again!' she called out.

Julian just smiled and scratched his head. Dear Elizabeth. What was she up to *now*? It seemed to be something new. At least she didn't seem to have exams on the brain any more!

Elizabeth left the school building and hurried to the stables. She wanted to speak to the stableman. He was a real countryman and a fount of knowledge.

She would ask him what a white cross on the trunk of a tree might mean. She would also ask him if he had ever put ropes round a tree and, if so, why. *We'll rope her up first thing in the morning* . . . That's what the men had said.

Of course, she mustn't let him suspect that she was asking about any *particular* tree. He might wonder how she knew so much about the oak tree when it didn't belong to Whyteleafe and was not even in the school grounds. She shouldn't really know anything about it at all!

But she had to speak to him urgently. It was *her* tree and she had to know if anything was going to happen to it in the morning.

She desperately hoped not. Perhaps the stableman could give a simple explanation. Then she would hurry back and tidy up her cubicle for dormitory inspection.

Silly old dormitory inspection! This was much more important.

'Where has Elizabeth got to *now*?' said Miss Ranger angrily. 'Her behaviour is very strange at the moment.'

The dormitory inspection was in full swing.

Once a fortnight, the dormitories at Whyteleafe School were checked for tidiness. The class teacher concerned would accompany Matron on a tour of inspection.

All the other girls in Number Six stood to attention

by their cubicles. Beds had been beautifully made, rugs straightened. The number of items on top of chests of drawers was limited to six, as school rules ordained. So far, Matron and Miss Ranger had been well pleased.

But now they were staring into Elizabeth's empty cubicle in annoyance. It was a mess. And the naughtiest girl herself was nowhere to be seen! Where was she?

She was climbing the stairs at that very moment, taking them slowly, one at a time. She was deep in thought and feeling trembly.

Mr Tucker, the stableman had not been at the stables. It had taken her some time to track him down. But now, at last, she had the answer to her questions.

It's not fair! It's horrible! she raged to herself, over and over again. *It's not in the least bit fair and I shall make them stop!*

She was already forming a plan in her mind.

She walked into Dormitory Six, her face very tense and pale.

In something of a daze she noticed that Miss Ranger and Matron were standing in her cubicle.

'Elizabeth! This is a disgrace!' said Matron. 'Look at all the books on your chest of drawers—'

'And don't add your English book to the pile!' scolded Miss Ranger, as she saw Elizabeth take the small volume out of her pocket. 'Your schoolbooks should be in your desk, not up here!'

'I've been reading it this evening for the exams,' protested Elizabeth.

She was still feeling in a daze.

'You should have been tidying up your cubicle!' said Miss Ranger, standing by the bed. 'What's your music case doing, just dumped on top of the bed? And you haven't even bothered to put your music away.'

The teacher gathered up the score and opened the brown leather case, intending to slip it neatly inside. But there was something in the way.

'Even your music case needs a tidy-up,' she complained.

She pulled out a crumpled sheet of paper that had been stuffed just inside the case. She straightened it out and stared at it in disbelief. 'Elizabeth!'

The teacher's shocked cry brought everybody running to the scene.

Miss Ranger was holding something aloft, between thumb and forefinger. She was waving it in front of the naughtiest girl.

Gasps of surprise echoed round Dormitory Six. It was the stolen exam paper.

'What was this English examination paper doing hidden in your music case, Elizabeth?' asked Miss Ranger.

Elizabeth gazed at the printed sheet in total

astonishment. It was an exam paper sure enough. Even from here she could see a list of questions about the English set book. She was speechless.

'Is that why you have been reading so avidly this evening?' continued the teacher in acid tones, glancing at the book in Elizabeth's hand. 'To plan your answers to the exam questions in advance?'

'No!' protested Elizabeth angrily. 'Of course not, Miss Ranger!'

'I repeat: how did this exam paper come to be hidden in your music case?' asked the teacher.

Matron was trying to usher the other girls out of earshot. But they were hanging on to every word.

'Answer me, Elizabeth!' rapped Miss Ranger.

'I have no idea!' exclaimed Elizabeth hotly.

'Come, come, Elizabeth. Think carefully before you speak. You must have *some* idea of how a stolen exam paper could be found in your music case,' said the teacher calmly. 'Just think about it for a moment. It must have got there somehow, must it not?'

Elizabeth's sense of outrage began to subside. Miss Ranger's comment was perfectly fair. How *had* it got in her case? She took a deep breath, to try to calm herself. It had been such a shock! The little girl frowned deeply for a few moments as she tried to think clearly.

Slowly, the truth dawned on her.

'Well, Elizabeth?'

The naughtiest girl had become pink with excitement.

'I – I think I know the answer,' she said. 'You see, my music case has been in somebody else's possession all day.'

'Somebody else's possession?'

Elizabeth's room mates glanced at each other, uncomfortably. What a silly thing to say! The music case had been lying under her bed all day. They had noticed it there and wondered if she had forgotten about dormitory inspection tonight.

'Whose possession, Elizabeth?'

'I – I'd rather not say, Miss Ranger.'

It sounded very feeble. The teacher glanced at her watch.

'It is nearly bedtime. You are to tidy up your cubicle, this instant. Then if, as you say, there is somebody else involved in this matter, you are to bring them to the staffroom before you go to bed. I will wait to see you there. If for any reason you cannot find this other person, there is nothing more we can do about it tonight. Miss Belle and Miss Best will see you in the morning.'

It was clear, realised Elizabeth, that Miss Ranger found it very difficult to believe her story.

'Yes, Miss Ranger!' she replied confidently.

Very soon the teacher would see that her story was true.

CHAPTER NINE

ELIZABETH DISAPPEARS

ARABELLA SAT primly on her bed in pyjamas, pretending to read a book. The curtains of her cubicle were drawn. She knew that would hardly deter Elizabeth. She was expecting her at any moment.

Next door, in Room Six, Matron had supervised Elizabeth while she tidied up her cubicle. In those ten minutes the dramatic news had spread like wildfire. The boys alone, away to their own quarters by then, knew nothing of the unfolding drama. But the news had very quickly reached Arabella's dormitory.

The excited chatter had raged all around her.

'The paper was in Elizabeth's music case! She was caught red-handed!'

'She tried to pretend someone else used her music case today. Miss Ranger says she'd better produce them!'

'I knew it was funny the way she didn't come to the

Meeting! I *said* that was weird.'

'Poor Elizabeth! We knew she was in a bad way!'

'It was silly of her to waste all that time on the piano!'

'It's not a *bit* like Elizabeth to cheat. I'm so amazed!'

Arabella, already in pyjamas, had quickly drawn the curtain round her cubicle. She had peered inside her music case in horror.

The truth had dawned. They must have got their cases muddled up yesterday. Elizabeth had come and swopped them back this evening without checking inside and now everybody thought that she had stolen the exam paper.

Suddenly, now, the curtains parted.

'So there you are!' exclaimed Elizabeth, stepping into the cubicle. 'Just the person I want to speak to.'

Arabella's heart was thumping. She noted the fierce glitter in Elizabeth's eye.

'Am I?' she asked innocently, looking up from her book. 'And why would that be, Elizabeth?'

'You know perfectly well! It's about you stealing that exam paper and then putting it into *my* music case by mistake!' hissed Elizabeth. 'We've got to go and see Miss Ranger straight away. The two of us. You had my music case all day, not your own! You will have to confess to her.'

'I'm sure I don't know what you're talking about!'

exclaimed Arabella, deliberately raising her voice. 'How dare you accuse me of stealing something. I haven't touched your silly music case!'

It brought Rosemary on to the scene at once.

'Elizabeth's saying I haven't had my music case all day, Rosemary. She says I've been using hers! Did you ever hear such nonsense?'

'Arabella's case has been here since yesterday evening. I've seen it!' protested Rosemary. 'Look, there it is! It's never budged.' She pointed to its position on the floor tucked between bed and chest of drawers. 'Whatever would she want *yours* for?'

Elizabeth stared at Arabella in disbelief. Arabella was refusing to own up. She must by now be perfectly well aware of what had happened. But she was not going to admit it.

'So you don't agree that you sneaked into the school office some time today and took that exam paper?' asked Elizabeth scornfully. 'And then crept up here and hid it in the music case by your bed? Thinking it was your own! If I hadn't come in here after tea and swopped it for your proper case, the exam paper would still be there *now*!'

Arabella had gone very white.

Rosemary, thinking it was because of the outrageous things being said, turned on Elizabeth.

'You came and swopped it, did you?' she jeered. 'Did anybody see you?'

'Well, no. It's just that I . . .'

Elizabeth's voice trailed away. For the first time she realised that she had not one single witness to support her story.

'It's just that you are sick with jealousy at Arabella being chosen for the concert!' said Rosemary, finishing Elizabeth's sentence in her own way. 'And, not content with stealing the exam paper, you're now trying to pin the blame on *her* so that you'll play in the concert instead of her!'

Arabella was breathing heavily. She was racked with emotion.

Elizabeth had guessed the truth exactly. And, faced with the fierce candour of what Elizabeth had been saying, Arabella had come within an ace of confessing. Until Rosemary's words had reminded her of how much she stood to lose . . .

The Leavers' Concert! Her great moment of triumph was just one week away. So many times Elizabeth had had the last laugh and she, Arabella, had been made to look stupid. All that would change now. People would look up to her. They would respect her. Perhaps they would even start to like her, the way they always liked Elizabeth. She had surprised herself, how well she could play the piano! She had worked so hard for her moment of glory next week. Nothing was going to rob her of that!

'I really don't know anything about a silly exam paper, Elizabeth,' she said, her face expressionless. 'You seem to have made a mistake.'

The naughtiest girl looked at her sorrowfully.

'You're a hopeless case, Arabella,' she said quietly. 'There is no point in talking to you.'

She left and returned to her own dormitory.

The room fell silent at her arrival, but she cared not. She went into her cubicle and drew the curtains. Then she lay down on top of the bed, still fully clothed.

She turned on her back, head resting on hands, staring at the ceiling. Outside dusk began to fall. None of her room mates came to see her, or said goodnight. Her friends were too embarrassed. Poor Elizabeth, they were thinking. So worried about the exams, to creep into the school office like that. And caught red-handed! Trying to pretend that it must have been somebody else!

Miss Ranger too. Waiting in vain for Elizabeth to appear with 'somebody else'. Thinking exactly the same thing.

They will have to think what they like, decided Elizabeth, with a deep sigh. *I can't prove my story is true and I expect Arabella will never confess. Never, ever! But then life is not fair. No. Nothing is fair!*

The amazing sequence of events since teatime had convinced her of that. She was not thinking of her own plight but of something of even greater concern.

Soon she heard steady breathing from every corner of the dormitory. The others were all asleep at last. It was time to put her plan into action.

When the rising bell sounded next morning, Elizabeth did not appear from her cubicle.

Kathleen walked over and pulled back the curtain. 'Wake up, Elizabeth. It's late!'

Then she gasped. The sun's morning rays slanted across Elizabeth's neat, empty bed. Kathleen could see at once that it had not been slept in.

Elizabeth had disappeared.

CHAPTER TEN

A HUE AND CRY

'ELIZABETH'S RUN away!' cried Kathleen in great alarm. 'Look, she must have done. Her bed's not been slept in!'

The others rushed over.

'I don't believe it!' exclaimed Jenny in astonishment. 'Perhaps she just got up early!'

'No, Kathleen's right.' Belinda checked the bed carefully. 'Look, the covers have never been pulled back. And do you notice something? One of the pillows has gone.'

'Yes, and so's the spare blanket!' realised Jenny.

They all looked at one another in horror. Poor Elizabeth! Overcome with shame, she had run away from Whyteleafe School. They had a sudden vision of her wandering the dark country lanes with blanket roll and pillow, sleeping in ditches, trying to make her way back home.

'We should have been nicer to her,' moaned Kathleen. 'We should have been more understanding . . .'

As the word spread to the next dormitory, other pyjama-clad girls thronged in. They gathered round Elizabeth's empty bed, pale and shocked. Nobody looked more shaken than Arabella who already had dark rings under her eyes from a bad night's sleep.

The first-form girls held an emergency meeting on the spot.

'She'll never get home safely! It's more than a hundred miles. And she hasn't any money!' said Tessa.

'I wonder where she slept last night?'

'Some smelly old barn, I expect.'

'What should we do?' asked Belinda. 'Do you think we should go and report this to the Beauty and the Beast straight away?'

'It's not like Elizabeth to run away when she's got a problem!' decided Jenny, after giving it due thought. 'Perhaps this is just one of her pranks, to give us all a fright! Perhaps she's hiding around the school somewhere.'

'And, if we go and tell the joint heads, she'll be in even deeper trouble,' realised Kathleen. 'More than she was already!'

'Yes, you're right!' exclaimed Arabella eagerly. 'We mustn't worry any of the teachers about this at the moment. That would be silly. Let's search the school buildings.'

'Perhaps she's asleep in one of the storerooms?' suggested Rosemary.

The first-form girls rushed to get dressed. Then they fanned out in all directions, scouring the school buildings.

Arabella scurried up and down the corridors, looking in the empty classrooms, opening and shutting each door with growing unease. Nobody had managed to find Elizabeth yet. Where *was* she?

'I expect she'll turn up at breakfast time,' said Rosemary, to comfort her friend. 'She hasn't any money and she's bound to be starving hungry. It's not your fault, Arabella, if Elizabeth Allen has decided to do something idiotic.'

These were not the words to bring comfort to Arabella.

Elizabeth did *not* turn up at breakfast.

Sitting in the dining hall, staring at that empty place, Arabella's serious unease turned to panic.

The naughtiest girl really had run away! And it was all her fault. She should have confessed about the exam paper while she still had the chance. Now Elizabeth felt hopeless about things and was sure that nobody would ever believe her. If only

Rosemary had not butted in, thought Arabella, she might have admitted the truth. She had been on the point of doing so.

Now she was seized by a feeling of dread. Elizabeth could be in danger. Something dreadful might have happened. Supposing she had been run over? And really, when she thought about it, Elizabeth was not *that* bad. She had her good points after all. As she toyed with her breakfast cereal, Arabella's eyes kept straying to the door. How lovely it would be to see the naughtiest girl come strolling in through that open door, right now, laughing at them all and enjoying her silly joke . . .

Come back, Elizabeth, she kept thinking. *Oh, do please come back!*

But still Elizabeth did not appear and by the end of breakfast there was a great hue and cry. Daniel went racing off to see if she might be sleeping in the school stables.

'We must go and see the joint heads right away,' said Joan, turning pale, as soon as Kathleen had explained things to her. The second-form monitor had looked across and noticed that her best friend's place at table was empty. 'Oh, poor Elizabeth! I am perfectly certain she would never have stolen an exam paper. She must be feeling very angry and upset at being misjudged.'

'Hear! Hear!' agreed Julian.

Kathleen reluctantly rose to her feet. She was beginning to feel very guilty.

'Will the heads ring the police, do you think, Joan?'

'I'm sure they will,' replied Joan. She looked across at Julian. 'Do you want to come with us, Julian?'

He just sat there, spooning down the last of his cereal. He shook his head. He was frowning.

'I might follow on in a minute,' he muttered. 'I'm just trying to have a good think.'

There was a great buzz of excitement round the dining hall as Joan and Kathleen went off together. By now, nearly everybody knew what had happened. Elizabeth Allen's bed had not been slept in. It looked as though she must have run away from school! Now Joan and Kathleen were going to report it to Miss Belle and Miss Best. The joint heads would have to telephone the police!

Julian put his spoon down, his brow deeply furrowed. The naughtiest girl was always full of surprises. Even so, he found this one most baffling. If she *had* taken that exam paper, she would have owned up at once except that she would never have taken it in the first place! She had been unjustly accused. But, in that case, the last thing she would do would be to run away. Not the bold, bad Elizabeth. She would stay to fight her corner, to the bitter end. It was such a riddle. There must be some other reason for her vanishing trick. Something different altogether . . .

He was trying hard to remember a remark she had made two days ago. It was to do with her swotting for the exams, without wanting people to know how worried she was.

'Got it!' he whispered suddenly. 'I remember what she said.'

I've got a secret place, you see!

A secret place! Was that why they couldn't find her for the Meeting yesterday? And was this now the explanation? Had the crazy Elizabeth been up all night, swotting for the exams in some secret hideout?

And still there! thought Julian. *Probably fast asleep! But where is it?*

At that moment Daniel returned.

'She's not in the stables,' he said miserably. 'I think it was very catty of those girls last night, not accepting her word. Elizabeth would never cheat. No wonder she was upset. But it's all my fault,' he confessed. 'You see, I spilt the beans, Julian. About her being so worried about the exams. That's why they didn't believe her. I didn't mean to but I did.'

'Oh, do shut up, Daniel,' said Julian absently. 'Can't you see I'm trying to think?'

When Joan and Kathleen arrived at the school office,

they were amazed to see that Arabella had beaten them to it.

'Come in, please,' called the joint heads.

They each sat behind a desk and Miss Ranger stood by the window. She had arrived earlier to report back on the matter of the stolen exam paper. The culprit had been found.

'Elizabeth Allen? Oh dear. How very disappointing!' the joint heads had exclaimed.

Arabella, accompanied by Rosemary, was already in there. They were both seated.

Joan and Kathleen stared at them. Why had Arabella got there ahead of them? She seemed to be crying. Rosemary looked distressed too, and was biting her lip.

'Please ring the police, Miss Belle!' Arabella was pleading tearfully. 'I'm so worried about Elizabeth! I'm so frightened that something could have happened to her. And, if it has, it's all my fault. I drove her to this. I drove her into running away! I could have owned up about the exam paper when I had the chance and I didn't.'

'You have owned up now, Arabella,' said Miss Belle calmly. She nodded towards some more chairs. 'Sit over there, please, Joan and Kathleen. You may join us.'

The two headmistresses were very composed.

'We will have to contact the authorities, which will

be very bad for Whyteleafe,' Miss Best began. 'Before we do so, we need to be quite sure the child has run away. Have you all had a good look for her?'

'We've searched high and low, Miss Best,' replied Kathleen, only just beginning to take it all in.

Elizabeth had been telling the truth all along. Somehow her music case *had* been in somebody else's possession yesterday. Arabella's! And it was Arabella who had stolen the English exam paper. She had come and confessed to Miss Ranger and the joint heads!

As Miss Belle and Miss Best asked further probing questions, Kathleen found it difficult to take her eyes off the fair-haired Arabella. It was strange to see her vain, doll-like face streaked with tears, to see her genuinely caring about somebody else for the first time, somebody other than herself.

'*Please* telephone the police,' she implored again.

The joint heads glanced at one another. It seemed that they had no choice.

'We'll speak to them right away,' said Miss Best, reaching out for the telephone.

'No!' cried a boy's voice from the doorway. 'Please don't ring them yet!'

Julian walked eagerly into the room. Everybody stared at him.

'I might be able to find Elizabeth! I've got a hunch,

but I'll need some time! Could you just give me fifteen minutes, please? We can ring the police after that!'

Miss Best took her hand away from the telephone. She glanced at Miss Belle and then nodded. They both knew that Elizabeth's friend was a brilliant boy.

'Very well, Julian. Fifteen minutes.'

'And not a minute longer,' added Miss Belle.

CHAPTER ELEVEN

WELL DONE, THE NAUGHTIEST GIRL!

'DON'T WORRY, big brown moth. Don't worry, friendly little robin!' whispered Elizabeth, as down below the men took the ropes off the back of the lorry. *Don't worry, chattering squirrels and cooing doves and busy little insects and creepy-crawlies!* 'This is your house. I won't let them chop it down, I promise!'

Hidden in the oak tree, Elizabeth had the fierce light of battle in her eye. She had slept fitfully in its warm boughs. It had been a much lighter sleep than usual. The sleep of a soldier at the battlefront, ready for the enemy and poised for action. And since dawn she had been wide awake. She knew that the woodmen might start work very early. That was why she had not dared to sleep in her proper bed last night.

They had arrived at long last, not as early as she feared but early enough. They parked their lorry on the wide grass verge below and began to sort through their equipment. She was ready for them. She tensed every muscle now. She was preparing to make her stand.

At the same time Julian was walking briskly round the grounds of Whyteleafe School. He was looking urgently about him. It was a chance remark of Daniel's that had given him his clue.

Mr Tucker, the stableman hasn't seen Elizabeth since last night, Julian. She was asking him all about trees or something.

So that was the person Elizabeth had rushed off to speak to last night. Mr Tucker. To ask him about trees. Why *trees*?

Trees . . . secret place.

Could Elizabeth's secret hideout be in a tree? And, in that case, which one? What sort of tree?

And then, in a flash of inspiration, Julian had remembered the piece of oak that Elizabeth had found him. That splendid piece of oak for his wood carvings . . .

But where had it come from? She had never explained. He had occasionally looked for oak himself and never found any. The reason being, as far as he could recall, that there were no oak trees in the school grounds. But there must be one somewhere, one that he had missed . . . And could that be where she had made her secret hideout?

He walked round to the back of the stable block, looking up at all the trees there. Then he stared at the meadow beyond. There was not an oak tree in sight. He hurried back by way of the cricket pitch. He was almost giving up hope. Then, suddenly, he saw it.

'It's been right under my nose!' he realised. 'Only it's growing *outside* the school, on the other side of the wall. That's why I didn't notice it!'

He stood back and surveyed it. Elizabeth could have got into that tree by climbing up the boundary wall . . .

'And she has!' gasped Julian, as Elizabeth's head suddenly poked out of the middle of the tree. She was shouting! She seemed to be looking down at some people in the road.

'Go away, please! Go away and take your horrid chainsaw with you! I'm staying here and I'm not going to budge. I won't let you cut this tree down. Never, ever! Don't you realise lots of little creatures live here? This is their home!'

Julian goggled for a moment – and then came to a swift decision. He turned away and sprinted back towards the school buildings. At top speed. His fifteen minutes was almost up.

'Julian!' exclaimed Miss Ranger in relief, as he burst back into the school office, his face shining. 'You have some news?'

'I've found her!' he exclaimed. 'I know why she disappeared now. It had nothing to do with the exam paper or anything like that!'

He told them all that was happening.

At first there were cries of joy and relief that Elizabeth had been found safe and well. But, after that, some anxious frowns appeared on the teachers' faces.

'That beautiful old oak tree? The one that we can see from the school grounds? It's being taken *down*?' said Miss Belle. 'Oh, Miss Best, we must do something about it. And quickly.'

'We certainly must,' agreed Miss Best. 'I will ring the tree department as soon as the council offices open.'

She rose to her feet and rapped out an order.

'Julian, you are to return to the tree immediately. You are to join Elizabeth there. She needs reinforcements. Under no circumstances are either of you to come down from that tree until we give you permission. And please tell Elizabeth that refreshments are on their way.'

'Oh, Julian, I'm so glad you turned up when you did,' said Elizabeth. 'I was getting so tired of arguing with those men. I don't think I could have stuck it out much longer up here. Not on my own. Not without any breakfast.'

'Another hour should do it,' grinned Julian.

Seated comfortably in the tree, the two friends munched the last of the delicious sandwiches that Joan and Arabella had brought out to them. They offered the robin a few crumbs.

It was morning break and quite a crowd of boys and girls was starting to gather below.

The woodmen had long since retreated. They had parked their lorry some distance away down the road. They were sitting in the cab, drinking tea from a flask, waiting helplessly for further instructions.

'They tried to tell me the tree needed to come down for a road-widening scheme!' said Elizabeth indignantly. 'A beautiful, healthy tree like this with no disease at all! Who wants the silly road widened? Drivers can go a bit slower as they always have done and still have a lovely old tree to look at.'

The tree department people agreed with Elizabeth entirely. It turned out that the powers that be hadn't got all the correct paperwork, so the men weren't allowed to cut the tree down. Within the next hour an official arrived and pinned a notice to the old oak. It was an emergency Tree Preservation Order. It would go to appeal, of course, but, now Miss Belle and Miss Best were involved, Elizabeth was confident the tree would survive.

The doves cooed and all the little birds sang, as though in gratitude. Elizabeth's heart sang loudest of all as, aching with tiredness, she and Julian were given permission to descend from the tree at long last. Everybody cheered.

'Well done, Elizabeth!'

Well done, the naughtiest girl!

CHAPTER TWELVE

GOODBYE TO WILLIAM AND RITA

NEVERTHELESS, ELIZABETH had been in breach of school rules. The big oak tree was out of bounds. She had visited it not once but several times. And she had spent an entire night away from her dormitory, causing everyone great alarm and anxiety. That was a most serious offence.

At the big School Meeting the next day it all had to be written down in the Book. It was the last Meeting of the summer term and the last one ever for William and Rita. There were serious matters to discuss and the head boy and girl were determined that they should be dealt with fairly and wisely. All their conclusions would be written in the Book, offering help and guidance to future Meetings after they had gone.

'As soon as you suspected the tree was in danger, Elizabeth, you should have reported it to a monitor,' said William. 'Even though, to do so, would have meant confessing that you had been out of bounds. Another time you must try not to take matters into your own hands.'

'Yes, William,' agreed Elizabeth contritely. 'I'm sorry.'

'On the other hand,' said Rita, busily writing in the Book, 'this was one of those very rare occasions when breaking a school rule had a beneficial outcome. If you had not been exploring the tree in the first place, you would never have discovered that it was to be felled. It would have been lost. Although you should not have acted alone, your action was brave and so that must go in the Book too.'

The Meeting had to deal with Arabella's crimes, too. That was more difficult.

At the behest of the joint heads Miss Ranger had started giving Arabella some extra lessons in preparation for Monday's English exam. She would have to spend the entire weekend on difficult exercises. There would be a completely new paper set, of course. The Beauty and the Beast had reasoned, correctly, that the girl must be beside herself with panic to have stooped so low. She clearly needed help. At the same time cheating was a serious offence at Whyteleafe School and so was letting someone else take the blame. These were things that the Meeting must deal with.

There was also the very difficult matter of next week's Leavers' Concert to think about. Should Arabella still be allowed to play – or should Elizabeth take her place?

'Why did you practise so hard for the concert, Arabella,' asked Rita, as the fair-haired girl stood up, 'when you should have been working for your summer exams?'

'At first I just wanted to be chosen to spite Elizabeth,' replied Arabella truthfully. 'She always seems to be better at things than me and then she laughs at me. I don't know why nobody likes me and everybody likes Elizabeth.'

'Elizabeth can be very naughty, but she has a warm heart and that is why people like her,' explained Rita. 'She cares for others whereas you are sometimes thought not to.'

'It wasn't a bit warm-hearted of her to make such a contest of it,' complained Arabella. 'She knew I was better than her, but she started practising so hard, I didn't dare slack off after that. I was so worried about the exams, but I *couldn't* let Elizabeth beat me and I knew she wanted to. It was my big chance to shine, you see,' she blurted out. 'I did so want to be chosen. That – that was the only reason I took so long to confess about the exam paper.'

'Is this true, Elizabeth?' asked William. The whole school was listening in fascination. 'That you knew Arabella was better than you, but decided to make a battle of it? Even when you both had exams coming up?'

For the first time Elizabeth felt a twinge of shame.

'Yes, it is true,' she said, hanging her head. 'I did realise Arabella was better, quite early on. But I still wanted to beat her. Even though I'd been in the school play and she hadn't. And even though it meant skimping all my revision. And so, in a way, I suppose I stopped her revising as well.'

Sitting down again, next to Julian on the first form benches, Elizabeth began to think deeply about things.

Poor Arabella! Elizabeth had been working hard and was starting to lose her fear of the exams. But she could tell that Arabella was as worried as ever. It must be dreadful to be the oldest in the form and always struggling near the bottom.

On the platform, with the other monitors, Joan put her hand up.

'Please, William, don't just blame Elizabeth! I think it was wrong of me, but I heartily encouraged her at the time.'

'And I encouraged Arabella!' exclaimed Rosemary, jumping to her feet. 'I tried to mention the exams sometimes, but most of the time I just egged her on.'

The head boy looked from Joan to Rosemary and nodded.

'Thank you both for speaking up,' he said. 'There's an important lesson to be learnt here. The rest of the school, please take note. We always want to please our friends, don't we? We like to say to them the things that they want to hear. But sometimes the thing that is *best* for them is the very last thing that they want to hear. The finest friendship you can give someone is to stand up to them sometimes and tell them when you think they are doing the wrong thing.'

Joan at once nodded agreement. Rosemary sat down, feeling very ashamed at the way she always pretended to agree with Arabella, even when she knew she was wrong. Elizabeth glanced at Julian admiringly. He had told her several times that she was overdoing things with the piano business.

Rita wrote all this down. Then she, in turn, addressed the school.

'There is something else I would like to point out. To both Elizabeth and Arabella. But it applies to the rest of us too. It is very easy to care about people whom we like. To care equally for those people whom we don't like is much more difficult, but is something we must strive for.'

Shyly, Kathleen put her hand up.

'Please, Rita, Arabella was really upset when she thought something had happened to Elizabeth. Even though she doesn't like her! She was crying.'

The naughtiest girl's eyes opened wide at this surprising piece of news. She turned to look at Arabella, but the other girl turned her head away, embarrassed.

'Thank you for pointing that out, Kathleen,' said Rita. 'And this brings us to the final business of the Meeting. We have given everything a good airing and now we have to decide about the Leavers' Concert. Should Arabella still be allowed to represent the first form or should Elizabeth take her place?'

'This is going to be a very difficult decision,' added William. 'Rita and I will talk it over with the monitors.'

Everybody on the platform went into a huddle. There seemed to be a long argument going on. Elizabeth sat very tense and still. So did Arabella. All around them the hall buzzed with conversation, as the boys and girls discussed among themselves which of the two girls should be allowed to play.

Then William banged the gavel on the table for silence.

'We are finding it impossible to reach agreement,' he announced. He gazed towards the back of the hall where, as always, Miss Belle, Miss Best and Mr Johns sat in on the Meeting. They never joined in unless their advice was sought. 'We would like the heads to tell us what they think.'

Miss Belle at once rose to her feet. She was smiling.

'While you have been discussing this difficult problem, we have been discussing it too. We have decided that you should let Elizabeth and Arabella use their own good sense in the matter. Let them discuss it together privately. Let *them* decide which of them should play at the Leavers' Concert.'

It was the end of summer term at Whyteleafe, the very last day of the school year. William and Rita and the others were leaving today! Exams were over and the results posted on the board.

Elizabeth had passed! She would be going up into the second form next term! She would be reunited with Joan. She would be going up with Julian and Patrick and Kathleen and Belinda and Jenny . . . and Arabella! Somehow Arabella had managed to scrape through the English exam and had passed in maths, and French as well. She had failed some other papers, but because of her tremendous progress in music this term had been given some useful bonus marks for that instead. So she was being allowed into the second form.

'As a matter of fact, I really like my piano practice now,' she had confided to the music master. 'I never realised how satisfactory it could be, to find out that there's something one is really good at!'

Mr Lewis was delighted.

It was time for the Leavers' Concert. He was up on the platform in the hall now, smiling at Sophie as she waited nervously with her flute. She would be the first to perform. All the parents had arrived and the hall was crammed full.

The girl from the junior class soon got over her nerves. She gave a faultless performance. Everybody applauded. William and Rita, sitting in the front row, sat very still. They glanced at each other, moist-eyed, for they knew that this concert would be their last memory of Whyteleafe.

'And now,' announced Mr Lewis, 'to represent the first form we have one of our most gifted pupils, Arabella Buckley.'

Sitting between her parents, near the front, Elizabeth watched Arabella as she walked on to the platform. She put her music in place on the grand piano which had been brought into the hall for this special occasion. How magnificent it looked. Arabella looked quite small against it. She looked different today, thought Elizabeth, her fair hair brushed and gleaming, a spot of colour in each cheek, her eyes sparkling.

As she started to play, a deep hush descended over the audience. The pictures came again to Elizabeth, conjured up by the music. Those lovely visions of green fields, grass blowing, clouds scudding across blue sky, wooded hills . . . What a fine player Arabella was!

William and Rita listened, enraptured. All too soon it was over.

Children from other classes came and went. Richard played his fine new piece. Then Courtney Wood, the well-known concert pianist, performed for the rest of the programme, as planned.

It had been a wonderful Leavers' Concert this year and yet, for Elizabeth, it was Arabella's music that lingered in the mind. Had the head boy and girl enjoyed it as much as she had? She did hope so!

Afterwards she and Julian went to say goodbye to them. They were deeply touched when Julian presented them with the little wood carvings.

'They are quite beautiful, Julian!' exclaimed Rita.

'Father Bear rather looks like me, doesn't he?' laughed William in delight.

He turned to face Elizabeth and smiled approvingly.

'So you and Arabella sorted it out then? How did you decide?'

'It was easy,' replied Elizabeth. 'I just thought Arabella's piece would be the best memento for you, better than mine actually. I – I'm just sorry that I haven't got anything of my own to give you.'

'But we heard your music drifting out one evening, Elizabeth, and that was lovely too,' said Rita quietly. 'I will never be able to hear "Greensleeves" in future without its reminding me of you.'

Elizabeth blushed with pleasure.

'Naughtiest girl in the school – best girl in the school!' laughed William. 'You have no need to give us a memento—'

He bent and kissed her on the cheek. Then Rita did likewise.

'Memento? Please don't be silly!'

'Dear Elizabeth! How could we ever forget you?'

BONUS BLYTON

Enid Blyton has been one of the world's best-loved storytellers for over seventy years. Her interest in writing began as a child and, before she loved receiving letters from the children who read her books, she enjoyed working with them as a teacher. The Naughtiest Girl stories are inspired by real schools and experiences. Turn the page to learn more about Enid as a child and as a teacher. Afterwards you might like to write about your school and teachers and the people in *your* class!

THE LIFE AND TIMES OF ENID BLYTON

11 August 1897	Enid Blyton was born in East Dulwich, London. Two brothers are born after her – Hanly (b. 1899) and Carey (b. 1902).
1911	Enid enters a children's poetry competition and is praised for her writing. She's on the path to becoming a bestselling author . . .
1916	Enid begins to train as a teacher in Ipswich. By the time she is 21, she is a fully qualified Froebel teacher, and starts work at a school in Kent.
1917	Enid's first 'grown-up' publication – three poems in *Nash's Magazine*.
June 1922	Enid's first book is published. It's called *Child Whispers*.
1926	Enid begins editing – and writes – the phenomenal *Sunny Stories for Little Folks* magazine. (She continues in this role for 26 years!)

1927	So vast is Enid's output that she has to learn to type. (But she still writes to children by hand.)
1931	Having married Hugh Pollock in 1924, the couple's first child, Gillian, is born. Imogen, their second daughter, was born in 1935.
1942	The Famous Five is launched with *Five on a Treasure Island.*
1949	The first appearance of *The Secret Seven* and of *Noddy* mark this year as special.
1953	Enid moves away from *Sunny Stories* to launch *Enid Blyton's Magazine.* She is now renowned throughout the world – she even established her own company, called Darrell Waters Limited (the surname of her second husband).
1962	Enid Blyton becomes one of the first and most important children's authors to be published in paperback. Now, she reaches even more readers than ever before.
28 November 1968	Enid dies in her sleep, in a nursing home in Hampstead.

Enid's death wasn't the end of her remarkable legacy. In the 1970s the Famous Five became TV stars (Noddy having already hit our screens in 1955). In 1996 the Enid Blyton Society was formed so that fans across the world could share their enthusiasm for Enid's work (www.enidblytonsociety.co.uk) In 2012 the Famous Five celebrated seventy years of continuous publishing, with special editions featuring covers by top illustrators, led by Quentin Blake. New book, film and merchandising deals are being struck all the time. Enid's work is definitely here to stay!

MY SCHOOL DAYS: AN INTERVIEW WITH ENID BLYTON

What did you like most about school?

I loved school, every minute of it. I loved learning. The things I liked at kindergarten were the things I have liked best all my life: stories, music, nature and games.

What do you remember about school?

I remember everything about it: the room, the garden, the pictures on the wall, the little chairs, the dog there, and the lovely smells that used to creep out from the kitchen into our classroom. I remember how we used to take biscuits for our mid-morning break and swap them with one another – and how we used to dislike one small boy who was clever at swapping a small biscuit for a big one.

What was your best subject?

Essay and composition and story-writing.

What about your worst?

Sums. I hadn't the right kind of brain for figures and I used to look on in awe when I saw other boys and girls doing the most complicated sums.

We know you loved stories. Tell us about some of your favourites?

My favourite book as a child was called *The Princess and the Goblin* by George Macdonald, and I also loved *Coral Island* by R. M. Ballantyne. Other books I enjoyed include:

Alice in Wonderland and *Alice Through the Looking-Glass* by Lewis Carroll.

Black Beauty by Anna Sewell (even though parts of it were sad).

The Water Babies by Charles Kingsley.

Arthur Mee's Children's Encyclopedia – which I read from end to end. Nature books. Annuals. Magazines too.

Myths and legends from all around the world.

I liked poetry – even when I didn't really understand it.

I quite liked comics, but found they were like sweets – you sucked them for a few minutes, then they were gone, and you didn't think about them any more.

Were there any books you *didn't* enjoy?

I didn't like *all* stories. Some I found dull and boring, just as you do. There were no real children as characters, and it was children I badly wanted to read about. There were no lively conversations in the books. Nothing to really make me laugh.

The responses to those questions are based on comments by Enid Blyton in her autobiography, The Story of My Life *© Hodder & Stoughton, 1952.*

WHAT THEY DID AT MISS BROWN'S SCHOOL

In 1920 Enid Blyton became a governess to the four Thompson children, whose ages ranged from four to ten. The family lived in Surbiton, in Surrey, in a house called 'Southernhay'. Enid had a small room which overlooked the garden, and it was there that she wrote many of her stories. Enid's tiny class often had lessons outdoors in the summer months.

Enid was very popular with her students, because her lessons were both practical and creative. She worked with them to put on performances for which they made props, costumes and invitations – and even sold tickets.

In 1941 she published a long story called 'What They Did at Miss Brown's School', which was divided into monthly episodes. It's been hard to find for many years, but you can read extracts in these new editions of *The Naughtiest Girl* books. The character of Miss Brown and her tiny class is very much based on Enid Blyton and her school at the Thompsons' . . .

Here's the ninth extract . . .

9. September. Planning for the Springtime. Bulbs for the Classroom

WHEN THE children came back to school at the beginning of September, they were delighted to see that Miss Brown had set out a good many of their seashells on cards.

'You must print the names neatly underneath and let me see how many you remember,' said Miss Brown. 'And Mary shall hang the seaweed up outside the window and tell us each day what the weather is going to be!'

John saw that Miss Brown had put up a big blank Nature Chart on the wall. It was headed WINTER TERM.

'Oh, Miss Brown!' he said, making a face. 'Winter term! How horrid that sounds! Here we are still in summery weather, with the blue sky above and the sun so hot that I can't wear a coat – and you are going to make us keep a chart for the winter term!'

Miss Brown laughed. 'You will find it is winter when

the middle of November comes,' she said, 'and our swallows and martins are gone, and there are few flowers left and few leaves on the trees!'

'I like the spring best of all,' said Mary. 'I wish we could have a bit of spring in the middle of winter, Miss Brown – wouldn't it be lovely?'

'Well, I don't see why we shouldn't,' said Miss Brown unexpectedly. 'How would you like to smell the delicious sweetness of hyacinths in December, and to see the gold of daffodils and the red of tulips in the New Year?'

'Oh, yes, let's!' cried the children.

'How can we do that?' asked Mary.

'We'll plant all kinds of bulbs in bowls,' said Miss Brown. 'If we do them this month, the first of them will be out by Christmas, and we shall really feel that spring can't be very far off, even if snow is thick on the ground!'

'I can bring two bowls, Miss Brown,' said Susan. 'I've got two of my own at home.'

'Well, if you will all try to bring the bowls, I will buy the bulbs and the fibre to plant them in,' said Miss Brown. 'A friend has kindly given me some money to spend on flowers and I think it would be a fine way to spend it – to buy bulbs that will give us flowers in the middle of winter.'

Well, that week the children brought six bowls, big and small. There were two blue bowls, two green ones, a yellow one and a brown one. Miss Brown was so pleased. She brought out from the cupboard four tall glass vases, nipped in at the neck, which she said were hyacinth glasses.

'They are rather like acorn glasses, but much bigger,' said Susan. 'Do we just put the bulb at the top here, Miss Brown?'

'Yes, and we put water in up to the neck,' said Miss Brown, 'with a bit of charcoal to keep the water sweet – and the hyacinth bulb will put its roots out into the water and grow well.'

'Can we come with you to buy the bulbs?' asked John. 'What are you going to buy?'

'Well, we will have some white Roman hyacinths for one bowl,' said Miss Brown. 'They will be out in December. We will also have a bowl of paper white narcissi – they flower very early too.'

'And let's have some red tulips!' begged Mary.

'Very well,' said Miss Brown, 'and we must have some ordinary hyacinths as well – we'll get bright blue for this blue bowl.'

'And can we have some daffodils?' asked Peter. 'I do love those.'

'Yes, this deep, tall bowl will do for those,' said Miss Brown. 'They grow a bit leggy.'

'That leaves one empty bowl,' said Susan. 'Can I

choose something for it, Miss Brown? I'd like crocuses!'

'Yes, crocuses would be lovely in that little green bowl,' said Miss Brown. 'And we will grow red, white, blue and pink hyacinths in the glasses – one for each of you! We can set those on the windowsill and watch them. We shall not need to put them away in the dark, as we shall with the other bowls.'

'Let's go and buy the bulbs tomorrow!' cried John. So the next day they set out to get them. They soon arrived at the same shop where they had bought their garden seeds and Mr Millet, the shopman was pleased to see them.

'I've some fine bulbs,' he said, 'all ready prepared for growing early. It's no good growing ordinary garden bulbs in bowls, you know, Miss Brown – they won't come out any earlier than the ones out-of-doors. You want to buy specially prepared bowl bulbs.'

'Yes, I know,' said Miss Brown. 'Now, children, here are the hyacinths – big, round, fat bulbs with purplish-brown scales. Feel them and choose one good solid one for yourselves, any colour you like. Be sure the bulbs don't feel soft or pulpy – they will not grow if they are.'

Susan chose a fat hyacinth bulb that would have a blue flower. Mary chose a pink one, Peter chose a white one and John had a red one. Mr Millet put each into a small bag and wrote the colour on in pencil.

Miss Brown had chosen fifteen small Roman hyacinth bulbs. They were not nearly so big as the children's bulbs. 'But you see,' said Miss Brown, 'Roman hyacinths are almost like white bluebells – not really like the big hyacinths you see in gardens. The flowers are smaller, so the bulbs are smaller.'

Then she chose six fine blue hyacinths. They were for another bowl. Then she and the children picked out six brown-skinned daffodil bulbs, and six neat red-brown tulips.

'There are the paper white narcissi,' said Mr Millet, bringing some bulbs that looked rather like small daffodil bulbs. 'These will flower very early. How many will you have?'

They chose six. And then they looked at the little rounded crocus corms.

'These are not bulbs but corms,' explained Miss Brown. 'A corm is quite solid inside, but if you cut a bulb open you would see that it is more like an onion, and right in the middle you would fine the hidden leaves and flowers, waiting to grow. Now, we'll have twelve of these crocus corms – purple crocus, please, as the yellow corms do not seem to be very good.'

Then they bought a bag of brown fibre to grow the bulbs in, and off they went back to school, very happy indeed.

The next day they set to work to plant all their bulbs. They did have a fine time. Miss Brown emptied the fibre into a big enamel bowl.

'Now,' she said, 'you must pour water into the fibre, and work it about with your hands until it is thoroughly wet. It is just wet enough if you can squeeze it in your hands without water coming out. When it is all ready, pack it neatly into the bowls, about halfway up.'

This kept the children very busy. How they loved to feel the wet fibre in their hands! At last they had wet it enough, and they put some in the bowls.

'And now we will plant the bulbs,' said Miss Brown. 'Mary, put the Roman hyacinths into that green bowl. Settle them firmly on the fibre. Then neatly pack the bowl full to about an inch from the top. John, do the same with the narcissus bulbs. Peter, plant the daffodils, and Susan, you can do the tulips.'

Very soon four bowls were packed full. Miss Brown planted the blue hyacinths, and then the children found that there was not enough fibre for the sixth bowl!

'It doesn't matter,' said Miss Brown. 'We can grow crocuses in stones and water very nicely indeed – and we can put them straight away on the windowsill, and watch them grow instead of putting them away in the dark! John, go outside and collect about thirty little pebbles and wash them.'

John soon came in with thirty clean pebbles and he arranged some of them at the bottom of the crocus bowl. Miss Brown poured water in. It just reached to the top of the pebbles, but no more. Then John set the twelve crocus corms neatly on the stones. After that he packed the rest of the stones round the corms, so that only the tiniest bit of the little white shoots at the top could be seen.

'Good!' said Miss Brown. 'Now we will do our other hyacinth bulbs – the ones we want to grow in the hyacinth glasses.'

Mary filled each hyacinth glass with water. Then the children each put a bit of charcoal in the water and carefully set their fat bulbs at the top of the glass. They rested there nicely, just touching the water underneath.

'Set them on the windowsill,' said Miss Brown. 'The crocuses can go there too. I will put the other bowls away into a dark, airy cupboard. There is one in the kitchen. Carry the bowls, children, please.'

There was a little dark cupboard off the kitchen that had plenty of fresh air from an outside ventilator. Miss Brown set all the bowls on a shelf there.

'They must stay for some weeks in the dark,' she said, 'so that they will make plenty of root growth. Then, when their roots are well grown, and the shoot is beginning to sprout, we will put them in the classroom.

Once a week we must feel the fibre and, if it is dry, we must give a little water.'

It wasn't long before the hyacinths in the glasses put out tiny white roots into the water. After that they grew very quickly, and soon the water was full of roots! Susan's had the first and biggest roots. She was very proud.

The crocus corms grew roots too. Miss Brown took up a few of the top stones and showed the children how the roots were twining round and between the pebbles. She added a little more water, for the warmth of the classroom was drying it up.

'The white crocus shoots look like white animal's teeth growing up,' said Susan. And so they did!

It was very exciting when Miss Brown brought the bowls of bulbs out into the classroom in November. They had all grown fine strong roots and were now sending up fat green shoots.

'Miss Brown!' said Susan one day in December. 'Look! Is this a bud in the paper white narcissi – down here in between the leaves?'

It was! Everyone was very pleased, and when they saw how quickly the leaves and buds grew they were astonished. Then the Roman hyacinths put up buds too, and as Christmas drew near the children anxiously watched to see if the flowers would open.

All their own hyacinths were budding too, but would not be out till the New Year. The tulips would be out just at the beginning of January and the daffodils later still.

The week before the holidays the white Roman hyacinths were out in full flower! How lovely they were – just like white bluebells, with a very sweet scent indeed. They made the whole classroom smell nice. Then the paper white narcissi opened their sweet-smelling stars, and the classroom smelt twice as sweet! Really, it was lovely!

'You were right when you said that we would have a bit of spring in the middle of winter, Miss Brown,' said Mary, sniffing the hyacinths. 'This was a lovely thing to do! And how pleased I shall be when the purple crocuses are all out too, and the tulips shine red, and the big hyacinths hang out their scented bells! And how lovely the classroom will look when the bowl of golden daffodils is out!'

'The only thing I'm sorry about is that we can't use our bulbs again for bowls next year,' said Peter. 'The man said they wouldn't be any use.'

'Ah, but we can plant them out in the garden and they will flower for us there!' said Miss Brown. 'We will have a little bulb corner, shall we? And plant our bowl bulbs there each year! Isn't that a good idea!'

Enid Blyton®

THE FAMOUS FIVE

Join the Adventure!

Have you read them all?

Enid Blyton®

THE SECRET SEVEN

SOLVE THE MYSTERY!

HAVE YOU READ THEM ALL?

Enid Blyton

THE SECRET SEVEN

SOLVE THE MYSTERY!

Don't miss…

Two action-packed Secret Seven stories from prizewinning author **PAMELA BUTCHART**!

Enid Blyton®

THE

SECRET SEVEN

SOLVE THE MYSTERY!

Solve every puzzle, just like the Secret Seven, in this fun book of 100 tricky codes, puzzles, sudokus, crosswords and more!

THE MYSTERY SERIES

Read all 15 classic stories!

ENIDBLYTON.CO.UK

IS FOR PARENTS, CHILDREN AND TEACHERS!

Sign up to the newsletter on the homepage for a monthly round-up of news from the world of

Enid Blyton®

JOIN US ON SOCIAL MEDIA

EnidBlytonOfficial BlytonOfficial

Illustration by Laura Ellen Anderson.

Enid Blyton®

is one of the most popular children's authors of all time. Her books have sold over 500 million copies and have been translated into other languages more often than any other children's author.

Enid Blyton adored writing for children. She wrote over 700 books and about 2,000 short stories. *The Famous Five* books, now 80 years old, are her most popular. She is also the author of other favourites including *The Secret Seven*, *The Magic Faraway Tree* and *Malory Towers*.

Born in London in 1897, Enid lived much of her life in Buckinghamshire and loved dogs, gardening and the countryside. She was very knowledgeable about trees, flowers, birds and animals. Dorset – where some of the Famous Five's adventures are set – was a favourite place of hers too.

Enid Blyton's stories are read and loved by millions of children (and grown-ups) all over the world. Visit enidblyton.co.uk to discover more.

Illustration by Laura Ellen Anderson.

The NAUGHTIEST GIRL Saves the Day

Have you read them all?

1. The Naughtiest Girl in the School
2. The Naughtiest Girl Again
3. The Naughtiest Girl is a Monitor
4. Here's the Naughtiest Girl
5. The Naughtiest Girl Keeps a Secret
6. The Naughtiest Girl Helps a Friend
7. The Naughtiest Girl Saves the Day
8. Well Done, the Naughtiest Girl
9. The Naughtiest Girl Wants to Win
10. The Naughtiest Girl Marches On

Enid Blyton®

The Naughtiest Girl Saves the Day

WRITTEN BY
ANNE DIGBY

HODDER

HODDER CHILDREN'S BOOKS

First published in Great Britain in 1999 by Hodder & Stoughton
This edition published in 2021
For further information about the editorial history of this book, see enidblyton.co.uk/books

5 7 9 10 8 6

Enid Blyton® and Enid Blyton's signature are registered
trade marks of Hodder & Stoughton Limited
Text © 2021 Hodder & Stoughton Limited
Illustrations by Claire Powell © 2021 Hodder & Stoughton Limited

No trade mark or copyrighted material may be reproduced without the
express written permission of the trademark and copyright owner.

The moral right of the author has been asserted.

All characters and events in this publication, other than those clearly in the public domain, are fictitious and any resemblance to real persons, living or dead, is purely coincidental.

All rights reserved.
No part of this publication may be reproduced, stored in a retrieval system, or transmitted, in any form or by any means, without the prior permission in writing of the publisher, nor be otherwise circulated in any form of binding or cover other than that in which it is published and without a similar condition including this condition being imposed on the subsequent purchaser.

A CIP catalogue record for this book is available from the British Library.

ISBN 978 1 444 95866 9

Printed and bound in Great Britain by Clays Ltd, Elcograf S.p.A.

Typeset in Caslon by Avon DataSet Ltd, Alcester, Warwickshire

The paper and board used in this book are made from wood from responsible sources.

FSC www.fsc.org MIX Paper | Supporting responsible forestry FSC® C104740

Hodder Children's Books
An imprint of Hachette Children's Group
Part of Hodder & Stoughton
Carmelite House
50 Victoria Embankment
London EC4Y 0DZ

An Hachette UK Company
www.hachette.co.uk
www.hachettechildrens.co.uk

CONTENTS

INTRODUCTION

by Cressida Cowell

bestselling author of the
How to Train Your Dragon series

Like so many, many children before and after me, Enid Blyton's books played a crucial role in turning my nine-year-old self into a passionate reader.

That is because Enid Blyton had an extraordinary knack for writing the kind of books that children actually *want* to read, rather than the kind of books that adults think they *should* read.

Enid Blyton could tap into children's dreams, children's desires, children's wishes, with pinpoint accuracy. She knew that every child, however good and well-behaved they might look on the outside, secretly longed to be Elizabeth Allen, the naughtiest kid in the school. I'm afraid I entirely cheered Elizabeth on, as she defied her parents, the headmistresses, her schoolmates, and the very serious School Meetings. If anything, I wanted her to be even naughtier.

But *The Naughtiest Girl* books were really my favourite of Enid Blyton's school stories because of Whyteleafe, a very different school from Malory Towers or St Clare's. What if there could be a school in which discipline was administered by the children rather than the adults? In which all money was given in at the start of the term and distributed among the children along socialist lines? Wouldn't this be the kind of school that children would actually *want* to go to, rather than the kind of school that children *have* to go to?

It was an interesting proposition to a nine-year-old, and it remains an interesting proposition.

I hope you enjoy this story as much as I did when *I* was nine years old.

Cressida Cowell

CHAPTER ONE

ELIZABETH AND JULIAN ARE TOGETHER AGAIN

'PERHAPS THE train from London's running late!' said Elizabeth impatiently. 'Do you think so, Joan? Or perhaps the coach from the station has broken down! Do you think it could be stuck halfway up the hill with a flat tyre? Just imagine all the boys and girls having to sit inside the stuffy, hot coach waiting for the wheel to be changed . . .'

Elizabeth jigged from one foot to the other restlessly. She was at the top of the stone steps, outside the main doors of Whyteleafe School. Her gaze kept darting to the big stone archway through which the school coach was due to appear.

'. . . what do *you* think, Joan?' she finished.

Joan was Elizabeth's best friend at Whyteleafe School, although slightly older and in the second form. She was as calm and sensible as Elizabeth was excitable and impulsive. She shook her head and smiled at her friend.

'*I* think you have a vivid imagination, Elizabeth. That's what *I* think!' she said quietly. 'The coach is hardly late at all yet.'

'But it was due at half past one and that was five minutes ago!' protested Elizabeth. 'And I'm starving hungry, aren't you, Joan? And none of us can go into the dining hall and have dinner until everyone's back from half-term!'

It was true that Elizabeth was hungry and regretted the fact that dinner would be late today. The delicious smell of savoury pies baking in the big ovens had wafted over to her from the kitchens. And, much earlier, she had seen the domestic staff preparing heaps of new potatoes and carrots from the school gardens. They would no doubt be steaming merrily away by now. There was always an especially good meal after a holiday, when many boys and girls were hungry at the end of a long journey back to their boarding school.

But there was more to it than that.

'As a matter of fact, I'm really looking forward to seeing my class again, Joan,' she confessed. 'Especially Julian. I'm longing to tell him about the notice that Miss Ranger has put up on the noticeboard. It's going to make our English lessons really exciting!'

ELIZABETH AND JULIAN ARE TOGETHER AGAIN

Most of the first form had gone home for the half-term holiday, including Elizabeth's special friend, Julian. Elizabeth had stayed on at school for a summer camp in the grounds. There had been lots of ups and downs, but all in all it had been a wonderful adventure. Now she was looking forward to the second half of the summer term, sleeping in a proper bed again and life getting back to normal.

'Hello, Daniel! You're one of the last back!' she called out cheerfully, as an open-topped car cruised by. Daniel Carter was one of her classmates and only lived in the next village. As with any child who lived near Whyteleafe, he was being brought back to school by car. 'You should have been one of the first!'

The pale, fair-haired boy was sitting in the back of the open car, reading a book. He looked up briefly and returned Elizabeth's wave, then immediately turned his attention back to his book.

'Have you seen the coach?' she shouted. But the car had passed them now and her words were carried away on the breeze.

'It must be such fun to ride in an open car like that,' commented Joan. 'What an unusual boy Daniel is, nose stuck in a book as his father drives him along!'

'Yes, he does seem to prefer his books to the sights and sounds of the real world and to having friends,' agreed Elizabeth. 'I think shyness has a lot to do with it.'

'But he's a great one for complaining about people at School Meetings,' Joan pointed out. 'That's not the best way to make friends.'

'Yes, wasn't it funny that time he grumbled about Arabella making faces at him?' laughed Elizabeth. 'He makes himself sound such a baby when he stands up with silly grumbles and complaints. It's such a shame he can't learn to be a good mixer because then people would like him more.'

'I expect Whyteleafe will lick him into shape in time,' smiled Joan. 'You know that better than anyone, Elizabeth. When you first came here, you were the naughtiest girl in the school!'

'Yes. I've been trying to live it down ever since!' groaned Elizabeth. Her naughtiest girl nickname had stuck and no doubt always would! 'Oh, Joan, wasn't I horrid?' she sighed.

She stared across the green lawns to the trees beyond. A bird wheeled above them in the cloudless blue sky. It was so lovely at Whyteleafe, thought Elizabeth.

'I did everything I could think of to get myself sent home, didn't I?' she continued. 'From the best school in the whole world!'

'I'm so glad you didn't succeed,' said Joan quietly,

giving her friend's hand a squeeze. 'I really am.'

A few moments later a large coach with WHYTELEAFE SCHOOL on the front came nosing through the archway.

'It's here!' whooped Elizabeth. 'Hurray! Now *everybody's* back!'

The coach pulled up at the foot of the steps. All the boys and girls who had been on the London train came tumbling out. Elizabeth ran down to greet them. Joan, as befitted a second-form monitor, followed at a more dignified pace to meet some of her own classmates.

'Julian!' squealed Elizabeth, her brown curls bouncing.

'Hello, naughtiest girl!' grinned the dark-haired boy, his cousin, Patrick, just behind him. 'How was camp then?'

'It was wonderful! But listen, Julian, such an exciting notice has gone up on the board. Wait till you see it! Miss Ranger's just put it up this morning. It's our form's turn to put on the summer play this year! It will be performed outside, in the school grounds! If we want to try for a part, we've got to sign up on the notice. The auditions are going to take place during English lessons!' Elizabeth had been bottling this news up for over an hour and it was now pouring out like a torrent.

'Oh, Julian, wouldn't it be fun if you and I could get the lead parts? The play's called *A Woodland Adventure* and it's been written by the joint heads!'

She tugged at Julian's hand. 'Come on, let's run. If we hurry, we'll be the first to get our names on the list—'

'Hey, steady on, Miss Whirlwind—' began Julian, looking amused.

'Yes, steady on, Elizabeth,' smiled Miss Thomas, as she shepherded the last of the children off the coach. She could see that the naughtiest girl was trying to whisk Julian away! 'Julian's not allowed to disappear off anywhere at the moment. Everyone from the London train's been given strict instructions to go straight to the dining hall, as soon as they've washed their hands and faces. I suggest you do the same, Elizabeth. We're all very hungry. Whatever it is it will have to wait.'

Elizabeth sighed and knew that she would have to be patient.

CHAPTER TWO

ELIZABETH'S HOPES ARE KEPT ALIVE

JULIAN REFUSED to hurry through dinner. He was very hungry and wanted second helpings of everything. Elizabeth had to agree that the savoury pie was one of the tastiest that Cook had ever baked. The new potatoes and carrots were mouthwatering. And pudding was treacle tart and custard, one of their favourites.

It was a very jolly meal, with everyone catching up on everyone else's news. Some of the children had been to see shows in London. Ruth and Tessa had been taken to Regent's Park Zoo by Tessa's mother. Patrick had been at Lord's all week with his father, watching the cricket. Patrick was slightly boring on the subject but Elizabeth didn't mind at all, feeling happy to be surrounded by her classmates once again. Julian claimed that he had done absolutely nothing apart from laze around and go swimming once or twice.

Elizabeth, Belinda and Kathleen enjoyed telling the others about school camp. Arabella, who had behaved badly at camp and got into trouble, was suitably subdued.

'What's the matter, Arabella? Didn't you enjoy camping out very much?' asked Julian lightly. He was always very quick and shrewd. 'You don't seem to be saying very much about it.'

The spoilt girl screwed up her dainty, doll-like face and gave a little shrug.

'It was all right,' she murmured.

Elizabeth had no intention of telling tales on Arabella, but she felt a quiet satisfaction. Arabella not saying much made a very pleasant change!

However, this happy state of affairs didn't last long.

At the end of the meal the conversation turned to the exciting news about the first-form play. Kathleen, like Elizabeth, had seen the notice that Miss Ranger, their form teacher, had placed on the noticeboard and she had been spreading the news.

'Let's all go and put our names down for it!' she said. 'Oh, won't it be fun, doing the auditions in English lessons?'

'I've put my name down already,' announced Arabella. 'And I've read the play! As soon as Miss Ranger put the notice up, I asked to borrow a copy. It's absolutely brilliant.'

'It's all about a little girl called Fay who falls asleep in the woods!' interrupted Arabella's friend, Rosemary. She was very excited. 'When Fay wakes up, she's turned into a beautiful fairy queen and she has all these wonderful adventures with a goblin called Jonkin and they meet all these woodland creatures . . .'

'Miss Belle and Miss Best wrote the play themselves,' said Arabella knowledgeably. 'They wrote it especially for us. Apparently it's five years since the first form had a turn of performing the summer play and they want it to be really special. Oh, aren't the joint heads clever to have written a whole new play?'

'And the part of Fay is just *made* for Arabella!' gabbled Rosemary. 'Can't you just see her as a fairy queen? I can. Of course,' she added quickly, 'there will be lots of other parts for everyone and lots of things to do, like making costumes and things. I'm hoping to be chosen as prompter,' she added modestly.

Elizabeth listened to all this in stunned silence.

Arabella and Rosemary were now getting up from the table, keen to be off. Rosemary was still gabbling in excitement.

'Shall we go and get the play from your desk, Arabella? We'll take it outside as you suggested! I'm longing to hear you read bits out loud. It will be good practice for you! I wonder which boy will be chosen to play Jonkin? Oh, that's going to be a good part too, isn't it—'

Arabella turned back and gave Julian a dazzling smile.

'I think Julian would make a wonderful Jonkin!' she simpered. 'Jonkin wears a mask in the play, but he has green eyes, just like Julian, and he's very funny and clever. I do hope you'll put your name down, Julian!'

As the two girls left the dining hall, Elizabeth bent her head over the last of her treacle tart, struggling to keep calm. In a blur she heard some of the others chattering as they started to drift away from the table . . .

'My goodness! Arabella's staked her claim quickly, hasn't she?'

'Trust her!'

'You have to admit she *might* make a good fairy queen. She'd look the part at least, with that dainty little face of hers.'

'Too doll-like. Not vivacious enough.'

'Well, let's go and have a look at this notice.'

'Might as well put our names down. It's going to be fun.'

Before long, only Elizabeth, Julian and Patrick were left sitting at the long table, all on their own.

'I *knew* we should have rushed and put our names on the list, Julian!' she said crossly, trying hard not to scowl.

Arabella had got her name down first. Probably right at the head of the list! Not only that, she'd got hold of a copy of the play already. She'd read it through and was about to start practising for the auditions. 'Now Arabella's got a head start on everybody else!'

'Well, blowed if I would want to play the part of a fairy queen!' said Julian. He was laughing at her. 'And, if *you* want to, Elizabeth, you'd better stop scowling and looking like a Bold, Bad Girl and practise looking pretty!'

'I don't know *what* I want now,' said Elizabeth sulkily. 'Perhaps Arabella *would* be best. Perhaps I wouldn't be any good. And besides she's got her name at the top of the list now.'

'You silly bumpkin.' Julian tweaked her hair. 'As if that makes the slightest difference to anything! Miss Ranger will just give out the parts to whoever reads them best when the auditions take place. I should think Arabella would be much too wooden. Now, you just run along, and sign up as you said you were going to.'

Elizabeth immediately felt cheerful again.

'I will too!' she exclaimed, smiling and clapping her hands. 'But . . .'

She looked at Julian anxiously.

'. . . what about you, Julian? Surely you want to be in the play too? It won't be half as much fun if you're not in it. Arabella's probably right about you being the goblin. I can just imagine you!'

Julian yawned. 'I don't think acting's quite my line, Elizabeth,' he said gently.

Patrick, sitting further along the table and toying with the last of his treacle tart, suddenly looked up when Julian said that.

Elizabeth was about to start arguing with Julian. She knew perfectly well that her friend was a natural actor, brilliant at voices and imitations and altogether very funny. What he really meant was that the idea of being in the first-form play bored him. How typical. How mean of him!

But, before she could open her mouth to protest, Patrick spoke for the first time. He had been looking rather gloomy, but now he had suddenly perked up. He couldn't help being a little jealous of his cousin, who was so full of talent, so good at everything he touched. To hear Julian being praised, even by Arabella, had made him smart.

'Glad to hear you've got some sense in your head after all, Julian,' he said. 'Wouldn't like to see my dear cousin make a complete fool of himself.'

'Oh, so that's what you think, is it?' asked Julian sharply.

He suddenly got to his feet. 'Come on, Elizabeth.

Let's go along and sign up for this play then.'

Patrick watched them go, open-mouthed.

'I thought you didn't want to be in it!' he said crossly.

Julian glanced back over his shoulder. 'I've changed my mind,' he said carelessly. 'It should be fun. A chance to make a complete fool of myself!'

As the two of them left the dining hall and headed towards the school noticeboard, Elizabeth felt rather sorry for Julian's cousin. She might have guessed that, whatever Patrick wanted, Julian would want to do the exact opposite.

As they wrote their names up on the list, she felt hopeful all over again. It would be wonderful to be chosen for the lead part and to play opposite Julian. He would make everything such fun.

Who else had signed up? She looked at the names. There were slightly more girls than boys so far. But there was one name that was rather unexpected.

'Look, Julian!' she exclaimed. 'Daniel Carter's signed up.'

All through dinner he had, as usual, sat furtively reading a book under the table and not taken the slightest interest in the conversation about the play. Daniel never joined in any activities that he could possibly avoid.

'What a surprise,' said Julian. 'Do you think he's hoping for the main boy's part, the goblin?'

Elizabeth laughed happily.

'With you around, Julian,' she replied, 'I'm afraid he'll just have to hope away!'

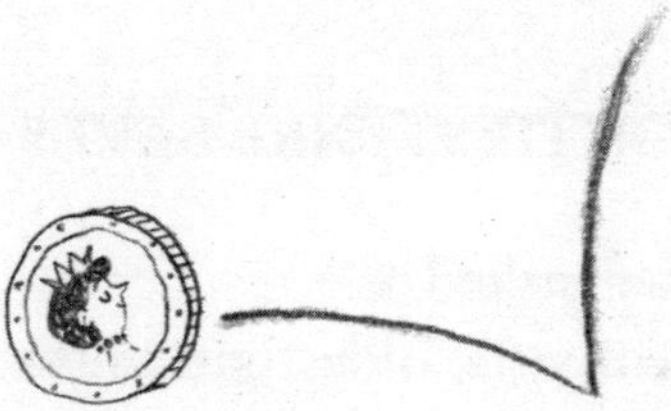

CHAPTER THREE

DANIEL DROPS A MYSTERIOUS HINT

IN THE English lesson the next day Daniel hardly looked like somebody hoping to land a good part in the play. He seemed rather glum about the whole thing!

'Here's yours, Daniel,' said Miss Ranger brightly, as she finished handing out copies of the play to those who had signed up. 'When you read it, you will find it's a very good play. I want you to study it carefully over the next few days and decide which part to try for. You must learn some lines from your favourite part. And –' the teacher looked up and smiled round at the class – 'the same thing applies to the rest of you. Please try to learn some of the lines you wish to speak when we have the auditions next week. You'll be able to act a part so much better if you do not have to read it from the script.'

'I've learnt some of my lines already!' piped up Arabella smugly.

'Are you sure?' asked the teacher kindly. She knew how much difficulty the oldest girl in the form had with memorising things.

Elizabeth was pleased that the auditions were still a few days away. They would be held during English lessons next week and the joint heads would be sitting in on some of the judging! Arabella had tried to steal a march, but now they all had a chance to catch up. It was very pleasing.

Daniel, however, did not look in the least bit pleased. Elizabeth, sitting on the corner of Julian's desk and eagerly leafing through the play, had noticed how reluctantly the fair-haired boy had collected his copy, the last member of the class to do so. Now he walked back to his desk, opened the lid and placed it inside without even glancing at it. Then he sat down and folded his arms.

As Miss Ranger addressed the class, he looked glummer than ever. She was telling them how, later on, rehearsals for the play would have to take place out of school hours – and in the fresh air. As the summer play was always held out-of-doors, it would be good practice for the children to get used to acting outside!

Daniel hated any form of outdoor activity. He was one of the few children at Whyteleafe to have his own tiny room, up on the attic floor above the main dormitories. Summer or winter, he loved his cosy little room under the eaves, where he could read his favourite storybooks to his heart's content.

'So be prepared to give up some spare time, those of you who are chosen,' concluded the teacher. 'We have so much other work to get through in English lessons. Remember, you have exams at the end of term and very important ones too, for those who wish to go up to the second form in September. So now –' she clapped her hands briskly – 'stop talking, everyone, please, and return to your desks and get out your spelling books.'

But by now Elizabeth was chattering away non-stop to Julian.

'Doesn't the story look fun, Julian? I *can* just see you as Jonkin! I don't in the least mind giving up my spare time if I'm chosen, do you? I'll have to skip some of my piano practice! But have you noticed something?' She lowered her voice to a whisper. 'Have you noticed how grumpy Daniel looks about the whole thing? I can't imagine anyone who would hate acting more, especially out-of-doors! So why did he put his name down?'

'I think there's probably a very simple answer,' Julian whispered back. He too had noted carefully Daniel's attitude. 'I don't think the poor boy wants to be in the play at all. I think one of the teachers *ordered* him to put his name down for it. Perhaps Miss Ranger herself.

It must worry them a bit, the way he never joins in anything.'

'Oh, Julian! You are clever!' responded Elizabeth. 'Yes, that must be the answer—'

'ELIZABETH!' exclaimed Miss Ranger. 'Please stop talking and get off Julian's desk. Julian, please get your spelling book out as you have been asked to do. I think I will have to separate you two.'

The teacher looked round the room and then pointed to an empty desk, all on its own, at the back of the classroom under the open window.

'Elizabeth, please get your books and move to that desk at the back. You love talking so much that I think it will be better for you.' She spoke to the little girl quite kindly. 'You will be out of temptation's way there and I know I can trust you to pay attention and work hard, even right at the back there.'

'Yes, Miss Ranger,' replied Elizabeth.

Julian looked at his friend apologetically, but Elizabeth did not mind in the least. She knew that Miss Ranger was acting for the best and, besides, it was a lovely place, there by the open window. There were soft summer scents wafting in on the warm breeze. The last thing Elizabeth wanted to do at present was to blot her copybook by talking to her friends in class. Now any temptation to do so had been removed.

She pondered upon what Julian had said. *Poor Daniel!* she thought.

But the very same day, at the end of the afternoon, Daniel caused them another surprise.

Once lessons were finished for the day Elizabeth and Julian went for a short ride in the grounds on the ponies. Emerging from the trees afterwards, they dismounted and walked the horses back to the school stables. A boy was leaning against one of the stable doors, as though enjoying the sunshine. He waved cheerfully when he saw them and hurried forward to greet them.

'Hello, Julian! Hello, Elizabeth!' he exclaimed, while patting the horses' necks. 'Isn't it a lovely day! Have you had a good ride?' It was Daniel.

The two friends unsaddled their horses and rubbed them down, at the same time glancing at each other in astonishment. It was such a surprise to see Daniel out in the fresh air! He looked so happy too. His cheeks were flushed and there was an air of suppressed excitement about him. What could have happened to bring about such a change in him? It was most perplexing.

'Isn't it a grand day?' he repeated, once the ponies were unsaddled. 'Here, I'll put the tack away for you and shut the ponies up for Mr Tucker, the stableman.'

'Will you really?' said Julian gratefully.

'That's sweet of you, Daniel,' said Elizabeth.

They dumped the tack and were about to leave when—

'Do you two know when the next School Meeting is?' the boy blurted out eagerly.

'Friday,' replied Elizabeth. 'Why?'

'Planning a complaint, Daniel?' asked Julian teasingly. 'Or possibly a grumble?'

The boy flushed. 'No, not at all. Nobody's done anything to annoy me at present,' he said solemnly. 'I've got a special request to make to the Meeting, that's all. A *very* special request!'

'Whatever's that?' asked Elizabeth, fascinated.

'I – I'm sorry, I can't tell you. Not yet . . .'

'Oh, please do!' begged Elizabeth. 'Why can't you tell us?'

'I – I've got to see how things go,' mumbled the boy. 'I'm sorry. I shouldn't have said anything. I didn't mean to intrigue you . . .'

He looked apologetic.

'Fair enough,' said Julian, turning to walk away.

Daniel hurried forward and grabbed Julian's arm. 'But please, if I do . . . when I do ask the Meeting this thing, I do hope you two will support me. Please.'

Elizabeth was more intrigued than ever. 'I'm sure we will if we can, Daniel.'

'Once we know what it is!' laughed Julian.

It was such a surprising episode. The two friends

talked about it all the way back to the school building. Daniel had seemed so very different from his usual self.

'Whatever's happened to him?' wondered Julian. 'Can that be the same chap who looked so glum in English this morning?'

An anxious thought suddenly crossed Elizabeth's mind.

'You don't think it's because he's read the play by now? And he's realised what a brilliant play it is and how brilliant the part of Jonkin is, and how this is his big chance to shine . . . ?'

She hated the idea of anyone other than Julian having the part.

'Hardly! He'd be up in that little room of his, learning it off by heart, not enjoying himself in the fresh air for a change,' replied Julian. 'No, I'm sure it's not that. But something's transformed him all right.'

'Can it be to do with this mysterious request he wants to put to the School Meeting?' pondered Elizabeth. 'I can't think what it's going to be.'

'We'll find out,' said Julian airily, 'soon enough.'

CHAPTER FOUR

AN INTERESTING SCHOOL MEETING

ON FRIDAY, lessons over for the week, Elizabeth ran up to the dormitory and got ready for the School Meeting. She washed her hands and brushed her hair and decided that today she would wear her school blazer, even though it was still a bit big for her. As she did up the shiny silver buttons and looked in the mirror, she felt a happy, belonging sort of feeling.

She was proud to wear the blazer and to be a member of Whyteleafe School. She admired the way that William and Rita, the head boy and head girl, ran the Meetings with the pupils themselves making all kinds of important decisions about any problems that arose, without any help from the teachers.

As she filed into the gym with Belinda, Kathleen and Jenny, she looked at her watch. They were early. But somebody else had got there ahead of them.

Daniel, usually one of the last, was seated very near the front at the far end of an empty bench. The girls took their places alongside him and Elizabeth noticed how spruce he looked. He was sitting upright, arms folded, waiting for the Meeting to begin. He seemed very alert. There was still the same air of suppressed excitement about him that had been there for some days.

Others, as well as Elizabeth and Julian, had noticed the change in Daniel. Although he still took a book with him everywhere, he was spending much more time out-of-doors. He looked happier and more lively. He had even begun to take an interest in the summer play. Apparently he'd learnt bits from several different parts and had shyly asked Martin to test him.

Well, now we shall find out more at last, thought Elizabeth. *He looks quite keyed up about this special request of his, whatever it is!*

The twelve school monitors came and took their places on the platform behind William and Rita, who were seated at a special table. There was a big book on the table. Important things that happened at Meetings were always written down in the Book. The scene never failed to remind Elizabeth of a courtroom, with William and Rita as the Judges and the monitors, the Jury.

The hall soon filled up as all the classes came in. Miss

Belle and Miss Best, the joint heads, and Mr Johns, the senior master, slipped quietly into their special chairs, right at the back. They were there to observe proceedings, but never joined in unless their advice was requested.

When everybody was seated and the hubbub of chatter was reaching a crescendo, William picked up a small hammer and struck the table loudly.

'Silence, please! The Meeting will now begin.'

As the gavel went down, Elizabeth, as always, felt a frisson of excitement. There was an instant hush all around her. What would today's Meeting bring?

'First of all, finance,' said William. 'A lot of you will have brought money back with you. Thomas is passing the school box along the rows. Please place all your money inside.'

There came the rustle of banknotes and the merry rattle of coins going into the big box as the children cheerfully parted with their money. Some of the campers had been sent postal orders. They went into the box too. It was a strict rule at Whyteleafe that all spending money was pooled and then shared out fairly, so that no pupil had an unfair advantage over another.

After that every child in the school was handed two shillings. This was their spending money for the week.

'Now, are there any requests for extra money?' asked the head girl.

Eileen put her hand up.

'Please, Rita, I broke a string in my racket at team practice yesterday. We've got a match soon, but Mr Warlow has had a look at it and he feels the racket's so worn that I really need to have a new one and just keep the old one as a spare.'

Rita had a quick word with William and they both nodded.

'That tennis racket of yours has had a lot of wear and tear this term in the service of the school, Eileen,' smiled Rita. 'No wonder it's worn out. You will be allocated some money to buy a new one.'

Patrick, who was in the second tennis team with Eileen, looked pleased for her sake. Now she would play even better.

The next request was rather more difficult to deal with.

A member of the junior class (which always sat cross-legged on the floor in the front of the first-form benches) rose to his feet.

'Please, I'm getting very keen on tennis now we're starting to learn, but I haven't got my own racket. There's one in the school second-hand shop and it only costs five shillings. Could I have some extra money to help me buy it?'

The head boy and girl went into a huddle with

the monitors to discuss the request. After two or three minutes they returned to the table and William called for silence.

'We don't think we can donate you any money from the pool, Henry, because it wouldn't be fair on any other juniors who don't own a racket. What we are prepared to do is to advance you your next two weeks' pocket money. With today's money that would mean you have six shillings.'

The little boy looked very disappointed. 'But then, please, William, that would only leave me a shilling for sweets and things to last me three whole weeks!'

'Yes, Henry,' said Rita kindly. 'So this offer is a good test for you. It will help you to decide just *how* keen you are on tennis and how much you want your own racket, rather than using the school ones while you're learning. Think about it for a while. Then let us know at the end of the Meeting what you have decided.'

'Yes, Rita.'

'Any more requests for money, anybody?' she asked.

Elizabeth glanced sidelong at Daniel. But he remained silent.

So whatever he intended to ask for then did not require spending money.

The Meeting moved briskly on to discuss the school camp. William proposed a vote of thanks for the tent monitors, explaining that they had all done an excellent job. Sitting on the platform, Joan looked proud and gave Elizabeth a grateful wave. Only they knew about the problems she had had as a tent monitor and how they had been overcome.

After that came grumbles or complaints. There were none at all this week.

'Good,' said William. 'We have just one more important matter to deal with. After that we will finish up with Any Other Business . . .'

'Nearly there, Daniel,' whispered Elizabeth behind her hand, smiling. 'You'll soon be able to ask what you want to ask.'

'I know!' nodded Daniel, looking eager and excited.

Elizabeth suddenly noticed how solemn William was looking.

'I'm sorry to have to tell you,' William was saying, 'that the matter we now have to deal with is a serious one. John, would you please stand up and tell the Meeting what you have told Rita and me?'

John Terry, the head boy of the school garden and one of Elizabeth's favourite people, rose to his feet. He was a blunt, straightforward boy who had great gifts as a gardener, but none for public speaking.

'Some little idiot's been vandalising the strawberry beds!' he blurted out, dark spots of anger on his cheeks.

'Somebody too greedy to wait for the fruit to get ripe! Pulling up the plants to see if any of the underneath berries are red yet, I dare say. Uprooting the plants with all the berries still green!'

There were shocked gasps around the hall. Whispers rippled up and down the rows of children. What a mean thing to do! Another month of ripening sun and the school gardens always produced big, luscious red strawberries – heaps of them. Strawberries and cream for tea . . . They all loved strawberry time! But any plants pulled up by the roots would die now before the fruit could ripen properly.

'How greedy and silly!' whispered Elizabeth.

'Greedy and silly and ignorant,' agreed Kathleen.

William banged the gavel for silence. There was more drama to come. He held something up between his thumb and forefinger. Everybody looked at it.

It was a shiny silver blazer button.

'Here is something very interesting,' he said. 'The person concerned lost their blazer button while they were hunting for strawberries. John found this lying among the uprooted plants. Would the person responsible now own up,' he said, with heavy irony, 'and we can give them their blazer button back.'

There was silence.

'Stand up and own up, please,' repeated William.

They all held their breath and waited. A half-minute ticked by. But still nobody moved.

'Very well,' said William at last. 'Whoever behaved in this stupid way will no doubt have friends and classmates. *They* will notice that someone has a blazer button missing. Will they please persuade the person concerned to come to our study and own up? John has a great number of jobs in the garden waiting for them. Now, is there any other business, please, before we close the Meeting?'

In the drama of what had just taken place Elizabeth had forgotten all about Daniel's special request. But she glanced at him now. He too seemed to have forgotten it! He was just sitting there, staring into space.

'Come on, Daniel!' she whispered, giving him a nudge.

The boy gave a start. Then, slowly, he put his hand up.

'Yes, Daniel?' asked Rita.

'I . . . I—' The fair-haired boy got to his feet, looking very self-conscious. Now that his big moment had come, he seemed embarrassed and tongue-tied. Poor Daniel! Elizabeth felt sorry for him. It was obviously something very important to him. It was daunting to have to ask in front of the whole school like this.

'Go on!' she encouraged.

'Please can I help with the horses and muck out the stables and things?' he blurted out. 'I know Robert helps sometimes and I'd like to as well.'

Rita looked at Daniel in surprise. This was hardly something that needed to be brought to a School Meeting.

'Well, only Mr Tucker can decide that, Daniel,' she said gently. 'I'm sure he'll be pleased to have some extra help and can find you some jobs to do. You must go and talk to him about it.'

Daniel sat down. His face was bright red.

Elizabeth stared at him in amazement. He had never taken the slightest interest in the school stables before. He was one of the few children in the class who never rode. But, above all, she felt cheated somehow. A sense of disappointment. Whatever had Daniel been making such a fuss about?

'What a let down!' she said to Julian, after the Meeting. 'What was so special about that? Why did he beg us to support him the other day? What a fuss about nothing! Oh, Julian, I do think Daniel is peculiar!'

'He's certainly a puzzle,' said Julian, with a shrug. 'But I'm more interested in this strawberry mystery.'

CHAPTER FIVE

THE AUDITIONS TAKE PLACE

'THE MYSTERY of who pulled up the strawberry plants? You're right, Julian,' nodded Elizabeth. 'That *is* rather interesting!'

It was annoying of Daniel to have been so tantalising about something so tame. But now the Meeting had given them something different to think about! Poor John. What a shock it must have been to find some of his plants uprooted. Elizabeth fully intended to spend some time in the school gardens this weekend and ask for some jobs to do. Could any of the plants be rescued?

'What puzzles me is why they didn't own up,' said Julian. 'People usually do.'

'Too scared, I suppose!' sighed Elizabeth. 'Too scared and cowardly.'

'But they must know they're going to be found out,' reasoned Julian, digging his hands deep in his pockets.

He looked at the three gleaming silver buttons on Elizabeth's blazer. 'Our school blazers only have three buttons on them. If you've lost one of them, you can't exactly hide the fact!'

'Yes,' agreed Elizabeth. 'And wasn't it funny to be wearing a blazer in the first place? I know I wouldn't wear mine if I was just messing about in the school gardens.'

'That's exactly what I was thinking,' replied Julian.

'But it's lucky they were!' said Elizabeth cheerfully. 'That blazer button is a wonderful clue. It's bound to catch them out before long. We could do some detective work ourselves, Julian. We'll start looking at everybody who's wearing a blazer.'

'Quite wrong, Elizabeth!' replied Julian.

'Wrong, why?' asked Elizabeth indignantly.

Julian looked amused. 'We must start looking at everybody who *isn't* wearing a blazer. There will be somebody, somewhere, who never wants to wear their blazer for some reason!'

'Because they're too scared?' realised Elizabeth. 'Oh, of course.'

'Yes. And that's going to be much more difficult. An interesting challenge.'

They both agreed to keep their eyes open. They were not the only ones.

The mystery of the vandalised strawberry plants

was a major talking point as they went into tea that day. Everybody wearing a blazer was subjected to scrutiny, Elizabeth included! She quickly became tired of people making teasing remarks about her being the 'naughtiest girl', as they came up and counted the buttons on her blazer!

The following morning she went along to the school gardens. She found John Terry netting the strawberry beds. He was very pleased to see her.

'Hello, Elizabeth. How good to see my best little helper! This job can be done quite quickly now there are two of us.'

Elizabeth was relieved to see that the majority of the strawberry plants remained untouched and were bushing out well, with plenty of green fruit. The uprooted ones from the first row had now been tidied up into a small heap beside the path. They were already withering and well beyond being saved. They were mostly poor, thin things, she noticed, with not many berries on them. So the damage to the strawberry crop had not been as bad as feared then. How stupid of someone to expect to find some ripe fruit in this way.

'I don't usually net the plants so soon,' explained John, as they unrolled the lengths of fine green netting and placed them carefully over the beds. 'They're to stop the birds getting at the ripe fruit – especially the blackbirds! They take not the slightest interest until they see a strawberry that's red and luscious and at its very peak! If you see a blackbird pecking at one, you can be quite sure that it has just reached its very moment of perfection!'

'How very clever of them!' laughed Elizabeth, her mouth watering as she remembered the days of strawberries and cream at the end of term last summer. 'I wonder how they know? So you've decided to prepare the defences well in advance?'

'Yes,' nodded John.

Once the nets were laid in place they staked them down by driving small pegs in the ground all the way round the edges. The birds, John explained, would try to wriggle under them if they saw any good gaps.

'Then, as often as not, they can't find their way out again!' he explained. 'They get in such a panic before they manage to escape. Sometimes you find an especially silly one tangled in the netting and you have to release it. However, that won't happen for a while yet.'

When they had finished, Elizabeth straightened up and arched her back. It had been hard work. She surveyed the covered beds with a sigh of satisfaction.

'Did you decide to net them early because of what one of the children has done, John?' she asked quietly.

He nodded. 'Yes. If anyone's ever tempted to meddle

with the strawberry plants again, it will remind them not to,' he said. 'Silly young idiots. I'm very surprised that nobody's owned up yet. But that blazer button is going to give them away.'

'It certainly is,' agreed Elizabeth. 'And I'm sure they won't dare to do it again!'

When she found Julian later, she learnt that he had been going round with Harry, questioning people about blazer buttons.

'We've been getting lots of rude answers, I'm afraid,' he said, with a grin. He yawned. 'This could prove to be quite a long job.'

'The damage isn't quite as bad as John made it sound,' said Elizabeth. 'There should still be plenty of strawberries for tea when it comes to end-of-term time! Perhaps we should wait a while and see if the person owns up. Oh, Julian, surely they will?'

For by now Elizabeth's mind was turning back to the summer play.

On the way back from helping John Terry she had seen Arabella, with the faithful Rosemary, over by the cedar tree, trying to say some lines off by heart while Rosemary held the script and acted as prompter.

Now that Elizabeth had read *A Woodland Adventure* through from beginning to end, she longed more than ever to be chosen for the leading girl's role. There were such sparkling lines for Fay to speak, especially in the scenes with Jonkin, the funny goblin who – surely! – could only be played by Julian.

And the two main parts would be auditioned first, on Monday! The joint heads were coming along and would give their opinions to Miss Ranger, although leaving her with the final decision. Later in the week, in other English lessons, the rest of the parts would be given out.

'Julian, we must decide which bits we want to act out on Monday,' said Elizabeth, 'and then we'd better learn the lines off by heart. Will you test me when I've learnt mine?'

'I'll test you tomorrow,' promised Julian, who had arranged to play tennis with Harry for now. 'Mind you learn them well!'

By Sunday evening Julian had still not bothered to learn any lines of his own and treated the whole thing in his usual casual way.

'Stop fussing, Elizabeth. I haven't decided which bit I want to act out yet. I'll get something together by tomorrow, I dare say.'

Elizabeth, on the other hand, had learnt three different sections of Fay's part, skimping most of her prep that weekend in order to do so.

'I'll act out each bit in turn, Julian, and you tell me which one you think is best.'

Julian watched and listened attentively and gave her some good acting tips too, as she went along.

'I liked the first one best,' he said, at the end. 'When Fay wakes up in the woods and finds that she's turned into a fairy queen and she thinks she's all alone until Jonkin peeps out from behind the tree! You do it very well. Do you know something? I think you could be a real star!'

He looked really proud of her as he said it. Elizabeth's mouth went dry with excitement. She could hardly wait for the auditions to begin.

When Elizabeth arrived for English the next day, she noticed Julian already in his place, casually flicking through the pages of the script. So he still hadn't learnt any lines! By the look of him, he was only just starting to think about it. Elizabeth felt cross. But she knew that she must concentrate hard now and not let anything distract her.

'We will start with Fay's part,' the teacher was saying. 'Belinda, would you like to go first, please?'

Miss Belle and Miss Best, the joint heads, were sitting at the front with Miss Ranger. Belinda stood up and launched into her lines. It was all very exciting. Elizabeth watched and held her breath and wondered how well Belinda would do.

She had chosen a tender scene in the play where Fay

finds the injured Mr Badger in the woods. She acted it out quite well, though she did forget her lines once or twice. When she sat down, everybody clapped her.

'Your turn now, Elizabeth,' smiled Miss Ranger.

'May I sit on the floor, under the window here, please?' asked Elizabeth. 'You will all have to imagine I'm sitting under the big tree, just waking up from a sleep, right at the beginning of the play.'

The joint heads nodded in approval. They were enjoying seeing their play start to come alive. Everybody in the class turned round to watch Elizabeth's performance. Somehow she riveted the attention.

She began by stretching and yawning and then opening her eyes. She stared all around her in wonderment.

'*Why am I here? Where have I been?*'

Then she stood up and ran her hands down her clothes.

'*Why am I dressed as a fairy queen?*'

Elizabeth continued her monologue, word perfect, acting it out as she went. She sighed, she gasped, she pirouetted, as she discovered the beautiful woods for the first time. It all seemed so real. She ended by subsiding back down to the floor again, once more under her 'tree', her voice a little sad.

'. . . *but when nightfall comes I'll be all alone.*

And missing my dearest friend from home.'

She gave a big sigh, as the script had directed.

Her performance should have ended at that point. But suddenly Julian stood on his chair, jumped off, hopped lightly over to Elizabeth's desk then ducked behind it. He peered at her round the corner, pretending the desk was a tree. Face screwed up like a goblin's, green eyes sparkling, he launched into Jonkin's part.

'*Alone my foot, alone my thumb,*

Come, my Royal Highness. Come!'

He pulled Elizabeth to her feet and danced her round the desk.

'*You'll meet new friends in this wood so green*

And all of them love their fairy queen!'

It was so unexpected that Elizabeth laughed in excitement. Her audition really was over now and her classmates were cheering and clapping. The teachers were smiling too. But then Miss Ranger held up a hand for silence.

'Very good, Julian. But we're not auditioning for Jonkin's part yet. Your turn will come in a few minutes. Thank you, Elizabeth. Now let us see what Arabella can do, please.'

Arabella was the third and final girl asking to be considered for the part of Fay. She rose to her feet, face pale with tension.

'Please, Miss Ranger, I've learnt the same bit as Elizabeth. The opening bit. And I was planning to sit and lean against the wall, just as she did.'

'That's perfectly all right, Arabella,' said Miss Ranger gently.

The fair-haired girl, looking as pretty as a picture, went and sat on the floor under the window – very much as Elizabeth had done.

Biting her lip in annoyance, Elizabeth had to watch and listen as her rival repeated all her actions. She stretched, she yawned, she opened her eyes . . .

'*Why am I here? Where have I been?*'

Arabella was striving hard to be expressive. It was a good effort – and there was no doubt that she looked the part.

But then, on her second line, she made a silly mistake. Carefully imitating Elizabeth's action and smoothing down her clothes, she said,

'*Why am I queened as a fairy dress?*'

Snorts and giggles broke out round the classroom and Miss Ranger had to bang the table for silence. Stumblingly, Arabella corrected herself and carried on through the opening monologue.

In spite of fluffing some more lines, and forgetting one line completely, it was quite an impressive effort. The boys and girls gave Arabella a good round of applause at the end. The teachers joined in. As Arabella returned to her seat, pink with excitement, Elizabeth began to feel very tense.

'We will now audition for the part of Jonkin,' announced Miss Ranger. 'After that I shall have a private chat with Miss Belle and Miss Best and then at the end of the lesson the parts will be given out.'

Elizabeth could hardly bear the suspense.

CHAPTER SIX

ELIZABETH IS OVEREXCITED

SEVERAL BOYS wanted to be in the play, especially in the roles of Mr Badger and Mr Grasshopper. They were both such good characters! Those two roles would no doubt be fought over, later in the week. But only two boys wanted to try for the Jonkin part as it looked quite daunting.

The other one was Daniel. He was called first and even he seemed hesitant.

'I – I'm not that sure I want to try for it,' he said awkwardly. 'Not really.'

'Oh, come along, Daniel,' chided Miss Ranger. 'You know you can do it.'

Elizabeth could see that the fair-haired boy was embarrassed. It was odd how Daniel had returned to his old ways lately. He had been so different last week, lively and cheerful, even asking Martin to test him for the play! Since then he had become his usual self again. It was true that he was spending a lot of time at the school stables, after speaking to Mr Tucker, the stableman. But Robert had complained that he was not really helping much. He read his books all the time, or simply lazed around, exactly as before. He might just as well have been in his room! What a funny boy he was, thought Elizabeth.

But now she felt uneasy. She remembered Julian's idea that the teachers had forced Daniel to put his name down for the play. Was it possible there might be favouritism?

Daniel began his first line, still embarrassed.

'Wait, Daniel!' said Miss Ranger, holding her hand up. Smiling gently, she rummaged in a bag. 'Look, this might help you. In the play Jonkin always wears a mask. A lot of the animal characters will wear masks too. Let's see you put this mask on, as you act out your lines. You may find that it helps you get into the spirit of things!'

The teacher handed the boy a face mask. It was not the actual goblin mask that would be used in *A Woodland Adventure*. That would not be ready until later. It was just an old mask from the school dressing-up chest, but it was a funny one, with an upturned nose and rosy cheeks.

As Daniel put the face mask on, the children

laughed and clapped. Elizabeth became even more uneasy. She was sure that Julian was right. The teachers wanted Daniel in the play; they very much wanted him to succeed.

Now, as he acted out the part from behind his mask, the improvement was very marked. He had learnt his lines well and his shyness was dropping away. He was much more carefree. His performance was not too bad at all.

'Congratulations, Daniel,' said Miss Belle afterwards. 'You did that well. Didn't he, Miss Best?'

The joint heads looked pleased.

'Now, Julian, your turn,' said Miss Ranger. 'And you must wear the face mask too, so we can judge you both fairly!'

Everybody cheered as Julian put the mask on and went straight into a goblin-like pose, crouching on his chair.

'I'm afraid I haven't learnt any lines yet,' he said, carelessly picking up the script. 'Apart from the little bit I did with Elizabeth. But – let me see – there's a scene here that's rather good, I think.'

Before Elizabeth had time to feel angry with Julian again for being so casual, he had launched forth. It was a passage from the play where Jonkin has decided, secretly, to bake a cake for the fairy queen.

'Here's a pinch of aniseed;
I'll find the other things I need;
Flower where the sweet bees suckle
And honey from the honeysuckle;
Butter from the buttercups . . .'

The class watched and listened in delight. It was hard to remember that Julian was reading from a script, so fluent was his performance. As he spoke the words, he did all the right actions as he went along! He ended up with a handstand, as required by the script.

Everybody clapped. It was a most excellent performance!

'Thank you, Julian,' nodded Miss Ranger, as Julian handed in the face mask. 'You should really have learnt your lines, though, like the others.'

Then Miss Ranger told the class to get out their English set books and read them in silence. She wished to confer with the joint heads.

As the three grown-ups went into a huddle, Elizabeth strained her ears, trying to catch what they were saying. But they spoke in very low, soft voices. Soon after that the joint heads departed from the classroom. Who had the Beauty and the Beast liked best? she wondered. They, after all, had written the play.

Nevertheless, Miss Ranger was in charge of the first form and was the play's producer. The final decisions on casting must be left to her, for she knew her pupils best.

After seeing Miss Belle and Miss Best out Miss Ranger came back and stood in front of the class and made her announcement.

'Elizabeth will play the part of Fay,' she said. 'And Arabella will be her understudy . . .'

Elizabeth gave a gasp of pleasure.

'And we will try Julian in the Jonkin part as long as he behaves properly and learns his lines. Daniel will be the understudy.'

Elizabeth felt weak with happiness as her classmates crowded round and clapped her on the back. 'Well done,' said Belinda sportingly. 'You were really good.' Julian was being congratulated too. There was noise and chatter all around.

As the bell went for the end of the lesson, Miss Ranger clapped her hands for silence.

'I can see you are all very excited,' she said. 'But remember, please, that this is school time. We have plenty of hard work to get through, if you are all to do well in summer exams at the end of term. The next lesson is geography. I am just slipping out to collect our weather map from Mr Johns . . .'

She looked at them sternly.

'When I return to the classroom, I expect to see you all sitting at your desks in absolute silence, please.

You will have your geography books out and be ready to start the next lesson.'

It was rather too much to ask. As soon as the teacher had left, the buzz of chatter broke out afresh. Elizabeth, in particular, was rather overexcited.

It had been such a strain, waiting to hear the results of the auditions. Now her dearest wish had been granted. She would play the part of Fay, Julian the part of Jonkin! With Julian cast opposite her the summer play was going to be tremendous fun. She was already looking forward to rehearsals. It was going to be the best thing they had ever done at Whyteleafe School!

She noticed that Daniel was congratulating Julian. He did not seem to resent the fact that he would just be understudy. The same could not be said of Arabella. She was the only person in the class not to congratulate Elizabeth. She was sitting at her desk, head bent, looking out her geography books.

'Cheer up, Arabella,' she called out boisterously. 'I might fall and break a leg!'

'Yes, you'll make a good understudy, Arabella,' giggled Belinda. 'You copied everything that Elizabeth did to perfection.'

Elizabeth winced. Nothing would have induced her to raise that herself. But she was touched that some of the others had noticed it.

Arabella looked up sulkily. 'I did nothing of the sort! I had everything planned already. It wasn't my fault that I had to go last . . .'

Belinda just laughed and then Arabella lost her temper. She sprang to her feet and pointed at Elizabeth.

'She cheated! She got Julian to help her! I saw them practising together last night. They had it all planned. It's not fair! It was Julian joining in at the end that got her the part!'

'Rubbish!' exclaimed Julian.

Elizabeth felt a temper coming on. She would get her own back on Arabella for saying that. What a mean girl she was!

As Miss Ranger came along the corridor with the map two minutes later, she could hear a commotion in the classroom. What was going on? She stood in the doorway and gazed at the scene.

Elizabeth Allen was standing on her desk, declaiming loudly, her face flushed with excitement. She was imitating Arabella.

'*Why am I here? Where have I been?*

Why am I dressed as a hairy fiend?'

Some of her friends had crowded round, hooting and stamping their feet at Elizabeth's impromptu performance.

'SILENCE!' came the voice from the doorway.

The children all scrambled back to their desks.

Elizabeth quickly jumped off hers and sat in her place. There was a hurried shuffling of paper and banging of desk lids as they all got their geography things out. Then came complete silence, broken only by muffled snorts as some children struggled hard to stop laughing.

But Miss Ranger's eyes were fixed only on Elizabeth, whose cheeks were still very flushed with excitement.

'I am surprised at you, Elizabeth. Do you not realise that anyone can fluff their lines in a play, even you? Do you not realise that you were being rather cruel and silly?'

Elizabeth opened her mouth to speak. She wanted to tell Miss Ranger how cruel and silly Arabella had been to her. Not just today either, but from the very first moment they had met. That dreadful moment in the Christmas holidays when Arabella had come to stay at her house just because their parents knew each other. And Elizabeth's mother had informed her that Arabella was coming to Whyteleafe and would be a nice companion for her, with her beautiful manners and lovely clothes! Why, Elizabeth had hated the spoilt girl on sight.

But, with her mouth still open, Elizabeth remained silent.

'Do you not realise?' repeated the teacher.

'*Cor!*' came the cheeky reply.

It was very loud and sounded deliberately silly and insolent.

There was a moment's shocked silence and then snorts of nervous laughter broke out. That *Cor!* coming from Elizabeth like that had been such a surprise. And now the naughtiest girl was looking all around her, pretending to be surprised herself.

'Who said that?'

'You did, Elizabeth,' replied Miss Ranger. She did not find it in the least bit funny. 'Stop showing off, Elizabeth. You have just been extremely cheeky to me. You will apologise at once, please.'

'It wasn't me, Miss Ranger!' protested Elizabeth in bewilderment. She turned and looked out of the open window, which was right behind her. 'It must have been someone fooling around outside!'

She opened the window very wide and leant out of it, looking right and then left. Several of her classmates rushed from their desks to the back of the room and crowded round her.

'That's funny, there's nobody there,' Elizabeth was saying.

'Ooops! Nobody there!'

'Can you see anybody, Martin?'

'Not a sausage.'

'Must have been a ghost!'

Some of the boys, in particular, were enjoying the distraction. This was the naughtiest girl as she used to be! It was good fun and better than geography.

'Sit down, all of you,' exclaimed Miss Ranger. 'Elizabeth, shut that window at once. Now turn round, sit down and face me.'

'Yes, Miss Ranger.'

The teacher spoke in icy tones.

'I see that getting the star part in the play has made you overexcited, Elizabeth. You have got completely carried away. If you cannot calm down, I will have to think again about my decision. Now, for the last time, will you please own up and apologise for speaking to me in that rude way.'

The whole class fell silent. The joke was over. They waited to see what Elizabeth would say.

CHAPTER SEVEN

A VERY BAD QUARREL

'I HAVE no intention of apologising, Miss Ranger,' said Elizabeth. 'How can I when it wasn't me?'

The boys and girls looked at the naughtiest girl in surprise. Of course it was her! Who else could it have been? They had all heard her. How silly of her to speak to Miss Ranger like that. Now she would lose her part in the play.

Elizabeth did not mean to sound ill-mannered, but she had a very hot temper. It was really horrid not to be believed like this. Even if it meant losing the precious part in the play, she thought angrily, she was not going to pretend she had made that cheeky comment when she had not.

'Really, Elizabeth,' began the teacher in exasperation. 'You will leave me with no other choice—'

There was a sudden sound.

ZZZZZZZZZZZZZZ.

It seemed to be coming from Elizabeth's direction, near the window.

ZZZZZZZZZZZZ.

There it was again. But this time it was over by the door. Was there a bumblebee flying round the room?

ZZZZZZ. ZZZZZZZ.

It was buzzing here, there and everywhere. But where was it? Nobody could see it.

'Julian!' realised Patrick.

And suddenly Julian was grinning and everybody in the class remembered. Julian had done this before! He was absolutely brilliant at imitations. He could throw his voice too. He could make sounds appear to come from anywhere, without moving his lips . . .

Julian, thought Elizabeth, in horror. *Of course.*

She was not amused. Nor was Miss Ranger.

'You have been misjudged, Elizabeth,' she said. 'I apologise for that. We had forgotten all about your friend, Julian, hadn't we, and the clever things he can do with his voice? However, I'm afraid there is one clever thing that Julian will *not* be doing with his voice in future. Please stand up, Julian. And take your hands out of your pockets while I am speaking to you.'

She lectured Julian sternly about disrupting the lesson and almost getting Elizabeth into further disgrace.

'I can see that you and Elizabeth are going to be very overexcited and silly if you are in the play together,' she concluded. 'I'm afraid I have changed my mind about the part of Jonkin. It will be played by Daniel. You will be Daniel's understudy.'

'Yes, Miss Ranger.'

For the rest of the lesson the class was very subdued, even Arabella and Daniel.

Elizabeth was subdued too, but inside she was boiling. She had briefly felt relief when the mystery was cleared up. She had been completely baffled as to where that voice had come from. She thought it must have come through the window just behind her, but, of course, there was nobody there! She never dreamt it had been one of Julian's tricks. It would have been too stupid of him.

But it *had* been him! And, if he hadn't let it be known, she could have lost her part in the school play.

Her relief quickly changed to anger, as she thought about his silly behaviour and his own part being taken away from him, which was no more than he deserved. Now she would have to play opposite Daniel instead. How dull that would be. She had been so looking forward to acting in the play with Julian.

'How could you be so stupid?' she raged at him, after lessons, as soon as they were alone. 'Now Daniel's got your part! You and your silly voices. You've ruined everything!'

Julian's green eyes glittered for a moment. 'If that's what you think, Elizabeth, I don't call you much of a friend.'

'What else am I supposed to think?' exploded Elizabeth. 'Even friendship has its limits!'

'Somebody must have been trying to get you into trouble and it wasn't me,' replied Julian coolly. 'I was trying to get you *out* of trouble.'

'Oh *really*? When nobody else in the class can throw their voice like that except you, Julian? Please don't make me any crosser than I am already!'

Now Julian's own temper snapped.

'In that case there can be only one explanation, can't there? I mean to say, it's the only answer . . .'

'What?'

'Miss Ranger was right all along. You were completely overexcited and you cheeked her yourself. So overexcited you don't even remember doing it!'

'How dare you!'

Elizabeth turned her back on Julian and stalked away. 'If that's what you think, I have nothing more to say to you.'

'Nor I to you,' Julian retorted, as he turned on his heel and headed in the opposite direction.

It was a very bad quarrel.

In the days that followed Elizabeth thought about it many times. But she always reached the same conclusion. Julian *must* have been responsible for that silly voice. There was just no other explanation! He probably realised he had been very foolish indeed. Was it pride that stopped him owning up and saying sorry so that they could be friends again?

But it was mean of him to try to persuade her that *she* had been the silly one, so overexcited that she didn't know what she was doing! That would make *her* responsible for him losing his part in the play!

She decided not to speak to Julian again until he apologised.

Julian felt exactly the same way about Elizabeth.

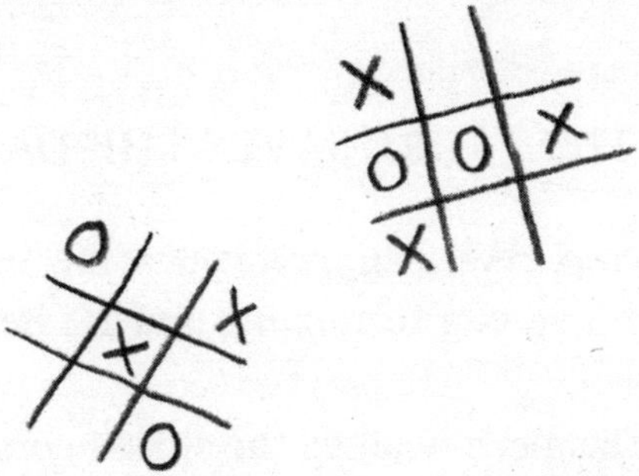

CHAPTER EIGHT

THE BUTTON'S OWNER IS FOUND

ELIZABETH WAS unhappy for the next few days. It was horrible not being on speaking terms with Julian. She had other friends in the first-form, but it was with Julian that she got on best. She would like to have seen more of Joan during this troubled time. But with the two girls in different forms that was not possible.

Arabella quickly took advantage of the situation. The vain little girl had no idea why Elizabeth and Julian had mysteriously fallen out, but it gave her quiet satisfaction. She was tired of the way everybody liked Elizabeth and nobody liked her.

'We may only be understudies, Julian,' she told him, 'but that still means we have to learn out parts. It's a very important job being an understudy. If anything happens, we could easily be called upon.' She gave him a winsome smile. 'I'm an absolute ninny at learning lines. Please help me. We can practise some of the scenes together. I'd love you to test me and I'll be only too pleased to test you.'

One evening Elizabeth walked into the common room and found them rehearsing some of the play together. Rosemary was their prompter. Arabella was giggling happily.

'Oh, Julian, you are naughty. You're peeping at the script, I can see you. You still haven't bothered to learn it.'

Elizabeth turned on her heel and walked straight out again. It was infuriating. Arabella seemed to be having more fun just being an understudy than she was having in the real play! Julian was allowing her to help him over that blazer button mystery too. It had still not been solved.

Much of Elizabeth's zest for acting had gone.

The other auditions had taken place and the full cast chosen. Rosemary had been made prompter. Elizabeth was pleased when Belinda, Kathleen and Jenny were all given good supporting roles in the play. John McTavish was picked to play Mr Grasshopper who had some very funny lines to speak. And Patrick, of all people, had landed the part of the poor, sickly Mr Badger. He seemed to be enjoying himself already, all the more so now that Julian had been kicked out of the play.

Elizabeth had vowed to put Julian right out of her

mind and throw herself into the play with gusto. After all, Daniel had been rather good as Jonkin, once he wore that funny mask.

But, from the very first rehearsal, her spirits sank. It was all Daniel's fault. He had memorised his lines well. He was good at English and had no difficulty with learning by rote. But his acting was so half-hearted! His mind always seemed to be elsewhere. She could strike up no rapport with him. In the scenes they had to act out together he refused to meet her gaze, but just kept glancing shiftily around.

Worst of all, he kept on apologising.

'I'm really sorry you've got me, Elizabeth,' he said, at that very first rehearsal, which took place after school on the terrace. 'I feel terrible that Julian had the part taken away from him.'

'I shouldn't bother to feel terrible about Julian!' retorted Elizabeth sharply. 'It was no more than he deserved.'

But the boy looked guilt-stricken all the same, and the apologies kept on coming.

'I'm sorry, that wasn't very good. I'm sure Julian would have done it much better . . .'

By the third rehearsal Elizabeth was ready to snap.

'If you mention Julian again, I'll scream! Stop being such a drip, Daniel. We've got to make a success of this!

I'm begining to think we're going to make complete idiots of ourselves in front of the whole school. Put some verve into it, *please* . . .'

What was the matter with the boy?

It was the weekend and Elizabeth was feeling particularly irritable.

On her way to rehearsal she had noticed Julian, Harry and Arabella talking to some of the juniors. At this week's School Meeting William and Rita had asked the assembled children to renew their efforts to find out who had vandalised the strawberry plants. Elizabeth would have loved to have been helping Julian track down that missing blazer button. Instead he and Harry were allowing Arabella to tag along with them.

In fact, Julian was simply filling in time. Secretly, he was still very hurt and angry at Elizabeth's behaviour – and puzzled too. As he saw her pass by, he wondered how long it was going to be before she finally came to her senses and apologised to him.

After the rehearsal on the terrace Elizabeth trudged back into school, her spirits at a low ebb. She was sorry she had lost her temper with Daniel. It was the worst thing she could have said to him! It was silly of her to frighten him like that. At least he had managed not to mention Julian's name again. He had just acted like a frozen rabbit instead.

I don't think the play's going to be any fun at all, Elizabeth concluded. She decided to go upstairs and read a book. She was walking towards her dormitory when suddenly she heard her name being called.

'I've been looking for you, Elizabeth.'

Assistant Matron came out of the little sewing room and greeted Elizabeth in the corridor. She carried a small blazer over her arm. Elizabeth recognised the strawberry jam mark on the front! It was hers – one she had outgrown and handed in at the beginning of term. She had a much bigger one now that would last longer, she hoped.

'I'm checking over all the second-hand uniforms this week, Elizabeth,' smiled Assistant Matron. 'I want to send it all to the cleaners next week. We need everything back in good time for the school-uniform sale at the end of term!'

The school second-hand shop did a good trade at the end of the school year, when parents came to collect their children from Whyteleafe. New uniform was so expensive and the children grew so quickly. Some parents were always pleased to have the chance to kit them out in good second-hand items for the new school year ahead.

Elizabeth stared dreamily at her first blazer. She felt quite fond of it now. She remembered her governess, Miss Scott, taking her to the big store to buy the brand-new uniform and, afterwards, reinforcing the blazer buttons with some extra-strong blue thread. 'You treat your clothes so roughly, Elizabeth,' Miss Scott had said. 'We don't want the buttons coming off.'

Elizabeth had cheeked Miss Scott at the time, telling her that she would not be at Whyteleafe School long enough for that to happen. She did not *want* to go to a horrid boarding school and would make sure that she was sent home as soon as possible! How silly and childish she had been, thought Elizabeth. She loved her school uniform now. She was very proud to wear it.

Elizabeth realised that Assistant Matron was looking at her expectantly. 'Did you want something, please?' she asked politely.

'The button, Elizabeth! You promised to give it to me weeks ago.'

Elizabeth's hand flew to her mouth.

In her relief at handing in the uncomfortably small blazer she had forgotten all about that button! It was the blazer becoming so tight that had made the middle button burst off, in spite of Miss Scott's best efforts. Elizabeth had put the button in a safe place, but then promptly forgotten all about it. Now she apologised.

'I'll go and find it straight away. I think I remember where I put it.'

'I have to go to the village now,' said Assistant

Matron, smiling. 'Just put it on my sewing table when you've found it, Elizabeth.'

'I will. I promise.'

She hurried into the dormitory and went to her cubicle. A white-painted chest of drawers stood there with pretty blue wooden handles. All the girls had one, next to their beds. On top of her chest of drawers, at the back, was a small china bowl in which Elizabeth kept oddments. A foreign coin, some hairgrips, a mouldering bath cube. She was almost certain that she had put the button there for safe keeping, all those weeks ago.

But there was no sign of it now. Elizabeth poked inside the bowl in puzzlement. Where *had* she put it then? She began to search through the drawers below, turning them out, one by one.

'Lost something, Elizabeth?' asked Kathleen cheerfully, coming into the dormitory.

At the same moment Arabella was passing the open door. She paused and peered inside, glancing at Elizabeth. She had just been indulging in a happy daydream. Her faithful friend, Rosemary, had told her what a poor performance Daniel and Elizabeth had put on at today's rehearsal; that Elizabeth had snapped at Daniel and Miss Ranger had not looked very pleased.

Surely it was only a matter of time before she and

Julian would be asked to step into the breach? Instead of being a flop the summer play would be the most brilliant success! In her mind's eye the sun was shining brightly. She and Julian, hand in hand, were being given a standing ovation . . .

Now Arabella heard Elizabeth speaking crossly to Kathleen.

'Just a silly old button! I was sure I put it in my little bowl. Assistant Matron needs it! Oh, Kathleen, do help me look for it. It's a silver blazer button with some bright blue thread hanging from it.'

Arabella nearly gasped out loud. She quickly tiptoed away down the corridor, feeling surprised and excited. She must tell Rosemary about this and they must think what to do.

Less than half an hour later, Jenny came up to the dormitory.

Elizabeth looked hot and bothered. It seemed to be one of those horrid days when *nothing* would go right. She and Kathleen had ransacked the cubicle. They had even pulled the chest of drawers away from the wall, no easy task, to see if the button could have slipped off the top and down the back. They had looked under Elizabeth's blue rug. They had even crawled under her bed. It was nowhere to be found.

The loss of the button somehow filled Elizabeth with

uneasiness, although she could not think why. And now Jenny had appeared in the doorway and was looking at her rather strangely.

'Can you come down to the common room, please, Elizabeth?' she asked unhappily. 'Something important's cropped up.'

When Elizabeth entered the common room, Arabella was sitting at one of the little tables. A few of their classmates sat nearby, watching with interest. There was a sense of expectancy in the room.

Something was lying on the table. Arabella placed it on the palm of her hand. Then, with a flourish, she held it out towards Elizabeth.

'Was this what you were looking for?'

Elizabeth stepped forward and examined the object closely. It was a silver blazer button with some bright blue thread hanging from it.

'My button!' she exclaimed. 'Where did you find it, Arabella?'

'William and Rita had it,' said Arabella, with a meaningful look. 'Rosemary and I heard you were looking for one. We've just been along to their study and borrowed it from them!'

'It's the button that John found in the strawberry beds!' said Rosemary solemnly. 'We were all asked to find out who owns it, remember? And now we have!'

Elizabeth looked at the button in complete astonishment.

'You surely don't think I was the person trying to steal strawberries?' gasped Elizabeth.

'We all like strawberries,' said Arabella, pursing her lips.

'I haven't worn my old blazer for weeks! Ask Assistant Matron if you don't believe me!' snapped Elizabeth, her temper flaring up. 'I'd never wear it to the school gardens anyway. I've absolutely no idea how the button got *there*! I put it in the little bowl on top of my chest of drawers weeks ago, and that was the last time I saw it!'

'Perhaps you just *meant* to do that,' suggested Arabella. 'Perhaps you actually had it in a pocket and it fell out one day when you were messing about in the gardens . . .'

'How dare you!' raged Elizabeth.

Before she could lunge at Arabella, Rosemary stepped between them. She spoke soothingly.

'Now it's no use getting angry with Arabella, Elizabeth. William and Rita said that if you *did* recognise the button you were please to go and see them in William's study at four o'clock. You can explain it all to them in the proper way.'

'Indeed I shall!'

She stormed out of the common room.

CHAPTER NINE

JULIAN MAKES IT FIVE

FOR ALL her bravado Elizabeth felt scared as she tapped on the door of William's study at four o'clock. How had her button got there? It was dreadful to be under suspicion like this. Surely the head boy and girl knew her too well to believe that she would damage young plants? Surely they must know that, although she might be tempted to pick the occasional ripe strawberry, she would never pull young plants out of the ground to look for fruit! It would be such a stupid and ignorant thing to do.

'Come in, Elizabeth.'

Still quaking, she walked into the cosy little study. William and Rita were waiting for her.

There was somebody else in the room with them, seated in the visitor's armchair. It was John Terry.

Elizabeth felt somehow reassured by the sight of

John, as he stood up and offered the chair to her. She sat down. Everybody seemed very calm.

'John's just been telling us how you helped him net all the strawberry beds, after the plants had been vandalised,' said William approvingly. 'But you do recognise the button then?'

Elizabeth nodded.

'We know you're one of his best little helpers,' stated Rita. 'We thought we should have a chat with John first about this button business.'

'Don't look so worried, Elizabeth,' smiled William. 'None of us thinks for one moment that you pulled up those plants.'

'Oh, thank goodness,' replied Elizabeth.

'But have you any idea how your button could have got there?' asked Rita. 'Is it possible that you lent it to somebody?'

'Definitely not,' said Elizabeth, with a firm shake of the head. 'I mean, who would want to borrow an old blazer button? Besides, I had to keep it safe because I'd promised to give it to Assistant Matron. It was just that I'd forgotten all about it until she asked me today.' Elizabeth explained about handing in the old blazer without it. 'The missing button should have been in the little bowl on top of my chest of drawers,' she finished.

At that Rita smiled and shook her head.

'You must be mistaken there, Elizabeth. You really must! Now try to think very carefully. You *forgot* to give it to Assistant Matron. Is it not possible that you *forgot* to put it in a safe place too? That you were just carrying it around in a pocket?'

'Well . . .' Elizabeth frowned. She was convinced that she had put the button in the bowl. 'I don't think so. But . . .'

'But it *is* possible, isn't it?' chuckled William. He was looking very relieved. 'Well, I think that's the beginning and the end of your involvement. John has told us how often you help in the garden. You must have been weeding the plants one day and the button fell out of your pocket! The whole thing is a complete coincidence and has nothing to do with the fact that, at a later stage, somebody vandalised them.'

'I – I suppose so,' said Elizabeth reluctantly. She was still frowning. When had she last worked in that part of the garden?

'You gave us a red herring when you produced that button, John!' chided Rita.

'It was wrong of me to jump to conclusions,' agreed John, with a wry smile. He scratched his head. 'I thought I'd found a grand clue and I'd found nothing of the sort.'

There was a thoughtful expression on his face as he

tried to work it out. He had been so sure that the lost button and the damaged plants were closely linked. But if the two things were unconnected . . . why, perhaps he had been on the wrong track altogether. He must start to keep his eyes and ears open . . .

As Elizabeth left to go to tea, she felt pleased that William and Rita and John believed in her. It did make her feel a little better.

However, as she walked into the dining hall, she could feel the tension in the air as many of the children glanced her way. The whispers had spread very quickly. The mystery of the blazer button had been solved! It belonged to the naughtiest girl. She had just been hauled up in front of the head boy and girl!

Her classmates were less chatty than usual. But her best friend Joan kept looking across from the next table and giving little smiles and waves, to show solidarity.

Elizabeth began to get a horrid feeling in the pit of her stomach. How very bad it must look to everybody, her blazer button having been found where the plants had been vandalised! Even worse was the feeling that somebody must have put it there deliberately. The more she thought about it, the more certain she became that she *had* left the button in the bowl and that things could not have happened in the way that William and Rita had suggested.

At the far end of the table Julian was eating his tea. He was deep in thought, a moody expression on his face.

Elizabeth had lost her own appetite. She had to force herself to eat the tuna salad, usually a favourite. She left her raspberry yoghurt. She could feel a hot pricking sensation behind the eyes and, just as soon as they were allowed to get down from table, she fled. She hurried out into the school grounds, her eyes blurred with tears. She was unaware of footsteps following her. She reached the lovely weeping ash tree, where the summer play was going to be performed. She crept under its secret canopy of leaves that almost touched the ground. She wanted to hide, like a wounded animal.

She sat down, leant against the tree trunk and buried her face in her hands. Everything was going wrong!

It had all started with Julian putting on that silly voice! Since then nothing had gone right. And he *still* wouldn't own up and say he was sorry. How she wished that he would. She needed his friendship so badly now.

'Elizabeth?'

Startled, she looked up and saw Julian ducking under the cascading fronds and coming to join her.

'Hello, bad girl. Now, at last, I hope you will believe me!'

He sat down and put an arm round her shoulders to comfort her. 'There's nothing to cry about.'

'There is! There is! William and Rita and John believe in me and so does Joan. But that's only four people in the whole school. Nobody else knows what to think.'

'Only four?' said Julian. 'Don't you mean five?'

'Five?'

'Yes, you forgot to count me. I believe in you.'

She stared at him in relief. She dried her eyes.

'Do you really? But Julian, what did you mean just then—'

'Elizabeth, somebody is trying to get you into trouble. I told you that a week ago. Now perhaps – at *last* – you'll believe me!'

Elizabeth gasped as it dawned on her what Julian was saying.

'Listen, Elizabeth. I did *not* put on that silly voice! Somebody else did. And that button could hardly have *walked* on its own to the school gardens. Somebody placed it there. But do you believe me now?' he asked urgently.

'Yes,' replied Elizabeth in a very small voice. 'Yes. I do.'

Her mind was in a turmoil. She still did not understand who else in the class could be clever enough to throw their voice in that amazing way. But now she was sure that it was not Julian.

I was trying to get you out of trouble was what he

had claimed at the time. And she had refused to believe him!

If that's what you think, I don't call you much of a friend, Elizabeth, he had told her angrily.

Now she turned to him, her cheeks hot with shame.

'You were right about me not being much of a friend, Julian,' she admitted. She felt bitterly angry with herself for misjudging him so. 'You took the blame to save me from losing my part in the play – and ended up losing your own. And that was all the thanks you got from me! Oh, Julian, I don't know how you can ever forgive me. Why have I got such a silly temper? I'm not surprised if you like Arabella better than me. I can be such a horrid person!'

Julian looked at Elizabeth's grief-stricken face. He stood up, then took her hands and pulled her to her feet.

'Up you get, Elizabeth. Stop moping. It doesn't suit you. Not a Bold Bad Girl like you! Arabella? You must be joking!' he said cheerfully. He had waited so long for Elizabeth to apologise and now she had. Everything was all right again. 'Come on, let's see if the ponies are free and go for a ride. It will clear our heads and help us to think.'

As they strolled towards the stables, the warm breeze whispering in the grass, Elizabeth felt like a new person.

'It's horrid to think someone's trying to make trouble for me,' she said, as they saddled up the horses. 'But nothing seems so bad now, Julian. Oh, I'm so glad we've made up our quarrel!'

'We'll soon get to the bottom of this peculiar business,' replied Julian confidently.

At that moment Robert appeared with Daniel.

'As you don't ride, would you like to walk Captain round the meadow, to give him some exercise?' Robert was saying to the fair-haired boy. 'I've got to go and give Patrick some tennis practice now.'

'If you want me to,' replied Daniel dully.

'What a strange boy he is,' Elizabeth remarked to Julian, as they set off on horseback. 'Let's take the bridle path, shall we? He still hasn't bothered to learn to ride. All that fuss about wanting to help at the stables. He doesn't seem to enjoy it very much! He doesn't seem to enjoy being in the play much either! Oh, Julian, we've got to find out who really cheeked Miss Ranger – and then she'll have to admit she was wrong. About us not being sensible if we act in the play together! She'll have to give you your part back!'

'Oh, I'm not worried about that,' shrugged Julian. He had only put his name down to annoy Patrick!

'Well, I'm worried if you're not!' exclaimed Elizabeth. 'It's really hard work doing it with Daniel.'

'I expect he'll improve,' said Julian.

They had a lovely ride together and talked a lot about the mystery. It was a very puzzling one. Elizabeth hated the idea that someone had a grudge against her. She could not think who it might be.

'The only person with a motive would be Arabella,' she mused. 'She would so love my part in the play. But I'm quite sure it isn't her.'

'So am I,' agreed Julian. 'She could never throw her voice like that. And she was really surprised about the blazer button, I could tell.'

On their return they rode back through the meadow.

Daniel was sitting by the hedge, reading a book, while Captain grazed peacefully nearby. A bird was sitting on the old horse's back, pecking at Captain's coat.

'You're supposed to be looking after him!' scolded Elizabeth, as they rode past. 'Can't you shoo that crow away?'

'Captain likes it,' mumbled Daniel, without even looking up from his book.

'Isn't he hopeless?' grumbled Elizabeth, as they passed out of earshot. 'Anything rather than put his book down for a minute. How can he possibly say Captain likes it!'

'But he's right!' laughed Julian. 'Horses are really grateful when members of the crow family sit on their backs! I think that one was a rook.'

'Grateful? Whatever for?' exclaimed Elizabeth.

'The birds search through their coats and get rid of little insects and parasites for them, that's what,' replied Julian, still amused at her indignation. 'Elizabeth, I'm beginning to think you've got a down on Daniel. The poor boy can't do anything right.'

Later, as they rubbed down the ponies, Elizabeth said, 'I haven't really got a down on Daniel. He would be nice if he wasn't so odd. But he is hopeless in the play, Julian! We've got to make sure you play Jonkin and not him.'

'You've got *your* part, Elizabeth,' replied Julian contentedly. 'So that's the main thing. You're going to be a star, I tell you!'

But he spoke too soon.

That same night the bane of Elizabeth's life struck yet again.

CHAPTER TEN

FIRE! FIRE!

IT TOOK Elizabeth a long time to get to sleep. She tossed and turned, listening to the gentle breathing of the other girls in Dormitory Six. She was so excited about the play and what Julian had said about her being a star. But she was also fearful. Why should someone be trying to get her into trouble? Who could it be?

Soon it was dusk outside and every other child in the school was fast asleep. At last Elizabeth began to feel sleepy. Her eyes closed. She started to drift away into a light, fitful sleep . . . Then a sudden raucous cry reverberated in her head:

Fire! Fire!

Was it a bad dream?

Fire! Fire!

There it was again! It seemed to be coming from

outside. Someone was screeching a warning. The school was on fire!

Half asleep and half awake, Elizabeth tumbled out of bed in a panic.

'Wake up, everyone! Please wake up! I think the school's on fire!'

She stumbled out into the corridor and rang the fire bell.

CLANG! CLANG! CLANG! CLANG!

The fire bell rang out all over the building.

There was great excitement as sleepy children emerged from dormitories in dressing gowns, rubbing their eyes.

'Fire!' cried Elizabeth. 'There's a fire somewhere in the school!'

They all formed orderly lines, as they had often been drilled to do, then left the building by the special fire exits.

Elizabeth led the way. 'Keep calm, everyone!' she cried. 'Make sure everybody's out of your dormy.'

As they milled around on the lawns outside, there was much chattering and ado. Where was the fire? They couldn't see any smoke! But there *must* be a fire somewhere. Elizabeth had rung the fire bell! Oh, thank goodness – it could only be a small one . . .

Now the teachers were appearing. None of them

had gone to bed yet. They were still fully dressed.

'There's a fire somewhere, Miss Ranger!' cried Elizabeth. 'I heard someone screaming—'

'Are you sure, Elizabeth?'

While the children waited outside on the chilly lawns, the teachers carried out a full inspection of the school premises. There was no fire.

Mr Johns returned and spoke to the assembled pupils. 'Back to bed, all of you! A false alarm, I'm pleased to say. Form into lines and go quietly back to your dormitories. There is no sign of a fire anywhere. You are quite safe.'

When Elizabeth reached Dormitory Six, she found Miss Ranger waiting for her. The expression on the teacher's face gave her a feeling of intense foreboding.

'Go straight back to bed, Elizabeth. That was a very silly joke. I will see you in the morning, after I have had a chat with Miss Belle and Miss Best.'

The next day, in spite of all her protests, Elizabeth had her part in the school play taken away.

'I am extremely surprised at you, Elizabeth. I accept your word that you did not deliberately set out to play a joke. But your imagination is obviously in a feverish state. From the moment you were given the star part in the summer play you have been much too overexcited. It is a great shame, but I have decided to give Arabella her chance. I am sure she will be more sensible. You will be the understudy.'

Tears came to Elizabeth's eyes. But this time they were tears of pure anger.

She went to find Julian.

'I know jolly well that I didn't imagine those cries. They were real as could be. Oh, Julian, don't you see? Somebody else must have heard them. Not just *me*.'

'Yes, surely,' agreed Julian. 'And somebody made them too. Which direction did they come from? Can you remember?'

'I was half asleep . . .'

'Think hard,' coaxed Julian.

Elizabeth frowned in concentration.

'Well, my window was open. It was somewhere outside . . . but sort of *above*. As though there was a fire on the floor above and somebody was leaning out of their window up there and screeching down to me, in a panic.'

'The attic floor, eh?' said Julian calmly. 'Well, we'll question all the children who sleep in Dormy Ten. That's the one upstairs, isn't it?'

'Yes,' said Elizabeth eagerly. 'And three or four children have their own little rooms as well. Oh, surely *someone* up there will have heard something?'

'Lucky it's Sunday. No lessons. It gives us all day to investigate. We're going to get to the bottom of this, Elizabeth, don't you worry,' he said airily.

It was a great comfort to have Julian by her side that day. Joan too was very loyal.

'I am quite sure you will be vindicated, Elizabeth,' she said sweetly. 'Somebody else must have heard something, as you say. Is there anything I can do to help? Would you like me to question everybody in the second form?'

'Oh, would you, Joan? That would be such a help. Julian and I are going to quiz everyone who sleeps on the top floor. I *think* the cries came from above. But, of course, I can't be certain.'

Most of Elizabeth's classmates were very impressed by her sincerity, as she went around with Julian, talking to people. They were puzzled and bewildered by the whole affair, just as they had been about the blazer button. They hoped, for the naughtiest girl's sake, that everything was going to turn out all right for her in the end. It had been rather exciting, hearing the fire bell go off like that! But of course the teachers did not see it that way. And now she had lost her part in the play.

Arabella should have been in a sunny mood that day. But she felt oddly tense and irritable. It was extremely annoying that Julian and Elizabeth, who had mysteriously quarrelled, had now just as mysteriously made it up.

It had been such a triumph when Miss Ranger told her that she, Arabella, was to play the part of Fay in *A Woodland Adventure* and must do her very best to make a success of it. She fully expected some of her classmates to come and find her and congratulate her and wish her luck. But she waited in vain. They all seemed more interested in Elizabeth's predicament and the detective work that she was doing with Julian. As the day wore on, Kathleen and Harry joined in, too, trying to help Elizabeth.

'Did you hear anyone shout "Fire!", Arabella?' asked Kathleen.

'Of course I didn't!' replied Arabella scornfully. 'Elizabeth just made it up.'

'What a waste of time!' agreed Rosemary.

'We're having a play rehearsal soon,' said Arabella. 'Are you coming to support me? I'm a little bit nervous because Rosemary says Daniel's the most terrible actor. You won't find anybody who heard any shouts in the night because nobody did.'

On that point at least Arabella was correct.

One by one, Elizabeth and Julian tracked down all the children who slept on the top floor. It was a long task. They were all out and about, enjoying their various weekend activities. And it was a fruitless task, too. For, one by one, the children shook their heads when questioned.

'Think *very* hard, James,' urged Julian. His room, like Daniel's, was almost directly above Elizabeth's window. 'Did you hear someone cry out? In their sleep perhaps? Someone having a bad dream about a fire?'

'I was dead to the world,' said James. 'I didn't hear a thing – except the fire bell. And I didn't even hear that at first.'

It was the same old story.

'Why don't you try Daniel?' he suggested. 'I often hear him moving around after lights out. I think he reads in bed.'

After that Elizabeth and Julian went to look for Daniel. He was their last hope. But they had not seen him all day.

'I expect he's reading a book in the stables,' commented Julian. 'That's where he usually is these days.'

'Or else *under the haystack fast asleep*, like Little Boy Blue!' said Elizabeth witheringly.

He was nowhere to be found.

'Surely he can't be spending all day in his room?' suggested Elizabeth suddenly. 'He used to sometimes. Even on lovely sunny days like today.'

Sure enough, they found Daniel in his small bedroom

under the eaves. He was not even reading. He was lying on the bed, staring up at the skylight. His play script lay on the bedroom floor.

'Daniel!' exclaimed Elizabeth. 'You lazy lump!'

The boy sat bolt upright, with a guilty start.

'I – I'm just learning my lines,' he said feebly. He picked the script up off the floor and pretended to flick through it. 'What do you want?'

There seemed to be a strange pallor about his face.

'I didn't hear anything, no!' he burst out, as Julian questioned him. He seemed rattled and upset. 'I was fast asleep. Cross my heart and swear to die.'

Julian's interest quickened. He was sure that Daniel was speaking the truth. So why was he looking so upset?

'But you have an idea who it might have been then?' he asked probingly.

'It – it could have been . . .' Daniel began to blurt out.

'Yes?' asked Elizabeth eagerly.

The boy clammed up. 'I don't know,' he said worriedly. 'It could have been anything, I suppose.'

At that moment Rosemary burst into the room.

'So there you are, Daniel! Miss Ranger sent me to find you. You're supposed to be at play rehearsal!'

'Do I have to be?' he asked miserably. 'Can't Julian have a turn? I don't feel like it today.'

'Don't be silly!' said Rosemary. She grabbed him by the arm. 'You're keeping everybody waiting.'

As she hustled him out of the room, Julian and Elizabeth followed them downstairs. Julian was humming to himself cheerfully.

'I think we're getting somewhere at last,' he said. 'I think Daniel knows something.'

'Yes,' agreed Elizabeth. 'So do I.'

Again she found it difficult to get to sleep that night. The dramatic events of the weekend were spinning round in her head. But now she was beginning to feel a glimmer of hope.

Arabella and Daniel were never going to last out in the play! She had heard from Kathleen that today's rehearsal had been a shambles!

Daniel's confidence had suddenly gone completely. And Arabella could not be of any help to him. She was a bag of nerves herself. She kept fluffing her lines. She had come back from the rehearsal with her face like a thundercloud. It was gradually dawning on her how much she was taking on and that failure stared her in the face.

Meanwhile, thought Elizabeth, she and Julian were getting to grips with the mystery. They had tried to pump Daniel again this evening, without success. But it was perfectly obvious that he suspected who the culprit was. He was shielding somebody! They would have to be patient, but surely they would discover the truth soon? Then she and Julian would be able to clear their names. Their parts in the play would be given back to them!

Elizabeth was just drifting off to sleep when there came a sudden thump at the door. She sat bolt upright in bed. There was another thump, followed by a tapping sound . . .

This time she was wide awake!

Fire! Fire! came the choking cry. It was coming from the corridor. What an eerie sound!

'They're trying to trick me again!' she gasped. 'They're in the building this time. They're hoping I'll ring the fire bell again!'

Trembling, she slipped out of bed. She donned her dressing gown and tiptoed towards the door. *Tap . . . tap . . . tap.* There was that noise again. She was frightened. But of one thing she was certain:

I'm not going to be caught out a second time! I know perfectly well there isn't a fire! she decided. *I've got to catch them, whoever it is!*

CHAPTER ELEVEN

THE NAUGHTIEST GIRL SAVES THE DAY

AS ELIZABETH edged open the door, she heard rapid movements outside. She peered into the dimly lit corridor. There was nobody there. They had moved along the corridor and disappeared round the corner. She could hear little bumps and thuds coming from the direction of the attic staircase.

She raced along in pursuit, turned the corner and bounded up the first few stairs in the gloom.

Suddenly, with a whoosh and a flutter, a black shape hurled itself at her legs and tried to peck at them.

'*Krrraaaa! Krrraaaa! Fire! Fire!*' it seemed to cry.

'A crow!' she gasped. 'A big black crow! How did it get indoors? Whatever's the matter with it?'

It was one of the most startling moments of Elizabeth's life. The bird was extremely agitated. It was still trying to peck at her legs.

'*Krrraaaa! Fire!*'

It was uncanny how human it sounded.

After that first shock Elizabeth felt a sudden rush of relief. Her 'enemy' of the previous night had been no more than a silly black crow! A crow whose cries sounded almost like human ones. It must have alighted very briefly on her windowsill last night. Right by her open window. No wonder none of the sleeping children had heard the noise.

'I must get the teachers quickly!' decided Elizabeth. 'They'll help get the bird out of the building. And now they'll see that I was *not* imagining things!'

As she tried to leave, the crow flew at her legs again.

'Do stop it—!' began Elizabeth crossly. Then she stopped.

A tiny wisp of smoke came curling down the attic staircase. Then another. And another.

She caught a faint, acrid smell . . .

'There is a fire up there!' she realised in horror. 'There really is a fire!'

She went hurtling up the long staircase to the very top. The bird was fluttering and flapping round her head the whole time, in full cry. '*Kraa! Kraa! Kraa! Kraaa!*'

'The smoke's coming from Daniel's room!' she realised.

His door was only slightly ajar, but, even from here,

the smell was now becoming overpowering. It was the most horrid smell, like burning chemicals . . .

She pushed open the door and then reeled back. There were no flames, but the room was full of suffocating smoke. The fair-haired boy lay prone on his bed, overcome by the fumes.

Daniel's passed out! Elizabeth thought. *I've got to get him out of there, quickly.*

But the acrid smoke was already filling her mouth and nostrils. She felt as though she would pass out too. She closed Daniel's door for a moment and dived into the bathroom next door. She held a towel under the cold-water tap until it was soaking wet.

Then, with the wet towel wrapped firmly round her face, she returned to the smoke-filled room and pulled Daniel to the floor. Her eyes were not covered by the towel and were already smarting painfully. She tried to ignore the pain.

Above their heads the panic-stricken bird wheeled out of the open skylight. It flew high into the sky and away into the distance. The skylight – *so that was how it had got in!* realised Elizabeth.

'Get flat on your tummy, Daniel!' she gasped. 'So we're down below the level of the fumes . . .'

But the boy was still unconscious.

Slithering slowly backwards towards the door,

Elizabeth dragged him, inch by inch, across the polished wooden floor. It took less than a minute, but that minute seemed like an hour. Several times Elizabeth started to choke. She was having to keep her eyes tightly shut now. She became scared that she too might lose consciousness before she could get Daniel to the door.

Then, at last, they were safely outside.

She slammed the door shut on the smoke-filled room. She knew that it would help to contain the fire. She rubbed the wet towel over her smarting eyes and then over Daniel's face, trying to revive him.

'Daniel. Daniel. Are you all right?'

His face twitched. 'Where am I? What's happened?'

'You passed out!' whispered Elizabeth, through her coughs. 'There's some horrible kind of fire in your room. This bird came and told me about it. A black crow—'

Daniel's eyes opened wide.

'You mean Rookie? He came and fetched you? Then it *was* Rookie last time. I wondered if it could have been. And tonight there really *was* a fire—?'

'Rookie?' asked Elizabeth in surprise. Daniel seemed to know all about the bird! 'Why do you call him that?'

'He's my pet. He's my tame rook. He's the brightest, best little rascal that ever lived.'

Daniel gulped. 'But I'm so ashamed, Elizabeth. He's brought you and Julian nothing but trouble. And, now I can't keep him secret any more, the teachers will send him away. He'll have to go, won't he?'

'I've got a funny feeling inside me that he's gone already,' whispered Elizabeth.

Suddenly she heard voices below and clattering footsteps.

The teachers had seen the plume of smoke coming out of Daniel's skylight. Now, armed with fire extinguishers, they came running up the stairs.

'What's happened? Are you all right, Daniel?' asked Mr Warlow.

'We'll soon put the flames out!' exclaimed Mr Johns, extinguisher at the ready.

'Please, Mr Johns, there aren't any flames yet,' warned Elizabeth, 'just these horrible poisonous fumes. You'll need wet towels round your faces!'

It was good advice. The two teachers were grateful for it as they charged into the room and squirted a smouldering toy on the bedside locker, then swiftly retreated. There was no risk of a fire spreading now. They had found the cause of all the smoke.

It was against school rules to have foam-filled toys, but Daniel had brought a teddy mascot from home without knowing it was stuffed with the forbidden material.

It was also against school rules to read after lights

out. It was even more strictly forbidden to read by candlelight. Daniel had been doing both. Nor had he remembered to blow the candle out. As he slept, the lighted candle had overbalanced. It had fallen against the teddy bear which had smouldered away, releasing the clouds of acrid fumes into the little bedroom.

'You won't be sleeping in there tonight, Daniel,' Mr Johns told the boy. 'It will take some hours for the room to air.'

Matron decided that both Daniel and Elizabeth should sleep in the sanatorium that night. She wanted to keep a watchful eye on them.

'Daniel has been very silly and Elizabeth has been very brave,' she stated. 'But they have both had a nasty shock. What they both need now is some medicine and a good night's sleep.'

By the following morning, both children were fit and well again.

And James, who had been rudely awakened by the commotion on the attic landing, was soon spreading the dramatic news all around the school.

Elizabeth had heard those cries again! Why, he had half heard them himself. They had woken him up. And this time there really *had* been a fire. It was in Daniel Carter's room. Daniel had passed out in the smoke and fumes. He might have *died*!

Elizabeth had dragged him to safety. The naughtiest girl had saved the day!

'You must have had a premonition on Saturday night, Elizabeth,' whispered Kathleen in awe, when Elizabeth appeared for French. 'Isn't it weird?'

'Please do not talk in my lesson, Kathleen!' exclaimed Mam'zelle '*Silence, s'il vous plaît.*'

Elizabeth and Julian exchanged secret smiles.

Over a delicious breakfast that Matron had cooked for them that morning, Daniel had told Elizabeth everything. After that she had wasted no time in finding Julian. He had been so quick to spot that Daniel was trying to shield someone. Now she was able to tell him who it was!

Very soon the whole school would hear about it too.

CHAPTER TWELVE

WILLIAM AND RITA HAVE A STORY TO TELL

IT WAS very unusual for a School Meeting to be called in the dinner hour. But then this was going to be a very unusual Meeting.

'We may have to decide upon a punishment for somebody,' William told the rows of assembled pupils. 'But first we have a story to tell you.'

'Once upon a time,' began Rita, 'there was a boy who was not very happy at his boarding school. He liked to read a lot and he liked to have privacy. In fact, his mother and father requested he be given a little room to himself. As things turned out, that, perhaps, was not such a good idea . . .'

The audience listened, fascinated, as the head boy took up the thread of the story.

'He liked going home for the holidays and last Easter holidays were especially enjoyable. You see, on the first day of the holidays he found a baby bird that had fallen from its nest. He took it indoors and nursed it back to health. It was a baby rook, so he called it Rookie. He hand-reared it. First of all, he fed it with bread and milk. Soon it needed a richer diet and he went out every day and dug up worms for it to eat. It grew very fast indeed . . . Your turn now, Rita.'

The head girl smiled at the spellbound children.

At the very back of the hall Miss Belle, Miss Best and Mr Johns sat listening quietly. They had given their permission for Daniel's story to be told.

'Members of the crow family cannot really be tamed. Rookie was no exception. He was soon into everything, jumping into the butter in the kitchen, pecking at the soap in the bathroom. Outside he would dive-bomb the bonfire in the garden, trying to attack the smoke! The family would cry, '*Fire!*' to warn him. Unlike the magpie, or the jay, or the hooded crow, the rook can make a *great* variety of sounds if it wants to, not just the usual cawing,' explained Rita. She smiled again. 'Soon Rookie could scream "*Fire!*" himself. But he still kept attacking the bonfire smoke in the same foolish way!'

'He was finally cured of the habit,' interrupted William, 'when he flew too close to the flames one day and almost singed his feathers. He had a healthy respect for smoke after that! By this time, his young owner was back at boarding school for the summer term.'

'While the boy was away at school, he often thought about Rookie,' continued Rita. 'He did love his wicked pet so. He missed him. He could hardly wait for half-term. When he got home, he found that Rookie was now full-grown and was becoming very boisterous. In fact, unmanageable. He would wait for the postman in the front garden and try to peck at his legs! And, that very half-term week, something dreadful happened. Rookie took a liking to the young strawberry plants growing in the next-door garden. He kept pulling them out of the ground. The next-door neighbour would have been pleased to shoot him!'

Some of the pupils gasped. The story was getting very exciting. Strawberry plants! A bird with a warning scream! Now they were certain that they knew what this was all about.

'What happened next?' cried some of the juniors.

'What happened next,' said William gravely, 'was that the boy's parents realised that they could cope with Rookie no longer. At the end of the boy's half-term holiday, before they took him back to school, they told their son that he must say goodbye to Rookie. For good. Very soon now they would release the bird somewhere in the countryside, back into the wild.

'So for the first day back at school the boy was very

sad, as you can imagine . . . Until, by the stables the following afternoon, a bird flew down from a treetop nearby and settled on the boy's shoulder. It was Rookie! The bird had followed the car back to school. It had secretly taken up residence at its young master's school!'

It was Rita who brought the story to its conclusion.

'The boy was overjoyed. The bird loved him! It had refused to be parted from him! He plucked up his courage. At the first School Meeting he fully intended to beg for permission to keep Rookie at school. He was just about to put his request to that fateful Meeting when . . .'

Rita looked round the hall. 'What happened?'

The juniors called out the answers.

'You said about the strawberry plants!'

'Daniel knew it must be Rookie!'

'He was scared Rookie would be sent away. So he made it up about helping in the stables instead!'

'He knew Rookie was living down there and he wanted to be with him sometimes.'

The head girl nodded. 'The bird must have flown in through Elizabeth's window one day and stolen her button,' Rita explained. 'And then he saw the strawberry plants to play with instead.'

'So he dropped it!' concluded William.

A buzz of conversation rippled through the hall.

Sitting near the back, John Terry scratched his head and smiled to himself. He had been so sure that the button had been linked to the crime – and he was right after all! When it had looked as though there was *not* a link, he had begun to wonder if a large bird or even an animal could have been responsible. He had been watching out for signs ever since, but had seen nothing. So he had been on the right track both times – but had failed to make the vital connection!

As the noise level in the hall began to rise, William rapped his little hammer sharply on the table.

'Silence, please. Everyone be quiet now. You have all guessed who the story is about. And now Daniel himself wants to stand up and speak to us.'

Elizabeth saw the fair-haired boy nervously clench and unclench his fists. He rose slowly to his feet. Then he took a deep breath. He spoke timidly.

'I want to tell everybody I'm sorry for the bad things I've done. I know we're not allowed to have matches or candles and I could easily have set the school on fire. I'm very ashamed about that. I'm also *very* ashamed . . .'

He gulped and glanced at Elizabeth. His voice seemed to be drying up in his throat. She gave him an encouraging nod. *Go on, Daniel.*

'. . . that I was so deceitful. I wanted to have Rookie at school with me so badly that I kept quiet and let other people suffer. I *guessed* it was Rookie who made a noise outside our classroom window. I expect he was looking for me. It was one of his cheeky sort-of-human sounds. But I let Julian take the blame! And Elizabeth getting into trouble for ringing the fire bell was even worse! I couldn't be sure, but I guessed she must have heard Rookie. And I didn't own up. I was so miserable about it. I just sat in my room all day. And the worst thing of all has been play rehearsals! How could I enjoy being in the play when I had made other people lose their parts?'

He sat down hurriedly and buried his face in his hands.

William then asked Elizabeth and Julian to stand up.

'You two have had the worst of Daniel's behaviour,' he said. 'Especially Elizabeth. Can you, Elizabeth, suggest to the Meeting what *you* think his punishment should be?'

There was an expectant hush in the hall, as Elizabeth opened her mouth to speak. School waited to hear what she would say.

CHAPTER THIRTEEN

THE SUMMER PLAY – AND AFTER

ELIZABETH HAD already consulted Julian. The two friends had discussed things very carefully just before the Meeting.

At the end of morning lessons they had gone with Daniel to the school stables to help him look for Rookie. But the glossy black bird with the white blaze above its beak was not there. It was so sad to see Daniel walking around and looking up at the trees, calling out, 'Rookie?' over and over again.

'You were right, Elizabeth,' he had said tearfully. 'He *has* gone. And I don't think he'll be coming back.'

Julian had put an arm round the boy's shoulders as the trio walked slowly back to school for dinner.

'It's hard for you to accept, Daniel. But it will be good if he never comes back. Rooks are not meant to live on their own. No wonder he was so anti-social!

They like to live with other rooks, in colonies. It will mean he's been accepted back into the wild.'

Now Elizabeth spoke up at the Meeting.

'Daniel *should* be punished for the fire in his room last night,' she said. 'But he already *has* been. The worst punishment of all. His bird was terrified. The fire and all the commotion frightened Rookie away! He's gone, you see. Daniel's been punished for everything else too. He's not had a moment's peace since Julian and I lost our parts in the play. His own guilty conscience saw to that!'

She sat down, out of breath.

There was a moment's silence. Then suddenly everybody was clapping Elizabeth's little speech. It was very fair of her. She had said exactly the right thing.

The head boy and girl both nodded in approval. So did the monitors on the platform. Joan felt very proud of Elizabeth.

William held up a hand for silence again. He fixed Daniel with a calm, kindly gaze.

'Love of books is a wonderful thing, Daniel. Favourite storybooks are like dear friends. But they must never be a substitute for caring for *real* people too. Lost in your storybook last night, burning that candle, you gave no thought to all the real boys and girls here at Whyteleafe and the possible danger of fire.'

Daniel hung his head.

'And caring for birds and animals. That too is a grand thing,' William ended. 'But neither should that ever be a substitute for caring for people. In your desire to keep Rookie you allowed *people* to suffer. You caused Elizabeth, in particular, a lot of pain and unhappiness.'

'Please, William, I know you are right, but it was just so amazing that Rookie liked me so much!' blurted out Daniel. 'The way he followed the car, all the way from our village, just so he could stay with me! You see –' he shook his head – 'the trouble with "real people" is that they don't seem to like *me* very much.'

Elizabeth leapt to her feet indignantly. 'That's not true, William. Julian and I like Daniel. We really do!'

She sat down, embarrassed.

Then, languidly, Julian got to his feet. 'There's something else that needs clearing up,' he said casually. 'About *my* having suffered over the play. That's not quite true. The part of Jonkin is such a long one. Surely I can't be expected to start learning it now? I would much rather Daniel kept it.'

'Only Miss Ranger can decide that, Julian,' replied Rita pleasantly. 'She is the play's producer. Miss Belle and Miss Best will have a say too. After all, it's their play.'

But the joint heads – and Mr Johns – were already nodding their approval. It was what the teachers had wanted all along for Daniel. They were worried that he never mixed. Julian's surmise had been correct. Furthermore, Daniel should never have been allowed a single room in the first place, the joint heads decided. They would have to rectify the matter.

It was a disappointment to Elizabeth. Julian was not to be her co-star in the summer play, after all. Arabella was left with that consolation at least.

But Daniel's performance just got better and better. Although he was still pining for the bird, the boy started to throw himself into rehearsals. It was fun that John McTavish was in the play, as Mr Grasshopper. Since moving in right next to John, in the big dormitory, the two had become good friends.

Julian was in the same dormitory and gave Daniel a lot of coaching. There was no doubt that helped too.

Most of all, Daniel did not want to let Elizabeth down. She soon began to get over her disappointment.

The great occasion itself took place on a beautiful midsummer's evening. *A Woodland Adventure* was enacted in the prettiest corner of the school grounds. The weeping ash tree with its trailing fronds made a perfect stage set for Jonkin and the Fairy Queen. Everyone loved the bemasked 'woodland animals' that appeared, disappeared and reappeared among the greenery.

The whole school sat transfixed, not least Miss Belle and Miss Best. They had worked so hard writing a new summer play in time for the first form's turn this year. And how well they were doing it! What a success for their play.

Elizabeth was the star of the show. She had to make several curtain calls. But Daniel too had some curtain calls for a fine performance. The Beauty and the Beast were delighted with both of them.

Elizabeth lingered in the grounds long afterwards. She wanted this evening to last forever.

So did Daniel. He was standing by the big sundial at the top of the lawn. Suddenly he looked up into the sky.

'Hello, Dan. What are you looking at?'

He pointed. A cloud of rooks was flying overhead, but one of the birds had dropped back. It circled above their heads for a moment. They both held their breath and waited.

Then, dipping one wing towards them, as if to say goodbye, it flapped away and caught up with its companions.

Elizabeth and Daniel continued to watch as the cloud of birds headed for the distant horizon. Soon the little cloud became no more than a moving speck against the lowering red sun. Then the birds were gone, and there was only the sun.

BONUS BLYTON

Enid Blyton has been one of the world's best-loved storytellers for over seventy-five years. Her interest in writing began as a child, and before she loved receiving letters from the children who read her books, she enjoyed working with them as a teacher. The Naughtiest Girl stories are inspired by real schools and experiences. Turn the page to learn more about Enid as a child and as a teacher. Afterwards, you might like to write about your school and teachers and the people in *your* class!

THE LIFE AND TIMES OF ENID BLYTON

11 August 1897	Enid Blyton was born in East Dulwich, London. Two brothers are born after her – Hanly (b. 1899) and Carey (b. 1902).
1911	Enid enters a children's poetry competition and is praised for her writing. She's on the path to becoming a bestselling author . . .
1916	Enid begins to train as a teacher in Ipswich. By the time she is 21, she is a fully qualified Froebel teacher, and starts work at a school in Kent.
1917	Enid's first 'grown-up' publication – three poems in *Nash's Magazine*.
June 1922	Enid's first book is published. It's called *Child Whispers*.
1926	Enid begins editing – and writes – the phenomenal *Sunny Stories for Little Folks* magazine. (She continues in this role for 26 years!)

1927	So vast is Enid's output that she has to learn to type. (But she still writes to children by hand.)
1931	Having married Hugh Pollock in 1924, the couple's first child, Gillian, is born. Imogen, their second daughter, was born in 1935.
1942	The Famous Five is launched with *Five on a Treasure Island*.
1949	The first appearance of *The Secret Seven* and of *Noddy* mark this year as special.
1953	Enid moves away from *Sunny Stories* to launch *Enid Blyton's Magazine*. She is now renowned throughout the world – she even established her own company, called Darrell Waters Limited (the surname of her second husband).
1962	Enid Blyton becomes one of the first and most important children's authors to be published in paperback. Now, she reaches even more readers than ever before.
28 November 1968	Enid dies in her sleep, in a nursing home in Hampstead.

A NOTE FROM ENID BLYTON'S DAUGHTER

Enid had two daughters, Gillian and Imogen, both of whom read all her stories, often before they were sent to the publishers. Sadly, Gillian has died, but she wrote an introduction to *The Naughtiest Girl* which tells us something of her mother's life . . .

Enid Blyton was not only a writer for children, she was also involved in the editing and writing of books for teachers. She was a trained Froebel and Montessori teacher and had run her own school before she married.

She was very interested in the world of education and especially a mixed boarding school called Summerhill, which was opened by A. S. Neill in 1921. He believed that the school should be governed by the children themselves with the teachers only taking part if asked by the children.

In The Naughtiest Girl stories Whyteleafe School

was run in the same way with a meeting held every week in the school hall. The head boy and girl presided over the meeting aided by twelve monitors chosen by the other children. It was a kind of school parliament where the children made their own rules, heard grumbles and complaints, judged one another and punished bad behaviour. All problems were discussed and decided by the children and only in very difficult situations were the head teachers asked for their advice.

Does your school have a student council? Do you know who its members are?

Summerhill, in Suffolk, is still a school today and, over its ninety-year history, has influenced many schools around the world. The school prides itself on children's 'right to play' and lessons are optional. Why not find out more about it by looking on the internet?

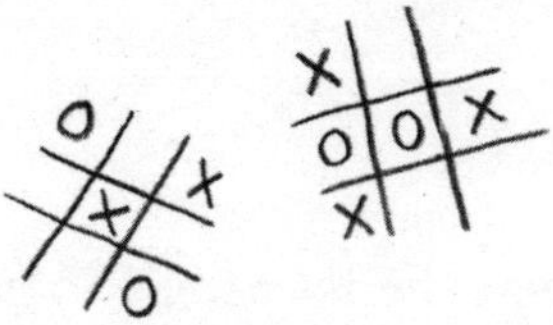

ENID AS A CHILD: ON THE PATH TO BECOMING A WRITER – PART TWO

When she was young, everyone thought Enid would follow a musical path. But when she was fourteen, her life changed. She submitted work to a poetry competition in a magazine. It was run by Arthur Mee, whose encyclopaedia Enid loved! He liked her poem, and printed it and – best of all – said, 'Perhaps one day you will *really* write.'

But it took a long time – and many setbacks – before Enid regularly began to be published. Her first publication as an adult was in *Nash's Magazine* in 1917.

When Enid decided she wanted to be a children's writer, she decided to train to be a kindergarten teacher, so that she would be surrounded by children. She said, 'I would see naughty children and good children, and I would learn what the children wanted to read.'

Enid's father was amazed when she told him she wanted to train to be a teacher, instead of following her music studies. And he said, 'How like you, Enid, to tell me these things over the *telephone*! Why must you be so headstrong?' He said he'd have to think about giving Enid permission, but, in the end, said yes.

At the end of her teacher training, she was given a glowing report by the headmistress . . .

She has very good ability, is both musical and artistic and has shown teaching capacity of a high order. Enthusiasm and energy are marked characteristics. She had a real love of children and handles them well . . . As one of the best students we have had for some years, I can recommend her warmly for a responsible post.

In January 1919 Enid took on her first teaching job, at Bickley Park School for boys.

You can read the first part of Enid's journey in the new edition of *The Naughtiest Girl Helps a Friend*.

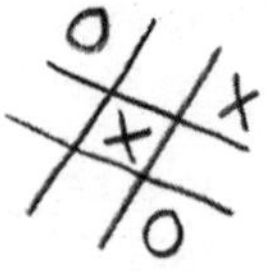

WHAT THEY DID AT MISS BROWN'S SCHOOL

In 1920 Enid Blyton became a governess to the four Thompson children, whose ages ranged from four to ten. The family lived in Surbiton, in Surrey, in a house called 'Southernhay'. Enid had a small room which overlooked the garden, and it was there that she wrote many of her stories. Enid's tiny class often had lessons outdoors in the summer months.

Enid was very popular with her students, because her lessons were both practical and creative. She worked with them to put on performances for which they made props, costumes and invitations – and even sold tickets.

In 1941 she published a long story called 'What They Did at Miss Brown's School', which was divided into monthly episodes. It's been hard to find for many years, but you can read extracts in these new editions of *The Naughtiest Girl* books. The character of Miss Brown and her tiny class is very much based on Enid Blyton and her school at the Thompsons' . . .

Here's the eighth episode . . .

8. August. A Day by the Sea

THE FOUR children at Miss Brown's school were quite sad when the summer holidays came.

'Miss Brown, you said we would have something lovely to do each month of the year, but we shan't in August, because we shall not be at school!' said Susan.

'Good gracious, can't you find something nice to do in August by yourselves?' asked Miss Brown.

'It's more fun to do something with *you*,' said Peter. 'You see, you know about things, so you can answer our questions.'

'Well now, I'll tell you what we'll do, if you are all at home,' said Miss Brown. 'I am not going away until the second week in August – and, if you like, I will take you all for a day by the sea, and show you what to look for when you go away for *your* holidays!'

'Oh, Miss Brown! Will you really?' cried all the children.

'I've always wanted to know about the sea creatures!'

said John. 'They are so strange. It will make my seaside holiday so much nicer if I know something about the creatures there.'

'Well, ask your mothers if you can come with me next Wednesday,' said Miss Brown. 'The motor coach leaves Farmer Straws' Corner at eight o'clock. Be there in time, for the coach won't wait for sleepy heads!'

So the next Wednesday all the children were climbing into the big red coach with Miss Brown at eight o'clock. The sea was two hours' journey away. Each of them had a bag of sandwiches, apples and chocolate, and they were all so excited that they couldn't stop talking for one minute.

'Now listen,' said Miss Brown, when the big, wide sea came into sight, as blue as a forget-me-not, sparkling in the sunshine. 'We will all go and have a glass of milk and a bun, and then we will go straight down to the beach and look for what we can find. I shall sit in the shade and wait for you to bring me your treasures. You can take off your shoes and stockings and paddle all you like today, for it is very hot.'

So the children were soon splashing in and out of the sea. Then they began to look for something to take to Miss Brown.

'I've found a starfish!' cried Susan in delight. 'It's got five fingers!' Susan put it into her pail and carried it to Miss Brown.

'Ah! A fine starfish!' said Miss Brown. 'He is nothing but five fingers and a mouth! Turn him upside down and you will see his mouth in the middle – and do you see these funny little fleshy-looking things jutting out from all these pinholes underneath? They are his suckers – he uses them when he wants to get about!'

'Is it true that a starfish will grow new fingers if it is cut in half?' asked John.

'Quite true,' said Miss Brown, 'but I hope you are not thinking of trying such a thing, John!'

'Of course not. I couldn't be so cruel,' said John. 'Miss Brown, let's put the starfish into this pond and see if it uses its sucker-legs to crawl away?'

So Susan slipped it into the pool – and sure enough the starfish crawled quickly away on his dozens of funny little sucker-legs!

'Now come and find something else!' cried Peter. 'Look, there's a crab!'

So the crab was taken to Miss Brown and she told them that it was a shore or green crab. She told them how it changes its coat. 'It cracks its shell across the back and leaps out!' said Miss Brown. 'It has a soft shell underneath and this quickly becomes hard. After it has sprung out of its old small shell it grows to twice the size in about twenty-four hours.'

'I wish we could take one home and see if we could watch it changing its shell,' said Mary longingly. But

Miss Brown said that nothing but shells and seaweed were to be taken home.

'Miss Brown! Look in this rock pool!' cried John. 'There are shrimps – and prawns too, I do believe!'

'So there are!' said Miss Brown.

'But I thought shrimps and prawns were pink,' said Susan in astonishment. 'In our shop at home they are, I know.'

'They go pink when they are cooked, silly!' said John, and they all laughed. 'They are grey when they are alive – a sort of sandy-grey to match the pool.'

'They are rather like tiny lobsters,' said Peter, watching them.

'Catch a few and put them in your pail,' said Miss Brown. So Peter caught a prawn and two shrimps and everyone looked at them closely.

'Do you see their legs at the front,' said Miss Brown, 'and their false legs, called swimmerets, at the back? And see their two stalked eyes! How would you like to have eyes on stalks? You would look very funny!'

'How can you tell the difference between a big shrimp and a small prawn?' asked Susan. 'I should never know which was which!'

'Do you see that long spike sticking out at the front of their heads?' asked Miss Brown. 'Well, if it is saw-edged, you have caught a prawn. If it is smooth, you have a shrimp. That's how you can tell. Shrimps and prawns are the dustmen of the pools. They eat up the rubbish.'

'Oh! What's that!' suddenly cried Mary, as a curious jelly umbrella bobbed across the deep part of the pool.

'A jellyfish!' cried Peter in excitement. 'Look, we can see it beautifully, Miss Brown. It is opening and shutting its umbrella-like body. I suppose that's how it gets along. What are those long threads hanging down, Miss Brown?'

'Those are sting threads,' said Miss Brown. 'If any small creature touches them, poison darts spring out and shoot the victim! This one is not a dangerous jellyfish to us, but the big brownish-yellow one can sting us very painfully indeed.'

'There's a jellyfish on the sand over there,' said John. 'Will it melt?'

'Yes, if you don't put it into the water,' said Miss Brown. 'It will melt right away and leave only a ring-shaped mark on the sand.'

John put the melting jellyfish into a pool, where it once more spread out its jelly-umbrella very thankfully indeed.

'We're finding a fine lot of things,' said Susan, pleased. 'I think I'll collect some shells now.'

'So will we,' said the others, and off they ran over

the smooth sand, which was dotted with all kinds of shells. They soon had a good collection to bring back to Miss Brown. She spread them out in her lap.

'You have univalves and bivalves,' she said. 'Who knows what I mean by that?'

'Univalves are one-shelled creatures and bivalves have two shells, like oysters,' said John at once. 'I know "bi" means two, because of "*bi*-ennial" and "*bi*-cycle".'

'Good boy,' said Miss Brown. 'Well, let's take your univalves or one-shelled creatures first. Now here is what looks like a nice little pointed hat. It is a limpet, and clings so tightly to the rock that even the biggest wave cannot move it – but it can crawl about if it wants to.'

'And what's this?' asked Susan, holding up a pretty little coiled shell of yellow.

'That is a sea-snail's shell,' said Miss Brown. 'And here is another in black and one in brown and another in orange. When the creature is alive, it feeds on seaweed, and if we could see its tongue under a microscrope we should see that it is set with hundreds of little hooked teeth that rasp away the seaweed.'

'This is a whelk's shell, isn't it?' said Mary, holding up a big spiral shell in white. 'Oh, Miss Brown, there's something inside it – look!'

Everyone looked, and Miss Brown laughed. 'There is

a hermit crab inside that shell,' she said. 'A hermit crab has a long, soft tail, and is always afraid that an enemy will come along and nibble it off. So he finds an empty whelk shell, creeps inside backwards, hangs on to the end with his pincers, and puts his claws here at the front door to frighten off enemies! No, don't try to pull him out, Susan – you may make him break his tail. Put him into a pool.'

So the hermit crab went into a pool and was most grateful. The children looked at the other shells. They knew the periwinkle, for they had seen it in the shops. Miss Brown showed them two or three more univalve shells they had – the quaint cowry, with its saw-edged slit underneath, the pretty shell called the painted top, cone-shaped and coloured brightly, and the graceful, tapering wentle trap or turning-stair shell.

'Now for the bivalves, the two-shelled creatures,' said Mary, and she picked up a dark blue double shell, which she could open and shut by the hinge at the back. 'This is a mussel, isn't it?'

'Yes,' said Miss Brown, 'there are thousands on the rocks over there. They cling tightly by means of many strong little threads. And this is half of an old oyster shell – and here is a pretty cockle shell. Cockles have a curious kind of "foot", and they can jump with this if they want to. And now here is a lovely scallop, rayed like the sun! Well, do you think you know them all? We'll take them home with us, and you shall see if you have remembered their names next time we meet!'

'I want to get some seaweed,' said Mary. 'I'd like to take a nice long ribbon of it home, Miss Brown, and then we'll hang it up outside the window. If it's dry, the weather will be fine, but if it hangs limp and wet the weather will be bad!'

Soon the children came back with long fronds of ribbon-like brown seaweed that they dragged behind them. It was very pretty, with frilled edges.

'You have brought one of the seaweeds called tangles,' said Miss Brown. 'There are a good many of them. We will take your frond home, Mary. It is the longest and finest, and has such pretty curled edges.'

'And look at this seaweed – it has little bladders that go pop when I squeeze them!' said Peter.

'That is the bladderwrack,' said Miss Brown. 'And just look in this little pond here – do you see that pretty purple-red seaweed waving graceful, misty fingers about? That is the coralline seaweed. And there is some sea lettuce over there, its bright green leaves reminding us of our own green lettuce at home.'

'I saw some sea grass too, in another pool,' said Mary. 'It was just like grass growing in the water.'

After that it was dinnertime and the children ate

every single thing they had brought with them. They bought lemonade and ice creams too, and had a perfectly lovely time.

'And now you have two hours more to paddle and play,' said Miss Brown. 'Enjoy yourselves and we'll start back home with all our treasures!'

When they climbed into the red motor coach that afternoon, the children were tired but very happy. They had two pails full of shells, and a beautiful big frond of brown seaweed.

'Well, that was a lovely thing to do for August!' said Susan. 'Thank you, Miss Brown. We loved it! Now, what's for September?'

'Oh, let's get the holidays over first!' laughed Miss Brown. 'I promise you I'll have something good for September – you just wait and see!'

Enid Blyton®

THE FAMOUS FIVE

Join the Adventure!

Have you read them all?

Enid Blyton®

THE

SECRET SEVEN

SOLVE THE MYSTERY!

HAVE YOU READ THEM ALL?

Enid Blyton®

THE

SECRET SEVEN

SOLVE THE MYSTERY!

Don't miss...

Two action-packed Secret Seven stories from prizewinning author **PAMELA BUTCHART**!

Enid Blyton®

THE
SECRET SEVEN

SOLVE THE MYSTERY!

Solve every puzzle, just like the Secret Seven, in this fun book of 100 tricky codes, puzzles, sudokus, crosswords and more!

THE MYSTERY SERIES

Read all 15 classic stories!

ENIDBLYTON.CO.UK

IS FOR PARENTS, CHILDREN AND TEACHERS!

Sign up to the newsletter on the homepage for a monthly round-up of news from the world of

Enid Blyton®

JOIN US ON SOCIAL MEDIA

EnidBlytonOfficial BlytonOfficial

Illustration by Laura Ellen Anderson.

Enid Blyton®

is one of the most popular children's authors of all time. Her books have sold over 500 million copies and have been translated into other languages more often than any other children's author.

Enid Blyton adored writing for children. She wrote over 700 books and about 2,000 short stories. *The Famous Five* books, now 80 years old, are her most popular. She is also the author of other favourites including *The Secret Seven*, *The Magic Faraway Tree* and *Malory Towers*.

Born in London in 1897, Enid lived much of her life in Buckinghamshire and loved dogs, gardening and the countryside. She was very knowledgeable about trees, flowers, birds and animals. Dorset – where some of the Famous Five's adventures are set – was a favourite place of hers too.

Enid Blyton's stories are read and loved by millions of children (and grown-ups) all over the world. Visit enidblyton.co.uk to discover more.

Illustration by
Laura Ellen Anderson.

The NAUGHTIEST GIRL Helps a Friend

Have you read them all?

1. The Naughtiest Girl in the School
2. The Naughtiest Girl Again
3. The Naughtiest Girl is a Monitor
4. Here's the Naughtiest Girl
5. The Naughtiest Girl Keeps a Secret
6. The Naughtiest Girl Helps a Friend
7. The Naughtiest Girl Saves the Day
8. Well Done, the Naughtiest Girl
9. The Naughtiest Girl Wants to Win
10. The Naughtiest Girl Marches On

Enid Blyton®

The Naughtiest Girl Helps a Friend

WRITTEN BY
ANNE DIGBY

HODDER

HODDER CHILDREN'S BOOKS

First published in Great Britain in 1999 by Hodder & Stoughton
This edition published in 2021
For further information about the editorial history of this book,
see enidblyton.co.uk/books

3 5 7 9 10 8 6 4

Enid Blyton® and Enid Blyton's signature are registered
trade marks of Hodder & Stoughton Limited
Text © 2021 Hodder & Stoughton Limited
Illustrations by Claire Powell © 2021 Hodder & Stoughton Limited

No trade mark or copyrighted material may be reproduced without the
express written permission of the trademark and copyright owner.

The moral right of the author has been asserted.

All characters and events in this publication, other than those clearly in the public domain, are fictitious and any resemblance to real persons, living or dead, is purely coincidental.

All rights reserved.
No part of this publication may be reproduced, stored in a retrieval system, or transmitted, in any form or by any means, without the prior permission in writing of the publisher, nor be otherwise circulated in any form of binding or cover other than that in which it is published and without a similar condition including this condition being imposed on the subsequent purchaser.

A CIP catalogue record for this book is available from the British Library.

ISBN 978 1 444 95865 2

Printed and bound in Great Britain by Clays Ltd, Elcograf S.p.A.

Typeset in Caslon by Avon DataSet Ltd, Arden Court, Alcester, Warwickshire

The paper and board used in this book are made from wood
from responsible sources.

MIX
Paper | Supporting responsible forestry
FSC® C104740

Hodder Children's Books
An imprint of Hachette Children's Group
Part of Hodder & Stoughton
Carmelite House
50 Victoria Embankment
London EC4Y 0DZ

An Hachette UK Company
www.hachette.co.uk
www.hachettechildrens.co.uk

CONTENTS

INTRODUCTION

by Cressida Cowell

bestselling author of the
How to Train Your Dragon series

Like so many, many children before and after me, Enid Blyton's books played a crucial role in turning my nine-year-old self into a passionate reader.

That is because Enid Blyton had an extraordinary knack for writing the kind of books that children actually *want* to read, rather than the kind of books that adults think they *should* read.

Enid Blyton could tap into children's dreams, children's desires, children's wishes, with pinpoint accuracy. She knew that every child, however good and well-behaved they might look on the outside, secretly longed to be Elizabeth Allen, the naughtiest kid in the school. I'm afraid I entirely cheered Elizabeth on, as she defied her parents, the headmistresses, her schoolmates, and the very serious School Meetings. If anything, I wanted her to be even naughtier.

But *The Naughtiest Girl* books were really my favourite of Enid Blyton's school stories because of Whyteleafe, a very different school from Malory Towers or St Clare's. What if there could be a school in which discipline was administered by the children rather than the adults? In which all money was given in at the start of the term and distributed among the children along socialist lines? Wouldn't this be the kind of school that children would actually *want* to go to, rather than the kind of school that children *have* to go to?

It was an interesting proposition to a nine-year-old, and it remains an interesting proposition.

I hope you enjoy this story as much as I did when *I* was nine years old.

Cressida Cowell

CHAPTER ONE

A BIG RESPONSIBILITY FOR JOAN

'LOOK, JOAN!' exclaimed Elizabeth, as they emerged from behind the stables. 'Look at all the tents! The teachers and the seniors must have put them up for us. There were only bushes and trees and grass and buttercups here this morning. Oh, Joan, I do hope Miss Ranger will let me be in your tent. I'm so proud you've been made a tent monitor!'

The two friends paused, out of breath. Their kitbags, stuffed full of spare clothes and camping equipment, were heavy. They each carried a pillow and a sleeping bag too. They were making their way from the school buildings across to the campsite. Putting everything down for a moment, they leant against the stable wall and gazed at the scene beyond.

'To think that's where we'll live for the next few days!' laughed Elizabeth, clapping her hands. 'Oh, won't it be fun? I'm so glad neither of us is going home for half-term. Isn't it just like a little secret village?'

For all children staying on at Whyteleafe School over half-term, a summer camp had been organised in the school grounds. And this wild corner, beyond the stables, made a perfect campsite. The school tents had been brought out of storage. They were ex-army bell tents. Supported by a central pole, their roofs tapered to a point and they were high enough to stand up in. The tents were dotted along both banks of an old dried-up stream bed. On a washing line, strung between two willow trees, some bright tea towels billowed gently in the sunshine.

'Why, yes, it does look half like a village,' Joan agreed quietly. 'The brown tents are like little houses. Except they haven't got any windows in them, of course,' she added. She touched the large torch that was sticking out of the top of her kitbag.

'At least this torch will be useful at night when it gets dark inside.' All the tent monitors had been told to bring a torch – only one was allowed per tent.

That reminded Elizabeth.

'I'll *die* if I haven't been put in your tent!' she repeated. 'I begged and begged Miss Ranger to say I could be. I wonder what she's decided?'

'Hadn't we better go and find out?' asked Joan, with her gentle smile.

'Yes, let's!'

The two friends humped their kitbags over their shoulders once more. With their pillows and sleeping bags rolled under their arms they staggered onwards. The ground was uneven here, with large tussocks of grass to step round. But they went as fast as they could. Elizabeth was beginning to feel tense now. Joan too looked rather anxious. What would Miss Ranger have decided?

Elizabeth and Joan were best friends. At one time they had been in the first form together. In those days Elizabeth had been called the naughtiest girl in the school and Joan had been her only true friend. Joan was older than Elizabeth and had gone up into the second form some time ago. In fact, she was a second-form monitor. It meant that the friends saw far less of each other in term time than they used to. It was going to be marvellous fun being at camp together, thought Elizabeth, and even better if she could be in Joan's tent.

Miss Ranger, Elizabeth's form teacher, was to be in charge of the girls at camp, assisted by Rita, the head girl. The boys, whose tents were pitched on the other side of the dried-up stream, would be answerable to Mr Leslie, the science master, and William, the school's head boy.

'You will sleep four girls to a tent,' Miss Ranger had explained to some of them. 'There will be a school monitor, or one of the senior girls, in every tent. She will be known as Tent Monitor. She will be responsible for the happiness and wellbeing of everyone in her tent. As there will be a little junior girl to look after in most of the tents, it will be an important responsibility.'

The boys' side of the camp would be run on similar lines.

'Will we still have Meetings, so we can air our complaints and grumbles?' Arabella Buckley had asked eagerly. She would have loved to have been a tent monitor herself, able to boss people around. But, as there was no hope of that, she was uneasy. 'I mean, if there are any problems that the tent monitor can't solve?'

'Oh, yes, there will be the usual Meetings, with William and Rita in charge,' Miss Ranger had assured her. 'But they will be held in the open air. I hope you can keep them nice and short.'

And now, as the two friends reached the campsite, here was Miss Ranger coming to greet them.

'Hello, Elizabeth. Hello, Joan. You are almost the last to arrive! My goodness, you're certainly heavily laden, Elizabeth. Here, let me take your pillow and sleeping bag.'

'It's my fault we've taken so long, Miss Ranger,' confessed Elizabeth. 'I couldn't decide which books to bring, or whether to bring my yo-yo, and then I couldn't get everything into my kitbag—'

'Never mind!' replied the first-form teacher. 'Follow me.'

She led them past the nearest tents and through to a large clearing. Here the ground was level. Groundsheets had been spread out, with bags and bedding piled high. Lots of girls were milling around Rita, the head girl. Rita was holding a list and directing the girls to their various tents. Beyond, a brick barbecue had been built and a fire lit. The delicious smell of toasted muffins mingled with woodsmoke drifted towards Elizabeth. Beyond the barbecue, a camp kitchen had been set up. In fact, it was still being built. Thomas, a senior boy, was banging some stakes into the ground with a mallet, while Mr Leslie sawed some rough planks.

The two friends dumped their things on a groundsheet and gazed round at all the activity with interest.

'This is Camp Centre!' explained Miss Ranger. 'It's a very busy place, as you can see.'

Elizabeth stared across at the list in Rita's hand.

'Please, Miss Ranger, will I be in Joan's tent?' she blurted out.

'Yes, indeed, Elizabeth,' replied the teacher lightly. 'I've decided that Joan will be the best person to keep you in order.'

The friends exchanged joyful looks.

'Oh, I'm so pleased,' said Joan quietly. She rarely showed emotions, but the relief on her face was unmistakable. 'I'm sure Elizabeth will be a great help to me.'

'Joan will *not* have to keep me in order, Miss Ranger!' said Elizabeth. Even though the teacher had made the remark lightly, it had stung just a little. She was *not* the naughtiest girl any more. She was going to be as good as good could be.

'Of course not,' replied the teacher. 'Joan, may I have a quiet word with you, please? It's just about your junior.'

As the teacher took Joan to one side, Elizabeth went and stood by the kitbags and gazed about her. She was in a happy little dream. She was definitely going in Joan's tent! Life was perfect. It was a sunny day and they had been promised more good weather to come. The sky was completely blue. And how fine the big bell tents looked! Much better than those low ones that you had to crawl into. It would be like living in their own little house!

Which tent would they be given? And which of the younger girls were they being asked to look after? Miss Ranger had warned them there would be a junior in most of the tents.

'Elizabeth!'

Joan walked across and joined her. The teacher had departed.

'Miss Ranger has told me where our tent is. She says we can just pick up our things and go straight there. You see,' she explained, 'it seems that Teeny's been here quite a while. She's sitting in the tent, waiting to get to know me.'

'Teeny Wilson? Is that who we've got?' asked Elizabeth cheerfully. Noticing that her friend looked rather pale, she added: 'What's the matter, Joan? Teeny won't be any trouble for you to look after. I'm sure she couldn't say boo to a goose!'

Tina Wilson was new at Whyteleafe School this term and small for her age. She was the smallest member of the junior class, which was why everybody called her Teeny. Elizabeth had noticed the timid little girl standing alone at playtime, her glasses too big for her small, round face.

Miss Ranger had confided to Joan that Teeny was not settling down well at her new school. She seemed rather shy and nervy. She would no doubt find sleeping in a tent rather strange at first, even a little scary. The teacher had reasoned that calm, gentle Joan was exactly the reassuring presence at camp that Teeny needed. She had told Joan as much.

'It's going to be a big responsibility looking after Teeny,' was all Joan would say.

'No, it isn't. It's going to be fun!' replied Elizabeth, as they headed along the bank towards the last group of tents. 'We'll make sure she has a good time. Am I going to be a big responsibility too?' she teased her friend. 'I promise I'll be good. You know I'm not the naughtiest girl in the school these days!'

Joan barely smiled.

'Sh,' she said. 'That's our tent at the end. She mustn't hear us talking about her. And wait, Elizabeth, there's something else I have to tell you. Let's put our things down a minute.'

Obediently, Elizabeth propped her things up against a willow tree, but she was hardly listening.

'What, Joan?' she asked, staring impatiently towards the brown bell tent that was to be their home for the next few days. The flap was partly open. She was longing to peep inside, see what it was like in there and make friends with Teeny. She and Joan would soon put the little junior at her ease. 'What a glorious position!' she exclaimed. 'We're right in the corner.'

The tent was pitched by the school's high boundary wall. The crumbling old wall's dark red brickwork was almost hidden in places by cascading honeysuckle. Elizabeth could smell the sweet scent wafting on the warm breeze, even at this distance. By the wall, the bank of the old stream dropped down to where the dried-up watercourse came to an end at a culvert. The culvert, an old brick-built tunnel, would once have carried the flowing water underground for a short distance. Now the stream bed was just dry, powdery dust and the entrance to the culvert choked with rubble and weeds.

'It's about the other person in our tent,' Joan was saying. 'It's going to be Arabella.'

'Arabella Buckley?'

As Joan's words sunk in, Elizabeth groaned.

'Oh, no, not Arabella!'

Then she suddenly giggled. She was too happy today to let anything dismay her for long. She thought of her rich, spoilt classmate, with her pretty, doll-like face. Arabella was always perfectly groomed and thought a great deal of herself.

'Miss High-and-Mighty at camp!' she exclaimed. 'Having to slum it in my tent. Oh, Joan, this should be funny!'

'Now, promise me you two won't quarrel—' began her friend.

'Don't be so tent-monitorish!' laughed Elizabeth. 'It depends how badly Arabella behaves whether we quarrel or not. Come on, Joan, what are we waiting for? Let's go and investigate the tent right now! As long as Arabella doesn't do anything silly and make me lose my temper, there's nothing to fret about!'

She grabbed Joan's hand and bounded towards the last tent.

She was far too excited to notice the frown on her friend's face or to hear her soft reply.

'Knowing Arabella, I'm worried she might.'

And that was not the only thing that Joan was worried about.

CHAPTER TWO

ARABELLA ACCUSES ELIZABETH

AS THE face peered in at her, the tiny, bespectacled girl in the tent gave a nervous start.

'Peepo! Hello, Teeny!' cried Elizabeth boisterously. Then she ducked into the tent, followed by Joan.

The small child shrank back into the shadows, just inside the tent. Her hands were shaking a little.

'Oh, I'm sorry,' she apologised. 'You made me jump.'

Teeny was on her own. Arabella had gone off somewhere.

'Isn't it lovely in here?' said Elizabeth, as her eyes got used to the gloom. She danced round the tall, stout tent pole in the centre. 'Look, Joan! You can stand up straight and walk around in the middle! Isn't this fun?'

'I've put my things over there,' Teeny was telling Joan shyly. She pointed to the far side of the tent. 'It's nice and dark and cosy over there. Is that all right, Joan? Am I allowed?'

Joan at once gave permission.

'What a good idea, Teeny,' said Elizabeth. 'I think I'd like to sleep that side too. Unless you want to, Joan?'

'Oh, no, I'll be quite happy here,' said Joan sweetly. She was crawling around near the open tent flap, in the very small space that Arabella had left clear. 'I like to be near the fresh air!'

'Arabella's taken up far too much room, though,' Elizabeth pointed out. Arabella's sleeping bag was already fully unrolled, with her personal belongings piled all around. 'She's been in and unpacked then, Teeny?'

'She was here very early,' replied the junior. 'She wanted to bag a good place in the tent, she said. She's gone to get a muffin now. Please may I go and get one as well, Joan?'

'Of course, Teeny,' replied Joan gently. 'Off you go. And, while you're out, Elizabeth and I will bring our stuff in and sort it out.'

'We'll get the tent shipshape!' added Elizabeth, eyeing Arabella's things. There was a glint in her eye. Did Arabella really think she was going to get away with having twice as much space as the rest of them? Not if Elizabeth could help it!

The two friends went outside to collect their belongings. They watched the figure of Teeny hurrying off through the tents, looking this way and that as she went.

'What a jumpy little thing!' observed Elizabeth. 'But she really likes you, Joan. I can tell that already. She really looks up to you.'

'I do believe she does,' agreed Joan.

When the two friends had finished sorting things out, they sat outside the tent in the sunshine to take a rest. It was then that Arabella appeared.

'I've had to move a few of your things, Arabella,' Joan said pleasantly. 'You hadn't left me quite enough room. And would you mind rolling your sleeping bag up, please?'

'Whatever for?' asked the fair-haired girl. 'I've arranged it just how I want it for bedtime tonight.'

'Because it's a camp rule,' replied Joan quietly. 'Kitbags must be kept packed during daytime and sleeping bags rolled up. With four people using the tent during the day we have to leave enough space for people to be able to move around.'

'Oh, sorry. I didn't know,' replied Arabella. 'Though I can't think who will want to spend time in the tent during the day when it's so sunny outside. I certainly won't.'

Giving Elizabeth a rather pointed stare, she ducked into the tent to attend to her sleeping bag. Elizabeth smiled to herself. *What good news*, she thought.

'Come on, Elizabeth,' said Joan, rising to her feet. 'If we're going to the village, we'd better stroll down there now. I've got my purse.'

'Are you sure we've got time?' asked Elizabeth. Reluctantly, she too got to her feet. 'We could always go tomorrow.'

'I've looked at the rota. We've got plenty of time!' replied Joan. 'We're down for kitchen duties at six o'clock and that's two whole hours away.'

Joan had discovered that her torch batteries were getting low. She wanted to go to the village and buy some spare ones. It was a strict rule at Whyteleafe School that, if pupils wished to walk down to the shops during free time, they must always go in pairs. Naturally, Elizabeth had agreed to accompany Joan. But in truth she would have much preferred to spend the free time exploring the campsite. There was so much jollity and excitement going on. There was going to be a barbecue round the campfire that evening!

'If you say so—' began Elizabeth.

And then suddenly there came a loud screech from inside the tent.

A moment later Arabella burst out, hurling her

sleeping bag on the ground in front of her.

'What have you put in my sleeping bag, Elizabeth Allen?' she shrieked. 'Take it all out, whatever it is. If you put it in, you can take it out! I suppose I was meant to feel all that stuff in the dark when I climbed into my sleeping bag at bedtime!'

'How dare you!' exclaimed Elizabeth in amazement. Her own voice rose in anger. 'Whatever are you talking about? How dare you start screaming at me!'

Girls from nearby tents were now peering out, to see what the rumpus was about.

Arabella turned to Joan for support.

'When I started to roll my sleeping bag up, it felt all lumpy!' she screeched. 'Then I put my hand inside and there was something all wet and yukky. And there was something prickly as well. Feel inside, if you don't believe me!' Her voice rose to a high-pitched squeak. 'I'm sure anybody in the *world* would scream at Elizabeth, if she did the same thing to them!'

As Joan bent down to unzip the sleeping bag, Elizabeth could feel herself starting to boil with rage.

She hardly cared what Joan was pulling out of the sleeping bag. A wet sponge, Arabella's hairbrush, a bar of sticky soap, a little nailbrush . . .

'Oh dear. Poor Arabella,' Joan was saying, rather helplessly. 'Somebody's been playing a joke on you . . .'

Elizabeth was too busy fighting to control her hot temper. Then—

Arabella walked up to Elizabeth!

'I suppose you think it's funny? I suppose you were really looking forward to watching me get into bed tonight—'

She gave Elizabeth a hard push. And at that point Elizabeth boiled over.

'Why should I want to bother to play a joke on you, you stupid creature!' she shouted. 'Everybody knows you've got no sense of humour. I don't know anything about your silly sleeping bag—'

'Fibber!'

'I expect you did it yourself to get me into trouble!'

'Fibber! Fibber! Fibber!' shrilled Arabella.

'Don't you dare call me a fibber!'

Elizabeth made a lunge at Arabella while Joan stood there, looking aghast, just as the next-door tent monitor came racing over.

'*Stop it!*' she cried. It was Philippa, one of the senior girls. 'Who's the tent monitor around here? Can't they keep order?'

It was the sight of Joan's ashen face that calmed Elizabeth down. She took a step backwards. Arabella too backed away.

'That's better,' nodded Philippa. 'If you've got a

disagreement, just learn to settle it in a civilised way.'

She returned to her tent.

Then a tiny figure tiptoed out from behind the nearby willow tree. It was Teeny Wilson.

She looked very white and trembly. She walked straight up to Arabella.

'Please don't blame Elizabeth,' she said. Her voice was barely more than a whisper. 'It wasn't her who played the joke on you.'

Arabella looked startled. 'Who was it then?' she asked.

'It was me,' said Teeny.

They all gasped. Then Teeny turned to Elizabeth miserably.

'It was only going to be a – a bit of fun. I didn't mean somebody else to get the blame.'

Elizabeth stared down at the small, upturned face in astonishment.

Arabella's mouth was opening and closing. No words would come out.

'Teeny, some people don't mind jokes and some people hate them,' explained Joan gently. 'You must please apologise to Arabella at once.'

The child went over and said sorry.

'I suppose you're only a kid,' muttered Arabella. 'But please don't do anything like that again. You will now be so kind as to spread my sleeping bag out in the sun and sit with it until it dries off. When it's completely dry, you will then roll it up and put it back in the tent.'

Arabella turned to Elizabeth. 'Sorry,' she said.

'I should think so!' replied Elizabeth.

Flouncing off, Arabella then called back over her shoulder to Joan, 'You could at least have stopped us two shouting at each other. No wonder Philippa didn't know who the tent monitor was supposed to be!'

It was so cruel that it brought tears to Joan's eyes.

As the two friends walked slowly away from the tent together, arm in arm, Elizabeth tried to comfort her.

'Arabella often says unkind things, Joan. You mustn't take any notice of her.'

Elizabeth was thinking hard. Her head was still spinning from the dramatic events of the past few minutes. She was astonished that Teeny had dared to play such a trick on Arabella. Teeny was such a shy, nervous little thing! It didn't make sense somehow.

But Joan had other things on her mind.

'I can't *help* but take notice of what Arabella said. The truth is I'm really worried, Elizabeth,' she confessed. 'Teeny looks up to me so and I know she will want to lean on me. I'm quite frightened . . . that I'm not going to make a success of things.'

Joan looked so agitated that Elizabeth's heart went out to her.

She suddenly felt full of remorse that she had teased Joan earlier. She had not taken her friend's worries seriously. She was also very cross with herself for losing her temper with Arabella, however much she had been provoked. Arabella wasn't worth it! Nothing was worth seeing Joan unhappy. She made a solemn vow.

'Joan, from now on I'm going to be as sweet and good-tempered with Arabella as anything. And I'll help you to make sure that Teeny doesn't do anything silly again either. You just wait and see. Everyone in the whole camp will soon realise that you're the finest tent monitor there's ever been! I'm going to back you up all the way.'

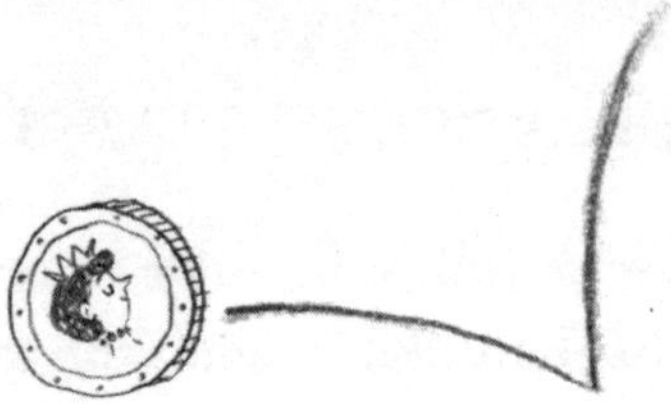

CHAPTER THREE

JOAN MAKES A SILLY MISTAKE

AS ELIZABETH made her solemn vow, Joan's face lit up with pleasure. Whatever her worries, it was a great comfort to have such a loyal friend.

'Thank you, Elizabeth,' she said softly. 'And I must try to live up to your hopes of me. I shall try not to let down any of the people in my tent.'

'You will be a fine tent monitor, just you see,' repeated Elizabeth, pleased to see that Joan looked calm and happy again. 'We'll both have to keep an eye on Teeny, though, won't we? Do you think she had just *finished* filling Arabella's sleeping bag when we surprised her in the tent? She was right next to it, wasn't she? And her hands shook with fright when we appeared!'

'Why, yes, so they did,' remembered Joan. 'That must have been the reason! I had been warned to expect her to be nervy, but—'

'Nobody could be as nervy as that!' agreed Elizabeth.

The two girls were walking along the top of the bank, deep in conversation.

On the opposite bank, where the boys' tents were pitched, some juniors were running along together, laughing and shouting boisterously. The girls gave them hardly a glance.

'Don't you think the whole thing was odd?' continued Elizabeth. 'It was such a strange thing for Teeny to do. She is such an unconfident little thing. Fancy her daring to try to play that trick on Arabella, of all people! You only have to look at Arabella to know that she's not the sort of person to play jokes on.'

'A girl in a higher form as well!' agreed Joan. 'Yes, it's puzzling. But I wonder if I can guess the reason? Miss Ranger has explained to me that Teeny is desperate to make some friends. Do you think she could have read storybooks about camping and the jolly jokes friends play on each other? Perhaps she thought we'd all like her and think she was fun and be pleased to have her in the tent?'

'Oh, Joan, that's a clever theory!' exclaimed Elizabeth. Then she began to laugh. 'You mean, perhaps she was trying to *make friends* with Arabella—?'

'Well, at least to break the ice.'

Even Joan began to laugh now, as she saw the

funny side.

'The trouble is,' sighed Elizabeth, when they had stopped laughing, 'I can see a flaw in that theory. If Teeny thought it was such a fun thing to do, why was she looking so scared—'

She got no further. 'Look out, Joan!' she cried.

Two figures were hurtling through the air towards them. They had launched themselves from the opposite bank and were heading straight for them!

The girls leapt back only just in time, as the flying figures thudded on to the grass in front of them, sprawled out like starfish.

'Are you all right?' gasped Joan anxiously.

'Of course they're all right!' said Elizabeth, as a boy and girl from the junior class scrambled to their feet. 'Look where you're going, you two! You nearly landed on top of us.'

Duncan and Kitty smiled cheekily. They were two very tough little juniors, both athletic. Elizabeth glanced at the huge leap they had made and was secretly rather impressed. The two opposing banks of the old stream were high at this point, the drop between them a steep one. Why, she would rather like to try that herself!

'You're lucky you haven't hurt yourselves!' Joan was saying. 'You could have missed your footing.'

'It's easy as pie,' boasted Duncan.

'Well, you're not to do it again,' Joan told them.

'There's a footbridge down by Camp Centre,' Elizabeth pointed out, anxious to give Joan full backing. 'What's wrong with using that?'

'It's the wrong way,' grumbled Kitty, rather sulkily. 'We're going to visit one of the tents up this end.'

'Yes, that's right, we are,' agreed Duncan, looking equally put out. 'We're going to see somebody in our class, aren't we, Kitty?'

'In that case you should have scrambled down the bank and up the other side,' Joan told them. 'And that's what you must do in future when you don't want to use the footbridge. Is that understood?'

'Yes, Joan!'

'And turn your collars down neatly!' added Elizabeth, for good measure. 'They look messy turned up like that!'

The two friends scampered off. Joan and Elizabeth watched them for a while.

'Thanks for backing me up,' said Joan gratefully.

'I think you managed them really well!' replied Elizabeth, turning on her heel then, impatient to be on their way. 'I wonder if we've got time to have a toasted muffin before we go to the village? I can smell them from here!'

'I'm sure we have—' Joan began. She stopped. 'Look, Elizabeth!' she said eagerly.

'What?' asked Elizabeth, turning back. 'Something interesting?'

'In a way, yes. Look there – can you see our tent?'

Joan was pointing back the way they had come. Through a gap in the tents they could just see their own, nestling under the high brick wall. Teeny was sitting cross-legged outside the tent. She was obediently watching over Arabella's spread-out sleeping bag, waiting for it to dry. And Duncan and Kitty were running up to speak to her!

'Teeny! That's who they were on their way to see!' exclaimed Elizabeth.

'Yes, isn't it good!' said Joan in relief. 'Teeny must be making some friends after all.'

'Perhaps we'll be able to stop worrying about her soon,' smiled Elizabeth. 'Let's go and get our muffins now!'

As Elizabeth stood by the campfire, swallowing delicious mouthfuls of warm muffin, she remembered some words from a famous poem that her father had once read to her. Something about – Bliss . . . was it . . . in that dawn to be alive . . .

This, she decided, was indeed bliss. How she loved it here at Whyteleafe School! How silly she'd been when she had first arrived last summer, trying to get herself sent home by being the naughtiest girl in the school . . . It was such a nuisance that she still had to live down that nickname. She was sorry that Philippa had overheard the quarrel with Arabella. That must have earned her a black mark! But everything was going to be all right now surely?

Camp Centre was abuzz with activity. Some of the boys had been collecting firewood for the barbecue. Mr Leslie had finished building a fine table in the camp's kitchen area. Cook had arrived in her old jeep and boxes of bread rolls were being stacked on the table. Although some of their meals would be eaten in the school building, there was to be a first night barbecue outside this evening.

There would be sausages and grilled bacon, eaten in the open air between crusty buttered rolls, and washed down with plenty of orange juice, apple juice or lemonade.

Elizabeth was looking forward to it with great excitement. She turned to the boy standing next to her.

'Poor old Julian, having to go home for half-term!' she told Martin. Julian Holland was her great friend in the first form. 'He has no idea what he's missing!'

'There's plenty of work to do,' replied Martin, who was also in the first form. He could be rather earnest at times. He pointed to the big table. 'You and Joan are doing kitchen duty with me and Arabella. We've got all those bread rolls to butter!'

'Have we really?' asked Elizabeth, with interest. She had wondered what job they would be given.

Joan had been talking to Susan, the other second-form monitor. They had been in a huddle together over their timetables. All the tent monitors had been given one of the typewritten lists in advance. It was their responsibility to see that the members of their tent were at all times punctual for camp duties.

'Elizabeth! Here a minute!' Joan called, as Susan walked away.

As soon as Elizabeth rejoined her friend, she could see that something was wrong.

'I've made a silly mistake,' she said, looking agitated. She handed Elizabeth the timetable and pointed to the first-day rota. 'I looked so quickly, I thought that was a six. But it isn't! It's a five—'

'So it is,' replied Elizabeth, peering at it. 'It's a bit smudgy. You could easily mistake it for a six—'

'So we've got to report for kitchen duty not at six o'clock but at five!' Joan was saying. 'And that's less than half an hour away!'

'Well, don't look so worried, Joan. We all make mistakes!' said Elizabeth cheerfully. Secretly she felt rather pleased. A trip to the village today had never been high on her list, not when they were still enjoying settling into camp! 'We'll just have to go and get your new torch batteries tomorrow after all,' she smiled. 'It was lucky you noticed in time—'

Because I don't want any more black marks against my name! Elizabeth was thinking privately.

'Oh, don't be feeble, Elizabeth!' interrupted Joan sharply. 'Of course we must get the batteries today. We can't possibly leave it till tomorrow!'

'But—'

'No buts! Come on quickly – we've got to hurry!'

Joan grabbed hold of her friend's hand and hauled her towards the footbridge which joined up the two halves of the camp.

'If we go up past the boys' tents, there's a short cut through to the back drive! Then it's only a few minutes down to the village. I've got my purse with me!'

'Joan, I don't think we've got enough time!' protested Elizabeth, puffing to keep up with her friend. 'Even if the batteries do run out tonight, it won't really matter, will it?'

'Of course it will!' exclaimed Joan. She seemed in a slight panic. 'Supposing Teeny wakes up in the night and wants something . . . If you're tent monitor, you *must* have a working torch. I'm sure it's one of the rules. Please, Elizabeth!' Joan shot her friend an imploring glance. 'We can run all the way there and all the way back. You know what a fast runner you are! You promised you'd help me to be a good monitor—'

'Of course,' nodded Elizabeth. She could see now that this was really important to Joan. 'Let's run really fast then. Let's break the world speed record!'

They pelted over the wooden footbridge and up the field, past the boys' tents, the summer breeze blowing through their hair. It was really exhilarating running as fast as this, thought Elizabeth.

But it took them some time to find the short cut through bushes that led into the school's back drive. The leaves had grown and all the bushes looked the same. By the time they reached the school gates, Elizabeth knew they were not going to make it to the village and back by five o'clock.

CHAPTER FOUR

ELIZABETH REMEMBERS HER VOW

AS THEY came through the school gates and pounded along by the road, on the grass verge, Elizabeth glanced at her watch with a sinking heart. This was such a mad idea of Joan's. They had not even reached the first corner yet!

But Joan was striding out, keeping just ahead of Elizabeth, her teeth gritted.

Then, rounding the first corner, Elizabeth let out a whoop of joy.

Of course! The garage shop!

'Look, Joan, the garage is open!' she cried out in relief. 'We won't have to go all the way to the village after all!'

'I always get my batteries at the hardware store—' began Joan.

'I tell you, the shop at the garage sells them!' protested

Elizabeth. 'How silly of me to forget. I went there once with Julian! He needed some for a model he was making.'

Recovering their breath, the girls picked their way through the forecourt of the petrol station. It was very busy indeed today, packed with cars waiting for petrol.

The hopeful look on Joan's face quickly faded when she saw the long queue of people in the garage shop.

'Oh, Elizabeth, it will take all day! Are you sure they sell them? Don't you think it would be better if we just raced straight on to the village—?'

'No, I don't!' said Elizabeth firmly. It was such a warm afternoon. The run had already made her hot and sticky. 'It will be much nicer standing in a queue than running along by the dusty old road. Have you got any spare money, Joan? Perhaps we can get an ice cream as well.'

'I really think we *should* run on—'

But Elizabeth looked resolute and went and stood at the back of the queue. On this matter, at least, she felt that Joan was being unreasonable. Joan had no choice but to come and stand beside her. She could see that Elizabeth had no intention of budging. And, of course, it was strictly forbidden for children to go to the village on their own.

The queue moved at a snail's pace. Joan fretted and frowned the whole while. At one point the shop manager disappeared for minutes on end to help a driver who was having trouble with the air machine.

'Sorry about that, folks,' he apologised when he returned. 'The poor man had a flat tyre!'

When Joan and Elizabeth finally got to the front of the queue, a horrible shock awaited.

'I'm sorry, girls,' said the man, coming back with some batteries. 'These are the only ones we stock here. If you need the bigger ones, you'll have to go down to the village.'

Elizabeth could have died of shame! Joan was wonderfully sporting about it.

'Don't be upset!' she said sweetly. 'It's no use crying over spilt milk. We'll just have to run all the harder now, won't we?'

Joan had no intention of being defeated. She was still determined to buy her new batteries!

They ran all the way to the hardware shop in the village, where there was no queue at all and the correct batteries were in stock. Then they raced all the way back to school.

They were terribly late. It was long past five o'clock.

Martin and Arabella had buttered a whole mountain of rolls without them. They were standing by the big table in the kitchen area, with the buttered rolls piled high in front of them.

'We were waiting and waiting for you to come!' complained Martin.

'We've just this minute finished. We had to do them all on our own, every single one!' said Arabella. 'It's not fair. You were supposed to be here at five o'clock!' she added very loudly.

Miss Ranger appeared. 'So there you are, Joan. Where *have* you been this past half-hour?' She looked very angry.

'I needed some new batteries for my torch, Miss Ranger,' began Joan. 'I'm so sorry, I—'

'That's no excuse, Joan. You know how important it is we keep to the timetable at all times, if camp is to run smoothly. And you a tent monitor! You're supposed to set a good example—'

Arabella was listening in the background, looking smug.

But it was not Arabella's face that Elizabeth was glancing at. It was Joan's. To see the distress on her best friend's face was almost unbearable!

Elizabeth remembered her solemn vow. She pushed herself forward.

'Please, Miss Ranger, it wasn't Joan's fault,' she burst out. 'It was entirely *my* fault! I made Joan stop at the garage shop and there was a long queue and they didn't have the right batteries! I should have listened to Joan. We should have headed straight for the right shop, in the village, the way she wanted us to, instead of me being so lazy, and then we would have been back here much quicker!'

'I see,' replied the teacher, gazing at Elizabeth and recalling her naughtiest girl nickname. For a moment Elizabeth wondered if she was going to be punished. But then—

'Thank you very much for owning up, Elizabeth,' said Miss Ranger, with a nod. 'That was quite the right thing to do.'

Elizabeth felt a warm glow. It was worth getting into trouble herself, to have helped Joan. Now nobody would think Joan was a bad tent monitor and Arabella could wipe the smug smile off her face.

But, to Elizabeth's dismay, Miss Ranger turned back to Joan immediately. And she proceeded to give her a stern lecture.

'You should know by now, Joan, that Elizabeth can be headstrong. And she is younger than you too. Just because she is your friend, that is no reason to forget that you are also her tent monitor. At camp, where everybody has more freedom, that carries very special responsibilities. You must remember those responsibilities in future and assert your authority at all times.'

For Joan it was mortifying. For Elizabeth it was completely infuriating.

She had got herself into trouble, and earnt a black mark, all for nothing! It had not helped to get Joan out of trouble after all. If anything, it had got her in deeper! It was *not* the outcome that Elizabeth had intended.

The pleased expression on Arabella's face didn't help her temper either. She would no doubt be spreading the story round the camp with glee.

Was Teeny really going to wake in the night, wondered Elizabeth, as Joan feared? Was Joan *really* going to need those silly new torch batteries? After all, it looked as though Teeny had already made friends with Duncan and Kitty at camp. Now that the junior girl had made some friends of her own, reasoned Elizabeth, she would soon stop being so dependent on Joan. She would stop going around looking so nervous and fearful, and Joan would be able to relax!

But Joan did not relax. She didn't seem to enjoy the barbecue at all. It was not just the telling-off from Miss Ranger. There was more to it than that. Elizabeth felt sure she knew what the reason must be.

Duncan and Kitty had not made friends with Teeny after all.

CHAPTER FIVE

QUITE A DIFFERENT TEENY

THE OTHER juniors all ignored Teeny. Duncan and Kitty rushed happily around at the barbecue with their friends. None of them took the slightest notice of the little girl.

At one point Duncan bounded up to Elizabeth, munching a bacon roll, looking cheeky.

'Mr Leslie says we can if we want to, Elizabeth!' he said, through a mouthful of bread.

'Don't speak with your mouth full, Duncan!' said Elizabeth. 'Can do *what* if you want to?'

'While we're at camp!'

'Do what while you're at camp?' repeated Elizabeth.

'Wear our collars up, of course!' he said, and went bounding off again.

As Duncan rejoined his friends, Elizabeth saw that at least five of them were following the same fashion.

Their blue school sports shirts were buttoned to the neck and the collars turned up. The rest of the school wore the shirts open-necked, the collars neat and flat. How silly, thought Elizabeth. She smiled to herself. It must be the latest craze in the junior class. But she had neither noticed nor cared this time. Her eyes were elsewhere, watching Teeny closely. They returned to Teeny now.

What was wrong with the child? She was so nervous and jumpy. She seemed frightened of her own shadow! She stuck close to Joan's side all the time, following her around like a puppy dog! Poor Joan looked more strained by the minute, weighed down by the responsibility.

Elizabeth felt guilty that she had questioned Joan's decision to get the batteries. Perhaps it really was important after all. It was Teeny's first night at camp tonight. If she had a bad, sleepless night, then Joan would need the torch, to be able to attend to her.

And, if that happens, I shall speak to Miss Ranger about it in the morning! decided Elizabeth. *Joan's much too brave to go bleating to Miss Ranger on her own behalf, but I shall say something. And then Miss Ranger will realise how important it was for us to run down to the village and how responsible Joan was being!*

That thought cheered Elizabeth up considerably.

A little fantasy ran through her mind in which Teeny was tossing and turning in her sleeping bag that night, until Joan came and sat beside her and held her hand, quietly reading her a story by the light of the torch. The child then dropped off into a deep, contented sleep . . .

Come the morning, fantasised Elizabeth, she would find Miss Ranger and quietly explain how wonderful Joan had been and how important it had been that her torch was working. And Miss Ranger would run anxiously to find Joan, to apologise. 'Please forgive me, Joan. What you and Elizabeth did was much more important than buttering bread rolls. I can see you are a very fine tent monitor indeed . . .'

'Elizabeth! There are some sausages left!' cried Kathleen, breaking into the reverie. The rosy-cheeked first-former ran over and grabbed Elizabeth's hand. 'Come on, hurry – they'll soon be all gone!'

Elizabeth enjoyed herself after that.

Food tasted so delicious eaten out of doors, round the campfire. The sweet smell of woodsmoke made her feel thirsty, but there were plenty of cold drinks to be had. Elizabeth liked the apple juice best. They were all being spoilt tonight, as a special treat. There was some excitement when little Kitty was stung by a huge bumblebee. But she was very brave and didn't cry at all. Rita took her to the first-aid tent, where

Matron treated the sting and soon made it better.

After that Mr Lewis, the school music master, came down to Camp Centre with an accordion that he squeezed and played jolly tunes on. Then they had a singsong round the dying embers of the fire. It was all very exciting.

At the end of the evening Elizabeth and Joan each took one of Teeny's hands and led her back to the tent. They were careful to step over the guy ropes of Miss Ranger's tent on the way. The teacher had her own private tent, a smart little green one.

'It's nice to think we have Miss Ranger so close at hand, isn't it, Teeny?' said Joan.

'I'm not scared,' said Teeny. 'Not when you're going to be in the tent with me, Joan.'

Soon Joan was settling the girl down into her sleeping bag. The juniors had been allowed to stay up late tonight. Teeny Wilson had had a long day.

'It's going to be a busy day tomorrow, Teeny,' said Joan, looking at her timetable. 'After breakfast we are going to have a Meeting.'

'A proper Meeting, with William and Rita in charge?' asked Teeny, wide-eyed. 'Just like we have in school?'

'That's right,' nodded Joan. 'Except we will sit on groundsheets, in rows, and there won't be a platform. And also Miss Ranger hopes the Meeting will be nice and short. There hasn't been much time for any complaints or grumbles yet, has there?'

'No.' Guiltily, the child stole a glance at Arabella's sleeping bag. It was neatly rolled up in the tent now. Arabella had not got back yet. 'No, I suppose not.'

'And tomorrow afternoon, Teeny, we're going on a nature walk over in the woods. I will be in charge of you. We'll take paper bags with us and see how many interesting things we can collect. Won't that be fun?'

Teeny peered over the top of her sleeping bag. Elizabeth thought she saw sudden fear in the child's eyes.

'I don't think I want to go to the woods, Joan. Do we have to go? Couldn't we stay in the tent instead? I've got my playing cards with me. We could play a game of Snap.'

'No, Teeny.' Joan suddenly sounded very weary. 'We have to keep to the timetable. It's much more fun in the fresh air anyway! We can play Snap some other time, if it rains.'

Elizabeth felt sorry for her friend. Poor Joan! She had been stuck with Teeny all evening. She took her responsibilities so much to heart.

'Why don't you go off and have a chat with Susan now, Joan?' she suggested nobly. 'I'll stay here and keep Teeny company. Go on!'

'Perhaps I will!' she said gratefully. 'It would be

rather nice to see Susan. She's promised to lend me a book.'

As Joan ducked away out of the tent, Elizabeth picked up her rolled-up sleeping bag, placed it by Teeny and sat on it.

She was remembering the little day-dream she had had earlier.

'Have you got a favourite book with you, Teeny?' she asked. 'Would you like me to read you a bedtime story?'

It might help Teeny to get to sleep, being read a story, Elizabeth had decided. Though not by torchlight, of course, for it was still light outside and the tent flap was rolled back.

'Ooh, thanks, Elizabeth!'

In the next five minutes Elizabeth very quickly discovered that her earlier daydream was certainly not going to come true. In fact, it could not have been more wide of the mark!

After finding a book and handing it to Elizabeth the junior girl squirmed down happily into her sleeping bag. She smiled and gave a contented sigh. This was quite a different Teeny. For the first time all the strain seemed to have left her little face.

'Oh, I do love it in here!' she told Elizabeth. 'It's so warm and cosy and soon it will be dark. It's going to be lovely snuggled up in my sleeping bag in the dark. I wish I could stay snuggled up in our cosy house like this all the time!'

Elizabeth started to read out loud. She was only two pages into the story when she heard a very gentle snoring sound. Teeny's eyes were closed. She was already in a deep, sound sleep.

What a fuss about nothing, thought Elizabeth. *Teeny likes it in the tent!*

And Teeny remained sound asleep for the rest of the night.

The only person to enjoy the use of the torch was Joan! She had awoken suddenly, just after it had got dark, and had used her torch to read in bed.

Elizabeth woke in the night to hear Arabella complaining bitterly.

'How are the rest of us supposed to get any sleep with that wretched torch on!' she whispered loudly. 'I don't care if Joan is the tent monitor, it's not fair of her to keep other people awake.'

Bleary-eyed, Elizabeth sat up to see what the fuss was about.

Joan was fast asleep. Her book and torch had fallen from her grasp. The torch had rolled along and was lying next to the book. The torch had been left on, its powerful beam lighting up the tent!

Joan had been reading in bed and had carelessly fallen asleep without switching it off!

'It's all right, Arabella, I'll fix it!' whispered Elizabeth, squirming out of her sleeping bag into the cool night air. She tiptoed across to Joan's side, clicked off the torch, then stumbled her way back through the darkness to her sleeping bag.

As Elizabeth wriggled back into her sleeping bag and fumbled with the zip, she couldn't help feeling cross. Now she was cold!

It suddenly seemed even more ridiculous, all the fuss Joan had made about getting the new torch batteries. Why, they weren't needed at all! Teeny loved it in the tent. She was in a deep, deep sleep. Even Arabella's complaining hadn't woken her.

Meanwhile, Joan had not even been trying to conserve the new batteries. Far from it. She had been really careless.

It was really very lucky that the beam of light had woken up Arabella. Otherwise Joan's precious new batteries, which had caused them so much trouble, would have been completely dead by the morning!

Sometime later that night Elizabeth was again woken by Arabella. She was still complaining – and this time more loudly.

'I'm freezing!' came her petulant voice. 'I'm absolutely

freezing. Joan, can you hear me? I'm freezing, I tell you.'

Elizabeth blinked and sat up. Joan was awake herself this time. She too was sitting up. Only Teeny, at the back of the tent next to Elizabeth, snored on happily.

For a moment Elizabeth was puzzled. It was the middle of the night, the coldest and darkest time, and yet she could see! Instead of it being pitch-dark inside the tent, as it had been earlier, everything was bathed in a pale light. She could see Arabella and Joan clearly, sitting up in their sleeping bags on the other side of the tent.

'You've opened the tent flap!' Arabella accused Joan.

Even as Arabella said it, Elizabeth suddenly realised that the tent flap was rolled back and tied in its daytime position. She could see the moon and the stars outside, hanging in a bright, clear night sky! They were shining into the tent! It was a beautiful sky, thought Elizabeth.

'Teeny needs some fresh air, Arabella,' hissed Joan. 'Please keep your voice down. You'll wake the other two.'

'Fresh air? It's cold! It's coming right on my face.'

'Lie down and go to sleep at once, Arabella,' replied Joan. 'It's rather stuffy in the tent with four people sleeping in it. As tent monitor, I have decided to open the flap. I am in charge and I must ask you to lie down and go back to sleep.'

'How can I go to sleep—?' began Arabella, her voice getting squeaky. 'I'm right next to it!'

Elizabeth listened in consternation. It didn't seem to her to be stuffy in the tent, not in the least. But Joan was right: she *was* their tent monitor. Miss Ranger had told her to exert her authority. And now that was exactly what she was doing . . .

On the other hand, whatever the rights and wrongs of it, there was going to be an awful rumpus in a minute, if Joan wasn't careful.

'It's all right, Arabella!' hissed Elizabeth. 'We can change places. I don't mind some fresh air. May we change places, Joan?'

'Of course, Elizabeth,' replied her friend in gratitude. 'Arabella, please go and sleep in Elizabeth's place, now that you've woken her up. And do not wake Teeny up. You've made quite enough noise already.'

Grumbling quietly, Arabella did as she was told.

In her new place, next to the open tent flap, Elizabeth tried to settle down and get warm and go back to sleep. It took her quite some time.

I do think Arabella's got a point, she thought, shivering slightly. *It's much too cold here, with the tent flap open. Oh dear. I do hope Joan's not going to find the tent stuffy every night. I didn't think it was stuffy at all!*

Elizabeth slept fitfully and was the last person in the

tent to awake next morning. Gentle sunshine was now filtering in through the open tent flap. Joan and Teeny had gone to wash and clean their teeth. Arabella was about to follow suit.

'Fancy offering to sleep there, Elizabeth!' she commented. 'You should have backed me up. We should have insisted that Joan close the flap. I was still cold, even on the other side of the tent. I'm not going to put up with this every night.'

'You may have to. Joan's our tent monitor, not you, Arabella!' said Elizabeth loyally.

Arabella's mouth set in a thin, stubborn line.

'Have you forgotten there's a Meeting this morning, Elizabeth? I have every intention of making a complaint!'

CHAPTER SIX

ELIZABETH BEGINS TO LOSE PATIENCE

AT WHYTELEAFE School the children made many decisions for themselves. A weekly Meeting was held, attended by the whole school. The Meeting was run not by the teachers, but by William and Rita, the head boy and girl, assisted by twelve school monitors who sat just behind them.

It was a kind of parliament. Problems were discussed, rules and regulations made. At the same time it was a little 'court' too, with William and Rita as the Judges and the monitors the Jury. Wrongdoing had to be reported. If it was serious, it was written in the Book. The Meeting would then decide what action should be taken. Of course, the joint headmistresses and the senior master usually sat at the back of the hall, as observers. But they rarely took any part in the Meetings. The children were expected to face up to their own faults bravely and work out the best way of dealing with them.

Elizabeth had hated the Meetings when she first came to Whyteleafe School. They had made it so difficult for her to be naughty! These days, however, she rather enjoyed them.

But she feared that this morning's Meeting might be less enjoyable than usual.

It would be held at Camp Centre, as soon as the boys and girls had washed up their breakfast things. There had been cornflakes and milk this morning, followed by plenty more buttered rolls, washed down with a mug of hot tea. Each pupil was responsible for their own enamel mug, bowl and plate, as well as their cutlery. They queued at the two standpipes set up in the kitchen area and swilled their mugs and bowls clean in jets of cold water. Mr Leslie had linked the campsite into the mains water supply, which already ran to the nearby stables.

He had also constructed a simple drainage system that took the waste water down to the empty stream bed. Elizabeth thought it was very clever. It really was like a secret village here!

On this pleasant, sweet-scented morning Elizabeth could not bring herself to tell Joan what Arabella had said. She was hoping that Arabella would change her mind. Joan had enough to worry about, for already

Teeny was hanging around her again. Gone was the happy, relaxed little thing who had been in the tent last night. She was back to her usual jumpy self, with that funny, half-scared look behind the big glasses.

It occurred to Elizabeth that Teeny would not be looking forward to the Meeting either. She must be wondering if Arabella was going to make a complaint about the sleeping-bag joke or, at the very least, a grumble. As Elizabeth dried up her cereal bowl, flicking a fly away with the tea towel, she puzzled again about that strange incident.

Whatever possessed Teeny to try to play such a trick? she thought. *I still don't understand it.*

Would Arabella make complaints about both Joan *and* Teeny at the Meeting? Elizabeth was very much hoping that she would think better of it. There she was now, sitting on a log in the sunshine, talking cheerfully to Belinda. She seemed in a good mood. The night was over. It was the nice, warm daytime again!

I think I'll go and speak to her, and be friendly, Elizabeth decided, remembering her promise to Joan. *I'll suggest we ask Joan if the four of us can take a vote about having the tent flap open at nights. That would be a much better way of settling it.*

But, before she could get Arabella alone, the whistle blew. It was time for the Meeting.

All the children went and sat in rows, on the groundsheets. Facing them, William and Rita sat on upturned logs behind a camping table. The Big Book was on the table in front of them. Seated cross-legged alongside them, also facing the audience, were the sixteen tent monitors, Joan among them. On canvas chairs, somewhere at the back, sat three grown-ups. Instead of Miss Belle and Miss Best and Mr Johns, as it would have been indoors, it was Miss Ranger, Mr Leslie and Matron. Apart from that, and the fact that they were out-of-doors (and a great number of children had gone home for half-term), it was just like a proper Meeting! And William even had to bang on the table for silence as usual. He did this with a wooden mallet used for driving in tent pegs. He had forgotten to bring the gavel.

The Meeting was much shorter than usual. There was no money to be shared out. That had been done just before half-term. There was only one grumble.

'Please, the zip of my sleeping bag keeps sticking,' said John McTavish. 'It's such a nuisance.'

'Sort it out with your tent monitor. There's probably a piece of lining caught in it!' replied William at once. 'That's not a proper grumble, John. What can the Meeting possibly do about it?'

Everybody laughed and John hastily sat down.

But Arabella duly made her complaint, as promised. Just as Rita was about to close the Meeting, she rose hesitantly to her feet. Elizabeth noticed Teeny blanch. But Arabella had no intention of complaining about the sleeping-bag joke. She had better fish to fry.

'I'm sorry to have to bring this up, William and Rita,' she said, looking her demurest and most doll-like. 'It's really a little embarrassing because it's a complaint about something our tent monitor did last night.'

Elizabeth saw Joan stiffen.

'Very well, Arabella,' said the head girl. 'Let us hear your complaint.'

With considerable dramatic skill Arabella told the Meeting about the freezing cold draught that had woken her in the night, her shock at finding the tent flap had been tied back and her monitor's insistence that it should remain open for the rest of the night.

William and Rita exchanged uneasy glances. They were well used to Arabella's complaints. Often they were trivial and almost always shrill. But this morning her tone was calm and measured.

'That is a perfectly reasonable complaint, even though it is about a tent monitor,' agreed William. 'Let us first of all hear what Joan has to say. Sit down, please, Arabella.'

Joan seemed to be frozen. There was a helpless

expression on her face. Susan had to give her a nudge, to make her stand up.

'I – I just thought the tent seemed rather stuffy, that's all,' she said feebly. 'I thought perhaps it would be better for the four of us to have some fresh air.'

Elizabeth sat there, curling up with embarrassment on Joan's behalf. Some of the campers were whispering and giving Joan surprised looks. Instead of trying to put up a spirited defence, Joan had made her excuse very lamely. It was almost as though she, herself, thought that what she was saying sounded rather silly!

And, for the first time, Elizabeth realised it only too plainly. It *was* silly. It was ridiculous. It had been freezing in that draught last night!

As Joan sat down again, William and Rita asked the rest of the tent monitors to come into a huddle while they debated the issue.

Joan sat apart, looking abject, while the discussion took place. All around Elizabeth there was giggling and chattering, and people saying, '*Brrrrr!*' It always added spice to Meetings when somebody made a proper complaint.

Soon the tent monitors returned to their places. William banged the mallet on the table.

'Silence, please. We are all agreed that the bell tents are designed to be closed at night. This stops insects flying in. There are adequate fresh-air vents in the canvas. After all, they were made for the British Army's desert campaign! Stand up again, please, Joan.'

Joan did so.

'Arabella's complaint is upheld. If you find the tent a little stuffy, perhaps your sleeping bag is too heavy, Joan,' he added sympathetically. 'I'm sure Matron might be able to find you a lighter one, if you ask her.'

The Meeting broke up. Elizabeth hurried over to join Joan and linked arms with her. She hated to see her so upset.

'I should have warned you! Arabella told me she was going to make a complaint, but I was hoping she would think better of it.'

'It wouldn't have made any difference if you had,' said Joan in a dull voice. 'It was fair enough. Perfectly fair.'

'Oh, then you don't mind if we have the flap closed tonight?' asked Elizabeth, unable to hide her relief.

'It will have to be, won't it?' sighed Joan. 'I can't have some of you feeling cold . . .'

'But Teeny was perfectly all right, Joan!' exclaimed Elizabeth, to cheer her friend up. 'I know you were worried about the tent being stuffy for Teeny's sake. But she slept like a baby, didn't she? She was fine. You didn't even need the torch for her! That's good, isn't it—?'

Elizabeth broke off. Miss Ranger was walking up

to them. The teacher spoke quietly to Joan.

'Let me explain something,' she said. 'I know I told you yesterday that you must always be sure to assert your authority, to show exactly who is tent monitor. But by that I meant you must be sure to keep Elizabeth in order! If you try to assert your authority in an unreasonable way, as you appear to have done with Arabella, then you will lose your tent-mates' respect.'

'Yes, Miss Ranger,' replied Joan.

As the two friends walked back to the tent together, Elizabeth felt helpless. She was so determined that everyone should see what a fine tent monitor Joan was. She had even earnt a black mark with Miss Ranger, covering up for her. But she could see Joan's confidence ebbing away in front of her eyes. Had Elizabeth's best efforts all been in vain? Things had certainly got off to a very bad start.

As if to prove Miss Ranger's point, Arabella's respect for Joan was now very low. After the triumph of having her complaint upheld at today's Meeting there was no stopping her!

When the friends arrived back at the tent, they found her already arranging some of her things round the sides, humming cheerfully. Teeny was with her.

'Thank you for not telling on me at the Meeting,' the junior was saying gratefully.

'Oh, that's all right, Teeny,' replied Arabella nonchalantly. 'I think we should have my mirror here, don't you? We can prop it up in the middle, against the tent pole.'

The vain first-former had been feeling lost without her favourite mirror. Usually it hung by her bed in the dormitory. If she stood far enough back, she could almost get a full-length view in it. She had carefully wrapped it and staggered down to the campsite with it. She had been puzzling ever since whether she would need Joan's permission to put it up in the tent.

'Hey, you can't put a mirror up in here!' protested Elizabeth. 'It'll get in the way. We'll all trip over it.'

'But we *need* a mirror in here, don't we, Joan?' said Arabella, turning to the tent monitor.

Joan hesitated. Without even waiting for her reply Arabella knelt down by the central tent pole and carefully propped the mirror there. She preened herself in it.

'There!' she said. 'We all want to make sure we look nice, don't we, Teeny? Just because we're at camp, that's no excuse for looking scruffy. I've brought plenty of different clothes—'

'We can see that—' began Elizabeth hotly. They were stacked all round the sides of the tent. Then she stopped. She mustn't lose her temper with Arabella.

She had promised Joan that. It would only make Joan's life more difficult.

'Please let's have a mirror up in the tent, Joan!' begged Teeny, coming and holding her hand. 'It'll make it more like our little house than ever!'

'You can have it up if you want, Arabella,' decided Joan.

'Oh, thank you, Joan. I was sure you'd agree!' replied Arabella, smiling sweetly.

Elizabeth glowered and left the tent.

Later, Joan apologised to Elizabeth.

'I only agreed to please Teeny,' she said. 'Have you noticed how happy she is in the tent? She's like a different person. It's as though she feels safe when she's in our little house, as she calls it.'

So Joan had realised it too.

'I wonder why she doesn't mix with the other juniors,' continued Joan. 'Do you think she could be being bullied?'

'Surely not,' shrugged Elizabeth. 'She's been at Whyteleafe since the beginning of term. There would have been some sign of it by now. Somebody would have seen something.'

'But there is *something* not right,' sighed Joan.

In her present mood Elizabeth was not sure if she cared. Far from it being fun to have a little junior to look after in the tent, it had become a problem. Joan, so kind and conscientious, had become a hopeless worrier since being put in charge of Teeny! That was at the root of things. Everything that had gone wrong had been due, in one way or another, to Teeny, decided Elizabeth.

Drat the little creature, she thought crossly. *I'm beginning to wish Joan had never set eyes on her.*

That afternoon there was worse to come.

CHAPTER SEVEN

TEENY HAS AN UNHELPFUL FALL

ELIZABETH HAD not slept well that first night, but Joan had fared even worse. By the end of the morning, she began to look rather tired. Just how tired Joan was Elizabeth was soon to discover.

Elizabeth was sitting in the school dining hall, with Teeny, eating a delicious meal of hot pie, with buttered new potatoes and carrots. It tasted good. The joint heads had decided that every day, at one o'clock, the children should come indoors for their main hot meal of the day.

But where was Joan? wondered Elizabeth.

At midday Rita had announced to the campers that any girl who wished to have a hot shower before dinner could go up to school early. Joan had thought that seemed a fine idea and hurried off. Elizabeth wasn't bothered.

'I'll meet you in the dining hall then, Joan. I'll bring Teeny with me.'

'Save me a place! I expect there will be a long queue for the showers,' was Joan's reply.

Elizabeth had saved Joan a place, but her friend had still not appeared. All the other girls were back from their showers and were halfway through dinner! Whatever could have happened to Joan?

She'll miss out on the first course altogether, if she's not careful, thought Elizabeth in alarm. *The queue for pudding's starting to form now.*

She gobbled down her last new potato and got up from the table.

'I'm just slipping off to find Joan,' she told Teeny. 'Now, you be sure and eat up all your food.'

'She must have forgotten the time,' said Teeny solemnly.

But the showers were silent and deserted. There was no sign of Joan in there. Puzzled, Elizabeth scratched her brown curly head. Where should she look now?

Perhaps Joan had gone to her dormitory, to find something she had forgotten to pack? Perhaps she was having a problem finding it . . .

Elizabeth bounded up the stairs to Joan's dormitory and threw open the door.

'Joan!' she exclaimed in amazement.

Her friend lay on top of the bed, fast asleep!

'Joan, wake up! Wake up!' Elizabeth shook Joan's shoulder. 'You've fallen asleep! There's delicious hot pie for dinner and you'll miss it at this rate!'

Joan woke up, looked startled, and sat bolt upright.

'Whatever time is it? I felt so sleepy after my shower. I only meant to have a little nap – oh, Elizabeth! I'm so sorry you've had to come looking for me! The fact is I didn't sleep very well last night.'

'I wondered where you'd got to!' laughed Elizabeth in relief.

Except Joan's lack of sleep was no laughing matter, as Elizabeth soon came to discover. On the nature walk in the woods that afternoon she thought that she had never seen her friend so exhausted. She kept on yawning and there were dark rings under her eyes.

Poor Joan! she thought. *By the look of her, she hardly got a wink of sleep at all in the tent last night. Worrying about Teeny and everything, I suppose.*

Miss Ranger and Mr Leslie had escorted all the boys and girls along the country lane at the back of the school and into the woods. They all walked with the teachers for a time and had fun naming different flowers and watching birds. Then brown paper bags were handed out.

'You're all to scatter for half an hour,' smiled Miss

Ranger. 'See how many different leaves you can find.' The pretty little woods boasted a splendid variety of trees. 'When we get back to camp, we'll see if we can identify them all. Let's see who can find the most!'

'And no need to go up trees,' said Mr Leslie. 'You will find plenty of leaves growing low down and some on the ground as well. When I blow the whistle, you are all to return here.'

The teachers then reminded all members of the junior class that they must stay close to their tent monitors and obey their orders.

Teeny was full of energy after her good night's sleep. She kept running up to Joan and showing her the leaves she was finding. Elizabeth collected some as well. To her relief, Arabella had decided to go off with Philippa and Mandy, the junior in the next-door tent.

Joan, pleased to see that Teeny was enjoying herself after all, went and sat on a mossy bank. It was beneath an oak tree, in a lovely sunny spot, on the edge of a dell.

'I don't think I can go another step,' she said, leaning back against the tree trunk. 'Let's have a little rest.'

Elizabeth came and sat down beside her. Both girls tilted their faces towards the sun. It was lovely to feel its warmth on their cheeks and to hear the breeze rustling through the leaves of the oak tree. Teeny walked round the tree and found an oak leaf to add to her collection.

'Coming over here with us, Teeny?' called a voice.

Kitty and Duncan appeared on the other side of the dell. They were waving to Teeny to come and join them in a friendly fashion.

Elizabeth and Joan glanced at each other eagerly. Yesterday they had been disappointed when Duncan and Kitty's visit to the tent had come to nothing. But surely there could be no mistaking the situation today? The two children were trying to get to know Teeny better.

'Some friends from your class!' said Elizabeth, pleased.

'Would you like to go and play with them?' asked Joan gently.

The little girl stood motionless. She clenched and unclenched her fists two or three times, as though trying to screw up courage. Then, coming to a decision, she nodded. What a funny, nervous little thing she was, thought Elizabeth.

'Off you go then!' smiled Joan.

Even as the little girl walked slowly down into the bumpy dell to join her classmates, Joan gave a huge yawn and her eyes closed thankfully.

'If you don't mind, Elizabeth, I'm going to snatch a nap. Will you keep an eye on them for me?'

'Of course!' replied Elizabeth.

Within moments Joan had dozed off!

It was so comfortable and warm on the mossy bank, thought Elizabeth, she would have liked a snooze herself. She closed her eyes and leant against the huge tree trunk, enjoying the feel of the rough bark in the small of her back. With eyes closed she could hear the murmur of voices as Duncan, Kitty and Teeny talked together in the dell. What a happy sound, she thought. Was Teeny making a real effort to mix with her classmates at last?

In her sleepy state it was a few moments before Elizabeth realised that the murmur of voices was becoming fainter, fading into the distance . . . She opened her eyes instantly, in time to glimpse the three figures disappearing among some trees on the other side of the dell.

I'd better creep after them! she thought. *Just to keep an eye on them. I mustn't spoil any fun, though, not when Teeny's making friends at last.*

Leaving Joan fast asleep, Elizabeth tiptoed across the dell and into the trees. From the sound of the children's voices she could tell they had stopped somewhere. As she drew nearer, she darted from tree to tree, in order not to be seen. There was no sign of Kitty's tent monitor, nor of Duncan's.

The little imps must have given them the slip, thought

Elizabeth, smiling to herself. *But I don't suppose they can be very far away.*

She pulled up behind some rhododendron bushes and peered through the masses of leaves. Now she had a clear view of the children!

'I'll go first, then Kitty, then you!' Duncan was shouting.

Elizabeth stared. The three juniors were up a tree. They were all sitting astride a long, low bough, which stretched out horizontally a few feet above the ground. Duncan was moving into a crouching position.

'Watch me do it, Teeny!' he was shouting. 'It's easy-peasy!'

He jumped from the end of the bough and landed in the long grass below, quite comfortably.

'Now me!' cried Kitty excitedly, bumping along to the end of the bough and doing likewise.

Elizabeth was too far back to stop them. Besides, it looked a very easy jump and rather fun, she thought. Her main emotion was relief at the sight of Teeny having fun with her classmates at last!

'Now you, Teeny!' Kitty was calling up. 'Do it just like we did. Dare you!'

The bespectacled junior was bumping out along the bough very, very slowly. Halfway along, she looked down and seemed to freeze.

'Come on, Teeny!' encouraged Duncan.

From her hiding place Elizabeth silently urged her on. *Yes, come on, Teeny. What have you stopped for? It's easy!* She wanted to shout it out loud. 'Come on, Teeny. You know you can do it!' She could tell from the look on Duncan and Kitty's faces that they wanted Teeny to succeed too.

'I can't!' Teeny suddenly cried out. 'I can't do it!'

Panic-stricken, she tried to turn round on the bough, to go back the way she had come. Duncan and Kitty were shouting at her . . .

'Don't do that! Don't be a baby!'

'You'll fall if you try that! Don't be such a coward, Teeny!'

Teeny just carried on trying to twist round, getting her legs in a hopeless tangle. She slithered and slipped – and overbalanced.

'Aaah!'

'*Teeny!*'

Even as Elizabeth was running towards her, Teeny came toppling down off the bough, her glasses flying through the air.

'Teeny! Are you all right?' exclaimed Elizabeth.

Duncan and Kitty looked on in dismay.

Elizabeth helped the little girl to her feet and dusted her down. She was shaken but unhurt.

Elizabeth found her glasses for her.

'Thank you, Elizabeth,' said Teeny, taking them. She looked very shamefaced. 'I was such a coward! It wasn't Duncan and Kitty's fault.'

'I know it wasn't,' said Elizabeth. 'I saw what happened—'

Duncan and Kitty exchanged relieved glances.

'You should have jumped, Teeny!' Elizabeth told her. 'It was simple. It was silly and dangerous to try to turn back. You'd better not go climbing up trees at all in future.'

The other two juniors were nodding in agreement.

'Shoo away, you two!' Elizabeth said quickly. 'You should be with your tent monitors. Off you go now, and find them! I'll look after Teeny. And don't you go telling the other juniors about this and having them laugh at her. I think we should just pretend it never happened.'

The two children looked at Elizabeth gratefully and scampered off. They had been rather frightened that they might get into trouble, thanks to Teeny being such a coward. But Elizabeth knew that if she was to scold them, it would put them off befriending Teeny another time. Except she was not sure that there *would* be another time.

'I think we should give up on Teeny,' she overheard Kitty say.

'But she does like us so,' replied Duncan. 'Shall we just try . . .'

His voice faded into the distance. It sounded like 'the green ear'.

Elizabeth frowned, puzzled. Whatever was Duncan talking about? Green ear? Try the green ear? She must have misheard!

Teeny looked so sad as she watched them go. Elizabeth felt sorry for her, in spite of everything. Why did she have to be such a baby and so scared of everything? She was her own worst enemy!

They hurried back and woke Joan, just as Mr Leslie's whistle blew. On the way back to Whyteleafe Elizabeth whispered to Joan what had happened.

Joan was conscience-stricken.

'I shouldn't have gone to sleep like that! I should have watched the whole time. Oh, thank goodness she wasn't hurt.'

'If she had been, it would have been her own silly fault!' said Elizabeth crossly. 'Don't fret about Teeny so, Joan. We can forget about it now.'

Unfortunately, it did not prove possible to forget about it.

That evening Teeny's glasses kept slipping down her nose. She showed them to Arabella, who was in the tent at the time.

'Why, the frames are damaged!' said Arabella knowledgeably. 'Look, there's a little screw missing that should hold the earpiece tight in place. How on earth did that happen?'

'It must have been when I fell out of the tree,' Teeny responded.

'Tree? What tree?' asked Arabella sharply. 'Where was Joan when this happened?' She proceeded to question Teeny carefully.

Joan was upset to find out about the glasses. She took them straight to Matron, who was confident that Mr Leslie could mend them by morning. Matron also insisted on handing Joan a lightweight sleeping bag.

'I thought you must have come to collect this, Joan! William said you would probably want to try it out tonight.'

'Oh, I'm so pleased you won't have to sleep in the thick one tonight, Joan,' said Arabella pointedly when Joan brought it back to the tent. 'It will be so lovely for the rest of us to have the flap closed.'

Joan stared at her miserably.

A few minutes later her misery increased tenfold. They were all settled down in their sleeping bags for the night. Patiently, Arabella waited until Teeny was sound asleep. Then she launched forth.

'I was very shocked to find out how Teeny broke her

glasses, Joan,' she whispered indignantly. 'Fancy your just allowing her to run off on her own like that! Elizabeth tries to cover up for you all the time. But, if you don't mind my saying so, I do think you are turning out to be a hopeless tent monitor!'

Elizabeth ground her teeth in dismay. How very unhelpful of Teeny to be such a coward and to fall and break her glasses! Joan was such a fine tent monitor; she worried about Teeny all the time. How dare Arabella say such things! At the same time, realised Elizabeth, this looked like more trouble for her best friend.

Joan just lay there, rigid, saying nothing.

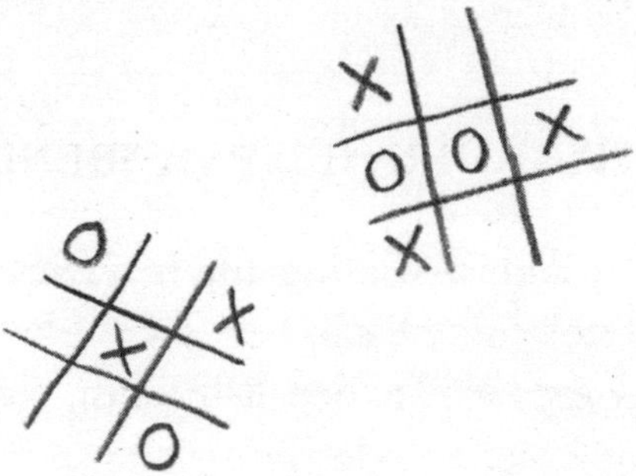

CHAPTER EIGHT

JOAN TELLS ELIZABETH THE TRUTH

ELIZABETH FOUND it difficult to get to sleep. She was too churned up, feeling exasperated with Teeny, furious with Arabella and above all worried about Joan. She lay there for some time, as outside the dusk slowly faded and the tent grew ever darker.

At last, when it was pitch-black inside the tent, her eyes began to close . . . And suddenly were wide open!

Had she dreamt it just now, or had Joan left the tent?

Surely not. The flap was securely tied; the tent was still in pitch-darkness.

'Joan?' she whispered. There was no reply.

Elizabeth wriggled out of her sleeping bag and crawled across to Joan's. She felt it with her hands. It was empty. So she hadn't dreamt it!

It was strictly forbidden to leave the tent at night without very good reason. Was Joan feeling ill? Elizabeth lay there for a few minutes, waiting for her friend to return. But Joan did not come back.

I must go and look for her! decided Elizabeth, feeling alarmed.

As quietly as possible, she struggled into her dressing gown, then crawled out of the tent. She was very careful all the while not to disturb Arabella. That would be a disaster!

What *was* Joan up to?

It was a warm night outside. There was more cloud cover than last night, but with just enough moonlight to see by. Elizabeth gazed around. Where should she begin to look?

She tiptoed round to the back of the tent, glancing this way and that, her ears attuned to the merest sound.

Down in the cutting, where clumps of grass grew beside the empty stream bed, she could hear the whirring of crickets. Then, suddenly, something else – a tiny sobbing sound!

She ran up over the top of the bank, then dropped down the other side.

'Joan!' she whispered.

She could see a forlorn figure down there, in a dressing gown, huddled up near the culvert that led beneath the boundary wall. Her shoulders were gently heaving. In some alarm Elizabeth ran to her and placed an arm round her shoulders.

'Joan, what are you sitting down here for?' she whispered. 'Whyever aren't you in the tent?'

'I can't go back in there!' Joan sobbed quietly. 'I keep trying to pluck up courage, but I can't. It's pitch-black in there, you see, Elizabeth.'

'Joan, I don't understand—'

'I'm so ashamed,' sobbed Joan. 'I can't bear anyone in the world to know. Not even you, Elizabeth . . .'

But now she blurted out the truth.

'I didn't want the torch batteries for Teeny. I wanted them for my own sake. Then, when I realised none of you wanted the torch on, I lay awake for hours, terrified. That's why I opened the tent flap in the end. Not for Teeny's sake. It was for myself. I just knew I would never sleep if I couldn't have any light in the tent. Elizabeth, I can't get to sleep if it's pitch-dark. Never, ever!'

'Oh, Joan!' gasped Elizabeth, struggling to take all this in.

Her friend was frightened of the dark! Elizabeth would never have guessed it. How well Joan had kept her secret!

'But Joan, how can you get to sleep in the dormy at nights?'

'Because there's always a light in the corridor. The

teachers always leave it on for us, don't they? So a nice crack of light comes under the door and that's all I need, Elizabeth. As long as I can see some light, I'm all right.'

'Poor Joan!' whispered Elizabeth. She took her handkerchief out of her dressing-gown pocket and dried her friend's eyes for her. 'You mustn't cry. It's not your fault! Can't we explain to somebody about it?'

'How can we?' asked Joan in despair. 'First of all, I can't bear anyone to know. You *must* understand that, Elizabeth. And secondly they would never let me be tent monitor. How can they allow someone who's frightened of the dark to be in charge of a junior? Especially a nervy little thing like Teeny. The poor child looks up to me so. If she found out about my silly fears, she would be frightened too. It would put the idea into her head that the dark is something scary when it's not. What sort of example would I be setting?'

At the mention of Teeny's name Elizabeth felt a moment's annoyance. Oh, no, not Teeny again!

But then, of course, it dawned on her. She had been blaming Teeny quite unfairly. All the things that had gone wrong so far had not been Teeny's fault, after all. Even the accident with the glasses this afternoon would never have happened if Joan had had a proper night's sleep and been awake enough to look after her!

The root of it all, Elizabeth was forced to admit

to herself, was Joan's secret fear. Teeny had not been to blame.

'I'm afraid, if we told anybody, there would be only one outcome,' Joan was saying calmly. In spite of everything it had given her comfort to confide in Elizabeth at last. 'I would probably be asked to sleep up at school at nights. And Arabella would probably be made tent monitor in my place.'

Elizabeth realised that this was true. At once, her eyes glinted. She was not going to allow that to happen! She had made a solemn vow to help Joan make a success of things. She was not going to let anything defeat her, not even this.

'We've got to think of something, Joan.'

Surely there must be some way round the problem?

She left Joan's side for a moment and peered into the culvert. She crawled inside it for a short distance. She was looking into pitch-darkness. The old tunnel ran under the wide country lane that lay beyond the school's boundary wall. It would once have carried the bubbling waters of the stream beneath the road, then out into open farmland on the other side.

'It's lovely and warm just inside here, Joan!' she said, as she emerged. 'Come down here a minute!'

'What are you doing, Elizabeth?' asked Joan, coming and crouching down beside her.

Elizabeth was on her knees now, moving rubble and fallen brick away from the entrance to the culvert. She cleared a space, then lay down in a bed of dock leaves, just inside. She was excited.

'I've had a brilliant idea, Joan!' she whispered. 'Let's go and get your sleeping bag from the tent. You can sleep in here! It'll be warm and cosy, but you'll still be able to peep out and see the moon and stars above!'

Joan lay down for a moment in the space that Elizabeth had cleared. Suddenly she looked pleased.

'I really think I could sleep here, Elizabeth,' she said. 'I really think I would rather like it!'

'Come on then!' hissed Elizabeth, taking her friend's hand. 'Let's go and get the sleeping bag. You'll need the thick one. And – I know! When you've gone, I'll stuff your kitbag inside the other one! If anyone should chance to look at it in the early morning, they will think it's you lying there, sound asleep.'

'Of course!' said Joan in delight. 'But I shall be sure to creep back to the tent as soon as dawn breaks, and be safely back in my place by morning. Oh, Elizabeth. I can do this every night! What a glorious plan.'

'But now we must be as quiet as mice,' whispered Elizabeth, as they crept silently back up the bank. 'If Arabella wakes up, our plan will be ruined.'

Unbeknown to the two friends, Arabella was already

awake. She was not only awake but up and about.

She was a light sleeper. The slight draught that had been caused by Elizabeth's leaving the tent had roused her.

Gradually, she had become aware that she and Teeny were alone in the tent. So she had scrambled into her dressing gown and ducked out of the tent herself. Where were the other two? She would try to find out what on earth they thought they were doing!

'I can hear you!' she hissed in a loud, triumphant whisper. She was coming their way. 'I can hear you larking about down there!'

Just below the embankment, the two friends froze like statues. Arabella was coming. She knew they were there!

'I shall have to report this to Miss Ranger!' Arabella was saying.

Joan gazed at Elizabeth in dismay. Arabella had woken up. They were about to be discovered. Oh, what horrible luck!

In her desperation an idea came to Elizabeth. She whispered it into Joan's ear. This was an emergency. It was the only thing she could think of to do.

It was to be an example of the naughtiest girl at her most headstrong.

CHAPTER NINE

ARABELLA IS MADE TENT MONITOR

ARMS OUTSTRETCHED, like someone in a trance, Elizabeth appeared over the top of the bank. She was moving at speed. She would have crashed straight into Arabella if the other girl had not jumped clear.

Arabella stared in surprise as the figure shot past her in the pale moonlight.

Elizabeth was walking stiffly, her eyes tightly shut, her arms as straight as pokers in front of her. She appeared to be walking in her sleep, marching towards the area where the tents stood.

Joan was following along in her wake.

'Hey, you two—!' began Arabella, as Joan carried straight on past her. 'What's going on—?'

Joan put a finger to her lips.

'Sh, Arabella. Sleepwalking! Mustn't be woken up suddenly. Dangerous. Just trying to keep an eye on her . . .'

Elizabeth was playing the part with gusto.

She was striding past Philippa's tent now, her hands still outstretched as though feeling her way. Arabella frowned suspiciously and started to run to catch up with her. She must get a proper look at Elizabeth's face. Was she really asleep? Was it true that she was walking in her sleep? Arabella found it hard to believe *that*.

As Arabella came up alongside her, Elizabeth quickly screwed her eyes shut again. She quickened her pace. It was horrid not to be able to see where she was going! But she must get away from Arabella.

She strode on fast and then faster and then . . .

Whoomph! Crash!

She tripped over the guy ropes of someone's tent. She hit the guys with such force that the tent pegs came clean out of the ground!

As she fell heavily against the small green tent, there came a horrible creaking, crashing sound—

The smart little tent began to subside. She heard a strangled cry from inside.

'What is going *on*?'

The tent was lying on the ground now. Miss Ranger's angry face appeared from under the folds of limp canvas.

Elizabeth could only sit there and stare in horror. She had brought the teacher's tent down on top of her while she slept!

Miss Ranger struggled out from beneath the fallen tent, found her dressing gown and slipped it on over her pyjamas. She confronted Elizabeth, who had now got to her feet and been joined by both Joan and Arabella.

'What exactly is the meaning of this tomfoolery, Elizabeth?' she asked. 'What are you all doing out of your tent, may I ask?'

'I think Elizabeth may have been sleepwalking—' Joan began desperately.

'You fibber!' exclaimed Arabella. 'Elizabeth was only pretending. And you were only pretending to be looking after her! You just did it because I'd come to see where you were! I heard you talking together before that. I heard you larking around!'

'Are you saying, Arabella, that Joan and Elizabeth were out of the tent at night?' asked Miss Ranger. 'And that you had to go and look for them?'

'Yes, Miss Ranger. And Elizabeth *can't* have been sleepwalking!' Arabella continued triumphantly. 'Look, she's wearing her dressing gown! Whoever heard of someone remembering to put on their dressing gown before they start walking in their sleep?'

The teacher had only to look at the two guilty faces to know that Arabella was speaking the truth.

'I can see that camping has gone to Elizabeth's head,' observed Miss Ranger. 'I thought she was much more sensible these days. But I am shocked at *your* behaviour, Joan. That you, a tent monitor, should have been joining in Elizabeth's pranks! I am beginning to wonder if I did the right thing to put you in charge of Teeny Wilson.'

'Joan let Teeny go off and climb a tree in the woods this afternoon!' Arabella blurted out. 'And Teeny fell out of the tree and broke her glasses!'

Miss Ranger was taken aback. Telling tales was not encouraged at Whyteleafe School. But, occasionally, the teachers agreed, it could be justified.

'Is this true, Joan?' she asked.

Joan stared at the ground and said nothing. She was deeply mortified.

'It was only a low branch she fell off!' Elizabeth protested. 'And she didn't hurt herself at all.'

'Thank you, Elizabeth, that will do,' replied the teacher. 'I can see that what Arabella says is true then.'

Miss Ranger gazed at all three girls, wondering what was the correct thing to do. To give herself time to calm down, she asked them to help her right the tent.

Only when that was done did she speak again. The teacher had come to a decision.

'The three of you will now return to your tent in silence,' she said. 'I shall ask William and Rita to call a special Meeting for tomorrow afternoon, so that it can be decided whether Joan should remain as a tent monitor or not.'

Miss Ranger then placed a hand on Arabella's shoulder.

'Until the special Meeting takes place I appoint you, Arabella, to be acting tent monitor. Until then you are in charge of the tent and, in particular, I expect you to take good care of Teeny. Do you think you can rise to the challenge, Arabella?'

'Oh, Miss Ranger,' simpered Arabella, longing to gloat, but somehow managing to look humble, 'I'll try my very best not to let you down.'

Joan's face was ashen.

And Elizabeth could have screamed with rage.

Elizabeth went to sleep feeling very sorry for herself. It was bad enough that Arabella had been appointed acting tent monitor. But she felt angry too at being in disgrace. She dreaded the special Meeting. She had not set out to be naughty, not at all. Everything she had done had been to help her friend. From the moment she had taken the blame for their being late back from the village . . . it had all been for Joan's sake! She had wanted nothing more than for Joan to make the grade as a fine tent monitor. And it had all been in vain after all.

And now Arabella would tell everyone at the Meeting about the sleepwalking episode! She would be teased and laughed at and called the naughtiest girl again . . .

But then, shortly before daybreak, Elizabeth was awoken by Arabella's voice.

'I know perfectly well you've got your torch on inside that sleeping bag, Joan. I can see the light from here. As tent monitor, I must ask you to put it out, please.'

At once, a lump came to her throat.

Poor Joan! Her troubles were so much worse than Elizabeth's own. It seemed that she had managed to snatch a few hours' sleep only by keeping her torch on inside her sleeping bag. Elizabeth heard the torch click off and its feeble light was extinguished.

She longed to protest, but she knew that Joan would not thank her for it. How she would hate it if Arabella, of all people, knew about her fear. It would make her more superior than ever!

If only there were some way of curing *Joan's fear*, thought Elizabeth. Suddenly she dimly remembered staying at a cousin's house. He always had to have the light on at night. 'He will grow out of it,' she had heard her aunt say to someone. 'The doctor says when he is about eleven or twelve.' *Why, in that case, Joan should be growing out of her fear any moment now*, decided Elizabeth hopefully. How wonderful if that happened and they could enjoy the rest of camp!

But how *could* they enjoy the rest of camp, she realised dully, with Joan suspended as a tent monitor and the insufferable Arabella appointed in her place? That, surely, was the only possible outcome of this afternoon's special Meeting.

At that moment the first twittering of birdsong rose up outside. The dawn chorus was beginning. Soon the pitch-dark inside the tent was giving way to a softer gloom. Comforted by the thought that Joan would now be able to sleep, Elizabeth turned over and went back to sleep herself.

When she awoke, the sun was well up and the tent flap tied back.

Joan was outside somewhere.

Arabella and Teeny were up and dressed. Teeny was kneeling in the centre of the tent, in front of the mirror. Arabella was brushing her hair for her.

'Fifty strokes, morning and night, to make your hair shine, Teeny,' Arabella was saying. 'It will make it shine like mine does!'

The little girl's glasses had already been returned by Matron and were secure on her nose once more. Drowsily watching Teeny, Elizabeth noticed that she seemed to be preening herself in the mirror. She had buttoned her blue shirt up to the neck and had turned the collar up. She was staring at the image dreamily, as though she liked it.

Arabella's going to make Teeny as vain as she is herself, thought Elizabeth, as the child fiddled with the shirt, unbuttoned it and turned the collar down again. Now she was asking Arabella why Joan was no longer in charge of her.

'Because Miss Ranger thinks I will make a better job of looking after you,' said Arabella proudly. 'You'll hear all about it this afternoon. There's going to be a special Meeting.'

'Oh,' replied Teeny, looking disappointed.

But Arabella did not make a better job of looking after Teeny. She made a very bad job of it. That morning she forgot all about her and the consequences could not have been more dramatic.

CHAPTER TEN

TEENY IN DANGER

'WHERE'S TEENY?' asked Arabella tetchily. 'I'm waiting to take her for a shower.'

Elizabeth and Joan stared at her in surprise. It was now noon. The two friends had spent the morning at the stables, helping Robert to groom the horses. After that they had been for a short ride. Now, as they returned to their tent, they found Arabella waiting impatiently outside. She was wearing a different outfit from the one she had worn at breakfast.

'How should we know?' asked Elizabeth rudely. It was a relief not to have to be polite to Arabella any more. 'You're the important tent monitor in charge of everything. You should know where Teeny is, not us.'

'But I thought she must have spent the morning with you!' said Arabella. 'When did you last see her?'

'We haven't seen her since breakfast time,' replied

Joan, with a puzzled frown. What was this all about? 'You and she were washing up your breakfast things together.'

Both friends had noticed how forlorn the little girl looked this morning. She had not seemed to be enjoying Arabella's company very much. She had been gazing wistfully at Duncan and Kitty. Once again the two boisterous juniors had been taking no notice of her. Elizabeth had commented to Joan how tragic it was that Teeny had been too cowardly to jump off that branch the day before.

'How different things might have been!' Elizabeth had sighed. 'For all of us.'

'You mustn't call Teeny a coward,' Joan had replied gently. 'We all have things that we're scared of.'

Now a pallor was creeping over Arabella's face.

'Where is she then?'

'Do you mean to say you haven't seen her all morning either?' asked Elizabeth accusingly. 'But where have you been? You were supposed to be in charge of her!'

'I had important things to do . . .' began Arabella lamely. 'She was in the tent when I left her. I didn't mean to be gone very long . . .' Arabella pouted. 'In any case Teeny said she had something *she* wanted to do.'

'What?' asked Joan tensely.

'I've no idea,' said Arabella. She clammed up.

The truth was that Arabella had quickly become bored with Teeny's company. After breakfast she had decided to slip up to school, taking some of her clothes back to exchange for others. She felt that she had brought the wrong outfits to camp and that she would look better in some others.

She had been only too happy when Teeny declined to come with her, saying that she had something of her own to do. And she had left the little girl sitting cross-legged in the tent, shuffling those silly playing cards, lost in thought.

Once in her dormitory Arabella had soon forgotten about Teeny altogether. Admiring herself in a wardrobe mirror, she had tried on outfit after outfit and quite lost track of time. She had only just returned to the tent.

'You had better start looking for her,' said Elizabeth grimly. 'Hadn't you, Arabella?'

'Elizabeth and I will run to Camp Centre and see if she's there,' said Joan anxiously. 'If we can't find her quickly, we must tell Miss Ranger.'

Leaving the frightened Arabella peering, helplessly, into empty tents, the friends raced off.

When they reached Camp Centre, they dearly hoped to find Teeny there. Had the loneliness of being left on her own all morning made her force herself to come and mix with her classmates? Perhaps they would find her playing happily with some other juniors at last.

But there was no sign of her. Most children had already left with their tent monitors to have a shower before dinner. Duncan and Kitty were loitering about and chatting happily to two of their classmates. That was all.

'Have you seen Teeny, any of you?' asked Joan softly, as she and Elizabeth walked up. 'Arabella's waiting to take her for a shower.'

Joan spoke in a calm, quiet voice for she did not want to alarm the younger children in any way.

'Not since breakfast,' volunteered Kitty.

'We've been helping Mr Leslie build some plate racks this morning,' said Duncan. He pointed proudly into the kitchen area. A row of plate racks stood there, made from green twigs crisscrossed and lashed together. 'Now we won't have to do so much drying up. We can leave things to dry in the sun, Mr Leslie says. Do you like them?'

'Yes, very good,' said Joan absently, at the same time gazing everywhere for some sign of Teeny. 'Well done.'

Elizabeth, however, was staring at the children in fascination.

All four had their sports shirts buttoned up to the

neck and the collars turned up. It was the new fashion among some of the juniors, as Elizabeth was already vaguely aware. But today they also wore what looked like a fat sprig of grass tucked in behind the top button. It was worn discreetly, almost like a secret badge.

Then some tent monitors appeared in the distance, shouting to the juniors to come up to school with them for their showers.

'Well,' said Joan worriedly, as the four juniors went racing off, 'Teeny can't have been at Camp Centre all morning, or those four would have seen her. Oh, Elizabeth, it was very wrong of Arabella not to find out what it was Teeny wanted to do. If only we knew that, it would be much easier to find her.'

Elizabeth was thinking hard. A picture flashed into her mind of Teeny this morning – of her turning her collar up, admiring herself in the mirror.

'I thought the juniors' shirts were just some kind of fashion,' she told Joan excitedly. 'But now I'm not so sure. I think it might be some kind of club – and that Teeny wants to join it. And maybe being asked to jump from the branch yesterday was somehow connected with it—'

She stared at her friend. 'Joan, do you think she might have gone back there this morning? To try the jump again? On her own?'

'Why would she do that?'

'Well, hoping to be let into the club . . .' mused Elizabeth.

'If you're right, we'd better go and tell Miss Ranger straight away,' said Joan. 'But why should the juniors have a club? You know they get crazes about how to wear things . . .'

'But the stems of grass they were wearing!' replied Elizabeth. 'It was those as well. They could be some kind of badge!'

'Grass?' asked Joan. 'Oh, you mean those green ears of corn? I noticed them wearing them last night, round the campfire.'

Elizabeth gasped. *Green ears of corn.* Of course!

Excitedly, she told Joan what she had overheard Duncan say to Kitty in the woods yesterday. About Teeny.

'But she does like us so. Shall we just try the green ear . . .'

Joan now became very interested.

'So you think Duncan and Kitty are the club leaders and they decided to give Teeny another chance? They told her last night that she could go and get a green ear of corn, like theirs . . .? And that's where she's gone to this morning?'

'I'm sure of it!' exclaimed Elizabeth. 'But I'm sure

they don't know about it. Teeny's made up her mind this morning, all on her own, to try and do it. To prove she's not a coward. That means it must be somewhere quite difficult . . .'

'But where?' asked Joan. 'Oh, we have to *think* . . .'

The whole camp had been to the woods yesterday. But there was certainly no corn growing there. Nor had they passed any on the way back. And, of course, there was no corn growing anywhere in the school grounds.

Yet at no time were members of the junior class permitted to go out of the school grounds on their own. So how had they managed to get those fresh-looking ears of corn?

'The only place I've ever seen any corn growing is over there somewhere,' said Elizabeth. 'On the other side of the lane.'

She waved a hand vaguely in the direction they had just come from. Out riding last July, she had seen a huge field of golden corn and workers getting the harvest in. At the moment, of course, it would still be green. The field, she now realised, must lie opposite the high wall where their tent was pitched.

She gasped. 'I think I know how they did it!'

Joan had realised the same thing.

The two friends raced to the footbridge and swung themselves down into the dried-up stream bed. They ran all the way along the cutting, puffing and panting, until the mouth of the culvert came in sight.

'Listen!' cried Joan, as they neared its entrance.

From deep in the darkness came a faint whimpering sound. Teeny was trapped somewhere in the tiny tunnel!

Remembering the pitch-blackness in there, Joan hesitated. Only one of them would be able to squeeze in. But Teeny was in there. There was not a second to lose!

She wanted to do it. She had been Teeny's tent monitor. She *must* do it. But she knew that Elizabeth would stop her. And that would be more than enough to make her nerve fail . . .

Elizabeth glanced at her friend's face and saw everything that was going through her mind.

She ran forward, tripped and fell to the ground. She gave a cry.

'My ankle! I think I've done something!'

Now Joan could hesitate no longer. 'It's all right, Elizabeth. Don't try to move! I'm going in there to get Teeny!'

Joan dropped to the ground, dived through the gap, then crawled forward into the darkness and was gone.

Soon Elizabeth heard her voice echoing from deep inside the culvert.

'It's all right, Teeny. It's Joan here. Don't be

frightened. We'll get you out of here!'

Elizabeth got to her feet and tiptoed forward. There was nothing wrong with her ankle at all.

Peering into the blackness, she could hear the clunk of rubble being moved. The roof of the culvert must have collapsed. Joan must be clearing a path for Teeny, with her bare hands. The child had been overcome with panic. She had lain there, not daring to move, convinced that she was trapped.

The little tunnel, like an echo chamber, carried their voices out.

'We'll just move these last few bricks, Teeny, and there'll be a nice gap and I'll be able to pull you through. We must do everything very slowly and carefully, so that we don't make any more disturbance.'

'Yes, Joan. Oh, Joan, I've been so scared.'

Only Elizabeth knew just how scared *Joan* must be and how brave she was being. Feeling immensely proud of her friend, she raced away to find Miss Ranger and Mr Leslie.

When she returned with the teachers and with Rita as well, they were just in time to see Joan's rear view appearing. Crawling backwards, Joan was gently pulling Teeny by the hands, out of the culvert, into the fresh air.

'We didn't feel there was any time to waste!'

Elizabeth explained to Miss Ranger. 'We were both so frightened Teeny might suffocate.'

'I think the whole school is going to be very proud of Joan,' replied the teacher. 'She can take great pride in what she's done.'

'I think she does already,' replied Elizabeth, looking at Joan's happy, glowing face as she hugged Teeny close.

Teeny, in spite of her frightening ordeal, was also looking very proud. Her tear-stained face was, just like Joan's, glowing with happiness and a sense of achievement.

There was something clutched in her grimy fingers. She held it up to show Joan.

'Look! Duncan and Kitty will be friends with me now!' she blurted out. 'I shall be allowed to be a member of the Dare Club.'

It was a green ear of corn.

CHAPTER ELEVEN

A VERY GOOD SCHOOL MEETING

THE SPECIAL Meeting was about to begin. The campers sat on the groundsheets in rows again. A low buzz of conversation rippled up and down the rows. It was always very exciting and interesting when William and Rita called a special Meeting. It meant that there was something important to discuss.

Sitting with her classmates, Elizabeth wondered what exactly was going to be raised at the Meeting.

It was no longer going to be about who should be tent monitor between Joan and Arabella.

There was Joan, at the front, seated with the other tent monitors. Elizabeth smiled and waved to her friend. Proudly, Joan waved back. She was back in her rightful place.

As soon as Teeny's rescue had taken place, Miss Ranger had stripped Arabella of her acting monitorship and asked Joan to resume her duties. Arabella was in deep disgrace for neglecting the little junior in her charge when it was well known that Teeny had no friends to play with.

But Teeny certainly had friends now! thought Elizabeth, with a smile.

It had been wonderful to watch her at dinnertime, surrounded by the other members of the Dare Club. In clean clothes, after a hot shower, she had sat between Duncan and Kitty, in the place of honour at one of the junior tables. She was a member of the club at last, her collar worn turned up, like the rest of them, her green ear of corn displayed like a trophy in her top buttonhole. Having no idea of the danger she had been through, Duncan and Kitty were simply pleased that Teeny had finally proved that she was not a 'coward'.

She was still sitting with her new friends now, chattering happily in the front row, a child transformed.

Since arriving at Whyteleafe, the shy, nervous girl had longed only to be friends with Duncan and Kitty – she liked and admired them so. They had promised her that, once she had proved her courage with a successful 'dare', she would be allowed to join their secret club and play with them.

But, each time Teeny had been given a dare to do, her courage had failed and she had not completed it.

With each failure her confidence had ebbed away. The more desperate she became to join the club, the more scared and jumpy she was, dreading each new dare, yet longing to succeed. Her greatest battle had been with herself. This morning, sitting in the tent and struggling with her fears, she knew that the challenge, to crawl through the culvert and pick a green ear of corn in the field that was out of bounds, was her very last chance. Duncan and Kitty would not give her another. And she had won the battle!

'Silence, please!' called William, banging the mallet on the table. 'At the Meeting this afternoon we are going to talk about courage.'

There was an immediate hush. Rita then told the astonished Meeting about the fall of rubble in the dangerous old tunnel. She told how it was only thanks to the alertness of Elizabeth and the bravery of Joan that no harm had befallen Teeny Wilson.

The two friends stood up and were given a round of applause. Then William took over.

'We believe that Teeny's narrow escape had something to do with a dare,' he said. 'If so, would the person or persons who made the dare please stand up?'

Sitting in the front row, Duncan and Kitty had turned pale. They exchanged frightened glances, but remained sitting.

'Would they please stand and own up?' William repeated.

The two juniors sat very, very still. They were frozen with fear.

William sighed. 'In that case—' He banged the mallet sharply on the table, making everyone jump. 'Duncan and Kitty, I must ask you to stand up at once and come out here to the front.'

Trembling slightly, the little boy and girl got slowly to their feet and went and stood in the front. Their faces had turned red with shame.

'I see,' said William. He surveyed them. 'How very interesting. So even you two are frightened of something? You are frightened of Rita and me.'

Now Rita joined in. 'William and I have made a full investigation. We have discovered, though not from Teeny, that all term you have been calling her a coward. You have been setting her dares to do that were beyond her capabilities. In doing so all her confidence was destroyed. You did not mean it to be cruel. You wanted her to succeed. But cruel it was.'

Duncan and Kitty, and some other members of the Dare Club too, were beginning to feel extremely uncomfortable. Teeny's mouth was hanging open, in wonder, that the head boy and girl had found all this out.

From the rest of the campers there came not a sound. As William continued, they hung on to every word he said.

'What you must all learn and understand,' he said, 'is that there are many different forms of courage and many different forms of cowardice. Let me give you an example. One dare you set Teeny, when we all got to camp, was to play a joke on someone in her tent. Because she was discovered, you told Teeny that she had failed. But do you know why she was discovered?'

Kitty and Duncan shook their heads.

'She was discovered because another girl was blamed. So what did Teeny do? Rather than let the other girl take the blame, she owned up. Did that not take courage?'

Slowly, the juniors nodded.

'And not to have owned up – would that not have been cowardly?' prompted Rita. 'And should you not have owned up just now, when William asked you to?'

'So who are the real cowards, you or Teeny?' concluded William.

'We are,' said Duncan, looking deeply ashamed.

The lesson had been well and truly learnt. Rita spoke to them now, almost gently.

'It is not brave or clever to make sleeping-bag jokes, or to break school rules, or do dangerous things.

It must stop. But we want you all to put this behind you now and enjoy the rest of camp. And I think the monitors have decided that you must give your club a new name. Can any of you think of one?'

'Let's call it the Friendship Club!' exclaimed Kitty, taking hold of Teeny's hand. 'Would that be a good name, Teeny? Do you like it?'

Teeny loved it. They all did.

Afterwards the whole camp agreed that it had been a very good Meeting. They had all learnt something from it, including Elizabeth.

'In a way I'm as bad as those little juniors,' she confessed to Joan later, as they sunned themselves outside the tent. 'I thought Teeny was a terrible coward when she wouldn't jump off that low branch.'

'Yes, William and Rita were so right,' agreed Joan. 'There are so many different ways of being cowardly – and of being brave.'

'And still no one knows how brave *you* were, Joan,' said Elizabeth. 'Going into that pitch-black tunnel. It would have meant nothing to me. But for you, of all people—'

'And nobody is going to know either!' replied Joan quickly. 'It was a private battle and I know now that I have won it. I am going to sleep without any light in the tent tonight, Elizabeth! You wait and see!'

Then she turned to her friend.

'It was so lucky that you fell, at exactly the right moment. I don't think I would have had the courage to go on if that hadn't happened. I was convinced you must have twisted your ankle. Are you sure that it's really better now?'

'It seems absolutely fine,' replied Elizabeth solemnly. She bent forward, as though to examine it. In fact, she was making sure that Joan would not see the smile on her face.

After such a bad start camp turned out to be wonderful. There was no more trouble with Arabella, certainly none with Teeny and, true to her word, Joan found that she could manage the darkness after that. Everyone was to agree that Joan turned out to be a very fine tent monitor, just as Elizabeth had vowed that they would.

Joan wanted to tell Miss Ranger that, for private reasons, she – Joan – was to blame for the visit to the village and for the sleepwalking episode. But Elizabeth refused to allow her.

'It would all be too complicated,' she said, with a shrug. 'And besides the sleepwalking was such a terrible idea. I would rather we all forgot about it.'

It had not been one of the naughtiest girl's best. The last one, the falling over idea, had been much better.

Elizabeth was pleased about that. She could bear one or two black marks against her name just to see her best friend happy again.

Elizabeth was not without courage herself.

BONUS BLYTON

Enid Blyton has been one of the world's best-loved storytellers for over seventy-five years. Her interest in writing began as a child, and before she loved receiving letters from the children who read her books, she enjoyed working with them as a teacher. The Naughtiest Girl stories are inspired by real schools and experiences. Turn the page to learn more about Enid as a child and as a teacher. Afterwards you might like to write about your school and teachers and the people in *your* class!

THE LIFE AND TIMES OF ENID BLYTON

11 August 1897	Enid Blyton was born in East Dulwich, London. Two brothers are born after her – Hanly (b. 1899) and Carey (b. 1902).
1911	Enid enters a children's poetry competition and is praised for her writing. She's on the path to becoming a bestselling author . . .
1916	Enid begins to train as a teacher in Ipswich. By the time she is 21, she is a fully qualified Froebel teacher, and starts work at a school in Kent.
1917	Enid's first 'grown-up' publication – three poems in *Nash's Magazine*.
June 1922	Enid's first book is published. It's called *Child Whispers*.
1926	Enid begins editing – and writes – the phenomenal *Sunny Stories for Little Folks* magazine. (She continues in this role for 26 years!)

1927	So vast is Enid's output that she has to learn to type. (But she still writes to children by hand.)
1931	Having married Hugh Pollock in 1924, the couple's first child, Gillian, is born. Imogen, their second daughter, was born in 1935.
1942	The Famous Five is launched with *Five on a Treasure Island.*
1949	The first appearance of *The Secret Seven* and of *Noddy* mark this year as special.
1953	Enid moves away from *Sunny Stories* to launch *Enid Blyton's Magazine*. She is now renowned throughout the world – she even established her own company, called Darrell Waters Limited (the surname of her second husband).
1962	Enid Blyton becomes one of the first and most important children's authors to be published in paperback. Now, she reaches even more readers than ever before.
28 November 1968	Enid dies in her sleep, in a nursing home in Hampstead.

Enid's death wasn't the end of her remarkable legacy. In the 1970s the Famous Five became TV stars (Noddy having already hit our screens in 1955). In 1996 the Enid Blyton Society was formed so that fans across the world could share their enthusiasm for Enid's work (www.enidblytonsociety.co.uk) In 2012 the Famous Five celebrated seventy years of continuous publishing, with special editions featuring covers by top illustrators, led by Quentin Blake. New book, film and merchandising deals are being struck all the time. Enid's work is definitely here to stay!

YOUNG ENID

Enid, aged seven, 1904

Ipswich High School, where Enid studied, 1917

Bickley Park School, where Enid taught, 1919

Photos of Enid Blyton courtesy of Tony Summerfield, the Enid Blyton Society.

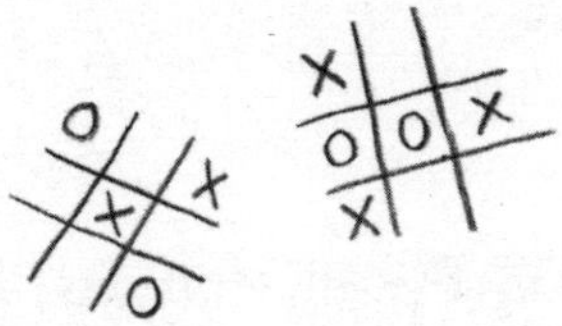

ENID AS A CHILD: ON THE PATH TO BECOMING A WRITER – PART ONE

Enid claimed that she was an ordinary child – except for *one thing*, which marked her out as a future writer. As soon as she lay awake at night, her imagination would fire up and stories would unfold in her head. She once said, 'They came out of nowhere – out of my imagination.' The stories weren't quite like dreams, which are often muddled and confusing. Enid's stories had their own threads, and . . . a beginning, a middle and an end.

Enid kept a diary, and wrote in it every single day. She also wrote lots of letters to people. Both of these things were excellent training for becoming a writer. Later on in life her advice to children wanting to write was, 'Fill your mind with all kinds of interesting things – the more you have in it, the more will come out of it.'

Enid also created a magazine called *DAB* – named after the last names of the three girls who contributed to it (Mirable Davis, Mary Attenborough and Enid Blyton, of course). Enid wrote stories, Mirabel wrote poems and Mary provided the illustrations. If you and your friends had a magazine, and named it after your initials, what would the title be?

The three friends sent each other postcards when they were away on holiday – but they were written in code, so the postman couldn't read them!

You can read more about Enid's journey to becoming a writer in the new edition of The Naughtiest Girl Saves the Day *– as well as more happenings at the school run by Miss Brown, who you will meet on the next page . . .*

Quotations from The Story of My Life *by Enid Blyton*
© Hodder & Stoughton Limited, 1952.

WHAT THEY DID AT MISS BROWN'S SCHOOL

In 1920 Enid Blyton became a governess to the four Thompson children, whose ages ranged from four to ten. The family lived in Surbiton, in Surrey, in a house called 'Southernhay'. Enid had a small room which overlooked the garden, and it was there that she wrote many of her stories. Enid's tiny class often had lessons outdoors in the summer months.

Enid was very popular with her students, because her lessons were both practical and creative. She worked with them to put on performances for which they made props, costumes and invitations – and even sold tickets.

In 1941 she published a long story called 'What They Did at Miss Brown's School', which was divided into monthly episodes. It's been hard to find for many years, but you can read extracts in these new editions of *The Naughtiest Girl* books. The character of Miss Brown and her tiny class is very much based on Enid Blyton and her school at the Thompsons' . . .

Here's the seventh episode . . .

7. July. A Few Pets Come to School

'MISS BROWN, you said that each month we could do something interesting,' said John. 'What are we going to do in July?'

'Well, you still have your silkworms growing day by day,' said Miss Brown, 'and your school garden to see to. Do you particularly want anything for July?'

'Oh, yes!' said Mary firmly. 'We must have something special for every month in the year, Miss Brown.'

Miss Brown laughed. 'Well,' she said, 'my cousin is going away to the seaside and she wants me to keep her rabbits for her. Shall we make July a month for keeping pets?'

'I'll bring my tortoise,' said Peter at once. 'That will be another pet.'

'It's no good bringing my cat,' said Susan. 'She wouldn't stay.'

'Nor would my dog,' said John.

'Well, we'll just have the rabbits and the tortoise!'

said Miss Brown. 'And maybe we'll find something else turning up as well!'

The rabbits arrived in a nice big hutch. They were pretty creatures, with noses that 'woffled', as Susan called it. 'I do love their woffly noses,' she said.

'Now who is going to clean the rabbits each day for me?' asked Miss Brown. 'Pets have to be seen to regularly every day, you know.'

'Let *me* clean the cage and feed them, please,' begged John eagerly. He loved all animals, and was longing to look after them.

'Very well, John,' said Miss Brown. 'Have a good look at the hutch, and see how easily it can be cleaned.'

John had a good look at the rabbits' home. It had a tray at the bottom that slid in and out so that it could easily be cleaned. At one end of the hutch was a box, put in upside down, with a hole cut in the side for the rabbits to go in and out.

'That's their bedroom!' said Susan. 'It's got hay inside! Isn't it a cosy room for them, John? They have a bedroom and a parlour!'

John gave the rabbits oats for breakfast. They liked those very much. Susan brought some bread for them, but Miss Brown said no, they were better without bread. Oats were best.

'But you can bring them a carrot to nibble if you like,'

said Miss Brown. 'That is good for them and they will enjoy it.'

'My mother says that warm tea leaves, squeezed nearly dry, mixed with pollard, are very good for rabbits,' said Mary. 'Can I bring some tea leaves, Miss Brown?'

'Of course,' said Miss Brown. 'And I have plenty of pollard. We might sometimes let the rabbits have a lettuce from our school garden too.'

The rabbits loved having the children to look after them. They were well fed, and their cage was beautifully cleaned by John every morning. Fresh hay was put into the hutch to keep it healthy and sweet.

'I think our rabbits might have a little exercise now,' said Miss Brown. 'They are quite tame and won't be frightened. Let them out of the hutch this morning at playtime, John, and they can have a run in the garden. But we must look after our lettuces!'

The children were so pleased when they saw the rabbits running free – and the rabbits were full of joy! The mother rabbit let Susan pick it up. Miss Brown showed Susan how to keep a firm hold of the rabbit's ears when she held it in her arms, in case something frightened the rabbit.

'You see, if it leapt suddenly from your arms, it might break its legs,' said Miss Brown. 'It won't leap if you hold its ears. It will be all right when it is used to you.'

Then Peter's tortoise arrived. He was a funny fellow who could put all his legs and his head too into his shell. Peter stood him on the grass.

'He'll soon put out his head and have a look around!' said Peter. And, sure enough, he did! Out came his funny head, with its two alert, sharp eyes, and the tortoise began to hurry off towards the lettuce bed as fast as ever he could!

'Oh, no, not that way, old fellow!' said Peter, and he turned the tortoise the other way round. But the tortoise was too clever to lose his way – he swung himself round and crawled quickly to the lettuce bed again.

'This won't do,' said Miss Brown. 'We will make him a nice little yard for himself. John, get the roll of wire netting out of the shed, and Peter, get four thick sticks. I want you boys to wire in a square piece of grass for the tortoise, and then he won't steal our plants!'

Very soon Crawler the tortoise had a nice big grassy playground for himself. He pulled at the grass when he was hungry. He gobbled up rose petals when the children dropped them into his pen. He chewed up lettuce leaves and young cabbage leaves hungrily.

'We'll give him a little wooden box to crawl into at night,' said Miss Brown. 'That shall be his home.'

So she got a wooden box, painted it green and put it into Crawler's pen. He loved it and crawled into it as soon as the sun went down, or if a sharp rainstorm came.

'He's a nice creature,' said Susan. 'He puts his head out for me to tickle him under the chin, Peter!'

The next person to bring a pet was Mary – and she brought such a funny one! What do you think it was? It was a prickly hedgehog!

'He crawled into our tennis net at home, and I did have a job untangling him, Miss Brown,' said Mary. 'Will he be a pet, do you think?'

'Oh, yes!' said Miss Brown, 'and a very useful one too! He will help to eat the grubs and caterpillars and beetles in our garden.'

'He's got a lot of horrid fleas on him,' said Susan.

'Yes, hedgehogs always have,' said Miss Brown. 'But you needn't bother about those – they are only hedgehog fleas, and won't hurt you. I'm afraid he won't be a very cuddlesome pet, Mary! He's too prickly.'

'Yes, he is,' agreed Mary. 'Let's call him Prickles. What shall we feed him on, Miss Brown? Do we have to collect beetles and things for him?'

'Oh, no!' said Miss Brown. 'He can collect those for himself. We will give him ordinary bread and milk, which he loves!'

'It's a good thing the school garden is wired all round,' said John. 'He won't be able to get out and he really will be a pet if he stays for long.'

They gave the hedgehog some bread and milk in a saucer. How he loved it! He lapped it all up and then, with a little grunt, he curled himself up under a bush and fell fast asleep!

'That's another pet!' said Mary, pleased. 'Now we've all got one except Susan.'

'And do you know I've got one for Susan!' said Miss Brown quickly, for she saw that Susan was beginning to look upset. The little girl couldn't bear to be the only one left out. 'Come along, Susan. It's a funny pet, but just as useful as the hedgehog!'

All the children followed Miss Brown. She took them to Susan's birdbath, and lifted up a stone by the edge. Underneath, curled up in a damp hollow, was a large toad!

'There you are, Susan!' said Miss Brown. 'A good, useful pet for you!'

Susan did not belong to the kind of children who can't bear frogs or toads. She liked all creatures, and she looked at the toad in surprise.

'Hasn't he got lovely eyes?' she said. 'Like jewels gleaming in his head!'

'Yes, aren't they!' said Miss Brown. 'All toads have beautiful eyes, but people seldom bother to look at them. Your toad will eat slugs and grubs and flies,

Susan, and will be a very useful friend to us. Find a few slugs for him and he will soon know you.'

The toad crawled out of his hiding place and looked up at Susan as if he knew who she was. A big bluebottle flew down beside him. The toad flicked out a quick tongue, blinked his eyes, swallowed – and the fly was gone!

'He just did that to show us how clever he was!' said Susan. 'Oh, Miss Brown, I like him. He's not at all an ordinary pet to have, is he? Do you think he'd like his back tickled?'

'I should think he'd love it!' said Miss Brown. So Susan got a straw and tickled his back gently and the toad wriggled with joy and tried to scratch his back too, with his front foot.

'Now we've all got pets!' said Susan. 'John's got rabbits; Peter's got a tortoise; Mary's got a hedgehog – and I've got a toad!'

The children looked after their pets so well that they were all as friendly and tame as could be. The rabbits lived free in the garden most of the time. The tortoise crawled round his pen and stretched out his neck to be tickled every time the children came by.

The hedgehog came into the schoolroom and curled himself up in the empty fireplace, where he slept soundly till the bell for playtime. He snored too – a dear little short snore that the children laughed to hear.

As for the toad, he soon crept out from his stone when he heard the voices of the children and crawled to meet them, for he knew that one of them would be sure to have a titbit for him.

And do you know, when Miss Brown's cousin came back, and said she would have her rabbits once more, there was such a surprise for her! There were seven rabbits instead of two!

'The mother rabbit has some dear little babies for you,' said Susan. 'But oh, we *shall* be sorry to part with them!'

'Well, you needn't part with them!' said Miss Brown's cousin, with a smile. 'I only want two rabbits – and I will give you the babies for yourselves, as you have been so good in looking after them for me!'

What do you think of that? The children were so excited that they could talk and think of nothing else – and do you know, when Susan was saying her money tables to Miss Brown, this is what she said: 'Two ha'pennies make a penny, four farthings make a penny, twelve pennies make a shilling, twenty rabbits make a pound!'

And how everybody laughed!

Enid Blyton®

THE FAMOUS FIVE

Join the Adventure!

Have you read them all?

Enid Blyton®

THE SECRET SEVEN

SOLVE THE MYSTERY!

HAVE YOU READ THEM ALL?

Enid Blyton®

THE

SECRET SEVEN

SOLVE THE MYSTERY!

Don't miss…

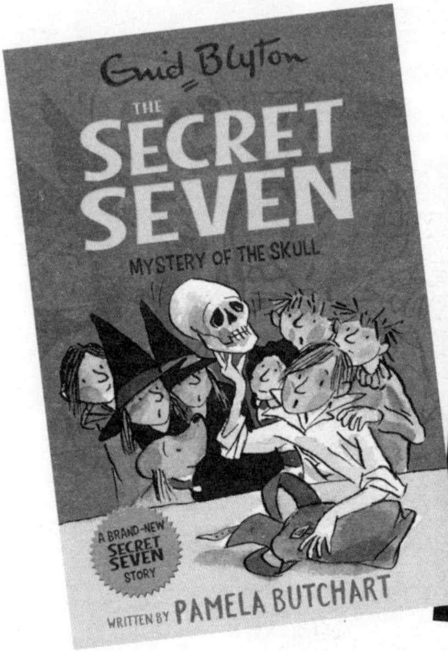

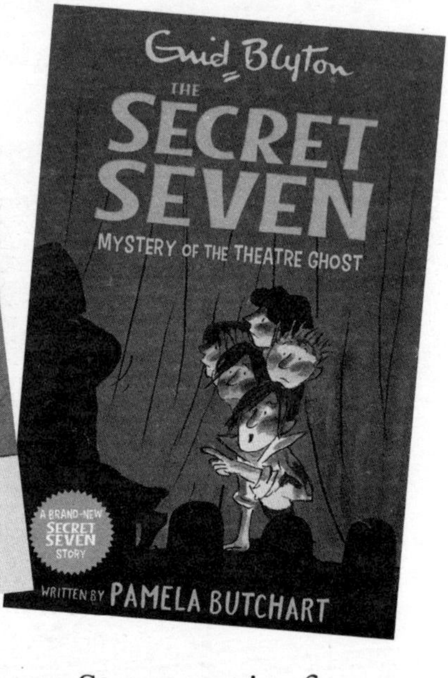

Two action-packed Secret Seven stories from prizewinning author **PAMELA BUTCHART**!

Enid Blyton

THE SECRET SEVEN

SOLVE THE MYSTERY!

Solve every puzzle, just like the Secret Seven, in this fun book of 100 tricky codes, puzzles, sudokus, crosswords and more!

THE MYSTERY SERIES

Read all 15 classic stories!

ENIDBLYTON.CO.UK

IS FOR PARENTS, CHILDREN AND TEACHERS!

Sign up to the newsletter on the homepage for a monthly round-up of news from the world of

Enid Blyton®

JOIN US ON SOCIAL MEDIA

EnidBlytonOfficial BlytonOfficial

Illustration by Laura Ellen Anderson.

Enid Blyton®

is one of the most popular children's authors of all time. Her books have sold over 500 million copies and have been translated into other languages more often than any other children's author.

Enid Blyton adored writing for children. She wrote over 700 books and about 2,000 short stories. *The Famous Five* books, now 80 years old, are her most popular. She is also the author of other favourites including *The Secret Seven*, *The Magic Faraway Tree* and *Malory Towers*.

Born in London in 1897, Enid lived much of her life in Buckinghamshire and loved dogs, gardening and the countryside. She was very knowledgeable about trees, flowers, birds and animals. Dorset – where some of the Famous Five's adventures are set – was a favourite place of hers too.

Enid Blyton's stories are read and loved by millions of children (and grown-ups) all over the world. Visit enidblyton.co.uk to discover more.

Illustration by Laura Ellen Anderson.

The NAUGHTIEST GIRL Keeps a Secret

Have you read them all?

1. The Naughtiest Girl in the School
2. The Naughtiest Girl Again
3. The Naughtiest Girl is a Monitor
4. Here's the Naughtiest Girl
5. The Naughtiest Girl Keeps a Secret
6. The Naughtiest Girl Helps a Friend
7. The Naughtiest Girl Saves the Day
8. Well Done, the Naughtiest Girl
9. The Naughtiest Girl Wants to Win
10. The Naughtiest Girl Marches On

Enid Blyton®

The NAUGHTIEST GIRL Keeps a Secret

WRITTEN BY ANNE DIGBY

HODDER

HODDER CHILDREN'S BOOKS

First published in Great Britain in 1999 by Hodder & Stoughton
This edition published in 2021
For further information about the editorial history of this book,
see enidblyton.co.uk/books

5 7 9 10 8 6

Enid Blyton® and Enid Blyton's signature are registered
trade marks of Hodder & Stoughton Limited
Text © 2021 Hodder & Stoughton Limited
Illustrations by Claire Powell © 2021 Hodder & Stoughton Limited

No trademark or copyrighted material may be reproduced without the
express written permission of the trademark and copyright owner.

The moral right of the author has been asserted.

All characters and events in this publication, other than those clearly in the public domain, are fictitious and any resemblance to real persons, living or dead, is purely coincidental.

All rights reserved.
No part of this publication may be reproduced, stored in a retrieval system, or transmitted, in any form or by any means, without the prior permission in writing of the publisher, nor be otherwise circulated in any form of binding or cover other than that in which it is published and without a similar condition including this condition being imposed on the subsequent purchaser.

A CIP catalogue record for this book is available from the British Library.

ISBN 978 1 444 95864 5

Printed and bound in Great Britain by Clays Ltd, Elcograf S.p.A.

Typeset in Caslon by Avon DataSet Ltd, Arden Court, Alcester, Warwickshire

The paper and board used in this book are made from wood
from responsible sources.

FSC www.fsc.org MIX Paper | Supporting responsible forestry FSC® C104740

Hodder Children's Books
An imprint of Hachette Children's Group
Part of Hodder & Stoughton
Carmelite House
50 Victoria Embankment
London EC4Y 0DZ

An Hachette UK Company
www.hachette.co.uk
www.hachettechildrens.co.uk

CONTENTS

INTRODUCTION

by Cressida Cowell

bestselling author of the
How to Train Your Dragon series

Like so many, many children before and after me, Enid Blyton's books played a crucial role in turning my nine-year-old self into a passionate reader.

That is because Enid Blyton had an extraordinary knack for writing the kind of books that children actually *want* to read, rather than the kind of books that adults think they *should* read.

Enid Blyton could tap into children's dreams, children's desires, children's wishes, with pinpoint accuracy. She knew that every child, however good and well-behaved they might look on the outside, secretly longed to be Elizabeth Allen, the naughtiest kid in the school. I'm afraid I entirely cheered Elizabeth on, as she defied her parents, the headmistresses, her schoolmates, and the very serious School Meetings. If anything, I wanted her to be even naughtier.

But *The Naughtiest Girl* books were really my favourite of Enid Blyton's school stories because of Whyteleafe, a very different school from Malory Towers or St Clare's. What if there could be a school in which discipline was administered by the children rather than the adults? In which all money was given in at the start of the term and distributed among the children along socialist lines? Wouldn't this be the kind of school that children would actually *want* to go to, rather than the kind of school that children *have* to go to?

It was an interesting proposition to a nine-year-old, and it remains an interesting proposition.

I hope you enjoy this story as much as I did when *I* was nine years old.

Cressida Cowell

CHAPTER ONE

A MESSAGE FROM WILLIAM AND RITA

'IT'S STILL lovely and sunny!' said Elizabeth happily, as she came out of the first-form classroom with her friend Julian and his cousin, Patrick.

It was four o'clock in the afternoon. Lessons at Whyteleafe School had finished for the day. Along the corridor, boys and girls were bursting out of other classrooms, laughing and chattering noisily. Soon everyone would change out of school uniform, go to tea, then race off to take part in all their summer-term activities.

There was always so much to do at Whyteleafe, thought Elizabeth. She loved it here now. She was still a monitor, though only an honorary one this term. There were no silly quarrels to worry about at present, no misunderstandings, no having to keep her temper. She and Patrick were just starting to get on reasonably well too. At the beginning of term they had been sworn enemies.

'This is my favourite time of year!' Elizabeth told Julian. 'The evenings are so light and long. It gives you time to fit everything in. I think I'll do some gardening later. I'm sure my lettuces need watering . . .'

'You've got to come and watch my tennis match first,' Patrick butted in.

Elizabeth nodded that she would, then continued.

'To think how much I hated it here at the beginning. It seems so strange now. I did everything I could to try and get myself sent home.'

'You mean last summer, when you were the naughtiest girl in the school?' asked Julian, his green eyes showing his amusement. 'Wish I'd been here then. Poor Elizabeth. You've been trying to live it down ever since.'

'Well, I *have* lived it down,' said Elizabeth firmly.

'She wouldn't be a monitor if she hadn't,' Patrick pointed out. 'Anyway, it wasn't all that strange. Hating it here at the beginning, I mean. Look at me: three weeks ago I couldn't stand the place!'

It was true. Julian's cousin was new this term. And, although the two cousins looked rather alike, their characters were very different. Julian was lively and jokey, full of a self-confidence that came from being so clever and good at everything. He didn't, for example, in the least mind Elizabeth being a monitor. Patrick, when he'd first arrived, had been sullen and lacking in confidence. And he had deeply resented a girl telling him what to do.

'But you do like it here now, don't you, Patrick?' said Elizabeth.

'Not so terrible having a school with girls in it, is it?' said Julian wryly. 'And you've got your trial for the second tennis team. Already! I call that good going.'

'Yes, not bad.' Patrick flushed with pride. 'Don't you two forget to come and watch me either. I need supporters.'

'We'll come and support you,' piped up a voice in the corridor, just behind them. It was Arabella Buckley, with a friend. 'We'll come and cheer Patrick on, won't we, Rosemary?'

'Of course we'll come!' said Rosemary, who always agreed with everything Arabella said.

'We'll be there, Patrick,' said Elizabeth quietly. 'You know you can do it. I'm sure you can beat Roger.'

Roger Brown was a big boy, in his last term at Whyteleafe. But, even so, he was only clinging on to his place in the school's second team by his fingertips.

Mr Warlow, the sports master, had watched Patrick play. He had also noted how hard the new boy practised each day. So a trial had been arranged.

After tea today Roger and Patrick were to play singles against each other. Everybody knew that, if Patrick proved to be the stronger player, he would be awarded that precious place in the second team.

'You'll need that special racket of yours, though, Patrick,' said Julian. 'Better not let Elizabeth get anywhere near it. You know what she's like.'

He kept a straight face as he said it. For a moment Elizabeth took him seriously.

'Julian Holland, what a hateful thing to say—'

Once, in a fit of rage with Patrick, Elizabeth had caused his lovely new racket to get soaked with rain. She hated to be reminded of it now.

It was Patrick who quickly smoothed things over. 'Don't worry! I'll guard it with my life!' he smiled.

Elizabeth smiled then too, and the awkward moment passed.

At teatime she even managed to make a joke at her own expense.

Patrick had changed into his tennis things and come over to join Elizabeth's table, carrying his precious tennis racket. It really was his pride and joy.

'If anything can bring me luck, it's this,' he told John McTavish. 'I'm useless with any other racket.'

'Better not leave it by my chair then, Patrick,' said

Elizabeth. 'I think you ought to padlock it to the table leg. You know what I'm like!'

All the boys and girls at the table laughed. Julian gave Elizabeth's arm an approving pinch. He was pleased to see his friend not taking herself too seriously.

Arabella, however, turned her pretty little doll-like face towards Patrick and smiled primly.

'It wasn't so funny at the time, though, was it, Patrick?' she said.

Elizabeth ground her teeth. She tried hard to think of something clever to say, to get back at Arabella. But, at that moment, someone came hurrying over to their table.

'Elizabeth?'

'Joan!'

Elizabeth was always pleased to see her special friend. But Joan was older and had gone up to the second form quite quickly, so the two girls saw less of each other these days. Elizabeth knew that if she did well at lessons this term she too would go up in September. Then she and Joan would be together again. Elizabeth was looking forward to that.

'I've got a message for you,' said Joan softly. She was always quietly spoken. 'It's from William and Rita. They would like you to come along to their study after tea, please.'

Elizabeth frowned in surprise. William and Rita were the head boy and the head girl of Whyteleafe School.

'Are you coming too? Are all the monitors coming?' Elizabeth asked. She was puzzled because there was no School Meeting due for a day or two yet.

Sometimes all the monitors were called in if there was something important to discuss before the Meeting. The Meeting was held once a week. All pupils had to attend. It was a kind of parliament. At Whyteleafe it was the boys and girls themselves who made many of the important rules and saw that they were applied fairly. When problems arose, they sorted them out themselves. The teachers rarely had to be involved.

'No, they just want you,' said Joan. 'I don't know what it's about.'

Elizabeth rushed through her tea after that. What did William and Rita want to see her about?

'Hey, Monitor, don't gobble your food. You're supposed to set a good example,' teased Julian. 'William and Rita aren't going to disappear down a big hole. They can wait,' he added carelessly.

'I'll finish up your scrambled egg if you can't manage it all, Elizabeth,' said her friend Kathleen, all smiles and rosy cheeks as usual.

'Would you really like it?' asked Elizabeth gratefully. 'Cook's given me too much. Then I can slip off and see what they want with me. I haven't done anything bad lately, have I, Kathleen?'

She picked up her remaining chocolate biscuits, put them in her pocket, scraped her chair back, then got up and left the table.

'If you'd done anything bad, it would have to wait for the Meeting, Elizabeth,' Julian called after her, 'and the whole school would have to hear about it! You know that's the system here. See you later!'

'Come straight on to the tennis courts!' Patrick added. 'I'll be playing soon.'

But Elizabeth, hurrying out of the hall, didn't hear them. The chatter and clatter from other tables filled her ears and drowned out the boys' voices.

There was only one thought in her mind at present.

Why had the head boy and girl asked her to come and see them?

CHAPTER TWO

ELIZABETH UPSETS PATRICK

'COME IN,' called the head boy, as Elizabeth tip-tapped nervously on the study door.

It was a lovely sunny room with a big window. William and Rita were sitting in armchairs.

Rita pointed to the visitor's armchair. 'Do sit down, Elizabeth.' She was smiling and speaking kindly. William was smiling too.

The little girl's heart stopped beating quite so fast. She sat down in the visitor's armchair with its cheerful chintz cover.

'We've got a problem,' explained William. 'We have discussed it with Miss Belle. But now we'd like your advice. We would like to know what you think.'

Miss Belle! Elizabeth's chest swelled with pride. Miss Belle and Miss Best were the joint headmistresses of Whyteleafe School. The children called them the

Beauty and the Beast. If Miss Belle was involved in this, then it must be an important matter on which Elizabeth's opinion was being sought.

Rita decided they should get it over with quickly.

'The fact is, we shouldn't really have thirteen monitors,' she said. 'It's always been the tradition that we have twelve. And, as I'm sure you've noticed at the Meetings this term, Elizabeth, it's almost impossible to get thirteen chairs on the platform. There's always one person practically falling off the end.'

Elizabeth nodded. She *had* noticed that.

It had all come about because, owing to lots of misunderstandings last term, Elizabeth had lost her position as monitor. A second-former, Susan, had been elected in her place. But then, at the end of term, when all the misunderstandings had been sorted out, the first form had asked for Elizabeth to be reinstated, as an honorary monitor.

'For once in a way we must have an extra one!' Miss Belle had agreed. For she knew how much Elizabeth wanted to prove herself a good, wise and sensible monitor, after some of the reckless things she had done.

'It seemed such a lovely idea to have an extra monitor at the time,' continued Rita. 'But we've discussed it with Miss Belle and we're all agreed that it can't be a permanent arrangement.'

William looked straight at Elizabeth.

'We've been wondering whether we should ask Susan to stand down, Elizabeth. What do you think?'

'Poor Susan! That wouldn't be fair!' exclaimed Elizabeth, without hesitation. 'She has had hardly any time as a monitor! And she *was* elected by the whole school, with proper votes and everything . . .'

Her voice tailed away. She swallowed very hard. There was no alternative.

'Let *me* stand down,' she said nobly, with a weak, wobbly smile. 'I've had a good turn as a monitor now. I wanted to prove myself—'

'You have certainly done that, Elizabeth,' said Rita.

'Good kid,' said William softly. 'Are you quite sure, Elizabeth? We could ask Susan, you know. She was only elected because of the misunderstandings about your behaviour.'

'I am quite sure,' said Elizabeth, somehow managing to keep that brave, wobbly smile in place. She wanted to rush away now, as fast as she possibly could.

'Well done, Elizabeth,' said Rita. 'William will announce it at this week's Meeting then.'

As Elizabeth left the study, William held open the door for her. He gave her a pat on the back as she went.

'You will be elected monitor again one day, Elizabeth. I am quite sure of that.'

'Thank you, William,' replied Elizabeth, feeling very noble.

She was proud of herself for being so calm and sensible in front of William and Rita, but, as soon as the study door closed behind her, she felt a hot prickling sensation behind her eyes. She was going to cry! She must run somewhere safe, where nobody could see her.

No longer a monitor!

She needed to be alone. She needed time to think, to get over the shock. Where could she go? Where was quiet and unhurried – peaceful?

The school gardens. She often went there when she wanted to think.

She made a beeline for the gardens at once. She shut herself in the furthest greenhouse. Then she let the tears flow.

'It's not fair!' she sobbed. 'It's not, not fair!'

She forgot all about Patrick and his tennis trial. She forgot that she had promised to come and support him.

Patrick's hopes and dreams had completely slipped her mind.

'Pull yourself together, Elizabeth Allen,' she told herself, some time later. 'Stop being a silly baby. It's perfectly fair and you know it is.'

She dried her eyes as best she could. She put her

sodden handkerchief away in her pocket. Then she peeped cautiously through the greenhouse windows.

There were very few people around. There was no sign of John Terry, the senior boy who ran the school gardens. Good. She did not feel like facing anyone yet, not even John. He was the most kind and understanding of boys, of course. He cared nothing for important positions, monitorships and the like, only for his beloved garden. John was a genius at growing things and at teaching others how to grow them. With his team of volunteers he helped to provide enough fresh fruit and vegetables to supply the kitchens at Whyteleafe School for much of the year.

Even so, she wanted a little more time on her own.

Elizabeth, she told herself, *you will no longer be a monitor after this week's Meeting. Just get that into your head! It's perfectly fair. And you've got to accept it!*

She felt rather cross with herself for not having foreseen this. It was quite true that since the beginning of term it had been uncomfortable and awkward having an extra chair on the platform at Meetings. She should have offered to stand down earlier! But it was such fun being a monitor, you wanted it to go on forever. So she had simply buried her head in the sand, as an ostrich does when it sees trouble ahead.

'All good things come to an end, Elizabeth,' her

last governess used to tell her. 'And sometimes sooner than you expect.'

Elizabeth had never listened to a word that Miss Scott said. She blushed to think how rude she had been and of all the awful things she had said, not only to Miss Scott but to the long line of governesses before her. Not surprisingly, none of them had ever stayed very long. But now she realised Miss Scott had been speaking sense after all.

But Rita says I've proved I can be a good monitor. And William says my turn will come again.

Elizabeth began to feel more cheerful. It was very warm in the greenhouse. She went and opened the door wide and stood there for a while, gazing out.

The sun was sinking lower. A gentle breeze was making rustling sounds in the blackcurrant bushes. Somewhere a blackbird was singing. A sweet, warm scent wafted from the wallflowers that bordered the nearest vegetable plot. There were butterflies settled there, sharing the flowers with the buzzing bees. In a reverie Elizabeth found her chocolate biscuits, rather warm and sticky by now. She ate them slowly, one melting mouthful at a time.

There's more to life than being a monitor, Elizabeth decided. *I shall have more time to myself. I must try and get good at lots of things. I shall make myself learn to be a brilliant gardener and grow wonderful things.*

She stared at the neat rows of broad beans that John and some of the younger boys had planted. How well they seemed to be doing. Although they did need weeding.

Most of Elizabeth's efforts to grow things so far had come to grief, usually because she had forgotten to look after them properly. But she knew that her lettuces were doing well. She closed the greenhouse door behind her and slowly walked round to have a look at them.

'They've grown again!' she exclaimed, as she came round the corner.

She had spent some of her own allowance on lettuce seeds. John had told her it was always worth getting the very best quality. She had planted the seeds out in neat rows, watched them grow into tiny lettuces, weeded them carefully once a week. Now she was beginning to get her reward.

The lettuces had suddenly burgeoned. Some of them had formed proper hearts. They were beginning to look like real lettuces. At this rate they would be ready before half-term. *Her* lettuces would be going into lots of school salads. That thought made Elizabeth feel very proud.

But they do *need watering, poor things*, she realised. *The ground all around them is quite parched-looking. I'll go and fill the watering cans.*

The two watering cans were lined up by the garden tap. Before filling them, Elizabeth turned on the tap and cupped some water in her hands. She washed the chocolate off her hands then doused her face clean. Now nobody would be able to see that she had been crying.

She filled the watering cans, but, when she reached her lettuce rows, she stopped. Was there still some heat in the sun? John had once explained to her that watering should be done in the cool of the day, morning or evening.

So Elizabeth set to work weeding between the rows of broad beans instead. It was hard physical work and it had a wonderfully soothing effect on her. By the time she had finished, she felt glowing with good health, and much more at peace with herself. She could face the world now.

I'm getting quite used to the idea of not being a monitor, she told herself. *I shan't tell anyone yet. I'll wait till it's announced at the Meeting. That will give me a bit more time to get really calm and strong about it. I expect Julian will tease me. I hope Arabella doesn't crow.*

The sun was now much cooler. Elizabeth returned to her lettuces and carefully watered each row. She had just finished when John Terry appeared.

There were other boys and girls arriving too. She could hear their voices beyond the yew hedge.

'That's well done, Elizabeth. Just the right amount of water,' he said. 'You don't want to drown them. They're doing well, aren't they?'

'Do you think so, John?'

'I'll tell you something, though. This is the last time you'll have to water them for a while.' He looked up at the sky. 'This is the end of the sunshine. There's going to be heavy rain for two or three days.'

Like any good gardener, John always took careful notes of the weather forecast.

'Oh. Is there? But it will save me a job then!' said Elizabeth cheerfully.

'Well, it will save you one job. But it could give you another. You see, Elizabeth—'

'John!' someone shouted.

Before John could finish, a boy came marching over, carrying a garden fork.

'Where exactly do you want this ground turned over?' asked the boy.

'I'll show you in a minute. I just want to explain something to Elizabeth.'

But Elizabeth was staring at the new arrival in dismay. He was a large, heavily built boy, one of the oldest in the school. He often came and helped in the gardens. He had big feet and big red hands and a gentle face. Elizabeth noticed how pale he looked, as though he was unwell. He was still in his tennis shorts. It was Roger Brown, Patrick's tennis opponent.

The match must be over!

Patrick's tennis trial! It had gone right out of her mind!

'It's all right, John, I've got to dash now!'

Elizabeth started running.

'Tell me another time. I've realised I shouldn't be here!' she called back.

She ran as fast as she could, all the way to the tennis courts.

Patrick was sitting on a bench near the courts with Julian, surrounded by first-formers. Elizabeth raced towards them, panting for breath.

'Did you win, Patrick?' she shouted.

'Of course he did!' shrilled Arabella.

'Elizabeth!' exclaimed Julian. 'What happened to you? Why didn't you come?'

Elizabeth went very red. 'I forgot,' she said.

'Patrick won!' cried Arabella triumphantly. 'He's going to be in the second team! It made all the difference to him having his friends here, cheering him on. Fancy you just forgetting to come, Elizabeth.'

Elizabeth thought how horrible it sounded, put like that.

She pushed past Arabella to get to Patrick, her hand

outstretched. She wanted to shake his hand.

'Congratulations, Patrick. You really deserve to be in the team after all your hard work! I truly meant to come and watch the match. I'm sorry. It's just that, after I'd been to see William and Rita, I had such important things—'

She broke off. She had been going to say 'such important things to think about'. But that sounded bad too, as though Patrick's tennis trial was *not* important.

In any case Patrick was ignoring her outstretched hand. He was getting to his feet.

'I've got important things to do as well,' he said. 'Now I'm in the second team, I've got to do some more work on my service action. I'm going to have a good go against the school wall. There's a match on Saturday.'

Without even glancing at Elizabeth he strode away. There was a sulky expression on his face. He was overjoyed to have beaten Roger and to have won his place in the team. But he had been wondering what had happened to Elizabeth. He had even, in fact, been worrying about her. Whereas she, it seemed, had simply forgotten all about him!

What were these important things anyway?

Later, he learnt from young Peter what Elizabeth had been doing while his match was in progress. She had been weeding some vegetable plot in the school gardens. Peter had seen her there.

That was all. Weeding! Even Julian's eyebrows shot up in surprise when Patrick passed on this information.

'She's good at heart, though, Patrick,' he shrugged. 'You'll find that out.'

Elizabeth had no intention of confessing to Julian, far less to Patrick, that she had been crying like a baby in the greenhouse. But she would go out of her way to be nice to Patrick, she decided. Then he would soon forget her lapse.

In fact, by cocoa time that evening, Patrick was already in a mood to forgive Elizabeth and give her another chance. His serving practice had gone well and he was very excited about the match against Woodville on Saturday.

'It's a home match, so you'll have to come and watch,' he told Elizabeth. 'Especially as you're a monitor.'

Elizabeth smiled wryly, thinking of the surprise in store for them all at the weekly Meeting. She chose her words with care.

'Monitor or not,' she said, 'I'll be there.'

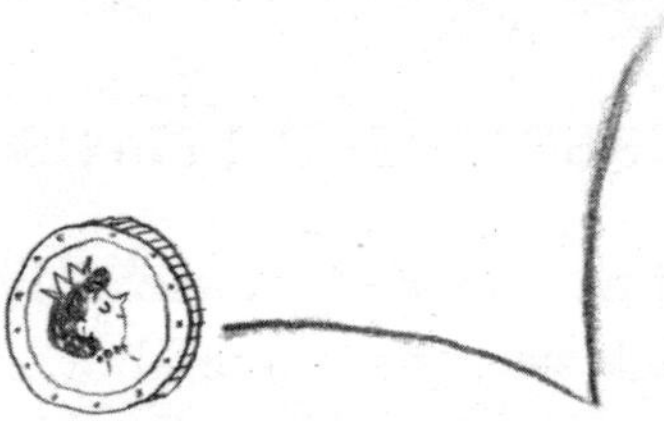

CHAPTER THREE

PATRICK MAKES A LITTLE JOKE

IT WAS time for the weekly Meeting. The whole school was required to attend. The boys and girls looked forward to it. It was the day their money was given out. After that there were always complaints and grumbles to be heard and interesting things to discuss.

It had been raining for two days and outdoor hobbies had been cancelled, even riding. They were pleased to have the Meeting coming up after tea to liven things up. The weather was supposed to get better by the evening, much to Patrick's relief. He was longing to get more practice before Saturday's match.

All the children trooped into the gym, which doubled as the school hall. In the Easter holidays a platform had been built at one end for the school's little plays and concerts. It made the Meetings much better too. There was a long row of chairs up on the platform, facing into the hall. There sat the school's twelve elected monitors, six each side of the head boy and girl.

William and Rita, in the centre, sat behind a small table. On the table was a big book, in which lots of things were written. By the book lay a small hammer, which they used like a judge's gavel. They *were* rather like judges, with their jury alongside them, Elizabeth always thought. This was not only the school's parliament, where problems were discussed and rules made, it was also its court. All complaints of bad behaviour or wrongdoing had to be brought to the Meeting. Problems were aired in public, punishments decided upon if necessary. Above all, boys and girls were made to face up honestly to their faults.

Miss Belle and Miss Best, the joint headmistresses, sat right at the back of the hall, with Mr Johns, the senior master. They rarely took any part in the proceedings and only then if their advice was requested.

Elizabeth had hated the Meetings when she first came to Whyteleafe School. She had thought them a perfectly silly idea. She had since changed her opinion.

But where was she today?

'That's funny,' said Julian, as he filed into the hall with the rest of the first form. He was staring towards the platform. 'Why isn't Elizabeth up there with the other monitors?'

'She must be late,' giggled Belinda.

'But there's no chair up there for her either.' Julian was always very quick to notice things. 'It's odd.'

Elizabeth had still not told anybody. It had been too early to tell people, she had reasoned. It would come out at the Meeting. She would be quite composed by then. That would be soon enough.

'I wonder what's going on?' mused Julian now.

He did not have to wait long to find out.

All the benches in the hall had filled up. Some of the younger children sat cross-legged on the floor. They were in the junior class, which was below the first form. The babble of whispering and chattering was getting louder and louder.

William stood up and banged the gavel. 'Silence, please.'

There was an instant hush.

'Before the Meeting starts, I have something to say.'

He smiled down at the person who was perched on the very end of a bench, in the front row.

'Stand up, please, Elizabeth. Come up here, on to the platform.'

As she stood up, for all her resolve, Elizabeth found her legs going wobbly. She felt butterflies in her tummy. The whole school was looking at her. She had so hoped that William or Rita would just make the announcement very quickly and quietly. This was awful.

Determined to look dignified, she walked slowly up on to the platform.

Julian and the others watched in surprise. It was their very own Elizabeth. The Bold Bad Girl. What was all this about?

'For much of last term Elizabeth was a monitor,' William told the school. 'This term, as a special dispensation, we asked her to stay on for a while – as an honorary monitor. We were so proud of her, weren't we? Well, she has done a really good stint and the time's come for Elizabeth to stand down now. I think we are all agreed that she has been a very fine monitor indeed. I want us all to show our appreciation.'

He gave a brief nod. Rita rose from her chair. Then all twelve monitors on the platform did likewise. As William shook Elizabeth by the hand, the head girl and monitors gave her a standing ovation.

The whole school joined in. With her head held high Elizabeth came down from the platform. As she walked down the hall to join her own form's benches, children on all sides started cheering loudly. After two days of being cooped up indoors it was good to have an excuse to shout and cheer!

Elizabeth felt weak with relief. The experience had

not been humiliating after all. It had been just the reverse. How tactfully William and Rita had handled it. She felt buoyed up, almost cheerful.

'You dark horse,' whispered Julian, as she sat down beside him. Belinda, Kathleen, even Patrick, all slapped her on the back. Patrick had reason to know how good a monitor she had been, but was secretly relieved. He would never get used to the idea of girls being allowed to boss boys around. This would be better, he felt.

Arabella was clapping politely, for quite the wrong reasons.

Julian squeezed Elizabeth's arm. 'Brave girl!' he hissed, green eyes twinkling. Alone among the first-formers, he had continued to be curious to know why William and Rita had summoned her the other day. He had been mystified that Elizabeth, usually so talkative, had never referred to it. Now he understood.

Elizabeth simply gave a huge sigh of relief. William was banging his gavel and calling for silence again; time to get on with the Meeting. Thank goodness *that* was all over!

Thomas held up the big money box now. All the children who had been sent money during the past week had to come forward and drop it inside. After that every member of the school was handed two shillings from the box, as their spending money for the week.

At Whyteleafe School they did not believe in some children having more money to spend than others. This was the way they shared it out fairly. If any pupil wanted extra money for a special purpose, they had to ask. The Meeting then decided if it was a proper reason.

'Please, I left all my stamps out in the rain and now they're useless,' said Peter, standing up. 'I need to write some letters this week. Can I have some extra money to buy more stamps?'

No, the stamps getting all messy and stuck together was due to Peter's own carelessness, the Meeting decided.

'You'll just have to go without a few sweets this week,' Rita said kindly.

Mary wanted the florist shop in the village to send some flowers to her aunt, who was very ill in hospital.

'Request granted,' said the head boy. 'Thomas, give Mary an extra five shillings from the box.'

After that there were three complaints to be heard. Two were proper complaints and one was silly.

'Arabella Buckley keeps making faces at me in class,' said Daniel Carter. 'She keeps trying to make me laugh. And, if I do laugh, I'll get into trouble.'

'That is not a proper complaint,' said William sternly. 'That is just telling tales. Sit down at once, Daniel.'

The first form were making spluttering sounds as they tried not to giggle.

'Try looking the other way, Daniel!' whispered Belinda.

'Arabella's not making faces!' hissed Julian. 'She always looks like that!'

Arabella, who had been feeling so triumphant, turned bright pink. She prided herself on her prettiness.

William banged the table again.

'Before we close the Meeting, some congratulations are in order. Roger, stand up, please.'

The big senior boy shambled to his feet. He was embarrassed to be in the limelight. His gentle face, even at the best of times, wore a slightly anxious look. It was just his normal expression.

'As we know,' said William, 'Roger is in the top class and in his last term at Whyteleafe. He has just heard recently that he has won a scholarship to Holyfield School. An academic scholarship. Well done, Roger. Can we give him a round of applause, please?'

As everyone clapped, Roger Brown gave a shy nod then quickly sat down.

'Isn't Holyfield the sporty school?' whispered a second-former to one of his classmates. 'Will he get on all right there?'

Everyone knew he'd lost his place in the second tennis team, to a mere first-former.

'They have other people as well,' the friend whispered

back. 'People who are musical or just plain brainy, like Rog. He should be all right!'

The first-formers, as they trooped out of the hall, were much more interested in the news about Elizabeth.

'You can be ordinary Elizabeth Allen now,' said Belinda kindly. 'It will give you more time for riding and everything.'

'Will it feel funny, not being a monitor any more?' asked Kathleen.

'Just for a while, I expect,' replied Elizabeth calmly.

The boys teased her a bit, especially Julian.

'Now you can go straight back to being the naughtiest girl in the school again!' he laughed.

'Never!' retorted Elizabeth. She was standing up to the teasing well.

But then Patrick struck a discordant note.

'Of course, there's no need for you to come and watch me play in the school match now,' he said. 'I won't want you there if you're not an important monitor.'

He was trying to make a joke. But Patrick's jokes were always rather heavy-handed.

His words really stung. For a moment Arabella and some of the others noted the look of dismay on Elizabeth's face.

By the time the little girl realised that he was not being serious, the main doors had been opened and everybody was whooping and rushing outside. It had stopped raining at last! It was going to be a fine evening.

'Hurray!' cried Patrick. 'I'll go and get my racket and practise my strokes.'

'I must go over to the stables and see the horses!' exclaimed Robert.

People were scattering in all directions.

My lettuces, thought Elizabeth. *I can go and look at them. I'm sure the rain won't have washed them away. They weren't little babies any more. I wonder if they've grown?*

Luckily, Elizabeth went and changed into her black wellies first, for there were puddles on all the paths in the school gardens. The big vegetable garden was all muddy and squelchy. She picked her way through the blackcurrant bushes, where the weak sunshine glistened on the wet leaves. Then on past the dripping yew hedges to where her lettuces lay . . .

She gave a gasp of dismay.

'Oh, no!'

She stood and stared at her rows of lettuce, unable to believe her eyes. Only three days ago they had been such fine specimens, all plumping out nicely and forming hearts. Now they were unrecognisable.

'They're all chewed up. They look horrible—'

UGH! As she bent to touch the nearest plant, a fat black slug slid off it. Gazing along the rows, she saw another slug, then another. They were feasting on her lettuces! They must have been feasting on them for days.

'Elizabeth?'

John Terry appeared, carrying a large white jug.

'Oh, John. Look! Look! Horrible slugs. Big, fat, black ones. They've eaten all my lettuces. They've ruined them!'

He came and put an arm round her shoulders.

'I know,' he said sadly. He looked down at her disappointed face. 'Poor Elizabeth! This was what I was trying to warn you about the other day when they said there was rain on the way. If only you hadn't been in such a hurry—'

'You mean you *knew* this might happen?'

'When it's very wet, we nearly always get an epidemic of slugs here. There are things you have to do about it.'

'But what, John? I don't understand.' Elizabeth frowned. Oh, *why* had she rushed away the other evening, just to hear about Patrick's silly tennis trial? Why hadn't she stopped and listened to John! 'What *can* you do?'

'Come with me and I'll show you.'

Still carrying the jug, he led her to a warm, sheltered part of the garden. There stood two rows of the finest-looking lettuces anyone could hope for. One row consisted of the round variety, the other of the cos variety.

'The slugs have hardly got to them at all!' exclaimed Elizabeth in surprise.

'These are mine,' said John quietly. 'They're extra special, so I've had to take good care of them. We get slugs in this part of the garden too, though not as many. But look, come along the rows with me and you'll see.'

For the first time, walking down the two rows with John, Elizabeth noticed there were old bowls placed at intervals, six of them in all. They were deep little bowls, old and chipped. Formerly school soup bowls, but long since thrown out. Elizabeth crouched down and peered inside one.

'It's full of dead slugs!' she shrieked.

'They all are,' replied John. 'They've all been drowned! Now, watch what I do, and I'll explain.'

John put down his jug. Then, working quickly, he gathered up the bowls two at a time. He tipped the bowlfuls of slimy, dead slugs on a nearby rubbish heap, then replaced the empty bowls in position.

'Some people put down pellets to kill slugs,' he told her. 'But that can be cruel. Pellets can harm other creatures too. This way is much better.'

He asked Elizabeth to hand him the jug.

'Is there milk in here?' she asked, sniffing. 'It smells a bit off.'

'It is,' smiled John. 'Cook always has plenty of old

milk left over. It doesn't matter if it's a bit sour. I cadge it off her.'

He went round his lettuces, slurping the clotting milk into the emptied bowls.

'The slugs love it. They even prefer it to lettuce. They climb into the bowls and drink till they're fat and bloated. Then they can't climb out again and they just quietly drown. They feel no pain.'

Elizabeth nodded. She was learning new things all the time.

She went to the rubbish heap and stared with interest at the mound of dead slugs there. It was very satisfying. *No more eating lettuce for any of you*, she thought.

'It does make extra work, though,' sighed John afterwards. Elizabeth noticed he looked rather tired. 'They say there's going to be a lot more wet weather next week. It's an extra job I could do without. That's what I was trying to explain to you, Elizabeth. That as soon as you stop having to water, there's a new job waiting to be done.'

They stood and looked at Elizabeth's lettuces, at the wreckage.

Elizabeth bit her lip, furious both with the slugs and with herself. If only she'd stopped and listened to John, her lettuces might still be all right. To make matters worse, she had boasted about them too. How the first form would laugh if they could see them now.

'You must ask for extra money at the next Meeting,' said John kindly. 'To buy new seeds with. It's not too late for a second planting. They would be ready by August.'

Elizabeth shook her head stubbornly. The next Meeting was a whole week away, August an eternity. It would be the summer holidays. Nobody would be here to see them! If she couldn't watch her *own* lettuces grow and flourish, she would just have to admire John's.

'I've got an idea, John!' she exclaimed suddenly. 'Let me look after *your* lettuces instead. You've got far too many jobs to do. You look really tired lately. And now you've shown me how to get rid of the slugs—'

'No! Certainly not!' said John sharply.

The little girl was speechless. It was as though she had been slapped.

'Are you going back now, Elizabeth?' he asked, more gently. 'Could you take the jug back to Cook for me, please?'

'No! Take it yourself!' she cried rudely. 'Aren't you frightened I might drop it and break it?'

With that she raced off, boiling with rage.

John, her friend John, was telling her she was useless. Not for one moment was she to be trusted with his precious lettuces! She could have wept with anger.

She was still feeling upset an hour later.

'Hello, Elizabeth! Where did you disappear to?' asked her friends, as she came into the common room.

It annoyed her that they all looked so cheerful and happy. They were building a castle out of playing cards.

'You're not supposed to use the best playing cards for doing that!' said Elizabeth, before she could stop herself. 'Only the old ones.'

'But it's more fun with these!' laughed Julian.

From the other end of the room Arabella was listening.

'You're not a monitor any more!' she called out. 'Has it slipped your mind, Elizabeth?'

Elizabeth turned away. She didn't feel like being friendly and sociable this evening. Or being teased.

'I'm tired,' she said truthfully. 'I'm going to have an early night.'

'Really!' said Arabella later. 'Did you notice? Elizabeth's face was like a thundercloud. It must be because you made that little joke this afternoon, Patrick. About her not being important and not needing to come to watch the match!'

'Perhaps she's sulking because she's not a monitor any more!' suggested Rosemary.

'Do you really think so?' wondered Patrick.

Across the room, Julian got up, stretched and yawned.

'Don't be stupid,' he said. His eyes were mocking. 'Elizabeth's made of stronger stuff than that. It will be something else, I expect. There will be something else going on in her head.'

He smiled to himself. With Elizabeth there nearly always was.

CHAPTER FOUR

JOHN TELLS ELIZABETH A SECRET

JULIAN WAS right, of course. Elizabeth went to bed that night still feeling cross about the slugs, but even angrier that John had insulted her.

The following morning, in the dining hall, she chose to ignore him.

'Good morning, Elizabeth,' he said, as they jostled to collect their cornflakes. 'Nice sunny one.'

Lower lip trembling slightly, she deliberately turned her back on him.

Back at her table, all the talk was about the tennis match against Woodville today.

'Isn't it lucky the weather's fine?' said rosy-cheeked Kathleen. 'Don't you think so, Elizabeth?'

Elizabeth said nothing. She could feel herself smouldering again. How could John behave as though nothing had happened?

Everybody noticed how quiet she was.

'I was only joking yesterday, Elizabeth,' Patrick said awkwardly when breakfast was over. 'You will come and watch the school match this afternoon, won't you?'

Elizabeth nodded, hardly taking in what he was saying. Her mind was elsewhere.

'Of course, Patrick.'

Then, as she came out of the hall, something unexpected happened.

She found John Terry lying in wait for her. He took her firmly by the arm.

'I've got to speak to you, Elizabeth.'

He propelled her round the corner, into the corridor, then gently pushed her into an empty classroom.

'Quick, in here. Nobody must hear.'

Elizabeth was too surprised to protest. Her bad feelings about John began to melt away. What was this all about? What did he want to say to her that was so important?

'Now look, Elizabeth,' he said, once the door was safely closed, 'I didn't mean to upset you last night. You must have thought me really rude and cruel. It was kind of you to offer to look after my plants. But I *had* to shut you up. I was frightened I might give something away.'

'Give something away?' asked Elizabeth, puzzled. But she was already feeling better, much better.

'Look, Elizabeth, can you keep a secret? A really important one. At least, it's important to me. There's not one person in the school knows. Nobody at all.'

Elizabeth began to feel excited and proud.

'Of course I can keep a secret!' she replied.

'Cross your heart and swear to die?'

Elizabeth did so.

'Right. Well, this is the position . . .'

Lowering his voice, he explained everything. He had filled in forms for a competition. He was hoping his two varieties of lettuce would win a very special cup at the village show. The show was in two weeks' time, just before half-term. As well as medals for crafts and woodworking, there was a silver cup for the best produce grown by a young person under sixteen. It could be fruit, flower, plant or vegetable.

John was a modest boy. He was not doing this in the hope of personal glory. That was the last thing on his mind.

'If, by any chance, my lettuces win the cup, it will be a great honour for the school. The local people sometimes grumble about us and think we have a soft life. This would show them that we don't. That we're not afraid to get our hands dirty and work the soil and grow good things.'

'It would be in the local newspaper as well,' said

Elizabeth, feeling excited. 'Then everybody would find out what a good school it is, and that we're allowed to do things for ourselves here . . .'

She paused. 'But why must it be such a secret, John? I'd love to tell everyone—'

'Don't you dare!' he said fiercely. Suddenly Elizabeth realised just how important this was to him. He could not bear the idea of failing. Nor would he be able to bear it for everyone to *know* he had failed. 'If, by any chance, I pull it off and win the cup, I want it to be a *complete surprise*. Now promise again that you'll keep my secret.'

'I promise,' said Elizabeth solemnly. 'I truly swear.'

'I've only told *you* because I wanted you to know why . . . last night . . . I wanted you to understand.'

'John, I'm so glad you have told me,' said Elizabeth. She looked ashamed. 'And I'm sorry I was so rude and hot-tempered. I do understand now. Of course you couldn't trust me to look after your plants when it's so important—'

John looked at her in surprise. He interrupted her.

'Oh, Elizabeth, you still don't understand. I suppose I haven't explained properly. I *would* trust you to look after them. You're one of my best young helpers. You make mistakes sometimes, but you learn fast. No, it's not that.'

Elizabeth was beginning to feel a warm glow of happiness spreading through her.

'It's the competition rules,' he said. 'I've signed the entry forms and I had to vouch that whatever I grow will be my own unaided work. Except for all the help nature gives me, of course,' he added, smiling. 'Don't you see, Elizabeth? Nobody is allowed to help me with these lettuces in any way. Don't you dare even try to water them for me!'

As they emerged from the empty classroom and went their separate ways, Elizabeth wanted to laugh out loud with happiness. She had completely misjudged John. She had been silly and hot-headed and jumped to conclusions. Now everything was all right again. She was so pleased he had shared his secret with her. She would keep it safe.

Later that morning Julian asked her to go out riding with him. He noticed how happy she seemed as they trotted along on their ponies, side by side.

'You were like a bear with a sore head earlier!' he remarked lightly. 'Was something the matter?'

'It was just a misunderstanding about something,' replied Elizabeth cheerfully.

'Oh!' Julian smiled. 'I might have guessed.'

At Elizabeth's dinner table all the talk was about the afternoon's match against Woodville. The visitors were due to arrive at two o'clock. The first-formers were all proud that Patrick was playing in the second team.

'I've got to find my best form!' said Patrick edgily. He was feeling nervous. It was quite understandable. 'I did well in the trial. But if I play badly today it will be me out and Roger back in again!'

'We're all going to come and cheer you on, Patrick,' said Elizabeth.

After dinner he left early to change into his tennis things. He now had a special badge sewn on his tennis shirt. It was a blue shield that showed that he was a second-team player. He kept his precious tennis racket in a special place. He would collect that first before he changed. He was planning to get in a few practice strokes before the match.

The others sat around chatting in the dining hall. They watched through the big windows as a minibus appeared in the drive.

'Here they come!' said Elizabeth. 'Watching this match is going to be fun.'

'Why are you in such a good mood all of a sudden?' asked Arabella.

'Am I?' asked Elizabeth. 'Well, it's none of your business even if I am.'

She stuck her tongue out at Arabella. Not being a monitor and having to set a good example had its compensations sometimes.

'Stop it, you two,' said Kathleen. 'Let's go and bag places near the courts. We want to have a good view.'

Coming out of the dining hall, they saw Patrick rushing towards them.

It was such a shock. He hadn't changed yet. His black hair was completely dishevelled. His face was pale and distraught.

'My tennis racket!' he croaked. 'I've been looking for it everywhere. It's gone. Somebody must have taken it.'

CHAPTER FIVE

ELIZABETH IS ANGRY

PATRICK CONFRONTED Elizabeth. He was extremely agitated.

'Elizabeth, is this some kind of joke?' he asked. 'Have you hidden my racket? If you have, *please* give it back,' he pleaded. 'The match is starting in less than fifteen minutes.'

She stared at him in surprise.

'I don't know what you're talking about, Patrick,' she replied coldly.

'Of course she doesn't!' Julian scolded his cousin. 'As if Elizabeth would hide your racket—'

'What about the time she threw it in the bushes!'

'That was completely different,' replied Julian. 'Look, stop saying stupid things, Patrick. Try to think clearly. You must have mislaid it.' He added, 'If the worst comes to the worst, I'll lend you mine—'

'I don't want your silly old racket!' exploded Patrick. 'Mine's the only one I can play with properly. You know that perfectly well. I haven't mislaid it. It should be on the top shelf in the sports cupboard. Everybody knows that's where I keep it. And it isn't there, I tell you!'

It was such an unexpected thing to happen. The first-formers all gathered round him, feeling worried and surprised. They so wanted to see Patrick do well in his first match. They had been looking forward to it.

Meanwhile, the two dark-haired, green-eyed cousins squared up to each other as if spoiling for a fight. Kathleen pushed the pair apart.

'Stop quarrelling, for goodness' sake. Let's all try and *do* something.'

'Yes, let's try and find Patrick's racket for him!' exclaimed Belinda.

Julian's anger at his cousin's rudeness suddenly passed. He could see how desperate he looked. He cooled down and took command of the situation.

'Patrick, dash and get changed,' he said, giving him a gentle push. 'You've only just got time! The rest of us will look for the racket. It can't be far away. I'm sure we'll find it.'

With a helpless shrug Patrick strode off.

Julian organised a search party. 'Martin, while he's in the changing rooms you go and hunt around his dormy.

He puts the racket under his bed sometimes, whatever he says. Kathleen, could you come with me? We'll search the sports cupboard. It might have slipped to the very back of the shelf. Elizabeth, would you go round to the south wall? He spends hours there, practising his strokes. He might have left it behind . . .'

Soon Julian had everybody rushing round the school, hunting for the missing racket, even some of the second-formers.

Elizabeth was not quite so forgiving. She felt hot and bothered inside at the way Patrick had insulted her. How dare he suggest that she might play a joke on him, just before his important match? As if she would do something like that, even to her worst enemy.

Nevertheless, she hurried out of the building and made her way to Patrick's favourite spot. He loved to come here, near the shrubbery, and bang tennis balls against the wall, over and over again. Julian had a point. He might have left the racket behind last time.

She ran up and down, looking for it. She even hunted round the corner. But there was no sign of it.

She stared towards the bushes. Was it possible that Patrick had used it to search for a ball? The holly, for example, was very prickly. It was easier to part the leaves with a racket than use one's hands.

Somewhere in the distance, she could hear children

coming outside, calling to one another despondently.

'It's no use! It's definitely not in the building!'

'He must have left it outside somewhere. Let's look round the field!'

If Patrick *had* used the racket to find a ball, reasoned Elizabeth, perhaps something had distracted him. A school bell even. He might have placed the racket on the ground, rushed off to lessons and then forgotten where he had left it. Well, it was a faint possibility.

She started to comb through the bushes diligently. There was still no sign of it.

She came out of the shrubbery, sucking her hand where the holly had pricked her. She stared across the school field towards the tennis courts. The team from Woodville School had arrived. They were filing on to the court, carrying their tennis rackets. The fifteen minutes was up!

She saw Patrick in his tennis whites. He was waiting by the entrance to the tennis courts. He was staring at the ground, the picture of dejection. Elizabeth's heart went out to him. She could hear Julian shouting from a window somewhere—

'It's no use, Patrick. We can't find it. I'll bring my racket out for you. I'm just coming.'

Elizabeth slowly began to circle the school buildings. Rather than go across to watch the match, her eyes searched out every nook and cranny. This was beginning to look very suspicious.

I was cross with Patrick for talking to me like that, she thought. *But, in one way, he was right. Somebody* has *played a horrid joke on him. Somebody's taken his racket and hidden it somewhere. It's the only explanation. Otherwise, surely, one of us would have found it by now? Oh, poor Patrick!*

If only she could find it for him, thought Elizabeth urgently. Her eyes scanned the big yard at the back of the school kitchens. It was out of bounds, but she crept in and searched around, even peering into some of the dustbins. Where would somebody hide a tennis racket? Not in a dustbin surely? She was being silly. Where else? She walked through the yard and out into the back drive. She was standing by some parked cars. The Woodville minibus was parked round here too.

There were garages beyond, most of them open.

That might be a good place to hide a tennis racket, decided Elizabeth. *In one of the teacher's garages. No one would dream of looking in there. Besides, we're not allowed round here.*

Should she go and search them? The situation was desperate.

She looked left and right. There was nobody about. She started to tiptoe past the back of the nearest car. It was Miss Best's car, a rather old-fashioned blue saloon, with shining paintwork and chrome. Miss Best's car always looked immaculate.

That's funny. She hasn't closed her boot properly! Elizabeth realised. It was open several inches. She found it hard to imagine the joint headmistress being so careless. She would be leaving the car lights on next. *I'd better close it for her.* The little girl took hold of the chrome handle and tried to close the lid of the boot. It would not shut. There was something in the way. She opened the boot wider to see what the obstruction was—

It was a tennis racket.

She pulled it out and looked at it in amazement.

'It's Patrick's!' she gasped. 'How extraordinary.'

Somebody had tried to hide it in the boot of Miss Best's car.

'Well, they haven't succeeded!' she realised joyfully.

Elizabeth slammed shut the boot. The noise brought Cook to the back door. *What's Elizabeth doing here?* she wondered. *I hope she's not being the naughtiest girl again.*

But Elizabeth had fled. With Patrick's racket in her hand she ran all the way to the tennis courts, her heart beating fast with excitement and triumph.

Patrick and his partner were at the far end of the first court, having a few practice strokes against the opposing pair from Woodville School. The match was due to start in two minutes' time. Patrick looked a picture of misery as he fluffed a stroke with the borrowed racket. He was by now totally convinced that Elizabeth had hidden his own. Then he heard her voice.

'Patrick!' she shouted through the wire netting. She was jumping up and down, waving the racket. 'I've found it!'

He raced off the court and came to meet her at the gate. Everybody was watching them.

'Oh, Patrick, isn't it lucky that I've found it in the nick of time?' she began, with a bright smile.

'Very funny, ha, ha. What a coincidence!' he hissed angrily.

He flung Julian's racket down at her feet and snatched his own. His face was like a thundercloud. The last few minutes had been the most miserable of his life. They had been almost unendurable.

'It's not amusing, Elizabeth,' he mouthed at her. 'I think you're beastly. I think this is the meanest trick I've ever come across.'

Elizabeth recoiled. She was speechless.

At that moment, atop the high green umpire's chair, Mr Warlow clapped his hands loudly.

'Time, please!' he called. 'Woodville won the toss and have chosen to serve. Back on court, Patrick, please. Let the match begin.'

Elizabeth slowly picked up Julian's racket and walked over to join the other first-formers. Belinda and Kathleen had saved her a place on the big grassy bank that overlooked the courts. They slapped her on the back. So did Julian. He took possession of his racket with a wry smile.

'I don't think I'll lend it to *him* again in a hurry.'

'Wherever did you find it?' whispered Kathleen.

'In the boot of Miss Best's car,' replied Elizabeth dully.

Belinda giggled out loud. 'The Beast's car boot? I don't believe it!'

Sitting just in front of them, Arabella turned her fair head scornfully.

'Don't tell fibs, Elizabeth Allen.'

'But it *was* in the boot of Miss Best's car,' Elizabeth hissed fiercely. 'It was, it *was*. I looked inside and there it was!'

'You just *happened* to be passing the Beast's car and decided to *look inside the boot*?' asked Rosemary in disbelief. She was sitting next to Arabella. 'You must have known it was there— You must have!'

'Seeing you'd hidden it there yourself!' suggested Arabella. She spoke primly. 'I think it was really mean to play a trick. And it's even meaner to pretend you didn't, now you feel scared. Now you see how serious it was. You had half the school looking for that racket!

If Patrick plays badly, it will be your fault, Elizabeth.'

'How dare you say that!' gasped Elizabeth.

'Please be quiet, children!' said Miss Ranger, their class teacher, who had just arrived to watch the match. 'You must not talk while play is in progress.'

Arabella studiously turned her well-groomed head away from Elizabeth and focused all her attention on the game. She clapped loudly every time Patrick won a point.

Far from playing badly, Patrick played a brilliant match. With his precious racket safely back in his hands all his confidence returned. But there was something else. He was fired up with anger at the joke that he believed had been played on him. He turned all that anger into hard, fierce strokes, beating the pair on the other side of the net time after time. He would show Elizabeth Allen a thing or two! She would see what a fine player he was, not someone only fit to have tricks played upon them.

Elizabeth hardly noticed how well Patrick was doing. For it was her turn to feel miserable now. She sat through the match in a blur. She was seething with anger towards Patrick. For Arabella, with her sarcastic comments, she had only contempt.

Soon the match was over. Whyteleafe's second pair had won by two sets to love! On the court Patrick was elated. Eileen, his partner, was handing round one of the school biscuit tins. She was hospitality monitor for the day. At Whyteleafe a different person was chosen to be hospitality monitor at every match. They were given the job of baking sweets, or biscuits, or little cakes, in the days before the match, to offer to all the players afterwards. Patrick was tucking into Eileen's fudge with relish.

He glimpsed the forlorn figure sitting on the bank. For the first time he wondered if he could possibly have misjudged Elizabeth. It would be terrible if her 'find' had been genuine. He must ask the others about it.

A cheer suddenly went up. Whyteleafe's first team pair had won *their* match as well. Eileen quickly hurried over with the tin, to offer more fudge around. Both matches were over. Whyteleafe had won the fixture.

The news about Patrick's racket had quickly spread. Arabella was claiming that Elizabeth must be telling stories. She was pretending she had found the racket in the Beast's car boot! It was all too far-fetched. Elizabeth had been sulky after Patrick teased her about not being a monitor. She must have decided to get her own back, most likely. The whole thing had got out of hand, so now she was trying to wriggle out of it . . .

Noting the funny looks, Elizabeth's anger deepened.

'Don't worry. *We* believe you,' said Kathleen sweetly.

But Elizabeth was scrambling to her feet. She had no intention of sitting around watching Arabella stir up mischief. She was even talking to Patrick now, as he came off court. She thought of the tremendous effort she had made to find his tennis racket for him. She had pricked herself on holly. It was outrageous!

She strode away, heading back to school.

Julian caught up with her by the main doors. He grasped her arm.

'Elizabeth!' He grinned. 'Don't get in a huff. You must admit it sounds a tall story, about the car boot. If you and I weren't such good friends, I'm not sure I'd believe you myself.'

'Thanks!'

'You know what Arabella's like. I don't know why she has to stir things up so,' he said, becoming serious for once. 'I'm not sure anyone's taking her seriously.'

'Some of them are.'

'Only the silly ones.'

'Patrick thinks I hid his racket. He will be quite sure of it now.'

'Well then, he's silly too. What a chap to have as a cousin. He's an embarrassment sometimes. I'm beginning to wish all over again that he'd never come to Whyteleafe. I was beginning to enjoy myself.'

'I hate him!' exclaimed Elizabeth.

Julian let go of Elizabeth's arm, put his hands in his pockets and frowned to himself. He turned over a small stone with the toe of his shoe. Then he looked her in the eye.

'The simple fact is, Elizabeth, that, as you did *not* hide Patrick's racket in the boot of the Beast's car, somebody else did. But who? And why? I think we should go straight over to the car and have a hunt around. We need to look for clues.'

'I can't be bothered!' said Elizabeth sulkily. 'If someone hates Patrick, it's no more than he deserves. Why should I care!'

'Except it would put you in the clear,' said Julian calmly.

'I *am* in the clear!' exclaimed Elizabeth. 'I don't have to prove myself to people like Arabella and Patrick. My *real* friends know I wouldn't play such a silly, mean trick and that's good enough for me.'

At that moment some first-formers appeared, Arabella among them.

Elizabeth turned her back on them and walked away.

She was tired of all this. She did not particularly want to see the rest of her classmates at the moment. Let them chatter away among themselves as much as they wished. She would go and do some gardening and enjoy some peace and quiet. She would go to the school gardens and find her dear John Terry and ask him to give her some jobs to do.

But, when she got there, there was no sign of him anywhere.

CHAPTER SIX

JULIAN LOOKS FOR CLUES

ELIZABETH WAS puzzled. She had never known John to be anywhere else but the school gardens on a fine Saturday afternoon. As well as the vegetable gardens, she looked for him in all the usual places: the greenhouses, the tool shed, the potting shed and round by the compost heap. He was nowhere to be found.

After looking for him all over she took a glance at his prize lettuces. They had grown some more and were hearting out nicely. She walked down the two rows, checking the bowls of milk. A few slugs had become trapped in them, but there was plenty of room for more. At present, the soil having dried out well, the slimy black creatures had gone to ground. It would need another spell of wet weather to bring them out again in force. At the end of one row a single dandelion was growing rather closer than it should to a cos lettuce. Elizabeth bent down to pull it out, then suddenly remembered.

She straightened up quickly. She had almost forgotten. She must do nothing to help John's plants before the competition for the cup, in two weeks' time. No, not even pull out a single weed! It was against the rules. She was proud to be the only person in the whole school who knew John's exciting secret.

'Peter! Sophie! Have you seen John?' she called, as two junior-class pupils appeared, carrying little forks and trowels.

'No,' replied Peter. 'Thomas is in charge today.'

'We're going to help put new straw round the tomato plants,' explained Sophie. 'The old straw got all wet. But first we're going to weed round the peas.'

The senior boy appeared then with the wheelbarrow laden with straw.

'That's the trouble when it's been wet,' laughed Thomas. 'It brings on the weeds faster than the things you're really *trying* to grow, don't you think, Elizabeth?'

'Yes.' Not to mention slugs and snails and other undesirables, Elizabeth thought. 'But Thomas, what's happened to John today? I've been looking for him everywhere.'

'Haven't you heard?'

The big boy stood the wheelbarrow down and walked over to her.

'He's stuck away in the san, poor chap. He's got German measles or scarlatina or something, I've forgotten what. But it's very infectious! He's in a room on his own. Nobody's allowed to go anywhere near him, in case the whole school catches it.'

'Oh, poor John,' Elizabeth gasped.

'It's all right, it's nothing serious. He'll be completely better in a week or ten days. Then Matron will let him out!'

Elizabeth digested the dramatic news. She remembered how tired John had looked the other evening; it must have been because the illness was coming on.

'Until he's let out of the san, I'm in charge of the school gardens,' said Thomas proudly. 'And, by the way, John gave Matron a message to give me. Nobody is to go near his private patch or touch any of his plants. Strictly forbidden.'

Elizabeth nodded. She knew the reason for that!

Her mind had already turned back to John's lettuces. She glanced at the sky, feeling anxious. A week or ten days! That was such a long time. Supposing it got very wet again and more slugs appeared and needed to be attended to? Or supposing there was a heatwave, with long, hot days, and the plants became parched and needed to be watered?

It did not bear thinking about.

'Have you come down to help?' Thomas was asking. 'Would you like to weed some peas, with Sophie and Peter?'

'Oh, please come and help us, Elizabeth,' said Sophie, running over and taking her hand. 'Look how many weeds have grown!'

Elizabeth smiled. 'I'll enjoy that, Sophie!'

After an hour's gardening Elizabeth felt much better. There was something deeply relaxing about working with the soil, in the gentle sunshine, the sights and sounds and smells of nature all around. It was impossible to feel anxious for long as you listened to the doves cooing in the dovecote, the bees buzzing round the wallflowers.

The following day at breakfast she was pleased to see through the windows that it was another mild day. Would the weather continue like this for the next ten days? With gentle sunshine and just the occasional sharp shower John's plants would be perfectly safe. Nature would take care of them for him, while he was locked away in the san.

That afternoon she went out riding with Julian again.

'I did go and look for clues yesterday, Elizabeth,'

he told her airily. 'After you went off. I wandered over and had a good hunt round the Beast's car.'

They both reined in their ponies.

'Oh? Did you find anything?'

'Just this old crisp packet blowing about under the car.' He produced a crumpled bag from the pocket of his jeans. It had stars and stripes on it and a picture of Uncle Sam. 'It's an American brand, *Southern Favorits*. Never heard of them, have you?'

Elizabeth glanced at the packet and shook her head.

'It could have blown over from the school dustbins. It doesn't mean anything.'

'True,' agreed Julian. He grinned. 'I've had a thought, though. Do you think the culprit could have been Roger Brown? Trying to upset Patrick, so he could get his place in the second team back?'

Elizabeth frowned and thought about the big, gentle senior boy. She simply could not imagine him creeping around and hiding Patrick's racket.

'Impossible,' she replied.

They looked at each other ruefully.

'In any case,' Elizabeth laughed, 'I'm not sure I care!'

The fact was that Elizabeth and Julian's cousin were no longer on speaking terms. They had simply decided to ignore each other. At the dinner table today Patrick had been rather full of himself. There was to be another home match next weekend. Whyteleafe would be playing St Faith's and Patrick had been picked for the second team again. After his good performance against Woodville his place was beginning to look very secure.

'And Mr Warlow has asked me to be hospitality monitor,' Patrick told Martin, 'as a reward for playing so well. Isn't that an honour!'

'You were brilliant,' said Martin, who was now a great admirer.

'It will be quite a tough match,' said Patrick. 'But the *really* big match will be the one after that, just before half-term.'

'You mean the match against Hickling Green?' said Rosemary knowledgeably.

Whyteleafe v. Hickling Green was always *the* big tennis fixture of the summer term. The two schools were long-standing rivals.

'Yes,' nodded Patrick. 'A lot of parents come to watch, if they're collecting us at half-term. I've got to play well against St Faith's, to make sure of my place for the big match.'

'I'm sure you will, Patrick,' cooed Arabella. 'Especially now you're keeping your racket safely locked up.'

Nobody else at the table had taken part in this conversation.

Unofficially the class was starting to divide into two factions.

There was a very small faction consisting of Patrick, Arabella, Rosemary and Martin. These four, together with one or two hangers-on, firmly believed that Elizabeth had played a mean trick on Patrick and was refusing to own up. She had not once been called the naughtiest girl in the school for nothing.

A much bigger faction, consisting of Julian, Belinda, Kathleen and many others, sided firmly with Elizabeth. They felt sure that if by any chance Elizabeth had played a joke, as a former monitor (and such a fine one), she would certainly have owned up.

'As a matter of fact, Julian,' Elizabeth said now, as they turned their ponies to head back to school, 'I really do *not* care. I mean, even if it *was* Roger wanting to get his place back in the second team. He deserves it more than Patrick does. He's much more decent than Patrick.'

'Yes.' Julian's green eyes twinkled. His friend was being illogical. 'Of course. And much too decent to have played such a trick in the first place. Well, Elizabeth,' he added airily, 'if you don't care, then why should I?'

There the conversation ended. They trotted briskly back to the school stables. After seeing to the pony Elizabeth decided to wander down to the school gardens. She had a compulsion to keep an eye on John's project.

I must just check that the plants are all right, she thought. *Even though there's nothing at all I can do about it if they're not.*

The prize lettuces looked as fine as ever. No more slugs had appeared. The few in the bowls remained thoroughly bloated and drowned-looking.

I suppose there's no chance they can somehow revive? Elizabeth fussed to herself. *It would be awful if they're just unconscious and could come back to life again.*

She walked round to the small rubbish heap where John had dumped all the dead creatures before. There was quite a mound of them. She turned them over with a twig, one by one, examining each one carefully. At first she screwed up her nose, but she soon got used to them. Poor fat things!

Yes, they're dead all right, she thought. *They're as dead as doornails. So the milk idea really, really works . . .*

'*UGH!*' came a voice at her shoulder.

Elizabeth sprang to her feet guiltily. She turned round.

Sophie was standing right behind her. The child's eyes were round as saucers.

'Why are you playing with those dead slugs, Elizabeth?' she asked, with a shudder.

Elizabeth hurriedly threw the twig away and laughed.

'It's my secret hobby, Sophie!' she joked. 'I like playing with dead slugs.'

'Do you really?' asked the child solemnly. She had been watching for some time.

'Look here, Sophie,' said Elizabeth briskly. She took her firmly by the hand. 'You know you're not allowed to come wandering down here on your own.'

'I just wanted to look at all the flowers again. They do smell lovely.'

'Well, you're coming back to school with me, right now.'

Sophie was reluctant to leave the flowers. Elizabeth decided to cheer her up.

'I'll teach you a funny song,' she said kindly. 'It's one my governess told me. You can make up any names you like to put in it.'

Soon they were chanting it together, all the way back to school.

'What is little Sophie made of? What is little Sophie made of?
Sugar and spice and all things nice
That's what little Sophie is made of!
What is little Patrick made of? What is little Patrick made of?
Slugs and snails and puppy dogs' tails
That's what little Patrick is made of!'

At the main doors, they parted, with peals of laughter. Sophie liked the song. She would use it for skipping!

Elizabeth felt cheerful too. She loved being at Whyteleafe School, in spite of the fact that she was no longer a monitor. She and Julian had been for such a good ride. And John's lettuces were looking fine. They were looking better than ever.

But the next day the rains came back.

CHAPTER SEVEN

ELIZABETH MAKES UP HER MIND

'WILL YOU please be so kind as to stop staring at me, Elizabeth?' requested Mam'zelle during French, the first lesson on Monday morning. 'Will you be so kind as to keep your eyes down and fixed on your work? Do you not know it is very rude to stare? What is the matter with you this morning? Is it that you have never before seen a person eating a biscuit?'

From the rest of the class there came muffled giggles as the boys and girls glanced up from their vocabulary sheets.

'Sorry, Mam'zelle,' Elizabeth apologised. 'I wasn't really staring at you. I was thinking about something else.'

'You will think about your French vocabulary while you are sitting in my lesson, if you please, Elizabeth.'

Elizabeth lowered her head obediently. She pored

studiously over her word sheet. Mam'zelle had given them ten minutes to learn some vocabulary while she herself marked some second-form essays over by the big window. Then there would be a test.

Elizabeth had not even noticed that Mam'zelle was eating a biscuit, it was so commonplace. The temperamental French teacher carried her school biscuit tin everywhere, full of Cook's homemade oatmeal biscuits. She needed them, she had explained to Miss Belle and Miss Best, to counteract the nervous dyspepsia she suffered when taking lessons. It helped to keep her digestive system calm. Everybody knew that. So naturally, first thing on Monday morning, out had come the biscuit tin.

I wish they would keep the rest *of her calm*, Elizabeth sighed to herself. She was embarrassed to have received a scolding in front of the whole class.

The little girl had been staring not at Mam'zelle but at the windowpanes beyond. There were large raindrops splattering on to them. Drip-drop. Drip-drop. They were getting louder and larger by the minute. Elizabeth had found it difficult not to watch the rain. Was this just the beginning or would it soon stop?

The rain did not stop. It poured down relentlessly until the middle of the afternoon.

This will bring the slugs out again, for sure, Elizabeth

thought in despair. *And with none of us able to do a thing about it.*

She now felt deeply anxious about John's project once again. The glimmerings of a plan began to form in the back of her mind.

After tea that day, when the rain had stopped, she walked down to the village with her friend, Joan. The children were only allowed to go to the village in pairs.

'What are you going to buy at the shops today, Elizabeth?' asked the second-former.

'I'm going to get some sweets for John Terry,' she replied. She still had sixpence left, even after paying Belinda back for some stamps she had borrowed. She had been planning to save the sixpence, but this was more important. 'John must be so miserable on his own in the san, day after day.'

'You are a very kind person, Elizabeth,' said Joan quietly, linking arms with her best friend as they walked along. 'Susan thinks so too.'

'Susan?'

'Yes. William and Rita told her how you stood down as an honorary monitor, so that she could have a proper turn. I was so proud of you when I heard that. You were being such a fine monitor.'

Elizabeth felt noble again. Then she suddenly blushed.

'Oh, Elizabeth, you've gone all red!' laughed Joan. 'I didn't mean to embarrass you.'

'It's not that,' confessed Elizabeth. 'The fact is, I'm quite pleased I'm *not* a monitor at the moment. I'm planning to do something rather un-monitorish. I wish I could explain to you, but I can't. It's to do with somebody else's secret, you see.'

'Try not to get into any scrapes then. But I am sure you will have a good reason for whatever it is you are planning to do.'

I have got a good reason, Elizabeth told herself an hour later, as she crept through the grounds towards the school sanitorium. John's sweets were in her hand. *I only hope his room is one of the ground-floor ones. And I only hope Matron doesn't see me!*

Unluckily for Elizabeth, the very first window she peered through found her looking straight into Matron's face!

Matron was sitting at her desk in her office and she looked up in surprise when she heard a rustle of bushes. Then she saw Elizabeth's face at the window. She quickly opened the window wide and leant out.

'Goodness gracious, Elizabeth Allen, you gave me such a scare!' she exclaimed. 'What are you doing, creeping round here like a burglar?'

Elizabeth was mortified.

'I wanted to give John a wave through his window, but I didn't know which room,' she said hurriedly. 'I was going to wave these sweets at him to cheer him up. I went and bought them for him after tea.'

'You won't be waving through any window at John for a while, you silly girl. He's upstairs and he's tucked up in bed fast asleep. He has to stay in complete isolation you know, Elizabeth. Just until the rash has gone and his temperature's back to normal.'

However, Matron took the sweets for him. Before closing the window on Elizabeth, she spoke much more gently.

'Everybody knows John's in quarantine! But you've got a good heart. It *will* cheer him up to know someone's come over with some sweets. He's been a real misery today, I can tell you. Fussing on about the rain and his blessed garden. A drop of rain, I ask you! It must be the fever, I expect.'

Elizabeth slipped away, feeling worse than ever. Her plan had come to nothing. Poor John! She had been so hoping she might get the chance to talk to him through the window. To tell him she thought that the competition rules were plain silly now and he must be prepared to let her help him a little bit. But she had been caught by Matron straight away!

Her feet began to drag as she struggled with her

conscience for a while.

It was very difficult to come to a decision. But it was the thought of John lying on his sickbed, fretting and unhappy, that finally persuaded her.

John's so great – I've got to help him. The competition rules are *silly now. I've got to look after his plants for him, without his knowing. And without anybody else knowing either. Nobody need* ever *know, not even John himself!* she realised. *All that will happen is he'll still win the special cup for the school, just as he's always hoped!*

Elizabeth broke into a run. Her mind made up, there was no time to lose. Recklessly, she ran immediately across to the school kitchens and found Cook.

'A jug of milk, Elizabeth? Whatever do you want a whole jugful for?'

Oh drat! thought Elizabeth.

Then, looking through the side window, she saw Fluff, the school cat, sitting outside on the low wall.

'I think Fluff looks thirsty,' she said, not untruthfully.

'Fluff always looks thirsty,' laughed Cook. 'Well, you're not going to give him a whole jugful. I'll pour some in a bowl for you.'

She found an old bowl under the middle sink and filled it from a jug.

'Off you go. And when you see Patrick could you give him a message? Tell him I shall have some more cooking chocolate on Thursday, if he wants to make his crispy cakes then.'

Elizabeth slipped out of the side door, walked straight past Fluff and headed for the school gardens. She carried the bowl carefully, for Cook had been generous. She did not notice Fluff stretch, yawn and decide to follow her.

I don't suppose this will be nearly enough, but at least it's a start, thought Elizabeth eagerly. She glanced around, anxious not to be seen.

Luckily, the grounds were deserted.

In fact, it was getting so late that Elizabeth should have been indoors. This was the time of evening when the first-formers were expected to read or play quietly in the common room.

'I wonder what's happened to Elizabeth?' Belinda was saying. 'I haven't seen her.'

'Perhaps she has a piano lesson,' shrugged Julian in his casual way.

'No, that isn't today,' said Kathleen.

'If you ask me,' Arabella intervened, 'Elizabeth is not exactly sociable these days. It's the shock of not being a monitor any more, I suppose.'

'*If* we ask you, we will be very interested to hear what you have to say,' replied Julian. 'But, as we haven't asked you, we are not.'

Elizabeth tiptoed through the school gardens and found John's vegetable patch. The ground was squelchy. She placed the bowl of milk carefully on the path and went to examine his salad plants.

It was such a relief to be doing something positive at last. From the moment she had made the decision to help John in secret a weight had lifted from her mind. There was nothing worse than sitting around, worrying and feeling helpless. This was going to be much more fun.

Half expecting to see the hearty green leaves ravaged by slugs, as her own had been, she was cheered to find them still intact.

She smiled as she thought of what Cook had said about Patrick and the cooking chocolate. Patrick had been going around saying it was sissy to have to make sweets or something, just because he was to be hospitality monitor at the St Faith's match on Saturday. A girl ought to make them and let him have the honour of handing them round. Even Arabella had drawn the line at that. In that case, he boasted, he would get hold of some of those biscuits like Mam'zelle's. But secretly he was making something after all!

Well, it would be difficult for *her* to give him the message. They were still not speaking. She would have to ask one of the others to tell him.

Elizabeth's mind turned back to the slug situation. Looking in the six bowls, one by one, she found that a lot more slugs were now trapped in them. The soil was very wet after today's rain and this had brought them out again.

Two of the bowls are nearly full! she realised. *Although the other four are all right.*

How lucky that she had got some milk from Cook straight away. There would be just enough to sort out the two nearly full bowls. Screwing up her nose, she carried them both over to the little rubbish pile and tipped them out on to the waiting slug mound. That was goodbye to some more fat slugs!

She came back, bent down and replaced the empty bowls in position.

Now to get the milk and tip half in each, she thought. Then she stopped. As she had straightened up, she had felt something rubbing against her legs. There came a loud purring sound. She looked down.

'Fluff!' she exclaimed. Then she saw the traces of milk on his mouth and whiskers. 'Oh, no!' squealed Elizabeth.

She ran over to find her milk. The bowl was empty. The big cat with the fluffy face had drunk every last drop.

Elizabeth trudged back to the school kitchens with

the empty bowl, feeling a sense of despair. Why did things have to go wrong? She had tried to help John, but in fact she had made matters worse. There had been six working slug traps and now there were only four. She had put two of them out of action. As those two bowls were now empty, the creatures would just ignore them. The four remaining bowls would not suffice very much longer. Given more rain, John's lettuces would soon be getting devoured! Oh, what should she do now?

The kitchens were deserted. Cook and her helpers had finished for the day. All the washing-up had been done, the floor swabbed down. Elizabeth crept over to the middle sink, carefully washed and dried the old bowl, then replaced it in the cupboard below. About to leave, she noticed that someone had carelessly left the pantry door ajar. She walked over to close it. It was a beautifully cool room, with a stone-flagged floor and marble shelves. Staring inside, Elizabeth glimpsed a long row of large jugs, each with a little square of muslin draped over the top.

On an impulse she slipped in, and peered inside the nearest jug.

It was full of milk. They all were. It was the milk for the children's breakfast cereal. As it was cool this evening, one of Cook's helpers had set them up in readiness for the morning.

'*Gallons and gallons of milk!* realised Elizabeth. She picked up the nearest jug. It was quite heavy. *Oh, nobody would ever miss one jug, would they? Not just one!*

It was a reckless thing to do. It was very hot-headed of Elizabeth.

She left with the jug, stealing along the corridors as quickly as she could without spilling the milk inside. She would hide the big jug in her bedside chest of drawers!

As she turned a corner, she paused. The common-room door was wide open and she would have to pass it before she could get up the stairs.

The only thing she could do was to make a dash for it!

'Elizabeth!' her friends cried, as she flashed by.

They crowded to the door, only to see her back view disappearing upstairs.

'Aren't you coming in?' they shouted.

'I'm sleepy, I'm going to bed!' came the muffled reply.

A minute later she was on her knees in the dormitory by her chest of drawers. She cleared a space for the jug of milk, placed it inside, then closed the drawer. Nobody ever looked in people's drawers. They were private.

To get her breath back, she flung herself on the bed and lay staring at the ceiling.

What have I done? she thought, feeling surprised at herself. *Well, there's no going back now.*

Slowly, very slowly, a feeling of relief crept over her. It could rain as much as it liked this week. The slugs could come marching out if they wanted to. She had plenty of ammunition now. She would be ready for them!

But, as so often happens in the scheme of things, there *was* no more heavy rain that week! The ground dried out nicely. Weather conditions for growing prize lettuces turned out to be quite perfect!

Elizabeth continued to keep a watchful eye on them and was thankful. Great secrecy and stealth would have been required, to help them along. Roger, no longer in the tennis team, was always working in the gardens these fine evenings, as was Thomas.

The large jug of milk remained hidden in her chest of drawers, untouched and, in time, forgotten.

So, when a second-former stood up at the next school Meeting, her words gave Elizabeth a shock.

'Please, I have a complaint. On Tuesday morning, when our table went up to collect our jug of milk, there was none left. Cook said staff always fill the right number of jugs, so one table must have been greedy and taken two. We had to share a jug with the next table and we all had a measly amount of milk on our cornflakes. I think the table that took two jugs of milk ought to own up.'

William and Rita, as Judges, looked around the crowded hall.

'Did any table help themselves to an extra jug of milk on Tuesday morning?' asked Rita pleasantly. 'If so, would they please own up now?'

There was silence.

The head boy and girl waited patiently for a few moments. There were rows of blank faces. It was obvious that no one was going to stand up.

At a nod from Rita, William looked relieved and banged the gavel on the little table.

'Very well,' he announced, with a smile. 'I think on this occasion we can be quite sure that one of the kitchen staff *did* make a little mistake. None of us is perfect! You must put the matter behind you, Chloe, and not be the last table to collect its milk next time!'

The whole school laughed.

Elizabeth felt very hot. As soon as the Meeting ended, she had to rush outside and gulp in some fresh air.

She had never in her life not owned up to something before. She felt terribly guilty. But how could she explain to the Meeting about the missing jug of milk without giving John's secret away?

She went for a walk in the grounds, to calm herself down.

Meanwhile, in the dormitory she shared with some

of the other girls a mystery was being investigated.

'I've noticed the funny smell for days,' said Jenny. 'But it's suddenly much worse. It's really bad today.'

'It seems to be coming from Elizabeth's chest of drawers!' exclaimed Belinda, sniffing around. 'Do you think we ought to look inside? I'm sure she wouldn't mind.'

When Elizabeth entered the dormitory, she found a crowd of girls waiting for her. Belinda was holding a large, empty milk jug in her hands. She had washed all the sour milk down the sink.

'So someone did take a jug of milk after all,' said Jenny. 'And it was you, Elizabeth. What did you take it for? It had all gone sour. You hadn't even drunk any!'

Elizabeth just stared at the empty jug in dismay and said nothing.

'Why didn't you own up at the Meeting?' asked Kathleen, looking upset.

'We've stuck by you all this time, Elizabeth!' exclaimed Belinda, who felt betrayed. 'But is it true what some people have been saying? That you do things and don't own up to them. That you can't be bothered to be good now you're not a monitor any more?'

'*Please* explain,' begged Kathleen.

'I can't explain, Kathleen!' Elizabeth blurted out. 'I just can't.'

Rosemary was standing in the doorway, listening.

'Arabella has been right about you all along!' she said smugly.

Elizabeth rushed past her and away down the corridor. She was feeling confused and upset. She had done something wrong. Now she had been found out. Even Belinda and Kathleen and Jenny were starting to turn against her. But she had only been trying to keep a secret.

She was thankful that the weekend lay ahead and she would not have to face the whole class again before Monday. She would spend some time with Joan.

First, in the morning, she would have a private talk with Julian.

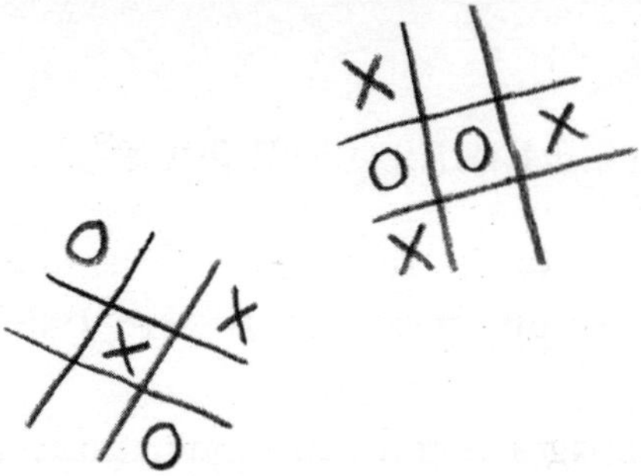

CHAPTER EIGHT

A PRIVATE LETTER ARRIVES

JULIAN WAS full of good advice the next morning.

'You're in a tight corner, Elizabeth, all because of this silly secret!' he said. 'Whatever is it? Has someone been asking you to make them some cheese? You can't keep that secret for long, it makes such a pong!'

His green eyes were laughing and full of mischief. Everything happened to Elizabeth!

'Of course not,' she replied. 'And, if they were, I wouldn't be able to tell you. But it's something much more important than that. And I've crossed my heart and sworn to die.'

'I know that. And so you can't go and confess to William and Rita, which is what the whole class expects you to do,' smiled Julian wryly. 'Even if you *could* confess, it wouldn't help much. The damage is done!'

'I know,' nodded Elizabeth. 'Now everybody thinks

that I played that trick on Patrick. That I hid his racket and was scared to own up about that as well. That's the thing I can't bear!'

'It's known as giving a dog a bad name,' said Julian. He patted her brown curly hair. 'Oh, poor Bold Bad Girl. Woof! Woof!'

'It's not funny,' protested Elizabeth. 'I didn't mind it when only two or three people sided with Patrick, but now *everyone* does. And the way Patrick looked at me this morning! I don't think he was *really* sure that I hid his racket – it was just Arabella winding him up. But now he's convinced!'

'Isn't it about time we found out who really did?' asked Julian quietly.

'Yes!' agreed Elizabeth. 'And I'm sorry, Julian. I didn't take it seriously before. I was proud and silly. I was just so cross, that's all. To think I was the one who had gone to all that trouble and *found* his beastly racket for him! But now I see I *do* have to put myself in the clear over that. It might even be – well – nicer for Patrick too,' she admitted ruefully. 'Oh, poor Patrick.'

Julian had very little time for his cousin, but now he looked thoughtful.

'Yes. I suppose so. He *was* pretty upset that you didn't come and watch his tennis trial. Then he must have thought you really disliked him – enough to play a mean trick just before his first match. Not very nice for him. I hadn't really thought about it much from Patrick's point of view,' he admitted airily.

'Nor me,' agreed Elizabeth.

She tried to concentrate hard. She thought of the crisp packet Julian had found, *Southern Favorits.*

'Arabella's parents are in America,' she said tentatively. 'That's why she's come to Whyteleafe. You don't think it's possible they send her goodies, like crisps and things?'

'She never hands them around, if they do,' frowned Julian. 'Besides, where's the motive? We have to find a motive.'

'Well, maybe to get me into trouble,' suggested Elizabeth.

'But she could never have planned that *you* would find the racket!'

'Maybe that was just a bonus?' sighed Elizabeth.

'The whole thing seems too imaginative for Arabella,' Julian replied, rather drily. 'Still. Interesting about her parents being in America. I didn't know that. Would you like to search her dormy?'

'Yes. This afternoon!' nodded Elizabeth. 'While she's safely at the match!'

Elizabeth had already decided not to watch the match against St Faith's this afternoon. She preferred to avoid her classmates at present. It was too horrid, the looks she was starting to get. She had arranged to go to the village with Joan instead. But Arabella would be at the match, no doubt sitting in the front row.

'The perfect opportunity!' agreed Julian, as they walked back to school together.

'I'll look in her desk as well,' said Elizabeth excitedly. 'What will you do, Julian?'

'I shall be at the tennis match,' replied Julian casually. 'Watching points.'

When she returned indoors, Elizabeth found an envelope in her pigeonhole. It was firmly sealed and marked ELIZABETH ALLEN PRIVATE.

She ran along to the girls' cloakroom and locked herself in a cubicle. Then she opened the envelope to see what was inside.

It was a note from John Terry. He had smuggled it out of the san with the help of one of the school cleaners!

Dear Elizabeth,

Thanks for the sweets. I am feeling much better and have enjoyed them. I shall be out of my 'prison' in a few more days, just in time for that IMPORTANT THING I am going to do. But I am dead worried. It says on the radio there will be heavy rain from Monday onwards. Please keep a close eye next week.

Remember do NOT do anything to help them along or we will break the rules. But I have an important job for you.

If they start getting attacked, please dig the very best specimens out of the ground. Wrap them in newspaper and hide them in the potting shed. There is a big, cool cupboard in there on the north-facing wall. Do NOT let anyone see you or they will ask questions. Thank you, special helper . . .

Your grateful friend,

John

P.S. When you have read this note, destroy it completely.

Elizabeth carefully memorised the note. Then, with trembling fingers, she tore it in into tiny pieces, dropped it down the lavatory pan and flushed it clean away.

It was so exciting to have received a secret message from John. Now she could only feel grateful that all her efforts to help the plants along had come to nothing. No rules had been broken after all. John would have been angry, if he had ever found out.

But at last, with the lettuces almost ready to pull, he had given her a very important job to do. He was placing his trust in her to do it well. After that he would soon be back in charge again, thank goodness. He would take his prize lettuces to the village show and win the cup and bring honour to the school! She took her place at dinner with her head held high.

Patrick and Eileen won their match again, although it was a much closer result than against Woodville, the week before. As Patrick proudly handed round his chocolate crispy cakes to the visitors from St Faith's, Miss Ranger and her class clapped and cheered loudly.

'Oh, well done, Patrick!' shouted Arabella. She turned to Julian. 'Wasn't your cousin marvellous?'

'Was he?' asked Julian.

He had not been following the rallies closely. He had spent most of the time studying the spectators, watching one face in particular.

Elizabeth, meanwhile, had found nothing of interest among Arabella's things.

She had been shocked to see how many clothes and pairs of shoes the spoilt little rich girl had smuggled back to school this term, even though it was against the rules. They were hidden under her bed. But of packets of American crisps, or indeed anything American, there was no sign.

I'd feel rather sorry for her, if I didn't dislike her so much, thought Elizabeth, her searches completed. She felt guilty for prying now. *It must be horrid being the oldest in the class and nearly always coming bottom and having your parents so far away.*

She went off to meet Joan and go to the village. She was lucky to have such a real and special friend, she decided. Arabella's friend Rosemary was very weak and just toadied to her.

Later she said to Julian, 'I'm afraid I drew a blank. How about you?'

'I spent most of the match watching Roger Brown's face,' replied Julian. 'And he looked pretty miserable, even when Patrick and Eileen were winning. It was written all over his face, even when his hands were clapping!'

'Upset to see Patrick playing well again? But that would be only natural,' mused Elizabeth. 'He must be secretly hoping to get his place in the team back. It's the big match next week against Hickling Green, when lots of parents come. He might have wanted to play in that and now it looks like being Patrick again.'

'I agree,' said Julian. 'It certainly doesn't prove he's done anything wrong.'

Neither of them wanted to think that about Roger.

'All the same,' sighed Julian, 'I think we should try and keep an eye on him.'

By Sunday night, Elizabeth remembered there was something else she would need to keep an eye on. This time with John Terry's permission.

It had started to rain again. It rained all that night, and when they trailed into French on Monday morning, it was still raining.

The lettuces have been doing so brilliantly, thought Elizabeth. *But there's still time for them to be ruined. I may have to start pulling them by tomorrow. I'll go down and have a look at them after tea today. Even if I have to take my umbrella with me!*

But Elizabeth never got the chance. Something terrible happened in the French lesson that morning, something truly amazing.

They were all sitting at their desks, their heads bent over their books as they copied down a passage from the blackboard. Mam'zelle quietly opened her biscuit tin and slid her hand inside to pull out her first biscuit of the week, then—

'*Aaaaagh!*'

She screamed, and dropped the tin. She had pulled out a handful of dead slugs.

CHAPTER NINE

THE MEETING DECIDES TO PUNISH ELIZABETH

MAM'ZELLE LEAPT to her feet, flinging the slugs away in horror. One hit Arabella on the nose and she screamed as well. The tin had clattered noisily to the floor, scattering dead slugs everywhere and a few snails too.

The classroom door was flung open and Miss Belle appeared.

'Whatever's the matter—?'

'This is the matter, very, very, *very* much the matter!' cried Mam'zelle, picking a slug off her skirt and holding it at arm's length, between thumb and forefinger, before letting it drop to the floor with the others. 'Look what horrible things have been put in my tin. There are some very wicked children in this class. They think they make everybody laugh—'

Some of the class were indeed stuffing their fists

in their mouths. The way Arabella had screamed! And Mam'zelle had looked so funny, holding up the slug like that . . .

One look from Miss Belle quelled their laughter. She was angry.

'Martin, go and find a school cleaner to come and clear up this mess at once for Mam'zelle. The rest of the class sit in silence.'

After Mam'zelle returned from washing her hands Miss Belle gazed at the children for a few moments.

'Whoever was responsible for that silly trick is to come and own up at dinnertime. That will be all.'

The class was very subdued after that. Elizabeth frowned in deep puzzlement, wondering how the mound of slugs on John's rubbish heap could have found their way into Mam'zelle's biscuit tin.

Was there a practical joker at work? Had the same person hidden Patrick's tennis racket?

'Well, Roger can't have done this,' she whispered to Julian, at dinnertime. 'There's no possible motive!'

'And can you see Arabella dare even look at a slug? I can't!' Julian whispered back. He was as puzzled as Elizabeth.

Miss Belle, Miss Best and Mr Johns were puzzled too. Nobody from the first form came to own up, as requested. The culprit must be elsewhere.

They asked the head boy and girl to call a special Meeting.

It took place immediately after tea, the same day.

'I hope the culprit owns up quickly,' whispered Belinda, as they filed into the hall. 'I want to play my new record in the common room.'

'I was hoping for a game of tennis, but it's still raining,' said Kathleen. 'I wonder who managed to get into the kitchens and get their hands on Mam'zelle's biscuit tin? At least it doesn't seem to have been anybody in our class.'

'Unless it was another of Elizabeth's little jokes,' said Jenny unhappily. 'And she's refusing to own up again.'

'Oh, I hope not,' said Belinda, biting her lip.

Of course, the rest of the form, especially Rosemary and Arabella, had been whispering about that possibility all day. Now they waited in keen anticipation to see what would happen at the Meeting.

Elizabeth was already in the hall, seated next to Julian. Her head was held high. She well knew what some of them were thinking, but she was confident that the truth would come out at the special Meeting. She was impatient for it to start. After that she would get on with the important job of examining John's plants for him.

The school monitors were seated on the platform,

with the head boy and girl. They all looked very serious. So did Miss Belle and Miss Best and Mr Johns, observing from the back of the hall.

The entire school was keyed up. A special Meeting was a rare event.

William banged the little hammer.

'I hope this matter can be dealt with quickly,' he told the assembly.

He explained, for the benefit of those who did not know (by now very few of them), exactly what had taken place during the first-form French lesson.

He gazed around the hall, slowly and carefully.

'The simple fact is that *somebody* in this hall invented this foolish joke. It is quite unfair that the first form should be the only ones under suspicion. Rita and I therefore ask the person responsible to stand up now and own up. The Meeting will then decide what their punishment should be.'

He waited. There was a breathless hush.

'Will the person please stand up?' he repeated.

He waited again. Still there was no movement in the hall.

William frowned. Then quietly he consulted Rita and all the monitors. A minute later he came back and banged the gavel, to stem the tide of whispering in the hall.

'Silence, please. As you know, at Whyteleafe School we do not believe in taletelling. But, if the person will not own up, we must get to the bottom of this in some other way. If anybody has any information, if they know anything at all that can shed some light on this, will they please stand up?'

Arabella could barely restrain herself, thinking of the previous incidents. She glanced at Patrick. But he gave a quick shake of the head and stared at the floor.

There then came a sound from the front of the hall. A member of the junior class, who had been sitting cross-legged on the floor, was scrambling to her feet. It was Sophie.

'What do you want to say, Sophie?' asked Rita gently.

'I know where the person must have stolen the dead slugs from,' she said importantly. 'They must have stolen them from Elizabeth.'

Elizabeth had a sinking feeling in the pit of her stomach. She could hear her classmates giving little gasps.

'From *Elizabeth*?' asked Rita.

'She's got a special place where she keeps them in the school garden,' explained Sophie. 'She likes playing with them sometimes, don't you, Elizabeth?' asked the child, in all innocence, at the same time turning round to look for Elizabeth.

'You may sit down now, Sophie,' said William. 'Elizabeth, stand up, please.'

Elizabeth did so, her cheeks aflame. Even Julian was looking at her in surprise.

'Is this true?' asked William. 'That you own some dead slugs?'

'I don't own them,' stated Elizabeth, her voice clear and decisive.

'But you know where there are some? You like playing with them?'

Some of the more senior pupils were snorting and trying not to laugh.

'I do know where there are some,' replied Elizabeth. 'But I don't really play with them. I was just messing about to see if they were properly dead.'

She stopped. If this line of questioning went on much longer, John's secret was bound to come out.

'Some of us might call that playing with them,' commented William.

Now the head girl stood up and took over.

'Elizabeth,' said Rita gently. She was puzzled beyond belief. 'Please just answer one simple question. Yes or no. Did you put some slugs in Mam'zelle's biscuit tin?'

'No, Rita. I did not,' replied Elizabeth in a loud, ringing voice. 'Somebody else must have found my slugs. That's what must have happened.'

That was too much for Arabella. She leapt to her feet.

'Fibber!' she cried indignantly. 'You must have done!'

'That will do, Arabella,' said William firmly. 'If you have something to say, please address the whole Meeting.'

Arabella took a deep breath. But, before she could compose a little speech, Patrick grabbed her arm.

'Shut up and sit down!' he hissed. 'You haven't any proof.'

Arabella subsided.

'Very well then,' said William, looking troubled. 'The time has come for Rita and I to discuss things with the monitors and then come to a decision.'

Everybody on the platform went into a huddle. In the hall the children whispered quietly among themselves. Julian gave Elizabeth's arm a squeeze.

'Don't they eat snails in France?' he grinned. 'Maybe that's why someone played the trick on Mam'zelle.'

'So what!' Elizabeth hissed back. She was in no mood for Julian's jokes. She was pent up, waiting to hear what the Meeting decided. She could see Joan up on the platform, speaking anxiously. She was quite sure that her best friend would be sticking up for her.

At long last William returned to the table and banged the gavel.

'We have reached our decision. The two second-form monitors are convinced that, whatever quarrels may be going on in the first form, Elizabeth Allen is very honest and has never been afraid to own up to wrongdoing. They know her best, of course, but Rita and I are of the same opinion. We have no evidence that Elizabeth played this trick and she has stated clearly to the whole Meeting that she did not. In due course we will discover the true culprit and until then let their own guilty conscience be their punishment.'

Elizabeth sighed with relief, proud to be a member of a school like Whyteleafe. But then her relief turned to dismay.

'Nevertheless, messing around with dead slugs is not something we would expect of a former monitor. It may even have given someone the idea for the trick played on Mam'zelle this morning. Please stand up again, Elizabeth. We have decided on your punishment.'

Elizabeth stood up, faced the platform and awaited her sentence.

'Until John Terry is released from the san and is able to supervise you again, you are forbidden from the school gardens. They are strictly out of bounds. That must be clearly understood.'

Elizabeth nodded and sat down. Her face was very pale.

The Meeting ended. Sophie was upset. She had not meant to get Elizabeth into trouble.

'If you ask me, you got off lightly, Elizabeth Allen!' scowled Arabella, as they came out of the hall. 'Who wants to do any gardening in this weather anyway!'

'Yes, what a swizz!' echoed Rosemary.

Patrick was looking thoughtful. He hurriedly steered Arabella and her friend away from Elizabeth. He badly wanted to have a talk with them.

Got off lightly? thought Elizabeth bitterly, as she stood and watched them go. She could have wept with frustration. She had been banned from the school gardens. She would never dare to defy such a ban, given out by the Meeting in front of the whole school, however unjust she knew it to be.

But it meant that she would be unable to follow John's secret instructions this week. She would be unable to save his prize lettuces for him. All the worry, all the trying to help, all the getting into trouble . . . it would all have been in vain.

The Meeting could not have decided on a worse punishment.

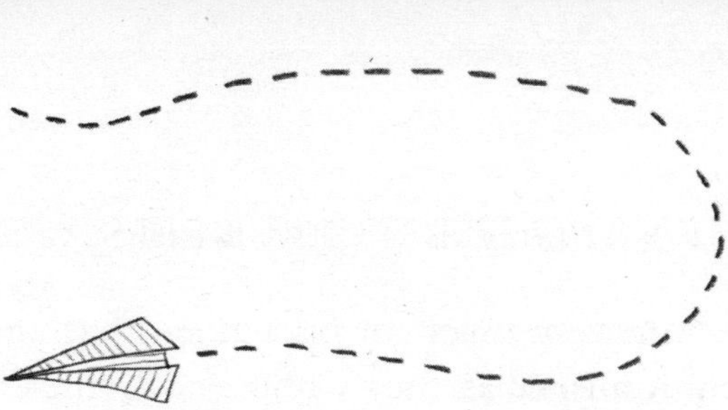

CHAPTER TEN

ARABELLA STIRS UP TROUBLE AGAIN

'COME ON, Rosemary. Let's go and talk to Cook,' said Arabella the following afternoon. 'You never know, she might have seen something.'

'Do you really think we should?'

'Of course we should. I don't think Elizabeth should be allowed to get away with playing that trick on Mam'zelle! Patrick says we haven't got any proof. Well, let us see if we can find some!'

Arabella was still smarting, even twenty-four hours later, from the conversation that had taken place with Patrick.

The fact was that poor Patrick was rather confused.

He had been rather impressed with Elizabeth's bearing at the special Meeting, with the clearness and candour of her voice. He was sure she had played that mean trick with his tennis racket. He felt she must dislike him very much to have done that and the idea made him miserable.

But surely Elizabeth did not dislike Mam'zelle too? They got on well. Why should she want to play an unkind trick on Mam'zelle? It did not make sense. At the special Meeting she had seemed to Patrick like someone telling the truth. So could there be an anonymous joker on the loose in the school? Somebody with a rather warped sense of humour, who chose their victims at random? To someone like that, putting his racket in the boot of the Beast's car could have seemed really amusing.

Could it be, reasoned Patrick, that Elizabeth really *had* found his racket for him, in the nick of time, that day? The thought chastened him, remembering the bad things he had said to her. On the other hand he found it strangely cheering. It would mean that Elizabeth did not dislike him after all.

'What are you suddenly talking about proof for, Patrick?' Arabella had asked scornfully. 'Have you forgotten about the missing jug of milk? She didn't own up about *that* either. And it was actually found in her chest of drawers!'

Patrick had no answer. Yet he had still felt uneasy.

'Let's see what we can find out, Rosemary!' said Arabella now. She felt excited as they walked over to the school kitchens together. She had discovered that Mam'zelle always left her empty biscuit tin with Cook at weekends, to be replenished for the new week ahead. 'Elizabeth could have got into the kitchens over the weekend and put her slugs inside the tin and shut the lid firmly. Then Mam'zelle could have come to collect her tin soon after. Picked up the tin, felt it was heavy and thought her biscuits were inside! Come to think of it,' frowned Arabella, 'I wonder what happened to the biscuits?'

'That's one of the things we can ask!' said Rosemary, who was not quite following all this.

Cook was on tea break, but one of the kitchen helpers, Molly, was there.

'No, I didn't see anybody suspicious, not over the weekend,' she said blankly.

Then Rosemary asked if she had seen any of Mam'zelle's special oatmeal biscuits lying around anywhere.

'Well, isn't it funny you should ask that?' replied Molly, looking unhappy. 'I found them all dumped in the wastebin on Saturday afternoon. I don't think Mam'zelle could have liked the look of them this week. Very wasteful, I thought it was.'

In the wastebin!

'Are you *sure* you didn't see somebody from our form

in here, on Saturday?' begged Arabella. 'Some time earlier? Before it was time for Mam'zelle to come to collect her tin? Think hard, Molly!'

'Well, only Patrick, of course,' said Molly. 'He came in to collect the tennis tin. He had made some nice chocolate crispy cakes for the tennis match. It was standing on the table, next to Mam'zelle's. I nearly gave him the wrong one. It's a blue tin, you see, very like hers.'

Arabella gasped out loud. Two blue tins. Of course!

'Thank you, Molly,' she said. 'You've been most helpful. If they didn't take all our money away from us at this school, I would give you a small gift.'

Then, grabbing Rosemary by the hand, she hurried out of the kitchens.

'Where are we going, Arabella?'

'To find Patrick, of course!' cried Arabella triumphantly.

The rain had stopped for a while. They found Patrick by the south wall, practising his tennis strokes. Arabella was careful not to show her true feelings.

'Patrick, I'm afraid I've got some rather unpleasant news,' she said sorrowfully.

She told him about the inquiries they had made in the school kitchens.

'So I'm afraid the slugs weren't meant for Mam'zelle,

at all, Patrick,' she said, her eyes cast down demurely. 'The person dumped the biscuits and replaced them with slugs because they thought it was the tennis tin. They were playing a mean trick on *you* again, Patrick. Nobody would dare play a trick like that on Mam'zelle.'

Patrick's face turned pale, as the words sank in.

A vivid picture of how it would have been came to his mind's eye. He, the hospitality monitor, proudly opening the blue tin, proudly offering round to the visiting team from St Faith's . . . the dead slugs! Elizabeth, sitting on the bank, waiting eagerly for this moment. Convulsed with laughter when she saw him humiliated . . .

So Elizabeth really did dislike him then. How he had fooled himself! The sense of disappointment turned to a sudden rush of anger.

'And nobody will dare play a trick like that on *me* again either!' he raged. 'Especially not Elizabeth Allen. Just wait till I find her.'

He pushed the two girls aside almost rudely and went racing round to the front of the school. Rosemary felt a twinge of anxiety. What was going to happen now? It was very unfortunate.

Elizabeth was standing at the top of some steps outside the main doors. She was standing on one leg, like a stork, staring into space and thinking about

John's lettuces. They were probably being chewed up right now, one by one, and there was nothing she could do . . .

Patrick came round the corner of the building, saw Elizabeth, then charged towards the steps, with his head down like an angry bull. He almost cannoned into Mr Johns on the way. He came bounding up the steps towards Elizabeth, shouting wildly and waving his arms—

'Those slugs and snails were meant for me, weren't they, Elizabeth! You wanted to make me look an idiot. You wanted to get me into trouble—'

His flailing arms caught Elizabeth's right elbow and she overbalanced. With a cry of surprise she found herself slithering all the way down the steps, to crash face downwards into a big muddy puddle at the bottom. She lay there, winded, gasping for breath. Whatever was the matter with Patrick? It had all been a dreadful shock.

Miss Ranger came running over. Both she and Mr Johns helped the girl to her feet. Elizabeth was covered in mud from head to toe. She was clearly shaken and tears were running down both cheeks.

Gently, Miss Ranger took hold of her hand.

Patrick stood, frozen, at the top of the steps, staring down at the scene in dismay.

'I'll see Elizabeth gets a hot bath and some fresh clothes,' said Miss Ranger. 'Oh, poor Elizabeth.'

'And *I* will deal with the boy,' said Mr Johns angrily. 'Patrick Holland, stay right where you are. I am going to have a word with you.'

As Elizabeth, still shaken and upset, was led indoors by her class teacher, the senior master spoke sternly to Patrick.

'We do not tolerate this sort of behaviour at Whyteleafe.'

'I didn't push her, sir. It was an accident—'

'Yes, because your temper was completely out of control,' replied Mr Johns. 'You behaved like a ruffian.'

'I had good reason to lose my temper!' protested Patrick. 'I've just found out something. Elizabeth tried to do something extremely bad to *me* . . .'

Mr Johns cut him short.

'You will report to the head girl's study in one hour's time,' he said. 'You may put your side of the story *then*. They will be very fair. But I shall be very surprised if you go unpunished, Patrick, whatever the provocation. Until you are called, please go and wait in your common room.'

Over the next hour, as he paced up and down the first-form common room, Patrick gradually began to feel calmer. His classmates had heard about the incident on the school steps. At Matron's insistence Elizabeth herself had been sent to bed after her hot bath. Luckily, she was unhurt, not even a bruise. But it was felt she should rest, have an early night. Now, as his classmates heard about the two blue biscuit tins, and how Elizabeth must have mistaken Mam'zelle's tin for the tennis tin, they began to understand why Patrick had lost his temper.

I'm sure William and Rita will understand too, thought Patrick. *I don't like telling tales, but I will have to explain it all to them. They will see what Elizabeth has been putting me through. It is hateful the way she can dislike me so much!*

However, on his way to Rita's study, he heard running footsteps behind him.

'Patrick!' puffed Kathleen, catching up with him. 'Wait! I've only just heard about it all and what you intend to say to William and Rita. But you can't. It's rubbish. Elizabeth could *not* have thought the oatmeal biscuits were the goodies for the tennis match. She could never have made that mistake. She *knew* you had made some chocolate crispy cakes.'

'How could she know?' asked Patrick. 'I kept it a secret. And besides we are not even on speaking terms.'

'I know you're not! That's why, when Cook gave her a message to give you about the cooking chocolate, she asked *me* to give you the message instead. To pretend that Cook had asked *me* to tell you. Elizabeth would never have put the slugs in the wrong tin. Either somebody from another form did it, or the trick was meant for Mam'zelle after all.'

Patrick's mouth fell open now.

'Thanks, Kathleen,' he croaked. 'Thanks for telling me this.'

He walked into the study in a bemused state.

When asked to put his side of the story, he could only mumble in embarrassment.

'It was just a misunderstanding. I thought Elizabeth had done something to me . . . but she hadn't. It was wrong of me to lose my temper.'

'You must learn to control it in future, Patrick. You must learn the hard way.'

At breakfast the following morning everyone at Elizabeth's table was very subdued. They had all heard the upsetting news. Patrick had lost his place in the tennis team. He was forbidden the honour of representing the school against Hickling Green, the most important fixture of the summer. He would have to be replaced by Roger Brown.

Patrick had moved to the furthest end of the table, away from Arabella. While he crunched his cornflakes he stared at her moodily.

She never once looked at him. She kept her eyes

fixed on her cereal bowl, her face pink with discomfiture.

Even Elizabeth was silent.

Patrick had apologised to her this morning. He had apologised handsomely. But he had lost his place in the second team. Nothing she could say would bring that back for him. As the little girl stared at Patrick's sad, crumpled face, she could only feel sorry for him. Poor Patrick!

John Terry was released from the san that afternoon, a day sooner than expected. The doctor had looked by and pronounced him fit. Luckily, nobody else at Whyteleafe had managed to contract the infection.

It was just before tea. With joy in his heart, after being cooped up for so long, John rushed down to the school gardens. He made straight for the potting shed. He knelt down by the big cupboard and opened the door. He peered inside. He expected to find some fine specimens of lettuce in there, carefully wrapped in newspaper. The cupboard was empty.

He hurried round to look at his lettuce patch. He stared at his plants in shock. They were almost drowning in pools of water. There were slugs crawling all over them. Most of the plants had been decimated.

Elizabeth never came and pulled any, even though I wrote to her! He was deeply disappointed in her. *She must have forgotten. I'm surprised.*

Deeply anxious, he hurried to the tool shed and found a trowel and some newspaper.

Then he worked his way up and down the two rows, examining each lettuce in turn. His shoes squelched in the mud. From his fine crop only a single lettuce in each row remained intact. One a round one, the other a cos. With nimble fingers he gently eased them out of the soil, careful not to damage any of the fine leaves. He wrapped them in newspaper and left them in the cool cupboard in the potting shed.

They were not the best two, he thought in despair. *They were not the two I would have chosen. I only hope they are going to be good enough. I'll take them to the church hall tomorrow. That is the day you are allowed to leave entries.*

He arrived at tea, very late. A big cheer went up. All the children were pleased to see John fit and well again. But Elizabeth saw him shoot her a puzzled look. She feared the worst.

'Are they all ruined?' she whispered when they found each other after tea.

'Nearly,' he said, with a brief nod. He looked hurt.

But, as Elizabeth explained about the special Meeting, and the dead slugs, and being banned from the school gardens, his face paled.

'Poor Elizabeth! Then . . . Oh! There's nothing else

I can do. I shall have to go and explain to William and Rita.'

'But you mustn't, John,' she pleaded. 'You know it's a secret! You always wanted it to be a complete surprise. At least wait and see if you win the cup.'

'I don't expect I will,' he sighed. But he looked at her gratefully. 'Thanks, Elizabeth. I'll find some way of putting things right for you. I promise.'

Elizabeth nodded. She had complete faith in John Terry.

Things were indeed put right for Elizabeth. It happened in the nicest possible way. John's two remaining lettuces won the cup!

At the last Meeting before half-term he was called up on to the platform by William and Rita. John held the silver cup aloft for the whole school to see. The children clapped and cheered and drummed their feet on the floor. It was such an honour for the school. There was going to be a photograph in the local newspaper. Everybody would see what fine things they did at Whyteleafe School.

'We have another announcement to make,' said William solemnly, when the cheering had died down. 'On behalf of the Meeting, I want to make a statement. Elizabeth Allen has been seriously misjudged. When Sophie saw her with the dead slugs last week, they had come from John's slug traps. She was worried about John's project, while he was in the san. She knew his secret plan, but also that it was against the rules of the competition for him to receive any help. She was simply turning the pests over with a twig, to check that they were properly dead. Stand up, please, Elizabeth.'

Elizabeth rose. With due ceremony Rita opened the Big Book in which everything that happened at the Meetings was written down. She was holding a pen.

'The Meeting wishes to delete all record of Elizabeth's supposed wrongdoing and punishment. Please accept our apologies for our hasty judgement, Elizabeth.'

As Rita wrote in the Big Book, Elizabeth was given a round of applause.

'So *that's* what you were up to!' whispered Julian, as she sat down. There was an amused light in his eyes. 'Did John use milk in his slug traps? Is that what the jug was for?'

Elizabeth smiled guiltily.

'I didn't use any, though!' she explained hastily. 'I'm so glad I didn't. It would have been breaking the competition rules.'

'Our Bold Bad Girl break any rules?' he mocked. 'Oh, no, never!'

An instant later they were serious again. For William had a final announcement to make.

'On one matter, I regret to say, the Book must remain open. We still do not know who played the unkind trick on Mam'zelle. Until the culprit owns up, or the truth comes out in some other way, none of us on this platform can rest.'

Nor could Elizabeth or Julian.

CHAPTER ELEVEN

THE CORRECT CONCLUSION

THE TWO friends longed to know who had really hidden Patrick's racket in the Beast's car boot. It had been at the root of so much trouble for Elizabeth and was still not resolved. Patrick no longer knew what to think. He was so forlorn about losing his place in the school team, through his own stupid behaviour, that he tried not to think about it at all. A few in the class still wondered, though.

Julian was by now deeply suspicious of Roger Brown.

Elizabeth was inclined to agree. 'I have to admit it was very clever of Arabella to realise that Mam'zelle's tin looked the same as the tennis tin and that one could be mistaken for the other. I had no idea she had so much brainpower. She proved herself a better detective than us.'

'Yes,' agreed Julian. Neither of them knew that it was

Molly in the kitchens who had pointed this out. 'Even if Arabella did get the wrong culprit! But you're right, Elizabeth. I feel quite miffed not to have thought of it myself. It does provide the perfect link with the mystery of the missing tennis racket.'

'Both tricks intended to get Patrick chucked out of the second team,' nodded Elizabeth. 'The first because he would have played so badly without his proper racket. The second to get him in disgrace for playing a stupid joke on St Faith's.'

'And Roger the only chap with a motive,' added Julian.

'Well, he's *got* his place back in the team now after all,' said Elizabeth. 'Oh, Julian,' she said impulsively, 'I do think it's such a shame about Patrick. I don't hate him any more. He was so silly letting himself be stirred up by Arabella. She's such a mischief-maker. But I wish he could get his place back from Roger. He's the better player anyway. I expect we'll lose against Hickling Green now!'

'You are very noble, Elizabeth,' grinned Julian. Then he sighed. 'But how can we prove that Roger's done anything wrong? How can we be sure? Wouldn't he have owned up by now anyway? He's such a decent chap.'

They both frowned. They had been over the same ground time and time again.

Soon it was the day of the big match.

Elizabeth and Julian were standing on the upstairs landing, gazing through the big window. Dinnertime was over and the tennis match against Hickling Green was due to start in exactly one hour. Last summer the match had been played away. Elizabeth remembered it was a good outing. This year it was the visitors' turn to come to Whyteleafe. The coach carrying the rival team and supporters would arrive in about forty-five minutes' time.

A few Whyteleafe parents were arriving already. Some of the pupils had a half-term exeat. There had been bustle and excitement all day as children packed their cases. Most parents would remain for the big match before driving them home. Elizabeth was staying on at school over half-term to camp in the grounds. Joan was staying on too. It would be such fun!

Watching the early cars roll up, Julian concentrated on naming all the different makes. Elizabeth, bored by this, was still fretting about Patrick, and the mystery, and whether Roger had been to blame. She knew that Julian had been keeping a careful eye on the senior boy.

'No, nothing suspicious, I'm afraid,' he reported, as Elizabeth returned to the subject yet again. 'In fact, just the reverse. Each time I watch him, he looks more down in the dumps than ever. It knocks a big hole in our theory, Elizabeth!'

She nodded. They had both noticed it. For someone who had got his place in the second team back Roger hardly seemed overjoyed. On the day it happened he was seen walking around school with an anxious frown. And the frown had just got deeper and deeper.

'Did you see him at dinnertime?' continued Julian. 'I thought *Patrick* looked miserable until I saw Roger's face. It just doesn't make sense.'

'And look at him now!' exclaimed Elizabeth, pointing. 'Look, Julian. There he is. I can see him. Look, over by the tennis courts.'

The big boy had just appeared, wearing his tennis whites. Racket in hand, he had begun pacing up and down, up and down by the empty tennis courts. He was waiting for the match. He was all ready to begin.

'But there's a whole hour to go yet!' exclaimed Julian. 'What strange behaviour!'

'Julian, why don't you go and talk to him?' asked Elizabeth suddenly. 'I'll stay here.'

'What, accuse him, you mean?' asked Julian. For a moment his usual sangfroid deserted him. How could he, a mere first-former, accuse one of the most senior boys in the school of wrongdoing, without a shred of evidence? 'Don't be silly, Elizabeth. It might just be his nerves.'

'It probably is. Which means he could be grateful for someone to talk to!' exclaimed Elizabeth. 'Of *course* I didn't mean accuse him! But you never know. He might open up a bit. You might find something out. I'll keep out of the way, though, or he'll be on his guard. He knows I got into trouble over the slugs and everything. But you can do it, Julian. You know how grown-up you can be!'

Julian smiled. He looked interested. 'It's worth a try,' he said.

He strolled nonchalantly over to the courts. Elizabeth watched from the window.

'Hello, Roger. Want a fruit gum?'

The big boy stopped in mid-pace, close to a wooden bench, blinking. His thoughts were far away. Someone was proffering a tube of sweets, waving it under his nose.

'Oh hello, Julian.'

'Here, have a fruit gum. Give yourself some energy for the big match.'

'Thanks.' Roger took the sweet and popped it in his mouth.

'Gosh, Roger. You do look nervous.'

'Do I?' He sucked hard on the gum. 'Matter of fact, I am a bit.'

Julian sank down on the wooden bench. Automatically,

Roger sat down beside him. It would seem unfriendly not to. Julian was a nice kid. Very intelligent.

'Well, you can only do your best,' said Julian comfortingly. 'That's what my mother always says.'

'I wish my father said the same! He says you've always got to play to win. You can't go through life being a loser!' Roger burst out. 'And he should know! There are so many of his old sports cups in our house it takes a week to clean the silver.'

Julian looked at Roger's big, gentle face with sudden interest.

He offered him another fruit gum. It was a black one this time, Julian's favourite, but he felt it might be a good investment.

'Is your father coming to watch you today?' he asked casually.

'Is he *coming*?' exclaimed Roger. 'He's flying in specially. He's cutting short a business trip. All the time I've been at Whyteleafe he's been longing for me to make the school teams. I tried and tried and never succeeded, till this term. As soon as Dad heard I'd made the second tennis team, he said it was a dream come true and he'd be here to watch me play in the Hickling Green match, no matter what. He thinks I must be a late developer and he says this will just be the beginning of my sports career . . .' There was a desperate look on Roger's face, as he said this. 'As a matter of fact, Julian, I'm pretty scared of letting my father down today. It will break his heart.'

Julian, with his bright, intelligent green eyes, looked at the boy beside him, at his ungainly feet and his large red hands.

'Won't he be pleased when he hears about your academic scholarship?' he ventured.

Roger shook his head. He was deep in thought.

'He thinks sport's more important. He's too old to play sport himself now. He wants to sort of live it through me. He knows about the scholarship already. The news came through just before he left on his last trip.'

'It must have been a bit of a worry for you,' said Julian, treading very carefully, 'when you lost your place in the team for a while?'

'A worry? It was a nightmare!' exclaimed Roger unguardedly. 'There was no way of letting Dad know. He was already in the States, you see, and there was nowhere I could telephone to stop him flying back today—'

Roger suddenly clammed up. He felt he was letting his tongue run away with him.

Julian was sitting very still. The word 'States' had sent a little tremor through him. So Roger's father made his business trips to America then?

Roger was lumbering to his feet.

'Well, that's enough. I can't sit here all day, eating all your fruit gums, can I, Julian?' he said awkwardly. He fished something out of his shorts pocket. 'Here – have a crisp. They're good ones. It's my last packet till Dad gets here.'

He produced an open crisp packet. Julian stared at it. The words on the front said *Southern Favorits*.

'I'm sorry, Roger!' he burst out. He truly did feel sorry for the big, gentle boy. 'I'm sorry. But I've guessed the truth. Even before you offered me a crisp!'

Julian produced the matching packet from his pocket, tattered and crumpled. He had been guarding it carefully, all this time. Just in case. 'You dropped this by Miss Best's car. The time you hid Patrick's racket in her boot. Then, when that didn't work, you tried to play another trick on him with the slugs. He thought Elizabeth had played those tricks. *That's* why he lost his temper with her and why you got your place back. But it should be Patrick playing today, shouldn't it? Not you!'

Roger sank back down on to the bench. He looked anguished. He buried his face in his hands. 'My father's coming!' he groaned. 'He'll be here soon! He's flown in from America specially. Please don't give me away,' he begged. 'I was honestly going to confess everything, after half-term, once this match was safely out of the way. I intend to own up at the next Meeting, I promise. But let me play today. Please.'

'I have to go and consult Elizabeth,' said Julian. He suddenly felt desperately torn. 'We'll decide this together.'

'Please let me play!' begged Roger, as Julian walked away.

Elizabeth said that there was no time to lose. They must go and find the head boy and girl and ask their advice. It was much too big a decision to make on their own.

William and Rita, without hesitation, reached the correct conclusion.

'It's all very sad,' said Rita. 'Of course Roger cannot be allowed to play. He has done such bad things, but, more to the point, it would solve nothing. He would simply be storing up more misery for himself in the future.'

'His father would expect him to get into teams at his next school,' agreed William. 'The misery would just go on and on forever! Mr Brown must be made to face up to the truth. Just because he was a sporting hero himself, it does not make Roger one. His talents lie in other directions. And he must be brave and tell his father the whole truth.'

Even as they were discussing it, Roger had come to the same conclusion.

Eyes blurred, he set off up the school drive. He would wait at the gates for his father's car. He would tell him the whole truth and ask to be taken home straight away.

William was about to leave the study to find Roger when there came some alarming sounds through the window.

A blaring horn – the scream of car brakes – a cry of pain.

They all rushed outside.

A heavily built man was kneeling on the school drive beside the prone figure of a boy. He had been driving fast. He had raced all the way from London Airport, anxious not to miss any of the match.

'It's Roger!' he cried out to them in horror. 'It's my own son. I've knocked down my own son.'

They all knelt round the boy while Rita rushed off to find Matron.

'Oh, let him be all right. Please let him be all right!' Roger's father kept saying. 'What was the matter with him? He was wandering alone, in such a daze. He was right in the middle of the drive. I couldn't stop in time—'

'He was very upset, sir,' Elizabeth said quietly. 'You see, he knew another boy should be playing in the match today. Somebody much better than him. He cheated to stay in the team, but it wasn't for himself. He did it all for you.'

'For me?' asked Mr Brown. He was stroking his son's head.

'He knows you want him to be good at sport,' said Julian. 'He couldn't face losing his place in the team and letting you down.'

There was a long silence.

'I've been a fool,' said Roger's father at last. 'Oh, please let him be all right!'

Matron arrived.

'Should we call an ambulance?' asked Mr Brown, looking fearful.

Matron kept everybody back while she examined Roger and took his pulse. Then she looked up, in very great relief.

'Pulse good and strong,' she said. 'No sign of any broken bones. I'm afraid his head must have struck the ground. He's concussed. I think he's just beginning to come round.'

Even as she spoke, Roger began to stir. He groaned once or twice and then opened his eyes and saw that it was his father who was bending over him.

'Dad, I've behaved stupidly. I've let you down. I'm so sorry—'

'Hush,' said his joyful father. He soothed his son's brow. 'I know all about it now. I'm the only one who's behaved stupidly. But I promise you, Roger, things will be very different in the future.'

There was just time for Patrick to change into whites, find his beloved tennis racket and fill the vacant place in the second team. Elizabeth had begged Mr Johns to allow him to play.

He was so happy to be back in the team. But he was sorry to hear that Roger had been knocked over by a car and had had to go to hospital for a check-up. He was very surprised to learn that Roger had been the person behind the beastly tricks, but relieved that none of it had been anything to do with Elizabeth.

So she did not dislike him after all!

Whyteleafe defeated their old rivals that day, and Patrick put up a very fine performance. There was much cheering and clapping as he came off the court. It was his play that had made all the difference.

Patrick walked up to Elizabeth and, in full view of everyone, gave her a big bear hug.

'Will you forgive me for being so beastly?' he asked, in embarrassment. 'It was so clever of you to find my racket that day. Fancy your noticing that the boot of the Beast's car was open, just a few inches. If you hadn't noticed that, I would have lost my place in the team. Everything would have been completely different.'

Over on the bank, Arabella watched and felt grumpy. Why did people always end up liking Elizabeth?

Elizabeth just stood in the sunshine and gave a happy little sigh. She was pleased that she was staying on at Whyteleafe over half-term. It was the best school in the whole world.

She thought of all the effort she had put into trying to help John Terry. In the end he had won the cup and surprised the whole school with no help from her at all! But she was proud to have kept his secret.

The person she had really helped was Patrick. And even that was an accident!

She still didn't know why the racket had been hidden in such an unlikely place. Though she learnt later that Roger had planned, in fact, to hide it in one of the garages – until Mr Leslie, the science master, suddenly appeared on the back drive. Roger, in a panic, had fled, thrusting Patrick's racket into the nearest car boot as he went!

But there was one thing that Elizabeth never did find out. The little song she had taught Sophie, about Patrick being made of slugs and snails and puppy dogs' tails, was the inspiration behind Roger's failed plan with the tennis tin. He had heard Sophie and her friends chanting it as they skipped one day and it had given him his brainwave.

With the naughtiest girl around these unfortunate things just seemed to happen!

BONUS BLYTON

Enid Blyton has been one of the world's best-loved storytellers for over seventy-five years. Her interest in writing began as a child, and before she loved receiving letters from the children who read her books, she enjoyed working with them as a teacher. The Naughtiest Girl stories are inspired by real schools and experiences. Turn the page to learn more about Enid as a child and as a teacher. Afterwards you might like to write about your school and teachers and the people in *your* class!

THE LIFE AND TIMES OF ENID BLYTON

11 August 1897	Enid Blyton was born in East Dulwich, London. Two brothers are born after her – Hanly (b. 1899) and Carey (b. 1902).
1911	Enid enters a children's poetry competition and is praised for her writing. She's on the path to becoming a bestselling author . . .
1916	Enid begins to train as a teacher in Ipswich. By the time she is 21, she is a fully qualified Froebel teacher, and starts work at a school in Kent.
1917	Enid's first 'grown-up' publication – three poems in *Nash's Magazine*.
June 1922	Enid's first book is published. It's called *Child Whispers*.
1926	Enid begins editing – and writes – the phenomenal *Sunny Stories for Little Folks* magazine. (She continues in this role for 26 years!)

1927	So vast is Enid's output that she has to learn to type. (But she still writes to children by hand.)
1931	Having married Hugh Pollock in 1924, the couple's first child, Gillian, is born. Imogen, their second daughter, was born in 1935.
1942	The Famous Five is launched with *Five on a Treasure Island.*
1949	The first appearance of *The Secret Seven* and of *Noddy* mark this year as special.
1953	Enid moves away from *Sunny Stories* to launch *Enid Blyton's Magazine.* She is now renowned throughout the world – she even established her own company, called Darrell Waters Limited (the surname of her second husband).
1962	Enid Blyton becomes one of the first and most important children's authors to be published in paperback. Now, she reaches even more readers than ever before.
28 November 1968	Enid dies in her sleep, in a nursing home in Hampstead.

SCHOOL RULES

Elizabeth is used to getting her own way, so it's a challenge to adapt to life at Whyteleafe where the students make their own rules. That said, the student council don't have many rules at all. Here are the ones explained to the new children in *The Naughtiest Girl in the School* . . .

'We place all the money we get into this box, and we draw from it two shillings a week each. The rest of the money is used to buy anything that any of you especially want – but you have to state at the weekly Meeting what you need the money for, and the Jury will decide if you may have it.

'The second rule is that if we have any complaint at all, we must bring it to the Meeting and announce it there, so that everyone may hear it, and decide what is to be done with it. Please be sure you understand the difference between a real complaint and telling tales, because telling tales is also punished. If you are not sure of the difference, ask your monitor before you bring your complaint to the Meeting.'

In that first book in the series we learn that, 'monitors are chosen for their common sense, their loyalty to the school and its ideas, and their good character.'

Do you think Whyteleafe's rules are fair?

What rules would you establish if you had a student council?

What do you think would be poor qualities in a monitor?

Why not discuss the answers with the people in *your* class or perhaps your family?

MY HAPPIEST TIMES

During her lifetime, Enid Blyton received many hundreds of letters from the thousands of children – all over the world – who enjoyed reading her books. She took great pleasure in replying to them. She also loved meeting children and it is said that the suggestion for an autobiography came from a young fan who presented Enid with a list of questions. He thought he might write a book about his favourite author, called *Enid Blyton – The Story of Her Life*, but his mother suggested that Enid might write it herself. And so she did. *The Story of My Life* was published in 1952. Enid wrote about her family, where she lived, the inspiration for her books and her writing process. She also talked about her childhood. Have you ever imagined what your favourite writers were like as children – and what important events may have shaped their future lives? Here is an extract from *The Story of My Life*, which takes us back to Enid's younger days . . .

* * *

My happiest childhood times were when I was reading and dreaming, when I was playing games with other children, and when I was out in the country or by the sea. Very much like your happiest times, I expect!

The games I played were Burglars and Police Officers, Making a House somewhere – behind a bush, or up a tree, or under a table. We had tops and hoops and marbles as the seasons came round.

We played a great many card games, because we all loved cards. So do my own girls. We played Snap and Happy Families, Old Maid and Beggar-My-Neighbour.

We also played board games such as Snakes and Ladders (and sometimes Ladders and Snakes – going up the snakes and down the ladders, instead of the other way round!). When I was six, my father taught me to play draughts and a little later he taught me to play chess. That was just before I was seven. He thought that all young children should learn to play chess. I enjoyed the games immensely.

I think my father was more of a naturalist than anything else. I didn't even know what a naturalist was at that time – all I knew was that my father loved the countryside, loved flowers and birds and wild animals, and knew more about them than anyone I had ever met. And what was more he was willing to take me with him on his expeditions, and share his love and his knowledge with me!

In those days it was considered quite ordinary to collect birds' eggs. Nowadays we teach children not to, because it distresses the birds and it might lead to many kinds gradually becoming extinct.

My father collected birds' eggs, and he had a cabinet of little drawers full of beautiful eggs, neatly arranged and labelled. One of the things I had to do to help him was to insert my hand into holes in trees to see if any nests were there, and to feel for eggs.

I never did like taking the eggs. I did so hope the bird wouldn't mind. Fortunately my father never wanted more than one egg. He never knew how scared I was of putting my hand down into those small holes. Once I heard a hissing noise down a hole, and I was sure it was an adder hiding there. I was afraid of being bitten, but I didn't like to say so.

Weekend after weekend I went out with my father. Looking back, it seems as if those days were always warm, always sunny, and that the sky was always as deeply blue as the cornflowers in my garden, or as faintly blue as the harebells on the common.

We were lucky to have woods and commons, ponds and lanes so near. We explored everywhere and everything – watching the lizards play on the sunny banks, listening to the willow warblers singing, poking down a hole that my father said badgers had been in, looking for the white violets we knew always blossomed in a certain dell.

All my childhood was steeped in the sunshine of the woods and commons and lanes, and what I didn't find out from nature herself I read about in books, and then searched for it again. I was perfectly happy, even when I wandered about alone, finding flowers to look up in our reference books, trying to discover what bird was singing, learning the difference between a thrush's nest and a blackbird's, and a hundred other things.

'One day I'll put all these things into a book,' I said, though I didn't tell anyone that, of course.

WHAT THEY DID AT MISS BROWN'S SCHOOL

In 1920 Enid Blyton became a governess to the four Thompson children, whose ages ranged from four to ten. The family lived in Surbiton, in Surrey, in a house called 'Southernhay'. Enid had a small room which overlooked the garden, and it was there that she wrote many of her stories. Enid's tiny class often had lessons outdoors in the summer months.

Enid was very popular with her students, because her lessons were both practical and creative. She worked with them to put on performances for which they made props, costumes and invitations – and even sold tickets.

In 1941 she published a long story called 'What They Did at Miss Brown's School', which was divided into monthly episodes. It's been hard to find for many years, but you can read extracts in these new editions of *The Naughtiest Girl* books. The character of Miss Brown and her tiny class is very much based on Enid Blyton and her school at the Thompsons' . . .

Here's the sixth extract . . .

6. June. The Surprising Silkworms

'MISS BROWN, you've got a ladder all the way up the back of your stocking!' said Mary one morning.

'Oh dear! And these are my very best silk stockings!' sighed Miss Brown. 'How I wish I could spin pure silk like the silkworms do! Then I could make my stockings for nothing!'

The children laughed. 'Do silkworms *really* spin silk, Miss Brown?' asked John.

'John! Have you never kept silkworms and seen what they do?' said Miss Brown in surprise.

'Never,' said John. 'I've kept ordinary caterpillars, Miss Brown, but they didn't spin silk or anything exciting like that.'

None of the others had kept silkworms either. Miss Brown made up her mind at once that that should be June's fun.

'It is a little late to get silkworm eggs,' she said, 'but maybe we can still buy them. If not, we'll buy the caterpillars themselves. I'll write a letter now, straight away, and order them. It will be June tomorrow, so there is no time to lose.'

By a piece of luck, the man she wrote to still had silkworm eggs to sell. They were a shilling a hundred. Miss Brown bought a hundred. They arrived on June the second and the children looked at them with interest.

'They are round and flat, and not much bigger than a pin's head, Miss Brown,' said John.

'Won't the silkworms be tiny!' cried Susan.

'Yes, at first,' said Miss Brown, 'but later on they will be longer and fatter than your fingers, Susan!'

Susan couldn't believe it. 'What do we feed them on?' she asked.

'Well, they like mulberry leaves better than anything,' said Miss Brown. 'But they will eat lettuce too. If we could get mulberry leaves, we should find the boxes pleasanter to clean out each day, for mulberry-fed silkworms leave only a dry litter behind them, but lettuce-fed ones leave a moist, unpleasant litter to clear up.'

'Well, Miss Brown, *I* know where there is a mulberry tree!' cried John. 'In my grandpa's garden. I can go there each day and get fresh leaves.'

'Good, John,' said Miss Brown, pleased. 'Well, we had better have leaves each day now, for these eggs may hatch at any time.'

'Are we all going to share them?' asked Susan, who always liked to have something of her own.

'I'll tell you what we will do,' said Miss Brown. 'These eggs will not all hatch out at once, but in batches. We will say that the first-hatched batch shall be John's, because he is to bring the leaves. The next shall be Mary's, the next Peter's and the last Susan's, because she is the youngest.'

'That will be fun!' said John. 'We'll have to have four boxes. And shall we have to cover the silkworms with glass or something, Miss Brown, to stop them crawling away? I remember my caterpillars all crawled away last year when I forgot to cover them.'

'Oh, no,' said Miss Brown, 'silkworm grubs are not like ordinary caterpillars, John – they are "tame" and will not crawl away from their boxes. You see, for thousands of years they have been kept for their silk, so they have lost the ways of wild caterpillars. We don't need to cover them, but we must remember not to leave them by the open window or the birds may come in and steal them!'

The next day about twenty of the silkworm eggs hatched! The children were so pleased. They looked into the box lid, where Miss Brown had placed the batch of eggs, and saw what looked like tiny, short bits of black cotton crawling about!

'Gracious! Are those tiny black things the silkworms?' asked Susan. 'I can hardly see them!'

'Yes, some of the eggs have hatched,' said Miss Brown. 'The grubs ate their way out of the eggshell. Now, John, where is your first lot of mulberry leaves? Good! We will put them into this second box lid – and then I want you to watch me lift these tiny caterpillars with my paintbrush. I don't want to harm them by lifting them with my fingers, but I can easily lift them on to the fresh leaves with a brush. Each day you must do this, John, so watch carefully.'

John had placed his mulberry leaves into a second shallow box lid. Miss Brown carefully lifted up each tiny, black, thread-like caterpillar to the leaves. Then she took a magnifying glass from her desk and lent it to each child in turn so that they might see how the tiny caterpillars began to nibble the leaves.

No eggs hatched the next day, but another lot had hatched into tiny black threads the day after. Mary lifted them gently on to her leaves in a third box. There was a fourth box too – or rather box lid – and in this John placed his caterpillars while he cleaned out the other box.

'We must always have an extra odd box,' said Miss Brown. 'Because we can't clean out a box while the caterpillars are in it. Now I wonder when *your* caterpillars are going to hatch, Peter!'

They hatched the very next day, and Peter was delighted. He too had a box lid given to him and some mulberry leaves.

Poor Susan had to wait a whole week before the last lot of eggs hatched – but as there were thirty-four she was delighted. 'I've got the most!' she said. 'I had to wait the longest, but I've got the most.'

'Good for you,' said John. 'I say, Miss Brown, aren't my silkworms growing! They are three times the size of Susan's!'

'I've got twenty-two,' said Peter, counting.

'I've got twenty-one,' said John.

'I've got twenty-three,' said Mary.

'And I've got thirty-four,' said Susan. 'That makes exactly a hundred.'

How those silkworms grew! They became a pearly grey colour and ate all day long. The children soon found a quick way of changing them from one box to another. This is what they did.

When John came to school in the morning with his new mulberry leaves, each child put a few fresh leaves into his or her box. The caterpillars soon smelt out the new leaves and crawled on to them in delight. Then all that the children had to do when cleaning them was to lift the new leaves *and* caterpillars into the spare box and clean out the old box! They did their cleaning one by one, so there was always a spare box to move the silkworms into, and the spare box left over was clean and ready to use the next day.

One day Susan was very much upset because when she counted her caterpillars she found there were only thirty! 'Four have gone!' she said, almost in tears.

'I am afraid you must have thrown them away when you cleaned out the box,' said Miss Brown.

'I shall write down the number I have and always count them in future,' said Susan. The others did this too, for they were afraid of losing theirs like Susan.

Another really dreadful thing happened the week after. Somebody opened the window and forgot to shut it – and there, on the windowsill, were the fat silkworms, eating away at the mulberry leaves.

When the children came back from their play in the garden, they heard a scurry of wings in the schoolroom – and what do you think had happened? Some sparrows had peeped in at the open window and had seen the silkworms. And they had taken at least thirty or forty!

The children were so upset. Miss Brown was sorry too.

'Well, I did warn you not to leave this window open,' she said.

'It was my fault,' said John, very red. 'I'm so very, very sorry.'

'Being sorry won't bring back our poor silkworms,' said Mary sadly.

'Well, it's a thing that any of us might have done,' said kind-hearted Peter, sorry for John. 'It's a good thing we came in when we did – we've still got plenty. And, my word, aren't the silkworms enormous now!'

They certainly were – and they kept doing a most surprising thing. They split their skins, and worked their way out of them! The first time Peter saw one doing this he was quite alarmed and thought that his silkworm was ill!

'Oh, no,' said Miss Brown, laughing. 'They grow so fast that their skins become too tight, so they have to split them. But it doesn't matter because they have a fine new skin underneath!'

Four times the silkworms changed their skins, and they grew so enormously that, as Miss Brown had said, they were longer and fatter than Susan's fingers.

'The silkworms always seem to feel a bit upset before they change their skins,' said John. 'But goodness, don't they eat afterwards! Miss Brown, I watched this one through the magnifying glass when it changed its skin. It was marvellous!'

After about six weeks had gone by the silkworms began to look a little different. The children all noticed the change.

'They seem to have gone a bit smaller,' said Mary, 'and they look rather transparent. Mine won't eat at all, Miss Brown, and look at that one shaking its head about as if it's giddy.'

'The time has come for them to change into chrysalises. We must help them,' said Miss Brown. 'Look, here is some new blotting paper. I want you to make some cone-shaped bags like those the grocer makes for currants. Make one for each silkworm. The silkworms are about to do their most marvellous work now – they are going to spin their silk!'

Miss Brown put a few twigs into each box. She told the children to watch which silkworms climbed up them. Any that did this were to be taken up gently and popped into a cone-shaped bag.

John had three silkworms to put into the blotting-paper bags.

'Write the date on the bags,' said Miss Brown. 'Now pin the bags up on the wall in a row, John. Pin under each one a piece of paper in case the silkworm sends out a flow of water and stains the wall. There – that's right!'

Soon more and more bags were pinned up on the wall as the silkworms came to the time when they must spin. How the children loved to peep into each bag and see the silkworms spinning, spinning, spinning! To and fro they moved their heads, and the children, looking through the magnifying glass, saw a thin thread of silk coming from their lower lips. Each silkworm had fastened itself to the bag, and was now winding the golden silk round itself.

At first the children could see each silkworm through the mist of thread, but after a while the silk was so thick that the silkworm had quite disappeared behind it. In a few days the cocoon was finished, a lovely golden case.

'Is the silkworm inside?' asked John.

'Yes, and there it changes its skin for the last time!' said Miss Brown. 'And if you could see the silkworm now it would no longer look like a caterpillar but a chrysalis. Its skin becomes hard, like a shell, and is red-brown. It lies quite still – and a miracle happens!'

'Yes, I know what it is,' said Mary. 'The caterpillar changes to a silk moth, with wings. I do wish I knew how it did that, Miss Brown. It's like magic.'

'Miss Brown, the silkworm I put into this bag yesterday is trying to get out,' called Susan. 'It won't spin.'

'Well, it isn't quite ready then,' said Miss Brown. 'Put it back into the box to eat a little longer. Now, John, when a week has gone by, we will unwind the silk from this cocoon and you will see how strong and fine the thread is – perfect for weaving into clothes.'

The silkworms all made their golden cocoons one by one – and then, when a week or so had gone by, Miss

Brown took a cocoon gently from a bag. She pulled off the loose outer silk, and found the end of the long thread that the silkworm used to spin its cocoon. Then she took a doubled-over piece of stiff paper and began to wind the silk round and round it.

The golden cocoon rolled about on the table with the pull of the silk. Miss Brown told John to go on winding off the silk till it was finished. It took him a long time! The cocoon became smaller and smaller as he wound the silk, which lay golden and fine round his paper. At last the last piece was wound and there, on the table, was nothing but a little hard-shelled chrysalis, and the last cast-off skin of the silkworm!

The children loved winding off their silk. They had such a lot. Mary said she was going to use it for sewing!

All the silkworm chrysalids were put into a box and then one day a surprising thing happened: from each chrysalis a cream-coloured moth came out. They had stout, furry-looking bodies, and they stood about, drying their wings.

'The big ones are the mother moths,' said Miss Brown. 'Now who would think that these pretty winged creatures could possibly grow from the tiny eggs we had at the beginning of June!'

The children took a big box and put the silk moths into it. First they lined the box with paper, as Miss

Brown told them to. They did not put on the lid as the moths could not fly. They did not even give them anything to eat, for the moths had no mouths!

'We'll leave them alone in peace in this shady corner of the classroom,' said Miss Brown. 'Then maybe they will lay their eggs for us, and next year we shall not need to buy any!'

The moths *did* lay their eggs – hundreds of them in neat batches on the lining paper. Miss Brown took out the paper, cut out the batches of eggs, left them exposed to the air for about four days, and then put them away in a cool cupboard till the next year.

'And next spring we'll hatch out our own eggs and keep silkworms all over again!' said Susan, pleased. 'Well, that *was* interesting, Miss Brown!'

Enid Blyton

THE FAMOUS FIVE

Join the Adventure!

Have you read them all?

ENIDBLYTON.CO.UK

IS FOR PARENTS, CHILDREN AND TEACHERS!

Sign up to the newsletter on the homepage for a monthly round-up of news from the world of

Enid Blyton®

Illustration by Laura Ellen Anderson.

JOIN US ON SOCIAL MEDIA

EnidBlytonOfficial BlytonOfficial

Enid Blyton®

is one of the most popular children's authors of all time. Her books have sold over 500 million copies and have been translated into other languages more often than any other children's author.

Enid Blyton adored writing for children. She wrote over 700 books and about 2,000 short stories. *The Famous Five* books, now 80 years old, are her most popular. She is also the author of other favourites including *The Secret Seven*, *The Magic Faraway Tree* and *Malory Towers*.

Born in London in 1897, Enid lived much of her life in Buckinghamshire and loved dogs, gardening and the countryside. She was very knowledgeable about trees, flowers, birds and animals. Dorset – where some of the Famous Five's adventures are set – was a favourite place of hers too.

Enid Blyton's stories are read and loved by millions of children (and grown-ups) all over the world. Visit enidblyton.co.uk to discover more.

Illustration by
Laura Ellen Anderson.

Here's The NAUGHTIEST GIRL

Have you read them all?

1. The Naughtiest Girl in the School
2. The Naughtiest Girl Again
3. The Naughtiest Girl is a Monitor
4. Here's the Naughtiest Girl
5. The Naughtiest Girl Keeps a Secret
6. The Naughtiest Girl Helps a Friend
7. The Naughtiest Girl Saves the Day
8. Well Done, the Naughtiest Girl
9. The Naughtiest Girl Wants to Win
10. The Naughtiest Girl Marches On

Enid Blyton®

Here's The NAUGHTIEST GIRL

HODDER

HODDER CHILDREN'S BOOKS

First published in Great Britain in *Enid Blyton's Omnibus!*
by George Newnes in 1952
This edition published in 2021 by Hodder & Stoughton
For further information about the editorial history of this book,
see enidblyton.co.uk/books

3 5 7 9 10 8 6 4

Enid Blyton® and Enid Blyton's signature are registered
trade marks of Hodder & Stoughton Limited
Text © 2021 Hodder & Stoughton Ltd
Illustrations by Claire Powell © 2021 Hodder & Stoughton Limited

No trade mark or copyrighted material may be reproduced without
the express written permission of the trade mark and copyright owner.

The moral right of the author has been asserted.

*All characters and events in this publication, other than those clearly
in the public domain, are fictitious and any resemblance to real persons,
living or dead, is purely coincidental.*

All rights reserved.
No part of this publication may be reproduced, stored in a retrieval
system, or transmitted, in any form or by any means, without the prior
permission in writing of the publisher, nor be otherwise circulated
in any form of binding or cover other than that in which it is published
and without a similar condition including this condition being imposed
on the subsequent purchaser.

A CIP catalogue record for this book is available from the British Library.

ISBN 978 1 444 95863 8

Printed and bound in Great Britain by Clays Ltd, Elcograf S.p.A.

The paper and board used in this book are made
from wood from responsible sources.

FSC www.fsc.org MIX Paper | Supporting responsible forestry FSC® C104740

Hodder Children's Books
An imprint of Hachette Children's Group
Part of Hodder & Stoughton
Carmelite House
50 Victoria Embankment
London EC4Y 0DZ

An Hachette UK Company
www.hachette.co.uk
www.hachettechildrens.co.uk

CONTENTS

INTRODUCTION

by Cressida Cowell

bestselling author of the
How to Train Your Dragon series

Like so many, many children before and after me, Enid Blyton's books played a crucial role in turning my nine-year-old self into a passionate reader.

That is because Enid Blyton had an extraordinary knack for writing the kind of books that children actually *want* to read, rather than the kind of books that adults think they *should* read.

Enid Blyton could tap into children's dreams, children's desires, children's wishes, with pinpoint accuracy. She knew that every child, however good and well-behaved they might look on the outside, secretly longed to be Elizabeth Allen, the naughtiest kid in the school. I'm afraid I entirely cheered Elizabeth on, as she defied her parents, the headmistresses, her schoolmates, and the very serious School Meetings. If anything, I wanted her to be even naughtier.

But *The Naughtiest Girl* books were really my favourite of Enid Blyton's school stories because of Whyteleafe, a very different school from Malory Towers or St Clare's. What if there could be a school in which discipline was administered by the children rather than the adults? In which all money was given in at the start of the term and distributed among the children along socialist lines? Wouldn't this be the kind of school that children would actually *want* to go to, rather than the kind of school that children *have* to go to?

It was an interesting proposition to a nine-year-old, and it remains an interesting proposition.

I hope you enjoy this story as much as I did when *I* was nine years old.

Cressida Cowell

CHAPTER ONE

BACK AT WHYTELEAFE SCHOOL

IT WAS the summer term at Whyteleafe School. All the children were back again – Elizabeth, Julian, Harry, John, Martin, Rosemary and the rest. They rushed round the school excitedly, glad to be back.

'Summer term! My favourite term!' said Elizabeth Allen, pleased. 'Hi, Julian – come and look at my new tennis racket!'

Julian came over, humming a little song. His green eyes twinkled at Elizabeth. 'Hallo,' he said. 'What are you going to be this term, Elizabeth? Naughtiest girl in the school? Best girl? Silliest?'

Elizabeth laughed and gave Julian a friendly punch. 'I'm a monitor, as you jolly well know,' she said. 'I'm going to do my best, and be a monitor all the term – not be chucked out in the middle, as I was last term. What about *you*?'

'Oh, I'm going to do my best too, but I've got all sorts of bests,' said Julian, grinning. 'I'll beat you at work this term, for one thing – and I'll beat you at tennis – and I'll beat you at thinking out a few little tricks to make life cheerful – and –'

'Oh, Julian, I *hope* you'll think of a few tricks,' said Elizabeth. 'But please don't put sneezing powder in the pages of my books again – honestly, it's awful to *have* to keep on and on sneezing without stopping.'

'Right,' said Julian, 'I'll make a note of it!'

Elizabeth was just going to say something more when she caught sight of a boy in the distance. He was so like Julian that she stared in surprise. Same black untidy hair, same green eyes – but what a sulky face!

'Look, there's somebody who looks very like you,' said Elizabeth. 'He must be a new boy.'

Julian turned. 'Yes, that's a cousin of mine. He's got rather a big opinion of himself, as you'll soon find out. He didn't want to come to Whyteleafe School at all.'

'Whyever not?' said Elizabeth, who simply couldn't *imagine* anyone not wanting to come.

'Well, he's not very fond of *me*,' said Julian. 'He doesn't like people who can do things better than he can – and he'll be in our form.'

'And when you use *your* brains you'll be top whenever you want to!' said Elizabeth. 'Even against *me!*'

'That's easy,' said Julian, and got another teasing punch. 'But quite seriously, Elizabeth, go slow with Patrick – he can be very spiteful. Don't play the heavy monitor with him too soon or too much.'

'I shall tick him off if he doesn't toe the line,' said Elizabeth at once. 'How will he behave, do you think?'

'A bit like *you* behaved when you first came!' said Julian, twinkling at her. 'Don't you remember? You were the naughtiest girl in the school – and you meant to be too! The things you did!'

Elizabeth went bright pink. 'You needn't keep reminding me of that first term,' she said. 'I was awful. I just can't think how I could have behaved like that.'

'Well, I wasn't there then,' said Julian, 'but I've heard plenty about it. I bet you'll always be known as the naughtiest girl, even if you go on being a monitor for the rest of your schooldays and end up as head girl!'

'Golly, I'd never be that,' said Elizabeth. 'Whoever heard of a naughtiest girl ending up as head? Here comes your cousin, Julian.'

Julian swung round. 'Hallo, Patrick,' he said. 'Finding your way about a bit? This is Elizabeth. She's a friend of mine and, if you want any help in anything, go to her, because she's a monitor.'

'I'm not likely to go to any friend of yours for help!' said Patrick in a high-and-mighty voice. 'And, by the way, you don't need to spread around the news that I'm your cousin – I'm not really proud of having you for a cousin! Too swollen-headed for my taste!'

He went off, hands in pockets. Julian glared after him. 'If he wasn't new, I'd shake him till his teeth rattled!' he said.

Elizabeth was indignant too. 'What cheek from a new boy!' she said. 'Well, he won't cheek *me*! If he does, I'll report him.'

A bell rang just then, and everyone hurried in to a meal. Elizabeth scrambled for her place at table. She beamed round at everyone. How good it was to be back among all her friends! John Terry grinned at her across the table.

'Going to help in the garden this term?' he called. 'Have you seen all the seeds that have come up since last term? We shall have a fine show this summer.'

John was partly responsible for the gardens of the school. He loved gardening and was very good at it. Elizabeth nodded back at him. 'Yes, of course I'll help. I love messing about in the garden.'

Elizabeth was going to be busy this term! She meant to ride each day on one of the school ponies. She meant to practise her tennis hard and get into one of the school teams. She meant to help John with the gardens. She was determined to beat Julian as top of the form whenever she could, and that meant a lot of hard work – and she meant to be a good monitor.

Somebody else meant to beat Julian too! That was Patrick, his cousin. Patrick was jealous of Julian – he had always been glad when he had heard that his cousin didn't work hard at school, and had continually been bottom. He knew that Julian had good brains, and it pleased him that he hadn't used them.

All the same, he hadn't wanted to go to Whyteleafe School. *Mixed boys and girls!* he thought, scornfully. *I'd rather go to an all-boys' school. Look at that Elizabeth now – fancy me having to take orders from a girl! Well, I shan't pay much attention to* her *anyway!*

He set himself to make a good impression on the others in his form. He entered into everything, and because he was good at games, and could be very comical when he tried, he was soon well liked.

He hadn't Julian's gift of making extraordinary noises, but how he wished he had! Julian could cluck exactly like a hen laying an egg, he could buzz like a bluebottle fly, drone like a bumblebee and make very strange noises like nothing at all.

Patrick had often tried to imitate noises, but he couldn't. For one thing everyone knew he was making them, and that gave the game away.

Nobody ever knows that Julian is doing the noises,

thought Patrick enviously. *Last Christmas, when he came to us for a party, he imitated a dog whining, and we all hunted round the house for ages – and, though I looked and looked at Julian, I* couldn't *see a single movement of his mouth or throat.*

Patrick soon found that Whyteleafe wasn't at all the 'sissy' kind of school he had expected. His class worked hard and played hard, practically every boy or girl had a hobby, and if anything went wrong it was reported at the big Meeting held by the school each week.

This was a kind of parliament, at which everything was discussed frankly by the children themselves. Complaints were heard, grumbles were made and set right, money was distributed evenly, plans were made.

Rita and William, the head boy and head girl, presided. If punishments had to be meted out, they said what they were to be. Twelve monitors sat on the platform with them – a kind of jury, Elizabeth always thought. She was very proud to be on the platform, sitting alongside the other monitors.

At first Patrick had been pleased to hear that he was to be in Julian's form. He had frequently heard his father and mother say what a pity it was that a boy with good brains like Julian should so often be bottom. He didn't know that the term before Julian had begun to use his brains well, and could always be top of the form if he wanted to be!

So it was a shock to him to find that in the first week's marks Julian was top, Elizabeth was second and he was tied third with somebody else.

'I thought you made a point of being at the bottom of the form,' he said to Julian. 'Or so I always heard.'

'You heard right,' said Julian quite amiably. 'I just didn't happen to want to be top, that was all. But I do now. Did *you* want to be top, Patrick? Bad luck that I happen to be using my brains this term, isn't it?'

Patrick turned away. All right, he'd work harder still. He wasn't going to play second fiddle to Julian. He pondered over his tennis. He was good at that. He would take special coaching and practise hard – Julian wasn't much good at tennis! It would do him good to be taken down a peg!

Then one day he came up against Elizabeth. She was the only person in the form he didn't try to be nice to. She was Julian's friend and a monitor – that was enough for Patrick! He hardly ever addressed a word to her, and if ever she came up to a group he was with he walked away.

Elizabeth laughed at first, but soon it infuriated her. She longed to pull him up for something, but the chance didn't come for three weeks.

Then a notice was put on the board for a meeting.

MEETING OF THE GARDEN COMMITTEE, AT FIVE O'CLOCK SHARP, said the notice. ALL THE FIRST FORM MUST ATTEND AS WELL, AS VOLUNTEERS ARE WANTED TO HELP WITH THE WEEDING.

Patrick was in the first form. He saw the notice and ignored it. Why should he go? He wasn't interested in gardening, he hated weeding and he certainly wasn't going to volunteer to do anything in the gardens!

He went off to have a quiet practice by himself, taking his racket and tennis balls with him. There was a wall at the side of the school against which he could hit the balls and strike them continually on the rebound.

So, when the meeting gathered, Patrick was not there! John, who was in charge, looked around. 'Are we all here?' he said.

'No. Patrick isn't,' said Elizabeth at once. 'I bet I know where he is too! Practising hitting balls against the side wall. I saw him pass the window with his racket.'

'Oh! Well, he's got to come,' said John. 'You are a monitor, Elizabeth. Fetch him, will you?'

'Right,' said Elizabeth, pleased at being able to make Patrick 'toe the line' for once. 'I can hear the thud-thud of the balls against the wall now. I'll bring him along at once!'

And off she went, quite sure she could make Patrick obey her!

CHAPTER TWO

PATRICK COMES UP AGAINST ELIZABETH

ELIZABETH HURRIED round to the side of the school. Thud, thud, thud, she heard the balls being hit regularly against the wall.

She turned the corner and called out to Patrick, 'Hey! You're supposed to be at the Garden Meeting. You'd better come at once.'

'Get out of my way, please,' said Patrick. 'I'm practising.'

Elizabeth glared. 'John sent me,' she said.

'All right. I send you back,' said Patrick, almost hitting Elizabeth with one of the balls, as he sent it against the wall near her.

'Don't be an idiot,' said Elizabeth, trying not to lose her temper. 'You know I'm a monitor, don't you? Well, you've *got* to come when you're told. It's no good having monitors unless they're obeyed, you know that.'

'I'm not obeying a girl,' said Patrick. 'Do go away. I shall get annoyed with you in a minute.'

Elizabeth promptly proceeded to get even more annoyed with the infuriating Patrick. She rushed at him and wrenched away his racket. He was so taken by surprise that he let it slip out of his hands.

Then Elizabeth raced away at top speed with it! Patrick tore after her in a rage. Elizabeth turned a corner and deftly threw the racket into the middle of a bush. Then on she went without stopping, back to the meeting.

She arrived there, panting. Before she could say a word to the startled meeting, Patrick arrived too, fuming. 'Where's my racket? How *dare* you snatch it like that? Elizabeth, what have you done with my racket?'

Elizabeth said nothing. John looked surprised, but pointed to a seat. 'Sit down, Patrick,' he said. 'We've been waiting for you.'

'I haven't come to your silly meeting,' said Patrick furiously. 'I've come after Elizabeth for my racket!'

'*Sit down*,' ordered John. 'You're at the meeting now, and here you'll stay. You won't get your racket till the meeting is over – and not then if you don't behave yourself!'

Patrick was so surprised at John's determined voice that he sat down. He looked all around for his racket, making up his mind to snatch it and go. But he couldn't see it, which was not surprising, as it was still outside in the bushes!

Patrick didn't hear a word of the meeting. He glared at Elizabeth's triumphant face. He scowled at the little smile on Julian's. Julian was amused at Elizabeth's method of bringing his unwilling cousin to the meeting, and he wondered where she had put the racket.

Elizabeth forgot about Patrick in her interest in the meeting, She was very fond of gardening, and John regarded her as one of his right-hand helpers. He kept consulting her, and she was pleased.

She didn't notice that the sky had clouded over and that it had begun to rain. It was only when it suddenly pelted against the window that she looked out and saw the torrents of rain that were falling. Even then she didn't think about the racket outside in the bushes.

She didn't think of it till the meeting was over. Then John turned to the bored and sulky Patrick. 'Now you can have your racket back from Elizabeth,' he said. 'And please remember if a meeting of the whole form is arranged, you've got to come to it.'

Patrick scowled. Elizabeth suddenly remembered where she had put his racket – in the middle of the bushes. Goodness, had it got wet in the rain? She knew it was a new racket, and that Patrick was intensely proud of it.

She wished she could go and get it out of the bushes and dry it before she gave it to Patrick. But he gave her no chance to do that. He followed close at her heels when she went out of the room. She walked out of the garden door and went to the wet bushes. It was still pouring with rain. She fished out the soaked racket.

Patrick stared at it in horror and anger. 'You beast! You flung my new racket there in the pouring rain! It'll be ruined.'

'It wasn't raining when I put it there, you know it wasn't,' said Elizabeth.

'Well, why didn't you go out and get it when the rain began?' said Patrick furiously. 'You left it there on purpose! You *meant* the rain to spoil it!'

'I *didn't* mean to spoil it!' said Elizabeth angrily. 'I didn't even notice it was raining till nearly the end of the meeting – and then I forgot all about your racket. It's your fault for not coming to the meeting, so that I had to fetch you!'

Patrick was wiping the strings with his handkerchief. He was trembling with rage and disappointment. His lovely new racket!

'*I* hate you for this,' he said. 'Now you'll go and laugh about it with Julian, and be glad you've ruined my racket – there wasn't a better one in the school! You'll both be glad it's spoilt!'

'Patrick, don't be silly,' said Elizabeth. 'Look, I'm very sorry I didn't think of your racket being out in the rain. If I'd remembered it, I'd have gone to get it at once. And of *course* Julian and I won't be glad if it's spoilt.'

'Yes, you will. I detest you both,' said Patrick, his face bright red, and his green eyes flaming like Julian's did when he was angry. 'I'll get even with you! You're just exactly the kind of mean, catty girl I'd expect my cocky cousin to be friends with!'

He tucked his racket under his arm, and walked off in a rage, the rain still pouring down as he went. Elizabeth shook back her wet curls. Blow! What an idiot she had been to forget the racket when it began to rain. She really was sorry about that.

Julian met her as she went back. 'Golly, you *are* wet!' he said. 'What happened? Where did you put his racket? *Not* out in the rain, I hope!'

'Yes, I did, but I didn't mean to,' said Elizabeth soberly, and she told Julian what had happened, and what Patrick had said. 'He never liked me before, Julian, and now he's really furious with me. He hates you too, doesn't he? Oh, dear, I do hope he won't do anything silly now. He really looked as if he'd like to hit me with his racket!'

'He probably would have if he hadn't thought his

racket would be hurt more than you would!' said Julian. 'Cheer up – what can he do to pay you back – or me either? Nothing that matters. Come on into the gym – there'll be games going on there.'

Patrick made a great fuss about his precious racket. He told everyone what had happened. He spoke of having to get all the strings replaced, and when the next School Meeting was held he actually got up and asked for the money to have his racket completely restrung!

He stood up when William said, 'Any complaints, please?' Anyone could then stand up and lodge a complaint, big or small. Patrick leapt to his feet before anyone else.

'I have a complaint!' he said. 'Against a monitor, Elizabeth Allen. She left my racket out in the rain and it's ruined. I want to ask for money out of the school moneybox so that I can pay for it to be restrung.'

'Elizabeth, perhaps you'd like to say something about this,' said William, the head boy, in surprise.

Elizabeth stood up, feeling embarrassed. She related truthfully what had happened, and added that she was very sorry about the racket being left out in the wet. 'But it wasn't for very long,' she said, 'and I'm sure, William, that it doesn't need restringing.'

'Have you the racket with you?' William asked Patrick. 'No? Well, go and get it. I know a good bit about rackets and I can tell you at once what wants doing.'

Patrick went to get the racket with a very bad grace. He came back and gave it to William. 'Look, there's a string gone already!' he said, pointing to the broken string. Elizabeth stared in dismay.

William examined the racket very carefully. Then he put it down and looked sternly at Patrick. 'That string is not frayed or split,' he said. 'It has been cut. The racket does not need restringing – only that one string needs putting in. Who cut it, Patrick? Tell me that?'

'How should I know?' said Patrick sulkily.

There was a short silence. 'Now listen,' said William, 'you yourself must pay for that one string being renewed. The rain had nothing to do with it being broken. I think you know that very well. Every other string is perfectly all right. If you still want the whole racket restrung, you can save up the two shillings you are allowed each week, and pay for it yourself, but it will take you more than a term's money!'

Patrick snatched up his racket without a word. He glanced at Elizabeth. She looked scornfully back. So he had actually cut a string in his own racket to try and make out that she had really spoilt it by leaving it for a few minutes in the rain! What a thing to do!

Patrick made a sudden face at her, and then left the

platform with his racket. He passed by Julian and saw a little smile on his face. He almost hit him with the racket! 'I'll pay you both back!' he said in a whisper, and marched right out of the hall.

'Don't call him back,' said Rita, the head girl, to William. 'He's a new boy. He's got to learn our ways! Now – any more complaints?'

There were none. Nor were there any grumbles. William hammered on the table as a little talking broke out.

'You may dismiss,' he said. 'The Meeting is over.'

Elizabeth sped to Julian. 'Oh, Julian – isn't Patrick *mean*! Did he really cut that string, do you think? It did look exactly as if it had been cut.'

'Of course he did,' said Julian. 'He's an idiot. We'd better look out for him now, Elizabeth. He may really try to pay you back!'

'Pooh! *I'm* not afraid of Patrick,' said Elizabeth. And she wasn't!

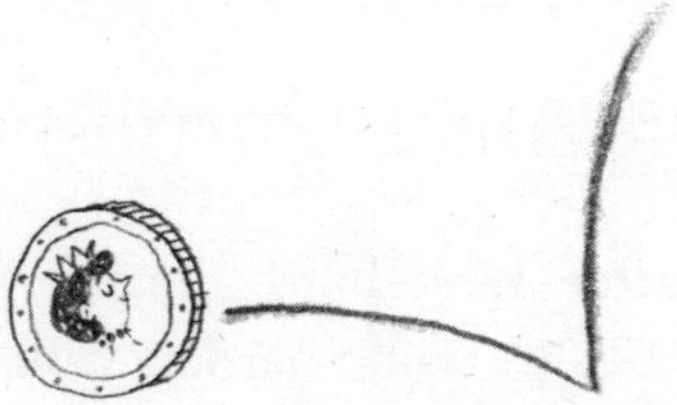

CHAPTER THREE

JULIAN'S LITTLE TRICK

PATRICK BROODED over the whole affair. He had a sulky nature and could not easily forget anything that upset him. He completely ignored Julian and Elizabeth, turning his back on them whenever they came near.

This only amused them, however, and in the end Julian turned the joke against Patrick by calling out warningly whenever he or Elizabeth went near him.

'Be ready to turn your back, Patrick. Here we come again! Hurry up and turn, or you'll see us!'

Patrick tried in vain to think of some big, triumphant way of getting back at Julian and Elizabeth. He was bitterly disappointed that Julian was so good at his classwork. His cousin had always been so don't-carish over that, so he had heard, and Patrick had looked forward to crowing over him and being top each week.

But, no matter how hard Patrick worked, Julian seemed to be able to work harder! Julian had brilliant brains, found learning easy and was determined that Patrick should not once beat him in marks.

Patrick was second one week – beating Elizabeth. But Julian was still triumphantly top, a full ten marks ahead of Patrick. Miss Ranger, the class mistress, was amazed at the high marks that Julian, Patrick and Elizabeth showed each week! She didn't know how hard they were vying with one another.

Patrick decided to concentrate on tennis, and beat Julian at that. Julian was good, but he wasn't keen on being in any of the school tennis teams. He said it meant too much hard work to keep in practice!

'All the same, Julian, you'd *better* get some practice in,' said Elizabeth, 'because that cousin of yours is getting jolly good. I watched him playing with some boys older than he is, and he was as good as they were. He'll be in one of the top teams if you don't look out – and won't he crow over you! Do, do beat him, Julian.'

'Blow you, Elizabeth,' said Julian, and pretended to sigh heavily. 'What with working hard to keep ahead of you and Patrick in class – and now having to tire myself out with tennis, to beat Patrick, my life's not worth living! What about *you* taking him on at tennis?'

'I do try, but he's got a much harder serve than

I have,' said Elizabeth honestly. 'Go on, Julian – you can be *much* better than Patrick, and I'd jump for joy if you got into the second team, which is what *he* wants to do!'

Julian tried – and Patrick had the disappointment of being well and truly beaten by his cousin when they played against each other two weeks after that! Patrick hadn't realised that Julian had become so good, and he was humiliated and disappointed.

If he gets into the second team instead of me, I'll rap him on the head! thought Patrick, going off the court with a very gloomy face. *He doesn't really care about tennis, and I do. He's only doing it to spite me.*

'Jolly good, Julian!' said Elizabeth, giving him a pat on the back as he came whistling off the court, having collected all the balls that Patrick had been too annoyed to pick up. 'Did you see his face? He looked as sick as a hen left out in the rain!'

'Oh well, it's rather a shame really,' said Julian. 'I don't care if I'm good at tennis or not, and he does. But, seeing that he only wants to have the pleasure of crowing over me if he beats me, I don't mind beating *him*!'

'Yes, and you *don't* crow!' said Elizabeth. 'I hope you get into the second team and go and play against Hickling Green School, Julian – that's always such a good outing.'

Julian began to get a bit bored with his extra efforts at lessons and tennis. He was also working very hard at making a model aeroplane, for he was very clever with his hands. All this concentration made him feel suddenly stale.

He began to plan a little pleasure for his form. Strange noises? Something weird up the chimney? He thought hard, and a sudden grin came on his face.

'The chimney! I sit fairly near the fireplace, and I could work something in the chimney. Now, let's see.'

When his classroom was empty, Julian went in cautiously. He crouched down by the chimney and looked up it. It was rather narrow. A broad mantelpiece was over the fireplace, and this Julian examined very carefully. He had noticed last winter that, when the wind was in a certain direction, little eddies of smoke came out from under the mantelpiece. He was looking for the crack from which they must have come.

There must be a crack or a hole somewhere, thought Julian, *or the smoke wouldn't get out from the chimney under the mantelpiece and into the room. Ah – here it is!*

He had found the crack where the cement had worn away. He took a chisel and made the hole considerably bigger. He poked the chisel some way through, and then decided that the hole was big enough for his purpose.

He took a piece of string and tied a penknife to one end. He poked the knife through the hole, and gave it a push. It clattered into the chimney, fell down and suddenly appeared in the hearth!

'Ha! Good!' said Julian, pleased. He still had hold of the string that went into the hole. He knocked a small tack in on the underside of the wooden mantelpiece and then tied the string to it firmly. He tested it. Yes, it held well.

He undid the knife from the other end of the string, which hung down the chimney into the fireplace. He then disappeared into the corridor and fetched a small bell that was kept there to summon Matron if she was needed in a hurry.

He went back into the classroom and carefully tied the bell to the end of the string that hung down the chimney. Then he undid the other end from the nail, and pulled it, so that the bell was dragged out of sight up the chimney!

Then Julian gave a little tug to the string he held, and a muffled and rather weird tinkle came from up the chimney!

Julian chuckled. He ran the end of the string under the mantelpiece and held it in place by little staples he drove into the wood. The string fell down the side of the fireplace just by his chair. Julian sat down and bent over his desk, holding the end of the string in his hand. He tugged it – and a mournful little jingle came from the inside of the chimney!

A nice little treat for the class this afternoon, thought Julian, and tied the string to one leg of his chair.

Miss Ranger took the class that afternoon. It was a geography lesson, rather dull. Julian waited for a moment of silence and then gave the string tied to his chair leg a little tug.

At once it pulled the bell hanging in the chimney and a sudden little jingle sounded in the room. Everyone looked up. Julian did too. He meant to be as surprised as anyone else!

He tugged the string again. *Jingle-tinkle-tink* went the bell obligingly.

'What's that noise?' asked Miss Ranger, puzzled. 'It sounds exactly like a bell somewhere. Where is it ringing? Has anyone got a bell with them this afternoon?'

'No, Miss Ranger!' chorused everyone except Julian. He tugged again, and the bell jangled quite loudly.

'Well, it *sounds* up the chimney!' said John. 'But how could a bell ring in the chimney?'

'It couldn't,' said Miss Ranger firmly. 'So we won't ask you or anyone else to go crawling up the chimney to look for bells there, John. Stand up, everyone, and put your hands above your heads. If anyone has a bell, and can ring it when their hands are above their head, they will be clever!'

Everyone stood with hands above their heads, Julian too. *Jingle-jingle-jing!* The bell rang again. Julian had managed to get his foot to the string and jerk it! A babble of noise broke out at once.

'Nobody's got a bell and yet it rang again! Miss Ranger, what is it? Miss Ranger, it's peculiar! Where is it, do you suppose? Can't we look for it?'

'No,' said Miss Ranger firmly, imagining a bevy of excited children crawling over the room and completely ruining the rest of the geography lesson. 'Bell or no bell, we go on with the lesson. Sit!'

They sat and the bell immediately rang a merry peal. 'Take no notice,' commanded Miss Ranger, who was just as puzzled as anyone else, but determined not to show it. 'I have only one more thing to say about this bell – and that is, if I find out that anyone in this class is plaguing us with a jingling bell, I shall do a bit of plaguing myself – and the culprit will be very, very sorry for themselves!'

After that they all settled down and, although the bell rang plaintively at intervals, and the children began to giggle each time, nobody dared to take much notice of it.

As soon as the class was ended and Miss Ranger was safely out of the room, John ran to the chimney. 'It sounded as if it came from here,' he said. 'I know it did!'

He put his hand up the chimney and groped about. *Tinkle, jing!* He had touched the bell!

'It *is* up here!' he cried. 'I thought so. But how on earth did it get there?' He turned and saw Julian's grinning face. He laughed. 'Julian! It's one of your ridiculous tricks – but *how* did you get the bell hanging there?'

'Easy!' said Julian, and showed the interested class how he had managed it. Only one of them sneered. That was Patrick, of course.

'What a childish trick! I'm sure Miss Ranger will be very scornful about it when I tell her.'

He was immediately pushed down hard on a chair and three or four children pinned him down firmly. 'Sneak! Tell-tale! We'll never speak to you again if you do that.'

'All right, all right. I was only joking,' said Patrick, trying to push them off, afraid of making them dislike him. They let him go.

John had pulled the bell down from the chimney and now it lay on the floor nearby. Patrick gave it a vicious kick, and it slid jangling over the floor. Julian smiled broadly. 'Taking it out on the bell instead of on me, I suppose?' he said. 'Pity you can't see a joke, Patrick.'

The next day a really peculiar thing happened. It was Miss Ranger's class again, this time in maths. All the children were copying sums down from the blackboard when once more there was a curious noise from the chimney.

Everyone raised their heads and grinned. Was this another trick of old Julian's? But he looked as surprised as they did.

The noise came again, a struggling kind of noise, then came a series of high squeaks, and a little soot fell down the chimney.

'Now whatever is *this*?' said Miss Ranger, exasperated. She suddenly thought of Julian and his tricks. She looked straight at him. 'Julian, is this one of your tricks? Answer me truthfully, please.'

'No, Miss Ranger. It isn't one of my tricks. I can't *imagine* what is going on in the chimney,' said Julian quite truthfully.

Squeak, squeak, chirri-chirri-chirrup!

Patrick got up. 'Julian's not telling the truth!' he said. 'It was *his* chimney trick yesterday – and it's his trick again today! Look up the chimney and you'll see his trick, Miss Ranger! He's a frightful fibber!'

CHAPTER FOUR

PATRICK IN TROUBLE

THE WHOLE class stared at Patrick in amazement and disgust. Julian shrugged his shoulders. 'I do assure you, Miss Ranger, I haven't the faintest idea what is going on up our chimney,' he said.

'You *do* know! You've put something up there again!' cried Patrick in a fury. 'Just to suck up to the class and make them think you're marvellous!'

'That's enough,' said Miss Ranger. And then, quite suddenly, with another series of squeaks and chirps, something fell down the chimney-place and came to rest with a little thud on the hearth!

'Chirrup!' it said feebly. The children stared at it. 'A baby starling – and golly, here comes another!' cried Harry, as a second black little creature arrived beside the other. 'There must have been a starling's nest up the chimney, and these two have wriggled out and fallen down. Poor little things!'

'Sucks to you, Patrick,' said Elizabeth in delight. 'You can't say that Julian built the starling's nest or turned out the young starlings, can you! Sucks to you!'

'Elizabeth, I don't like that vulgar expression,' said Miss Ranger coldly. 'John, take those two poor little creatures and put them outside in a bush where perhaps their starling parents may see them and feed them. Patrick, take that scowl off your face.'

'It was Julian who put the bell up the chimney yesterday anyhow!' blurted out Patrick. 'So what are you going to do about *that*?'

'Nothing,' said Miss Ranger calmly. 'Sit down in your places, everyone. We are now going on with our lesson – and I must warn you all that I do *not* feel in the mood for any more disturbances, whispers or giggles.'

The children bent over their books, but there were many scornful glances thrown at Patrick. He bent over his book too, kicking himself for thinking that was a trick of Julian's – and for being unable to prevent himself from blurting out about the bell trick.

He hurried out in front of the others afterwards, afraid that they would take him to task. He ran to get his racket, meaning to go and bang the balls at the side wall, to work off some of his anger.

But the class followed him, and soon he was

surrounded by an angry little company. Elizabeth advanced on him, her eyes gleaming. 'I may as well tell you,' she began, 'that sooner or later complaints will be made about you at the next School Meeting, and—'

'Shut up,' said Patrick, and threw a ball up into the air to hit against the wall. 'Go away, all of you. I'm fed up with this school – and most of all I'm fed up with my grinning, very-very-clever cousin and with Elizabeth, the cocky, high-and-mighty monitor!'

Elizabeth tried to grab his racket, to make him stop playing about – he should be *made* to listen to what was being said! But Patrick swung it away and then raised it again to hit another ball.

He hit Elizabeth instead! Crack! The racket descended heavily on her right shoulder and she yelled. Julian leapt at Patrick, his face blazing. *Coward!*

He caught Patrick by the shoulder, and held him tightly. 'We'll call a Meeting tonight!' he said. 'We'll say that for the rest of this term Patrick shall not play tennis again! We'll confiscate his racket for hitting Elizabeth.'

'Let me go! said Patrick fiercely. 'It was an accident, but I'm glad I hit her all the same. She deserved it! Call your Meeting if you like – I shan't be there! And I'll tell you this, Julian – you're only doing this to keep me out of the second team, because you want to be in it yourself, instead of me!'

He flung Julian off, made a dive under the arms held up to stop him and tore away at top speed.

'Let him go,' said Rosemary. 'Elizabeth, are you hurt?'

'No. Not really,' said Elizabeth. 'Only bruised. Isn't he a beast, though? Julian, it's bad luck on you to have a cousin like that!'

'We'll send him to Coventry! We won't speak to him for the rest of the term! We'll see that he doesn't touch a racket again!' said several voices.

'Telling a fib about Julian!'

'Wasn't it strange, though, those birds falling down the chimney the very day after Julian had put a bell up there!'

'Jolly decent of Miss Ranger not to say anything more about it when Patrick blurted out the truth,' said John.

A monitor from the second form appeared round the corner. 'I say! What's happening? Didn't you hear the bell, you idiots? You won't get anything to eat if you don't hurry up. I've been sent to find you.'

'Oh, goodness, we never even *heard* the bell!' said Elizabeth, still rubbing her shoulder. 'Come on, everyone. All this has made me feel jolly hungry.'

Patrick did not come in to the meal. Miss Ranger did not enquire about him. She knew that he was upset and probably did not want to appear in public just then.

Nobody bothered about him. Let him miss his meal if he wanted to. Do him good! That was what most of his class thought.

Elizabeth and Julian did not attempt to call a big School Meeting that night after all. When they had cooled down a bit it seemed rather silly to air the grievances of the first form in front of the whole school.

'After all, the next Meeting is on Friday,' said Elizabeth. 'If Patrick doesn't behave himself for the rest of the week, we'll make a formal complaint about him then, and deal with him. I don't really believe he *meant* to hit me, Julian.'

'Well, perhaps not,' said Julian. 'He's an unpleasant bit of work, though, isn't he? I wish he hadn't come here. It's hard enough to beat *you* in order to be top of the form – it's getting to be even harder to beat Patrick and I'm really a bit tired of practising my tennis at every moment, just so that he won't be in the second team!'

'It's jolly good for you to work hard at things!' said Elizabeth, remembering how don't-carish Julian had been the term before. 'I wonder where Patrick is? He hasn't shown up at all.'

'Good thing too,' said Julian. 'I expect he doesn't want to face the form. They'll do to him what he's been doing to you and me – they'll turn their backs whenever he appears!'

'Where did you put his racket?' asked Elizabeth. 'Have you hidden it so that he can't get it?'

'Yes. I've put a note in his desk to say that he can have it back if he apologises to you,' said Julian. 'Otherwise he won't have it.'

'Oh, dear, I don't really like all this upset,' said Elizabeth. 'It makes me have feelings that aren't at all suitable to a monitor. Even if Patrick comes and apologises – and I believe he'd rather lose his racket than do that – I shan't feel like accepting his apology. I might say something rude and begin the upset all over again.'

'Well, do,' said Julian, with a grin. 'I've no objection!'

'Come and have a game of tennis,' said Elizabeth. 'Let's slash out at the balls and work some of our crossness out of us. Come on!'

So out they went and were soon hitting the balls with a will. When they had finished they looked about for Patrick. Would he come and apologise? He must have seen the note in his desk by now.

But he was still nowhere to be seen!

CHAPTER FIVE

IN THE MIDDLE OF THE NIGHT

THE CHILDREN were allowed to take their tea into the garden that day and have little picnics in friendly groups. That was always fun. Elizabeth, Julian, John, Harry, Rosemary and Joan found a place in the shade by some bushes.

'Anyone seen Patrick?' asked Elizabeth, biting into bread and honey.

'Yes. I saw him coming out of our classroom,' said John. 'I don't know where he is now, though. Having tea by himself somewhere, I expect, brooding over his woes.'

'Oh, well, don't let's think about him any more,' said Elizabeth. 'He's keeping out of our way and I'm not surprised.'

They thought no more about Patrick. Elizabeth went back with the others to fetch her prep and do it out-of-doors that lovely warm evening. But it was difficult to learn French verbs when the swallows swooped and darted in the sky, and bees hummed happily in the flowers around. French verbs didn't go well with swallows and bees.

When they all went up to bed Elizabeth looked round once more for Patrick. She hated to go to bed without making up a quarrel, though she had often done so.

She called to Julian as he went to the boys' dormitory. 'Julian! See if Patrick is in your dormy.'

He wasn't. Julian began to feel a bit worried. Where was the idiot? Sulking somewhere? He debated whether or not to report that Patrick hadn't come up to bed. He decided that he wouldn't – not for a little while anyhow.

If I do report him, and he's hiding somewhere, waiting till we're all in bed because he's afraid of being jeered at, he'll get into more trouble, thought Julian. *And he'll think I've reported him just for that reason – to get him into a row. Blow him! Well, I'll get into bed, and wait till he comes before I go to sleep.*

He told this to John and Harry, who shared the dormitory with him and Patrick. They agreed to do the same as Julian – wait till Patrick came before they went to sleep. 'And we won't rag him at all,' said Harry.

'He's had a pretty poor day.'

But alas for their good resolve – every boy was fast asleep before five minutes had gone! The girls fell asleep too, but Elizabeth kept waking up and wondering about Patrick.

As she turned over for about the twelfth time, she thought she heard a rustling of paper. She sat up in bed and groped for what she had heard. Yes, there *was* a bit of paper somewhere in her bed. It must have slipped down there when she had got in. She pulled it out.

She put on her torch and read what was written there. It was a note from Patrick!

Elizabeth,

You can believe me or not, but I didn't *mean* to hit you, and I apologise for my racket slipping down on your shoulder like that. It was partly your fault for grabbing at it. I wish I hadn't blurted out about Julian's trick too, but I said it without thinking.

You won't be bothered with me any more. I'm fed up with Whyteleafe and I'm going away tonight as soon as it's dark. I'm going home. It was mean to take my racket away from me. I would have liked to take it with me. There's no use in staying at Whyteleafe – Julian is determined to outdo me in everything – but the tennis isn't fair, because I really *could* do well at that, and I might have got into the second team.

Nobody likes me now. I don't like anybody either, least of all you. I hope there's a good old upset about me running away – it will serve this beastly school right!

Patrick'

Elizabeth read this in the greatest horror. She sat staring at the letter in a panic. Patrick must have slid it under the sheet for her to find when she got into bed, and it had slipped down when she got in. What a pity she hadn't read it hours before – she might have stopped Patrick from being such an idiot as to run away!

She slipped on her dressing gown and went to Julian's dormitory. She put her head round the door and called softly, 'Julian! Julian!'

Julian was a light sleeper. He awoke at once. He went to the door. 'What are you doing here?' he said. 'You'll get into a frightful row.'

'It's about Patrick,' said Elizabeth. 'Come down into our classroom and read a note he's left in my bed. It's urgent, Julian.'

Julian put on his dressing gown and the two went down into their classroom. They did not dare to switch on the light, but shone their torches on to the note. Julian read it in dismay:

'I say! The fool! We'll have the police looking for him, and Whyteleafe in the papers, and there'll be a frightful disturbance,' he groaned. 'What in the world are we to do?'

'When do you suppose he went?' whispered Elizabeth. 'He wouldn't go till it was dark, would he? It can't have been dark very long because these summer nights are light for ages. Should we snoop around a bit and see if we can see anything of him?'

'We could. But he'll be gone,' said Julian, feeling most uncomfortable at the thought of having to go and wake Mr Johns and the two headmistresses, and show them the note. He began to feel that he hadn't come very well out of the affair himself. It was possible that the grown-ups might think him rather mean to have deliberately tried to outshine Patrick, and not give him a chance to make good at anything.

There was no sign of Patrick, so the two decided most reluctantly to go and tell someone in authority. They made their way down the back stairs of the school, meaning to go through to the hall and up the stairs to where the staff bedrooms were.

And then, as they went down the back stairs, they heard a sound. They stopped. What was that? Where did it come from?

'It's in the cupboard,' whispered Julian. 'Look – over there, where all the sports things are kept. But Patrick can't be there!'

Another sound came from the cupboard – a sound as if the door was being jiggled a little. The two crept up to it. The key was in the lock. Julian did not touch the key, but cautiously turned the handle. The door would not open. It was obviously locked on the outside.

'Whoever's in there is locked in,' whispered Julian. They looked at one another. 'It can't be Patrick. He wouldn't go to this cupboard – it's only got spare sports things in.'

Julian spoke quietly at the crack of the door. 'Who's in here?'

A voice answered at once. 'Who's that? I'm locked in here. I'm Patrick. Let me out.'

Elizabeth clutched at Julian joyfully. So Patrick hadn't gone! Julian was glad too. He put his mouth to the crack again.

'Patrick. It's me, Julian – and Elizabeth's here too. We found your note just now. You're an idiot. We are idiots too, so we're quits.'

There was a silence. 'You let me out at once,' came Patrick's voice, rather shaky.

'All right, on one condition,' said Julian. 'Do you promise to give up your mad idea of running off tonight, and will you go straight to bed?'

'No,' said Patrick.

'All right. We're off to bed,' said Julian.

A frantic voice came from inside the cupboard. 'Don't go! It's horrible in here – smelly and lonely and uncomfortable. Let me out. I won't run off. I promise.'

'How did you get locked in here?' asked Julian, still not turning the key.

'Well, I badly wanted to take my racket with me,' said Patrick's voice, 'and I didn't know where it had been hidden. So I looked everywhere. The last place I thought of was this old sports cupboard – but while I was looking someone came along, slammed the door and locked me in.'

'Matron, I expect,' said Julian. 'She's always slamming doors and locking them. Well, I'll let you out.'

He unlocked the door and shone his torch into the cupboard. Patrick was there, blinking, looking very tousled and untidy, and rather white in the face.

Elizabeth felt sorry for him. She slid her arm through his. 'Patrick! I know you didn't mean to hit me! Of *course* I know it. I think we all got silly and excited. We none of us behaved very well.'

'You didn't come to any meals,' said Julian, remembering. 'Aren't you hungry?'

'Yes,' said Patrick, going upstairs with them.

'Come and have some of my tuck then,' said Julian. 'But don't give me away, because we're not supposed to have food at night. Elizabeth, look the other way. Being a monitor, you can't approve!'

'Oh, dear, can't I? But I *do*,' said Elizabeth. 'Patrick, I'll give you back your racket. Julian, where have you hidden it?'

Julian whispered to her and she disappeared. The boys looked at one another. Julian shoved some more biscuits at Patrick. 'I don't *really* want to be in the second team,' said Julian in a casual, ordinary voice. 'I just thought I would be to show you I *could* be. But all this practising bores me. In any case you'll always be better than me in that. So go ahead.'

'Oh! Well, thanks,' said Patrick, seeing that this was Julian's way of patching up a quarrel. 'And *I* don't particularly want to work hard to be top of the form. You're welcome to that position. We'll – er – split our brains, shall we?'

'Not a bad idea,' said Julian, munching a biscuit himself. 'Easier for us both. Hallo, here's Elizabeth back again.'

Elizabeth came in with the racket. 'Here you are, Patrick – and don't you dare to hit me again with it!'

Patrick eagerly took his precious racket. Elizabeth suddenly realised what a tremendous lot he thought of it. She stared at him and he stared back. Then he suddenly smiled.

'Whatever would people think if they saw us all here, munching biscuits at this time of night!' he said. 'Now, don't you go reporting us at the next Meeting, Elizabeth!'

'Come on, we *must* go to bed!' said Julian, hearing a clock strike midnight. 'We shall all be bottom of the form if we go on like this – staying up till past midnight!'

They crept upstairs very quietly and said goodnight on the landing. Elizabeth got into bed, feeling at peace. Who would have thought things would turn out like this after all? Perhaps Patrick would settle down and be as proud of Whyteleafe as they all were.

Julian got into bed and was asleep at once. Patrick was in bed too, but he was rather uncomfortable: he had taken his racket with him, feeling that he really couldn't let it out of his sight now; and it was a very hard and knobbly bedfellow!

Whyteleafe School's not so bad, thought Patrick. *Julian's not so bad, either. And, as for Elizabeth, why, she's really quite nice. I'm very much afraid* – very *much afraid – I'm going to like her!*

BONUS BLYTON

Enid Blyton has been one of the world's best-loved storytellers for over seventy-five years. Her interest in writing began as a child, and before she loved receiving letters from the children who read her books, she enjoyed working with them as a teacher. *The Naughtiest Girl* stories are inspired by real schools and experiences. Turn the page to learn more about Enid as a child and as a teacher. Afterwards you might like to write about your school and teachers and the people in *your* class!

THE LIFE AND TIMES OF ENID BLYTON

11 August 1897	Enid Blyton was born in East Dulwich, London. Two brothers are born after her – Hanly (b. 1899) and Carey (b. 1902).
1911	Enid enters a children's poetry competition and is praised for her writing. She's on the path to becoming a bestselling author . . .
1916	Enid begins to train as a teacher in Ipswich. By the time she is 21, she is a fully qualified Froebel teacher, and starts work at a school in Kent.
1917	Enid's first 'grown-up' publication – three poems in *Nash's Magazine*.
June 1922	Enid's first book is published. It's called *Child Whispers*.
1926	Enid begins editing – and writes – the phenomenal *Sunny Stories for Little*

	Folks magazine. (She continues in this role for 26 years!)
1927	So vast is Enid's output that she has to learn to type. (But she still writes to children by hand.)
1931	Having married Hugh Pollock in 1924, the couple's first child, Gillian, is born. Imogen, their second daughter, was born in 1935.
1942	The Famous Five is launched with *Five on a Treasure Island.*
1949	The first appearance of *The Secret Seven* and of *Noddy* mark this year as special.
1953	Enid moves away from *Sunny Stories* to launch *Enid Blyton's Magazine.* She is now renowned throughout the world – she even established her own company, called Darrell Waters Limited (the surname of her second husband).
1962	Enid Blyton becomes one of the first and most important children's authors to be published in paperback. Now, she reaches even more readers than ever before.
28 November 1968	Enid dies in her sleep, in a nursing home in Hampstead.

WHAT THEY DID AT MISS BROWN'S SCHOOL

In 1920 Enid Blyton became a governess to the four Thompson children, whose ages ranged from four to ten. The family lived in Surbiton, in Surrey, in a house called 'Southernhay'. Enid had a small room which overlooked the garden, and it was there that she wrote many of her stories. Enid's tiny class often had lessons outdoors in the summer months.

Enid was very popular with her students, because her lessons were both practical and creative. She worked with them to put on performances for which they made props, costumes and invitations – and even sold tickets.

In 1941 she published a long story called 'What They Did at Miss Brown's School', which was divided into monthly episodes. It's been hard to find for many years, but you can read extracts in these new editions of *The Naughtiest Girl* books. The character of Miss Brown and her tiny class is very much based on Enid Blyton and her school at the Thompsons' . . .

Here are the next episodes . . .

4. April. Planning the School Garden

THE CHILDREN loved the soft, warm days of April when the sun shone from a brilliant sky, and great clouds like bunches of cotton wool swept overhead. Sometimes the rain poured down as the sun shone and then a rainbow arched itself among the clouds, and the children watched it in delight till it slowly faded.

They had been saving up for seed-buying, and one morning Miss Brown asked them to bring their money in to see how much they had. Miss Brown said she would buy the vegetable seeds herself – that would be her share.

'Oh, are we going to grow vegetables too?' asked Susan in delight. 'As well as planting the beans and peas we grew in our germinators?'

'Oh, yes,' said Miss Brown. 'We must have some lettuces and some radishes, and we will plant some mustard and cress again too – plenty of it, so that we can have it for tea three or four times.'

Well, that afternoon the four children went shopping with their teacher. They were excited, because they had been looking out for seed packets and they had seen such a lot in the shops, all so colourful and bright, with pictures of flowers on the front.

'Now we must *not* buy cheap seeds,' said Miss Brown. 'That is quite certain. It always pays, in gardening, to buy the best we can afford, because then we shall get finer flowers and better vegetables.'

So they asked the man at the shop which were his *best* seeds, and he showed them the packets. There were so many, of all sorts and kinds, that the children simply didn't know which to choose. So Miss Brown had to help them.

'No, don't have wallflowers,' she said. 'They would not flower till next year. No, Susan, it's no use looking longingly at sweet williams – they wouldn't flower till next year either. You want *annuals*. Look for annuals – seeds that will flower this same year – not biennials, which will only flower the second year.'

So then the children examined the packets carefully and looked for the word 'annuals'. The shopman helped them.

'You can have Shirley poppies, and what pretty things they are,' he said. 'Or here is candytuft, as sweet as its name. And there's marigold that will grow anywhere, and nasturtium which isn't particular either. And clarkia that Miss Brown will love for cutting. And you should really have this Virginian stock to edge your little garden – it grows as thick as grass, and is as pretty as a picture!'

'Oh, Mr Millet, we don't know *which* to have!' said the children. 'Which shall we choose, Miss Brown?'

'Whichever you like!' laughed Miss Brown. 'Hurry up and choose – I'm going to buy my radish seed.'

'Now, see here,' said Mr Millet the shopman, in a low voice, as Miss Brown went to another counter. 'I happen to know that Miss Brown likes a sweet smell – so what about a little mignonette? She'll love a bit of that in the classroom when it's out. And she's very fond of cornflowers too.'

'Well, we'll have both of those then,' said Mary at once, for she was fond of Miss Brown and wanted to please her. 'Look, Mr Millet – here is all the money we have. How many packets will it buy?'

Mr Millet counted it. 'Oh, quite a lot of packets,' he said. 'You choose which you'd like and I'll see if your money will buy them all.'

So this is what they chose – Virginian stock, marigolds, nasturtiums that climbed, cornflowers, Shirley poppies, clarkia, mignonette and candytuft.

'Yes, you can have all those,' said Mr Millet, counting

the packets. 'And one more too. Look, here is love-in-a-mist, a pretty blue flower that grows in a mist of fine green leaves – or what about giant sunflowers? They grow taller than I am, and will give you seeds for the birds in the winter.'

'Oh, giant sunflowers, please!' said the children at once. So the nine packets were wrapped up, and then Miss Brown had to hear all about them. She showed them her packets – one of mustard, one of cress, one of radishes and one of lettuce. 'What fun we are going to have!' they all said, as they went out of the shop.

'We will have a look at the garden this afternoon,' said Miss Brown, 'and decide what we must do before we plant our seeds.'

So they had a look at it. Miss Brown had dug it over in the autumn, but it now looked untidy and full of weeds.

'It wants raking and weeding well,' said Miss Brown. 'Who will come after tea and help?'

'I will!' shouted everybody. And everybody came. They took out every weed, and then John raked the whole bed with Miss Brown's big rake. Soon it was smooth and soft, ready for the seeds. The frost had got into the earth and had broken it into powder. Now it was fine and dry in the April sun.

'We will wait for a shower and then plant our seeds

when the ground is moist,' said Miss Brown.

The very next morning there was a sharp shower. Mary looked out into the garden. 'Miss Brown!' she cried, 'The garden looks just right for planting!'

'I believe it is!' said Miss Brown. 'Come along out and bring your seeds.'

They all trooped out joyfully. Miss Brown stopped and looked at the seed packets. 'Please sort these packets out into low-growing plants and taller ones,' she said to John. 'It is no use our putting giant sunflowers at the front and the tiny Virginian stock at the back!'

It wasn't long before the children decided that the Virginian stock must come right at the front for an edging. The mignonette and candytuft could come just behind, for they did not grow very tall. The marigolds could go in that row too. Then must come the cornflowers, the Shirley poppies and the clarkia. At the back would be the nasturtiums climbing up Miss Brown's trellis, and also the big sunflowers.

'That should make a lovely bed,' said Miss Brown. 'Now we'd better begin at the back. John, the giant sunflower seeds must be planted one by one, please, in holes that you can make with this tool called a dibber.'

John took the pointed piece of wood called a dibber, and dibbed holes at the back of the bed. He dropped a sunflower seed into each one and covered them up. They were large, long, flattish seeds. Then Mary was told to plant the nasturtium seeds so that they could climb up the trellis. She had to plant those one by one too, for they were large and rounded.

John was sent to write wooden labels for all the seeds while some more were being planted. He came out with a pencil and sat down on Miss Brown's barrow to write the wooden labels.

Then Peter was told to plant the Shirley poppies and the clarkia in one long row. Miss Brown showed him how to make a shallow drill or furrow with a stick. Then he shook the seeds very carefully out of the packet of poppies, and then out of the clarkia packet.

'If the wind happens to blow, just wait a minute,' said Miss Brown. 'We don't want our seeds blown all over the garden.'

Susan planted the cornflowers, and then the others planted the rest of the seeds – Virginian stock all along the front edge, and candytuft, marigolds and mignonette separately behind. John produced the labels, and each row or patch was labelled correctly.

Then Miss Brown went to her little vegetable bed, and the children helped her to plant the lettuce seeds, the radishes and the mustard. She said she would plant the mustard two days later because it took a shorter time to grow than the cress.

'We will plant the cress in the shape of an S for Susan,' she said. 'It will be fun to see it growing into a green letter!'

'Susan sowed the Virginian stock very thickly,' said John. 'You told us not to shake the seeds out thickly, Miss Brown.'

'I know,' said Miss Brown. 'If people cannot sow seeds thinly, it is best to mix fine sand with the seeds and sow them mixed with that. But Virginian stock likes to be sown thickly, and it will make a lovely thick edging. We shall not thin its seedlings out at all.'

'What is thinning out?' asked Peter.

'Well,' said Miss Brown, 'you will find that, although you have sown your seeds as thinly as you could, the seedlings will come up too thickly, too close together – so we shall have to pull up a good many of them, because it is much better to have a few beautifully grown, strong plants than many poor weak ones. There will be plenty to do in our garden, Peter! We must water it if it gets dry. We must weed it – and we must thin out the seedlings.'

The children were most impatient to see their seeds grow, but it was not until two weeks had gone by that they saw the first hint of green in their flowerbed. The candytuft and Virginian stock pushed up first and the others followed quickly. The giant sunflowers and nasturtiums were last, but they grew very fast once they were up, and it was not long before the first nasturtium began to climb up the trellis.

The garden was the greatest fun! The children watered it when they came to school. They weeded it when it wanted weeding. They thinned out the thick seedlings carefully and watched the rest grow into sturdy and beautiful plants.

Miss Brown's mustard and cress grew well and, the first time it was ready to cut, Miss Brown asked the children to tea and gave them good thick sandwiches of the delicious green stuff. The lettuces grew too, and would soon be ready for salad, and the radishes grew large and red. The children tasted these and loved them, though Susan said hers had burnt a hole in her tongue, it was so hot!

The peas and beans they had grown came into flower and smelt very sweet.

And oh, what a joy it was when the flowers blossomed! The Virginian stock was a mass of pink, white and yellow. The poppies danced in all colours. The nasturtiums gave brilliant flowers for the classroom. The candytuft held up heads of red and pink and white, and the clarkia grew rosettes of red and pink and lasted for weeks in the schoolroom vases.

The marigolds bloomed on and on and on, and the

cornflowers were made into a bunch for Miss Brown's bedroom. The classroom smelt of mignonette every day when that quaint red-brown flower bloomed, and everyone loved it.

'Its name is French for "little darling" and it's a jolly good name!' said Mary, sniffing its fragrance.

'The giant sunflowers will be out soon,' said John. 'Miss Brown, one looks right over the wall! Their faces are simply enormous – as big as my dinner plate!'

'They will give us many seeds for the finches and sparrows!' said Miss Brown. 'We will save them and dry them when the flowers are over.'

'What fun we've had with our garden!' said Susan. 'I'd like to begin it all over again, Miss Brown.'

'Well, so you shall!' said Miss Brown, with a laugh. 'Every year you can begin again – that's what gardeners love, Susan!'

5. May. Having Fun with the Birds

THE FOUR children at Miss Brown's school all loved the birds. They loved hearing them practising their spring songs in February and March, they enjoyed watching for the first swallows and house martins in April, and they were most excited when they knew where a nest was.

'Miss Brown, couldn't we hang up a nesting box somewhere?' asked John. 'The garden is full of tits, and I am sure they would nest here if they had a proper box.'

'Well, we'll buy one,' said Miss Brown. 'They are quite cheap.'

'I've just had two shillings from one of my uncles,' said John. 'Would that buy a nesting box?'

'Oh, yes!' said Miss Brown. 'You shall go with me to buy it after tea, John.'

So John went proudly with Miss Brown to buy the nesting box. It had a little hole near the top for the tits to go in and out, and the overhanging lid could be lifted up and down so that John might see if any birds had begun to build later on.

'Where shall we put it?' said John next morning.

'Let's go into the garden and see,' said Miss Brown. So she and the children trooped out and had a good look around. There was a spruce fir tree not too far from the schoolroom window and Miss Brown stopped underneath it.

'This tree will do well,' she said. 'Now we will put the box under this bough here, close to the trunk – and we will make it face north-east, as driving rain seldom comes from that direction. Where's that big nail, John? Hammer it in.'

John hammered in the nail, and Miss Brown hung

up the box. It was brown, and matched the colour of the tree trunk. John lifted up the lid and peeped in.

'Nothing at all inside,' he said. 'Won't it be exciting when I lift up the lid and see a nest beginning to be made!'

'It will,' said Miss Brown, 'but you will have to remember that if you do too much peeping *then*, John, the birds may desert the nest.'

'Miss Brown, Miss Brown, when will the birds come and look at the box to see if it is a good nesting place!' cried Susan.

'Oh, today, I hope,' said Miss Brown.

'Can't we let them know we've put a fine nesting box here for them?' wondered Peter. 'Miss Brown! Why couldn't we hang a nice bone under the nesting box? Then the tits would be sure to find that and would look inside the box too.

'That's a very good idea, Peter,' said Miss Brown. She sent Peter for a bone and he hung it under the box. Then they all trooped indoors to lessons.

'I wish I could have a nesting box too,' sighed Peter. 'But I haven't any money. I suppose if I tried to make a nest and put it in a tree, it wouldn't be much good, would it, Miss Brown?'

'I'm afraid not,' said Miss Brown. 'But I will tell you what you can do, if you like, Peter – you can bring an old tin, or an old kettle to school and we will put it under the hedge at the bottom of the school garden. There are two robins hunting about there for a nesting place – maybe they will choose your kettle! They love to build in something like that, you know.'

'Oh, good!' said Peter, and when he arrived at school that afternoon he brought with him two tins, an old saucepan and a kettle too!

Everybody laughed. 'I'm surprised you didn't bring a coal scuttle and a dustbin as well!' said John.

'Well, I thought I'd give the birds a good choice of nesting places,' said Peter happily. 'May I choose my hiding places for them at playtime, Miss Brown?'

'Of course,' said Miss Brown. So at eleven o'clock the four children ran to look for good places to put the tins. Peter put one halfway up a hedge. He put the saucepan in a ditch. He put the other tin on a bank, and the kettle he threw among some nettles.

'There!' he said. 'Robins! Choose which you like to nest in – and mind you do choose one, or I shall be most disappointed.'

The two girls felt a little left out of all this, and they wondered how they could have fun with the birds too.

'What can *I* do?' said Mary.

'I will tell you something nice to do,' said Miss Brown. 'Yesterday, as I went along the lane I saw a post where cows rub themselves and sometimes leave their hairs. And, goodness me, how the birds were quarrelling about those hairs! Then a little further on I came to Farmer Straws' hen yard, and there were about twenty sparrows there squabbling over the few feathers that the hens had let fall. And . . .'

'But Miss Brown, what did they want the hairs and the feathers for?' interrupted Susan.

'They wanted them for a nest lining,' said Miss Brown. 'And while it is easy to find moss, roots, fibres, dead leaves and so on, to make the nests themselves, it is quite difficult to find the softer material for a lining – hair, wool, feathers and fluff.'

'What was the something nice you said I could do then?' asked Mary. 'Find some nest linings?'

'Yes,' said Miss Brown. 'I have an old net bag here in my desk. Look!' She pulled it out. 'Well, would you like to collect all the soft things you can, Mary, and fill the bag with them? It will be a lucky bag for the birds then and they can come and pull out whatever they want.'

'Oh, I'd simply love to do that!' cried Mary, pleased. 'I shall collect all the feathers I can – and ask Mummy for the fluff out of the carpet-sweeper each day – and get the wool off the hedges, where the sheep have scraped against it – and I can get the hairs out of my hairbrush!'

'And I'll give you mine too!' cried Susan.

'And my mother has been making a rug, and she has got lots of little bits of wool left over!' said Peter. 'You shall have those, Mary. Oh, your lucky bag will soon be full!'

Mary took the net bag home and crammed it full of all the soft things she could think of – hairs from everyone's brushes, strands of wool from her work basket, feathers from the hen run, wool from the brambles, fluff from the carpet-sweeper, snippings from the ragbag, and even hairs brushed out of her dog's coat.

The others brought things too and soon the bag was full of soft bits and was ready to put up. Miss Brown tied it flat to a branch of a tree near the window, and then the children kept an eye on it.

'Good gracious!' said Peter in the middle of the next lesson. 'There are seven birds on Mary's lucky bag already, Miss Brown. Do look!'

Everyone looked. There were three sparrows, a robin, two chaffinches and a hedge sparrow all pulling busily at the contents of the bag. The sparrows flew off with feathers. The robin took a mouthful of hairs. The chaffinches took the fluff from the sweeper and the hedge sparrow took a beakful of everything!

'Oh, isn't it a success!' said Mary, pleased. 'Oh, Miss Brown, isn't it funny to think that some of the nests round about are lined with my hairs! I like to think of that.'

'Miss Brown! There's a tit gone right into my nesting box!' cried John suddenly. 'I saw it. Oh, do you think it is going to nest there?'

'We'll see,' said Miss Brown. Then she suddenly saw that seven-year-old Susan was looking very red, as if she were going to cry. 'Whatever's the matter, Susan?' she asked.

'Everybody's done something for the birds except me,' said Susan, a tear rolling down her cheek.

'Oh, don't be silly, dear,' said Miss Brown. 'You are sharing everything with the others.'

'It isn't the same as having something all to myself,' said Susan. 'John's got his nesting box. Peter's got his tins and things. Mary's got her lucky bag. I've got nothing.'

'Well, you shall give the birds their bath,' said Miss Brown. 'I was thinking that now the hot weather is coming we must put out a bath for them. Have you anything at home that would do for a bath?'

'Miss Brown, Susan's mother has had a new sink put into her scullery!' cried John. 'Couldn't Susan have the old sink for a birdbath? We could dig a hole for it in the ground and put it there so that it looked like a little pond!'

Everyone was most excited about this, and after tea that day Susan's father wheeled the old sink to school, and dug a hole for it in the middle of the lawn. It just fitted the sink. Then Susan's father dug out a little narrow bed round the sink, and gave Susan a shilling to go and buy some double daisy plants to put round the sink.

'It looks exactly like a pond with flowers growing round it!' cried Susan, as she and Miss Brown planted the pink and white button daisies. 'Oh, I'm so happy, Miss Brown. I think I've got the nicest thing of all to do for the birds.'

'Well, you must keep your pond nicely filled with water,' said Miss Brown. 'Not too deep, or you won't get the smaller birds bathing in it.'

And now all the children were pleased because they were each having fun with the birds in their own way. A pair of tits were already nesting in John's box, and he lifted up the lid very gently to see how the nest was getting on. The box was soon half full of nesting material, mostly moss, and hairs taken from the lucky bag.

One of the greatest excitements was on the day that Peter went to examine his tins for the sixth time to see if any robin was nesting – and he found the kettle half full of dead leaves and moss. He spied a robin nearby with a leaf in its mouth and he rushed off to Miss Brown in delight.

'They've chosen the kettle, they've chosen the kettle!' he shouted. 'The robins are beginning to build.'

'Well, that's lovely,' said Miss Brown. 'We have tits building in John's nesting box, robins building in your old kettle, all the birds of the garden pulling treasures from Mary's lucky bag, and any amount of them splashing in Susan's birdbath all day long!'

'Yes, it's lovely,' said Susan happily. She was so proud of her bird pond. The double daisies had grown well around it, and the birds looked sweet, splashing away in the water, sending drops all over the daisies. The robin loved a bath and was always splashing there. The thrushes and blackbirds came every morning and evening. The chaffinches came when the bath was empty, and the sparrows hopped in and out all day long. It was the greatest fun to watch.

And there was more fun to come too, for both robin and tit laid eggs, and hatched them into tiny birds. How proud Peter and John were when they saw their young families hopping about the garden, learning to look after themselves!

'This is another thing we'll do every year!' said Mary. 'We'll always have fun with the birds in the springtime!'

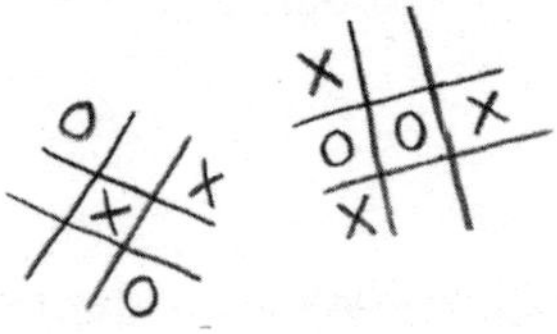

THE NAUGHTIEST GIRL QUIZ

If you've read all four of Enid Blyton's original stories about the naughtiest girl, then you will have no problem with this quiz by Tony Summerfield . . .

1. The uniform of Whyteleafe School is in which colours?
a) brown and orange
b) blue and silver
c) blue and yellow

2. Which boy looks after the gardens at Whyteleafe?
a) Martin Follett
b) John Terry
c) Julian Holland

3. What is the name of Elizabeth Allen's governess?
a) Miss Scott
b) Miss Thomas
c) Miss White

4. Who is the first-form teacher in *The Naughtiest Girl?*
a) Miss Ranger
b) Miss Stevens
c) Miss Timms

5. In *The Naughtiest Girl is a Monitor* who organises a midnight feast, but doesn't invite Elizabeth?
a) Arabella Buckley
b) Belinda Green
c) Helen Marsden

6. In *The Naughtiest Girl* books what is the name of the music master who takes Elizabeth for piano lessons?
a) Mr Johns
b) Mr Lewis
c) Mr Warlow

7. In *The Naughtiest Girl is a Monitor* what is the name of the Allen's cook?
a) Mrs Jenks
b) Mrs Marks
c) Mrs Tonks

8. In *The Naughtiest Girl Again* who is reprimanded at the meeting for not feeding her guinea pigs?
a) Dora
b) Doris
c) Dorothy

ANSWERS

1. a); 2. b); 3. a); 4. a); 5. a); 6. b); 7. a); 8. b)

THE NAUGHTIEST GIRL THROUGH THE YEARS . . .

1940

1962

1967

1971

1973

1979

1986

1999

2007

Enid Blyton®

THE FAMOUS FIVE

Join the Adventure!

Have you read them all?

Enid Blyton®

THE

SECRET SEVEN

SOLVE THE MYSTERY!

HAVE YOU READ THEM ALL?

THE MYSTERY SERIES

Read all 15 classic stories!

ENIDBLYTON.CO.UK

IS FOR PARENTS, CHILDREN AND TEACHERS!

Sign up to the newsletter on the homepage for a monthly round-up of news from the world of

Enid Blyton®

JOIN US ON SOCIAL MEDIA

EnidBlytonOfficial BlytonOfficial

Illustration by Laura Ellen Anderson.

Enid Blyton®

is one of the most popular children's authors of all time. Her books have sold over 500 million copies and have been translated into other languages more often than any other children's author.

Enid Blyton adored writing for children. She wrote over 700 books and about 2,000 short stories. *The Famous Five* books, now 80 years old, are her most popular. She is also the author of other favourites including *The Secret Seven*, *The Magic Faraway Tree* and *Malory Towers*.

Born in London in 1897, Enid lived much of her life in Buckinghamshire and loved dogs, gardening and the countryside. She was very knowledgeable about trees, flowers, birds and animals. Dorset – where some of the Famous Five's adventures are set – was a favourite place of hers too.

Enid Blyton's stories are read and loved by millions of children (and grown-ups) all over the world. Visit enidblyton.co.uk to discover more.

Illustration by Laura Ellen Anderson.

The NAUGHTIEST GIRL is a Monitor

Have you read them all?

1. The Naughtiest Girl in the School
2. The Naughtiest Girl Again
3. The Naughtiest Girl is a Monitor
4. Here's the Naughtiest Girl
5. The Naughtiest Girl Keeps a Secret
6. The Naughtiest Girl Helps a Friend
7. The Naughtiest Girl Saves the Day
8. Well Done, the Naughtiest Girl
9. The Naughtiest Girl Wants to Win
10. The Naughtiest Girl Marches On

Enid Blyton®

The NAUGHTIEST GIRL is a Monitor

HODDER

HODDER CHILDREN'S BOOKS

First published in Great Britain in 1945 by George Newnes
This edition published in 2021 by Hodder & Stoughton
For further information about the editorial history of this book,
see enidblyton.co.uk/books

3 5 7 9 10 8 6 4

Enid Blyton® and Enid Blyton's signature are registered
trade marks of Hodder & Stoughton Limited
Text © 2021 Hodder & Stoughton Limited
Illustrations by Claire Powell © 2021 Hodder & Stoughton Limited

No trade mark or copyrighted material may be reproduced without the
express written permission of the trade mark and copyright owner.

The moral right of the author has been asserted.

All characters and events in this publication, other than those clearly in the public domain, are fictitious and any resemblance to real persons, living or dead, is purely coincidental.

All rights reserved.
No part of this publication may be reproduced, stored in a retrieval system, or transmitted, in any form or by any means, without the prior permission in writing of the publisher, nor be otherwise circulated in any form of binding or cover other than that in which it is published and without a similar condition including this condition being imposed on the subsequent purchaser.

A CIP catalogue record for this book is available from the British Library.

ISBN 978 1 444 95862 1

Typeset by Avon DataSet Ltd, Arden Court, Alcester, Warwickshire

Printed and bound in Great Britain by Clays Ltd, Elcograf S.p.A.

The paper and board used in this book are made
from wood from responsible sources.

MIX
Paper | Supporting
responsible forestry
FSC® C104740

Hodder Children's Books
An imprint of Hachette Children's Group
Part of Hodder & Stoughton
Carmelite House
50 Victoria Embankment
London EC4Y 0DZ

An Hachette UK Company
www.hachette.co.uk
www.hachettechildrens.co.uk

CONTENTS

INTRODUCTION

by Cressida Cowell

bestselling author of the
How to Train Your Dragon series

Like so many, many children before and after me, Enid Blyton's books played a crucial role in turning my nine-year-old self into a passionate reader.

That is because Enid Blyton had an extraordinary knack for writing the kind of books that children actually *want* to read, rather than the kind of books that adults think they *should* read.

Enid Blyton could tap into children's dreams, children's desires, children's wishes, with pinpoint accuracy. She knew that every child, however good and well-behaved they might look on the outside, secretly longed to be Elizabeth Allen, the naughtiest kid in the school. I'm afraid I entirely cheered Elizabeth on, as she defied her parents, the headmistresses, her schoolmates, and the very serious School Meetings. If anything, I wanted her to be even naughtier.

But *The Naughtiest Girl* books were really my favourite of Enid Blyton's school stories because of Whyteleafe, a very different school from Malory Towers or St Clare's. What if there could be a school in which discipline was administered by the children rather than the adults? In which all money was given in at the start of the term and distributed among the children along socialist lines? Wouldn't this be the kind of school that children would actually *want* to go to, rather than the kind of school that children *have* to go to?

It was an interesting proposition to a nine-year-old, and it remains an interesting proposition.

I hope you enjoy this story as much as I did when *I* was nine years old.

Cressida Cowell

CHAPTER ONE

ARABELLA COMES TO STAY

IT WAS in the middle of the Christmas holidays that Mother sprang a surprise on Elizabeth. Christmas was over, and Elizabeth had been to the pantomime and the circus, and to three parties.

Now she was beginning to look forward to going back to boarding school again. It was dull being an only child, now that she had got used to living with so many girls and boys at Whyteleafe School. She missed their laughter and their chatter, the fun and games they had together.

'Mother, I love being at home, but I do miss Kathleen and Belinda and Nora and Harry and John and Richard,' she said. 'Joan has been over here to see me once or twice, but she's got a cousin staying with her now, and I don't expect I'll see her any more these hols.'

Then Mother gave Elizabeth a surprise.

'Well,' she said, 'I knew you would be lonely – so I have arranged for someone to come and keep you company for the last two weeks of these holidays, Elizabeth.'

'Mother! Who?' cried Elizabeth. 'Somebody I know?'

'No,' said Mother. 'It is a girl who is to go to Whyteleafe School next term – a girl called Arabella Buckley. I am sure you will like her.'

'Tell me about her,' said Elizabeth, still very surprised. 'Why didn't you tell me this before, Mother?'

'Well, it has been decided in a hurry,' said Mother. 'You know Mrs Peters, don't you? She has a sister who has to go to America, and she does not want to take Arabella with her. So she wanted to put the child into a boarding school for a year, perhaps longer.'

'And she chose Whyteleafe School!' said Elizabeth. 'Well, it's the best school in the world, *I* think!'

'That's what I told Mrs Peters,' said Mother. 'And she told her sister – and Mrs Buckley at once went to see the headmistresses, Miss Belle and Miss Best . . .'

'The Beauty and the Beast,' said Elizabeth, with a grin.

'And it was arranged that Arabella should go to Whyteleafe this term,' went on Mother. 'As Mrs Buckley had to leave for America almost at once, I offered to have Arabella here – partly as company for you, and partly so that you might be able to tell her a little about Whyteleafe.'

'Mother, I do hope she's a decent sort of girl,' said Elizabeth. 'It will be fun sharing hols with someone I like, but awful if it's someone I don't like.'

'I have seen Arabella,' said Mother. 'She was a very pretty girl with most beautiful manners and she was dressed very nicely too.'

'Oh,' said Elizabeth, who was often untidily dressed, and was sometimes too impatient to have very good manners. 'Mother, I don't think I like the sound of her *very* much. Usually beautifully-dressed girls aren't much good at games and things like that.'

'Well, you'll see,' said Mother. 'Anyway, she is coming tomorrow – so give her a good welcome and tell her as much about Whyteleafe as you can. I am sure she will love it.'

Elizabeth couldn't help looking forward to Arabella coming, even if she did sound rather goody-goody. She put flowers into the room her new friend was to have, and put beside the bed some of her own favourite books.

It will be rather fun to tell someone all about Whyteleafe School, she thought. *I'm so proud of Whyteleafe. I think it's marvellous. And oh – I'm to be a* monitor *next term!*

Impatient, hot-tempered Elizabeth had actually been

chosen to be a monitor for the coming term. It had been a great surprise to her, and she had been happier about that than about anything else in her life. She had often thought about it in the holidays, and planned how good and trustworthy and wise she would be next term.

'No quarrels with anyone – no bad tempers, no silly flare-ups!' said Elizabeth to herself. She knew her own faults very well. Indeed, all the children at Whyteleafe knew their faults, for it was part of the rule of the school that every child should be helped with their faults – and how could anyone be helped if those faults were not known?

The next day Elizabeth watched from the window for Arabella to come. In the afternoon a rather grand car drew up at the front door. The chauffeur got out and opened the car door – and out stepped someone who looked more like a little princess than a schoolgirl!

'Golly!' said Elizabeth to herself, and thought of her own school tunic of navy blue with its bright yellow badge. 'Golly! I shall never be able to live up to Arabella!'

Arabella was dressed in a beautiful blue coat with a white fur collar. She wore white fur gloves and a round white fur hat on her fair curls. Her eyes were very blue indeed and had dark lashes that curled up. She had a rather haughty look on her pink-and-white face as she stepped out of the car.

She looked at Elizabeth's house as if she didn't like it very much. The chauffeur rang the bell, and put a trunk and a bag down on the step.

Elizabeth had meant to rush down and give Arabella a hearty welcome. She had decided to call her 'Bella' because she thought Arabella rather a silly name – *like a doll's name*, thought Elizabeth. But somehow she didn't feel like calling her 'Bella' now.

Arabella suits her better after all, thought Elizabeth. *She* is *rather like a doll with her golden curls and blue eyes, and lovely coat and hat. I don't think I like her. In fact, I think I feel a bit afraid of her!*

This was strange, because Elizabeth was rarely afraid of anything or anyone. But she had never before met anyone quite like Arabella Buckley.

Although she's not much older than I am, she looks rather grown-up, and she walks like a grown-up – all proper – and I'm sure she talks like a grown-up too! thought Elizabeth. *Oh dear, I don't want to go down and talk to her.*

So she didn't go down. The maid opened the door – and then Mrs Allen, Elizabeth's mother, came hurrying forward to welcome the visitor.

She kissed Arabella, and asked her if she had had a tiring journey.

'Oh, no, thank you,' said Arabella in a clear, smooth voice. 'Our car is very comfortable, and I had plenty of sandwiches to eat halfway here. It is so kind of you to have me here, Mrs Allen. I hear you have a girl about my age.'

'Yes,' said Mrs Allen. 'She ought to be down here giving you a welcome. She said she would be. Elizabeth! Elizabeth, where are you? Arabella is here.'

So Elizabeth had to go down. She ran down the stairs in her usual manner, two at a time, landing with a bump at the bottom. She held out her hand to Arabella, who seemed a little surprised at her very sudden appearance.

'Do come down the stairs properly,' said Mrs Allen. It was a thing she said at least twelve times a day. Elizabeth never seemed able to remember to go anywhere quietly. Mrs Allen hoped that this nice, well-mannered Arabella would teach Elizabeth some of her own quietness and politeness.

'Hallo,' said Elizabeth, and Arabella held out a limp hand for her to shake.

'Good afternoon,' she said. 'How do you do?'

Gracious! thought Elizabeth, *I feel as if she's Princess High-and-Mighty come to pay a call on one of her poor subjects. In a minute she'll be offering me a bowl of hot soup or a warm shawl.*

Still, it might be that Arabella was only feeling shy. Some people did go all stiff and proper when they felt shy. Elizabeth thought she had better give Arabella a chance before making up her mind about her.

After all, I'm always making up my mind about people – and then having to unmake it because I am wrong, thought the little girl. *I've made an awful lot of mistakes about people at Whyteleafe School in the last two terms. I'll be careful now.*

So she smiled at Arabella and took her up to her room to wash and have a talk.

'I expect you didn't like saying goodbye to your mother when she went off to America,' said Elizabeth in a pleasant voice. 'That was bad luck. But it's good luck for you to be going to Whyteleafe School. I can tell you that!'

'I shall be able to judge whether it is or not when I get there,' said Arabella. 'I hope to goodness there are decent children there.'

'Of course there are – and, if they are horrid when they first come, we soon make them all right,' said Elizabeth. 'We had one or two boys who were awful, but now they are my best friends.'

'Boys! Did you say *boys*!' said Arabella in the greatest horror. 'I thought this was a girls' school I was going to. I hate boys!'

'It's a mixed school – boys and girls together,' said Elizabeth. 'It's fun. You won't hate boys after a bit. You soon get used to them.'

'If my mother had known there were boys at the school, I am sure she would not have sent me,' said Arabella in a tight, prim little voice. 'Rough, ill-mannered creatures – dirty and untidy, with shouting voices!'

'Oh, well, even the girls get dirty and untidy sometimes,' said Elizabeth patiently, 'and as for shouting – you should just hear *me* when I'm watching a school match!'

'It sounds a terrible school to me,' said Arabella. 'I had hoped Mother would send me to Grey Towers, where two of my friends had gone – it's such a nice school. They all have their own pretty bedrooms and wonderful food. In fact, the girls are treated like princesses.'

'Well, if you think you'll be treated like a princess at Whyteleafe, you'll jolly well find out you're wrong!' said Elizabeth sharply. 'You'll be treated as what you are – a little girl like me, with lots of things to learn! And, if you put on any airs there, you'll soon be sorry, let me tell you that, Miss High-and-Mighty!'

'I think you are very rude, considering that I am a visitor, and have only just come,' said Arabella, looking down her nose in a way that made Elizabeth feel very angry. 'If that's the sort of manners they teach you at Whyteleafe, I am quite sure I shan't want to stay there more than a term.'

'I jolly well hope you don't stay a week!' said hot-tempered Elizabeth at once. She was sorry the moment after.

'Oh dear!' she said to herself. 'What a bad beginning! I really must be careful!'

CHAPTER TWO

OFF TO WHYTELEAFE SCHOOL AGAIN

ARABELLA AND Elizabeth did not mix well at all. There was nothing that Elizabeth liked about Arabella, and it seemed that Elizabeth was everything that Arabella most despised and hated.

Unfortunately Mother liked Arabella – and certainly the little girl had most beautiful manners. She always stood up when Mrs Allen came into the room, she opened and shut the door for her, and fetched and carried for her in a very kind and polite manner.

The politer Arabella was, the noisier Elizabeth became. And then Mrs Allen began to say things that made Elizabeth cross.

'If only you had as nice manners as Arabella, dear! I do wish you would come into a room more quietly! And I wish you would wait till I have finished speaking before you interrupt . . .'

All this made Elizabeth rather sulky. Arabella saw it and, in her smooth, polite way, she enjoyed making the differences between her and Elizabeth show up very clearly.

A week went by. Everyone in the house by this time liked Arabella, even Mrs Jenks, the rather fierce cook.

'She only likes you because you suck up to her,' said Elizabeth when Arabella came up from the kitchen to say that Mrs Jenks was making her very favourite cake for her that afternoon.

'I don't suck up to her,' said Arabella in her usual polite tones. 'And I do wish, Elizabeth, that you wouldn't use such unladylike words. *Suck up!* I think it's a very ugly saying.'

'Oh, shut up,' said Elizabeth rudely.

Arabella sighed. 'I wish I wasn't going to Whyteleafe. If you're the sort of girl they have there, I'm not going to like it at all.'

Elizabeth sat up. 'Look here, Arabella,' she said, 'I'm just going to tell you a bit about my school, then you'll know exactly what you're in for. You *won't* like it – and the school won't like you. So it's only fair to prepare you a bit, so that you don't feel too awful when you get there.'

'All right. Tell me,' said Arabella, looking rather scared.

'Well, what I'm going to tell you would please most children,' said Elizabeth. 'It's all so sensible and fair and kind. But I dare say a Miss High-and-Mighty like you will think it's all dreadful.'

'Don't call me that,' said Arabella crossly.

'Well, listen! At Whyteleafe we have a head boy and a head girl. They are called William and Rita, and they are fine,' said Elizabeth. 'Then there are twelve monitors.'

'Whatever are they?' asked Arabella, wrinkling up her nose as if monitors had a nasty smell.

'They are boys and girls chosen by the whole school as leaders,' said Elizabeth. 'They are chosen because we trust them, and know them to be kind and just and wise. They see that we keep the rules, they keep the rules themselves, and they help Rita and William to decide what punishments and rewards the children must have at each weekly Meeting.'

'What's the weekly Meeting?' asked Arabella, her blue eyes round with surprise.

'It's a kind of school parliament,' said Elizabeth, enjoying telling Arabella all these things. 'At each Meeting we put into the moneybox any money we have had that week – that's the rule . . .'

'What! Put our own money into a school moneybox!' said Arabella in horror. 'I have a lot of money. *I* shan't do that! What a mad idea.'

'It seems mad at first if you're not used to it,' said Elizabeth, remembering how she had hated the idea two terms ago. 'But actually it's a very good idea. You see, Arabella, it doesn't do for one or two of us to have pounds and pounds to spend at school – and the rest of us only a few shillings. That's not fair.'

'I think it's quite fair,' said Arabella, knowing that she would be one of the few very rich ones.

'Well, it isn't,' said Elizabeth. 'What we do is – we all put our money in, and then we are each given two shillings out of the box, to spend as we like. So we all have the same.'

'Only two shillings!' said Arabella, looking quite horrified.

'Well, if you badly want some more, you have to tell the head boy and girl, and they will decide whether you can have it or not,' said Elizabeth.

'What else do you do at the Meeting?' asked Arabella. 'I think it all sounds dreadful. Don't the headmistresses have a say in anything?'

'Only if we ask them,' said Elizabeth. 'You see, they like us to make our own rules, plan our own punishments and give our own rewards. For instance, Arabella, suppose you are too high-and-mighty for anything, well, we would try to cure you by—'

'You won't try to cure me of anything,' said Arabella

in a very stiff tone. 'You're the one that ought to be cured of a lot of things. I wonder the monitors haven't tried to cure you before now. Perhaps they will this term.'

'I've been chosen to *be* a monitor,' said Elizabeth proudly. 'I shall be one of the twelve jurymen, sitting up on the platform. If a complaint is made about *you* by anyone, I shall have power to judge it and say what ought to be done with you.'

Arabella went very red. 'The very idea of a tomboy like you judging *me*!' she said. 'You don't know how to walk properly, you don't know your manners and you laugh much too loudly.'

'Oh, be quiet,' said Elizabeth. 'I'm not prim and proper like you. I don't suck up to every grown-up I meet. I don't pretend, and put on airs and graces and try to look like a silly, beautifully dressed doll who says "Ma-ma" when you pull a string!'

'Elizabeth Allen, if I were like you, I'd throw something at your head for saying that!' said Arabella, standing up in a rage.

'Well, throw it then,' said Elizabeth. 'Anything would be better than being such a good-little-girl, Mummy's-precious-darling!'

Arabella went out of the room, and so far forgot her manners as to slam the door, a thing she had never done in her life before. Elizabeth grinned. Then she looked thoughtful.

'Now,' she said to herself, 'you be careful, Elizabeth Allen. You're very good at making enemies, but you know quite well that leads to nothing but rows and unhappiness. Arabella's an idiot – a conceited, silly, empty-headed doll – but you let Whyteleafe deal with her, and don't try to cure her all at once by yourself. Try to be friends and help her.'

So Elizabeth tried to forget how much she disliked vain little Arabella and her doll-like clothes and manners, and treated her in as friendly a manner as she could. But she was very glad indeed when the day came for her to return to school. It was dreadful to have no other companion but Arabella. At Whyteleafe she would have dozens of others round her, all talking and laughing. She need never speak to Arabella unless she wanted to.

She's older than I am, and perhaps she will be in a higher form, she thought, as she put on her school uniform with delight. It was a nice uniform. The coat was dark blue with a yellow edge to the collar and cuffs. The hat was also dark blue, and had a yellow band. On her legs Elizabeth wore long brown stockings and brown lace-up shoes on her feet.

'How I hate these dark school clothes,' said Arabella in disgust. 'What a dreadful uniform! Now at Grey

Towers, the school I wanted to go to, the girls are allowed to wear anything that suits them.'

'How silly,' said Elizabeth. She looked at Arabella. The girl seemed different now that she was in the ordinary school uniform, and not in her expensive, well-cut clothes. She looked more like a schoolgirl and less like a pink-faced doll.

'I like you better in your uniform,' said Elizabeth. 'You look more real somehow.'

'Elizabeth, you do say extraordinary things,' said Arabella in surprise. 'I'm as real as you are.'

'I don't think you are,' said Elizabeth, looking hard at Arabella. 'You're all hidden away behind airs and graces, and good manners and sweet speeches, and I don't know if there is a real You at all!'

'I think you're silly,' said Arabella.

'Girls! Are you ready?' called Mrs Allen. 'The car is at the door.'

They went downstairs, carrying their small night-bags. Each girl had to take a small bag with the things in it that she would need for the first night, such as a nightdress, toothbrush, and so on, for their big trunks were not unpacked till the next day.

They carried lacrosse and hockey sticks, though Arabella had said she hoped she wouldn't have to play either game. She hated games.

They caught the train up to London, and at the big station there they met the girls and boys returning to their school. Miss Ranger, Elizabeth's form mistress, was there, and she welcomed Elizabeth.

'This is Arabella Buckley,' said Elizabeth. All the boys and girls turned round to look at Arabella. How new and spick and span she looked. Not a hair out of place, no wrinkles in her brown stockings, no smut on her cheek!

'Hallo, Elizabeth!' cried Joan, and put her arm through her friend's.

'Hallo, Elizabeth! Hallo, Elizabeth!'

One by one all her friends came up, smiling, delighted to see the girl who had once been the naughtiest in the school. Harry clapped her on the back and so did Robert. John asked her if she had done any gardening. Kathleen came up, rosy-cheeked and dimpled. Richard waved to her as he carried a violin case to the train.

Oh, it's lovely to be back with them all again, thought Elizabeth. *And this term – this term I'm to be a monitor! And won't I be a success! I'll make that stuck-up Arabella look up to me all right!*

'Get in the train quickly!' called Miss Ranger. 'Say goodbye, and get in.'

The guard blew his whistle. The train puffed out. They were off to Whyteleafe once more.

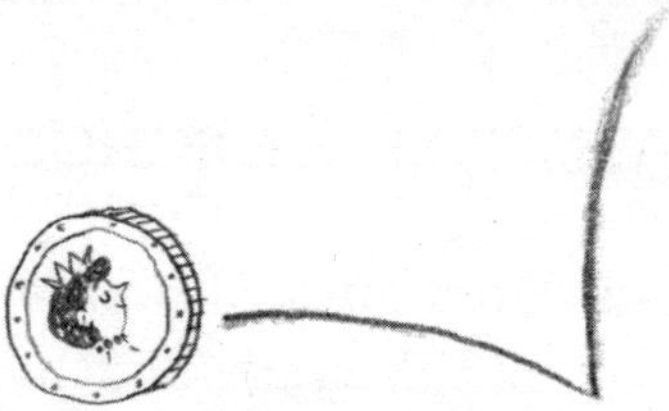

CHAPTER THREE

FOUR NEW CHILDREN

ONE OF the exciting things about a new term is – are there any new children? What are they like? Whose form will they be in?

All the old children looked to see who was new. Arabella was, of course. Then there were three more, two of them boys, and one a girl.

Elizabeth, as a monitor, made it her business to make the new children feel at home. As soon as they arrived at Whyteleafe, she set things going.

'Kathleen, show Arabella her dormitory, and tell her the rules. I'll help the other three. Robert, will you give a hand too? You will have two new boys to see to today.'

'Right,' said Robert, grinning. He had grown in the holidays and was tall and burly now. He was glad to be back at school, for at Whyteleafe were the horses he loved so much. He hoped that he would be allowed to take charge of some of them, as he had been the term before.

Elizabeth turned to the new children. Arabella had already gone off with Kathleen, looking rather scared. The other three new ones stood together, one boy making rather a curious noise, like a hen clucking.

'That's just like a hen clucking,' said Elizabeth. 'You sound as if you've laid an egg!'

The boy grinned. 'I can imitate most animals,' he said. 'My name's Julian Holland. What's yours?'

'Elizabeth Allen,' said Elizabeth. She looked at the new boy with interest. He was the untidiest person she had ever seen. He had long black hair that fell in a wild lock over his forehead, and his eyes were deep green, and brilliant, like a cat's. 'He looks jolly clever,' said Elizabeth to herself. 'I bet he'll be top of the class if he's with Miss Ranger.'

The boy made a noise like a turkey gobbling. Mr Lewis, the music master, was passing by, and looked round, startled. Julian at once made a noise like a violin being tuned, which made Mr Lewis hurry into the nearest music practice room, thinking that someone must be there with a violin.

Elizabeth gave a squeal of laughter. 'Oh! You *are* clever! I hope you're in my form.'

The other boy, Martin, was quite different. He looked

very clean and neat and tidy. His hair was well brushed back from his forehead, and his eyes were a very clear blue. They were set a little close together, but they had a very wide and innocent expression. Elizabeth liked him.

'I'm Martin Follett,' he said in a pleasant voice.

'And I'm Rosemary Wing,' said the new girl, rather shyly. She had a pretty little face, with a smiling mouth, but her eyes were rather small, and she did not seem to like to look anyone full in the face. Elizabeth thought she must feel very shy. Well, she would soon get over that.

'Robert, you take Julian and Martin to the boys' dormitories,' she said, 'and I'll take Rosemary to hers. Hang on to them till they know their way about, won't you, and show them where they have their meals and things like that.'

'Right, Monitor,' said Robert, with another grin. Elizabeth felt proud. It was grand to be a monitor.

'Oh, are you a monitor?' asked Rosemary, trotting after Elizabeth. 'That's something very special, isn't it?'

'It is rather,' said Elizabeth. 'I'm *your* monitor, Rosemary. So, if ever you are in any difficulty or trouble, you must come to me and tell me – and I'll try and help you.'

'I thought we had to bring our troubles or complaints to the weekly Meeting,' said Rosemary. She had heard about this in the train that day.

'Oh, yes, but at first you had better tell *me* what you'd like to bring before the Meeting,' said Elizabeth, 'because, you see, we are only allowed to bring *proper* difficulties or complaints to the Meeting – not just tales. You might not know the difference between just telling tales and bringing a real complaint.'

'I see,' said Rosemary. 'That's a very good idea. I'll do that.'

She's a nice little thing, thought Elizabeth, as she showed Rosemary where to put her things and told her to put out her toothbrush, hairbrush and nightdress. 'By the way, Rosemary, we are only allowed to have six things out on our dressing tables, not more. You can choose what you like.'

It was fun to give out the rules like this. Elizabeth remembered how Nora, her own monitor two terms ago, had told *her* the rules – and how she had disobeyed them at once by putting out eleven things! She wondered now how she could have been so silly – how she could have dared!

'Yes, Elizabeth,' said Rosemary obediently and she counted the things to put out.

In the next dormitory Kathleen was having trouble with Arabella, who was very scornful about all the rules told her.

'Well, there are not many,' said Kathleen, 'and, after

all, we make the rules ourselves, so we ought to obey them, Arabella. I'll fetch Elizabeth here, if you like – she is the monitor and can tell you the rules properly.'

'I don't want to see Elizabeth,' said Arabella at once. 'I saw her quite enough in the holidays. I only hope I'm not in the same form.'

Kathleen had a great admiration for Elizabeth, although she had hated her part of the term before. She spoke up at once.

'You'd better not say things like that about our monitors. We choose them ourselves because we like and admire them. Anyway, it's bad manners to talk like that about somebody whose guest you have just been.'

Arabella had never in her life been accused of bad manners before. She went quite palc and could think of nothing to say. She looked at Kathleen and decided that she didn't like her. In fact, she didn't think she liked anyone at all so far, except that little pretty girl called Rosemary – the one who was new. Perhaps she could make friends with her. Arabella felt sure that Rosemary would be most impressed with her tales of wealth, rich clothes and marvellous holidays.

The next few days everyone settled down. A few were homesick, but Whyteleafe was such a sensible school and the children were so jolly and friendly that even new boys and girls found it hard to miss their homes.

There was laughter and chatter to be heard everywhere.

All the new children were in Elizabeth's class. Good! It was fun to have new children and, now that Elizabeth was a monitor, it was nice to impress Julian and the others. Joan had gone up into the next class, so Elizabeth was the only monitor in hers.

Miss Ranger, the form mistress, soon sized up the new children, and talked them over with Mam'zelle.

'Julian is a lazy boy,' she said. 'A pity, because I'm sure he has a wonderful brain. He thinks of plenty of clever things to do *outside* lessons. He can make simply anything with his hands. I saw him showing the others a little aeroplane he had made – it flies beautifully. All his own ideas are in it, none of them copied. He'll spend hours thinking out things like that – but not one minute will he spend on learning his geography or history!'

'Ah, that Julian,' said Mam'zelle in a tone of great disgust. 'I do not like him. Always he makes some extraordinary noise.'

'Noise?' said Miss Ranger in surprise. 'Well, I must say he hasn't tried out any extraordinary noises on me yet. But I dare say he will.'

'Yesterday, in my class, there was a noise like a lost kitten,' said Mam'zelle. '"Ah, the poor thing!" I said. "It has come into our big classroom and got lost." And for ten minutes I looked for it. But it was that boy Julian doing his mews.'

'Really?' said Miss Ranger, making up her mind that Julian would not do any mews or barks or whines in *her* class. 'Well, thanks for the tip. I'll look out for Julian's noises!'

The talk passed on to Arabella. 'A silly, empty-headed doll,' said Miss Ranger. 'I hope we can make something out of her. She really ought to be in the next class, but she is rather behind, so I must push her on a bit before she goes up. She seems to have a very high opinion of herself! She is always doing her hair or smoothing down her dress – or else trying to show us what perfect manners she has!'

'She is not bad, that one,' said Mam'zelle, who was quite pleased with Arabella because the girl had lived for a year in France and could speak French well. 'In my country, Miss Ranger, the children have better manners than the children here – and it is pleasant to see one with manners as good as Arabella's.'

'Hm,' said Miss Ranger, who knew that Mam'zelle would rarely have anything to say against children who spoke French well. 'What do you think of Martin – and Rosemary?'

'Oh, the sweet children!' said Mam'zelle, who loved Rosemary's willingness to please, and to obey her in everything. 'The little Martin now – he is so good; he tries so hard.'

'Well, I'm not so sure about him,' said Miss Ranger. 'Rosemary is all right, I think – but she's a weak little thing. I hope she'll make the right friends. I wish Elizabeth Allen or Jenny would make friends with her.'

So the teachers sized up their new children – and the old children sized them up too. Julian was an enormous success. He was a real daredevil, with most extraordinary gifts that he used when he pleased. He had a wonderful brain, inventive and brilliant, and he could make all kinds of things, and think of all kinds of amusing tricks which he was quite prepared to perform in class as soon as he had settled down a bit.

'It's a shame you are so low in the form, Julian,' said Elizabeth at the end of a week. 'You've got such marvellous brains. You ought to be top!'

Julian looked at her with his brilliant green eyes. 'Can't be bothered,' he said in his slow, deep voice. 'Who wants to learn history dates? I'll forget them all when I'm grown. Who wants to learn the highest mountains in the world? I'll never climb them, so I don't care. Lessons are a bore.'

Elizabeth remembered that she was a monitor. She spoke earnestly to Julian.

'Julian, do work hard. Do try to be top.'

Julian laughed. 'You're just saying that because you've remembered you're a monitor! You can't catch *me* with goody-goody talk like that! You'll have to think of some jolly good reason for me to work hard before I do!'

Elizabeth went red. She didn't like being called goody-goody. She turned away.

But Julian came after her. 'It's all right, I'm only teasing,' he said. 'Listen, Elizabeth – Joan, your best friend, has gone up into the next form so why can't *we* be friends? You've got the best brain in the form – after mine, of course – and you're fun. You be my friend.'

'All right,' said Elizabeth, rather proud that the brilliant and unusual Julian should ask her. 'All right. We'll be friends. It will be fun.'

It *was* fun – but it brought a lot of trouble too!

CHAPTER FOUR

THE SCHOOL MEETING

ARABELLA AND the other new children waited with much interest for the first Meeting. At none of their other schools had they had a kind of school parliament, run by the children themselves. They wondered what it would be like.

'It sounds a good idea,' said Martin.

'I think so too,' said Rosemary in her timid little voice. She always agreed with everyone, no matter what they said.

'Stupid idea, *I* think,' said Arabella. She made a point of running down everything at Whyteleafe if she could, because she had so badly wanted to go to the grand school her friends had gone to – and she looked down on Whyteleafe, with its sensible ideas.

Julian unexpectedly agreed with her, though he usually had no time for Arabella, with her silly airs and graces. 'I can't say *I* shall bother much about the School Meeting,' he said. 'I don't care what it says or does. It will never make any difference to me. As long as I can do what I like I am quite willing to let others do what *they* like too.'

'Oh, Julian – you say that, but you don't mean it,' said Kathleen. 'You'd hate it if someone broke one of the things you are always making, you know! Or told tales about you, or something like that. You'd go up in smoke!'

Julian did not like being argued with. He tossed his long black hair back, and screwed up his nose in the way he always did when he was annoyed. He was making a tiny boat out of an odd bit of wood. It was like magic to see it form under his hand.

'Anyone can tell tales of me as much as they like!' said Julian. 'I don't care about anything so long as I can do what I like.'

'You're a funny boy, I think,' said Jenny. 'You are either terribly stupid in class, or – just sometimes – terribly bright.'

'Why? What did he do that was so bright?' asked Joan, who was listening. She was in the next form, and so did not see Julian in class.

'We were having mental arithmetic,' said Jenny. 'And usually Julian gets every single thing wrong in maths. Well, for some reason or other – just because he wanted to show off, I think – he answered every single question right, straight off, almost before Miss Ranger had got them out of her mouth!'

'Yes, and Miss Ranger was so astonished,' said Belinda. 'She went on asking him harder and harder ones – things we would have to think about and work out in our heads for a minute or two – but Julian just answered them pat. It was funny.'

'It made Miss Ranger awfully cross with him next time, though,' said Kathleen, 'because, at the next maths lesson, he seemed to go to sleep and wouldn't answer a thing.'

Julian grinned. He really was an extraordinary boy. The others couldn't help liking him. He was so exciting. They all begged and begged him to make some of his amazing noises in Miss Ranger's class, but he wouldn't.

'She's watching out for them, I know she is,' he said. 'It's no fun doing them if people know it's me. It's *really* fun when people honestly think there's a kitten in the room – or something like that – like Mam'zelle did the other day. You wait. I'll give you some fun one day soon, but I'd like to choose the person myself to try my tricks on.'

Elizabeth was longing for the first School Meeting.

She wanted to go and sit up on the platform with the other monitors, in front of the whole school. She was not vain about being made a monitor, but she was rightly proud of it.

'It really is an honour,' she said to herself. 'It does mean that the school trusts me and thinks I'm worthwhile. Oh, I do hope this term will go well, without any upsets or troubles.'

The children filed into the big gym for the first Meeting. Then in came the twelve monitors, serious-faced. They took their places, and sat, like a thoughtful jury, in front of all the children. Arabella gazed at Elizabeth with dislike. Fancy that tomboy, with her bad manners, being made a monitor!

Then in came William and Rita, the head boy and girl, the Judges of the whole Meeting. All the children rose to their feet as they came in.

At the back sat Miss Belle and Miss Best, the two headmistresses, with Mr Johns, one of the masters. They were always interested in the Meetings, but, unless the head boy and girl asked them to, they did not enter into it in any way. This was the children's own parliament, where they made their own laws, their own rules, and where they themselves rewarded or punished any child who deserved it.

There was very little to talk about at that first

Meeting. Every child was told to put what money it had into the big school moneybox. Elizabeth looked with interest at Arabella, when she was sent round with the box. Would Arabella do as she had said and refuse to put in her money?

Arabella sat looking as if butter would not melt in her mouth. When the box came to her she put in a ten-shilling note and two separate shillings. She did not look at Elizabeth.

Most of the children had quite a lot of money to put into the box at the beginning of term. Parents, uncles and aunts had given them shillings, half-crowns and even notes to go back to school with, and the box felt nice and heavy when Elizabeth took it back to William and Rita.

'Thank you,' said William. The children were all talking together, and William knocked on the table with his little hammer. At once there was silence – except for a curious bubbling noise, like a saucepan boiling over.

It seemed to come from somewhere near Jenny, Julian and Kathleen. William looked rather astonished. He knocked again with his hammer, but still the noise went on, a little louder, if anything.

Elizabeth knew at once that it was one of Julian's extraordinary noises. She looked at him. He sat on the form, his green eyes looking over the heads of the others, his mouth and throat perfectly still. How *could* he do noises like that? Elizabeth felt a tremendous giggle coming and she swallowed it down quickly.

I mustn't giggle when I'm sitting up here as monitor, she thought. *Oh dear, I wish Julian would stop. It's just like a saucepan boiling over, but louder.*

By this time one or two children were giggling, and William knocked sharply with his hammer again. Elizabeth wondered if she ought to say that it was Julian who was making the noise and holding up the Meeting.

But I can't. He's my friend. And I'm not going to get him into trouble, even if I am *a monitor*, she thought. She tried to make Julian look at her, and he suddenly did. She glared at him, then frowned.

Julian made one last loud bubbling noise, and then stopped. William had no idea at all who had made the noise. He gazed round the Meeting.

'It may be funny to hold up the school Meeting *once*,' he said. 'But it would not be funny a second time. We will now get on with the money-sharing.'

Each child came up to take two shillings from the monitors, out of the school box. William had brought plenty of change with him, which he put into the box, taking out the notes instead.

When each child had their two shillings for spending, William spoke again.

'The new children probably know that out of this two shillings they must buy their own stamps, sweets, hair ribbons, papers, and so on that they want. If any extra money is needed, it can be asked for. Does anyone want any extra this week?'

John Terry stood up. He was in charge of the school garden, and was a very hard and very good worker. He, with those other children who helped him, managed to supply the school with fine vegetables and flowers. Everyone was proud of John.

'William, we could do with a new small barrow,' he said. 'You see, there are one or two of the younger children who are helping in the garden this term, and the old barrow is really too heavy for them.'

'Well, how much would a smaller one cost?' asked William. 'We've got plenty of money in the box at the moment, but we don't want to spend *too* much money.'

John Terry had a price list with him. He read out the prices of various barrows.

'They seem very expensive,' said William. 'I almost think we had better wait a bit to see if the younger children are going to go on being keen, John. You know what sometimes happens – they start so well, and then get tired of it. It would be a waste of a barrow if we bought it and then no one used it.'

John looked disappointed. 'Well,' he said, 'it's just as you like, William. But I do think the youngsters are keen. Peter is anyway. He worked hard last term, and I really couldn't do without him in the garden now. He's got his two friends with him now, helping us.'

Small Peter glowed red with pleasure at hearing John say this. His two small friends at once made up their minds that they would work hard in the garden too, and make John as proud of them as he seemed to be of Peter.

'Has anyone anything to say about a new barrow?' asked Rita. Nobody spoke – until Julian suddenly opened his mouth and spoke in his deep voice.

'Yes. Let the youngsters have their barrow, but I'll make it for them. I can easily do that.'

Julian had not stood up to speak. He lolled on the form in his usual lazy fashion.

'Stand up when you speak,' said Rita. Julian looked as if he was not going to. But at last he did, and then repeated his offer.

'I'll make a barrow, a small one. If I can go into the sheds, I can easily find everything I want. You don't need to spend any money then.'

Everyone was interested. Elizabeth spoke up eagerly.

'Let Julian do it, William! He's *awfully* clever at

making things. He can make *anything*!'

'Very well. Thank you for your offer, Julian,' said William. 'Get on with the job as soon as you can. Now – any other business to discuss?'

There was not. William closed the Meeting and the children filed out.

'Good, Julian!' said Elizabeth, slipping her arm through his. 'I bet you'll make the finest barrow in the world!'

CHAPTER FIVE

ARABELLA GETS INTO TROUBLE

ALL THE new children settled down as the days went on. Julian set about making the new barrow in a very workmanlike way. He explored the various sheds, and brought out an old rubber wheel that had once belonged to somebody's tricycle. He found some odd bits of wood and other odds and ends, and took them all to the carpentering room.

The children heard him whistling there as he hammered away. Then they heard the creaking of a barrow being wheeled up and down.

'Golly! Has he finished it already?' said Harry in surprise. 'He's a marvel!'

But he hadn't, of course. He was only making one of his noises. His green eyes twinkled as the children peeped round the door. He loved a joke.

The boys and girls crowded round him, exclaiming

in admiration.

'Julian! It's going to be a marvellous barrow! Julian, how clever you are!'

'No, I'm not,' said Julian, laughing. 'I was bottom of the form this week. Didn't you hear?'

'Well, the barrow is fine anyway,' said Belinda. 'It's just as good as a real one.'

Julian cared for neither praise nor blame. He had not offered to make the barrow because he was sorry that the youngsters hadn't one. He had offered to make it simply because he knew he could, and he would enjoy making it.

Julian was very well liked, for all his don't-care ways. But Arabella was not. She would make friends with no one but the little, meek Rosemary. Rosemary thought the lovely, well-mannered girl was like a princess. She followed her everywhere, listened eagerly to all she said and agreed with everything.

'I think this is a stupid school,' Arabella said to Rosemary many times. 'Think of the silly rules it has – all the sillier because they are made by the children themselves.'

Up till then Rosemary had thought that the reason the rules were so good was because they *had* been made by the boys and girls. But now she agreed with Arabella at once.

'Yes. They *are* silly.'

'Especially the one about putting all our money into the school moneybox,' said Arabella.

This had not mattered much to Rosemary, who had only had two shillings and sixpence to put in. Her parents were not very well off, and she had not been given much money at any time. Still, she agreed with Arabella, of course.

'Yes, that's a very silly rule,' she said. 'Especially for people like you, Arabella, who have to give up so *much* money. It's a shame. I saw you put in the ten-shilling note and the two shillings.'

Arabella looked at Rosemary and wondered if she could trust her – for Arabella had a secret. She had not put in all her money! She had kept a whole pound note for herself, so that, with the two shillings she had been allowed, she had twenty-two shillings. She was not going to give that up for anyone! It was hidden in her handkerchief case, neatly folded up in a hanky.

No, she thought. *I won't tell Rosemary yet. I don't know her very well and, although she is my friend, she's a bit silly sometimes. I'll keep my own secret.*

So she told no one. But she and Rosemary went down to the village together that day to buy stamps, and a hair grip for Rosemary – and Arabella could not help spending some of her money!

'You go to the post office and buy your stamps, and I'll go and buy some chocolates at the sweet shop,' she said to Rosemary. She did not want the other girl to see her buying expensive chocolates, and handing over three or four shillings for them.

So, while Rosemary was buying a tuppenny-ha'penny stamp in the post office, Arabella slipped into the big sweet shop and bought a pound of peppermint chocolates, the kind she loved.

She saw a bottle of barley sugar too, and bought that. Lovely! Then, as Rosemary didn't come, she went into the shop next door, and bought herself a book.

The two girls wandered round the village a little while, and then went back to school. 'You know,' said Arabella, linking her arm in Rosemary's, 'that's another silly Whyteleafe rule – that no one is allowed to go down to the village alone unless they're in the higher forms.'

'Awfully silly,' agreed Rosemary.

Arabella undid the bag of chocolates. 'Have one?' she said.

'Oooh, Arabella – what a lovely lot of chocolates!' said Rosemary, her rather small eyes opening wide. 'Golly, you must have spent all your two shillings at once!'

They went in at the school gate, munching chocolates.

They were really delicious. Arabella shut up the bag and stuffed it into her winter coat pocket. She did not want the others to see what a lot of chocolates she had, in case they might guess she had spent more than two shillings on them.

She went to take off her hat and coat. Jenny was putting hers on, and when Arabella put the book she had bought down on the bench between them Jenny picked it up.

'Hallo! I always wanted to read this book. Lend it to me, will you, Arabella?'

'Well, I haven't read it myself yet,' said Arabella. 'I only bought it this afternoon.'

Jenny looked at the price inside the cover, and whistled. 'It's a three-and-sixpenny book. How could you buy that with two shillings?'

'I got it cheap,' said Arabella, after a moment's pause. She went red as she said it, and sharp-eyed Jenny saw the blush. She said no more, but went off, thinking hard.

The mean thing! She didn't put all her money into the box! thought Jenny.

Rosemary annoyed Arabella very much that evening when they were in the common room together, because she gave away the fact that Arabella had bought the chocolate peppermints! She did not mean to, of course – but she did it, all the same!

The children were talking about the sweet shop, which they all loved, and where they all spent money each week.

'I think those boiled sweets are the best bargain,' said Jenny.

'Oh, no – those clear gums last much the longest,' said Belinda.

'Not if you chew them,' said Harry. 'I bet if you sucked a boiled sweet properly, right to the end without crunching it up, and after that sucked a clear gum without chewing at all, there wouldn't be much to choose between them.'

'Let's have a competition and see,' said John.

'It's no good *me* trying,' said Jenny. 'I always crunch everything, and it goes like lightning down my throat.'

'*I* think the best bargain of all is chocolate peppermints,' suddenly said Rosemary's meek little voice.

Everyone laughed scornfully. 'Idiot!' said Julian. 'You only get about five for sixpence. They are most awfully expensive.'

'They're not,' said Rosemary, 'really they are not. Arabella, show them the enormous bagful you got today at the shop.'

This was the last thing that Arabella wanted to do. She frowned heavily at Rosemary.

'Don't be silly,' she said. 'I only got a few. They *are* expensive.'

Rosemary was amazed. Hadn't she taken one herself from an overflowing bag? She opened her mouth to say so, but caught sight of Arabella's warning face and stopped.

The others had listened to all this with much interest. They felt perfectly certain that Arabella had spent a lot of money on the chocolates, and Jenny remembered the book too. She looked sharply at Arabella.

But Arabella was now looking her usual calm self, rather haughty. *You're a deceitful person, in spite of your grand, high-and-mighty ways*, thought Jenny to herself. *I bet you've got those chocolates hidden away somewhere, so that no one shall know you spent a lot of money on them. I'll find them too – just see if I won't!*

Arabella got up in a few minutes and went out. She soon came back, carrying a small paper bag in which were six or seven chocolate peppermints. 'These are all I got for my money,' she said graciously. 'I'm afraid there isn't enough for one each, but we could divide them in half.'

But nobody wanted any. It was an unwritten rule at Whyteleafe that if you didn't like a person, you didn't accept things from them. So everyone except Rosemary said no. Rosemary took one, feeling puzzled and astonished. She *knew* she had seen a much bigger bag of chocolate peppermints before. Could she have been mistaken?

Jenny grinned to herself. Arabella must think they were all stupid if she thought she could make the other boys and girls believe she had only bought a few sweets – when that silly little Rosemary had given the secret away! She wondered where Arabella could have hidden the rest of the chocolates.

She thought she knew. Arabella learnt music and had a big music case. Jenny had seen her go to it that afternoon, although she had neither lesson nor practice to do. Why?

Because she wanted to put her chocs there, thought Jenny. She slipped off to the music room, where everyone kept their music. She took up Arabella's case and peeped inside it. The chocolate peppermints were there, where Arabella had hurriedly emptied them.

Richard came into the room while she was looking. 'See, Richard,' said Jenny in a tone of disgust. 'Arabella has kept some money back – and bought heaps of chocs and a book – and told all kinds of lies.'

'Well, make a complaint at the Meeting then,' said Richard, taking up his case and going out.

Jenny stood and thought for a moment. 'Would a complaint at the Meeting be thought a tale?' she wondered. She had better ask the others before saying anything. But she wouldn't tell Elizabeth – not yet, anyhow – because Arabella had been staying with Elizabeth, and it might be awkward for the new monitor if she knew about Arabella.

So Jenny told the others, when Elizabeth, Rosemary and Arabella were not there. They were really disgusted.

'I'm sure it would be a proper complaint,' said Harry. 'All the same, it's rather awful to have your name brought up at the Meeting quite so soon in the term, just when you're still new. Let's just show Arabella that we think her jolly mean. She'll soon guess why – and at the next Meeting I bet she'll pop *all* her money into the box!'

Then poor Arabella was in for a bad time! For the first time in her life she knew what it was to be with children who didn't like her at all, and who showed it!

CHAPTER SIX

ARABELLA MAKES A COMPLAINT

ARABELLA HAD turned up her nose at the boys and girls of Whyteleafe School from the first day she had arrived. She had told Rosemary that she didn't care whether they liked her or whether they didn't.

But it was difficult not to mind when everyone seemed to turn up their noses at her! It gave Arabella a very important, superior sort of feeling to despise all her class except Rosemary. But it gave her quite a different kind of feeling when she felt *she* was despised!

The children would not have been so thorough about it if Arabella had not behaved so stupidly from the beginning. Now they couldn't help feeling they were getting a bit of their own back!

'They treat me as if I was a bad smell!' Arabella complained to the faithful Rosemary. 'Why, that horrid boy Julian actually holds his nose when he passes me.'

This was quite true. Julian did hold his nose with his finger and thumb every time he came near Arabella. It annoyed her dreadfully. She was so used to being looked up to and admired by children, and to being praised by grown-ups that she simply didn't understand this sort of behaviour. It made her very angry indeed.

Arabella did not guess why the children were treating her like this. She had no idea that it was because they thought she had been dishonest and deceitful over her money. She felt sure she had been so clever about that that no one knew about it. She did not know that Jenny had peeped into her music case and seen the chocolates there.

Jenny entered into the fun of teasing Arabella too. Her way of teasing her was to talk in a very smooth, polite voice, exactly like Arabella's, of amazing riches and wonderful holidays, in the very same way that Arabella loved to talk.

Jenny was a very good mimic. She could imitate anyone's voice, and anyone's laugh. It made the children giggle to hear her talking just like Arabella, when Arabella was there.

'And my dears,' Jenny would say, '*last* hols were the most marvellous of all. We actually took three cars with us when we went away – and the last one held nothing but my party clothes! Oh, and I really must tell you of the time when I went to stay with my grandmother. She allowed me to stay up to dinner *every* night, and we had fifteen different courses to eat, and four different sorts of – of – ginger beer!'

Shrieks of laughter followed all this. Only Arabella did not laugh. She did not think it was at all funny. She thought it was simply horrid. At her old school everyone had loved hearing her tales. Why did they make fun of them at this nasty school?

Another very annoying thing happened to Arabella too. She would be sitting in the common room, sewing or writing, and suddenly Jenny or someone would say, 'Oh, look – is that an aeroplane?' Or, 'I say – is that a moth?' pointing at the same time out of the window or up to the ceiling.

Everyone would at once turn their heads, Arabella as well, and when poor Arabella turned back to her sewing or her writing she would find her pen gone, or her scissors. She would hunt on the floor for them until she suddenly heard a giggle.

Then she would know that someone had quickly snatched them up and put them on the windowsill or on a desk in the corner, just to tease her.

She told Rosemary about all the teasing, and the other girl listened with sympathy. 'It's too bad, Arabella,' she said. 'I don't know why they do it.'

'Well, you ask them, and find out,' said Arabella. 'See? Now, don't forget – and don't say *I* asked you to find out.'

So, when Arabella was next out of the room Rosemary found courage enough to speak to Jenny.

'Why are you so beastly to Arabella?'

'Because she deserves it,' said Jenny shortly.

'Why does she deserve it?' asked Rosemary.

'Well, don't you think she's a stuck-up, deceitful creature?' said Jenny. 'I know you're always hanging round her like a little dog, but you must surely know it's dishonest to keep back money from the school box and spend it on herself – and then tell lies about it.'

Jenny's sharp eyes were fixed on timid Rosemary. The other girl dropped her gaze and did not look at Jenny.

She was too weak to stick up for her friend, or even to say that she did not know that what Jenny said was true – though now that Jenny had said it, it did seem to Rosemary that Arabella *had* been deceitful.

'Yes. That was bad,' said Rosemary at last. 'Oh dear. Is that why you are so horrid to her?'

'Well, she must know why we are,' said Jenny impatiently. 'She's not so stupid as all that surely.'

Rosemary did not like to say that Arabella had no idea why everyone was horrid to her. Neither did she like to tell Arabella why the others were annoying her so. She was like a leaf in the wind, blown this way and that – 'Shall I tell her? I'd better. No. I can't, she'd be angry. Well, I won't tell her then. Oh, perhaps I'd better. No, I really can't.'

So, in the end Rosemary did not tell Arabella, and when Arabella asked her what the others had said she shook her head.

'They're – they're just teasing you because they think it's fun,' she said. 'Just because they're horrid.'

'Oh!' said Arabella, red with anger. 'Well, I shall complain to the Meeting. I just won't have this happen!'

'Oh, Arabella, don't do that,' said Rosemary in alarm. 'They might say it was telling tales – and you'd get into worse trouble! Tell your monitor first, and see if she thinks it would be telling tales to tell the Meeting.'

'I certainly shan't say anything to Elizabeth!' said Arabella. 'Go and ask advice from *her*? No thank you!'

And so silly Arabella, not guessing the trouble that would come to her, boiled away inside all the week, hating the others and longing for the Meeting to come!

It came at last. Arabella's lips were tightly pressed together as she looked round at the children of her form. 'Just wait!' her eyes seemed to say. 'Just wait and see how I will show you up!'

The school moneybox was handed round, but not very much was put in. Arabella put nothing in. Then the two shillings were handed to everyone, and the usual business began.

'Any requests?'

'Please can I have fivepence extra, William?' asked Belinda, standing up. 'A letter came for me this week without a stamp on – so I had to pay double postage on it, and it cost me fivepence. It was from one of my aunts. I expect she forgot to put a stamp on.'

'Fivepence for Belinda,' ordered William. 'It wasn't her fault that she had to pay extra.'

Fivepence was handed out to Belinda, and she sat down, pleased.

'Could I have sixpence to buy a new ball, please?' said a small boy, standing up rather shyly. 'Mine rolled down the railway bank and we're not allowed to go on the line.'

'Go to Eileen, and she will sell you one of our old balls for tuppence,' said William. 'You will have to pay it out of your own money.'

There were no more requests. The children were whispering between themselves and William knocked on his table with his little hammer. Everyone stopped talking.

'Any complaints?'

Arabella and another girl stood up almost at the same moment.

'Sit down, Arabella. We'll hear you next,' said Rita. 'What is it, Pamela?'

'It's a very silly complaint,' began Pamela, 'but it's an awful nuisance. You see, my cubicle is by the big window in my dormitory, and my monitor says it must be kept open when we are not there – and it must, of course – but on windy days all the things on my dressing table blow out of the window and I'm always getting into trouble because they are found outside!'

Everyone laughed. Rita and William smiled. Joan, who was in Pamela's form, spoke to Rita. She was Pamela's monitor.

'Pamela is quite right,' she said. 'Anyone who has that cubicle has the same trouble. But we could move the dressing table out of the window, if Matron wouldn't mind.'

'Ask her tomorrow,' said Rita. Matron was the one who saw to things of that sort, and she would see that the table was moved.

'Now, Arabella,' said William, noticing the angry, flushed face of the little girl, waiting her turn. Arabella stood up gracefully, not forgetting her little airs even in her rage.

'Please, William,' she said in her smooth, polite

voice, a little shaken now by nervousness and anger, 'please, I have a very serious complaint to make.'

Everyone sat up straight. This was interesting and exciting. Serious complaints were worth listening to. All the first form looked at one another and pulled faces. Was Arabella going to complain about them? Well, she was very silly then, because her own secret would be bound to come out!

'What is your complaint?' asked William.

'Well,' said Arabella, 'ever since I have come to this school the children in my class – all except Rosemary – have been absolutely horrid to me. I can't tell you the things they do to me!'

'I think you must tell me,' said William. 'It's no use making a complaint and not saying what it really is. I can't believe that the whole form have been horrid to you.'

'Well, they have,' said Arabella, almost in tears. 'Julian is the worst. He – he holds his nose whenever he comes near me!'

There were a few giggles at this. Julian laughed loudly too. Arabella glared at him. Elizabeth, up on the monitors' platform, looked most surprised. She was the only one who did not know the real reason for the first form's treatment of Arabella, and she thought it was very foolish of the girl to complain of ordinary teasing. She had not known there was a real reason behind it all. But now she guessed that there was.

Arabella went on with her complaints. 'Then there is Jenny. She mimics me and mocks me whenever she can. I'm a new girl and it's very unkind. I haven't done anything to make them so unkind to me. It makes me very unhappy. I shall write to my mother. I shall . . .'

'Be quiet,' said Rita, seeing that Arabella was working herself up in a real tantrum. 'Be quiet now, and sit down. We will go into this. You shall have another chance to speak later, if you want to. But wait a minute – have you told your monitor about this?'

'No,' said Arabella sulkily. 'She doesn't like me either.'

Elizabeth went red. That was true. She had *shown* that she didn't like Arabella too – and so Arabella hadn't come to her for help or advice before putting everything before the Meeting. Oh, dear – that was a pity!

'Oh,' said Rita, glancing at Elizabeth. 'Well now, let me see. We'll hear Jenny first. Jenny, will you please explain your unkind behaviour, and tell us if you have any real reason for it?'

Jenny stood up. Well, Arabella had brought all this upon herself! She began to tell what she knew.

CHAPTER SEVEN

THE MEETING DEALS WITH ARABELLA

'YOU SEE,' said Jenny, 'Arabella really brought all the trouble on herself. She didn't keep the rules, and we knew it, and so we didn't like her, and we teased her. That's all.'

'Oh, you storyteller!' said Arabella. 'I *have* kept the rules!'

'Arabella, be quiet,' said William. 'Who is Arabella's monitor? Oh, you are, Elizabeth Allen. Will you tell us, Elizabeth, if, in your opinion, Arabella has kept the rules?'

'Elizabeth doesn't know what we know,' said Jenny, interrupting. 'We know the deceitful and dishonest thing that Arabella did, but Elizabeth doesn't.'

Elizabeth looked very upset. How was it she hadn't known? She spoke to William.

'I'm afraid I don't know what Jenny is talking about, William,' she said. 'I know I ought to – because I'm a monitor and I should see all that goes on in the form – but I really don't know this.'

'Thank you,' said William gravely. He turned to Jenny. 'What have you to complain of about Arabella, Jenny?' he asked, with a glance at the fiery-red face of Arabella. The girl was full of horror now – whatever was Jenny going to say? She, Arabella, had meant to make a complaint, but she had never guessed that anyone else would complain about *her*.

Then, of course, it all came out.

'Arabella didn't put all her money into the box last week. We know, because she bought a three-and-sixpenny book in the village and a lot of expensive chocolates,' said Jenny. 'She hid some in her music case so that we wouldn't know. She told lies about it too. So you see, William, we don't like her and we showed it. We thought perhaps she would be ashamed of herself if we teased her, and be honest next time and put all her money in.'

'I see,' said William. 'Sit down, Jenny.'

Everyone was now looking at Arabella. She didn't know what to say. How she wished she had never made her complaint! Whatever was she to do! This was simply dreadful.

'Arabella,' said Rita, 'what have you to say to this? Is it true?'

Arabella sat quite still and said nothing. Then a tear trickled down her cheek. She felt very, very sorry for herself. Why had her mother sent her to this horrid school where they had Meetings like this every week, and where no fault could be kept hidden?

'Arabella,' said Rita, 'please stand up. Is this true?'

Arabella's knees were shaking, but she stood up. 'Yes,' she said in a low voice. 'Some of it is true. But not all. You see – I didn't quite understand about putting *all* my money in. I did put in most of it. I wanted to ask my monitor, Elizabeth, about lots of things, but she seems to dislike me too, and – and . . .'

Elizabeth felt angry. Arabella was trying to put some of the blame on to *her*. She scowled at the girl and disliked her all the more.

'That's nonsense,' said Rita briskly. 'Elizabeth would always tell you anything, even if she did dislike you. Now listen, Arabella, you have behaved very foolishly, and you have only yourself to blame for the others' treatment of you. You will have to put things right.'

The head girl turned to William and spoke in a low voice for a moment or two. He nodded. Rita spoke again. The whole school listened with interest.

'It is sometimes difficult for new children to understand and fall in with our rules,' said Rita in her clear voice. 'But, after they have been here for a while, every boy and girl agrees that our rules are good. After all, we make them ourselves *for* ourselves, so it would be silly of us to make bad rules. We haven't very many anyway. But what we have must be kept.'

'I see that,' said Arabella, who was still standing up. 'I'm sorry I broke that rule, Rita. If the others had told me I had broken the rule, and just scolded me and given me a chance to put *all* my money in next time, I'd have done it. But they didn't. They were just horrid and I didn't know why.'

'You will go to your monitor after this Meeting and give her all the money you have got, every penny. She will put it into the box. You will be allowed only sixpence this week, for stamps, as you had so much extra last week.'

Arabella sat down, her cheeks flaming red again. Give her money to Elizabeth! Oh, dear, how she would hate that.

Rita had not quite finished with the matter. She spoke to the first form rather sternly.

'There is no need for you to take things in hand yourselves and do any punishing,' she said. 'After all, your monitors are there to give advice, and we have the Meeting each week to put anything right. You first-formers are not sensible enough to know how to treat a thing of this sort. You should have gone to Elizabeth.'

The first-formers looked uncomfortable and felt small.

'It is all rather a mountain made out of a molehill,' said William. 'Arabella is a new girl and didn't understand the importance of our rules. Now that she does she will keep them.'

A little more business was done at the Meeting and then the children filed out. Elizabeth went to Jenny.

'Why didn't you tell me about Arabella? It was mean of you not to. I did feel an idiot, sitting up there on the monitors' platform, hearing all this and not knowing a thing about it!'

'Yes, we ought to have told you,' said Jenny. 'I'm sorry. But, you see, we knew Arabella had been staying with you, and we thought it might be rather awkward, if she was a friend of yours.'

'Well, she's not,' said Elizabeth in a fierce tone. 'I can't bear her. She quite spoilt the last two weeks of my holidays for me.'

'Sh, you idiot!' said Kathleen, giving her a nudge. Arabella was coming by, and must have overheard what was said.

'Arabella! You'd better get your money now and give it to me,' said Elizabeth hastily, hoping that Arabella hadn't overheard what she had just said. 'I'd like it now, while the school box is out.'

Arabella was rather white. She said nothing, but

went to her dormitory. She took out all the money she had hidden in various places.

She went downstairs again and found Elizabeth. Elizabeth, feeling rather awkward, held out her hand. Arabella crashed all the money into her palm, making Elizabeth cry out in pain. Some of the money went on the floor.

'There you are, you horrid thing!' said Arabella, her voice full of anger and tears. 'I suppose you were pleased to see me made fun of at the Meeting! Well, you didn't come out of it so well yourself, did you? The only person who didn't know anything! I'm sorry I spoilt your holidays – you may as well know that you spoilt mine too! I hated your home and everything in it, you most of all!'

Elizabeth was shocked and angry. She stared at Arabella, and spoke sharply.

'Pick up the money you've dropped. Pull yourself together, and don't talk to your monitor like that. Even if we don't like one another, we can at least be civil.'

'I can't imagine why anyone made *you* a monitor!' said Arabella in a scornful voice. 'Ill-mannered tomboy! I hate you!'

Arabella went quickly to the door, went through it and slammed it after her. Elizabeth was left alone to pick up the money and put it into the box. She was astonished at Arabella's fierceness, and worried too.

Oh, dear, it's going to be very difficult to be a monitor in the first form if this sort of thing is going to happen, thought Elizabeth, rattling the money into the box.

As she went down the passage Arabella met Rita. The head girl saw her tear-stained face and stopped her kindly.

'Arabella, we all make mistakes at first so don't take things too much to heart. And do go to your monitor for advice and help,' said Rita. 'Elizabeth is a very wise little person, and very fair and just. I am sure she can always help you.'

This was not at all what Arabella wanted to hear at that moment. She was glad to have Rita's kind word, but she did not want to hear praise of Elizabeth. As for going to Elizabeth for advice – well, she would never, *never* do that!

Rita went on her way, rather worried about Arabella, for she did not really feel that she was sorry for her mistake. If a person was really sorry, it was all right – they did try to do better. But if they were not sorry, only angry at being found out, then things went from bad to worse.

Elizabeth went to find Julian. 'I say, *you* might have warned me about Arabella,' she said. 'You really might. Why didn't you?'

'Couldn't be bothered,' said Julian. 'I don't care whether she puts her money into the box or not – and I certainly don't care if she's teased or not. I like to do as I like, and I'm not interfering with other people. Let them do as *they* like.'

'But Julian,' said Elizabeth earnestly, 'you must see that we *can't* all do as we like, when we live so many together. We—'

'Now don't start that goody-goody monitor talk,' said Julian at once. 'That's the only thing I don't like about you, Elizabeth – that you're a monitor. You seem to think it gives you a right to lecture me and make me into a Good Boy, and put everything right the way *you* think it should be.'

Elizabeth stared at Julian in dismay. 'Julian! How horrid of you! I'm very *proud* of being a monitor. It's mean of you to say it's the one thing you don't like about me. It's the thing I'm proudest of.'

'I wish I'd known you when you were the naughtiest girl in the school,' said Julian. 'I'd have liked you better then, I'm sure.'

'You wouldn't,' said Elizabeth crossly. 'I was silly then. Anyway, I'm just the same girl now as I was then, only I'm more sensible, and a monitor.'

'There you go again!' said Julian, heaving an enormous sigh. 'You simply can't forget for one moment that you are one of those grand, marvellous and altogether wonderful beings – a *monitor*!'

He stalked away and left Elizabeth looking after him angrily. How stupid it was to have a friend who didn't like the thing you were proudest of! Really, Julian was most annoying at times!

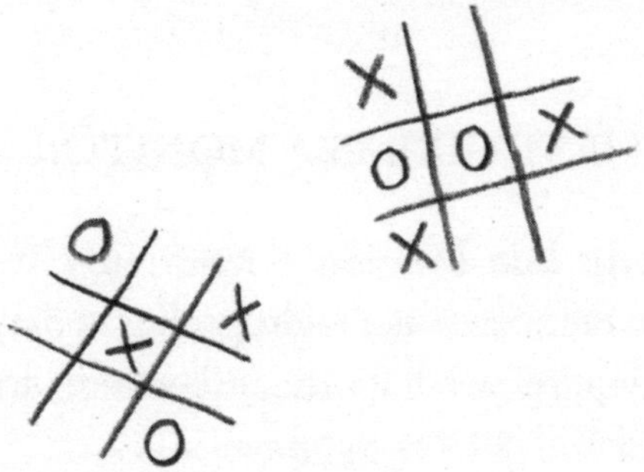

CHAPTER EIGHT

ELIZABETH LAYS A TRAP

SCHOOL LIFE went on its jolly way in that Easter term. Games were played and matches were won and lost. Many of the children who liked riding rode out every morning before breakfast. Robert always rode with Elizabeth, and the little girl chattered away to him as they rode.

'Do you like being a monitor, Elizabeth?' asked Robert one morning not long after the second Meeting of the school.

'Well,' said Elizabeth, and stopped to think. 'It's funny, Robert, I felt terribly proud when I was made a monitor – and I do still – but somehow it's set me a bit apart from the others, and I don't like that. And Julian will keep saying I'm goody-goody, and you know I'm not!'

'No, that's the very last thing you are,' said Robert, with a grin. 'Well, I've never been a monitor or leader of any sort, Elizabeth, but I've often heard my uncle say that being set over others isn't altogether a happy thing at first – till you're used to it, and shake down into your new position.'

'I didn't like not being told about that Arabella business,' said Elizabeth. 'I felt left out. Last term I'd have been in the middle of it and heard everything. I think someone might have told me.'

'Well, we will next time, I expect,' said Robert.

Elizabeth worked in the school garden as hard as ever with John Terry. The crocuses they had planted together came up by the hundred, and looked wonderful in the early spring. The yellow ones came out first, and opened out well in the sunshine. Then the purple ones and the white ones came out together.

Julian's barrow was a great success. It was strange-looking, but strong and well made. The smaller boys loved using it.

'Thanks, Julian,' said John. 'That has saved us quite a large amount of money. I shall come to you when I want anything else!'

There was a great deal to do in the garden that term. There always was in the spring term. There was a good deal of digging to finish, and many things to plant. The children, under John's direction, sowed rows and rows of broad beans.

'Oh, dear, *must* we sow so many thousands, John?' groaned small Peter, standing up to straighten his back.

'Well, the whole school likes broad beans,' said John. 'It's nice to grow what people like.'

The children could keep pets if they liked, although they were not allowed to have cats or dogs, because these could not be kept in cages. Any child who had a pet had to look after it, and look after it well. If he or she did not, the pet was taken away from them, but that rarely happened, because the children were fond of their guinea pigs, mice, budgies, pigeons, and so on, and took a great pride in keeping them clean and happy.

Arabella did not give Elizabeth any trouble in the next week or two, but she did not speak to her or have any more to do with her than she could help. She and Rosemary went about together, sometimes with Martin Follett. Julian made friends with everyone – or rather everyone made friends with him, for he did not seem to care whether people were nice to him or not, but the boys and girls thought him an exciting and very clever person.

His only real friend was Elizabeth, and the two laughed and joked together a great deal. He did not say any more about her being a goody-goody monitor, and slowly Elizabeth began to get used to the idea that she was set over the others. In fact, she sometimes forgot it altogether.

She was reminded of it when Rosemary came to her in trouble. 'Elizabeth, can I speak to you about something?' said the girl timidly.

'Of course,' said Elizabeth, remembering at once that she was a monitor, and must help, and act wisely.

'Well, I keep missing money,' said Rosemary, looking upset.

'*Missing* money!' said Elizabeth. 'What do you mean? Losing it, do you mean!'

'Well, I did think I was losing it at first,' said Rosemary. 'I thought I must have a hole in my pocket, but I haven't. I missed tuppence last week. And yesterday a whole sixpence went – and you know what a lot that is out of two shillings, Elizabeth. And today a penny has gone out of my desk.'

Elizabeth was very astonished. She stared at Rosemary, and could hardly believe her ears.

'But Rosemary,' she said at last, 'Rosemary, you don't think anybody *took* your money!'

'Well, I do,' said Rosemary. 'I hate to say anything, Elizabeth, really I do. But I haven't any money left now except threepence, and that has to last me till the next Meeting, and I really must buy some stamps.'

'This is awful,' said Elizabeth. 'It's – it's stealing,

Rosemary. Are you quite, quite sure of what you say?'

'Yes,' said Rosemary. 'Shall I make a complaint at the next Meeting?'

'No,' said Elizabeth grandly. 'I may be able to settle it myself. Then we can bring it before the Meeting, and we can tell them we settled the matter between us.'

'All right,' said Rosemary, who had no wish to get up and say anything before the Meeting. She was far too timid and weak! 'How will you settle it?'

'We'll lay a trap,' said Elizabeth. 'I'll think about it, Rosemary, and tell you. Don't tell anyone else.'

'Well, I did tell Martin Follett,' said Rosemary. 'I couldn't very well help it, because I was looking all over the place for my sixpence yesterday, and feeling very miserable at losing it – and he came in and was awfully kind. He helped me hunt for ages, and he offered me tuppence of his own. So then I told him that I couldn't understand what was happening to my money. But I haven't told anyone else.'

'Well, don't,' said Elizabeth. 'We don't want to put anyone on their guard. I must say it was kind of Martin to offer you tuppence, though.'

'He's very generous,' said Rosemary. 'He bought John Terry a packet of very special beans for the garden, you know. He said he wasn't keen on gardening himself, so that was his only way of doing his bit.'

I wonder – I do wonder who could possibly be mean enough to take anyone's money, thought Elizabeth as Rosemary went out of the room. *What a horrible thing to do! Now, this really is a problem for me, and I must think about it. I'm a monitor, and I must try to put it right.*

She sat down and thought hard. She must find out the thief. Then she could deal with her – or him – and prove to everyone what a fine, sensible monitor she was. But how could she catch him?

'I know what I'll do,' said Elizabeth to herself. 'I'll show everyone the fine new shilling I got out of the school box last week, and then I'll put it in my desk, but I'll mark it first, so that I shall be able to know it again – and then watch to see if it disappears.'

So, the next day, when the children were playing in the gym at break, because it was raining out-of-doors, Elizabeth took out her brand-new shilling and showed it round.

'Look,' she said. 'It must have come out of the mint only last week, I should think! Isn't it bright and new?'

Ruth had a new penny as bright as gold, and she brought that out of her purse too. Robert had a new threepenny bit.

'I shan't keep my shining shilling in my pocket, in case I get a hole there,' said Elizabeth. 'I shall put it in my desk, just under the ink hole. It will be safe there.'

Before she put it there she marked a little cross on it with black Indian ink. Then she placed it under the ink hole, in front of everyone, just before Miss Ranger came to take the class.

She glanced at Rosemary. The girl nodded her head slightly to tell Elizabeth that she knew why she had shown off her shilling and put it into a safe place in front of everyone.

Now we'll just see, thought Elizabeth glancing round the class and wondering for the hundredth time which boy or girl could possibly be mean enough to take it.

The children left the schoolroom after morning lessons were finished and went to have a quick run and play in the garden. Then they had to come in to wash before dinner.

Elizabeth ran into the classroom to see whether her shilling was still in its place. She opened her desk. Yes, her shilling was still there. She felt glad. Perhaps Rosemary was mistaken after all!

It was still there when afternoon school began. Rosemary looked across at her and Elizabeth nodded her head to tell her that the money was still there. Suppose the thief did not take it? Elizabeth would have to think of something else.

The shilling was still there after tea. Rosemary came up to Elizabeth. 'Don't leave your shilling there any more,' she said. 'I don't want it to be taken. You might not get it back – and a whole shilling lost would be dreadful.'

'I'll leave it there till tomorrow,' said Elizabeth. 'Just to see.'

In the morning, before school, the little girl slipped along to the classroom. She opened her desk and felt for the bright new shilling.

It wasn't there. It was gone. Although she had half expected this, Elizabeth was really shocked. So there was a thief in the class – a mean, horrible thief. Who was it? Well, wait till she saw that marked shilling – then she would know!

CHAPTER NINE

ELIZABETH GETS A SHOCK

IT WAS one thing to mark a coin so that she would know it again when she saw it, but another thing to make a plan to find it in someone's keeping! Elizabeth wondered and wondered how she could manage this.

After tea that day it was still raining and the children gathered together in their common room. It was a cheerful room with wide windows, a big fireplace, a gramophone and a wireless, and lockers for all the children to keep their things in. It was the room the children liked best and felt to be really their own.

There was a merry noise that evening. The wireless was going, and the gramophone too, so that the one or two who wanted to read groaned aloud, and went to turn off either the wireless or the gramophone.

But as these were immediately turned on again by somebody else it was a waste of time to turn them off!

'I say! Let's play a game of some sort,' said somebody. 'I've got a good race game here. Let's all play it. There are twelve horses to race.'

'Right,' said the children, and watched Ruth put out the big game. It almost covered the table. There was a little squabbling over which horses to choose, and then the game began.

It was fun to be playing a game all together like this, and it was exciting to move the horses along the big board.

'Blow!' said Harry. 'I've landed in the middle of a ditch. I've got to go back six. One – two – three – four – five – six!'

The game was played to the end. Belinda won, and was presented with a bar of chocolate. Then Kathleen got out a game of her own. It was a spinning game. There were many little tops, all of different colours to be spun. They spun beautifully, making a tiny whirring sound as they did so.

Seeing the tops spinning gave Elizabeth an idea. She banged on the table.

'Let's all see if we can spin coins. Who is the best at it?'

The children put their hands into their pockets and brought out money. Some had pennies, some ha'pennies, some sixpences, and one or two of them had shillings.

Julian had been far and away the best at spinning

the tops. He could make them jump and hop across the table in a marvellous way. Now he showed how clever he was with coins.

'See my penny hop!' he cried, and spun it deftly on the polished tabletop. It hopped and skipped as it spun in a marvellous way. Nobody else could do the trick.

'Watch me spin a shilling on the top of a glass!' said Julian. 'It will make a peculiar noise. Fetch a glass, somebody.'

A glass appeared and was put on the table. Everyone watched Julian. His green eyes gleamed with pleasure as he saw the admiring looks around him. He spun the shilling on the bottom of the upturned glass, and it made a very funny noise.

'Like singing a little song,' said Ruth. 'Let *me* try, Julian.'

The shilling fell off the glass, and Ruth picked it up. She tried her best to spin it, but it hopped off the glass at once and rolled off the table beside Elizabeth. The little girl bent to pick it up.

It was a bright new one. Elizabeth glanced at it, thinking it was funny that there should be a second brand-new shilling in the form – and then she saw something that gave her a terrible shock.

She saw the tiny black cross she had made on the shilling! She stared at it in the greatest dismay. It was her own shilling, her very own, the one she had shown everyone, the one she had marked and put into her desk.

'Come on, Elizabeth – hand over the shilling!' said Ruth impatiently. 'Anyone would think you had never seen a shilling before, the way you are staring at it!'

Elizabeth threw the shilling across to Ruth. Her hand was trembling. Julian! *Julian* had her shilling. But Julian was her friend. He couldn't have her shilling. But he had – he had! He had taken it out of his pocket. Elizabeth herself had seen him. The little girl stared miserably across at Julian, who was watching Ruth with his deep-set eyes, a lock of black hair over his forehead as usual.

Rosemary had noticed Elizabeth's face. She had seen her staring at the shilling. She knew that it must be the same one that the little girl had marked. She too looked in amazement at Julian.

Elizabeth was not going to say anything to Julian just then, but she could hardly wait for a chance to speak to him alone. She waited about that evening, hoping that she would find a chance. She thought and thought about the whole affair.

Of course, I know Julian does just as he likes, and says so, thought Elizabeth. *He just doesn't care about anything or anybody. But, after all, I am his friend, and he should care about what he does to* me. *He could have had my shilling if he had asked me. How* could *he do such a thing?*

Then another thought came into her mind. *I mustn't judge him till I hear what he says. Somebody may have lent it to him – or he may have given someone change for a shilling. I must be careful what I say. I really must.*

Just before bedtime her chance came to speak to Julian alone. He went to get a book from the library, and Elizabeth met him in the passage as he came back.

'Julian,' she said, 'where did you get your nice bright shilling from?'

'From the school box last week,' said Julian at once. 'Why?'

'Are you sure?' said Elizabeth. 'Oh, Julian, are you quite, quite sure?'

'Of course I am, idiot. Where else can we get money from?' said Julian, puzzled. 'What are you looking so upset about? What's the matter with my shilling?'

Elizabeth was about to say that it was *her* shilling when she stopped. No, she mustn't say that, or Julian would know she was accusing him of taking it from her. He was her friend. She couldn't accuse him of anything so dreadful. She must think about it.

'Nothing's the matter with the shilling,' she answered at last, thinking that something must be dreadfully the matter with Julian.

'All right then, don't look so peculiar,' said Julian,

getting impatient. 'It's *my* shilling – out of the school box – and that's that.'

He stalked off, looking puzzled and annoyed. Elizabeth stared after him. Her mind was in a complete muddle. Of all the people in the form, the one she had never even thought of for one moment as the thief was Julian.

She slipped into a music room by herself and began to play a sad and gloomy piece on the piano. Richard, who was passing, looked in in surprise.

'Gracious, Elizabeth! Why are you playing like that? Anyone would think you had lost a shilling and found sixpence!'

This old saying was half true at the moment, and Elizabeth gave a choky laugh. 'Well, I *have* lost a shilling – but I haven't found sixpence,' she said.

'Golly, Elizabeth, you're not making yourself miserable over a shilling, are you?' said Richard. 'I've never heard you playing so dolefully before. Cheer up.'

'Richard, listen – I'm not silly enough to be miserable over a shilling,' said Elizabeth. 'It's something else.'

'Well, tell me then,' said Richard. 'I shan't tell anyone else, you know that.'

This was true. Elizabeth looked at Richard, and thought perhaps he could help her.

'Suppose you had a friend, and suppose he did

something simply terribly mean to you – what would you do?' she asked.

Richard laughed. 'If it really was my friend, well, I wouldn't believe it!' he said. 'I'd know there was some mistake.'

'Oh, Richard, I think you're right,' said Elizabeth. 'I just won't believe it!'

She began to play the piano again, a happier tune. Richard grinned and left Elizabeth. He was used to her troubles by now. She was always getting into some difficulty or bother!

Richard is right, thought Elizabeth. *I shan't believe it. It's some accident that Julian has got that shilling. I'll have to begin all over again and find some way to catch the real thief.*

So she was just as friendly to Julian as ever, though Rosemary, who knew what had happened, was very puzzled to see it. She spoke to Elizabeth about it.

'It couldn't have been Julian,' said Elizabeth shortly. 'It must have been someone else. He got that shilling out of the school box. He said he did when I asked him. There is some mistake.'

The next day Rosemary came to Elizabeth again. 'Listen,' she said, 'what do you think has happened? *Arabella* has lost some money now! Do you suppose it's the thief at work again?'

'Oh, golly!' said Elizabeth. 'I was so hoping that nothing more would happen. How much has Arabella lost?'

'Sixpence,' said Rosemary. 'She put it into her mac pocket, and left it there – and when she went to get it it was gone. And Elizabeth, Belinda left some chocolate in her desk – and that's gone too. Isn't it awful?'

'Yes, it is,' said Elizabeth. 'How hateful it all is! Well, I'm absolutely determined to find out who the thief is now – and I'll haul him or her in front of the Meeting at once!'

The next thing that disappeared was sweets out of Elizabeth's locker. She went to get them – and they were not there!

'Blow!' said Elizabeth, angry and shocked. 'This is getting worse. I wish I knew who had my sweets.'

She soon knew. In class that afternoon Julian screwed up his face as if he wanted to sneeze. He pulled a hanky out of his pocket quickly, and something fell out. It was a sweet.

'One of *my* sweets!' said Elizabeth angrily to herself. 'The beast! He's taken my sweets. Then he must have taken that shilling too. And he calls himself my friend!'

CHAPTER TEN

A DREADFUL QUARREL

THE MORE Elizabeth thought about the stolen money and sweets, the angrier she felt with Julian. It *must* be Julian – but how could he do such a thing?

He's always saying he does as he likes, so I suppose he takes other people's things if he wants them, thought the little girl. *He's bad. I know he's clever and amusing and jolly, but he's bad. I shall have to speak to him.*

She could hardly wait till the afternoon class was over. She paid no attention whatever to her lessons and Miss Ranger glanced at her sharply two or three times. Elizabeth did not seem to hear any questions at all, but simply gazed into space, with an angry look in her eyes.

'Elizabeth, I suppose you know you are in class?' said Miss Ranger at last. 'You have not answered a single question for the last half-hour.'

'I'm sorry, Miss Ranger,' said Elizabeth hastily. 'I – I was thinking of something else.'

'Well, will you kindly think of what you are supposed to be doing?' said Miss Ranger.

So Elizabeth had to try and forget Julian's misdeeds for a while, and think of Mary, Queen of Scots. But somehow her thoughts always slid away to Julian.

She looked at the boy, who sat in front of her. He was writing, his lock of black hair falling over his face. He brushed it impatiently away from time to time. Elizabeth wondered why he didn't have his hair cut shorter. Then it wouldn't worry him so. He looked round and grinned at her, his green eyes rather like a goblin's.

Elizabeth would not smile back. She bent her head down to her book, and Julian looked surprised. Elizabeth was usually ready with her smiles.

The class went rushing off at four o'clock – all except Elizabeth, who had to stay in and copy out some work for Miss Ranger. She was annoyed at this, but not really surprised, for she knew she had not done any work at all that afternoon. So she raced through it, her mind still thinking of what she should say to Julian. She must get him alone somewhere.

It was teatime when she had finished. She went to have her tea, but because she was upset she could not eat much, and the others teased her.

'She's sickening for measles or something,' said Harry. 'I've never seen Elizabeth off her food before. There must be something wrong with her!'

'Don't be funny,' said Elizabeth crossly.

Harry looked surprised.

'What's the matter? Are you all right?'

Elizabeth nodded. Yes, *she* was all right, but something else was all wrong. Oh, dear. She didn't want to tackle Julian, and yet she wouldn't have any peace of mind till she did.

She went to Julian after tea. 'Julian, I want to talk to you. It's very important.'

'Can't it wait?' asked Julian. 'I want to finish a job I'm doing.'

'No. It can't wait,' said Elizabeth. 'It's really important.'

'All right,' said Julian. 'I'll come and hear this terribly important thing.'

'Come into the garden,' said Elizabeth. 'I want to talk to you where we can't be overheard.'

'Well, I'll come to the stables,' said Julian. 'There won't be anybody about there now. You're very mysterious, Elizabeth.'

They walked together to the stables. No one was to be seen there at all. 'Now, what is it?' said Julian.

'Hurry up, because I want to get on with my job. I'm mending a spade for John.'

'Julian. Why did you take that money – and the chocolate and my sweets?' asked Elizabeth.

'What money – and what sweets?' said Julian.

'Oh, don't pretend you don't know!' cried Elizabeth losing her temper. 'You took my shilling – and you must have taken Rosemary's money too – and I *saw* one of my sweets drop out of your pocket this afternoon when you pulled out your hanky to sneeze.'

'Elizabeth, how *dare* you say these things to me?' said Julian, his face going red, and his green eyes getting very deep in colour.

'I dare because I'm a monitor, and I know all about your meanness!' said Elizabeth in a low, angry voice. 'You called yourself my friend and—'

'Well, I like that! *You* call yourself *my* friend, and yet you say these hateful things to me!' said Julian in a loud voice, also losing his temper. 'Just because you're a monitor you think you have the right to go around accusing innocent people of horrible tricks. You're not fit to be anyone's friend. You aren't mine any longer.'

He began to walk off, but Elizabeth ran after him, her eyes blazing. She caught hold of his coat sleeve. Julian tried to shake her off.

'You've got to listen to me, Julian!' almost shouted

Elizabeth. 'You've got to! Do you want all this to be brought out at the next Meeting?'

'If you dare to say anything to anyone else, I'll pay you out in a way you won't like,' said Julian, between his teeth. 'All girls are the same – catty and dishonourable, making wild statements that aren't true and not even believing people when they do tell the truth!'

'Julian! I don't want to bring it up at the Meeting,' cried Elizabeth. 'I don't – I don't. That's why I'm giving you this chance of telling me, so that I can help you and put things right. You always say you do as you like – so I suppose you thought you could take anything you wanted and . . .'

'Elizabeth, I *do* do as I like but there are many many things I don't like, and would never do,' said Julian, his green eyes flashing, and his black brows coming down low over them. 'I don't like stealing – I don't like lying – I don't like tale-telling. So I don't do those things. Now I'm going. You're my worst enemy now, not my best friend. I shall never, never like you again.'

'I'm not your worst enemy, I want to help you,' said Elizabeth. 'I saw my own marked shilling, I tell you. I saw my own sweet come out of your pocket. I'm a monitor, so I . . .'

'So you thought you had the right to accuse me, and you thought I'd confess to something I don't happen to have done, and you thought I'd cry on your shoulder and promise my monitor to be a good little boy,' said Julian in a horrid voice. 'Well, you are mistaken, my dear Elizabeth. Why anyone made you a monitor I can't think!'

He walked away. Elizabeth by now was in a real temper, and she tried to pull him back once more. Julian turned in a rage, took hold of Elizabeth by the shoulders and shook her so hard that her teeth rattled in her head.

'If you were a boy, I'd show you what I really think of you!' said Julian in a low, fierce voice. He suddenly let Elizabeth go and walked off, his hands deep in his pockets, his hair untidy and his mouth in a straight, angry line.

Elizabeth felt rather weak. She leant against the stable wall and tried to get back her breath. She tried to think clearly, but she couldn't. What a dreadful, dreadful thing to happen!

Footsteps nearby made her jump. Martin Follett came out of the stable, looking very white and scared.

'Elizabeth! I couldn't help hearing. I didn't like to come out and interrupt. Elizabeth, I'm so sorry for you. Julian had no right to be so beastly when you were trying your hardest to help him.'

Elizabeth felt grateful for Martin's friendly words,

but she was sorry he had overheard everything.

'Martin, you're not to say a word to anyone about this,' she said, standing up straight again, and pushing back her curls. 'It's very private and secret. Do you promise?'

'Of course,' said Martin, 'but Elizabeth, let me help a bit. I'll give you some of my sweets. And I'll give you a shilling to make up for the one you lost. That will put things right, won't it? Then you needn't bother Julian any more, or quarrel with him. You needn't bring the matter up at the Meeting either.'

'Oh, Martin, it's all very kind of you,' said Elizabeth, feeling very tired suddenly, 'but you don't see the point. It's not my shilling or my sweets I mind, silly – it's the fact that Julian has been taking them. You can't put *that* right, can you! Giving me a shilling and your sweets won't help Julian to stop taking what isn't his. I should have thought you could have seen that.'

'Well, give him a chance,' said Martin earnestly. 'Don't report him at the Meeting. Just give him a chance.'

'I'll see,' said Elizabeth. 'I'll have to think it all out. Oh, dear, I wish I wasn't a monitor. I wish I could *go* to a monitor for help! I don't seem much use as a monitor myself. I can't even think what I ought to do.'

Martin slipped his arm through hers. 'Come and

have a talk with John about the garden,' he said. 'That will do you good.'

'You're kind to me, Martin,' said Elizabeth gratefully. 'But I don't want to talk to John. I don't want to talk to anybody just now. I want to think by myself. So leave me, please, Martin. And Martin, you do *promise* not to tell anyone about this, don't you? It's Julian's business and mine, not anybody else's.'

'Of course I promise,' said Martin, looking straight at Elizabeth. 'You can trust me, Elizabeth. I'll leave you now, but, if I can help you any time, I will.'

He went, and Elizabeth thought how nice he was. *I'm sure he won't tell anyone*, she thought. *It would be so awful if the others got to know about this. I simply don't know what to do. Julian will really hate me now. If only things would blow over!*

But they didn't blow over. They got very much worse. Julian was not the kind of boy to forget and forgive easily, and he was certainly not going to make things easy for Elizabeth. She had been his best friend – now she was his worst enemy! Look out then, Elizabeth!

CHAPTER ELEVEN

JULIAN PLAYS A TRICK

EVERYONE SOON noticed that Julian and Elizabeth were no longer friends. Elizabeth looked thoroughly miserable and upset, and Julian took no notice of her at all.

Arabella was pleased. She liked and admired Julian tremendously, for all his careless, untidy ways. She had been annoyed when he had chosen Elizabeth for his friend. She would have liked to have been chosen instead.

'He's got simply marvellous brains!' said Arabella to Rosemary, who, not having many herself, sincerely admired those who had. 'He could do anything, that boy! I think he will be a wonderful inventor when he grows up – really *do* something in the world!'

'Yes, I think so too,' said Rosemary, agreeing with Arabella, as she always did. 'Arabella, I wonder why Elizabeth and Julian have quarrelled. They haven't spoken a word to one another all day – and, whenever

Julian does take a look in Elizabeth's direction, it's really fierce!'

'Yes, I'd like to know too why they've quarrelled,' said Arabella. 'I think I'll ask Julian. Perhaps he would like to be friends with us, now that's he's quarrelled with Elizabeth.'

So Arabella asked Julian that afternoon. 'Julian, I'm sorry to see that you and Elizabeth have quarrelled,' she said in her sweetest voice. 'I'm sure it must have been Elizabeth's fault. Why did you quarrel?'

'Sorry, Arabella, but I'm afraid that's my own business,' said Julian rather shortly.

'You might tell me,' said Arabella. 'I am on your side, not Elizabeth's. I never did like Elizabeth.'

'There aren't any "sides", as you call it,' said Julian.

And that was all that Arabella could get out of Julian. She felt cross about it and more curious than ever. Whatever could the matter be? It must be something serious or Elizabeth wouldn't look so worried.

'I do wish we could find out,' she said to Rosemary. 'I really do wish we could.'

'What do you want to find out?' asked Martin, coming up behind them.

'Why Elizabeth and Julian have quarrelled,' said Arabella. 'You haven't any idea, have you, Martin?'

'Well, I do know something,' said Martin. Arabella stared at him in excitement.

'Tell us,' she said.

'Well,' said Martin, 'it's a dead secret. You mustn't tell anyone at all. Promise?'

'Of course,' said Arabella, not meaning to keep the secret at all. 'Who told you, Martin?'

'Well, Elizabeth told me herself,' said Martin.

'Then you can quite well tell us,' said Arabella at once. 'If Elizabeth told *you*, she will be sure to tell the others too.'

So Martin told the secret – how Elizabeth had accused Julian of stealing money and sweets, and how he had denied it angrily. Arabella's big eyes nearly fell out of her head as she listened. Rosemary could hardly believe it either.

'Oh, how beastly of Elizabeth!' said Arabella. 'How could she, Martin? I'm sure that however don't-carish Julian is, he is honest!'

Soon the secret was out all over the form. Everyone knew why Julian and Elizabeth had quarrelled. Everyone spoke about stolen money and sweets, Julian and Elizabeth.

'I think Julian ought to know that Elizabeth has spread the tale about him,' said Arabella to Rosemary. 'I really do. It's not fair.'

'But did she spread it?' asked Rosemary doubtfully. 'It was Martin that told us.'

'Well, he said Elizabeth told *him*, didn't she – and, if she told him, she would probably have told others,' said Arabella. 'After all, everyone knows now, so I expect Elizabeth did a lot of the telling.'

Rosemary felt a little uncomfortable. She knew how much Arabella herself had told, and she knew too that Arabella had added a little to the story. But Rosemary was too weak to argue with her friend. So she said nothing.

Arabella spoke to Julian the next day. 'Julian,' she said, 'I do think it is mean of Elizabeth to spread that tale of you taking things – you know, money and sweets. I do really.'

Julian looked as if he could not believe his ears. 'What do you mean?' he asked at last.

'Well, it's all over the form now that you and Elizabeth quarrelled because she said you took things that belonged to other people, and you denied it,' said Arabella. She slipped her arm through Julian's. The boy had gone very pale.

'Don't worry, Julian,' she said. 'We all know what Elizabeth is! Goodness knows why she was made a monitor! Who would go to *her* for help, I'd like to know! She's not to be trusted at all.'

'You're right,' said Julian, 'but I thought she was. I never imagined for one moment she would spread such a story. A monitor too! She's a little beast. I can't think why I ever liked her.'

'No, I'm sure you can't,' said Arabella, delighted. 'Fancy her going all round the form, whispering these horrible things about you – and you haven't said a word about *her*!'

Of course, Elizabeth had not said a word either, but Julian did not know that. He had not known that Martin had overheard everything, and he thought that if the story got round, it could only have been told to the others by Elizabeth herself. He thought very bitterly of her indeed.

'I'll pay her back for that,' he said to Arabella.

'I should,' said Arabella eagerly. 'As I told you before, Julian, I'm on your side, and so is Rosemary. I expect lots of others are too.'

This time Julian did not say anything about there being no sides. He was hurt and angry, and the only thing he wanted to do was to get back at Elizabeth and hurt her.

And then many curious things began to happen to Elizabeth. Julian used all his clever brains to think out tricks that would get her into trouble – and when Julian really used his brains things began to happen!

Julian sat just in front of Elizabeth in class. In one lesson, history, the children had to have out a good many books, which they put in a neat pile on the back of their desks, so that they might refer quickly to them when they needed to.

Julian invented a curious little gadget like a spring. He twisted the spring up in a peculiar way so that it took a long time to untwist itself. He slipped it under Elizabeth's pile of books.

The lesson began. Miss Ranger was not in a good temper that day, for she had a headache, so the children were being rather careful not to make noises. Nobody let their desk lids fall with a slam; nobody dropped anything.

Julian grinned to himself, as he worked quietly in front of Elizabeth. He knew that the peculiar little spring was slowly untwisting itself under the bottom book. It was extremely strong, and when it reached a certain twist it would spring wide open and force the books off the desk.

Sure enough, this happened after about five minutes had gone by. The spring gave itself a final twist and the books moved. The top one fell, and then the others, all in a pile to the floor.

Miss Ranger jumped. 'Whose books fell then?' she said crossly. 'Elizabeth, don't be careless. How did that happen?'

'I don't know, Miss Ranger,' said Elizabeth, puzzled. 'I really don't.'

Julian bent to pick up the books, which had fallen just behind. He put another twisted spring under the bottom one again, pocketing the first one, which had fallen to the floor with the books.

In five minutes' time that spring worked too. It was a stronger one, and the books shot off the desk in a hurry. Crash, crash, crash, crash, crash!

Miss Ranger jumped violently, and her fountain pen, which she was using, made a blot on the book she was correcting.

'Elizabeth! Are you doing this on purpose?' she cried. 'If it happens again, you will go out of the room. I will not have you disturbing the class like this.'

Elizabeth was extremely puzzled. 'I'm very sorry, Miss Ranger,' she said. 'Honestly, the books seemed to jump off my desk by themselves.'

'Don't be childish, Elizabeth,' said Miss Ranger. 'That's the kind of thing a child in the lower school might say to me.'

Julian picked up the books, grinning. Elizabeth gave him a furious look. She had no idea that he was playing a trick on her, but she didn't like the grin. Once more Julian placed one of his curious springs under the bottom book.

And once again all the books jumped off the desk in a hurry. This time Miss Ranger lost her temper.

'Go out of the room,' she snapped at Elizabeth. 'Once might have been an accident – even twice – but not three times. I'm ashamed of you. You're a monitor and should know how to behave.'

With scarlet cheeks Elizabeth went out of the room. In her first term she had *tried* to be sent out of the room, but now she felt it to be a great disgrace. She hated it. She stood outside the door, almost ready to cry for shame and anger.

It wasn't my fault. My books really did *seem to jump off by themselves. I never even touched the beastly things!* she thought.

And then, how dreadful! Who should come by but Rita, the head girl herself. She looked in the greatest surprise at Elizabeth, standing red-faced outside the door. 'Why are you here, Elizabeth?' she asked gravely.

CHAPTER TWELVE

ELIZABETH IN DISGRACE

'I WAS sent out of the room, Rita,' said Elizabeth, 'but it was for something that wasn't my fault. Please believe me.'

'Don't let it happen again, Elizabeth,' said Rita. 'You know that you are a monitor, and should set an example to the others. I am not very pleased with various things I have heard about you and the first form this term.'

She walked down the passage and Elizabeth stared after her, wondering what Rita knew. She felt suddenly very sad and gloomy. *I looked forward to this term so much*, she thought, *and now everything is going wrong*.

She was called back into the room at the end of the lesson, and Miss Ranger spoke a few stern words to her. Elizabeth knew that it was no good saying again that she had not made the books fall, so she said nothing.

The next trick that Julian thought of was most extraordinary. He grinned with delight when it came into his mind. He went into the laboratory, where the children did most of their science work, and mixed up various chemicals together. He made them into a few wet little pellets and put them into a box. Then, before afternoon school, he slipped into the empty classroom, moved Elizabeth's desk and put a table in its place.

He stood a chair on top of the table and then climbed up and stood on it. He could reach the ceiling then. He arranged the little wet pellets close together on the white ceiling. He brushed them quickly over with a strange-smelling liquid. This would have the effect of making the little pellets gradually swell and burst, letting out a large drop of water which would fall straight downwards.

This is a good trick, thought Julian, as he jumped down from the chair, put it back in its place and pulled the table away. He put Elizabeth's desk back, arranging it exactly under the pellets on the ceiling. They were white and hardly noticeable.

That afternoon Mam'zelle came to take French. Elizabeth and the others had learnt French verbs and some French poetry. Mam'zelle was to hear it. All the children gabbled it over to themselves just before the lesson, making sure they knew it. Mam'zelle was heard coming along the passage and Elizabeth sprang to hold open the door.

Mam'zelle was in a good temper. The children were glad. Miss Ranger didn't get cross unless there really was something to be cross about, but Mam'zelle often got cross about nothing. Still, this afternoon she looked very pleasant indeed.

'And now we will have a very nice afternoon,' she said, beaming round. 'You will all say your verbs without one single mistake, and you will say your poetry most beautifully. And I shall be very pleased with you.'

No one made any reply to this. It would be nice if nobody made any mistake, but that was too much to be hoped for! Someone always came to grief in the French class.

Julian chose that afternoon to use his brains in the proper way. He rattled off his verbs without a single mistake. He addressed Mam'zelle in excellent French, so that she beamed all over her face with pleasure.

'Ah, this Julian! Always he pretends he is so stupid, but he is very clever! Now we will see if he knows his poetry well! Speak it to me, Julian.'

Julian began reciting the French smoothly and well. But no sooner had he begun than there came an interruption. It was Elizabeth.

She had been sitting down, her head bent over

her French book. And right on the top of her head had come a big drop of water! Elizabeth was most astonished. She gave a small cry and rubbed the top of her head. It was wet!

'What is the matter, Elizabeth?' asked Mam'zelle impatiently.

'A drop of water fell on my head,' said Elizabeth, puzzled. She looked up at the ceiling, but there did not seem anything to be seen there.

'You are silly, Elizabeth,' said Mam'zelle. 'You do not expect me to believe that.'

'But a drop of water *did* fall on my head,' said Elizabeth. 'I felt it.'

Jenny and Robert began to giggle. They thought Elizabeth was making it up in order to have a bit of fun. Mam'zelle rapped sharply on her desk.

'Silence!' she said. 'Julian, go on with your poetry. Begin again.'

Julian began again, knowing that another drop or two would fall on Elizabeth's head shortly. He wanted to laugh.

'Oh! Oh!' said Elizabeth suddenly from behind him! Two drops had fallen splash on to her hair. The little girl simply couldn't understand it. She rubbed her head.

'Elizabeth! Once more you interrupt!' said Mam'zelle angrily. 'Are you trying to spoil Julian's work? He is doing it so well. What is the matter now? Do not tell me again that it is raining on your head!'

'Well, Mam'zelle, it *is*,' said Elizabeth, and she rubbed her hand in her wet hair. Everyone roared with laughter. Mam'zelle began to get really angry.

'Silence, everybody!' she cried. 'I will not have this noise. Elizabeth, I am surprised at you. A monitor should not behave like this.'

'But Mam'zelle, honestly, it's very odd,' began Elizabeth again – and then another drop fell on her hair. She gave a jump and looked up at the ceiling. She really felt very puzzled indeed.

'Ah! You look at the ceiling as if it was the sky? You think it is raining on you! You think you will play me a silly joke!' cried Mam'zelle, her eyes beginning to flash. Everyone sat up, enjoying the fun. It was exciting when Mam'zelle lost her temper.

'Well, can I sit somewhere else?' asked Elizabeth in despair. 'Something does keep dropping on my head and I don't like it.'

'You can go and sit outside the room,' said Mam'zelle sternly. 'This is the silliest joke I have ever heard of. You will ask next if you can bring an umbrella into my class and sit with it over your head.'

The whole class squealed with laughter at the thought of this. But Mam'zelle had not meant to be funny, and she banged angrily on her desk.

'Silence! I do not make a joke. I am very angry. Elizabeth, leave my class.'

'Oh, please, Mam'zelle, no,' said poor Elizabeth. 'Please don't send me out of the room. I won't interrupt again. But, honestly, it's very strange.'

Another drop fell on her head, but she said nothing this time. She could not bear to be sent out of the room a second time, she really couldn't! She would rather get soaked through than that!

'Well, one more word from you and you will go,' threatened Mam'zelle. Elizabeth thankfully sat down, and made up her mind not even to jump if another of those unexpected drops landed on her hair.

But there was no more to come. Soon Elizabeth's hair was dry again, and nothing fell to wet it. She recited her verbs and poetry in her turn, and was allowed to remain in the room for the rest of the lesson.

Afterwards most of the children crowded round her. 'Elizabeth! How did you dare to act like that? Let's feel your head!'

But it was now dry, and no one would believe Elizabeth when she said over and over again that drops of water *had* fallen on her. They rubbed their hands over her hair, but not a bit of wetness was left.

'Why don't you own up to us and say it was a good

joke?' asked Harry. 'You might just as well.'

'Because it *wasn't* a joke, it was real,' answered Elizabeth angrily.

The children went off. They all thought Elizabeth had played a joke, but they also thought it wasn't right not to own up to it afterwards.

'She's telling untruths,' said Arabella to Rosemary. 'Well, all I can say is she's a funny sort of monitor to have!'

One or two of the others agreed. They had enjoyed the joke, but they really did think that Elizabeth had made up the story of the falling drops, and they felt rather disgusted with her when she denied it.

Mam'zelle related the story to Miss Ranger in the mistresses' common room that day. 'It is not like Elizabeth to be so silly,' she said.

Miss Ranger looked puzzled. 'I don't understand her,' she said. 'She is not behaving like herself lately. She was very stupid in my class too – kept pushing piles of books over! So childish.'

'I thought she would make a good monitor,' said Mam'zelle. 'I am disappointed in Elizabeth.'

Arabella spoke against Elizabeth whenever she could, and some of the children listened. Arabella was clever in the way she spoke.

'Of course,' she said, 'I like a joke as much as anyone,

and it's fun to play a trick in a dull lesson. But honestly I don't think a *monitor* should do that. I mean, I don't see why any of *us* shouldn't play the fool a bit if we like, but not a monitor. You do expect a monitor to behave or why make them monitors?'

'She was called the naughtiest girl in the school two terms ago, wasn't she?' said Martin. 'Well, it must be difficult to stop being that really. I think it was silly to make her a monitor. She couldn't have been ready to be one.'

'Look at the beastly stories she spread about poor Julian too,' said Arabella. 'A monitor should be the first to stop a thing like that, not start it. Well, I always did say I couldn't imagine why Elizabeth was a monitor.'

'Perhaps she won't be for long!' said Martin. 'I don't see why we should put up with someone who behaves like Elizabeth. How can we look up to her or go to her for advice? She oughtn't to *be* a monitor!'

Poor Elizabeth. She knew the children were whispering about her – and she couldn't do anything about it.

CHAPTER THIRTEEN

ARABELLA'S SECRET

THE NEXT School Meeting came and went without anything being said by Elizabeth. The girl was so miserable and so puzzled as to what she should do for the best that she had made up her mind to say nothing, at least for the present.

Meanwhile Arabella was soon going to have a birthday. Her mother had promised to send her a big birthday cake, and whatever else she liked to ask for to eat or drink. Mrs Buckley was now in America, but Arabella could order what she liked from one of the big London stores.

Arabella talked about it a good deal. She loved to boast, and she talked of all the good things she would order.

Then she had an idea. She told it to Rosemary. 'What about a midnight feast, Rosemary? We had one once at my old school and it was such fun. We should have plenty to eat and drink – and think how exciting it would be to have it in the middle of the night!'

Rosemary agreed. 'Should we have it at midnight?' she asked. 'We couldn't very well have it earlier, because some of the mistresses and masters might be up.'

'Yes, we'll have it just after midnight,' said Arabella. 'But we won't ask Elizabeth! She's such a horrid thing she might give the secret away and spoil the feast!'

'All right,' said Rosemary. 'Well, who will you ask then?'

'Everyone – except just a few who are Elizabeth's old friends,' said Arabella. 'We won't ask Kathleen – or Harry – or Robert. They still stick up for Elizabeth. Anyway, I suppose Elizabeth wouldn't come, even if we did ask her, because she might think a midnight feast was against the silly rules, and she's a monitor.'

So the first form once more had a secret that was whispered from one to the other. Elizabeth heard the talking, and noticed that it died down when she passed. She thought they must be whispering about her again, and she was angry and sad.

Julian was asked, of course, and Martin. Julian's green eyes gleamed when he heard of the midnight feast. This was just the sort of daring thing he liked.

The children discussed where they should hide the

food and drink. They did not want the mistresses to guess what they were going to do.

'We'll show the birthday cake around, and have some of it for tea,' said Arabella, 'but we won't say anything about the other things.'

'Hide the ginger beers in one of the garden sheds,' said Martin. 'I know a good place. I'll put them there. I can fetch them on the night.'

'And put the biscuits in the old games locker in the passage,' said Julian. 'It's never used, and no one will see it there. I'll take them along.'

So the goodies were hidden here and there, and the children began to feel most excited. The few that were left out did not know what was happening. They only knew that it was Arabella's secret, and that a great fuss was being made of it.

Arabella always made a point of talking in a low voice about the party whenever she saw Elizabeth coming near. Then she would give a jump when she looked up and saw Elizabeth, nudge the person she was talking to and change the subject quickly and loudly.

This annoyed Elizabeth very much. 'You need not think I want to hear your stupid secret,' she said to Arabella. 'I don't. So talk all you like about it – I'll shut my ears!'

All the same, it was not pleasant to be left out.

Neither was it pleasant to see Julian talking and laughing to Arabella and Rosemary. Elizabeth did not know that he did it sometimes to annoy her. He could not bring himself to like the boastful, vain little Arabella very much. But, if his friendship with her annoyed Elizabeth, then he would certainly go on with it!

Arabella's birthday came. The children wished her many happy returns of the day and gave her little presents, which she accepted graciously, with pretty words of thanks. There was no doubt that Arabella knew how to behave when she was getting her own way!

Elizabeth gave Arabella nothing – neither did she wish her a happy birthday. She saw Julian give her a beautiful little brooch he had made with his own clever hands. Arabella pinned it on joyfully.

'Oh, Julian!' she said loudly, knowing that Elizabeth could hear. 'You *are* a good friend! Thank you ever so much.'

The midnight feast was to be held in the common room. This room was well away from any of the mistresses' bedrooms, and the children felt they would be safe there. They all felt excited that day, and Miss Ranger wondered what could be the matter with her class.

Quite by chance Elizabeth opened the old games locker in the passage. She was hunting for a ball to practise catching with on the lacrosse field, and she thought there might possibly be one there. She stared in surprise at the bag of biscuits.

I suppose Miss Ranger put them there, she thought. *Perhaps she has forgotten them. I must tell her. She may want them for the biscuits to give out at break.*

But Elizabeth forgot all about them and didn't say anything to Miss Ranger. She had no idea that they belonged to Arabella, and were going to be eaten at the feast.

Arabella's secret was well kept. The children who had been asked really were afraid that if Elizabeth got to know it she might try to stop it, as she was a monitor. So they carefully said nothing at all to her. She and a few others were quite in the dark about it.

When midnight came all the children but Arabella were asleep. She had said she would keep awake and tell everyone when it was time. She was so excited that she had no difficulty at all in keeping her eyes wide open until she heard the school clock strike midnight from its tower.

She sat up in bed and groped for her dressing gown. She put on her slippers. Then, taking a small torch, she went to wake her friends, giving them little nudges.

They awoke with jumps. 'Sh!' whispered Arabella to each one. 'Don't make a noise! It's time for the midnight feast.'

Elizabeth was sound asleep, and so was Kathleen. They did not wake when the others padded out of their room to meet the boys, who were now coming from their own part of the school to the common room. There was a lot of whispering, and choked-back giggles could be heard all the way down the passages.

The children crowded into the common room and lit candles. They were afraid to put on the electric light in case the strong light showed through the blinds.

'Anyway, it's more fun to have candles!' said Arabella gleefully. This was the kind of thing she liked. She was queen of the party! She wore a beautiful silk dressing gown and blue silk slippers to match. She really looked lovely, and she knew it.

The children set out the food and drink. What a lovely lot there was!

'Sardines! I love those!' said Ruth.

'Tinned peaches! Oooh! How lovely!'

'Bags I some of those chocolate buns! They look as if they would melt in my mouth!'

'Pass that spoon, someone. I'll ladle out the peaches.'

'Don't make such a noise, Belinda. That's twice you've dropped a fork! You'll have Miss Ranger here if you don't look out.'

Pop! A ginger-beer bottle was opened and another and another. Pop! Pop! The children looked at one another, delighted. This was really fun. It was past midnight and here they were, eating and drinking all kinds of lovely things!

'Where are the biscuits?' said Arabella. 'I feel as if I'd like a biscuit to eat with these peaches. I can't see the biscuits. Where are they?'

'Oh, I forgot to get them,' said Julian, getting up. 'I'll fetch them now, Arabella. I won't be a minute. They are in that games locker.'

He went out to fetch the biscuits, groping his way along the passage, then up the stairs to where the locker stood in a corner.

He had no torch and it was dark. He stumbled along, trying to be as quiet as possible. He walked into a chair, and knocked it over with a crash. He stood still, wondering if anyone had heard.

He was not far from the room where Elizabeth slept. When the chair went over, the little girl awoke with a jump. She sat up in bed, wondering what the noise was.

I'd better go and see, she thought. She slipped out of bed and put on her dressing gown. She did not notice that half the beds were empty in the dormitory. She put on her slippers and crept to the door with her torch not yet switched on.

She went into the passage and stood there. She walked along a little way and thought she heard the noise of someone not very far in front of her. She padded softly down the passage.

The Someone went to the old games locker. Elizabeth distinctly heard the creak as it was opened. Who could it be? And what were they doing at that time of night?

Elizabeth walked softly up to the locker. She switched on her torch very suddenly, and made Julian almost jump out of his skin.

'Julian! What are you doing here? Oh, you horrid, mean thief – you're stealing *biscuits* now! I think you're too disgusting for words! Put them back at once!'

'Sh!' hissed Julian. 'You'll wake everyone, you idiot.'

He did not attempt to put back the bag of biscuits. He meant to take them to the feast. But Elizabeth did not know that, of course. She honestly thought he had come there to steal the biscuits in the middle of the night.

'Well, I've really caught you this time!' she cried. 'Caught you with the stolen goods in your hand! You can't deny *that*! Give them to me!'

Julian snatched them away. The lid of the locker fell with a terrific bang that echoed all up and down the passage.

'Idiot!' said Julian in despair. 'Now you've woken everyone!'

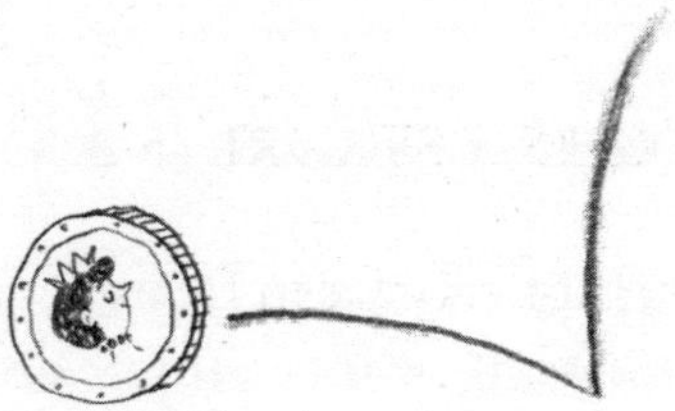

CHAPTER FOURTEEN

SNEEZING POWDER

THE CRASH of the locker lid certainly had awakened a good many people. There came the sound of footsteps and of doors being opened. The mistresses would soon be on the scene.

Julian fled to warn the others, giving Elizabeth a furious push as he passed her. She almost fell over. She did not know where he had gone, so she ran back to her own dormitory, excited to think that she really had caught Julian in the very act of stealing the biscuits.

Now I'll report him! she thought, as she climbed into bed. *I jolly well will!*

Julian ran to the common room and opened the door. 'Quick!' he said. 'Get back to your beds. Elizabeth caught me as I was getting the biscuits, and made an awful noise. If you don't get back quickly, we'll all be caught.'

Hastily the children stuffed everything into their lockers round the wall, or into empty desks. Then they blew out the candles and fled, hoping that they had not left too many crumbs about.

The boys raced for their own dormitories. The girls rushed to theirs.

'Blow Elizabeth!' panted Arabella as she took off her dressing gown and slipped into bed. 'We were just in the middle of everything. Now it's all spoilt!'

The mistresses had been asking one another what the noise was. Mam'zelle, who slept nearest to the first-form dormitories, was a sound sleeper, and had heard nothing at all. She was surprised when Miss Ranger opened the door and woke her.

'Perhaps it is the girls in the first-form dormitories playing tricks on one another,' said Mam'zelle sleepily. 'You go and see, Miss Ranger.'

But, by the time that Miss Ranger went into the dormitories and switched on the lights, not a sound was to be heard. All the children seemed to be sleeping most peacefully. Too peacefully really, Miss Ranger thought!

Elizabeth saw the light switched on, and out of the corner of her eye she watched Miss Ranger. Should she tell her what had happened? No, she wouldn't. She would spring it on the School Meeting tomorrow, and make everyone sit up and take notice!

Miss Ranger switched off the light and went quietly back to bed. She couldn't imagine what the noise had been. Perhaps the school cat had been chasing about and upset something. Miss Ranger got into bed and fell asleep.

Elizabeth lay awake a long time, thinking of Julian and the biscuits. She was quite, quite sure now that Julian was a disgusting thief. All that talk about doing what he liked and letting others do what *they* liked! It was just a way of excusing himself for his bad ways.

He'll get a shock when I stand up at the Meeting and report him, thought Elizabeth.

The children were angry that Elizabeth should have brought their fun to such a sudden end. 'Shall we give her a good scolding?' said Arabella primly.

'Well, she doesn't know about the feast,' said Julian, 'though she must have wondered what you had all been up to when you crept back to bed so suddenly.'

Elizabeth *had* wondered, but she knew that Arabella had had a birthday and she had simply thought that the girls had visited her that night, and had a few games. She had not thought of a feast.

'Don't let's tell her,' said Julian. 'We could finish the feast tonight and she might stop it if she guessed.'

So no one told Elizabeth that she had spoilt the feast,

but they gave her many dark looks, which puzzled her very much.

Julian thought of a way to pay back Elizabeth for spoiling the fun of the night before. He told the others.

'Look,' he said, 'I've made some sneezing powder. I'll scatter some between the pages of Elizabeth's French book and we'll all watch her get a sneezing fit in Mam'zelle's class.'

'Ooh, yes!' said everyone in delight. This was a joke after their own hearts.

Julian slipped into the classroom before afternoon school. He went to Elizabeth's desk and opened it. He found her French book, and lightly scattered the curious sneezing powder over it. He had discovered it when he was inventing something else, and had found himself suddenly sneezing. Julian was always inventing something new, thinking of something that no one had thought of before!

He scattered the pages full of the white powder, then shut the book carefully and put it back. He slipped out of the classroom, grinning. Elizabeth would get a surprise in the French class. So would Mam'zelle.

The children went to their form rooms when the bell rang for afternoon school. 'French!' groaned Jenny. 'Oh dear. I'm sure I shall forget everything if Mam'zelle is in a bad temper.'

'I feel so sleepy,' whispered Arabella to Rosemary, who also looked tired, after the midnight feast. 'I hope Mam'zelle doesn't pick on me if she wants to be cross. I hope she'll pick Elizabeth. Won't it be fun if she *does* start sneezing!'

There was oral French for the first ten minutes. Then Mam'zelle told the class to get out their French reading books. Elizabeth got out hers and opened it.

It was not long before the sneezing powder did its work. As the little girl turned over the pages, some of the fine white powder flew up her nose and tickled it. She felt a sneeze coming and got out her hanky.

'*A-tish-oo!*' she said. Mam'zelle took no notice.

'*A-tish-oo!*' said Elizabeth, wondering if she had got a cold. '*A-TISH-OOOOOO!*'

Mam'zelle looked up. Elizabeth hastily tried to smother the next sneeze. There was a pause, in which Jenny read out loud from her French book. She came to the end of the page, and turned over. Everyone did the same.

The turning of the page sent more of the powder up Elizabeth's nose. She felt another sneeze coming and hurriedly put up her hanky. But she couldn't stop it.

'*A-TISH-OOOOOO! A-TISH-OOOOOO!*' The sneezes were quite loud enough to drown Jenny's reading. One or two of the children began to choke back giggles. They waited for Elizabeth's next sneeze. It came. It was such a loud one that it made Mam'zelle jump.

'Enough, Elizabeth,' she said. 'You will sneeze no more. It is not necessary. Do not disturb the class like this.'

'I can't – *a-tish-ooo* – help it,' said poor Elizabeth, with tears streaming down her cheeks, for the powder was very strong. '*A-tish-tish-tish-oooo!*'

Mam'zelle became angry. 'Elizabeth! Last week it was drops falling on your head – this week it is sneezes. I will not have it.'

'*A-tish-ish-ish-ooo-ooo*,' said poor Elizabeth. The class began to laugh helplessly. Mam'zelle flew into a temper and banged on the desk.

'Elizabeth! You are a monitor and you behave like this! I will not have it. You will stop this sneezing game at once.'

'*A-tish-OOOOOO!*' said Elizabeth. The children laughed till the tears ran down their cheeks. This was the funniest thing they had ever seen.

'Leave the room, and do not come back,' ordered Mam'zelle sternly. 'I will not have you in my class.'

'But oh, Mam'zelle, please – *tishoo*, *tishoo* – *tishoo* – oh, Mam'zelle,' began Elizabeth. But Mam'zelle came over to her, took her firmly by the shoulders and walked her to the door.

She shut it behind Elizabeth and turned to face the class sternly.

'This is not funny,' she said. 'Not at all funny.'

The boys and girls thought it was. They tried their hardest to swallow down their giggles, but every now and again someone would choke, and that would set the whole class giggling again.

Mam'zelle was very angry indeed. She set them a page of poetry to copy out that evening as a punishment, but even that did not make the class stop giggling.

Elizabeth stood outside the door, upset and puzzled. 'Whatever made me sneeze like that?' she wondered. 'I'm not sneezing at all, out here. Am I starting a very bad cold? I simply could *not* stop sneezing in the classroom. It was mean of Mam'zelle to send me out here.'

And then, to Elizabeth's horror, William, the head boy, came along, talking to Mr Lewis, the music master. Elizabeth tried to look as if she wasn't there at all. But it was no use. William knew at once she had been sent out of the room.

'Elizabeth!' he said. 'Surely you haven't been sent out of the room *again*! Rita told me you had, last week. Are you forgetting you are a monitor?'

'No,' said Elizabeth miserably. 'I'm not. Mam'zelle

sent me out because I couldn't stop sneezing, William. She thought I was doing it on purpose. But I wasn't.'

'Well, you are not sneezing now,' said William.

'I know. I stopped as soon as I came out here,' said Elizabeth.

William walked on, thinking that Elizabeth must have been playing a silly joke. He would have to speak to Rita about it. They could not have monitors being sent out of the room like that. It was not right to have monitors setting a bad example.

Elizabeth had no idea that Julian had played a joke on her. She really thought she had been sneezing because she was beginning a cold. She was surprised when no cold came.

Well, I shall go to the Meeting tonight, she thought. *And it will serve Julian right to be shown up in front of everyone. I know they will believe me, because I am a monitor.*

CHAPTER FIFTEEN

A STORMY MEETING

THE CHILDREN filed into the big gym for the usual school Meeting that night. Elizabeth was excited and strung up. She longed to get the Meeting over, and have everything settled.

'Any money for the box?' said William, as usual. Ten shillings came in from a boy who had had a postal order from an uncle. Arabella put in two pounds – her birthday money. She had learnt her lesson about that! She was not going to be reported for keeping back money again.

Two shillings were given to everyone. Then William and Rita dealt with requests for more money. Elizabeth could hardly keep still. She felt nervous. She glanced at Julian. He sat as usual on the bench, a lock of hair falling into his eyes. He brushed it back impatiently.

'Any complaints?' The familiar question came from William, and a small boy sprang up before Elizabeth could speak.

'Please, William! The other children in my class are always calling me a dunce because I'm bottom. It isn't fair.'

'Have you spoken to your monitor about it?' asked William.

'Yes,' said the small boy.

'Who is your monitor?' asked William.

A bigger boy stood up. 'I am,' he said. 'Yes, the others do tease James. He has missed a lot of school through illness, so he doesn't know as much as the others. But I spoke to his teacher, and she says he could really try harder than he does, because he has good brains. He doesn't need to be bottom very long.'

'Thank you,' said William. The monitor sat down.

'Well, James, you heard what your monitor said. You yourself can soon stop the others teasing you, by using your good brains and not being bottom! You may have got so used always to being at the bottom that it didn't occur to you you could be anything else. But it seems that you can!'

'Oh,' said James, looking pleased and rather surprised. He sat down with a bump. His form looked at him, not quite knowing whether to be cross with him or amused.

They suddenly nudged one another and grinned. James looked round, smiling too.

'Any more complaints?' asked Rita.

'Yes, Rita!' said Elizabeth, and jumped up so suddenly that she almost upset her chair. 'I have a very serious complaint to make.'

A ripple of whispering ran through the school. Everyone sat up straight. What was Elizabeth going to say? Arabella went rather pale. She hoped Elizabeth was not going to complain about *her* again. Julian glanced sharply at Elizabeth. Surely, surely she wasn't going to speak about him!

But she was, of course. She began to make her complaint, her words almost falling over one another.

'Rita, William! It's about Julian,' she began. 'I have thought for some time that he was taking things that didn't belong to him – and yesterday I caught him at it! I caught him with the things in his hand! He was taking them out of the old games locker in the passage.'

'Elizabeth, you must explain better,' said Rita, looking grave and serious. 'This is a terrible charge you are making. We shall have to go deeply into it, and unless you really have proof you had better say no more, but come to me and William afterwards.'

'I *have* got proof!' said Elizabeth. 'I saw Julian take the biscuits out of the locker. I don't know who they belonged to – Miss Ranger, I suppose. Anyway, Julian must have found them there, and when he thought we were all asleep at night he went to take them. And I heard him and saw him.'

The whole school was quite silent. The first-formers looked at one another, their hearts beating fast. Now their midnight feast would have to be found out! Julian would have to give away their secret.

William looked at Julian. He was sitting with his hands in his pockets, looking amused.

'Stand up, Julian, and tell us your side of the story,' said William.

Julian stood up, his hands still in his pockets. 'Take your hands out of your pockets,' ordered William. Julian did so. He looked untidy and careless as he stood there, his green eyes twinkling like a gnome's.

'I'm sorry, William,' he said, 'but I can't give any explanation, because I should give away a secret belonging to others. All I can say is I was not stealing the biscuits. I was certainly *taking* them, but not stealing them!'

He sat down. Elizabeth jumped up, like a jack-in-the-box. 'You see, William!' she said. 'He can't give you a proper explanation!'

'Sit down, Elizabeth,' said William sternly. He looked at the first-formers, who all sat silent and uncomfortable, not daring to glance at one another. How good of Julian not to give them away! How awful all this was!

'First-formers,' said William gravely, 'I hope that if any one of you can help to clear Julian of this very serious charge, you will do so, whether it means giving away some secret or not. If Julian, out of loyalty to one or more of you, cannot stick up for himself, then you must be loyal to him, and tell what you know.'

There was a silence after this. Rosemary sat trembling, not daring to move. Belinda half got up then sat down again. Martin looked straight ahead, rather pale.

It was Arabella who gave the first form a great surprise. She suddenly stood up, and spoke in a low voice.

'William, I'd better say something, I think. We *did* have a secret, and it's decent of Julian not to give it away. You see it was my birthday yesterday and we thought we'd have a – a – a midnight feast.'

She stopped, so nervous that she could hardly go on. The whole school was listening with the greatest interest.

'Go on,' said Rita gently.

'Well, well, you see, we had to hide the things here and there,' said Arabella. 'It was all such fun. We didn't tell Elizabeth – because she's a monitor and might have tried to stop us. Well, Julian hid my biscuits in the old games locker and he went to get them after midnight, when the feast had begun. I suppose that's when Elizabeth means. But they were *my* biscuits, and I asked him to get them, and he brought them back to the common room where we were. And I think it's jolly mean of Elizabeth to accuse Julian of stealing them. She's done that before. The whole form knows she's been saying that he takes money and sweets that don't belong to him.'

This was a very long speech. Arabella finished it suddenly, and sat down, almost panting. Julian looked at her gratefully. He knew that she would not at all like telling the secret of the midnight party, but she had done it to save him. His opinion of the vain little girl went up sky-high – and so did everyone else's.

William and Rita had listened closely to all that Arabella had said. So had Elizabeth. When she had heard the explanation of Julian's midnight wanderings she went very white, and her knees shook. She knew in a moment that in that one thing, at any rate, she had made a terrible mistake. William turned to Elizabeth, and his eyes were very sharp and stern.

'Elizabeth, it seems that you have done a most unforgivable thing – you have accused Julian publicly of something he hasn't done. I suppose you did not even ask him to explain his action to you, but just took it for granted that he was doing wrong.'

Elizabeth sat glued to her seat. She could not say a word.

'Arabella says that this is not the only time you have accused Julian. There have been other times too. As this last accusation of yours has been proved to be wrong, it is likely that the other complaints you have made to the first form are wrong too. So we will not hear them in public. But Rita and I will want you to come to us privately and explain everything.'

'Yes, William,' said Elizabeth in a low voice. 'I'm – I'm very, very sorry about what I said just now. I didn't know.'

'That isn't any excuse,' said William sternly. 'I can't think what has happened to you this term, Elizabeth. We made you a monitor at the end of last term because we all thought you should be, but this term you have let us all down. I am afraid that already many of us are thinking that you should no longer be a monitor.'

Several boys and girls agreed. They stamped on the floor with their feet.

'Twice you have been sent out of your classroom,' said William. 'And for the same reason – disturbing the class by playing foolish tricks. That is not the behaviour of a monitor, Elizabeth. I am afraid that we can no longer ask you to help us as a monitor. You must step down and leave us to choose someone else in your place.'

This was too much for Elizabeth. She gave an enormous sob, jumped down from the platform and rushed out of the room. She was a failure. She was no good as a monitor. And oh, she had been *so* proud of it too!

William did not attempt to stop her rushing from the room. He looked gravely round the well-filled benches. 'We must now choose another monitor,' he said. 'Will you please begin thinking who will best take Elizabeth's place?'

The children sat still, thinking. The Meeting had been rather dreadful in some ways, but to every child there had come a great lesson. They must never, never accuse anyone of wrongdoing unless they were absolutely certain. Every child had clearly seen the misery that might have been caused, and they knew that Elizabeth's punishment was just.

Poor Elizabeth! Always rushing into trouble. What would she do now?

CHAPTER SIXTEEN

ELIZABETH SEES WILLIAM AND RITA

A NEW monitor was chosen in place of Elizabeth. It was a girl in the second form, called Susan. Not one child outside the first form had chosen a first-former. It was clear that most people felt that the first form would do better to have an older girl or boy for a monitor.

'Arabella, it *was* brave of you to own up about the midnight feast,' said Rosemary admiringly. All the others thought so too. Arabella felt pleased with herself. She really had done it unselfishly, and she was rather surprised at herself for doing such a thing. It was nice to feel that the rest of the form admired her for something.

One person was feeling rather uncomfortable. It was Julian. He felt very angry with Elizabeth for making such an untruthful and horrible complaint about him, but he did know that it was because of his tricks she had been sent out of the room twice, and not because of her own foolishness. Partly because of his tricks and their results, Elizabeth had lost the honour of being a monitor.

'Of course, William and Rita might have said she couldn't be because she complained wrongly about me,' said Julian to himself. 'But it sounded as if it was because of her being sent out of the room. Well, she doesn't deserve to be a monitor anyway – so why should I worry?'

But he did worry a little, because, like Elizabeth, he was really very fair-minded and, although he did not like the little girl, he knew that dislike was no excuse at all for being unfair. He had come very well out of the whole affair, thanks to Arabella. But Elizabeth had not. Even Harry, Robert and Kathleen, her own good friends, had nothing nice to say of her at the moment.

The Meeting broke up after choosing the new monitor. The children went out, talking over what had happened. You never knew what would come out at a School Meeting.

'Nothing can be hidden at Whyteleafe School!' said Eileen, one of the older girls. 'Sooner or later everyone's faults come to light, and are put right. Sooner or later our good points are seen and rewarded. And we do it all ourselves. It's very good for us, I think.'

Miss Belle and Miss Best had been present at the Meeting, and had listened with great interest to all that had happened. William and Rita stayed behind to have a word with them.

'Did we do right, Miss Belle?' asked William.

'I think so,' said Miss Belle, and Miss Best nodded too. 'But William, have Elizabeth along as soon as ever you can, and let her get off her chest all that she has been thinking about Julian – there is clearly something puzzling there. Elizabeth does not get such fixed ideas into her head without *some* reason. There is still something we don't know.'

'Yes. We'll send for Elizabeth now,' said Rita. 'I wonder where she is.'

She was out in the stables in the dark, sobbing against the horse she rode each morning. The horse nuzzled up to her, wondering what was upsetting his little mistress. Soon she dried her eyes, and sat down on an upturned pail in a corner.

She was puzzled, deeply sorry for what she had said about Julian, very much ashamed of herself and horrified at losing the honour of being a monitor. She felt that she could never face the others again. But she knew she would have to.

'What is the matter with me?' she wondered. 'I make up my mind to be so good and helpful and everything and then I go and do just the opposite! I lose my temper. I say dreadful things – and now everyone hates me. Especially Julian. It's funny about Julian. I did see that he had my marked shilling. I did see that one of my sweets fell out of his pocket. So that's why I thought he was stealing the biscuits, and he wasn't. But did he take the other things?'

Someone came by, calling loudly. 'Elizabeth! Where are you?'

Messengers had been sent to find her, to tell her to go to Rita and William. She could not be found in the school, so Nora had come outside to look for her with a torch.

At first Elizabeth thought she would not answer. She simply could not go in and face the others just yet. Then a little courage came to her, and she stood up.

I'm not a coward, she thought. *William and Rita have punished me partly for something I* haven't *done – because I really didn't play about in class – but the other thing I* did *do. I did make an untruthful complaint about Julian, though I thought at the time it was true. So I must just face up to it and not be silly.*

'Elizabeth, are you out here?' came Nora's voice again.

This time the little girl answered. 'Yes. I'm coming.'

She came out of the stables, rubbing her eyes. Nora flashed her torch at her. 'I've been looking everywhere for you, idiot,' she said. 'William and Rita want you. Hurry up.'

'All right,' said Elizabeth, feeling her heart sink. Was she going to be scolded again? Wasn't it enough that she should have been disgraced in public without being scolded in private?

She rubbed her hanky over her face and ran to the school. She made her way to William's study. She knocked at the door.

'Come in!' said William's voice. She went in and saw the head boy and girl sitting in armchairs. They both looked up gravely as she came in.

'Sit there,' said Rita in a kindly voice. She felt sorry for the headstrong little girl who was so often in trouble. Elizabeth felt glad to hear the kindness in Rita's voice. She sat down.

'Rita,' she said, 'I'm terribly sorry for being wrong about Julian. I did think I was right. I honestly did.'

'That's what we want to see you about,' said Rita. 'We couldn't allow you to say any more about Julian in public, in case you were wrong again. But we want you to tell us now all that has happened to make you feel so strongly against Julian.'

Elizabeth told the head boy and girl everything – all about Rosemary's money going and Arabella's; how her own marked shilling had gone – and had appeared in Julian's hand when he was spinning coins; and how her own sweet had fallen from his pocket.

'You are quite, quite sure about these things?' asked William, looking worried. It was clear to him that there was a thief about – somebody in the first form – but he was not so sure as Elizabeth that it was Julian! He and Rita both thought that whatever the boy's faults were, however careless and don't-carish he was, dishonesty was not one of his failings.

'So you see, William and Rita,' finished Elizabeth earnestly, 'because of all these things I jumped to the idea that Julian was stealing the biscuits last night. It was terribly wrong of me, but it was the other things that made me think it.'

'Elizabeth, why did you think you could put matters right yourself when the money first began to disappear?' asked Rita. 'It was not your business. You should not have laid a trap. You should have come straight to us, and let us deal with it. You, as a monitor, should report these things to us, and let us think out the right way of dealing with them.'

'Oh,' said Elizabeth, surprised. 'Oh. I somehow thought that as I was a monitor I could settle things myself – and I thought it would be nice to put things right without worrying you or the Meeting.'

'Elizabeth, you must learn to see the difference

between big things and little things,' said Rita. 'Monitors can settle such matters as seeing that no one talks after lights out, giving advice in silly little quarrels and things like that. But when a big thing crops up we expect our monitors to come to us and report it. See what you have done by trying to settle the matter yourself. You have brought a terrible complaint against Julian, you have made Arabella give away the secret she wanted to keep and you have lost the honour of being made a monitor.'

'I felt so grand and important, being a monitor,' said Elizabeth, wiping away two tears that ran down her cheek.

'Yes, you felt *too* grand and important,' said Rita. 'So grand that you thought you could settle a matter that even Miss Belle and Miss Best might find difficult! Well, there is a lot you have to learn, Elizabeth, but you do make things as hard for yourself as possible, don't you!'

'Yes, I do,' said Elizabeth. 'I don't think enough. I just go rushing along, losing my temper – and my friends – and everything!' She gave a heavy sigh.

'Well,' said William, 'there is one thing about you, Elizabeth – you *have* got the courage to see your own faults, and that is the first step to curing them. Don't worry too much. You may get back all you have lost if only you are sensible.'

'I think we had better get Julian here and tell him all that Elizabeth has said,' said Rita. 'Perhaps he can throw some light on that marked shilling – and the sweet. I feel certain he didn't take them.'

'Oh, let me go before he comes,' begged Elizabeth, who felt that Julian was the very last person she wanted to meet just then. She pictured his green eyes looking scornfully at her. No, she couldn't bear to meet him just then.

'No, you must stay and hear what he has to say,' said Rita firmly. 'If Julian didn't take these things, there is something peculiar about the matter. We must find out what it is.'

So Elizabeth had to sit in William's study, waiting for Julian to come. Oh dear, what a perfectly horrid day this was!

CHAPTER SEVENTEEN

GOOD AT HEART!

JULIAN CAME at once. He was surprised to see Elizabeth in the study too. He gave her a look, and then turned politely to William and Rita.

'Julian, we have heard a lot of puzzling things from Elizabeth,' said William. 'We are sure you have an explanation for them. Will you listen to me while I tell you them – and then you can tell us what you think?'

Julian listened while William told all that Elizabeth had poured out to him and Rita. Julian looked surprised and puzzled.

'I see now why Elizabeth thought I was the thief,' he said. 'It did look very odd, I must say. Did I really have the marked shilling? And did a sweet of Elizabeth's really fall out of my pocket? I heard something fall, but as the sweet wasn't mine I didn't pick it up. I saw it on the floor, but I didn't even know it had fallen from my pocket. I certainly never put it there.'

'How did it get there then?' said Rita, puzzled.

'I believe I've got that shilling now,' said Julian suddenly. He felt in his pockets and took out a brand-new coin. He looked at it closely. In one place a tiny black cross could still be seen. 'It's the same shilling,' said Julian.

'That's the cross I marked,' said Elizabeth, pointing to it. Julian stared at it thoughtfully.

'You know, I'm sure, now I come to think of it, that I didn't have a bright new shilling like this out of the box that week,' he said. 'I'd have noticed it. I'm sure I got two old shillings. So someone must have put this new shilling into my pocket – and taken out an old shilling. Why?'

'And someone must have put one of Elizabeth's sweets into your pocket too,' said William. 'Does any boy or girl dislike you very much, Julian?'

Julian thought hard. 'Well, no – except, of course, Elizabeth,' he said.

Elizabeth suddenly felt dreadfully upset when she heard this. All her dislike for Julian had gone now that she felt, with Rita and William, that Julian hadn't taken the money or sweets, but that someone had played a horrible trick on him.

'Elizabeth just hates me,' said Julian, 'but I'm sure

she wouldn't do a thing like that!'

'Oh, Julian, of course I wouldn't,' said poor Elizabeth, almost in tears again. 'Julian, I don't hate you. I'm more sorry than I can say about everything that has happened. I feel so ashamed of myself. I'm always doing things like this. You'll never forgive me, I know.'

Julian looked gravely at her out of his curious green eyes. 'I have forgiven you,' he said unexpectedly. 'I never bear malice. But I don't like you very much and I can't be good friends with you any more, Elizabeth. But there is something I'd like to own up to now.'

He turned to William and Rita. 'You said, at the Meeting, that Elizabeth had twice been sent out of the room for misbehaving herself,' he said. 'Well, it wasn't her fault.' He turned to Elizabeth. 'Elizabeth, I played a trick on you over those books. I put springs under the bottom ones and they fell over when the springs had untwisted themselves. And I stuck pellets on the ceiling just above your chair, so that drops fell on your head when the chemicals in them changed to water. And I put sneezing powder in the pages of your French book.'

William and Rita listened to all this in the greatest astonishment. They hardly knew what Julian was talking about. But Elizabeth, of course, knew very well indeed. She gaped at Julian in the greatest surprise.

Springs under her books! Pellets on the ceiling that turned to water! Sneezing powder in her books! The little girl could hardly believe her ears. She stared at Julian in amazement, quite forgetting her tears.

And then, very suddenly, she laughed. She couldn't help it. She thought of her books jumping off her desk in that peculiar manner. She thought of those puzzling drops of water splashing down – and that fit of sneezing. It all seemed to her very funny, even though it had brought her scoldings and punishments.

How she laughed. She threw back her head and roared. William, Rita and Julian could not have been more surprised. They stared at the laughing girl, and then they began to laugh too. Elizabeth had a very infectious laugh that always made everyone else want to join in.

At last Elizabeth wiped her eyes and stopped. 'Oh, dear,' she said, 'I can't imagine how I could laugh like that when I felt so unhappy. But I couldn't help it. It all seemed so funny when I looked back and remembered what happened and how puzzled I was.'

Julian suddenly put out his hand and took Elizabeth's. 'You're a real sport,' he said. 'I never for one moment thought you'd laugh when I told you what I'd done to pay you out. I thought you might cry or fly into a temper or sulk, but I never thought you'd laugh. You're a real sport, Elizabeth, and I like you all over again!'

'Oh,' said Elizabeth, hardly believing her ears. 'Oh, Julian! You *are* nice. But oh, what a funny thing to like me again just because I laughed.'

'It isn't really funny,' said William. 'People who can laugh like that, when the joke has been against them, are, as Julian says, good sports, and very lovable. That laugh of yours has made things a lot better, Elizabeth. Now we understand one another a good deal more.'

Julian squeezed Elizabeth's hand. 'I don't mind the silly things you said about me, and you don't mind the silly things I did against you,' he said. 'So we're quits and we can begin all over again. Will you be my friend?'

'Oh, *yes*, Julian!' said Elizabeth happily. 'Yes, I'd love to. And I don't care if you make hail or snow fall on my head, or put any powder you like into my books now. Oh, I do feel happy again.'

William and Rita looked at one another and smiled. Elizabeth seemed to fall in and out of trouble as easily as a duck splashed in and out of water. She could be very foolish and do silly, hot-tempered, wrong things – but she was all right at heart.

'Well,' said William, 'we have cleared up a lot of things, but we still don't know who the real thief was – or is, for he or she may still be taking other things. We can only hope to find out soon, before any other trouble is made. By the way, Elizabeth, if your first accusation of Julian was made privately and secretly, as you said, how was it that all the first form knew? Surely you did not tell them yourself?'

'No, I didn't say a word,' said Elizabeth at once. 'I said I wouldn't, and I didn't.'

'Well, *I* didn't say anything,' said Julian. 'And yet the whole form knew and came to tell me about it.'

'Only one other person knew,' said Elizabeth, looking troubled. 'And that was Martin Follett. He was in the stables, Julian, while we were outside. He came out when you had walked off, and he offered me a shilling in place of mine that had gone. I thought it was very nice of him. He promised not to say a word of what he had heard.'

'Well, he must have told pretty well everyone, the little sneak,' said Julian, who, for some reason, had never liked Martin as much as the others had. 'Anyway, it doesn't matter. Well, thanks, William and Rita, for having us along and making us see sense.'

He gave his sudden, goblin-like grin, and his green eyes shone. Elizabeth looked at him with a warm liking. How could she *ever* have thought that Julian would do a really mean thing? How awful she was! She never gave anyone a chance.

'He's always saying he does as he likes, and he's not going to bother to work if he doesn't want to, and he doesn't care what trouble he gets into, and he plays the most awful tricks – but I'm certain as certain could be that he's good at heart,' said Elizabeth to herself.

And Julian grinned at her and thought, *She flies into the most awful tempers, and says the silliest things, and makes enemies right and left – but I'm certain as certain can be that she's good at heart!*

'Well, goodnight, you two troublemakers,' said William, and he gave them a friendly push. 'Elizabeth, I'm sorry about you not being a monitor any more, but I think you see yourself that you want to get a bit more common sense before the children will trust you again. You do fly off the handle so when you get an idea into your head.'

'Yes, I know,' said Elizabeth. 'I've failed this time, but I'll have another shot and do it properly, you see if I don't!'

The two went out, and William and Rita looked at one another.

'Good stuff in both those kids,' said William. 'Let's make some cocoa, Rita. It's getting late. Golly, I wonder who's the nasty little thief in the first form. It must be somebody there. He's not only a nasty little thief, but somebody very double-faced, trying to make someone else bear the blame for his own misdeeds by putting the marked shilling into Julian's pocket!'

'Yes, it must be someone really bad at heart,' said Rita. 'Someone it will be very difficult to deal with. It might be a girl or a boy – I wonder which.'

Julian and Elizabeth went down the passage to their own common room. It was almost time for bed. There was about a quarter of an hour left.

'I'm coming into the common room with you,' said Julian, and Elizabeth squeezed his arm gratefully. He had sensed that she did not want to appear alone in front of all the first form. It was going to be hard to face everyone now that she had been disgraced, and was no longer a monitor.

'Thank you, Julian,' she said, and opened the door to go in.

CHAPTER EIGHTEEN

JULIAN IS VERY FUNNY

THE FIRST-FORMERS had been talking about Elizabeth most of the time, wondering where she was, and saying that it served her right to be punished. Everyone was on Julian's side; there was no doubt about that.

'I shall tell Julian just what I think of Elizabeth,' said Arabella. 'I never did like her, not even when I stayed with her in the hols.'

'I must say I think it was a pity that Elizabeth accused Julian without being certain,' said Jenny.

'I suppose she was feeling annoyed because she had been left out of my party,' said Arabella spitefully. 'So she got back at Julian like that.'

'No. That wouldn't be like Elizabeth,' said Robert. 'She does do silly things, but she isn't spiteful.'

'Well, I shan't speak a word to her!' said Martin. 'I think she's been mean to Julian.'

'Sh. Here she comes,' suddenly said Belinda. The door opened, and Elizabeth came in. She expected to see scornful looks and even to hear scornful words, and she did. Some of the children turned their backs on her.

Close behind her came Julian. He saw at once that the first-formers were going to make things difficult for Elizabeth.

'Julian,' said Arabella, turning towards him. 'We all feel sorry to think of what you had to face at the Meeting tonight. It was too bad.'

'You must feel very sorry about it,' said Martin. '*I* should.'

'I did,' said Julian in his deep and pleasant voice, 'but I don't now. Come on, Elizabeth – we've still got about ten minutes before bedtime. I'll play a game of double patience with you. Where are the cards?'

'In my locker,' said Elizabeth gratefully. It had been dreadful coming into the room and facing everyone, but how good it was to have Julian sticking up for her like this – her friend once more. She fumbled about for the cards in her locker.

Every boy and girl stared in the greatest astonishment at Julian. Had he gone mad? Was he being friendly to the person, the very person, who had said such awful things about him? It was impossible. It couldn't be true.

But clearly it *was* true. Julian dealt the cards, and

soon he and Elizabeth were in the middle of the game. The others were so surprised that they watched silently, not finding a word to say. Arabella was the most surprised, and it was she who found her tongue first.

'Well!' she said. 'What's come over you, Julian? Don't you know that Elizabeth is your worst enemy?'

'You're wrong, Arabella,' said Julian in an amiable voice. 'She's my best friend. Everything was a silly mistake.'

There was something in Julian's voice that warned the others to say nothing. They turned to their own games, and left Julian and Elizabeth alone.

'Thanks, Julian,' whispered Elizabeth.

His green eyes looked at her with amusement. 'That's all right,' he said. 'Count on me if you want any help, Worst Enemy!'

'Oh, Julian!' said Elizabeth, half laughing and half crying. Then the bell went for bedtime and everyone cleared away books and games and went upstairs.

Things were not very easy for Elizabeth the next few days. The other children did not forgive and forget as easily as Julian did, and they treated her coldly. One or two were nice to her – Kathleen was, and Robert, and Harry. But most of them took no notice of her, and seemed to be glad she was no longer monitor.

Joan, of the second form, who had been Elizabeth's

friend in the first term, came to find her. She took Elizabeth's hand and squeezed it. 'I don't quite know the rights and wrongs of it all,' she said, 'but I do know this, Elizabeth – that you wouldn't have said what you did if you hadn't really thought it was true. It will all blow over and you'll be made monitor again, you'll see!'

Elizabeth was glad of the kind words that her real friends gave her. *Now I know what it is like when people are kind to others in trouble,' she thought. 'I shall remember how much I like kindness now, when things have gone wrong – and I shall be the same to others if* they *get into trouble.*

Elizabeth looked very serious these days. She worked very hard, was very quiet and her merry laugh did not sound nearly so often. Julian teased her about it.

'You've gone all quiet, like Rosemary,' he said. 'Come on – laugh a bit, Elizabeth. I don't want a gloomy friend.'

But Elizabeth had had a shock and had to get over it. Julian wondered what he could do to make her her old happy self. He began to think out a few jokes.

He told the children what he was going to do. 'Listen,' he said, 'when Mr Leslie, the science master, takes us for science in the laboratory, I shall make some of my noises. But you must none of you make out that you hear them. See? Pretend that you hear nothing, and we'll have a bit of fun.'

Science was a bit dull that term. Mr Leslie was rather

boring, and very strict. The children did not like him much, so they looked forward with the greatest glee to Julian's idea. They rushed to the lab that morning with much eagerness.

'What noises will you make?' asked Belinda.

'Wait and see,' said Julian, grinning. 'We will have a bit of fun – and Mr Leslie will get a few surprises.'

He certainly did. He walked stiffly into the room, nodded to the children and told them to take their places.

'Now, this morning,' he said, 'we are going to test potato slices for starch. I have here . . .'

He went on talking for a while, and then handed out small slices of potato. Soon all the children's heads were bent over their experiment.

A curious noise gradually made itself heard. It was like a very high whistle, so high that it might have been the continual squeak of a bat, or of a bow drawn over a very highly strung violin string.

Eeeeeeeee, went the noise. *Eeeeeeeee*.

All the boys and girls stole a look at Julian. He was bending over his work, and there was not a single movement of mouth, lips or throat to be seen. Yet they all knew he must be making that weird noise.

Mr Leslie looked up sharply. 'What is that noise!' he asked at once.

'Noise?' said Jenny, with an innocent stare. 'What noise, Mr Leslie?'

'That high squeaking noise,' said Mr Leslie impatiently.

Jenny put her head on one side like a bird, pretending to listen. All the other children did the same. From outside the window there came the sound of an aeroplane in the sky, and in a moment the plane came in sight.

'Oh. It was the aeroplane you heard, Mr Leslie,' said Jenny brightly. Everyone giggled.

Mr Leslie frowned. 'Don't be absurd, Jenny. Aeroplanes do not make a high squeaking noise. There it is again!'

Eeeeeeeeeee! Everyone heard the noise, but pretended not to. They bent their heads over their work, badly wanting to giggle.

Julian changed his noise. Into the room came a deep, growling noise. Mr Leslie looked startled.

'Is there a dog in the room?' he asked.

'A dog, Mr Leslie?' said Belinda, looking all around. 'I can't see one.'

Elizabeth exploded into a giggle, which she tried to turn into a cough. The growling noise went on, sometimes hardly to be heard, sometimes very loud. Mr Leslie couldn't understand it.

'Can't you hear that noise?' he said to the nearest children. 'Like a growl.'

'You said it was a squeak just now, sir,' said Harry, looking surprised. 'Is it a squeaky growl, or a growly squeak?'

Elizabeth exploded again, and Jenny stuffed her hanky into her mouth. Mr Leslie grew very cross.

'There is nothing funny to laugh at,' he snapped. 'My goodness – what's that now?'

Julian had changed his noise, and a curious, muffled *boom-boom-boom* sound could be heard. It did not seem to come from anywhere particular, least of all from Julian!

Mr Leslie felt scared. He glanced at the children. Not one of them seemed to be hearing this new boom-boom noise. How strange! It must be his ears going wrong. He put his hands up to them. Perhaps he wasn't well. People had noises in their ears then.

Boom-boom-boom went the strange, muffled sound. 'Can you hear a *boom-boom* noise?' said Mr Leslie in a low voice to Harry. Harry put his head on one side and listened. He listened with his hand behind one ear. He listened with it behind the other. He listened with both hands behind both ears.

Elizabeth gave a loud giggle. She really couldn't help it. Jenny giggled too. Mr Leslie glared at them.

Then he turned to Harry.

'Well, if you can't hear it, it must be something wrong with my ears,' he said. 'Get on with your work, everyone. Stop giggling, Jenny.'

The next noise was like a creaking gate. It was too much for poor Mr Leslie. Muttering something about not feeling very well, he fled out of the classroom, telling the children to get on with their work till he came back.

Get on with their work? That was quite impossible! Peals of laughter, roars of mirth, squeals and giggles filled the room from end to end. Tears poured down Jenny's cheeks. Harry rolled on the floor, holding his aching sides. Elizabeth sent out peal after peal of infectious laughter. Julian stood in the middle of it and grinned.

'Oh, that *has* done me good!' said Elizabeth, wiping the tears from her eyes. 'I've never laughed so much in my life. Oh, Julian, you're marvellous! You *must* do it again. Oh, it was gorgeous!'

It did everyone good. Those gusts of laughter had cleared the air of all spitefulness, scorn and enmity. Everyone suddenly felt friendly and warm. It was good to be together to laugh and to play, to be friends. The first form was suddenly a much nicer place altogether!

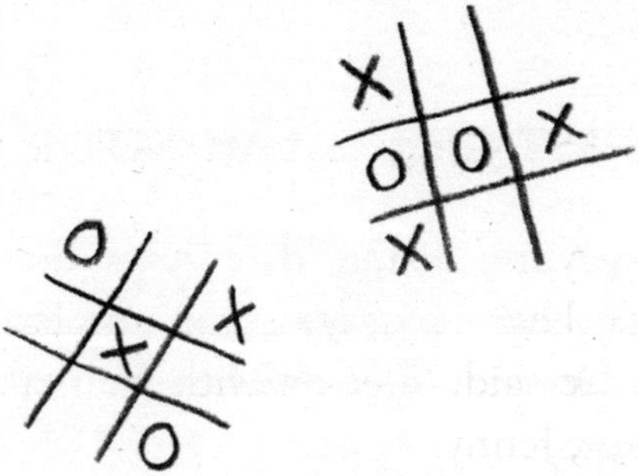

CHAPTER NINETEEN

JULIAN HAS SOME SHOCKS

JULIAN'S SUCCESS in Mr Leslie's class rather went to his head. He tried several other noises in Mam'zelle's class, and in the art class too. He tried a mooing noise in Mam'zelle's class, not knowing how terrified she was of cows.

Poor Mam'zelle honestly thought that a cow was wandering about in the passage outside, and she stood trembling in horror. 'A cow!' she said. 'It is nothing but a cow that makes that noise.'

'*Moo-ooo-oo*,' said the cow, and Mam'zelle shuddered. She could not bear cows, and would never go into a field where there was one.

'I'll go and shoo the cow away, Mam'zelle,' said Jenny, enjoying herself. She rushed to the door and there began a great shooing, mooing noise that sent the class into fits of laughter. Then Mam'zelle suddenly came to the conclusion that cows do not usually wander about school passages, and she looked sharply at Julian. Could that dreadful boy be making one of his famous noises?

The first form had a wonderful time with Julian's noises and tricks. There seemed no end to them. His brilliant brains invented trick after trick, and they were so clever that no mistress or master seemed able to guess that they were tricks until it was too late.

Julian used the sneezing powder again, this time on Mr Lewis, the music master, when he was taking a singing lesson. He took two or three forms together for singing, and the lesson quickly became a gale of laughter as poor Mr Lewis sneezed time after time, trying in vain to stop himself. Julian was quite a hero in the school for his many extraordinary jokes and tricks.

But he was not a hero to the teachers. They often talked of him, sometimes angrily, sometimes sadly.

'He's the cleverest boy we've ever had at Whyteleafe,' said Miss Ranger. 'Far and away the cleverest. If only he would work, he would win every scholarship there is. His brains are marvellous if only he would use them.'

'He thinks of nothing but jokes,' said Mr Leslie angrily. He was now firmly convinced that the extraordinary noises he had heard in the science lesson had been made by Julian, and he was angry every time he thought of it. And yet that boy, as if to make up for playing such a trick, had written out a really brilliant essay for Mr Leslie, an essay that he himself would have been proud to write. He was an odd fellow, there was no doubt about it.

At the school Meeting following the one in which Elizabeth had lost her position as monitor, the little girl, now no longer on the platform with the Jury, but down in the gym with the others, had got up to speak.

'I just want to say that I know now I was completely wrong about Julian,' she said humbly. 'I have said so to him, and he has been very nice about it – and we are good friends again, so that shows you how nice he has been. I'm sorry I was such a bad monitor. If ever I am a monitor again, I will do better.'

'Thank you, Elizabeth,' said William, as the little girl sat down. 'We are very glad to have Julian absolutely cleared of the charge against him – and glad to know that he has been big enough to forgive you and to be friends so quickly.'

There was a pause. Julian grinned at Elizabeth, and she smiled back. It was good to be friends once more. Then William spoke again, and a graver note was in his voice.

'But I have something else to say to Julian,' he said. 'Something not quite so pleasant, Julian. All your teachers are displeased with you. It is not so much that you play the fool in class, and play tricks and jokes, but that you only use your brains for those things and for nothing else. According to everyone, you have really wonderful brains, inventive and original – brains that could do something for the world later on – but you only use them for nonsense and rubbish, and never for worthwhile work.'

He stopped. Julian flushed and put his hands deeper into his pockets. He didn't like this at all.

'It's all very well to keep your class in fits of laughter, and to be a hero because of your jokes,' said William, 'but it would be much better to work hard also, and later on become a hero in the world of science, or in the world of inventions.'

'Oh, I don't care whether I'm famous or not when I'm grown-up,' said Julian rather rudely. He was always rude when he felt awkward. 'I just want to have a good time, do what I like and let others do what *they* like. Hard work is silly, and—'

'Stand up when you speak to us, and take your hands out of your pockets,' said William.

Julian frowned, stood up and took his hands out of his pockets.

'Sorry, William,' he said, his green eyes looking rather angry. 'I haven't any more to say – only that they're *my* brains, and I can choose how to use them myself, thank you. All this goody-goody talk doesn't mean a thing to me.'

'I can see that,' said William. 'It's a pity. It seems you only care for yourself and what you want yourself. One day you will learn differently, but what will teach you, I don't know. I am afraid it will be something that will hurt you badly.'

Julian sat down, still red. Use his brains for hard work when he could have a good time and laze around, playing tricks and jokes to make his friends laugh! No thank you. Time enough to use his brains when he had to go out into the world and earn his living.

Elizabeth said nothing to him about William's talk. It was a little like she herself had once said to him when she was a monitor. It wasn't goody-goody talk. It was common sense. Julian was silly not to work. He could win marvellous scholarships, and do all kinds of fine things when he grew up. It was odd that he didn't want to.

The only effect that William's talk had on Julian was to make him even lower in the form than before! He was nearly always bottom, but the next week his marks were so poor that even Julian himself was surprised when they were read out. He grinned round cheerfully. *He* didn't care if he was bottom or not!

The week went on, and soon half-term came near. The children began to talk about their parents coming to see them. Elizabeth spoke to Julian about it.

'Will your parents come, Julian?'

'I hope so,' said the boy. 'I'd like you to see my mother. She's simply lovely. She really is – and so pretty and merry and sweet.'

Julian's eyes shone as he spoke of his mother. It was clear that he loved her better than anything on earth. He loved his father too, but it was his pretty, happy mother who had his heart.

'It's because of Mother I wear my hair too long,' he said to Elizabeth, with a laugh. 'She likes this silly haircut of mine, with this annoying lock of hair always tumbling over my forehead. So I keep it like that to please her. And she loves my jokes and tricks and noises.'

'But isn't she disappointed when she knows you are always bottom of the form?' asked Elizabeth curiously. 'My mother would be ashamed of me.'

'Oh, mine likes me to have a good time,' said Julian. 'She doesn't mind about places in class, or whether I'm top of exams or not.'

Elizabeth thought that Julian's mother must be rather odd. But then Julian was odd too – very lovable and exciting, but odd.

Half-term came at last – and with it came most of

the children's parents, eager to see them. Mrs Allen arrived and Elizabeth gave her a great hug.

'You're looking well, darling,' said Mrs Allen. 'Now, we must ask Arabella to come with us, mustn't we, because no one is here to see her.'

'Oh,' said Elizabeth, '*must* we, Mother?'

She caught sight of Julian, and called to him. 'Julian, here's my mother. Has yours come yet?'

'No,' said Julian, looking a little worried. 'She hasn't – and she said she would be here early. I wonder if the car has broken down.'

Just then the telephone bell rang loudly in the hall. Mr Johns went to answer it. He beckoned to Julian and took the boy into the nearest room. Elizabeth wondered if anything had happened.

'Mother, I must just wait for Julian to come out before I go and get ready to come with you,' she said. She hadn't long to wait. The door opened, and Julian came out. But what a different Julian!

His face was quite white, and his eyes were full of such pain that Elizabeth could hardly bear to look at them. She ran to him.

'Julian! What's the matter? What has happened?'

'Go away,' said Julian, pushing her away blindly, as if he could hardly see. He went into the garden by himself. Elizabeth ran after Mr Johns.

'Mr Johns! Mr Johns! What's the matter with Julian? Please – please tell me.'

'It's his mother,' said Mr Johns. 'She's very ill – desperately ill. His father is a doctor, you know, and he is with her, and some other very clever doctors too. She is too ill for him even to see her. It's rather a blow for him, as you can see. Maybe you can help him, Elizabeth. You're his friend, aren't you?'

'Yes,' said Elizabeth, all her warm heart longing to comfort the boy. He was so proud of his mother – he loved her so much. She was the most wonderful person on earth to him. Oh, surely, surely she would get better!

She ran to her mother. 'Mother, listen. I can't come out today. I'm so sorry, but Julian's mother is desperately ill and I'm his friend, so I must stay with him. Could you just take Arabella out, do you think? I think I really must stay with Julian.'

'Very well,' said her mother, and she went to find Arabella. Elizabeth herself went to hunt for Julian. Goodness knew where he would hide himself. He would be like a wounded animal, going to some hole. Poor, poor Julian – what could she say to comfort him?

CHAPTER TWENTY

JULIAN MAKES A SOLEMN PROMISE

JULIAN WAS nowhere to be seen. Wherever had he gone? Elizabeth called to Harry. 'Harry! have you seen Julian anywhere?'

'Yes, I saw him tearing down to the gates,' said Harry. 'What's the matter with him?'

Elizabeth didn't answer. She rushed down to the big school gates too. She wondered if Julian had thought of catching a train and going to his mother. She ran out of the gates and stood looking down the road.

Some distance away, hurrying fast, was a boy. It must be Julian. Elizabeth tore after him, panting. She must get hold of him somehow. He was in trouble, and she might be able to help him.

She ran down the country lane and turned the corner. There was no one in sight. How could Julian have gone so far in such a short time! He couldn't possibly have turned the next corner yet! Elizabeth hurried along, feeling worried.

She came to the next corner. There was no one in sight on the main road either. Where could Julian have gone? She went back some way, thinking that he might have gone into a field through a gate a little way back. She passed a red telephone kiosk without thinking of looking inside it – and she was very startled when she suddenly heard the click of the kiosk door, and heard Julian's voice calling her urgently.

'Elizabeth! Oh, Elizabeth! Have you got any change on you?'

Elizabeth turned, and saw that Julian was in the telephone box. She ran to him eagerly, fumbling in her pocket for her money.

'Yes – here is a sixpence – and some pennies,' she said. 'What are you doing?'

'Telephoning my father,' said Julian. 'Mr Johns said I wasn't to, at school. He said my father wouldn't want to be worried by phone calls – and I dare say he's right – but I've *got* to ask him a few questions myself. But I haven't got the right money to put in the box for the call.'

He took the money Elizabeth offered, and shut himself in the telephone box again. Elizabeth waited outside. She had to wait for a long time.

It was a quarter of an hour before Julian could get

through to his father, and the boy was almost in despair with the delay. He kept brushing his long lock of hair back, and he looked so white and forlorn that it was all Elizabeth could do not to open the kiosk door and go in beside him.

But at last he got through to his father, and Elizabeth could see him asking urgent questions, though she could hear nothing. He spoke to his father for about five minutes, and then put down the receiver. He came out, looking very white.

'I think I'm going to be sick,' he said and went pale green. He took Elizabeth's hand, and went through the nearby gate into the field. He sat down, still looking green. But he wasn't sick. He slowly lost his green look, and a little colour came back to his cheeks.

'I'm an idiot,' he said to Elizabeth, not looking at her, 'but I can't help it. Nobody knows how much I love my mother – or how sweet and loving she is.'

Elizabeth saw that he was making a great effort not to cry, and she wanted to cry herself. She didn't know what to do or say. There didn't seem any words that were any use at all. So she just sat close to Julian and squeezed his hand.

At last she spoke in a low voice. 'What did your father say?'

'He said – he said – Mother had just got a tiny

chance,' said Julian, and he bit his lip hard. 'Only a tiny chance. I can't bear to think of it, Elizabeth.'

'Julian, doctors are so clever nowadays,' said Elizabeth. 'She will get better. They'll do something to save her – you'll see!'

'My father said they're trying a new drug, a new medicine on her,' said Julian restlessly, pulling up the grass that grew beside him. 'He said that he and two other doctors have been working on it for years and it's almost ready. He's getting some today, to try it on Mother. He says it's the last hope – it will give her a tiny chance.'

'Julian, your father must be very clever,' said Elizabeth. 'Oh, Julian, it must be marvellous to be as clever as that, and to be able to discover things that can save people's lives. Fancy – just fancy – if your father's clever work should save your mother's life. You must take after him in brains, I think, Julian. You're very clever too. Oh, Julian, one day *you* might be able to save the life of someone you love by using a great invention of your own.'

Elizabeth had said these words in order to comfort Julian, but to her dismay and horror the boy turned over on to the grass and began to sob.

'What's the matter? Don't do that,' begged Elizabeth. But Julian took no notice. After a while he sat up again, looked for a hanky, which he hadn't got, and rubbed his hands over his dirty face. Elizabeth offered him her hanky. He took it and wiped his face.

'If my father's new drug *does* save my mother's life, it will be because of his years of hard work; it will be because he's used his brains to the utmost,' said Julian, almost as if he were speaking to himself. 'I thought he was silly to work so hard as he did, and hardly ever have a good time or take long holidays.'

He rubbed his eyes again. Elizabeth listened, not daring to interrupt. Julian was terribly in earnest. This was perhaps the biggest moment in his life, the moment when he decided which road he was going to tread: the easy, happy-go-lucky road, or the hard, tiring road his father had taken – the road of hard work, of unselfish labour, always for others.

Julian went on speaking, still as if he were thinking aloud.

'*I've* been given brains too – and I've wasted them. I deserve to have this happen to me. There's my father using his brains all these years and maybe he can save my mother because of that. It's the finest reward he could have. Oh, if only I could still have my mother, how hard I'd work! It's a punishment for me. William said something would teach me sooner or later – and it might be something that would hurt me badly.' Julian brushed back his hair, and bit his trembling lip.

'You have got the most wonderful brain, Ju,' said Elizabeth in a low voice. 'I've heard the teachers talking about you. They said you could do anything you liked, anything in the world. And, you know, I do think if you've got a gift of any sort, or good brains, you can be very, very happy using them, and you can bring happiness to other people too. This isn't goody-goody talk, Julian, really it isn't.'

'I know,' said Julian. 'It's wise and sensible talk. Oh, why didn't I show Mother what I could do when I had the chance? She would have been so proud of me! She always said she didn't mind what I did, or how I fooled about, but she would have been so proud if I'd really *done* something. Now it's too late.'

'It isn't – it isn't,' said Elizabeth. 'You know your mother has a chance. Your father said so. Anyway, whatever happens, Julian, you can still work hard and use your brains and do something in the world. You could be anything you liked!'

'I shall be a surgeon,' said Julian, his green eyes gleaming. 'I shall find new ways of curing ill people. I shall make experiments, and discover things that will give millions of people their health again.'

'You will, Julian, you will!' said Elizabeth. 'I know you will.'

'But Mother won't be there to see me,' said Julian,

and he got up suddenly and went to the gate. 'Oh, Elizabeth, I see why this has happened to me now. It's about the only thing that could have made me really see myself, and be ashamed. I wish – oh, I wish . . .'

He stopped. Elizabeth knew what he wished. He wished that such a dreadful lesson need not have come to him. But things happened like that. The little girl got up and went through the gate with him.

They walked back to the school, and on the way they passed a small country church. The door was open.

'I'm going in for a minute,' said Julian. 'I've got a very solemn promise to make, and I'd better make it here. It's a promise that's going to last all my life. You stay outside, Elizabeth.'

He went inside the little, dim church. Elizabeth sat down on the wooden bench outside, looking at the early daffodils blowing in the wind.

I'd better pray too, she thought. *If only Julian's mother would get better! But I don't somehow think she will. I think poor Julian will have to work hard and do brilliantly without his mother to be proud of him, and love him for his big promise.*

After a short while Julian came out again, looking more at peace. He had a very steadfast look in his green eyes, and Elizabeth knew that, whatever happened, his promise of a minute ago would never be broken. Julian's brains would no longer be used only to amuse himself. Now, all his life long, he would do as his father had done, and use them for other people. Perhaps, as he had said, he would be a great surgeon, a wonderful doctor.

They walked back to the school in silence. There were no boys or girls there, for they all had gone out with friends or parents. Julian gave Elizabeth back her dirty hanky.

'Sorry you've had to miss your outing,' he said, with a crooked little smile, 'but I couldn't have done without you.'

'Let's take some food and go for a picnic,' said Elizabeth.

Julian shook his head. 'No,' he said, 'I want to be here – in case there's any news. There may not be, today, my father said – or even for a day or two. But there might be, you see.'

'Yes,' said Elizabeth. 'All right, we'll stay here. Let's go and do some gardening. John won't be there, but I know what to do. There are some lettuces to plant, and there is still a bit of digging to be done. Could you do that, do you think?'

Julian nodded. They went out together, and were soon working in the wind and the sun. How good it was to work in the wind and the sun! How good it was to have a friend, and stick by him in times of trouble!

CHAPTER TWENTY-ONE

MARTIN GIVES ELIZABETH A SURPRISE

NO NEWS came for Julian that day, except a message to say that his mother was about the same, no worse and no better. The other children were upset to hear of the boy's trouble, and everyone did their best to comfort him, in their various ways.

Strangely enough, Martin seemed the most upset. This was odd, Elizabeth thought, because Julian had never liked Martin very much, and had not troubled to hide it. Martin went to Elizabeth, looking very distressed.

'Can I do anything to help Julian?' he said. 'Isn't there *anything* I can do?'

'I don't think so,' said Elizabeth. 'It's kind of you to want to help, Martin, but even I can't do very much, you know.'

'Do you think his mother will get better soon?' asked Martin.

'I don't somehow think so,' said Elizabeth. 'It's going to be awful for him when the news comes. I wouldn't bother him at all if I were you, Martin.'

Martin shuffled about, fidgeting with books and pencils, and Elizabeth grew impatient.

'What's the matter with you, Martin? You are awfully fidgety!' she said. 'You keep shaking the table, and I want to write.'

There was only one person in the common room besides Elizabeth and Martin, and that was Belinda. She finished what she was doing, and then went out. Martin shut the door after her and came back to Elizabeth.

'I want to ask your advice about something, Elizabeth,' he said nervously.

'Well, don't,' said Elizabeth at once. 'I'm not a monitor any more. I'm not the right person to ask for advice now. You go to our new monitor. She's sensible.'

'I don't know Susan, and I do know you,' said Martin. 'There's something worrying me awfully, Elizabeth – and, now that Julian is in trouble, it's worrying me still more. I love my own mother very much too, so I know what Julian must be feeling. Please let me tell you what I want to, Elizabeth.'

'Martin, don't tell me,' said Elizabeth. 'Honestly, I shan't be able to help you. I'm not sure of myself any more – I keep doing the wrong things. Look how I accused poor Julian of stealing. I shall be ashamed of that all my life. He was so decent about it too. You go and tell Susan.'

'I can't tell someone I don't know,' said Martin in despair. 'I don't want you to help me. I just want to get it off my chest.'

'All right, tell me then,' said Elizabeth. 'Have you done something wrong? For goodness' sake stop shuffling about, Martin. Whatever's the matter with you?'

Martin sat down at the table, and put his face in his hands. Elizabeth saw that his face was getting red, and she wondered curiously what was up with him. He spoke in a muffled voice through his fingers.

'I took that money – quite a lot of it – from Arabella and Rosemary and you and other people too. And I took the sweets and the chocolate, and I took biscuits too and cake once,' said Martin in a funny, dull voice.

Elizabeth sat, staring at him, startled and shocked.

'You thief!' she said. 'You horrid, beastly thief. And yet you always seemed so kind and generous. Why, you even offered me a shilling in place of the one I lost – and all the time *you* had taken it! And you offered Rosemary money too, and she liked you awfully for it. Martin Follett, you are a very wicked boy, and a horrid pretender too, because you made yourself out to be so kind and generous and all the time you were a deceitful thief.'

Martin said nothing. He just sat there with his face in his hands. Elizabeth felt angry and disgusted.

'What did you tell *me* for? *I* didn't want to hear. I accused poor, unhappy Julian of doing what *you* did, you beast. And oh, Martin – was it *you* who put the marked shilling into Julian's pocket – and the sweet too – to make me think it was he who had taken them? Could you be so mean as that?'

Martin nodded. His face was still hidden. 'Yes. I did all that. I was afraid when I found that shilling was marked – and I never liked Julian because he didn't like me. I was afraid that if I was found out, none of you would like me. And I so badly wanted to be liked. Hardly anyone ever likes me.'

'I don't wonder,' said Elizabeth scornfully. 'Good gracious! It was mean enough to take the money and the other things – but it was much, much meaner to try and put the blame on somebody else. That's not only mean, but cowardly. I can't imagine why you've told me all this. It's a thing to tell William and Rita, not me.'

'I can't,' said Martin, with a groan.

'Think of all the damage you've done!' said Elizabeth, growing very angry as she thought of it. 'You made me think poor Julian stole – and I accused him – and he got back at me by getting me turned out of class and I lost my position as monitor. Martin Follett, I think you're the nastiest, most hateful boy I've ever met. I wish to goodness you hadn't told me.'

'Well, I can't bear to think that I got Julian into trouble, now that he's so – so desperately unhappy,' said Martin. 'That's why I told you. I had to get it off my chest. It seemed about the only thing I could do for Julian.'

'Well, I wish you'd confessed to somebody else,' said Elizabeth, getting up. 'I can't help you and I don't want to. You're mean and cowardly and horrible. You oughtn't to be at Whyteleafe. You're not fit to be. Anyway, I'm too worried about Julian just now to bother my head about *you*!'

The little girl gave Martin a scornful glance, got up and went out of the room. How disgusting! Fancy behaving like that – stealing, and then putting the blame on to others – and letting them bear it too!

Rosemary went into the common room as Elizabeth walked out. Elizabeth went to a music room, got out her music and began to practise, thinking of Julian and Martin and herself, as she played.

After a short while the door of the practice room opened and Rosemary looked in. Her pretty, weak little face looked rather scared as Elizabeth frowned at her. But for once in a way Rosemary was strong, and in spite of Elizabeth's frown she went into the music room and shut the door.

'What do you want?' said Elizabeth.

'What's the matter with Martin?' asked Rosemary. 'Is he ill? He looked awful when I went into the common room just now.'

'Good,' said Elizabeth, beginning to play again. 'Serves him right!'

'Why?' asked Rosemary in surprise.

Elizabeth would not tell her. 'I don't like Martin,' she said, and went on playing.

'But Elizabeth, why not?' said Rosemary. 'He's really awfully kind. You know, he's always giving away sweets and things. And, if ever anyone loses their money, he offers to give them some. I really think he's the most generous boy I know. He never eats any sweets himself – he only keeps them to give away. I think he's most unselfish.'

'Go away, Rosemary, please. I'm practising,' said Elizabeth, who didn't want to hear Martin praised just then.

'But Elizabeth, what *is* the matter with poor Martin?' said Rosemary, overcoming her timidity for once. 'He really did look dreadful. Have you been saying anything unkind to him. You know how unkind you were to poor Julian. You never give anyone a chance, do you?'

Elizabeth did not answer, and Rosemary went out of the room, going so far as to bang the door because she really felt cross with Elizabeth. She did not like to go back to Martin because he had turned his back on her, and told her to go away. It was all very puzzling.

I suppose Elizabeth has quarrelled with him *now!* she thought. *Well, I haven't done any good by going to her*.

But she had. As soon as she had gone, Elizabeth began to remember the things that Rosemary had said about Martin – and they suddenly seemed very strange to her.

'She said he was the most generous boy she knew,' said Elizabeth to herself. 'She said he never ate sweets himself but always gave them away. And when anyone loses their money he always offers them some. And it's quite true he offered *me* sweets and money. How odd to steal things and then give them away! I've never heard of that before.'

Elizabeth stopped practising, and began to think hard. How could Martin be mean and yet generous? How could he make people unhappy by taking their things, and make others happy by giving them things? It didn't seem to make sense. And yet he did – there was no doubt about it.

He doesn't steal for himself, thought Elizabeth. *I do think it's odd. I wish I could ask someone about it. But I'm not going to Susan, and I'm certainly not going to William and Rita again just now. I don't want them to think I'm interfering again – and anyway I'm not a monitor now. It was tiresome of Martin to tell me.*

She thought about it all for some time, and then something happened that made her forget. It was in the middle of the arithmetic class.

The children heard the telephone bell ring shrilly in the hall. It rang two or three times and then someone went to answer it. Then footsteps came down the passage, and a knock came at the classroom door.

A maid came in and spoke to Miss Ranger. 'If you please, miss, there's someone urgently wanting Julian on the telephone. It's a long-distance call, so I didn't go to tell Miss Belle, in case the call was cut off before Julian got to the phone.'

Julian was out of his seat almost before the maid had finished. With a face as white as a sheet he half ran out of the room and down the hall. Elizabeth's heart almost stopped beating. At last news had come for Julian. But was it good or bad? The whole class was silent, waiting.

'Let the news be good – let the news be good,' said Elizabeth to herself over and over again, and didn't even notice that she had made blots all across her book.

CHAPTER TWENTY-TWO

MARTIN REALLY IS A PUZZLE!

THERE CAME the faint tinkle of the telephone bell as the receiver was put down. Then came the sound of footsteps down the passage, back to the schoolroom – hurrying footsteps. The door was flung open, and Julian came in, a radiant Julian, with sparkling eyes and a smiling mouth.

'It's all right,' he said. 'It's good news. It's all right.'

'Hurrah!' said Elizabeth, most absurdly wanting to cry. She banged on her desk for joy.

'Good, oh good!' cried Jenny.

'I'm so glad!' shouted Harry, and he drummed with his feet on the floor. It seemed as if the children had to make some sort of noise to express their delight. Some of them clapped. Jenny patted Belinda on the back; she didn't know why. Everyone was full of joy.

'I'm very glad for you, Julian,' said Miss Ranger. 'It

has been a great worry. Now it's over. Is your mother much better?'

'Much, much better,' said Julian, his face glowing. 'And it was all because of that wonderful new medicine my father and his two friends have been working on for so many years. It gave my mother a chance, just a chance – and this morning she suddenly turned the corner, and she's going to be all right. Gosh, I don't know how I'm going to do any more lessons this morning!'

Miss Ranger laughed. 'Well, there are only five minutes left of this lesson before break. You had better all clear away your books and have five minutes' extra break, just to work off your high spirits. Everyone is glad for you, Julian!'

So the first form put away their books, chattering happily, and rushed out into the garden early. The other forms were surprised to hear them playing there before the bell had gone. Elizabeth dragged Julian to a quiet corner.

'Julian, isn't it marvellous? Are you happy again now?'

'Happier than I've ever felt before,' said the boy. 'I feel as if I've been given another chance – one more chance to show my mother she's got someone to be proud of. Golly, I'm going to work now! I'm going to take all my exams with top marks. I'm going to win any scholarship I can. I'm going to take my medical exams as young as possible. I'm going to use my brains in a way they've never been used before!'

'You'll be top of the form in a week,' laughed Elizabeth. 'But Julian, don't give up being funny, will you?'

'Well, I don't know about that,' said Julian. 'I'll perhaps think of jokes and tricks in my spare time, but I shan't waste my time or anybody else's now by being too silly. I'll see. I'm turning over a new leaf – going all goody-goody, like you wanted me to be!'

'No, I didn't want that,' said Elizabeth. 'I like good people; but not goody-goody. Save up some noises and jokes for us, Julian – you'll want a bit of rest from hard work sometimes!'

Julian laughed, and they went off to play with the others. The boy was quite mad with delight. All his fears were gone – his mother was better – he would see her again soon – there was time this term to work hard for her, and let her see what he could do.

For a time Elizabeth forgot about Martin. Then she noticed him now and again, looking, as Rosemary had said, very forlorn. He hung around Julian in an irritating way, and Julian, who didn't like him, had difficulty in shaking him off.

Oh blow, I'd forgotten about Martin, thought Elizabeth to herself. *Well, I shan't tell Julian what he told me. He's so happy today and I won't let Martin's meanness spoil his day. Anyway, I've been ticked off enough for trying to manage things my own way. I shan't bother about this. I should only get into trouble again.*

So she tried not to think any more about Martin. But soon he stopped trying to hang around Julian and began to hang around Elizabeth instead. He seemed completely lost somehow. Elizabeth was glad when bedtime came and she could get rid of him.

The excitements of the day were a bit too much for Elizabeth. She lay in bed that night and could not get to sleep. She turned this way, she turned that way, she punched her pillow, she threw off her eiderdown, she pulled it on again – but she couldn't go to sleep, no matter what she did!

She began to think about the puzzle of Martin. Again and again she thought, *How can a person be two different things at one and the same time? How can you be selfish and unselfish, mean and generous, kind and unkind? I wish I knew.*

She lay and remembered all the School Meetings she had been to. She thought of the odd things some children did, and how, when the reason for their actions was found, they could be cured.

There was Harry – he was a cheat – but it was only because he was afraid of being bottom of the form and letting his father down, thought Elizabeth. *And there was Robert – he was a bully last term – but it was only because he had once been dreadfully jealous of his small brothers, so he got rid of his jealousy by being beastly to other small children. And there's me – I was awful, but I* am *better now, even though I've been in disgrace this term.*

She remembered the big book in which William and Rita wrote down the accounts of every School Meeting. In it were the stories of many bad or difficult children who, through many a year at Whyteleafe, had had their faults and wrongdoings shown up, discussed kindly and firmly and, in the end, been helped to cure themselves.

I don't believe there's any cure for Martin anyway, thought Elizabeth. *I wonder if there's anything in William's Big Book that would explain Martin's funny behaviour. I'd like to see. Oh dear, I wish it was morning, then I could go and see.*

The children were allowed to refer to 'William's Big Book', as they called it, when they liked. There was so much sound common sense in it.

I'll go and read it now, thought Elizabeth suddenly. *I shall never go to sleep tonight. There won't be anyone about now, so I'll just pop on my dressing-gown, go down to the gym, and find the book. It will be something to do anyway.*

She put on her dressing gown and slippers. She crept out of the dormitory, where everyone was sound asleep, and went downstairs to the gym. On the platform was a table, and in the drawer of the table the big book was kept.

Elizabeth had a torch with her, for she dared not switch on the light. She opened the drawer and took out the book. It was filled with writing – different writing, for three or four head boys and head girls had kept the Book throughout the time that Whyteleafe School had been running.

Elizabeth dipped here and there. *She* was in the book too – here it was, 'the Bold Bad Girl' – that was what Harry had called her two terms ago when she was the naughtiest girl in the school. And here she was again, made a monitor because of fine behaviour – and oh dear, oh dear, here she was again, disgraced because of bad behaviour!

'Elizabeth Allen lost her position as monitor because she accused one of her form wrongly of stealing, and because her behaviour in class showed that she was unsuited to be a monitor,' she read in William's neat, small handwriting.

'I seem to appear in this book rather a lot,' said Elizabeth. She turned to the beginning pages of the book and read with interest of other children who had been good or bad, difficult or admirable – children who had left the school long ago. Then the story of a girl began to interest her. It seemed very much like Martin's story.

She read it through, then shut the book and thought hard. *What a peculiar story!* she thought. *Very like Martin's really. That girl – Tessie – she took money too, but* she *didn't spend any of it on herself – she gave it away as fast as she stole it. And she took flowers from the school garden, pretended she had bought them and gave them to the teachers. And it was all because nobody ever liked her, so she tried to buy their liking and their friendship by giving them things. She stole so that she might appear kind and generous. I do wonder if Martin does the same.*

She went back to her bed, thinking. *How awful to be so friendless that you've got to do something like that to get friends*, she thought. *I wonder if I'd better say something to Martin tomorrow. He did look pretty miserable today. Anyway, I've had enough with interfering with other people. I'll just ask him a few questions, and then leave it. He can do what he likes about himself. I don't care.*

She went to sleep after that, and was so tired in the morning that she could hardly wake up. She went yawning down to breakfast, grinned at Julian and sat down to eat her porridge. What had she been worrying about the night before? Her French? No, she knew that all right, thank goodness. Julian? No, that worry was gone now.

Of course – it was Martin she had been thinking

about. She took a look at his pale face, and thought that he looked rather small and thin.

He's a horrid boy, she thought. *Really horrid. Nobody* really *likes him, not even Rosemary, though they say he's kind and all that. It's funny he hasn't a single real friend. Horrid as I have sometimes been, I've always had real friends – somebody has always liked me.*

A chance came for Elizabeth to speak to Martin soon after breakfast. Elizabeth had rabbits to feed, and Martin had a guinea pig. The cages were side by side and the two children were soon busy.

'Martin,' said Elizabeth, going straight to the point, as she always did. 'Martin, why do you give away the sweets and money and things you steal, instead of keeping them for yourself? Why steal them if you don't want them?'

'Only because I want people to like me, and you can't make people like you unless you're kind and generous,' said Martin in a low voice. 'My mother has always told me that. It's not *really* stealing, Elizabeth – don't say that – I give the things away at once. It's – it's the same sort of thing that Robin Hood did.'

'No, it isn't,' said Elizabeth. 'Not a bit. It's stealing, and you know it is. How can you bear to know that you are so dishonest and mean, Martin? I should die of shame!'

'Well, I feel as if I'm dying of shame too, ever since you called me all those awful names yesterday,' said Martin in a trembling voice. 'I simply don't know what to do!'

'There's only one thing to do – and a little coward like you would never do it,' said Elizabeth. 'You ought to own up at the next Meeting that you took the things, and say that you put the blame on Julian! *That's* what you ought to do!'

CHAPTER TWENTY-THREE

A SCHOOL MATCH – AND OTHER THINGS

SCHOOL WENT happily on. A lacrosse match was played, and Elizabeth was in it. It was a home match, not an away match, so the whole school turned out to watch. Elizabeth felt most excited.

Julian was playing in the match too, and so was Robert. Julian was good at all games. He could run swiftly and catch deftly.

'We ought to put up a good show today,' said Eileen when she took the team out on to the field. 'We've got some strong first-form players this term. Now, Elizabeth, keep your head, pass when you can, and for goodness' sake don't go up in smoke if one of your enemies kicks you on the ankle! Julian, keep by Elizabeth if you can, and let her pass to you. You catch better than anyone else.'

It was an exciting match. The other school had

brought a strong team, and the two schools were very evenly matched. Elizabeth got a whack on the hand from someone else's lacrosse stick that gave her so much pain she thought she would have to go off the field.

Julian saw her screwed-up face. 'Bad luck!' he called. 'You're doing well, Elizabeth. Keep it up! We'll shoot a goal soon, see if we don't!'

Elizabeth grinned. The pain got better and she played well. The other school shot three goals, and Whyteleafe also shot three. The children who were looking on anxiously consulted their watches – only one minute more to go!

Then Elizabeth got the ball and tore for the goal. 'Pass, pass!' yelled Julian. 'There's someone behind you!'

Elizabeth threw the ball deftly to him, and he caught it. But another enemy was on him at once, trying to knock the ball out of his net. He passed it back quickly to Elizabeth. She saw yet another enemy coming to tackle her, and in despair she flung the ball hard at the goal.

It was a wild shot, but somehow or other it got there! It bounced on a tuft of grass, and just avoided the waiting lacrosse net of the goalkeeper. It rolled into the corner of the goal net and lay still.

Whyteleafe School went quite mad. The whistle blew for Time, and the two teams trooped off the field.

Julian gave Elizabeth such a thump on the back that she choked.

'Good for you, Elizabeth!' said Julian, beaming. 'Just in the nick of time. Jolly good!'

'Well, it was really a fluke,' said Elizabeth honestly. 'I couldn't see where I was throwing. I just threw wildly, and by a fluke it went into the goal!'

The first-formers crowded round her, cheering her and patting her on the back. It was very pleasant. Then the two teams went in and had a most enormous tea. It was all great fun.

'I think you ought to be a monitor all over again!' said Rosemary. 'I never felt so thrilled and proud in my life as when you shot that last goal, Elizabeth, just as the whistle blew. I almost forgot to breathe!'

Elizabeth laughed. 'Golly, if people were made monitors just for shooting goals, how easy it would be!'

Nobody felt like doing prep that night. Julian longed to make a few noises. The others looked at him, trying to make him start something. Mr Leslie was taking prep and it would be fun to have a bit of excitement.

Julian wanted to please the others. He wondered what to do. Should he make a noise like a sewing machine? Or what about a noise like bees humming?

He looked down at his book. He hadn't begun to learn his French yet. He remembered his promise, made so solemnly in the little country church a few days back. He was never going to forget that.

Julian put his hands over his ears and began to work. Maybe if there were a few minutes left at the end of prep he would do something funny – but he was going to do his work first!

Work was easy to Julian. He had a quick mind, and an unusual memory. He had already read a great deal, and knew a tremendous lot. He could easily beat the others if he tried. But it was not so easy to try at first, when he had let his mind be lazy for so long.

But, at the end of the first week of trying, Julian was top of the form! He was one mark ahead of Elizabeth, who was also trying hard. Everyone was amazed, especially Miss Ranger.

'Julian, it seems that you must either be top or bottom,' she said when she read out the marks. 'Last week you were so far at the bottom that I am surprised there were any marks to read out at all. This week you are a mark ahead of Elizabeth, who has been working extremely well. I am proud of you both.'

Elizabeth flushed with pleasure. Julian looked as if he didn't care a rap, but Miss Ranger knew that was only a pose. Something had changed him, and he cared now – he wanted to use his brains for the right things, not only for silly jokes and tricks.

I think perhaps his mother's illness must have had something to do with it, thought Miss Ranger. *I do hope this great change lasts! Julian is a joy to teach when he really works. I hope he won't be bottom again next week.*

But Julian would never be bottom again. He was going to keep that promise all his life. He was not going to waste his brains any more.

Only Martin did badly that week – even worse than Arabella usually did! He was right at the bottom and Miss Ranger spoke sharply to him.

'You can do better than this, Martin. You have not been bottom before. You seem very dreamy this week.'

Martin was not really dreamy. He was worried. He wished he had not told Elizabeth his secret now. She had said such hard things to him, things he couldn't forget. And she hadn't helped him at all.

Miss Ranger had a few words to say to Arabella also. 'Arabella, I am getting tired of seeing you so low in the form. You are one of the oldest – the very oldest in fact. I think if you gave a little more attention to your work and a little less to whether your hair is looking nice, or whether your collar is straight or your nails perfect, we might see a little better work.'

Arabella went red. She thought Miss Ranger was very unkind. 'She speaks more sharply to me than to anyone else in the form,' she complained to Rosemary.

This was quite true, but Miss Ranger knew that she could only get at thick-skinned Arabella by plain speaking. The vain little girl hated to feel small, hated to be scolded or put to shame in front of anyone. Whyteleafe School was very good for her. There was plenty of plain speaking there.

Arabella decided not to be bottom the next week. She stopped fussing about her hair and her dress – at least she stopped fussing in class.

'You'll soon be quite passably nice, Arabella,' said Robert, who hadn't much time for the vain little girl. 'I haven't heard you ask Rosemary once today if your hair is tidy. It's simply marvellous!'

And, for once Arabella laughed at the joke against herself, instead of sulking. Yes, she really was getting 'passably nice' in some ways!

The next School Meeting came. 'It won't last long,' said Elizabeth to Julian. 'There won't be much business done at it, Julian. Let's slip out quickly afterwards and bag the little table in the common room. I've got a big new jigsaw we can do.'

'Right,' said Julian.

But there was more 'business' to be done at that Meeting than Elizabeth thought, and there was no time for a jigsaw puzzle that night. It was all quite unexpected, and nobody was more surprised than Elizabeth when it happened.

The Meeting opened as usual. There was very little money to be put into the box, though a few children had postal orders. Then the money was given out.

'Any requests?'

'Please, William,' said one small boy, Quentin, 'the cage I keep my guinea pig in fell over yesterday, and one side of it broke in. Could I have the money for another cage?'

'Well, that's rather expensive,' said William. 'There isn't a great deal of money in the box at the moment. Can't you mend the cage?'

'I have tried, but I'm not very good at it,' said Quentin. 'I thought I'd done it all right, but I hadn't, and my guinea pig got out. I was late for school because I had to catch it. It's in with Martin's guinea pig now, but they fight.'

'I'll mend it for Quentin,' said Julian, actually remembering to stand up and take his hands out of his pockets. 'It won't take me long.'

'Thank you, Julian,' said William. 'There really isn't a great deal of money in the box at the moment. But I believe there are quite a lot of birthdays next week, so maybe we shall have a full box again soon. Any more requests?'

Nobody quite liked to ask for any more money as there wasn't much to spare.

'Any complaints?' said William. There was a dead silence. It was clear there were none.

'Well, there's nothing much to say this week – except that I am sure the whole school will like to know that Julian is top of his form, instead of bottom, this week,' said William, with a sudden smile. 'Keep it up, Julian!'

That is the nice part about Whyteleafe School, thought Elizabeth. *You get blamed – but you do get praised too, and that's lovely!*

'You may go,' said William, and the children got up to go. But, in the middle of the noise of feet, there came a voice.

'Please, William! I've got something to say!'

'Sit down again,' ordered William, and everyone sat in surprise. Who had spoken? Only one boy was on his feet – and that was Martin Follett, looking very green and shaky. 'What do you want to say, Martin?' asked William. 'Speak up!'

CHAPTER TWENTY-FOUR

MARTIN GETS A CHANCE

ELIZABETH LOOKED in astonishment at Martin. Surely he could not be going to tell his own secret – that it was he who had stolen the money and tried to put the blame on to Julian!

He's such a mean, deceitful, horrid boy, she thought, *and a real coward. Whatever is he going to say?*

Martin swallowed once or twice. He seemed to find it difficult to say a word now. William saw that he was dreadfully nervous and he spoke more kindly to him.

'What is it you want to say, Martin? Don't be afraid of saying it. We are always ready to hear anything at the School Meeting, as you know.'

'Yes. I know,' said Martin in rather a loud voice, as if he was trying to get all his courage together at once. 'I know. Well, I took that money – and all the other things – and I put that shilling into Julian's pocket, and the sweet too, so that nobody would think it was me – they would think it was Julian.'

He stopped speaking, but he didn't sit down. Nobody said a word. Martin suddenly spoke again. 'I know it's awful. I dare say I'd never have owned up except for two things. I couldn't bear it when Julian's mother was ill – I mean, it was awful to think I'd done a horrid trick to someone who was miserable. And the other thing that made me speak was because someone said I was a coward, and I'm not.'

'You certainly are not,' said Rita. 'It is a courageous thing to do – to stand up and confess to something mean. But why did you steal, Martin?'

'I don't really know,' said Martin. 'I know there's no excuse.'

Elizabeth had sat and listened to all this in the greatest surprise. Fancy Martin being brave enough to say all that in front of everyone! Now Julian was completely cleared of any blame. She looked at Martin and felt suddenly sorry for him.

He so badly wanted people to like him, and they don't, she thought, *and now he has had to own up to something that will make them dislike him all the more! Well, that was a brave thing to do.*

William and Rita were talking to one another. So were the monitors. What was to be done with Martin?

How was this to be tackled? Elizabeth suddenly remembered what she had read in the big book the night before. She stood up.

'William! Rita! I understand about Martin! He hasn't got any excuse for what he did, but there's a real reason; it wasn't just badness. It wasn't the usual sort of stealing.'

'What do you mean, Elizabeth?' asked William in surprise. 'Stealing is always stealing.'

'Yes, I know,' said Elizabeth, 'but Martin's sort was strange. He only took things from other people so that he might give them away! He never kept them himself.'

'Yes, that's quite true,' said Rosemary, most surprisingly forgetting her timidity, and standing up beside Elizabeth. 'He gave me money whenever I lost mine, and he is always giving away sweets. He never keeps any for himself.'

'William, there's a bit about the same sort of thing in our big book – the one on the table in front of you,' said Elizabeth eagerly. 'I couldn't help wondering why Martin seemed such a funny person – you know, kind and unkind, mean and generous – it seemed so odd to be opposite things at once – and there's a bit about a girl in our book who was just the same.'

'Where?' asked William, opening the book. Elizabeth walked up to the platform, bent over the book, turned the pages and found the place. 'There you are!' she said, pointing.

'How did you know it was here?' asked Rita.

'Well, Martin told me all he'd done, and I was disgusted,' said Elizabeth, 'but all the same I was puzzled about him and I wondered if there was anything about that kind of thing in our book – so I looked, and there was.'

William read the piece and passed it to Rita. They spoke together. Elizabeth went back to her place. Martin was looking very miserable, wishing heartily that he had never said a word now. He felt that everyone's eyes were on him, and it was not at all a nice feeling.

William spoke again, and everyone listened intently. 'Stealing is always wrong,' said William in his clear, pleasant voice. 'Always. People do it for many reasons – greed, envy, dishonesty. All bad reasons. But Martin did it for a different reason. He did it because he wanted to buy friendship. He did it because he wanted to buy people's liking and admiration.'

William paused. 'He took things in order to give them away to someone else. He may have thought to himself that because it is good to give to others, it was therefore not bad to take them away from someone else. But they were not his to give. It was stealing just the same.'

A tear trickled down Martin's cheek and fell on the floor. 'I want to go away from Whyteleafe,' he said in a low voice, without standing up. 'I shall never do any good here now. I've never done any good anywhere.'

'You can't run away like that,' said William. 'What's the good of trying to run away from yourself? You've got courage or you wouldn't have stood up and said what you did. We all make silly mistakes, we all have bad faults, but what really matters is – are we decent enough to try and put them right? You did have a reason for what you did, a silly reason. Now you see it was silly, and you see that what you did was bad. All right, that's the end of it.'

'What do you mean – that's the end of it!' said Martin in surprise.

'The end of your silly habit of taking what doesn't belong to you in order to buy friendship!' said William. 'You know quite well you *can't* buy it. People like you for what you are, not for what you give them. Well, if the reason for that bad habit is gone, the habit goes too, doesn't it? You'll never steal any more.'

'Well, I don't think I shall,' said Martin, and he sat up a little straighter. 'I've felt so guilty and so ashamed. I'll take another chance.'

'Good,' said William. 'Come and see me this evening and we'll get things a bit straighter. But I think you must pay back each week any money you have taken from different children, and you must also buy sweets to give back to those you took them from. That's only fair.'

'Yes, I will,' said Martin.

'And we'll give him a chance and be friendly,' suddenly said Elizabeth, eager to do her bit to help. How she had disliked Martin! Now she wanted to help him! What was there about Whyteleafe School that made you see things so differently all of a sudden? It was odd.

'It seems to me,' said Rita in her slow, distinct voice, 'it seems to me as if Elizabeth is a much better monitor when she isn't one than when she *is*!'

The children laughed loudly at this. Elizabeth smiled too. *Rita is right*, she thought, surprised. *I do seem to be wiser when I'm not a monitor than when I am! Oh, how topsy-turvy I am!*

The Meeting broke up at last. Martin went to Julian. 'I'm sorry, Julian,' he muttered, not looking at the boy at all.

'Look at me,' commanded Julian. 'Don't get into the habit of not looking at people when you speak to them, Martin. Look at me, and say you're sorry properly.'

Martin raised his eyes and looked rather fearfully into Julian's green ones, expecting to see scorn and anger. But he saw only friendliness there. And he said he was sorry properly.

'I *am* sorry. I was a beast. I've learnt my lesson and I'll never be two-faced again,' he said, looking straight into Julian's eyes.

'That's all right,' said Julian. 'I like you better now than I did before, if that's any comfort to you. Look, William is wanting you.'

Martin went off with William. What William said to him nobody ever heard, but Rosemary, who saw him coming from the study later, said that Martin looked much happier.

'I'm going to be really friendly to him,' she said. 'He'll want a friend. I never thought he was bad. I always thought he was nice. So I shall go on thinking it.'

Elizabeth looked in surprise at the timid Rosemary. Good gracious – that was another person changing! Who would have thought that Rosemary, who agreed with everyone, would say straight out that she was going to be friends with someone like Martin!

You simply never know about people, thought Elizabeth. *You think because they're timid they'll always be timid, or because they're mean they'll always be mean. But they can change awfully quickly if they are treated right. Golly, Arabella will be changing and forget to be vain and boastful! No, that could never happen!*

There was no time to do the jigsaw – only just time to clear away the things left out, and have some supper and go to bed.

'Things do happen here, don't they?' said Julian, with a grin. 'Come on down to supper.'

At supper Miss Ranger was continually annoyed by the buzzing of a bluebottle. She looked all down the table for it, but could see it nowhere.

'Where *is* that fly?' she said. 'It's very early in the year for a bluebottle surely! Get rid of it, somebody. We can't have it laying eggs in our meat.'

The bluebottle buzzed violently, and Mr Leslie, at the next table, looked all around for it. It really was becoming a nuisance.

Elizabeth looked suddenly at Julian. He grinned at her and nodded. *Oh, it's one of Julian's noises!* she thought, and exploded into a giggle. Then everyone knew – and how they laughed, even Miss Ranger.

'I thought it was a good time to play a joke,' said Julian when he said goodnight to Elizabeth. 'We had all had such a very serious evening. Goodnight, Elizzzzzzzzzzzzzabeth!'

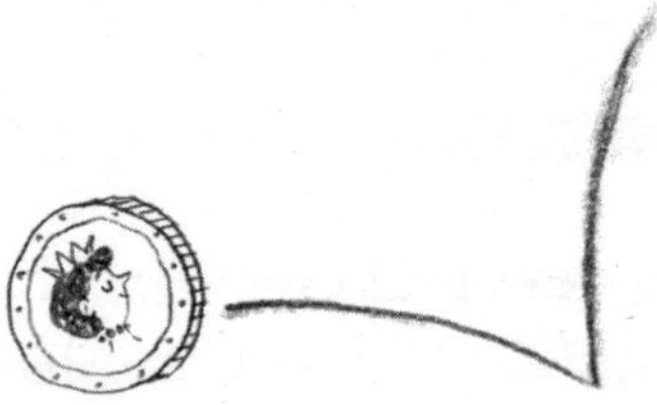

CHAPTER TWENTY-FIVE

AN ADVENTURE FOR ELIZABETH

THREE DAYS went swiftly by, days of work and play, riding and gardening, looking after pets, going for nature rambles – it was extraordinary the way the weeks flew by.

'Once the beginning of the term is past, the end seems to appear so quickly!' said Elizabeth. 'There doesn't seem to be much middle to a term!'

'Let's go for a nature walk this afternoon,' said Julian. 'We've got an hour and a half quite free. Don't garden with John – he's got plenty of helpers at the moment with that tribe of youngsters – we'll go over the hills and down to the lake.'

'All right,' said Elizabeth, looking out of the window at the brilliant April sunshine. 'It will be lovely on the hills – we might find primroses on our way.'

So, that afternoon, the two set off together. They

carried nature tins on their backs, for they meant to bring back many things for the nature class. 'We'll find frogspawn in the lake,' said Julian. 'I bet there's plenty there, and tadpoles too.'

They went over the hills together. 'We must be back by teatime,' said Elizabeth. 'That's the rule, unless we have permission to stay out later. My watch is right. I don't want to get into trouble again for anything just at present. I've not been too bad this last week or two!'

Julian grinned. He thought that of all the children in the form Elizabeth probably tried hardest to be good, and yet walked into trouble more often than anyone else. You never knew what was going to happen to Elizabeth.

She seems to make things happen somehow, thought Julian. *She's such a fierce little person, so downright and sincere. Well, we've both had our ups and downs this term. Let's hope we'll have a little peace till the end of term.*

They went over the hills, picking primroses in the more sheltered corners. The sun shone down quite fiercely, and Elizabeth took off her blazer and carried it.

'This is lovely,' she said. 'Julian, look, there's the lake. Isn't it beautiful?'

It was. It lay smooth and blue in the April sunshine. There seemed to be nobody there at all. The children were pleased to think they would have it all to themselves.

They began to look for frogspawn. There was none to be found, but there were plenty of tadpoles. They caught some and put them into their jars.

'I feel a bit tired now,' said Elizabeth. 'Let's sit down.'

'I'm going up the hill a little way,' said Julian. 'I want to find some special sort of moss. You sit here and wait for me.'

Julian disappeared. After a while Elizabeth thought she heard him coming back, but it was someone else. It was a child of about six, nicely dressed, with big blue eyes and very red cheeks. He was panting as if he had been running.

Elizabeth was surprised to see him all alone. He seemed rather small to be allowed near the lake by himself. She lay back and shut her eyes, letting the sun soak into her.

She heard the little boy playing about – and then she heard a loud splash. At the same moment she heard a terrified scream, and she sat up suddenly.

The little boy had disappeared. But a little way out on the lake some ripples showed, and then a small hand was flung up.

'Golly! That boy has fallen in!' said Elizabeth in dismay. 'He must have crawled out on that low tree branch, and tumbled off. I thought he oughtn't to be here by himself.'

Then a woman appeared, running. 'Where's Michael? Did I hear him scream?' she called anxiously. 'He ran away from me. Have you seen a little boy anywhere?'

'He has fallen into the water,' said Elizabeth. 'Can he swim?'

'No, oh, no! Oh, he'll be drowned,' cried the woman. 'Oh, let's get help quickly.'

There was no help to be got. Elizabeth quickly undid her shoes. 'I'll wade in and get him,' she said. 'If the water is too deep, I'll have to swim.'

She waded out, feeling the sand of the lake bottom just under her stockinged feet. Suddenly the sandy bottom fell away, and Elizabeth was out of her depth. She had to swim.

She was a good swimmer, and she struck out at once, but it was not easy to swim in clothes. They weighed her down dreadfully. Still, she managed somehow, and it was only a few strokes that she had to swim. Her quick mind remembered all she had learnt about life-saving.

She caught hold of the sinking child and pulled him towards her. At once he clung to her, almost pulling her under too.

'Leave go!' ordered Elizabeth. 'Leave go! I will hold *you*, not you me.'

But the child was too frightened to leave go. He pulled poor Elizabeth right under, and she gasped and spluttered. Somehow she undid his arms from round her neck, turned him over on his back, put her hands under his armpits and swam on her back to the shore, pulling the kicking child along.

Soon she felt the sandy bottom under her feet and she struggled to stand. The child slipped from her hands and went under again. He got caught in some weeds and did not float up to the top. Elizabeth was in despair. She went under the water herself to look for him, and caught sight of a leg. She got hold of it and pulled hard.

The child came out of the weeds. He was no longer struggling. *Oh dear, I believe he is drowned*, thought Elizabeth in horror. She dragged him to the shore. He was quite limp, and lay still.

The woman bent over him, moaning and quite terrified. Elizabeth thought she was silly. 'Look, we must work his arms up and down, up and down, like this,' she said. 'That will bring air into his lungs and make him breathe again. Look – work his arms well.'

The girl was tired, and she let the woman do the life-saving work, then she took her turn – and suddenly the child gave a big sigh and opened his eyes.

'Oh, he's alive – he's alive!' cried the woman. 'Oh, Michael, Michael – why did you run away from me?'

'You'd better get him home as soon as he can walk,' said Elizabeth. 'He's wet through. He'll catch an awful chill.'

The woman took the child off in her arms, weeping over him, forgetting even to say thank you to the little girl who had saved him. Elizabeth took off her dress and squeezed it dry. She began to shiver.

Suddenly Julian appeared down the hill. He stared in the greatest astonishment at Elizabeth. 'Whatever *have* you been doing?' he asked. 'You're wet through.'

'I had to pull a kid out of the water,' said Elizabeth. 'I couldn't help getting wet. I hope Matron won't be angry with me. Good thing I took my blazer off – I've got one dry thing to put on at any rate.'

'Come on home, quick,' said Julian, helping her on with her blazer. 'We're late anyway and now you'll have to change all your clothes. Oh, Elizabeth – you can't even go out for a walk without doing something like this!'

'Well, I couldn't leave the child to drown, could I?' said Elizabeth. 'He ran away from his nurse.'

They went home as quickly as they could. The tea bell went as they reached the school. 'I'll slip in to tea and say you are coming in a minute,' said Julian. 'Hurry up.'

Elizabeth hurried up – but she was cold and shivery, and wet clothes are not easy to take off. She put them in the hot-air cupboard to dry, hoping that Matron would not see them there before she herself had time to take them out.

'I don't see how I could help it, all the same,' said Elizabeth, drying herself on a towel. 'I just had to pull that child out of the water. I bet he would have drowned if I hadn't.'

Matron didn't notice the wet clothes. Elizabeth was able to take them out of the cupboard before she saw them. She had a sharp word from Miss Ranger for being late for tea, but otherwise it seemed as if things were all right.

'Oh, Julian – I left my jar of tadpoles by the lake,' said Elizabeth in dismay, after tea. 'Aren't I an idiot?'

'Well, you must share mine,' said Julian. 'I've got plenty. I suppose if you go about dashing into lakes, rescuing silly kids, you are bound to forget something or other.'

Elizabeth laughed. 'Don't tell anyone, please,' she said. 'Matron doesn't know my clothes were wet, and the others would only tease me if they knew I'd dashed into the lake like that.'

So Julian said nothing. He hadn't seen Elizabeth swim to the child's rescue, he hadn't known what a hard task it had been to get him safely to shore, or how Elizabeth had brought him back from death by showing the nurse how to work his arms up and down to make him breathe again. He just thought she had waded into the water, slipped and got wet, and pulled the child out.

So nobody knew, and Elizabeth forgot about it. She was working very hard indeed, trying to keep pace with Julian, who, now that he was using his brains properly, seemed likely to beat her easily every single week.

'It's most annoying!' said Elizabeth, giving him a friendly shove. 'I do my best to make you use your brains and work hard – and what happens? I lose my place at the top of the form! I shall complain about you at the Meeting tonight, Julian. I shall say that you are robbing me of my rightful place at the top of the form. So be careful!'

'There'll be no excitement at the Meeting tonight, old thing,' said Julian. 'We've all been as good as gold lately.'

But he was wrong. There was plenty of excitement!

CHAPTER TWENTY-SIX

HAPPY ENDING

THE CHILDREN always enjoyed the weekly School Meetings, even if there was not much business to be done. It was good to meet all together, good to share their money, good to see their head boy and girl on the platform, with the serious monitors nearby.

'You feel how much you belong to the school then,' said Jenny. 'You really feel part of it, and you know that what you are and do really matter to the whole school. It's a nice feeling.'

There were only two weeks to go till the end of the term. No one had any money at all to put into the box. But there had been several birthdays two or three weeks before, so there was still plenty of money to share.

It was given out as usual, and then William allowed ten shillings to go to John to buy two big new watering cans.

'One of ours has two holes in it and they can't be mended,' said John. 'The water drips out on to our feet and wets them all the time. And the other can is so small. Last summer we lost a lot of plants because we didn't do enough watering, and this time I want plenty of water if the weather's dry. So I'd be awfully glad to have two new cans.'

The garden had looked lovely that early spring. Crocuses had blazed on the school bank, daffodils were out everywhere, wallflowers were filling the air with their delicious scent and polyanthus had flowered along the edges of the beds. John and his helpers had done really well. The whole school was willing to buy him cans, barrows, spades – anything he wanted. They were very proud of John and his hard work.

Nobody else wanted any money. There were no complaints either. It looked as if it was going to be a short and rather dull Meeting. But no – what was this? Miss Belle and Miss Best were actually walking up from the back of the big gym! *They* had something to say, they had business to discuss! Mr Johns came with them.

In surprise William and Rita gave them chairs, wondering what was happening. The school looked up to the platform, wondering too. It couldn't be anything awful, because Miss Belle and Miss Best were smiling.

The headmistresses sat down. Mr Johns sat beside

them. They spoke a little and then Miss Belle got up.

'Children,' she said, 'it is not often that Miss Best, Mr Johns and I come up here to speak to you at a School Meeting – unless, of course, you ask us. But this time we have something to say – something very pleasant – and I want to say it in front of the whole school.'

Everyone listened eagerly. Whatever could it be? Nobody had the least idea.

Miss Belle took a letter from her bag and opened it. 'I have had a letter,' she said. 'It is from a Colonel Helston, who lives not far from here. This is what he says.'

Miss Belle read the letter and everyone listened with interest and excitement.

'Dear Madam,

Four days ago my little son, Michael, ran away from his nurse. He fell into the lake near your school, and would have been drowned if it had not been for a girl from Whyteleafe. This girl waded into the water, then swam to Michael. Michael struggled hard and pulled her under the water. She got him on his back, and swam towards the shore with him. He slipped from her hands and became entangled in some weeds. He was without any doubt drowning at that moment. The girl dived into the weeds and pulled him out. When she got him to shore she showed the nurse how to bring him back to life again, and herself helped to do this, with the result that he lived, and is now safe and well with me at home.

I was away at the time, and only came back today, to hear this amazing story. I do not know which girl it was. All I know is that the nurse saw she had a Whyteleafe school blazer on the ground nearby, and I would like you, please, to tell me the name of the child so that I may thank her myself, and give her some reward for her very plucky action. She saved the life of my little boy – he is my only child – and I can never be grateful enough to the little girl from Whyteleafe School, whoever she may be.

Yours sincerely,

Edward Helston'

The children listened in amazement. Who could it be? Nobody knew. But then, whoever it was must have come home with wet clothes – surely they would have been seen. The children looked from one to the other. Julian nudged Elizabeth. His green eyes shone with pride in his friend. Elizabeth was as red as a beetroot. *What a fuss about nothing!* she thought.

'Well,' said Miss Belle, folding up the letter, 'this surprising letter gave me and Miss Best very great pride and pleasure. We do not know who this girl is. We asked Matron if anyone had given her wet clothes to dry, but no one had. So it is a complete mystery.'

There was a silence. Elizabeth said nothing at all. Everyone waited.

'I should like to know who it is,' said Miss Belle. 'I should like to give her my heartiest congratulations on a brave deed that she said nothing about. The whole school should be proud of her.'

Elizabeth sat quite still. She simply could *not* stand up and say anything. For the first time in her life she really felt shy. She hadn't done anything much – only just pulled that child out of the water. Oh dear, what a fuss about it all!

Julian got to his feet. 'It was Elizabeth!' he said, so loudly that it sounded almost like a shout. 'Of course it was Elizabeth! Who else could it be? It's exactly like her, isn't it? It was our Elizabeth!'

The children craned their necks to look at Elizabeth. She sat on the floor, still very red, with Julian patting her on the shoulder.

Then the clapping and cheering began! It nearly brought the roof down. Elizabeth might be naughty and hot-tempered and often do silly, wrong things, but she was as sound and sweet as an apple in her character, and all the children knew it.

Clap, clap, clap, hurrah, hurrah, bang, bang, clap, clap! The noise went on for ages, until Miss Belle held up her hand. The sounds died down.

'Well, so it was Elizabeth!' she said. 'I might have guessed it. Things always happen to Elizabeth, don't they? Come up here on the platform, please, Elizabeth.'

Elizabeth went up, flaming red again. Miss Belle, Miss Best and Mr Johns actually shook hands with her solemnly and said they were very proud of her.

'You are bringing honour to the name of Whyteleafe,' said Miss Belle, her eyes very bright. 'And you bring honour to yourself at the same time. We would like to give you a reward ourselves, Elizabeth, for your brave deed. Is there anything you would like?'

'Well . . .' said Elizabeth, and paused. 'Well . . .' she said again. Julian wondered what she was going to say. Was she going to ask if she might be made a monitor again?

'I'd like you to give the school a whole holiday, please,' said Elizabeth in a rush, thinking that she was asking rather a big thing. 'You see there's a big fair on at the next town soon – and it would be such fun if you would give us a whole holiday, so that we could go to it. We've all been talking about it, and I know everyone would like to go. Do you think we could?'

There was another outburst of cheering and clapping.

'Good old Elizabeth!' shouted somebody. 'Trust her to ask something for the school, and not for herself!'

Miss Belle smiled and nodded. 'I think we might say yes to what Elizabeth wants, don't you?' she said, and Miss Best nodded too. Elizabeth smiled, very pleased. She might have been in great disgrace, and made the children think bad things of her that term, but anyway she had made up for it now by getting them a whole holiday to go to the fair.

She turned to go down into the gym again. But somebody was standing up, waiting to speak. It was Julian.

'What is it, Julian?' asked Miss Belle.

'I am speaking for the whole of the first form,' said Julian. 'We want to know if Elizabeth can be made a monitor again, now, this very night? We think *she* ought to have some reward. And we want her for our monitor. We all trust her and like her.'

'Yes, we do, we do!' cried Jenny, and a few others. Elizabeth's eyes shone like stars. How marvellous! To be made a monitor because the whole form wanted it, and wanted it so badly! Oh, things were wonderful!

'Wait, Elizabeth,' said Miss Belle, stretching out her hand and pulling the little girl to her. 'Do you want to be made a monitor again?'

'Oh, yes please,' said Elizabeth happily. 'I can do

better now. I know I can. Let me try. I won't let anyone down again. I'll be sensible and wise, really I will.'

'Yes, I think you will,' said Miss Belle. 'We won't pass round bits of paper and vote for you, Elizabeth, as we usually do – you shall be monitor from this very minute. Susan shall still be monitor too. For once in a way we must have an extra one! A very special extra one!'

So Elizabeth went to sit at the monitors' table, proud and pleased. Everyone was glad, even Arabella. How could anyone not be glad when Elizabeth had so generously asked for something for the whole school, instead of asking for something for herself alone, as she might so easily have done?

'Well, that was a good Meeting, wasn't it?' said Julian when the children at last filed out of the gym, chattering and laughing in excitement. 'This has been a thrilling term, I must say. I'm glad I came to Whyteleafe School. It's the best school in the world!'

'Yes, it is,' said Elizabeth. 'Oh, I do feel so happy, Julian.'

'You've a right to,' said Julian. 'Funny person, aren't you? Naughtiest girl in the school – and best girl in the school! Worst enemy – and best friend! Well, whichever you are, you're always our Elizabeth, and we're proud of you!'

BONUS BLYTON

Enid Blyton has been one of the world's best-loved storytellers for over seventy-five years. Her interest in writing began as a child, and before she loved receiving letters from the children who read her books, she enjoyed working with them as a teacher. *The Naughtiest Girl* stories are inspired by real schools and experiences. Turn the page to learn more about Enid as a child and as a teacher. Afterwards you might like to write about your school and teachers and the people in *your* class!

THE LIFE AND TIMES OF ENID BLYTON

11 August 1897	Enid Blyton was born in East Dulwich, London. Two brothers are born after her – Hanly (b. 1899) and Carey (b. 1902).
1911	Enid enters a children's poetry competition and is praised for her writing. She's on the path to becoming a bestselling author . . .
1916	Enid begins to train as a teacher in Ipswich. By the time she is 21, she is a fully qualified Froebel teacher, and starts work at a school in Kent.
1917	Enid's first 'grown-up' publication – three poems in *Nash's Magazine*.
June 1922	Enid's first book is published. It's called *Child Whispers*.
1926	Enid begins editing – and writes – the phenomenal *Sunny Stories for Little Folks* magazine. (She continues in this role for 26 years!)

1927	So vast is Enid's output that she has to learn to type. (But she still writes to children by hand.)
1931	Having married Hugh Pollock in 1924, the couple's first child, Gillian, is born. Imogen, their second daughter, was born in 1935.
1942	The Famous Five is launched with *Five on a Treasure Island*.
1949	The first appearance of *The Secret Seven* and of *Noddy* mark this year as special.
1953	Enid moves away from *Sunny Stories* to launch *Enid Blyton's Magazine*. She is now renowned throughout the world – she even established her own company, called Darrell Waters Limited (the surname of her second husband).
1962	Enid Blyton becomes one of the first and most important children's authors to be published in paperback. Now, she reaches even more readers than ever before.
28 November 1968	Enid dies in her sleep, in a nursing home in Hampstead.

Enid's death wasn't the end of her remarkable legacy. In the 1970s the Famous Five became TV stars (*Noddy* having already hit our screens in 1955). In 1996, the Enid Blyton Society was formed so that fans across the world could share their enthusiasm for Enid's work (www.enidblytonsociety.co.uk) In 2012 the Famous Five celebrated seventy years of continuous publishing, with special editions featuring covers by top illustrators, led by Quentin Blake. New book, film and merchandising deals are being struck all the time. Enid's work is definitely here to stay!

MY SCHOOL DAYS: AN INTERVIEW WITH ENID BLYTON

What did you like most about school?

I loved school, every minute of it. I loved learning. The things I liked at kindergarten were the things I have liked best all my life: stories, music, nature and games.

What do you remember about school?

I remember everything about it – the room, the garden, the pictures on the wall, the little chairs, the dog there, and the lovely smells that used to creep out from the kitchen into our classroom. I remember how we used to take biscuits for our mid-morning break and swap them with one another – and how we used to dislike one small boy who was clever at swapping a small biscuit for a big one.

What was your best subject?

Essay and composition and story-writing.

What about your worst?

Sums. I hadn't the right kind of brain for figures and I used to look on in awe when I saw other boys and girls doing the most complicated sums.

We know you loved stories. Tell us about some of your favourites?

My favourite book as a child was called *The Princess and the Goblin* by George Macdonald, and I also loved *Coral Island* by R. M. Ballantyne. Other books I enjoyed include:

Alice in Wonderland and *Alice Through the Looking-Glass* by Lewis Carroll.

Black Beauty by Anna Sewell (even though parts of it were sad).

The Water Babies by Charles Kingsley.

Arthur Mee's Children's Encyclopedia – which I read from end to end. Nature books. Annuals. Magazines too.

Myths and legends from all around the world.

I liked poetry – even when I didn't really understand it.

I quite liked comics, but found they were like sweets – you sucked them for a few minutes, then they were gone, and you didn't think about them any more.

Were there any books you *didn't* enjoy?

I didn't like *all* stories. Some I found dull and boring, just as you do. There were no real children as characters, and it was children I badly wanted to read about. There were no lively conversations in the books. Nothing to really make me laugh.

The responses to those questions are based on comments by Enid Blyton in her autobiography, The Story of My Life *© Hodder & Stoughton Limited, 1952.*

WHAT THEY DID AT MISS BROWN'S SCHOOL

In 1920 Enid Blyton became a governess to the four Thompson children, whose ages ranged from four to ten. The family lived in Surbiton, in Surrey, in a house called 'Southernhay'. Enid had a small room which overlooked the garden, and it was there that she wrote many of her stories. Enid's tiny class often had lessons outdoors in the summer months.

Enid was very popular with her students, because her lessons were both practical and creative. She worked with them to put on performances for which they made props, costumes and invitations – and even sold tickets.

In 1941 she published a long story called 'What They Did at Miss Brown's School', which was divided into monthly episodes. It's been hard to find for many years, but you can read extracts in these new editions of *The Naughtiest Girl* books. The character of Miss Brown and her tiny class is very much based on Enid Blyton and her school at the Thompsons' . . .

Here's the third extract . . .

3. Off to the Pond. Making the Aquarium.

MARCH CAME in with wind and sun, and the school garden was soon bright with golden crocuses. The east wind made the children fidgety, so, one morning when Susan had upset her paintbox, and John had upset the chalks, and even quiet Mary had spilt water all over the classroom, Miss Brown shut up her book and spoke firmly.

'My dears, I can see that if I keep you in the schoolroom this morning you will end up doing something dreadful! Wipe up the water, Mary, and then you can all get your hats and coats. We'll go to the pond and see what we can find there!'

'Ooooh!' said all the children at once, and their fidgets fell from them like magic. Mary mopped up the water, and then in a minute or two they were all ready to go with Miss Brown.

The pond lay in a little sheltered hollow at the end of a lane called Butterfly Lane, because there were so many butterflies there in the summer. Miss Brown told the children to bring along their small nets, and a jam jar each, with a string tied round the neck to make a handle. Then they made their way to the pond.

It lay there in the March sunshine, ruffled a little by the wind. It looked exciting.

'Now I am going to help you make an aquarium this week,' said Miss Brown to the children. 'And we shall want some creatures to live in it and some waterweed too. So do your best to fish for tadpoles, and to find snails and nice pieces of weed.'

'Last time we were here, Miss Brown, the pond was frozen,' said John. 'Oh look – what is that big piece of black-spotted jelly lying over there, Miss Brown?'

'It's frogspawn!' squealed Susan. 'The tadpoles haven't hatched out of it yet. Oh, Miss Brown, can we take some of the frogspawn home with us and see the tadpoles hatching out?'

'Of course,' said Miss Brown. 'Put some in your jar, John.' So John caught the slippery mass in his net and then jerked it into his jar – *plomp!* He put a little water in, and looked at the jelly. It was spotted with black comma-shaped eggs that would soon change to tadpoles and wriggle free.

Then Peter found water snails, and collected fifteen, all sizes. He was very pleased.

'Put them in your jar,' said Miss Brown. 'They will be useful in our aquarium, because they act like dustmen, and destroy all the rubbish. They will eat the slime from the walls of our aquarium too and will be very useful.'

'Look, Miss Brown, look!' suddenly cried Mary. 'There are two big black beetles at the top of the pond. One is smaller than the other. Can we catch those for our aquarium?'

'See if you can catch the bigger one of the two,' said Miss Brown. 'Don't catch the one that is about an inch long. He is the dytiscid beetle, and would eat all our tadpoles!'

'But won't the bigger beetle eat our tadpoles too?' asked Susan.

'No, he is the great black water beetle and he eats green stuff, not other creatures,' said Miss Brown. 'He would be a fine fellow to have in our aquarium – only we shall have to cover the top if we keep him, because he will fly away if we don't!'

'Can he fly as well as swim?' cried Mary in surprise. 'Come here, beetle – oh, he's gone.'

'There's another one there, look, Mary,' said sharp-eyed Susan. So there was. Mary's net slipped suddenly under it and the beetle found himself out of the water. Mary put him into her jar, very proud indeed. He was very large, about two inches in length.

'We are getting on well,' said Miss Brown. 'Some frogspawn and fifteen snails and a fine water beetle. What about some pondweed? There is some Canadian pondweed over there, Peter – pull some up and put it into your jar. It will grow beautifully in our aquarium and will help to keep the water pure.'

Peter put some in his jar. Susan found two more water snails, and pulled some weeds too – so they all had their jars full.

'Can't we find some toadspawn as well?' asked John.

'There isn't any yet,' said Miss Brown, peering down into the pond. 'It isn't like the frogspawn, you know, John – it's in long strings of jelly, and the strings are wound in and out of the stems of the waterweeds. It is not so easy to see as the frogspawn. We will come and find some later on.'

'Can we make the aquarium soon?' begged Mary, on the way back. 'It would be so lovely to see all these creatures swimming about happily.'

'Tomorrow we will begin it,' said Miss Brown. 'I must go into the town this afternoon and see if I can buy an old wireless accumulator cheaply. That will make a fine aquarium for us.'

Well, the next morning the children were most excited to see that Miss Brown *had* managed to get the old glass tank from a wireless shop. It was a nice big one and had cost four shillings. Miss Brown had already cleaned it well.

'Now,' said Miss Brown, 'what we want to do is to make our aquarium as much like a little pond as possible, so we shall all be busy this morning. Susan, go and find lots of little smooth pebbles, wash them under the tap and bring them to me. Mary, go to the cupboard and get the bird sand we use for the canary's cage. John, go and find some nice large flints, with holes in if possible, that we can build up in the tank to make shelters for our creatures.'

'What shall *I* do?' asked Peter.

'Fetch your jar of weed,' said Miss Brown. 'I want you to pick out the best and longest pieces and tie the bottom end of each to a little stone. Then, when we put the weed into our tank, the stone will hold it down to the bottom till it roots, and the weed will float prettily.'

The children were soon very busy indeed. It *was* fun! Mary put the bird sand carefully over the bottom of the tank till it was about an inch and a half deep. Then Susan came in with her tiny washed pebbles, and a row or two of those were put on top of the sand.

'Now, before we put in John's big flints, we had better fill the tank with water,' said Miss Brown.

'How are we going to do that without disturbing all the sand and pebbles?' asked Mary.

'Easily!' said Miss Brown. 'John, get me a sheet of brown paper, please, and cut it about the size of the inside of the tank.

John soon had the paper ready. Miss Brown laid it neatly over the sand and pebbles and then sent Susan for a jug of water from the water butt outside. She poured the water slowly and gently on to the brown paper. The paper prevented the sand and pebbles from being disturbed, and the water rose clear and silvery in the aquarium.

It took five jugs full of water to fill the tank to within about five inches from the top. Then Miss Brown gently put in her hand and removed the brown paper, which was now soft and soaking wet, then she allowed John to arrange his big stones to make archways and shelters.

'You must see that the top of one stone comes right out of the water,' said Miss Brown, 'because when our tadpoles turn into small frogs they will want to sit with their noses out of the water to breathe – so you must give them a sitting place!'

Then Peter dropped in his pieces of waterweed one by one. The stones on the end sank to the bottom, pulling the weed, which swayed beautifully in the water.

'It looks exactly as if it's growing!' cried Peter. 'Oh, Miss Brown, our aquarium really does look like a tiny pond! It's lovely!'

'Quick! Let's put in the snails!' cried Susan, and she went to fetch her two. She slipped them in and they sank to the bottom. They were too frightened to come out and crawl.

Peter put his snails in too. Then Mary's water beetle went in, and he enjoyed himself at once and swam all round the aquarium in delight, looking at John's flints and even swimming right through a hole in one of the big stones. John was very pleased.

Then the frogspawn was gently slipped in. Miss Brown would not put much in – she said that a small tank would only take about twenty tadpoles, and even that might be too many when they grew big.

'You can take the rest back to the pond,' she said. 'And every time we go to the pond we can bring back with us some of the pond water. We can then take out some of the old water and add the fresh.. It will be full of tiny water life, which the tadpoles will feast on later on. At first they will eat the weed. The water from the butt is good for our aquarium too, but not clear tapwater.'

The spawn floated at the top of the tank. The beetle swam busily around, sometimes going to the top to take in air bubbles. All the snails came to life and began to crawl around. Dear me, the aquarium looked very busy indeed.

'What fun it will be to watch all the creatures every day,' said John. 'Are you going to put the tank on the windowsill in the sun, Miss Brown?'

'Certainly not!' said Miss Brown. 'Do you want the creatures to be cooked in the sun, John? That's a mistake so many people make. You must keep water creatures somewhere away from the bright light or sunshine. Look – we will put it on this shelf over here, where the north window is. It will be just right there!'

Well, the children did have fun with that aquarium! Every day they watched it. They saw the snails crawling up the glass. They saw the beetle eating the weed. They watched the tadpoles hatch from the jelly, which Miss Brown then removed from the tank. The tadpoles were amusing to watch. They wriggled all over the place and grew larger and larger. The pondweed grew too, and made a green garden for the creatures in the tank.

'This is the nicest thing we've done this year so far!' said Mary. 'Can we keep goldfish in the tank when the tadpoles are frogs, and we've put them out into the garden, Miss Brown?'

'Yes, we will,' said Miss Brown. 'Well, we've not been dull this year so far, have we, children? Tracking snowprints in January and making germinators in February – and now a fine aquarium in March!'

'What's for April, Miss Brown?' cried the children.

'I shall set you to work in the garden then!' said Miss Brown, with a laugh. 'So look out your spades and forks and trowels!'

Enid Blyton

THE FAMOUS FIVE

Join the Adventure!

Have you read them all?

Enid Blyton

THE SECRET SEVEN

SOLVE THE MYSTERY!

HAVE YOU READ THEM ALL?

Enid Blyton®

THE

SECRET SEVEN

SOLVE THE MYSTERY!

Don't miss…

Two action-packed Secret Seven stories from prizewinning author **PAMELA BUTCHART**!

THE MYSTERY SERIES

Read all 15 classic stories!

ENIDBLYTON.CO.UK

IS FOR PARENTS, CHILDREN AND TEACHERS!

Sign up to the newsletter on the homepage for a monthly round-up of news from the world of

Enid Blyton®

JOIN US ON SOCIAL MEDIA

EnidBlytonOfficial   BlytonOfficial

Illustration by Laura Ellen Anderson.

Enid Blyton

is one of the most popular children's authors of all time. Her books have sold over 500 million copies and have been translated into other languages more often than any other children's author.

Enid Blyton adored writing for children. She wrote over 700 books and about 2,000 short stories. *The Famous Five* books, now 80 years old, are her most popular. She is also the author of other favourites including *The Secret Seven*, *The Magic Faraway Tree* and *Malory Towers*.

Born in London in 1897, Enid lived much of her life in Buckinghamshire and loved dogs, gardening and the countryside. She was very knowledgeable about trees, flowers, birds and animals. Dorset – where some of the Famous Five's adventures are set – was a favourite place of hers too.

Enid Blyton's stories are read and loved by millions of children (and grown-ups) all over the world. Visit enidblyton.co.uk to discover more.

Illustration by
Laura Ellen Anderson.

The NAUGHTIEST GIRL Again

Have you read them all?

1. The Naughtiest Girl in the School
2. The Naughtiest Girl Again
3. The Naughtiest Girl is a Monitor
4. Here's the Naughtiest Girl
5. The Naughtiest Girl Keeps a Secret
6. The Naughtiest Girl Helps a Friend
7. The Naughtiest Girl Saves the Day
8. Well Done, the Naughtiest Girl
9. The Naughtiest Girl Wants to Win
10. The Naughtiest Girl Marches On

Enid Blyton®

The NAUGHTIEST GIRL Again

HODDER

HODDER CHILDREN'S BOOKS

First published in Great Britain in 1942 by George Newnes
This edition published in 2021 by Hodder & Stoughton
For further information about the editorial history of this book,
see enidblyton.co.uk/books

3 5 7 9 10 8 6 4 2

Enid Blyton® and Enid Blyton's signature are registered trade marks
of Hodder & Stoughton Limited
Text © 2021 Hodder & Stoughton Limited
Illustrations by Claire Powell © 2021 Hodder & Stoughton Limited

No trademark or copyrighted material may be reproduced without the
express written permission of the trademark and copyright owner

The moral right of the author has been asserted.

All characters and events in this publication, other than those clearly in the public domain, are fictitious and any resemblance to real persons, living or dead, is purely coincidental.

All rights reserved.
No part of this publication may be reproduced, stored in a retrieval system, or transmitted, in any form or by any means, without the prior permission in writing of the publisher, nor be otherwise circulated in any form of binding or cover other than that in which it is published and without a similar condition including this condition being imposed on the subsequent purchaser.

A CIP catalogue record for this book is available from the British Library.

Typeset by Avon DataSet Ltd, Arden Court, Alcester, Warwickshire

ISBN 978 1 444 95861 4

Printed and bound in Great Britain by Clays Ltd, Elcograf S.p.A.

The paper and board used in this book are made from wood
from responsible sources.

FSC
www.fsc.org
MIX
Paper | Supporting responsible forestry
FSC® C104740

Hodder Children's Books
An imprint of Hachette Children's Group
Part of Hodder & Stoughton
Carmelite House
50 Victoria Embankment
London EC4Y 0DZ

An Hachette UK Company
www.hachette.co.uk
www.hachettechildrens.co.uk

CONTENTS

INTRODUCTION

by Cressida Cowell

bestselling author of the
How to Train Your Dragon series

Like so many, many children before and after me, Enid Blyton's books played a crucial role in turning my nine-year-old self into a passionate reader.

That is because Enid Blyton had an extraordinary knack for writing the kind of books that children actually *want* to read, rather than the kind of books that adults think they *should* read.

Enid Blyton could tap into children's dreams, children's desires, children's wishes, with pinpoint accuracy. She knew that every child, however good and well-behaved they might look on the outside, secretly longed to be Elizabeth Allen, the naughtiest kid in the school. I'm afraid I entirely cheered Elizabeth on, as she defied her parents, the headmistresses, her schoolmates, and the very serious School Meetings. If anything, I wanted her to be even naughtier.

But *The Naughtiest Girl* books were really my favourite of Enid Blyton's school stories because of Whyteleafe, a very different school from Malory Towers or St Clare's. What if there could be a school in which discipline was administered by the children rather than the adults? In which all money was given in at the start of the term and distributed among the children along socialist lines? Wouldn't this be the kind of school that children would actually *want* to go to, rather than the kind of school that children *have* to go to?

It was an interesting proposition to a nine-year-old, and it remains an interesting proposition.

I hope you enjoy this story as much as I did when *I* was nine years old.

Cressida Cowell

CHAPTER ONE

BACK AT WHYTELEAFE

ELIZABETH WAS excited. The long summer holidays were almost over, and it was time to think of going back to school. Her mother, Mrs Allen, was busy getting all her things ready, and Elizabeth was helping her to pack the big trunk.

'Oh, Mummy, it's fun to think I'll see all my friends again soon!' said Elizabeth. 'It's lovely to be going back to Whyteleafe School once more. The winter term ought to be great fun.'

Her mother looked at Elizabeth and laughed. 'Elizabeth,' she said, 'do you remember what a fuss you made about going away to school for the first time last term? Do you remember how you said you would be so naughty and disobedient that you would soon be sent back home again? I'm glad to see you so happy this term – looking forward to going back.'

'Yes, I was stupid and silly,' said Elizabeth, going red as she remembered herself a few months back. 'Goodness, when I remember the things I said and did! Do you know, I wouldn't even share the cakes and things I took back? And I was so awfully rude and naughty in class – and I just wouldn't go to bed at the right time or do anything I was told. I was quite, quite determined to be sent back home!'

'And after all you weren't sent back, because you found you wanted to stay,' said Mrs Allen, with a smile. 'Well, well, I hope you won't be the naughtiest girl in the school *this* term.'

'I don't expect I shall,' said Elizabeth. 'I shan't be the best either – because I do fly into tempers, you know, and I don't think before I speak. I'm sure to get into trouble of some sort! But never mind, I'll get out of it again, and I'll really do my best this term.'

'Good girl,' said her mother, shutting down the lid of the trunk. 'Now look, Elizabeth – this is your tuckbox. I've put a tin of toffees in, a big chocolate cake, a tin of shortbread and a large pot of blackcurrant jam. That's all I can get in. But I think it's enough, don't you?'

'Oh, yes, thank you, Mummy,' said Elizabeth joyfully. 'The others will love all those. I wonder if Joan's mother will give her a tuckbox this term.'

Joan was Elizabeth's friend. She had been to stay

with Elizabeth in the summer holidays and the two had had a lovely time together. Then Joan had gone back home again for a week or two before school began. Elizabeth was looking forward to seeing her friend again – what fun to sleep in the same dormitory together, to sit in the same form and play the same games!

Elizabeth had told her mother all about Whyteleafe School. It was a school for boys and girls together, and the children ruled themselves, and were seldom punished by the masters or mistresses. Every week a big School Meeting was held, and all the children had to attend. The head boy and girl were the Judges, and twelve monitors, chosen by the children themselves, were the Jury. Any grumbles or complaints had to be brought to the Meeting and, if any child had behaved wrongly, the children themselves thought out a suitable punishment.

Poor Elizabeth had suffered badly at the weekly Meetings, for she had been so naughty and disobedient, and had broken every rule in the school. But now she had come to see that good behaviour was best not only for herself but for the whole school too, and she was very much looking forward to everything. Perhaps this term she could show just how good she could be, instead of just how naughty!

She was to leave the next day. Everything was packed

up. She had a new lacrosse stick and a new hockey stick, for both games were played at Whyteleafe. Elizabeth was very proud of these. She had never played either game before, but she meant to be very good indeed at them. How she would run! What a lot of goals she would shoot!

Her mother took her up to London to catch the train that was ready to take her and the other girls and boys to the school. Elizabeth danced on to the London platform, and cried out in delight to see all her friends waiting there.

'Joan! You're here first! Oh, how do you do, Mrs Townsend! Have you come to see Joan off?'

'Yes,' said Mrs Townsend. 'How do you do, Mrs Allen? I'm glad to see the naughtiest girl in the school looking so delighted to be going back to Whyteleafe again!'

'Oh, don't tease me,' said Elizabeth. 'I'm not the naughtiest girl any more! Oh, look – there's Nora! Nora, Nora! Did you have good holidays?'

Nora, tall and dark, turned and waved to Elizabeth. 'Hallo, kid!' she said. 'So you're coming back again, are you? Dear, dear, we shall have to make a whole set of new rules for you, I expect.'

Mrs Townsend laughed. 'There you are, Elizabeth!' she said. 'Everybody will tease you. They will find it hard to forget how naughty you were in your first term at Whyteleafe!'

'Look! There's Harry!' cried Joan. 'Harry! You know those rabbits you gave Elizabeth and me last term? Well, they're grown up now, and they've got babies of their own. I've got two of them with me to take back to school for my own pets.'

'Good!' said Harry. 'Hallo, Elizabeth! How tanned you are! Hie, John – here's Elizabeth! You'd better start planning your winter gardening with her.'

John Terry came up. He was a tall, strong boy, about twelve years old, so fond of gardening that he was head of the school garden, under Mr Johns, a master. He and Elizabeth had planned all kinds of things for the winter term.

'Hallo, Elizabeth!' he said. 'Have you brought that gardening book you promised? Good! We'll have some fun this term, digging, and burning up rubbish!'

The two of them talked eagerly for a minute or two, and then another boy came up, dark-haired and serious-faced. He took Elizabeth's arm.

'Hallo, Richard!' said Elizabeth. 'You are a mean thing – you said you'd write to me and you didn't! I bet you haven't practised once during the holidays!'

Richard smiled. He was a splendid musician for his age and could play both piano and violin beautifully.

He and Elizabeth shared a great love for music, and the two of them had been twice encored when they played duets at the school concert.

'I went to stay with my grandfather,' he said. 'He has a really marvellous violin, and he let me use it. I just didn't think of anything but music all the time I was on holiday. Thanks for your card. The writing was so bad I could only read your name at the end – but still, thanks all the same!'

'Oh!' began Elizabeth indignantly, and then she saw the twinkle in Richard's eye, and laughed. 'Oh, Richard, I hope Mr Lewis lets us learn duets again this term!'

'Say goodbye to your people now,' said Miss Ranger, coming up to the little group. 'The train is just going. Find places as quickly as you can.'

Miss Ranger was Elizabeth's form mistress. She was strict, very just and quite a jolly person. Elizabeth and Joan were delighted to see her again. She smiled at them and went on to the next group.

'Do you remember how Miss Ranger sent you out of the room last term for flipping your rubber at people?' said Joan, with a giggle, as the two of them jumped into a carriage. Elizabeth laughed. She turned to her mother.

'Goodbye, Mummy darling!' she said. 'You needn't worry about me *this* term! I'll do my best, not my worst!'

BACK AT WHYTELEAFE

The engine whistled loudly. Every boy and girl was now safely in the train. The mothers, fathers, uncles and aunts waved goodbye. The train pulled out of the station and London was soon left behind.

'Now we're really off!' said Elizabeth. She looked round the carriage. Belinda was there, and Nora. Harry had got in, and John Terry too. John was already pulling out a bag of sweets. He offered them round. Everybody took one, and soon chatter and laughter filled the carriage, as the children told about their holidays.

'Is there anybody new this term, I wonder?' said Joan. 'I haven't seen anyone yet.'

'Yes, there are two or three newcomers,' said John. 'I saw a boy down the other end of the train, and a couple of girls. I should think they'd be in your form. I didn't like the look of the boy much – sulky-looking creature!'

'What are the girls like?' asked Joan. But John hadn't noticed. 'Anyway, we shall soon see what they're like when we arrive,' said Joan. 'I say, Elizabeth, what have you got in your tuckbox? My mother has given me a huge box of chocolates, a ginger cake, a tin of golden syrup and a jam sponge sandwich.'

'Sounds good!' said Elizabeth. The children began to talk about their tuckboxes, and the time flew past as the train roared on its way.

At last the long journey was over and the train came to a stop at a little country platform. The boys and girls jumped down from their carriages and ran to take their places in two coaches.

'Let's look out for the first glimpse of Whyteleafe School!' said Elizabeth, as the coaches rumbled off. 'Oh, look – there it is! Isn't it lovely!'

The children stared up the hill on the top of which was their school. All of them were glad to see it again. Here and there the creeper up the walls was beginning to turn red, and the windows shone in the autumn sun.

Through an enormous archway rumbled the coaches, and up to the front door. Elizabeth remembered the first time she had arrived there, five months before, at the beginning of the summer term. How she had hated it! Now she was glad to jump down the coach steps with the other children and race into the school.

She looked around for the new girls and boy. She saw them standing rather forlornly together, wondering where to go. Elizabeth took Joan's arm. 'Let's go and look after the new ones,' she said. 'They're looking a bit lost.'

'Right!' said Joan, and they went up to the three children. They were all about eleven or twelve years old, though the boy was big for his age.

'Come with us and we'll show you where to wash,

and where to go for dinner,' said Elizabeth. They all looked at her gratefully. Rita, the head girl, came by just then, and beamed at Elizabeth.

'So you've taken the newcomers under your wing,' she said. 'I was just coming to see about them. Good! Thanks, Elizabeth and Joan!'

'That's the head girl,' said Elizabeth to the boy and two girls. 'And look – that's William, our head boy. They're both fine. Come on. I'll show you the cloakrooms and we can all wash.'

Off they all went, and were soon washing and drying themselves in the big cloakroom downstairs. Then into the dining hall they went, hungry as hunters. How glad they were to smell a good stew, and see the carrots and onions floating in it!

'It's grand to be back again!' said Elizabeth, looking happily around, and smiling at all the faces she knew. 'I wonder what adventures we'll have this term.'

'Perhaps we shan't have any,' said Joan. But she was wrong. Plenty of things were going to happen that term!

CHAPTER TWO

SETTLING DOWN

EVERYONE SOON settled down. Except for a few new children, the girls and boys were the same as the term before. Some had gone up into a higher form, and felt rather grand for the first few days. The new boy and two new girls were all in Elizabeth's form.

Miss Ranger took down their names: 'Jennifer Harris, Kathleen Peters, Robert Jones.'

Jennifer was a jolly-looking girl, with straight hair cut short, and a thick fringe. Her brown eyes twinkled, and the other girls felt that she would be good fun.

Kathleen Peters was a pasty-faced girl, very plain and spotty. Her hair was greasy-looking, and she had a very unpleasant expression, almost a scowl. Nobody liked her at all, those first few days.

Robert Jones was a big boy for his age, with a rather sullen face, though when he smiled he was quite different.

'I don't like Robert's mouth, do you?' said Joan to Elizabeth. 'His lips are so thin and pursed up. He doesn't look very kind.'

'Oh well, we can't help our mouths!' said Elizabeth.

'I think you're wrong there,' said Joan. 'I think people make their own faces, as they grow.'

Elizabeth laughed. 'Well, it's a pity poor Kathleen Peters didn't make a better face for herself,' she said.

'Sh!' said Joan. 'She'll hear!'

The first week went by slowly. New books were given out, and lovely new pencils and pens. The children were given their places in class, and Joan and Elizabeth sat next to one another, much to their delight. They were by the window and could see out into the flowery garden.

Any child who wanted to could help in the garden. John Terry was willing to give anyone a patch, providing they would promise to keep it properly. These little patches, backing on to an old sunny wall, were interesting little spots. Some children liked to grow salads, some grew flowers, and one child, who loved roses better than anything, had six beautiful rose trees and nothing else.

Elizabeth didn't want a patch. She wanted to help John in the much bigger garden of which he was in charge. She was longing to make plans with him about it. She had all kinds of ideas about gardens, and had read her gardening book from end to end twice during the holidays.

The children were allowed to have their own pets, though not dogs or cats, as these were too difficult to deal with, and could not be kept in cages. Some children had rabbits, some had guinea pigs, a few had fantail pigeons that lived in a big pigeon house on a pole, and one or two had canaries or goldfish. It was fun having pets. Not all the children had them – only those who were fond of animals or birds. The pets were kept in a big, airy shed not far from the stables where the horses lived that the children were allowed to ride.

Hens and ducks were kept, of course and, although these belonged to the school, any child who wished could help to care for them and feed them. There were three beautiful Jersey cows in the meadow too, and one girl and boy milked these every day. They had to be up early in the morning, but they didn't mind at all. It was fun!

Jennifer Harris had some pets. They were small white mice, and she was very fond of them indeed. They were kept in a big cage, and she cleaned it out every day, so that it was spotless. No one else had white mice at that time, and Elizabeth and Joan went with Jennifer to see them.

'Aren't they sweet?' said Jennifer, letting a mouse run

up her sleeve. 'Do you see their pink eyes? Elizabeth, would you like to let that one run up your sleeve? It's such a lovely feeling.'

'Well, I don't think I will, thank you,' said Elizabeth politely. 'It may be a lovely feeling to you, but it might not be for me.'

'Hallo! Are these your white mice, Jennifer?' asked Harry, coming up. 'I say, aren't they lovely? Golly, you've got one peeping out from your neck – did you know?'

'Oh, yes,' said Jennifer. 'Take it, Harry. It will run up your sleeve and come out at your neck too.'

Sure enough it did! It ran up the boy's sleeve, and soon its tiny nose was peeping out behind his collar. Joan shivered.

'I really don't think I could bear that,' she said.

The bell rang and the mice were hurriedly put back into their cage. Joan went to have a last peep at her two rabbits. They were fat and contented. She shared them with Elizabeth and was very fond of them indeed.

Teatime and suppertime the first week were lovely, because the children were allowed to take what they liked from their tuckboxes. How they enjoyed the cakes, sandwiches, sweets, chocolates, potted meat and jams they brought back with them! Everybody shared, though the new boy, Robert, didn't look too pleased about it, and Elizabeth noticed that Kathleen Peters did not offer any of her sweets round, though she shared her potted meat readily enough.

Elizabeth remembered how selfish she had been about sharing her own things at the beginning of her first term, so she held her tongue and said nothing.

I can't very well blame other people for a thing I've done myself, she thought. *I'm jolly glad I'm different now!*

The big happening of each week was the School Meeting. The whole school attended, and any of the masters and mistresses who wished to. The two headmistresses, Miss Belle and Miss Best, always did, and Mr Johns usually came too. But they sat at the back, and did not take any part in the Meeting unless the children called upon them for help.

It was a kind of school parliament, where the children made their own rules, heard grumbles and complaints, judged one another and punished bad behaviour.

It was not pleasant to have one's faults brought before the whole school and discussed, but on the other hand it was much better for everyone to know their own failings and have them brought out into the open, instead of fearing them and keeping them secret, so that they grew bigger. Many a child had been cured forever of such things as cheating or lying by having the sympathy and help of the whole school.

SETTLING DOWN

The first School Meeting was held about a week after school began. The girls and boys filed into the gym, where a big table had been placed for the twelve monitors, who were the Jury. These had been chosen at the last Meeting of the summer term, and would remain monitors for a month, when they could either be chosen again, or others put into their place.

Everyone had to stand when William and Rita, the head boy and head girl, came into the gym. They sat down and everyone else sat too.

William knocked on the table with a small wooden hammer, and the children were quiet.

'There isn't much to say today,' said the head boy. 'I expect the new children have been told why we hold this big Meeting every week, and what we do at it. You see at this table our twelve monitors, and you all know why they are chosen. We chose them ourselves because we can trust them to be sensible, loyal and kind, and therefore you must obey them and keep the rules they make.'

Then Rita spoke. 'I hope you have all brought your money with you. As the new children probably know, any money we have is put into this big box, and out of it we take two shillings for every person each week. Out of that you must buy anything you need, such as stamps, sweets, ribbons, shoelaces, and so on. If you want any more than two shillings, you must say why, and it will be given to you if it is deserved. Now will you please get your money ready. Nora, take round the box.'

Nora got up. She took the big box and handed it down each row. The children all put in their money. The new boy, Robert Jones, looked most annoyed.

'I say,' he said, 'you know I've got a whole pound from my grandfather. I don't see why I should put it into the box. I shan't see it again!'

'Robert, some of us have too much money and some of us have too little,' explained William. 'It sometimes happens that we have a birthday and get lots of money, and sometimes we haven't any at all. Well, by putting *all* our money into the big box each week, we can always have two shillings to spend – the same for everyone, you see, which is quite fair – and if we need anything beyond that, we can always get it if the Jury give permission. So put in your money.'

Robert put his pound note in, and did not look at all pleased. His face looked even more sulky than usual!

'Cheer up!' whispered Elizabeth, but he gave her such a scowl that she said no more. Nora took the box back to the table. It was very heavy now.

Two shillings were given out to everyone, and the money went into pockets and purses. Rita and William had the same as everyone else.

'Any extra money wanted this week?' asked William, looking round the school.

Kenneth stood up. 'Could I have an extra sixpence?' he asked. 'I borrowed a book out of the school library and I can't find it, and I've been fined sixpence.'

'Take it out of your two shillings,' said William, and the Jury nodded in agreement. 'I don't see why the school's money should pay you for being careless, Kenneth! There are too many books lost. Pay the school library sixpence, and you can have it back when you find the book. No extra money granted!'

A girl stood up. 'My mother is abroad and I have to write to her each week, of course, but the letters have to have a sevenpence stamp on. Could I possibly have a little extra money allowed for that?'

The Jury discussed the matter. They agreed that it was hard luck on Mary to have to spend so much money on one letter each week.

'Well, you can have four ha'penny extra each week,' said Rita at last. 'That means you pay the usual twopence ha'penny for a stamp, and the school money pays the rest. That's quite fair.'

'Oh, yes,' said Mary gratefully. 'Thank you.' Fourpence ha'penny was given to her, and she put it into her purse.

'I think that's all the business for this week,' said Rita,

looking at her notes. 'You all understand that any bad behaviour, such as unkindness, disobedience, cheating, bullying, and so on, must be brought before this Meeting each week. But I hope that the new children will understand that this does not mean telling tales. Perhaps their monitor will explain everything to them.'

'Yes, I will,' said Nora.

'Now, any complaints or grumbles before we go?' asked William, looking up. But there were none. So the Meeting broke up, and the children filed out of the gym. Elizabeth was rather silent as she went. She was remembering the bad time she had had last term at the Meeting. How defiant and rude she had been! She could hardly believe it now.

She went off with Joan to feed the rabbits. One was so tame that it would lie quite peacefully in Elizabeth's arms, and she loved that.

'Isn't everything peaceful this term?' said Joan. 'I hope it goes on like this, don't you?'

But it wasn't going to be peaceful for long!

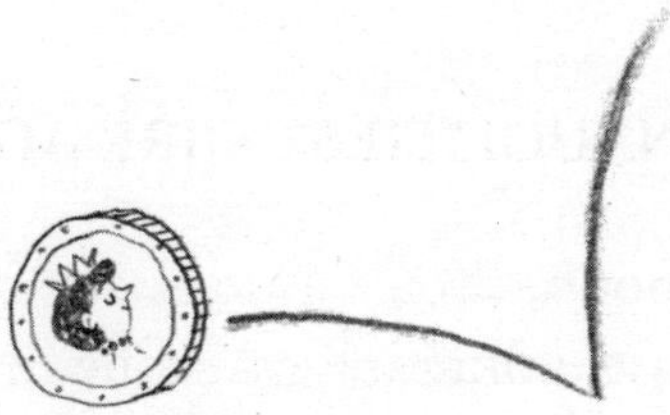

CHAPTER THREE

ELIZABETH MAKES AN ENEMY

IT WAS two of the new children who disturbed the peace of the form. When Robert had settled down and found his feet, the other boys and girls found that he was spiteful and unkind. And they discovered too that Kathleen Peters, the spotty girl, was so quarrelsome that it was really very difficult to be nice to her.

On the other hand, Jennifer Harris was great fun. She was a wonderful mimic and could imitate the masters and mistresses marvellously, especially Mam'zelle. Mam'zelle wagged her hands rather a lot, and her voice went up and down when she spoke. Jennifer could put on a face exactly like Mam'zelle's, and talked and wagged her hands in a manner so like her that she sent the class into fits of laughter.

'Jenny's fine,' said Elizabeth. 'But I simply can't bear Robert or Kathleen. You know, I think Robert's cruel, Joan.'

'Why do you think that?' asked Joan. 'Has he been unkind to you?'

'No, not to me,' said Elizabeth. 'But I heard someone squealing yesterday and I saw little Janet running away from him, crying. I called out to know what was wrong, but she wouldn't tell me. I believe Robert had been pinching her or something.'

'I shouldn't be surprised,' said Joan.

Belinda Green heard what they were saying and came up.

'I think Robert's a bully,' she said. 'He's always running after the smaller ones, and jumping out at them, and giving them sly pinches.'

'The hateful thing!' cried Elizabeth, who always hated any unfairness. 'Wait till I catch him! I'll jolly well report him at the very next Meeting!'

'Well, be sure to get your facts right,' said Belinda, 'or Robert will say you are telling tales, and then you won't be listened to.'

Robert came up at that moment and the three of them said no more. Robert bumped hard into Elizabeth as he passed and nearly sent her into the wall.

'Oh, I didn't see you!' he said, with a grin, and went on down the room. Elizabeth went red with rage. She took a step after Robert, but Joan pulled her back.

'He only did it to make you annoyed,' she said. 'Don't *be* annoyed!'

'I can't help being,' said Elizabeth furiously. 'Rude, clumsy thing!'

It was time to go into class then, and there was no time to do anything more. Robert was in Elizabeth's class, and she glared at him as she sat down. He made an extraordinary face at her – and they were enemies from that moment.

When Robert got nearly all his sums wrong, Elizabeth smiled with pleasure. 'Serves you right!' she said in a loud whisper. Unfortunately Miss Ranger heard it.

'Is there any need to gloat over bad work done by somebody else?' she said coldly – and then it was Robert's turn to grin with delight.

Each of them was pleased when the other did badly – though Elizabeth got more laughs out of Robert than he did out of her, for she was a clever girl and found lessons easy. Robert was much slower, though he was bigger and taller.

At games they did all they could to defeat each other. They were very often on opposite sides, and if Robert could give Elizabeth a whack over the hand with his lacrosse stick, or a blow on the ankle with his hockey stick, he would. Elizabeth was not an unkind girl, but she found herself lying in wait for Robert too, and giving him a hard blow whenever she could.

Mr Warlow, the games master, soon noticed this, and he called the two of them to him.

'You are playing a game, not fighting a battle,' he told them gravely. 'Keep your likes and dislikes out of hockey and lacrosse, please, and play fairly.'

Elizabeth was ashamed, and stopped trying to hurt Robert, but Robert took an even greater delight in giving Elizabeth a bruise whenever he could, though now he was careful to do it when Mr Warlow was not watching.

'Elizabeth, you really are stupid to make an enemy of Robert,' said Nora one day. 'He is much bigger than you are. Keep out of his way. You'll lose your temper one day and put yourself in the wrong. That's what he's hoping for.'

But Elizabeth would not listen to advice of that sort. 'I'm not afraid of Robert!' she said scornfully.

'That isn't the point,' said Nora. 'He's only doing all this to annoy you, and if only you'd take no notice of him, and not try to pay him back, he'd soon get tired of it.'

'He's a hateful bully!' said Elizabeth.

'You're not to say things like that unless you have real proof,' said Nora, at once. 'And if you *have* real proof, then you must make a complaint at the Meeting.

That's the place to accuse people of things. You know that quite well.'

Elizabeth made a sulky face and went off by herself. Why couldn't Nora believe her? Oh, well, Nora wasn't in her form and didn't know that hateful Robert as well as she, Elizabeth, knew him.

The next afternoon, after tea, Elizabeth went round to play with the rabbits. On the way she heard somebody calling out in a pleading voice, 'Please don't swing me so high! Please don't!'

Elizabeth peeped round at the swings. She saw a small boy on one, about nine years old. Robert was swinging him and, my goodness, wasn't he swinging him high!

'I feel sick!' cried the boy, whose name was Peter. 'I shall *be* sick! I shall fall off. Let me down, Robert, let me down! Don't swing me any more!'

But Robert took no notice of the small boy's shouting. His thin lips were pursed together and, with an unkind gleam in his eyes, he went on pushing the swing – high, high, higher!

Elizabeth was so angry that she had to blink her eyes to see clearly. She ran to Robert.

'Stop!' she cried. 'You're not to do that! You'll make Peter ill.'

'Mind your own business,' said Robert. 'He asked me to give him a swing and I'm giving him one. Go away, you interfering girl. You're always poking your nose where it isn't wanted.'

'Oh, I'm not!' cried Elizabeth. She tried to catch hold of the swing as it came down, to stop it, but Robert was too quick for her. He gave her a push and sent her spinning into a bush. Then he sent the swing even higher than ever.

'I'll go and tell somebody!' cried Elizabeth, picking herself up.

'Tell-tale, tell-tale!' chanted Robert, giving the swing another push. Elizabeth lost her temper completely and rushed at the aggravating boy. She caught hold of his hair and tugged at it so hard that she pulled a whole handful out! Then she slapped his face and gave him such a punch in his middle that he doubled himself up with a groan.

Elizabeth stopped the swing and helped the trembling Peter off the seat. 'Go and be sick if you want to,' she said. 'And don't let Robert swing you any more.'

Peter staggered off, looking rather green. Elizabeth turned to face Robert, but just then three or four children came up, and neither child felt inclined to go on with the quarrel in public.

'I'll report you at the very next Meeting!' cried Elizabeth, still in a great temper. 'You just see! You'll be punished all right, you cruel, unkind boy!'

She went off, raging. Robert looked round at the interested children who had come up. 'What a temper that girl has got!' he said. 'Look here – she pulled my hair out!'

He picked up some of his dark hairs and showed them to the others. They looked surprised.

'You must have been doing something awful to make Elizabeth lose her temper like that,' said Kenneth.

'I was only giving someone a swing,' said Robert. 'Elizabeth interfered, as usual. I wish she'd leave me alone. No wonder she was called the naughtiest girl in the school last term!'

'We pinned a notice on her once, calling her the Bold Bad Girl!' said somebody, with a laugh, as he remembered how angry Elizabeth had been. 'Did you hit Elizabeth, Robert? If you did, you're mean. Girls are awfully annoying sometimes, but you can't hit them.'

'I didn't touch her,' said Robert, though he knew quite well that if the others hadn't come up at that moment he would certainly have gone for Elizabeth and slapped her. 'She just went up in smoke and flew at me, the horrid girl!'

Elizabeth rushed off to tell Joan all that had happened. Joan listened gravely.

'Robert really is a horrid bully,' she said. 'He'll have to be stopped. But oh, Elizabeth, I do think it's rather a pity you lost your temper like that! You have got such a hot temper, you know!'

'Well, *anyone* would have lost their temper if they had seen Robert swinging that poor wretched little Peter almost over the top of the swing post!' said Elizabeth, still boiling with rage. 'He was quite green.'

'You don't suppose the Meeting will think it's telling tales if you report Robert, do you?' asked Joan doubtfully. 'If I were you, I'd ask Nora first.'

'I'll do no such thing!' cried Elizabeth. 'I'm the best judge of this! I saw what happened, didn't I? All right then – I'll report Robert at the Meeting tomorrow, and then we'll just see what the Jury say. He'll get a dreadful shock – and he'll deserve it too.'

Elizabeth was angry all day, and when the next day came she could hardly wait for the evening to come, to report Robert. Then he would see what happened to boys who did mean, unkind things!

Robert did not seem to be at all upset at the idea of Elizabeth reporting him. He made faces at her whenever he saw her, which made her very angry indeed.

'You'll get a shock at the Meeting tonight!' said Elizabeth. But there was a shock waiting for Elizabeth too!

CHAPTER FOUR

WHAT HAPPENED AT THE MEETING

THE TIME for the weekly Meeting came. Elizabeth sat down on the form next to Belinda and Joan, longing for the moment to come when she could make a complaint about Robert. Robert sat not far away, his sullen face unsmiling, but there was a gleam in his eye when he turned to look at Elizabeth.

'I shouldn't be surprised if Robert doesn't make a complaint about you too, Elizabeth,' whispered Joan. 'He looks as if he's got something up his sleeve.'

'I don't care,' said Elizabeth. 'Wait till the Meeting hears what *I've* got to say!'

William and Rita came in, with the headmistresses and Mr Johns. The children stood up. The head girl and boy sat down, and the Meeting began.

Money was collected, though there was not very much that week. Kenneth had had a birthday and had five shillings to put into the box. Janet had a shilling. Everyone was given their two shillings, and Mary got her fourpence ha'penny extra for her weekly stamp.

'Have you found the lost library book yet?' asked William, looking at Kenneth. 'We said you could have back your sixpence fine if you did.'

'No, I haven't found it,' said Kenneth. 'I've hunted everywhere.'

'Anybody want any extra money?' asked Rita, jingling the box to see how much there was in it.

'I suppose I couldn't have any extra?' asked Ruth, standing up. 'I lost all my two shillings last week. It was a dreadful blow because I badly wanted some stamps.'

'How did you lose it?' asked Rita.

'There was a hole in my pocket,' said Ruth. 'It fell out through that, goodness knows where.'

'Did you know there was a hole in your pocket?' asked Rita.

Ruth hesitated. 'Well,' she said, 'I did know there was one coming, as a matter of fact. It was just a tiny little hole. I didn't know it had got big enough to lose money.'

'Who's your monitor?' asked William. 'Oh, you are, Nora. Do you think it was Ruth's fault?'

'Well,' said Nora, 'quite truthfully, Ruth isn't awfully good at mending her clothes when she ought to. She lost a lovely pocketknife last term, through a hole in a pocket – didn't you, Ruth?'

'Yes,' said Ruth, looking rather uncomfortable. 'Yes, I did. I know I should have mended that hole. I'm untidy and careless about things like that. I jolly well won't get a hole again, though. I think I shouldn't have asked for extra money, as it was my own fault.'

She sat down. The Jury began to talk to one another. A girl sitting on one of the forms stood up. It was Eileen, a kindly girl with a mass of fair curls.

'May I say something?' she asked. 'I think that as Ruth has owned up that it was her own fault, and as she really is very generous with her money when she has it, couldn't she have an extra two shillings, just for once?'

'We are just discussing that,' said Rita. 'This is what we are going to do. We will let you have a shilling, Ruth, not two shillings, because we all believe you aren't quite so silly as to let a thing like this happen a third time, and you have been very honest about it. Come and take an extra shilling.'

'Oh, thank you,' said Ruth, going to the table. 'I had to borrow some stamps from Belinda, and now I can pay her back without using this week's two shillings. I'll be more careful in future, Rita!'

'Any more money wanted?' asked William, knocking on the table with his hammer, for the children had begun to talk to one another. Everyone was quiet.

'It's my granny's birthday this week,' said a small girl, getting up. 'I want to send her a card. Could I have extra money to buy it with, and for the stamp too?'

'No,' said William. 'That should come out of your two shillings. Not granted. Any more requests?'

There were none. Elizabeth knew that the time for complaints or grumbles would come next, and she went red with excitement. William said a few words to Rita about something and then knocked for silence again.

'Any complaints or grumbles?' he asked. Elizabeth stood up – and so did Robert – but Robert was just half a second before her.

'You first, Robert,' said William. 'Sit down and take your turn next, Elizabeth.'

Elizabeth didn't sit down. She didn't mean to let Robert speak first.

'Oh, please, William!' she said. 'I have such a serious complaint to make.'

'Well, it will keep,' said William. 'Sit down.'

'But William, it's about Robert,' began Elizabeth again, her voice rising.

'Elizabeth, do as you're told,' ordered Rita. 'You will have plenty of time to say all you want to.'

There was nothing for it but to sit down. Elizabeth was very angry. She glared at Robert, who didn't look at her at all, but stood patiently waiting to speak.

'Well, Robert, what have you to say?' asked William.

'I hope this isn't telling tales,' began Robert in a rather apologetic voice, 'but I really must complain about Elizabeth Allen's behaviour to me. I have always tried to be fair to her . . .'

'Oooooh!' cried Elizabeth indignantly. 'You know you haven't! You've . . .'

'Silence, Elizabeth!' ordered William sharply. 'You can say all you want to say in a minute. Don't interrupt. Go on, Robert.'

Elizabeth was boiling with rage. Joan put her hand on her friend's arm to try and calm her, but Elizabeth shook it off. Just wait till she had her turn to speak!

'I've always tried to be fair to her,' went on Robert in a very polite voice. 'But really, I can't let her pull my hair out and slap me in the face.'

There was an astonished silence. Everyone looked at Elizabeth. Robert went on, pleased at the surprise he had caused.

'I've got some of the hairs she pulled out in this envelope to show you, William, in case you don't believe me. And there are two or three children who will tell you it really happened. Of course, I couldn't hit her back. I know she was supposed to be the naughtiest girl in the school last term, and . . .'

'You can leave that out, Robert. It has nothing to do with this,' said William at once. 'We have always found Elizabeth to be just and fair and kind so far, no matter how naughty she once was. Will you please tell us *why* Elizabeth did these extraordinary things?'

'She didn't want me to swing somebody,' said Robert. 'She's always interfering with me, whatever I do. She laughs if I make a mistake in class. Well, never mind about that. I was just swinging Peter, and he was squealing with excitement, and she came and pulled out my hair, slapped me and punched me.'

'Thank you,' said William. 'Sit down. Elizabeth, perhaps you would like to tell us if these complaints are true. Did you pull out Robert's hair and slap him?'

Elizabeth stood up, her cheeks as red as fire and her eyes flashing. 'Yes, I did!' she said. 'And he deserved it! I wish I'd pulled out more of his hair. I wish . . .'

'That's enough, Elizabeth,' said Rita at once. 'If you can't control yourself enough to tell us properly what happened, there's no use in your saying anything.'

Elizabeth knew she was being silly. She tried her hardest to be sensible. 'Please, Rita, I'll tell my story properly,' she said. 'Then you'll see why I got so angry, and perhaps you'll say I was right to lose my temper with Robert. I was going to see my rabbits when I heard somebody squealing out. It was Peter on the swing, and he was shouting to Robert not to swing him so high, because he was frightened.'

'Go on,' said William gravely.

'Well, I rushed over to stop the swing, and Robert sent me right over,' said Elizabeth, feeling her temper rise again as she told what had happened. 'I got up and flew at Robert to stop him swinging Peter again, because he was quite green and I thought he would fall off. And oh, William and Rita, that's not the only time that Robert has bullied the younger ones. He's a real bully, unkind and mean.'

There was a silence again. Everyone in the school knew quite well that a very serious thing had happened. Which of the two children was right? Bullying was hateful. Bad temper and fighting were wrong.

Joan was very upset. She knew quite well that Elizabeth had made up her mind to be good and do as well as she could this term, and now here was the hot-tempered girl flying into trouble almost at once! It was just no good trying to stop her. If Elizabeth saw something unfair, she would rush at it in a temper and try to put it right that way. Joan couldn't see how this matter could be put right.

William and Rita spoke together in low voices. The Jury discussed the matter too. Robert sat on his form, not even red in the face. He did not look at Elizabeth.

William knocked for silence. 'We would like to ask the boys and girls who saw the affair to report on it,' he said. 'Who saw it?'

Three children stood up. They said shortly that they had seen the hairs that Elizabeth had pulled out and had seen how red Robert's face was where it had been slapped.

'Did Robert hit back at all?' asked Rita.

'Not that we saw,' said Kenneth, and sat down, feeling sorry for Elizabeth.

'And now we will ask Peter to tell us what happened,' said William in a kindly tone. 'Stand up, Peter, and answer my questions.'

The small nine-year-old Peter stood up. His knees shook beneath him, and he felt dreadful to have the eyes of the whole school on him.

'Was Robert swinging you high?' asked William.

Peter looked across at Robert. Robert gave him a strange look. Peter spoke in a trembling voice. 'Yes – he was swinging me quite high.'

'Were you frightened?' asked William.

'N-n-n-no,' said Peter.

'Did you squeal for help?' asked Rita.

'No,' said Peter, with a look at Robert. 'I was just – just squealing for fun, you know.'

'Thank you,' said William. 'Sit down.'

Elizabeth leapt up. 'Robert must have made Peter

promise to say all that!' she cried. 'Ask if there are any other young ones who would like to complain about Robert, Rita.'

Rita looked round where the younger children sat.

'Is there anyone who has a complaint to make about Robert?' she asked. 'If he has been unkind to you, or ill-treated you in any way, speak now.'

Elizabeth waited for half a dozen children to stand up and speak. But there was a complete silence! Nobody spoke, nobody complained. What a very strange thing! *Now* what was going to happen?

CHAPTER FIVE

ELIZABETH IS VERY CROSS

THE COMPLAINTS to the School Meeting were so serious that the two Judges and the Jury took a long time to discuss them. In the meantime, the rest of the children also discussed the matter among themselves. Not many of them were for Robert, for he was not liked, but on the other hand most of the boys and girls felt that Elizabeth had no right to lose her temper so fiercely.

'And after all,' whispered one child to another, 'she *was* the naughtiest girl in the school last term, you know.'

'Yes. We used to call her the Bold Bad Girl,' said another child. 'But she was quite all right after the half-term. She really did turn over a new leaf.'

'And I know quite well that she meant to do her very best this term,' said Harry. 'I've heard her say so heaps of times. She lost her temper with me last term, but she said she was sorry and has been absolutely decent to me ever since.'

So the talk went on, while Elizabeth and Robert sat up straight, hating one another, each longing to hear that the other was to be punished.

Meanwhile, the Judges and Jury were finding things very difficult. Some of the Jury felt quite certain that Robert was a real bully – and yet not even Peter would complain, so maybe there was not much truth in what they thought. All the monitors on the Jury were fair-minded and just, and they knew quite well that they must never judge anyone unless they had real, clear proof of wrongdoing.

Again, all the Jury knew quite well how bad Elizabeth had been the term before, and yet how marvellously she had managed to conquer herself and turn over a new leaf. They could not believe that she would fight Robert just for nothing. It was all very difficult. They did not feel that they wanted to punish Elizabeth in case by any chance Robert *did* turn out to be a bully.

At last William knocked with his wooden mallet for silence. The whole school sat up, eager to know what had been decided. Elizabeth was still fiery red in the face, but Robert looked quite pale and cool.

'We find this matter very difficult to decide,' said William in his pleasant voice. 'It is quite clear that Elizabeth did lose her temper badly, and flew at Robert, but it isn't quite as clear that Robert was bullying Peter. After all, we must take Peter's word for that. He should know! But we know enough of Elizabeth to realise that she is a very just person, and it is quite plain that she thought Robert was doing something very unkind.'

There was a pause. The school listened hard. William thought for a moment and then went on.

'Very well. Elizabeth may have been mistaken, but she really believed that Robert was being unkind. So she lost her temper and flew at him to stop him. That is where you were wrong, Elizabeth. Hot temper makes you see things all muddled instead of clearly, so when you see something you disapprove of you *must* try to keep your temper, so that you can judge things properly and not get them all exaggerated and twisted. You spoke as if you hated Robert just now, and that does *you* as much harm as it does Robert.'

'I do hate him!' burst out Elizabeth angrily.

'Well, to go on with this,' went on William, 'we have decided that unless we get much plainer proof that Robert is a bully, we can't very well either judge him or punish him. And as we are sure you really did think he was doing something mean we shan't punish you either, Elizabeth, but you must say you are sorry to Robert for behaving so badly to him.'

The whole school thought this was a good decision.

Nobody wanted Elizabeth badly punished, for they really did like the hot-headed girl. The school came to the conclusion that she must have been mistaken about Robert and therefore she really should apologise, and let the matter end there.

Elizabeth said nothing. She sat on the form, looking sulky. Robert looked pleased. This was grand! William and Rita spoke together for a moment or two, and then said a few more words to close the matter.

'Well, that is our decision, Elizabeth and Robert. You will apologise, Elizabeth, and you will accept the apology graciously, Robert. Elizabeth, guard your temper – and Robert, see that no charge of bullying is ever made against you. If it should be, you would not be judged lightly.'

Then William spoke of other things for a few moments and broke up the Meeting, for the time was getting late. The children were dismissed and filed out of the gym, all looking rather solemn. Bad temper and bullying! These were things not often dealt with at the Meeting.

Robert swaggered out, hands in pockets. He felt important and pleased. He had won *that* battle. Now Elizabeth had got to say she was sorry. Serve her right!

But Elizabeth had no intention of saying she was sorry. Joan looked in dismay at the angry face of her friend as she marched into the common room.

'Elizabeth! There's Robert over there. For goodness' sake go and apologise now, and get it over,' she begged the angry girl.

'But I'm *not* sorry!' said Elizabeth in a loud voice, tossing back her dark curls. 'Not a bit! I'm glad I flew at Robert. How can I say I'm sorry if it's an untruth?'

'Well, you can apologise,' said Joan. 'That's only good manners. Just go up and say, "I apologise, Robert." You don't need to say anything more.'

'Well, I'm not going to,' said Elizabeth. 'The Judges and the Jury were wrong for once! Nobody can make me apologise.'

'Elizabeth, no matter what you feel, you should be loyal to William and Rita,' said Joan, troubled. 'It isn't what you feel yourself that matters – it's what all the others feel to be right. You're one against a whole lot.'

'Well, I may be, but I'm the one who happens to be right,' said Elizabeth in a trembling voice. 'I know Robert is a bully.'

'Elizabeth, do what the Meeting says, and then we'll watch and see if we can't catch Robert at his horrid tricks,' begged Joan. 'Do it to please me. You'll make me so unhappy if you don't – and the whole school will think badly of you if you're afraid to apologise.'

'I'm not afraid!' said Elizabeth, with her eyes flashing angrily.

Joan smiled a little smile to herself. She turned away from Elizabeth. 'You *are* afraid,' she said. 'You're afraid of hurting your own silly pride.'

Elizabeth marched straight up to Robert. 'I apologise,' she said stiffly.

Robert gave a polite bow. 'I accept your apology!' he said. Elizabeth stalked off by herself. Joan ran after her.

'Leave me alone,' said Elizabeth crossly. She went into a music practice room and sat down at the piano. She played a piece she knew very loudly and fiercely. Mr Lewis, the music master, looked into the room in surprise.

'Good gracious, Elizabeth!' he said. 'I've never heard that piece sound so angry before. Get up, and let me play you something *really* fierce – something with a thunderstorm or two in it.'

Elizabeth got up. Mr Lewis took her seat and played a stormy piece of music, with the wind and the sea, streaming clouds, roaring trees in it – and then the storm died down, the rain sprinkled softly, the wind ceased, the sun shone, and the music became calm and smooth.

And as she listened the little girl felt soothed and softened too. She loved music so much. Mr Lewis glanced at her and saw that she looked peaceful instead of troubled. He played a little longer and then the bell went for Elizabeth's bedtime.

'There you are,' said Mr Lewis, shutting the piano. 'After the storm, the calm. Now go off to bed, sleep well, and don't worry your head too much about anything.'

'Thank you, Mr Lewis,' said Elizabeth gratefully. 'I do feel better now. I was all hot and bothered about something, but now I feel happier. Goodnight!'

CHAPTER SIX

JENNY'S WHITE MICE

ELIZABETH DID not sleep very well that night. She tossed and turned, thinking of the Meeting, of 'that hateful Robert', as she called him to herself, of the apology she had had to make – and she made plans to catch Robert when he was being unkind to any of the younger ones.

'Yes, I'll watch and wait and catch him properly,' said Elizabeth to herself. 'He *is* a bully, I know he is – and sooner or later I'll catch him!'

Elizabeth was heavy-eyed and tired the next day. She did her lessons badly, especially French, and Mam'zelle was cross with her.

'Elizabeth! How is it that you did not learn your French verbs yesterday?' scolded Mam'zelle. 'That is not good. You sit there, half asleep, and you pay no attention at all. I am not pleased with you.'

Robert grinned to himself, and Elizabeth saw him. She bit her lip to stop herself from being rude to both Robert and Mam'zelle.

'Well, have you no tongue?' asked Mam'zelle impatiently. 'Why did you not learn your verbs, I said?'

'I *did* learn them,' said Elizabeth truthfully. 'But somehow I've forgotten them this morning.'

'Then you will please learn them sometime today and remember them!' said Mam'zelle, her dark eyes flashing. 'You will come and say them to me when you know them.'

'All right,' said Elizabeth sulkily. But Mam'zelle would not let that pass. She rapped on the desk and spoke sharply.

'You will not say "All right" to me in that rude way! You will say, "Very good, Mam'zelle."'

'Very good, Mam'zelle,' said Elizabeth, knowing quite well that Robert was enjoying her scolding immensely, and wishing that she could pull some more hairs out of his dark head.

After that the lesson went on smoothly, for Elizabeth was determined not to give Robert any more chances to crow over her. But she did not do so well as usual in anything for, as soon as she had a moment to think, she began to plan how she might catch Robert being unkind to someone.

Belinda and Joan and Nora had a little talk together, while Elizabeth was having her music lesson that day.

'We'll have to keep Elizabeth away from Robert for a few days if we can,' said Joan. 'She just hates him, and, you know, she has such a quick temper that she's quite likely to fly at him again if he makes a rude face at her.'

'After a few days she won't feel so badly about it all,' said Nora. 'We'll try and get her to come down into the village with us, or to garden with John, or something like that – the less she sees of Robert, the better. I can't say I want to see very much of him myself!'

So for the next few days Elizabeth found that she was always being rushed off somewhere.

'Come and help me to choose a new ribbon, Elizabeth!' Joan would beg. 'I really must get one.' And down to the village the two would go.

'Elizabeth, come and practise catching the ball at lacrosse with me,' Nora would say. 'You're getting quite good. A little more practice and you'll be first-rate.'

Then Elizabeth would beam with pride and go to fetch her lacrosse stick.

'Elizabeth, John wants you and me to go and help him to pile up rubbish for a bonfire!' Belinda would call. 'Coming?'

And off Elizabeth would go again, so that she hardly

saw Robert at all, except in class. But she did not forget what she had planned to do, and when she had a chance she watched to see if any of the smaller children were being bullied.

But she saw nothing of the sort. Robert went about his own business and seemed to keep right away from the younger ones. He knew quite well that Elizabeth was watching for him to do something bad again, and he wasn't going to give her the chance to catch him. She would soon get tired of that.

Robert was immensely fond of horses, and rode as often as he could. He was not allowed to look after them, because only the bigger boys and girls were allowed to do that, but he spent as much time as he could hanging round the stables, and talking to the brown-eyed horses, who put their heads out over the stable doors when they saw him. Robert took no interest in the other animals at all, much to the annoyance of the other children, who always loved to show off their pets to anyone.

So, what with Robert going out riding and the other girls taking Elizabeth off with them as often as they could, the two enemies had few chances to meet and quarrel. It was only in class that they could show their dislike of one another.

Robert was so anxious not to give Elizabeth any

chance of jeering at him that he worked extra hard, and took enormous care with his homework. Miss Ranger, the form mistress, was surprised and pleased to find Robert making such progress with everything, and she praised him.

'Robert, you are doing very well,' she said. 'I shouldn't be surprised if you are top of the class one week this term, if you work like this!'

Robert went red with pleasure. He was really a lazy boy, and had never been anywhere near the top of his form, even at his old school. Elizabeth was annoyed to hear Miss Ranger say this. Why, she, Elizabeth, could easily be top of the form if she wanted to! She would work like anything and just show Robert he couldn't get to the top while she was in the form!

So she worked very hard too; but both children were working hard for the wrong reason – to spite one another! So they did not enjoy their work at all, which was a great pity.

Then for a time both Robert and Elizabeth forgot their quarrel in the interest of something else. Jennifer's white mice made a great disturbance, and Jenny nearly got into serious trouble!

Her white mice had a family of nine small baby mice, most adorable creatures with soft white fur, woffly noses, pink eyes and tiny tails. Jenny loved these very much indeed, and it was quite a sight to see the little girl with half a dozen mice running up and down her sleeves.

'Jenny, put them back, the bell's gone,' said Elizabeth one morning. 'Hurry! You'll be late, and Miss Ranger isn't in a very good temper this morning.'

'Oh, golly, I can't find them all,' said Jenny, feeling all over her body for the baby mice. 'Wherever have they gone? Is there one down my back, Elizabeth?'

'Oh, Jenny, how can you let them do that!' cried Elizabeth. 'No, there isn't one down your back. They must be all there in the cage now. Do come on. I shan't wait for you if you're a second longer.'

Jenny shut the cage door carefully and latched it. Then she ran off with Elizabeth and they arrived in their classroom, panting, just as Miss Ranger also arrived.

They took their places. The lesson was geography, and the class were learning about Australia and the big sheep farms there. Jenny had a seat in the first row, just in front of Elizabeth and Joan.

And, in the middle of the lesson, Elizabeth saw the nose of a white mouse peeping out at the back of Jenny's neck! Jenny felt it too. She wriggled, put up her hand and pushed the mouse down. It disappeared.

Elizabeth so badly wanted to giggle that she did not dare to look up at all. When she *did* look up, she saw the mouse peeping out of Jenny's left sleeve. It looked round at Elizabeth with pink eyes. Then it disappeared again.

Jenny found the mouse very tickly indeed. She wriggled about. She tried to make the mouse go up to her shoulder where it could be comfortable and go to sleep. But it wasn't at all sleepy. It was a very lively mouse indeed. It ran all round Jenny, sniffing here and there at shoulder straps and tapes, and Jenny couldn't stop wriggling.

Miss Ranger noticed her. 'Jenny! What in the world is the matter with you this morning? Do sit still.'

'Yes, Miss Ranger,' said Jenny. But a second later the mouse went under her left armhole, where Jenny really was very ticklish indeed, and the little girl gave a giggle and another wriggle. Miss Ranger looked up.

'Jennifer! You are behaving like a child in the kindergarten! And Elizabeth, what is the matter with *you*?'

There was nothing the matter with Elizabeth except that she simply could *not* help laughing at Jenny, because she knew so well why Jenny was wriggling. The mouse popped its head out of Jenny's collar and stared at Elizabeth and Joan. The two girls tried to stop their giggles, but the more they tried to stop, the worse they got.

'This class is a disgrace this morning,' said Miss Ranger impatiently. 'Come up here to the board, Jennifer, and point out some things to me on the map.

If you can't *sit* still, perhaps you can stand still!'

Jenny got up and went to the board. The mouse was pleased to find it was having a ride, and it scampered all round Jenny's back. Jenny put her hand behind her and tried to stop it.

'Jenny! What *is* wrong?' asked Miss Ranger. By this time the whole class knew about Jenny's mouse, and everyone was bending over their books, red in the face, trying their hardest not to giggle. A little squeal came from Kenneth, and Miss Ranger put down her book in despair.

'There is some joke going on,' she said. 'Well, let me share it. If it's funny, we'll all have a good laugh. If it isn't, we'll get on with the lesson. Now, what's the joke?'

Nobody told her. Jenny looked at the class with pleading eyes, begging them silently not to give her away. The mouse also looked out of Jenny's sleeve. Miss Ranger was really puzzled.

And then the mouse decided to explore the world a bit! So out it ran, jumped on to Miss Ranger's desk and sat up to wash its whiskers.

The class went off into shouts of laughter. Miss Ranger looked down in the greatest astonishment. She had not seen where the mouse had come from.

'How did this mouse come here?' she asked.

'It jumped from my sleeve, please, Miss Ranger,'

said Jenny. 'I was playing with my white mice when the bell rang, and I suppose I didn't put them all back into the cage. This one was still up my sleeve.'

'So that's the joke!' said Miss Ranger, beginning to smile. 'Well, I agree it's a good joke, and no wonder everyone laughed. But it's not a joke to be repeated, Jenny. It's funny this time – but, if it happens a second time, I shan't think it is at all funny. You quite understand that, don't you? White mice are very nice in their cage, but not at all suitable running round people's necks in a classroom.'

'Oh, yes, I do understand that, Miss Ranger,' said Jenny earnestly. 'It was quite an accident. May I put the mouse up my sleeve again?'

'I'd much rather you didn't,' said Miss Ranger. 'I feel this lesson will not be very successful as long as that mouse is in the room. Take it back to its cage. It will have plenty to tell all its brothers and sisters.'

So off went Jenny, and the class settled down again. But the laughter had done everyone good, especially Elizabeth. She felt almost her old happy self again after that!

CHAPTER SEVEN

KATHLEEN IN TROUBLE

ELIZABETH ENJOYED the games in the winter term very much indeed. She didn't know which she liked best, hockey or lacrosse!

'I almost think I like lacrosse best,' she said to Joan. 'The catching is such fun.'

'If you go on playing well, you'll be in the next match,' said Joan. 'I heard Eileen say so!'

'Did you really and truly?' said Elizabeth joyfully. 'Oh, I say! Nobody else out of our form has been in a school match yet. If only I could be!'

Somebody else in the form was extremely good at lacrosse too – and that was Robert! He had never played the game before, but he was very quick on his feet, and could catch marvellously. The game was played with a hard rubber ball which had to be thrown from one player's net to another, caught and sent hurtling at the goal net. The job of the other side was to knock the ball away, or make the player who had the ball toss it to someone else, when the enemy might perhaps be able to get it.

As soon as Robert saw that Elizabeth was becoming good enough to play in a school match, he made up his mind that he would be better than she was, and take her place in the match.

He knew that only one person would be chosen from their form, for only one was lacking in the numbers that made up the team. What sport it would be if he could play better than Elizabeth! So that was another thing for him to do – practise catching the ball whenever he could get someone to throw to him. But he wouldn't let Elizabeth guess that he was trying to be better than she was – no, he would let her think he wasn't trying very hard, else she would begin to practise as well.

In the meantime, school life went on much as usual. Elizabeth began to work very hard with John in the school garden. They cut down all the old summer flowers, and piled them in heaps on the place where they had their bonfires. They dug over the beds and made themselves very hot and tired, but very happy. They each made out plans for the spring and gave them to each other, and John actually said that Elizabeth's plan was better than his.

'It's not very *much* better,' said John, looking at the two plans carefully, 'but I do like one or two of your ideas very much, Elizabeth. For instance, your idea of having crocuses growing in the grass on that bank over there is lovely.'

'Well, your idea of having rambler roses over that ugly old shed is lovely too,' said Elizabeth. 'I say, John, won't it look marvellous!'

'I wonder if the School Meeting will allow us extra money this week for the crocus corms,' said John. 'We should want about five hundred crocuses to make any sort of a show. Let's ask, shall we?'

'Well, *you'd* better ask, not me,' said Elizabeth, her face going sulky. 'You know what happened at the last Meeting, John. It was horrid to me.'

'No, it wasn't, Elizabeth,' said John, leaning on his spade and looking at Elizabeth across the trench he was digging. 'I think the Meeting was quite fair. Don't be silly. You can be such a sensible girl, and yet you're such an idiot sometimes.'

'I shan't help you in the garden if you call me an idiot,' said Elizabeth.

'All right,' said John. 'I'll get Jenny. She's jolly good.'

But Elizabeth did not walk away in a rage as she felt inclined to do. She took up her spade and began to dig so hard that the earth simply flew into the air.

She wasn't going to let Jennifer take her place!

John burst out laughing. 'Elizabeth! You'll dig down to Australia if you're not careful! And really I'd rather you didn't cover me with earth while you're doing it.'

Elizabeth looked up and laughed too.

'That's better!' said John. 'You'll get a face like Kathleen Peters if you aren't careful!'

'I hope not!' said Elizabeth. 'That's another person I don't like, John. She's so quarrelsome, and she seems to think we are always saying or thinking nasty things about her – and honestly we just don't bother about her half the time.'

'Well, don't start making an enemy of her too,' said John, beginning to dig again. 'Friends are better than enemies, Elizabeth, old thing, so make those instead.'

'Well, nobody could make a friend of Kathleen!' said Elizabeth. 'Honestly they couldn't, John. You're not in her form, so you don't know what a tiresome person she is.'

It was quite true that Kathleen was tiresome. She was always grumbling about something, and she spent the whole of her two shillings each week on sweets, which she never shared with anyone else.

'No wonder she's spotty!' giggled Belinda unkindly. 'She's eating sweets all the time – and her mother sends her heaps too, only she never tells us, in case we might expect her to share them. Let her keep them! I don't want any!'

Kathleen was not only tiresome with the boys and girls, always trying to quarrel, and accusing them of saying nasty things about her, but she was always in trouble with the mistresses and masters too. If anyone found fault with her, she would argue back and try to make out that she was right.

Mam'zelle was not so patient with her as were the others. When Kathleen dared to say that Mam'zelle hadn't told her what homework to do the day before, the hot-tempered French mistress flared up at once.

'And now this Kathleen again!' she cried, wagging her hands at the ceiling. 'She thinks I am a goose, a cuckoo, a donkey! She thinks I do not know how to give homework! She thinks I am not fit to teach French to her!'

This was really rather funny, and the class sat up, enjoying the fun. When Mam'zelle got cross it was marvellous!

'But Mam'zelle,' said foolish Kathleen, who simply would not stop arguing with anyone, 'you did say . . .'

'Ah! I did say something then!' cried Mam'zelle. 'Truly, you think I did say something? Ah, my Kathleen, that is so, *so* kind of you! Perhaps if you think a little harder you will remember that I did give you some homework to do – though, of course, that is no reason why you should do it.'

'But you *didn't* give me any,' said Kathleen.

Belinda nudged her. 'Shut up, Kathleen,' she said. 'You *were* given some – but you didn't write down what you had to do.'

'Belinda! It is not necessary that you should interfere,' said Mam'zelle. 'Ah, this class! It will turn my hair white as snow!'

Mam'zelle had hair as dark as a raven's wing, and the class did not feel that anything would turn it white. They sat staring from Mam'zelle to Kathleen, wondering what was going to happen next. It ended in Kathleen being sent by herself to the common room to do the homework she had not done.

That girl will drive me mad, thought Mam'zelle to herself. *How she whines!*

The other mistresses were not quite so impatient, and Miss Ranger was really rather worried about Kathleen. The girl always looked so miserable – which, of course, was no wonder, because she was always arguing or quarrelling with someone.

Jennifer Harris enjoyed the scene with Mam'zelle very much. She watched all Mam'zelle's actions, listened carefully to the rise and fall of her excited voice, and then practised the whole scene by herself. First she was the whining Kathleen, then she was impatient Mam'zelle, and so on. It really made a very funny scene.

Jenny was most anxious to try it on the others to make them laugh. So the next evening, when most of her form were in the common room, playing the gramophone, reading books and writing letters, she began to mimic Mam'zelle.

The boys and girls looked up, interested. Belinda switched off the gramophone. Kathleen was not there.

In a moment or two the clever girl had the whole room roaring with laughter. She wagged her hands like Mam'zelle, and when she came out with 'I am a goose, a cuckoo, a donkey!' exactly as Mam'zelle had said it the children giggled in delight.

Jenny mimicked Kathleen's rather whining voice marvellously. It really might have been Kathleen speaking! But then Jenny went a bit too far. She said things that Mam'zelle had not said.

'Ah, truly, Kathleen, I do not like your spots, I do not like your greasy hair, I do not like your manners!' said Jenny, with a funny accent just like Mam'zelle's. And at that moment Elizabeth noticed something – Kathleen was in the room! No one had seen her come in. How long had she been there?

Elizabeth nudged Jenny, but Jenny took no notice. She was enjoying herself far too much. Everyone was listening to her, amused and admiring.

'Jenny! Shut up!' hissed Elizabeth. 'Kathleen's come in.'

Jenny stopped at once. All the children looked round, and felt rather uncomfortable when they saw Kathleen. Belinda started up the gramophone. Somebody began to whistle the tune. Nobody liked to look at Kathleen.

Elizabeth sat down in a corner, wishing that Jenny hadn't said quite such awful things in Mam'zelle's voice. Suppose Kathleen really thought that Mam'zelle had said them after she had been sent to the common room to do her forgotten homework? She stole a quick look at Kathleen.

At first it seemed as if Kathleen was going to turn off the gramophone and say something. But she thought better of it, and sat down with a jerk in a chair. She got out her notepaper, and sat chewing the end of her pen. Her face was pale as usual, and her eyes were small and angry. She looked spiteful and mean.

I guess she won't easily forgive Jenny for that, thought Elizabeth. *We ought to have stopped Jenny, because she went too far – but really she's so awfully funny. I wonder if Kathleen will complain about it at the next Meeting. I shouldn't be surprised.*

Kathleen didn't say a word about the affair to anyone. She spoke to no one at all that evening. Her bed was next to Elizabeth's in the dormitory, and when Kathleen did not reply when everyone called goodnight as usual Elizabeth poked her head between the blue curtains to speak to her, for she was sorry about the whole thing.

Kathleen did not see her. The girl was sitting on her bed, looking earnestly at her face in her hand mirror. She looked really sad, and Elizabeth knew why. Poor Kathleen was thinking how plain and ugly she was! She had always known it herself – but it was dreadful to know that everyone else knew it too, and laughed about it.

Elizabeth drew back her head and said nothing. Would Kathleen have the courage to repeat at the Meeting all that Jenny had said about her? Surely she couldn't do that!

Kathleen had her own plans. She was going to pay Jenny out in her own way. She got into bed and lay thinking about them. Jenny had better look out, that's all!

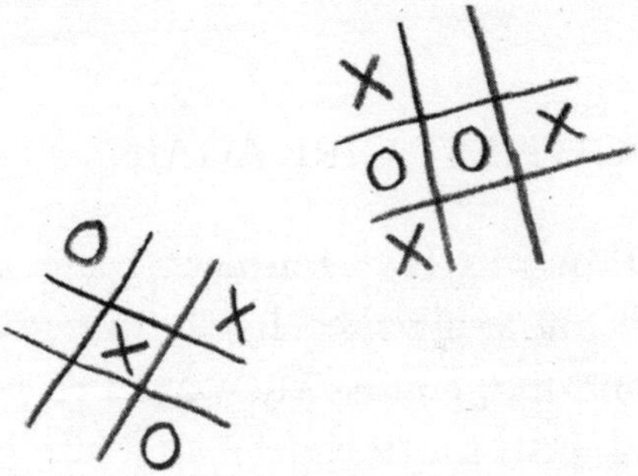

CHAPTER EIGHT

ANOTHER SCHOOL MEETING

THINGS WERE not very pleasant the next two or three days. There seemed to be rather a lot of bad feeling about. For one thing Kathleen simply would not speak to Jenny at all, which was not very surprising considering what she had overheard Jenny saying.

But, besides not speaking to her, Kathleen began to speak *against* her. Jenny was always very hungry, and she ate very well indeed – and Kathleen called her greedy.

'It makes me sick to see the way that greedy Jenny eats,' she said to Belinda after tea the next day. 'Honestly, she ate seven pieces of bread and butter, and three buns, besides an enormous piece of birthday cake that Harriet gave her.'

Belinda said nothing. She did not like rows, but Elizabeth overheard and flared up at once in defence of Jenny.

'That's a mean thing to say, Kathleen!' she said. 'Jenny *isn't* greedy! She's always terribly hungry at mealtimes – well, I am too, I must say – but I've never seen Jenny gobbling just for the sake of eating, or taking more than her share if there wasn't enough for everyone. And how awful of you to *count* how many pieces of bread and butter she had!'

'I shall count again,' said Kathleen, 'and you'll be surprised to find I'm right. Jenny is greedy. It's disgusting!'

'Kathleen! What about you and your sweets then!' cried Elizabeth. 'You're greedy over them – why, you never offer anyone any!'

'Stop it now, you two,' said Belinda, feeling uncomfortable. 'I don't know what's the matter with our form this term – somebody always seems to be quarrelling!'

Kathleen went off. Elizabeth took out her paintbox to paint a map, and set it down on the table with a crash. Her face was as dark as thunder.

'Elizabeth! I wonder you haven't broken that box in half!' exclaimed Belinda. 'My word, I wish you could see your face!'

'I think you might have stuck up for Jenny,' said Elizabeth, stirring her paint water so crossly that it slopped over on the table. 'I wouldn't let anyone say a word against a friend of mine without sticking up for them.'

'Well, you've made things much worse by sticking up than I have by saying nothing,' said Belinda. 'I don't know what's come over you lately – you're really bad-tempered!'

'No, I'm not,' said Elizabeth. 'Things have gone wrong, that's all. Anyway, I won't let that spotty-faced Kathleen say mean things about old Jenny. Jenny's a sport. Golly, how I laughed about that white mouse the other day! Miss Ranger was nice about that, wasn't she?'

About a quarter of an hour later Jenny came into the common room looking furious. She sat down in a chair with a bump. Belinda looked up from her sewing.

'My goodness! Another thunderstorm beginning!' she said. 'What's up, Jenny? One look at you and even the milk would turn sour!'

'Don't be funny,' said Jenny. 'It's that horrible Kathleen! She told Kenneth that I borrowed his bike yesterday without asking him. And I didn't. I took Harry's and I *did* ask him! Mine had a puncture!'

'Well, really, Kathleen's going a bit too far!' said Elizabeth indignantly. 'That's twice she's said nasty things about you today. I'll tell her what I think of her when I see her!'

'She's in the passage outside, still telling Kenneth about me,' said Jenny. 'Go and say what you want to – it will do her good!'

'No, don't, Elizabeth,' said Belinda. 'You are such a little spitfire. Don't interfere.'

But Elizabeth had already marched out of the room. She saw Kathleen and went up to her.

'Look here, Kathleen,' she said, 'if you don't stop saying unkind and untrue things about Jenny, I'll report you to the next Meeting!'

'And what about the unkind and untrue things that Jenny said about me in front of you all!' said Kathleen in a low and trembling voice. 'How dared she mock me like that!'

'Well, they might have been unkind, but they weren't untrue,' said Elizabeth. Then she was sorry she had said that. But it was too late to unsay it. Kathleen turned away and went off without saying another word.

She was really afraid that Elizabeth might report her, and she made up her mind that she had better not speak against Jenny. But she would do all kinds of little things to annoy her and get her into trouble – and she would do them to that interfering Elizabeth too.

I'll be very, very careful so that nobody guesses it's me, thought Kathleen to herself. *I'll hide their books – and make blots on their homework – and do things like that. I'll soon pay them out!*

The next School Meeting came along quickly. The children took their places as usual, and the Meeting began. A nice lot of money was put into the box, for three children had had birthdays and had many postal orders sent to them. That was lucky!

'We are rich today,' said William, jingling the box. 'Give out the ordinary money, Eileen – and fourpence ha'penny extra to Mary as usual. Now, any requests for extra money?'

Leonard, one of the bigger boys, stood up. 'May I have half a crown to pay for mending a window, please?' he asked. 'I broke one yesterday in the common room.'

'By accident, or were you fooling about?' asked William.

'I was playing with an old cricket ball,' said Leonard.

'Well, you know quite well that we made a rule last term not to bring balls into the common room,' said William. 'It only means broken windows.'

'I quite forgot that rule,' said Leonard. 'I *should* like the money, though – half a crown is a lot to have to pay. I'm sorry about it, William.'

The Jury discussed the matter. They quite saw that half a crown was a lot of money when each boy and girl only had two shillings each week. On the other hand, Leonard had broken a rule that he himself had helped to make last term, and why should the school money pay for his fooling about?

The matter was decided at last. William banged with

his hammer and the children were quiet.

'Was anybody else fooling about with you?' asked William. Leonard stood up again.

'Well, yes,' he said, 'but it was when *I* threw the ball that the window got broken.'

'The Jury think that the half crown shouldn't come out of the school box,' said William, 'but they also think that you shouldn't have to pay it all. You'd better discuss it with the children who were playing about with you at the time, and divide the payment between you. That's fair.'

A boy got up. 'I was fooling about too,' he said. 'I'll pay my share. I agree that it's fair.'

Two others got up, a boy and a girl. 'We will pay our share too,' they said.

'Right,' said William. 'Four into two shillings and sixpence – sevenpence ha'penny each. That won't ruin any of you. And please remember that as you all help to make the few rules we have, it's up to you to keep them.'

John nudged Elizabeth. 'Ask for the money for our crocuses,' he whispered. 'Go on. I'm not going to! It was your idea.'

'I'm sure the Meeting won't let me have anything after what they said last week,' said Elizabeth in a fierce whisper.

'Coward!' said John, with a grin. That was quite

enough to make Elizabeth shoot to her feet at once. She could never bear to be called a coward!

Kathleen looked at her rather anxiously. She was half afraid that Elizabeth was going to complain about her to the Meeting.

'What do you want, Elizabeth?' asked Rita. 'Extra money?'

'Yes, please,' said Elizabeth. 'John and I have got some fine plans for the school garden and we both think it would be lovely to have yellow and purple crocuses growing in the grass on that sloping bank near the gates. John says we'd want at least five hundred crocus bulbs. Please may we have the money to buy them, Rita?'

William and Rita spoke together for a moment and the Jury nodded their heads at one another. Everyone thought the money could be given.

'Yes, you can have what you want,' said William. 'The whole school will enjoy seeing the crocuses in the early spring, and it is quite fair that the money should come out of the school box. Find out how much the bulbs will be, Elizabeth, and we shall be very pleased to give you the money. Also I would like to say that the whole school appreciates the way that you and John work at our garden.'

Elizabeth blushed with pleasure. This was quite unexpected. She sat down with a word of thanks.

John grinned in delight at her. 'What did I tell you?' he whispered. 'You can always trust William and Rita to be absolutely fair!'

'Any complaints or grumbles?' asked Rita. A small boy got up promptly. He was a cheeky-looking child, and had his complaint all ready.

'I should like to make a complaint about Fred White,' he said. 'He's always borrowing my things and never giving them back.'

'That's telling a tale, not making a proper complaint,' said William at once. 'Go to your monitor to decide silly little things of that sort. Who is your monitor?'

'I am,' said a boy called Thomas.

'Well, please explain carefully the difference between telling tales and making a genuine complaint,' said William. 'We only decide serious things at this Meeting.'

'Any more complaints?' asked Rita. A boy called William Peace got up. He was in the form below Elizabeth, a serious-faced boy.

'I have a small complaint to make,' he said. 'I learn the violin and I see that my practice times have been altered to the times when my form goes for a nature ramble. I belong to the Nature Society, and I hate to miss the rambles. May the time of one of them be altered?'

'It would be quite easy,' said William. 'Discuss it with Mr Lewis, the music master, and see if there is anyone who can change practice times with you.'

'Thank you,' said the boy, and sat down. There were no more complaints. Kathleen did not get up and say anything at all, though the others in her form were almost sure that she would complain about Jenny. They did not know that the girl was going to punish Jenny in her own way.

'The Meeting is dismissed,' said William, and the school filed out, chattering as soon as the children got to their various common rooms. Elizabeth went to John.

'It's good that we can have the money for the crocuses, isn't it?' she said, with her eyes shining. 'We'll go down to the village tomorrow, John, and see how much they are. I'm longing to plant them, aren't you? October is the right month. They will look so lovely in the springtime.'

'Elizabeth, I wish you knew how much nicer you look when you are all happy and smiling like that,' said John. 'It is so horrid when you frown and sulk.'

'You're always lecturing me, John!' said Elizabeth. But she was glad all the same that John was pleased with her. Alas! He was not going to be pleased with her for long!

CHAPTER NINE

KATHLEEN PLAYS SOME TRICKS

KATHLEEN DID not change her mind about paying back Elizabeth and Jenny. She began to play all kinds of mean little tricks on them, and she played them so cleverly that they did not guess she had done them.

She slipped into the classroom after tea when there was no one there and went to Jenny's desk. She knew that Jenny had written out her French homework very carefully indeed, and she had seen her put the book back into her desk.

Kathleen took out the book and opened it at the place where the work had been done. She dipped a pen in the ink – and then she made three large blots on the page by shaking the pen hard!

She looked at it. The page was dreadful. Jenny would get into trouble, no doubt about that! She waited until the blots were dry and then shut the book. She slipped it into the desk and ran back to the common room. She saw Jenny there and gave her a sly look. *Ah, wait, Jenny! You'll have a shock tomorrow*, thought Kathleen.

Elizabeth was in the room too, putting one of her favourite gramophone records on. Kathleen wondered what she could do to her. She sat and thought for a while, then quietly got up. She slipped out of the room and put on her coat. It was dark outside, and she went out of the garden door into the school grounds.

She went to where Elizabeth kept her spade, fork and trowels. John always insisted that every tool used should be cleaned till it was bright and shining, before it was put away. Elizabeth was always particular about this, for she knew that well-kept tools did good work.

Kathleen took down the garden tools. She carried them outside, and went to a place where she knew that the earth was damp and muddy. She dug the tools into the wet soil and made them very dirty indeed.

Then she carried them back to the shed and put them into a corner. She shone her torch on to them. They were brown with mud. John would be furious when he found them – and as they were the ones that Elizabeth always used he would be sure to think that she had been careless.

Well, I'll soon teach Jenny and Elizabeth that it doesn't pay to be horrid to me! thought Kathleen to herself, as she went back to take off her coat. *They deserve to be punished! They've been mean to me. Now I'm being mean back to them. Serves them right!*

She went back to the common room. She couldn't help feeling rather victorious somehow, and she longed for the next day to come, so that she might see her two enemies getting into trouble.

The first one to get into trouble was poor Jenny. Mam'zelle asked Kenneth to collect the French books and Jenny gave hers up without even opening it. Mam'zelle set the class some translation to do, and then opened the French exercise books to correct them.

When she came to Jenny's and saw the three enormous blots across the page, blotting out some of the sentences, she threw up her hands in horror.

'What is this?' she cried. 'Whose book is this?' She looked quickly at the name, and gazed across at Jenny in astonishment.

'Jennifer Harris! How can you give in work like this! It is shocking!'

Jenny looked up in surprise. What *could* be the matter with her work? She had done it quite carefully. 'Why, Mam'zelle!' she said. 'Is there something wrong?'

'Jenny, my child, you do not belong to the kindergarten!' cried Mam'zelle, holding up the book for Jenny to see. 'Look at this page! Is it not disgraceful?

You know that you should have written out all this work again – work from this form cannot be given in covered with blots. I am truly ashamed of you!'

Jenny stared in the greatest surprise at her book. She knew quite well she hadn't made any blots at all. It couldn't be her book!

'That's not my book, Mam'zelle,' she said. 'It can't be. I didn't make any blots at all. I would never give in work like that.'

'Jenny, I can see clearly!' cried Mam'zelle, beginning to get excited. 'I read your name here, see – Jennifer Harris. It is most certainly your book. And, if you did not make these blots, how did they come? Blots do not make themselves, as you very well know.'

'I simply can't imagine how they came,' said poor Jenny really puzzled now. 'Honestly I can't, Mam'zelle, I'm most awfully sorry. I'll do the work again.'

'And you will be more careful in future,' said Mam'zelle, calming down. Jenny was upset and puzzled. She supposed that in some way she must have made the blots without noticing them, just as she shut the book. She did not see Kathleen looking at her with a spiteful gleam in her eyes. Kathleen was delighted at the success of her trick. She would play a few more on Jenny very soon!

There was half an hour that afternoon for any child

to go for a walk, practice lacrosse or do gardening. Elizabeth chose to go to the garden. There was one piece she hadn't quite been able to finish digging the day before. She could just finish it in the time.

So off she skipped, and called out to John who was already digging hard. But John did not look at all pleased with her.

'Elizabeth, you did do some digging and forking yesterday, didn't you?' he called.

'Rather!' said Elizabeth, stopping beside him. 'I used nearly all my tools, I was so busy. What's the matter, John? You look cross.'

'I *am* cross,' said John. 'Go and get your tools and you'll see why.'

Elizabeth couldn't *think* what he meant. She rushed off to the shed – and stopped in surprise and dismay when she saw her tools. They were all muddy and dirty! Not one of them shone bright and silvery. What a very extraordinary thing!

She went outside, carrying them with her. 'John!' she said. 'I'm quite sure I cleaned them as usual yesterday when I put them away.'

'You can't have,' said John in a cold sort of voice. 'Tools don't get dirty at night by themselves, Elizabeth. Have some sense.'

'I've got plenty!' cried Elizabeth. 'And my sense

tells me that if I *did* clean them, which I know I did, it's not *my* fault that they're dirty now.'

'Well, don't let's argue about it,' said John. 'I'd have thought a lot more of you, Elizabeth, if you'd owned up, and said you'd forgotten just for once. It's not like you to say you did a thing when you didn't.'

'John!' cried Elizabeth, shocked. 'How can you say such a thing about me! I'm never afraid of owning up. You know that. I tell you I *did* clean the tools.'

'All right, all right,' said John, going on with the digging. 'I suppose they all walked out of the shed in the middle of the night and went digging by themselves and forgot to have a wash and brush-up afterwards. We'll leave it at that.'

The two children dug in silence. Elizabeth was puzzled, upset and angry. She hated to think that John didn't believe her, and yet her common sense told her that it really did look as if she had forgotten to clean her tools. It was horrid to have John cross with her. She didn't know what to do.

'John,' she said at last, 'I really do think I cleaned the tools, but if I forgot, I'm very sorry. I've never forgotten before. I won't forget again.'

'All right, Elizabeth,' said John, lifting his honest brown eyes to hers. He smiled at her, and she smiled back. But in her secret heart she was very puzzled indeed.

Kathleen had been waiting about by the garden shed to see what would happen. She was pleased when she saw that John was cross with Elizabeth. She went away, planning to do something else to get Elizabeth into trouble. What should she do next? Perhaps in a day or two she would dirty the tools again. She had better not do that too soon, though, in case Elizabeth began to suspect a trick.

She decided to take two or three of Elizabeth's books and hide them somewhere. Miss Ranger would be cross if they couldn't be found. So once again Kathleen slipped into the classroom, and this time she went to Elizabeth's desk. She took out her geography exercise book, her arithmetic book and her history book. She slipped out of the room with them and went to a cupboard outside. On the top were kept old maps. Kathleen stood on a chair and threw the books right on the very top, among the old maps. Nobody was about to see her. She quickly put back the chair, and went away.

And now what should she do to Jenny? The naughty girl frowned, and thought hard. Then she smiled to herself. She would take two of the white mice and put them into Miss Ranger's desk! That would be marvellous! Miss Ranger would be quite sure to think that Jenny had put them there herself. Nobody would know who had done it.

To do this Kathleen had to wait till the next morning. She planned to get the mice before breakfast. No one would be about then. She lay in bed that night, thinking of what Miss Ranger would say when she opened the desk and found the mice.

She was up early the next morning. Nora was surprised, for Kathleen was usually one of the last out of bed. 'Hallo, turning over a new leaf?' she said.

Kathleen didn't answer. She slipped downstairs five minutes before the breakfast bell went, and ran to the big shed where the pets were kept. She went to the cage of white mice. She had with her a little box, and it took her only a second or two to pick up two of the tiny white mice and slip them into the box. Then she hurried to her classroom with them. She lifted up the lid of Miss Ranger's desk.

She opened the box – and out scurried the white mice into the desk. Kathleen shut down the lid. What a surprise Miss Ranger and Jenny were going to get!

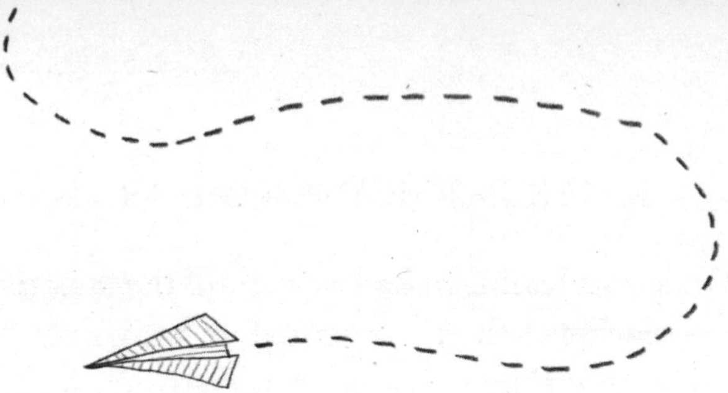

CHAPTER TEN

EXCITEMENT IN CLASS!

THE FIRST lesson that morning was arithmetic. Miss Ranger explained a new kind of sum to the class, and they listened hard.

'Now get out your books and we will do a few of these sums,' said Miss Ranger, beginning to put down a few on the blackboard. 'You should all be able to do them correctly, but if anyone hasn't quite understood what I have been saying, ask me first, before you begin the sums.'

Elizabeth opened her desk to get out her arithmetic exercise book. It wasn't on the top of the pile, where she usually put it. She hunted through her desk. How funny! The book wasn't there at all. Where could it be?

'Elizabeth! How much longer are you going to have your head in your desk?' asked Miss Ranger.

'I can't find my book,' said Elizabeth.

'Well, you had it yesterday,' said Miss Ranger. 'Did you take it out of the classroom?'

'No, Miss Ranger,' said Elizabeth. 'I hadn't any arithmetic homework to do. I just put the book back when I'd finished with it yesterday morning. But it really isn't here.'

'Take some squared paper from the shelf in the cupboard,' said Miss Ranger. 'We can't wait all morning for you to find the book.' So Elizabeth took some squared paper and did her sums on that, thankful that she hadn't got into trouble. She simply could *not* imagine where her book could be! She kept on and on thinking about it.

Kathleen wondered what would happen when Elizabeth couldn't find the other books! She was also longing for Miss Ranger to open her own desk and find the mice. But Miss Ranger had no reason to open her desk in the arithmetic lesson. So the mice remained undisturbed. They had curled up in a corner and gone to sleep.

The next lesson was French, and after that came geography. Miss Ranger wanted a map drawn, and the girls got out their exercise books. And once again Elizabeth couldn't find hers.

'Well, really, Elizabeth, you are surely not going to tell me that your geography book is lost too!' said

Miss Ranger impatiently.

'Miss Ranger, I just can't understand it, but it's gone,' said Elizabeth, putting her head above the desk lid to speak to Miss Ranger.

'It is very careless of you to lose both books,' said Miss Ranger. 'I am not pleased, Elizabeth. Perhaps I had better look through your desk myself to make quite sure that they are not there. I can't imagine that you could lose *two* of your exercise books when you say you did not even take them out of the classroom!'

But not even Miss Ranger's sharp eye could see the missing books, and she went back to her own desk. Robert was pleased to see Elizabeth getting into trouble. As for Kathleen, she was so delighted at the success of her mean trick that she did not dare to look at either Elizabeth or Jenny in case they saw how glad she was.

'I will give you some map paper, and you must pin the map you draw into your book when it is found again,' said Miss Ranger. She lifted up the lid of her desk to get some blank drawing paper – and awoke the two mice!

With squeals and squeaks they raced round the desk in fright, jumping over rubbers and books and rulers. Miss Ranger stared at them in amazement and anger.

She was about to shut down the desk and leave the mice there when they both leapt out, ran down Miss

Ranger's skirt and tore across the floor. All the girls and boys stared in the greatest astonishment.

Miss Ranger put on a very stern face and looked at the surprised Jenny.

'Jenny,' she said, 'I believe you are the only person in the school who keeps white mice as pets. Do you really think it is a funny joke to put the poor little things into my airless desk in order to play a foolish trick on me?'

Jenny couldn't say a word at first. She really was too amazed to speak. *Were* they her mice? How in the world could they have got into the desk?

'Miss Ranger, of *course* I didn't put them in there!' she said at last. 'Please, please believe me. I wouldn't do such a thing to my little mice. And anyway you were so decent to me when I came to class with one down my neck that I certainly wouldn't have been mean enough to play a trick on you after that.'

The mice fled all over the room. Jenny watched them anxiously, terrified that they would go under the door and escape – perhaps to get eaten by the school cat!

'You had better try to catch them,' said Miss Ranger. 'We can't have the whole lesson disturbed like this. I can't imagine how they could have got into my desk unless you put them there. I shall have to think about the whole thing. I am very displeased about it.'

Jenny leapt up from her seat to catch the mice.

But that was easier said than done. The frightened creatures tore all over the room, hiding under first one desk and then another. Some of the girls pretended to be frightened and squealed whenever a mouse came near to their feet. Elizabeth and Belinda tried to help, but those mice were too nimble to be caught.

And then, to Jenny's great dismay, they squeezed themselves under the schoolroom door, and escaped into the passage outside! Jenny ran to the door and opened it – but the mice had disappeared! Goodness knew where they had gone! The little girl ran down the passage, looking everywhere, but the mice were nowhere to be seen.

Jenny was really fond of her mice. Tears came into her eyes and she brushed them away. But others came, and she did not like to go back to the classroom, crying. So she leant against the passage wall for a minute, trying to fight back her tears. Someone had played a mean trick on her! Someone had tried to get her into trouble! Someone had made her lose two of her pets! It was horrid, horrid, horrid!

Footsteps came down the passage – and who should come round the corner but Rita, the head girl! She was most surprised to see Jenny standing there, crying.

'What's the matter?' she asked. 'Have you been sent out of the room?'

'No,' said poor Jenny. 'It's my white mice. They're gone – and I'm so afraid the school cat will eat them.' She poured out the whole story to Rita. The head girl looked very grave.

'I don't like the idea of somebody trying to get you into trouble like this,' she said. 'You are quite, quite sure you didn't play the trick yourself, Jenny?'

'Oh, Rita – I really couldn't treat my pets like that,' said Jenny earnestly. 'Do believe me.'

'Well, the matter must be brought up at the next Meeting,' said Rita. 'We'll have to get to the bottom of it. Now go back to your class, Jenny. Cheer up. Maybe the mice will turn up again!'

Jenny went back. Miss Ranger saw her red eyes and did not scold her any more. The bell went for the lesson to stop, and the class put away their books. Break came next. Thank goodness!

Robert bumped into Elizabeth as they went out of the classroom, and she glared at him. 'How many more books are you going to lose?' he asked.

Elizabeth tossed her head and walked off with Joan. But a thought came into her head. Could Robert have taken her books? It really was so very extraordinary that both her arithmetic book *and* her geography book should have gone! She went over to Jenny and pulled her into a corner.

'Do you think Robert has got anything to do with my losing my books and your mice being put into the desk?' she said. 'I know he'd like to get me into trouble.'

'Yes, but why should he get *me* into trouble too?' said Jenny.

'Oh, he might think that if he played tricks only on *me*, I would guess it was him,' said Elizabeth. 'But, if he played tricks on you and anybody else, we might not think it was him at all. See?'

'Well, he must be pretty horrid if he's as mean as all that,' said Jenny, troubled. 'Oh, Elizabeth, I wish I knew who it was. It's so awful having these things happen.'

It was even more horrid when the history lesson came and Elizabeth had to confess to Miss Ranger that that book had disappeared too!

'Elizabeth! This is really peculiar,' said Miss Ranger crossly. 'One book is enough to lose – but *three*! You must have taken them out of the classroom and left them somewhere. You must hunt for them well, and if you cannot find them you must come to me and buy new ones.'

Oh, bother! thought Elizabeth in dismay. *They are threepence each. That's ninepence out of my precious two shillings. It's too bad! If Robert has hidden my books I'll pull all the hairs out of his head!*

She said this to Joan. 'No, you won't do anything of the sort,' said Joan. 'You'll report him at the Meeting and let the school judge him. After all, that's what the Meeting is for, Elizabeth – for all of us to help to untangle the difficulties of a few of us. It's much better too to let the Jury and the Judges decide for us, because we have chosen them as being the wisest among us. Don't take matters into your own hands, Elizabeth. You're such an impatient person – you'll only do something silly!'

'I wish you wouldn't keep talking to me like that,' said Elizabeth, taking her arm from Joan's. 'You might back me up!'

'I *am* backing you up, if you only knew it,' said Joan, with a sigh. 'I would be a poor friend to you if I said, "Go to Robert and pull his hair out," even before you really know for certain whether he is playing these horrid tricks, or not.'

'Well, you've only got to see how pleased he is when I get into trouble to know that he's at the bottom of it all!' cried Elizabeth. 'Oh, if only I could catch him bullying someone again. Wouldn't I love to report him at the very next Meeting!'

Elizabeth hadn't long to wait. She caught Robert the very next day!

CHAPTER ELEVEN

MORE TROUBLE

FOR SOME time now Robert had not bullied anyone or been unkind, because he really had been afraid of being seen by Elizabeth. He knew that she was watching to catch him and he did not mean to give her any chance to report him again.

But two or three weeks had now gone by and he thought that she no longer bothered to watch. He did not know that she thought he had played the tricks on her and was watching very carefully indeed.

Robert had to go and get some water for his painting after tea. Elizabeth saw him go out of the common room and she looked at Joan.

'Joan! Do you think Robert has gone to take my books again, or do some horrid trick?' she said in a low voice. 'Let's follow him and see.'

So the two girls got up and followed Robert. He

went down the passage, and ran down the stairs to the cloakroom where the water taps were. And running round the corner came small, cheeky Leslie, the boy who had complained that another was always borrowing things and not giving them back. He ran full-tilt into Robert, and made him double up in pain.

Leslie giggled. It was funny to see big Robert panting like that! Robert put out a hand and caught him, holding the boy's arm so tightly that it hurt.

'Let me go,' said Leslie.

Robert looked up and down the passage quickly. No one was about. He pulled Leslie into the wash place and shook him hard.

'How dare you run into me like that!' he demanded. 'And I'll teach you to laugh at me, you little nuisance!'

'Robert, let me go!' begged Leslie again. He knew that Robert was a bully and he was afraid of him.

'Say "I humbly beg your pardon, and I will never, never do such a thing again!"' said Robert.

But Leslie, although he was afraid, was not a coward. He shook his head. 'I'm not going to be as humble as all that!' he said. 'You let me go, you big bully!'

Robert was angry. He shook Leslie hard again. 'You say what I told you to say, or I'll make you sit on the hot-water pipes!' he said.

Hot-water pipes ran all round the wash place to

warm it. Leslie glanced at them fearfully. But he still shook his head.

'No, I shan't beg your pardon,' he said obstinately. 'If you'd been decent to me, as any other of the big boys would have been, I'd have said I was sorry like a shot. Let me go!'

'You'll sit on the hot-water pipes first!' said Robert in a rage, and he dragged poor Leslie towards the pipes. They were not terribly hot, but hot enough to make Leslie shout.

Meantime, where were Elizabeth and Joan? They were just round the corner, listening to all that was said, and when they heard Robert pulling Leslie to the hot pipes they ran into the wash place at once. Leslie was just shouting.

Robert pulled the little boy off the pipes as soon as he saw Elizabeth and Joan. He went red and looked very angry. To think he had been caught by those interfering girls – and one of them Elizabeth too!

'We've caught you nicely, you horrid boy,' said Elizabeth scornfully. 'Leslie, we are going to report Robert at the next Meeting. Just see you tell the truth and back us up in what we say.'

'I'll do that all right,' said Leslie. 'I'm not a little coward like some of the others, who didn't dare to complain about Robert when they had the chance! As for Peter, you know why *he* didn't say that Robert was swinging him much too high, don't you? Robert went to him and threatened him with all kinds of punishment if he dared to say a word against him!'

'I did not,' said Robert angrily, though he knew perfectly well that what Leslie said was true. 'You wait till I get you alone again, that's all!'

'There you are, you see!' said Leslie. 'You would like to do exactly the same thing to me again. But you won't get the chance! I'll report you at the Meeting all right, even if Elizabeth and Joan don't!'

The small boy marched off. Elizabeth turned to Robert. She spoke fiercely. 'I know jolly well that it's you that has been playing those horrid tricks on me and on Jenny,' she said.

'I did not,' said Robert, this time speaking quite truthfully.

'Well, I don't believe you!' said Elizabeth. 'You are mean enough for anything. You're a perfectly horrid boy and I think you ought to be sent away from our school.'

'Just as *you* ought to have been sent away last term, I suppose!' said Robert mockingly. He had heard all about Elizabeth's naughtiness during the summer term. Elizabeth went red.

'Be quiet!' said Joan. 'It was a good deal because

Elizabeth wanted to be kind to *me* that she was disobedient and I won't have you sneering at her for that!'

'I shall say what I like,' said Robert, and went off by himself, hands in pockets, whistling as if he didn't care about anything at all.

'Well, now that he knows we know he played those nasty tricks, he won't dare to play any more,' said Elizabeth, pleased. 'So that's something!'

But, of course, it was Kathleen who had tried to get Elizabeth and Jenny into trouble, not Robert – and she saw no reason why she should stop being horrid to the two girls whom she so much disliked. Both girls were pretty, clever and amusing – three things that poor Kathleen was not – and she was jealous of their shining hair and bright eyes, their good brains and jolly jokes. She wanted to hurt the girls who had the things she hadn't and yet so much wanted to have.

Elizabeth told Jenny that she was sure it was Robert who had taken her mice, and put them in the desk. The mice had never been found again and Jenny had been sad ever since. Her eyes flashed when she heard Elizabeth say that it was Robert who had played the trick.

'And I suppose he blotted my French book too, so that I had to do the work again!' said Jenny angrily. 'And I shouldn't be surprised if he dirtied those garden tools of yours, Elizabeth – I could never understand that, you know.'

'Well, I guess we shan't have any more tricks played on us, because Robert will be afraid we'll tell them all to the Meeting,' said Elizabeth. 'And we will too!'

But next day another trick was played on her and on Jenny too. On Wednesdays their monitor had to look at all their drawers and their hanging cupboards to see that they were tidy. Nora was very strict about tidiness, and the girls in her dormitory had learnt to be very neat indeed – even Ruth, who was most untidy by nature, and found it difficult to keep any drawer neat.

'It's awful!' she complained about three times a week. 'I tidy my drawers so well – then I want a handkerchief in a hurry and can't find it, and turn the drawer upside down, and then it's all untidy again!'

Elizabeth and Jenny were quite tidy, and they always made a rule on Tuesday night to tidy everything beautifully so that their chest and cupboard were ready for Nora to inspect the next day. They had done this as usual – so on Wednesday, when Nora went to pull open their drawers and found everything in a most terrible muddle, they were too astonished to say anything.

'Jenny! Elizabeth! What *have* you been thinking of to get your things into such a disgraceful mess!' cried

Nora, looking at their drawers. 'Look, everything jumbled up – crumpled, untidy – honestly I've never seen such a mess. And you are usually so tidy, both of you. What have you been doing? Didn't you remember I always looked on Wednesdays?'

'Of course we remembered,' said Jenny. 'And we tidied them last night before we went to bed. Why, you must have noticed us, Nora.'

'I didn't notice,' said Nora. 'I was at the other end of the dormitory.'

The three girls looked into the drawers. Everything was upside down. Elizabeth and Jenny knew perfectly they could never have got their things into that muddle. Somebody had played a hateful trick again, to get them into trouble.

'It's Robert!' burst out Elizabeth. 'He's always playing horrid jokes on us, Nora. He dirtied my tools, and took my books, and put Jenny's mice into Miss Ranger's desk, and . . .'

'My dear girl, it couldn't have been Robert who did this,' said Nora. 'You know the boys never come into this part of the school. He would have been seen at once, because there is always somebody going up and down the passage outside.'

'Well, it must have been Robert,' said Elizabeth sulkily. 'If you're going to get anyone into trouble, for these untidy drawers, Nora, you ought to go and scold Robert.'

'I'm not going to scold anyone,' said Nora. 'You're neither of you so untidy as all that! I think someone *has* been mean to you. Anyway, tidy your things, for goodness' sake.'

The girls set to work. They were both angry. They did not notice how pleased Kathleen looked. *Ah*, she thought, *so Elizabeth and Jenny thought that it was Robert who had played tricks! Good!* Nobody would think it was she, Kathleen, who had done them all. She felt much safer now.

The next School Meeting was not until Friday night. On Thursday something happened that disappointed Elizabeth very much. The lacrosse match was to be on Saturday, and she had been practising very hard indeed to be good enough to play in it. Only one of her form was to be chosen for the school team, and Elizabeth felt certain she would be the one.

But when she went to look at the noticeboard, on which were pinned notices of matches, rambles, and so on, she found that Robert's name was set down for the match instead of hers!

There it was – ROBERT JONES HAS BEEN CHOSEN FROM FORM THREE TO PLAY IN THE LACROSSE MATCH ON SATURDAY AGAINST KINELLAN SCHOOL.

There was a lump in Elizabeth's throat. She had tried so hard! She did so badly want to play. She was very good, really she was! And now that horrid, hateful Robert had been chosen instead of her. She could really hardly believe it.

'Never mind,' said Joan. 'You'll get a chance next time, I expect.'

'I *do* mind!' said Elizabeth fiercely. 'He will crow over me now. Oh, how I hope that the School Meeting will punish him well and say he's not to play in the match!'

Robert was delighted to see his name down, but for all his pleasure he was really very anxious indeed. He knew Elizabeth and Joan were going to report him at the Meeting and he was not looking forward to that. He was a little coward at heart, and he was afraid.

So, when Friday came Robert looked rather anxious. If only the Meeting was after Saturday, so that he could play in the match first! How marvellous that he had been chosen and not Elizabeth! Serve her right, the interfering girl!

The time for the Meeting came. The children took their places, looking rather solemn, for they knew it was going to be a serious one.

CHAPTER TWELVE

A VERY SERIOUS MEETING

EVEN THE smaller children felt rather solemn, as the whole school took their places in the big gym. Leslie had told everyone in his form that he was going to report the big boy, Robert, and some of the younger ones, who disliked Robert very much, had made up their minds that they too would tell about him if they had the chance.

'I should have told the truth about him when I was asked at the other Meeting,' said Peter. 'He did swing me much too high and made me sick – and afterwards he came to me and said he would open the door of my guinea pigs' cage and let them escape, if I dared to say anything against him. So I didn't dare. But I wish I had now.'

William and Rita looked rather grave as they took their places at the table up on the platform. Rita had told William of the mean tricks that had been played on Jenny to get her into trouble, and the two Judges knew that they might have a rather difficult time trying to get at the bottom of things. Still, Miss Belle and Miss Best and Mr Johns too were at the back of the room. They could help if things got too difficult.

Robert looked pale. Elizabeth was red with excitement and so was Jenny. Joan was excited too, though she didn't show it.

The usual business was done with the box of money. The two shillings were given to everyone, and extra was allowed to two children for something they wanted. Then the Meeting got down to the real business of the evening.

'Any complaints or grumbles?' asked William, tapping on the table with his hammer.

Up jumped Elizabeth and Leslie, both together.

'Elizabeth was first,' said Rita. 'Sit down, Leslie. Your turn will come later.'

Leslie sat down. Elizabeth began to speak, her words almost tumbling over one another in her haste.

'William and Rita, I have a very serious complaint to make,' she said. 'It's the same one as Leslie was going to make. It's about Robert.'

'Go on,' said William, with a grave face.

'You will remember that I reported him for bullying

Peter,' said Elizabeth. 'And because there wasn't enough proof of that, and because I lost my temper with Robert, the Meeting didn't punish Robert, and made me apologise to him. Well, listen to this!'

'Keep calm, Elizabeth,' said Rita. 'Don't get so excited.'

Elizabeth tried to speak calmly, but she did dislike Robert so much that it was difficult not to sound in a rage all the time.

'Well, William and Rita, Joan and I actually *saw* Robert bullying Leslie,' said Elizabeth. 'He made him sit on the hot-water pipes! And another thing we have found out is that he made Peter promise not to complain about being swung so high. He said he would let all Peter's guinea pigs out of their cage if Peter dared to say anything against him at the Meeting. I was quite right – he is a horrid bully!'

'Don't call people names like that,' said Rita. 'Wait till the whole Meeting has judged, Elizabeth. Have you anything more to say?'

'Yes, I have,' said Elizabeth. 'And it's this: not only has Robert been unkind to the younger ones, but he has been perfectly horrid to me and Jenny too. He has got us into all kinds of trouble by playing mean tricks on us.'

'What tricks?' asked William, looking very worried.

'Well, he took three of my books and hid them somewhere where I can't find them,' said Elizabeth. 'He took my garden tools and dirtied them so that John scolded me. He put two of Jenny's white mice into Miss Ranger's desk and they escaped, and Jenny never found them!'

'Is that true, Jenny?' asked William.

Jenny stood up. 'It's quite true,' she said. 'I never found my poor little mice again. I don't mind a trick being played on *me*, William, but it's cruel to play it on my pets.'

'Sit down, Jenny,' said William. He spoke to Rita, and then turned to the school again.

'Leslie, stand up and say what you have to say,' he said.

The cheeky little Leslie stood up. He felt rather important. He put his hands in his pockets, and began rather cheekily, 'Well, it was like this—'

But William cut him short. 'Take your hands out of your pockets, stand up properly and remember that this is a serious affair,' he said. Leslie took his hands out at once, and went red. He lost some of his cheeky look, and began to speak in a polite tone. He related exactly what had happened, and the Judges and Jury heard him patiently to the end.

'And now we should like to hear what Peter has to

say,' said Rita. The small Peter got up. His knees were shaking again, for he was greatly in awe of the head boy and girl. He stammered as he spoke.

'P-p-please, William and Rita, Robert d-d-*did* swing me too high that time,' he said. 'And I was sick afterwards.'

'Then why did you tell an untruth about it when we asked you?' asked William.

'Because I was afraid to tell the truth,' said poor Peter. 'I was afraid of Robert.'

'You must never be a coward,' said William gently. 'It is much finer to be brave, Peter. If you had been brave and had told the truth, we could have stopped Robert from bullying others. Because you were afraid, you have been the cause of others being ill-treated, and you made us disbelieve Elizabeth, and made her unhappy. Remember to tell the truth always, no matter how hard it seems at the time. We shall all think much more of you if you do.'

'Yes, William,' said Peter, making up his mind that he would never be a coward again.

'You could have told your monitor about it, even if you were afraid to tell the Meeting,' said William. 'That is why we choose monitors – because we hope that their common sense will help us. Sit down, Peter.'

Peter sank down, glad that he hadn't to say any

more. William looked at Robert, who was sitting, looking sulky and unhappy.

'And now, Robert, what have you to say?' he asked. 'Serious complaints have been made against you. Are they true?'

'Only one complaint is true,' said Robert, standing up. He spoke in such a low voice that the Jury could not hear him.

'Speak up,' said William. 'What do you mean – only one complaint is true? Which complaint?'

'It is quite true that I made Leslie sit on the hot-water pipes,' said Robert, 'but anyway they weren't very hot. But I did *not* play any tricks on Elizabeth and Jenny. Not one! Not one!'

'Oooh!' said Elizabeth. 'You did, Robert! I saw how pleased you were each time I got into trouble!'

'Silence, Elizabeth!' said William. 'Robert, you say you did not play the tricks that Elizabeth described. Now, you did not tell us the truth last time, when you told us about Peter and the swing. It will be difficult for us to believe you this time, because we shall all think that again you may be telling us untruths to get yourself out of trouble.'

'Well, I *am* telling the truth this time!' said Robert fiercely. 'I didn't play those tricks. I don't know who did – I jolly well know *I* didn't! I don't like Elizabeth,

I think she's a horrid, interfering girl, but I'm not mean enough to play tricks like that to get her into trouble – and why should I play tricks on Jenny? I don't dislike Jenny. I tell you, somebody else is to blame for those tricks.'

Most unfortunately for Robert, there was not one person in the school, except Kathleen, of course, who believed him. They all remembered that he had told an untruth before, and they felt certain that he was doing so again. William knocked on the table with his hammer, for the children had begun to whisper together.

'Silence!' he said. 'Now, we have a very serious matter to attend to. Three charges have been made against one boy. First, that he bullies children smaller than himself. Second, that he has played mean tricks to get two girls into trouble. Third, that he tells untruths. The Jury and Rita and I are going to discuss the matter to see what must be done about this, and the rest of you can also discuss it among yourselves, so that if anyone has a good idea, they may bring it forward in a few minutes.'

The school began to chatter. The Jury and the Judges talked together in low tones. They all looked extremely serious. Robert sat by himself, for the boys next to him had gone to talk to the children behind. He felt dreadful. Why, oh why had he been stupid enough to bully the younger ones? Why must he always be so unkind to the little ones? Now perhaps he would be sent home and his mother and father would be very angry and upset.

Miss Belle and Miss Best looked very serious too. Mr Johns said a few words to them, and then the three of them waited to see what the Judges would say. They never interfered with the School Meeting unless they were asked to.

After a little while Rita and William knocked on the table for silence. The whole school sat up. Surely the Judges and Jury hadn't decided so quickly! What were they going to say?

'Miss Belle and Miss Best and Mr Johns, we feel we would like your help today,' said William gravely. 'Would you please give us your advice?'

'Of course,' said Miss Best, and the three of them came up on to the platform. And then began a strange talk that was going to make all the difference to Robert's school life!

CHAPTER THIRTEEN

ROBERT GETS A CHANCE

THE WHOLE school was now looking very solemn and serious. Not a smile was to be seen anywhere. Everyone stopped talking as the three teachers took their places on the platform, on chairs that the Jury quickly fetched for them.

'The matter had better be openly discussed,' said Miss Belle. 'Let us take one complaint at a time. First of all, this question of bullying the smaller ones. Now, have we ever had any cases of bullying since you became our Judges, William and Rita?'

'No,' said William. 'But I remember there was a case when I was much lower down in the school. Will it be in the Book?'

The Book was a record of all the complaints made by the children, and of how they had been dealt with, and what the results were. It lay on the table, a big brown volume half full of small writing. Each Judge had to enter in a report of the Meetings held, because Miss Belle and Miss Best said that sometime the Book might be a great help. Now William took up the Book and began to look back through the pages.

At last he found what he wanted. 'Here it is,' he said. 'A girl called Lucy Ronald was accused of bullying younger children.'

'Yes, I remember,' said Miss Belle. 'We found out the cause of her bullying. Read it, William, and see what it was. It may help us with Robert.'

William read it quickly to himself. Then he looked up. 'It says here that it was found out that Lucy had been an only girl for seven years, and then she had twin baby brothers brought to live with her in her nursery,' he said. 'And her mother and father gave all their attention to them, and so did the nurse, so that Lucy felt left out. She hated the babies because she thought that her parents gave them the love they had always given to her.'

'Go on,' said Miss Belle.

'Well, she couldn't hurt the babies because they were never left alone,' said William. 'So she worked off her feelings of dislike and jealousy on other children – she always chose the smaller ones because they couldn't hit back, and because they were small like her baby brothers.'

'And I suppose the habit grew and grew until she couldn't stop it,' said Rita, interested. 'Is that how bullies are made, Miss Belle?'

'It's one of the commonest ways,' said the headmistress. 'But now we must find out if Robert's fault is caused in the same way.'

The whole school had been listening with great interest to this discussion. Everybody knew what a bully was, and nobody liked bullies at all. The children looked at Robert to see if he was listening too. He was. He gazed at William, and didn't miss a word.

'Well,' said Mr Johns, 'we'll find out if Robert has anything to say now. Robert, have you any brothers or sisters?'

'I've two brothers, five years and four years younger than I am,' answered Robert.

'Did you like them when they were small?' asked William.

'No, I didn't,' said Robert. 'They took up everybody's time, and I didn't have a look in. Then I got ill, and nobody seemed to bother about me as they used to do, and I knew it was because of James and John, my little brothers. Well, when I got better, I just seemed to hate little children, and I began to pinch them and be unkind to them. I pretended they were James and John. I couldn't do it to them because nobody would let me, and I would have got into such a row.'

'And so a bully was made!' said Mr Johns. 'You made war on other children because you couldn't get rid of the two small brothers whom you thought took your place at home! Poor Robert! You make yourself much more unhappy than you make others.'

'Well, people have called me a bully ever since I was about five,' said Robert sullenly. 'So I thought I was one – something that couldn't be helped and that I couldn't stop!'

'Well, it can be helped, and you can stop it yourself,' said Miss Best. 'You see, Robert, once you understand how a bad habit began, and how it grows, you also understand how to tackle it. Now that we know why you became a bully, I am sure that none of us really blames you. It was just unlucky for you. You aren't really a bully – you are just an ordinary boy who took up bullying because you were jealous of two small brothers. You can stop any time, and change to something that is *really* you!'

'I remember being awfully jealous of my little sister,' said Belinda. 'I know how Robert felt.'

'So do I,' said Kenneth. 'It's a horrid feeling.'

'Well, it's quite a natural one,' said Miss Belle. 'Most of us grow out of it, but some don't. Robert just hasn't, but he will now that he sees clearly what has happened. It isn't anything very dreadful, Robert. But doesn't it seem rather silly to you that a boy of your age should be teasing and bullying Peter and Leslie just because years ago a feeling of jealousy grew up in your heart for your two young brothers? It's time you put all that behind you, don't you think so?'

'Yes, it is,' said Robert, feeling as if a light had suddenly been lit in the darkness of his mind. 'I'm *not* really a bully. I want to be kind to people and animals. I didn't know why I was the opposite – but now that I do know it will be easy to change. I feel different about it already. I'm sorry I was so beastly to other children all these years. But I'm afraid no one will trust me now – they won't help me!'

'Yes, we will, Robert,' said Rita earnestly. 'That is the great thing about Whyteleafe School – that we are all willing to help one another. There isn't a boy or girl in this school who would refuse to help you, or to give you a chance to show that you are quite different from what you have seemed.'

'What about Elizabeth?' said Robert at once.

'Well, we'll ask her,' said Rita. 'Elizabeth, what do *you* think about it?'

Elizabeth got up. Her mind was in a whirl. So Robert the bully wasn't really a bully – he was only a boy who had got a wrong idea about himself because of something that had happened years ago. It seemed very strange. Was it true? She didn't believe that Robert would change! And what about all those horrid tricks that had been played on her and on Jenny?

'Well—' said Elizabeth, and stopped. 'Well, of course I'll help if Robert wants to try. After all, you all helped *me* last term when I was dreadful. But I can't forgive him for playing those mean tricks on me and Jenny. I think he should be punished for those.'

'I tell you I didn't do them!' burst out Robert.

'Somebody must have done them,' said Rita. 'If Robert didn't do them, who was it? Is the boy or girl brave enough to own up?'

Nobody said a word. Kathleen went red, but looked down at the floor. She had begun to feel rather dreadful now that Robert had been accused of her tricks.

'William and Rita, you didn't believe me before when I complained about Robert,' said Elizabeth. 'And I was right. It isn't fair of you not to believe me now. I'm sure I'm right.'

The Jury and Judges talked together. They found it very hard to decide anything. Then William spoke.

'Well, Elizabeth, you may be right. We did not believe you last time – and this time we will not believe Robert. We will try to make things fair between you by saying that you may play in the match tomorrow instead of Robert. Nora says that you were disappointed that you were not chosen.'

'Oh, thank you!' said Elizabeth, thrilled.

Robert stood up. He looked unhappy.

'Very well,' he said. 'I quite see that it's my turn to give way to Elizabeth this time, as she had to apologise to me last time when I told untruths. But I do say again and again that I didn't play those tricks.'

'We won't say any more about that,' said William. 'Now, Robert, we've been talking about how we can help you. Mr Johns says that the best thing we can do for you is to let you take care of something or somebody, so that it's easy for kindness to take the place of unkindness. You love horses, don't you?'

'Oh, yes!' said Robert eagerly.

'Well, although your form are not allowed to have anything to do with the horses except ride them, we are going to make another rule just for you,' said William. 'You will choose two of the horses and make them your special care. You will feed them, water them and groom them. When your class goes riding, you may choose one of the younger children to ride the second horse and help them all you can.'

Robert listened as if he could not believe his ears. Good gracious! Choose two horses for his own special pets – look after them each day! This was a thing he had always longed to do, for of all animals the boy loved horses best – loved them with all his heart. He felt as if he could weep for joy. He didn't care about not playing in the match now! He didn't care about anything. He felt a different boy.

'Thank you *awfully*, William,' said Robert in a rather choky voice. 'You can trust me to take care of the horses – and you can bet I'll choose those kids that I've teased to take out riding first!'

'We thought you'd do that,' said Rita, pleased. 'Let us know at the next Meeting how you've got on, Robert. We shall all want to know.'

'I'll go riding with you, Robert!' called a small boy's voice. It was Peter. He had listened hard to everything that had been said, and in his generous heart he wanted to help Robert. He also felt a little guilty – for he remembered how once he had been jealous of his small sister and had shoved her when no one was looking. Good gracious, he might have turned into an unhappy bully like Robert!

'The Meeting must really break up now,' said Miss Belle. 'It has taken a long time and it is past the bedtime of the younger ones. But I think we all feel tonight that we have learnt something big – and once again you children have the chance of helping one of yourselves. It is grand to be helped, but it is even grander to help!'

'The Meeting is dismissed!' cried William, and knocked on the table with his hammer.

The children filed out, rather serious, but happy and satisfied. A difficult problem had been solved, and they were pleased.

Only one child was neither happy nor pleased. And that child, of course, was Kathleen! Robert had lost his place in the match because of her. Every child in the school was going to help him – but Kathleen had harmed him.

She was very miserable. But whatever could she do about it?

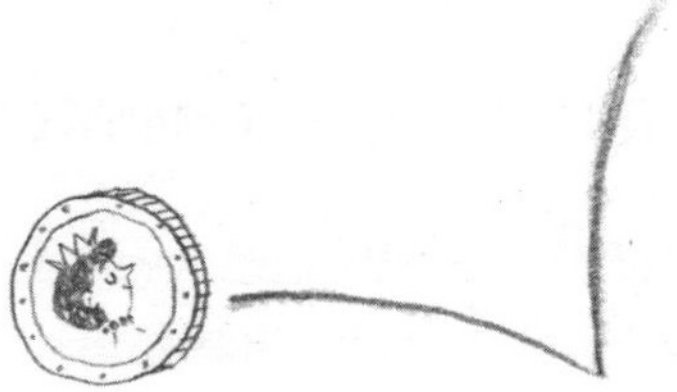

CHAPTER FOURTEEN

THE DAY OF THE MATCH

THE NEXT day was Saturday, the day of the lacrosse match. Elizabeth woke up early, and looked eagerly at the window. Was it a fine day?

It wasn't very fine. There were clouds across the sky. But at least it wasn't raining. Good! What fun it would be to play in her first match!

'Jenny!' whispered Elizabeth, as she heard the girl move in her bed. 'Jenny! It's the day of the match – and I'm playing instead of Robert!'

Jenny grunted. She wasn't sure if she was very pleased that Elizabeth should crow over Robert like that. Jenny thought Robert should certainly be punished, but crowing over him was another thing altogether.

Kathleen was awake too. She heard what Elizabeth said, and she felt guilty. She had thought that it was fine for another child to take the blame and the punishment for something she herself had done, but somehow she didn't feel like that now. Also she was angry that Elizabeth should have the pleasure of playing in the match – for she did dislike Elizabeth so very much! What a nuisance everything was!

And what about Robert? Well, Robert also awoke early, and he remembered at once all that had happened the night before. He sat up in bed, his eyes shining, as he thought of the two horses he would choose for his own special care. He felt quite different. It didn't matter now a bit that the whole school knew he had been a bully – because they also knew it wasn't really his fault, and in a week or two he would be able to show them what he really was. What a surprise they would get!

He remembered the lacrosse match, and a little sinking feeling came into his heart as he remembered that Elizabeth was to take his place.

I'd like to have played in the match, he thought to himself. *And it is jolly hard that the Meeting gave me that punishment for something I really didn't do, but I suppose they had to believe Elizabeth this time. I must put up with it and hope that the person who's really playing those tricks will be found out sometime. Then everyone will be jolly sorry they punished me for nothing!*

He sat and thought for a while, his chin on his knees. *Elizabeth is a funny girl. She's so fierce and downright, so keen on being fair and just – and yet she's been awfully unfair to me. She might know I wouldn't play mean tricks like that. I don't like her at all.*

Robert half made up his mind that he wouldn't speak to Elizabeth at all, or have anything to do with her. Then, as he thought of the lovely time he was going to have looking after the horses, his heart softened, and he couldn't feel hard even to Elizabeth! And anyway he was going to show everyone that he could be kind just as easily as unkind.

'I know what I'll do!' he said to himself. 'I'll go and watch the match – and if Elizabeth shoots a goal I'll cheer like the rest. That will be a hard thing for me to do, but I'll do it just to show everyone I can!'

Robert got up before the others in his dormitory that morning. He slipped out and went to the stables. He would talk to the two horses he was going to care for – and he would go riding over the hills on his favourite. He felt proud and important as he unlocked the stable door and spoke to the stableman.

'Can I talk to Bessie and Captain?' he asked. 'I've got permission to look after them.'

'Yes, I've been told,' said the man. 'All right – but I'll have to oversee your work with them the first week, young man. After that, if you're all right, you can carry on.'

Robert heard running footsteps and looked out into the yard. He saw Leonard and Fanny hurrying to the cowsheds. They were going to milk the cows. They saw him and shouted, 'Hallo, Robert! Have you chosen your horses yet?'

'Rather!' said Robert. 'Come and see the two that are going to be mine! Look, this is old Bess – she's a darling. And this is Captain. Rub his nose.'

Leonard and Fanny looked at the two horses and then they looked at Robert. They stared at him so hard that Robert was puzzled.

'What's the matter?' he said. 'Have I got a smut on my nose, or something?'

'No,' said Fanny. 'But you do look different, Robert. You used to look so horrid – sort of sulky and mean – but now you're smiling and your eyes are all shiny. We're staring because it seems rather strange to see somebody change in a night! Come and see our cows! Would you like a glass of warm milk?'

The children linked their arms in Robert's and pulled him over to the cowsheds, where the patient cows stood waiting to be milked. They chattered and laughed as they went, and Robert felt warmed by their friendly talk and looks. He began to chatter too, and soon he was standing drinking a glass of warm, creamy milk from the first cow.

This is fun! he thought. *I'll see Leonard and Fanny each morning when I come to look after my horses. I shall soon make friends!*

In five minutes' time he was galloping over the hills by himself, enjoying the wind in his hair and the bump of the horse's back beneath him. He talked to Bess, and she pricked back her ears to listen. All horses loved Robert. He had never had a great deal to do with them before, and now it seemed to him almost too good to be true to think that he could have as much to do with them as he liked.

'After tea I'll ask young Peter if he'd like to come riding on Captain,' he planned. 'I'll soon make that kid forget all about the teasing I gave him.'

Everyone who met Robert that morning had a grin for him, or a clap on the back. The whole school was keeping its word!

Neither Kathleen nor Elizabeth met him, for both girls were busy. Elizabeth was digging with John in the garden, and Kathleen had gone with some others for a nature ramble. Elizabeth was chattering to John about the match.

'It's a bit of luck for me that I'm playing, isn't it?' she said. 'I was so disappointed when I saw Robert's name up on the board, instead of mine.'

'I expect Robert is feeling just as disappointed

now,' said John, digging hard.

'Well, it serves him right,' said Elizabeth. 'He's been jolly mean to me and Jenny. Think how he dirtied my tools one night, John – and you blamed *me* for it.'

'I'm sorry I blamed you wrongly,' said John. 'I only hope you are right about Robert, Elizabeth, and that *he* is not being blamed for something he hasn't done either.'

'Well, he's a horrid boy anyhow,' said Elizabeth. 'I'm glad he's out of the match. I bet he won't come anywhere near it. He'll be so ashamed that he's not playing after all!'

But that was just where Elizabeth was quite wrong!

The children playing the match had to change into their gym clothes immediately after lunch. The matches usually began at half past two, so they hadn't a great deal of time. Kinellan School was arriving by bus at twenty past two, and the Whyteleafe team had to be at the gate to meet them and welcome them.

Elizabeth could hardly eat any lunch, she was so excited. She stole a look at Robert, and saw that he was looking quite happy. Elizabeth pushed her potatoes to the side of her plate.

'Miss Ranger! I just can't eat any more. I'm so excited!'

'Well, for once you may leave what's on your plate,' said Miss Ranger, smiling. 'I know what it feels like to be playing in your very first match.'

Elizabeth rushed off with the others to change. Then

she went to welcome the Kinellan team, and take them to the field. They put their clothes in the pavilion there.

'Look – almost the whole school has turned out to watch!' said Elizabeth to Nora, as she saw the children streaming up from the school.

'And there's Robert too!' said Nora, as she caught sight of him coming along with the others.

'Where?' asked Elizabeth in surprise. Then she saw him. Good gracious! Robert had come to watch the match he had hoped to play in! He had come to watch somebody play instead of him! The little girl could hardly believe her eyes. She suddenly felt rather small and ashamed. She knew she wouldn't have been able to do such a generous thing if she had been in Robert's place.

'I call it jolly decent of Robert to come and watch you play in his place,' said Nora. 'I think that's a big and generous thing to do. It's funny that a boy able to do a big thing like that should be mean enough to play horrid tricks. It makes me wonder if he really did do them after all.'

Elizabeth picked up her lacrosse stick. She had felt so sure Robert wouldn't come near the match. She was quite wrong. And now suppose that, as Nora said, Robert hadn't done all the things she thought he had – suppose he was being punished unfairly? And all because of her! It wasn't a very nice feeling.

'Oh, well, never mind! I'm jolly well going to enjoy my first match!' said Elizabeth to herself, and she ran out of the pavilion into the field.

But what a disappointment – it was beginning to rain! The teams stared up into the sky in dismay. Surely the rain wasn't going to be much? Surely it would soon stop? It would be too bad if they couldn't play.

The children all crowded into the pavilion to wait. The rain fell more and more steadily. It pelted down. The clouds became lower and blacker – there really was no hope at all!

'I'm afraid the match is off,' said Mr Warlow. 'Go to the gym and we'll arrange games for the visiting team.'

The children ran helter-skelter to the school. Elizabeth ran too, sadly disappointed. It was too bad! Her very first match, and the rain had spoilt it!

A voice spoke in her ear. 'Elizabeth! Bad luck! I'm sorry!'

The girl turned – and saw that it was Robert who had spoken! He had run off to join the others, so she couldn't answer. Elizabeth stood still, astonished. *Robert!* Fancy *Robert* saying that! She simply couldn't understand it.

'Elizabeth! Do you want to be soaked to the skin?' cried Miss Ranger's voice. 'What are you doing standing out there like that? Come along at once, you silly child!'

And into the school with the others Elizabeth went, very much puzzled, and not knowing quite what to do about it!

CHAPTER FIFTEEN

KATHLEEN OWNS UP

EVERYBODY WAS disappointed that the match was off, especially the players themselves.

The rain poured down all the afternoon. Mr Johns and Miss Ranger got some games going in the gym, and the visitors enjoyed themselves thoroughly.

Joan was sorry for Elizabeth's disappointment. She slipped her arm through her friend's. 'Elizabeth, never mind! There's another match next Saturday. Maybe you'll be able to play in that instead.'

'Perhaps,' said Elizabeth. 'But it really *is* bad luck that it rained today. I've been practising so hard, and really I'm getting quite good at catching the ball and shooting at goal!'

'I guess Robert was pleased that it rained so that you couldn't play,' said Joan.

'Well, Joan, that's the funny part. He was there

to watch – and when it rained and we all went off the field he came up and said it was bad luck and he was sorry,' said Elizabeth. 'I really was surprised. And somehow I felt rather mean.'

'Wait till he plays a few more tricks, then you won't feel so mean!' said Joan.

But no more tricks were played. Kathleen hadn't the heart to think of any more. She had seen somebody else publicly punished for her own wrongdoing, and she was beginning to despise herself. She hated Jenny and Elizabeth, but it was a miserable sort of feeling now, not a fierce red-hot feeling.

I'm a dreadful person! thought Kathleen in despair. *I'm plain and spotty and pale. I'm dull and slow, and now I'm mean and deceitful and cowardly! That's the worst of beginning to do horrid things – they make you feel horrid yourself, and then you can't ever be happy any more. I'm not fit to be at a school like Whyteleafe, where the children are happy and jolly – and where even a boy like Robert, who's been hateful to others, can turn over a new leaf and begin again!*

Poor Kathleen! It had seemed such fun, and so clever, at first, to think out nasty little tricks to get Jenny and Elizabeth into trouble – but, now that she had found that mean ways make a mean person, she hated herself.

And it's much worse to hate yourself than it is to hate

somebody else, thought Kathleen. *Because you can never get away from yourself. I wish I was a happy honest sort of person like Nora or John.*

Kathleen was really unhappy. She went about looking so miserable that the girls felt sorry for her.

'Don't you feel well?' asked Elizabeth.

'I'm all right,' said Kathleen, and walked off with her head drooping like a sad little dog.

'What's up, Kathleen? For goodness' sake smile a bit!' cried Belinda. 'You're enough to turn the milk sour! Have you had bad news from home, or something?'

'No,' said Kathleen. 'I just don't feel like smiling, that's all. Leave me alone.'

Her work was so bad that Miss Ranger began to be worried. What in the world could be the matter with the girl? She looked as if she was worrying about something. Miss Ranger managed to get Kathleen alone for a few minutes, and spoke to her gently.

'Kathleen, my dear – is there anything wrong? Your work has gone to pieces this week, and you look so miserable. Can't you tell me what's wrong? I may be able to help.'

Kathleen felt the tears coming into her eyes when she heard Miss Ranger speaking to her so kindly. She turned her head away.

'Nobody can help,' she said in a funny muffled voice.

'Everything's gone wrong. And nothing and nobody can put it right.'

'My dear child, there are very few things that can't be put right, if only you will give somebody a chance to help,' said Miss Ranger. 'Come now, Kathleen – what's wrong?'

But Kathleen wouldn't tell her. She shook her head obstinately, and Miss Ranger gave it up. She could not like Kathleen, but she felt very sorry for her.

Then Kathleen made up her mind to do a very foolish thing. She would run away – right away home – but first she would tell Elizabeth and Jenny all she had done. She would confess to them, so that Robert would be cleared of blame. She could at least do that. She wouldn't despise herself quite so much if she owned up.

Though it will be awfully difficult, thought poor Kathleen. *They will look at me in such a horrid way – they will call me names and everyone in the school will know how awful I have been. But still, I shall have run away by then, so I shan't mind.*

That evening, after tea, Kathleen went up to Jenny. 'Jenny,' she said, 'I want to speak to you and Elizabeth alone. Where's Elizabeth?'

'She's in the gym,' said Jenny, surprised. 'We'll go and get her. What do you want, Kathleen?'

'I'll tell you when Elizabeth is with us,' said Kathleen.

'We'll go into one of the music practice rooms. We'll be alone there.'

Very much puzzled, Jenny went with Kathleen to find Elizabeth. They soon found her and called her. Elizabeth went with them, surprised and rather impatient, because she had been having some fun with Belinda and Richard.

Kathleen closed the door and faced the other two. 'I've got something to say to you both,' she said. 'I've been very unhappy, and I can't bear it any more, so I'm going to go home. But before I go I want to own up to something. Don't blame Robert for all those tricks – *I* did them all!'

Elizabeth and Jenny stared at Kathleen as if they couldn't believe their ears. *Kathleen* had done all those things – hidden the books, taken Jenny's mice, dirtied the garden tools, muddled the drawers? Oh, the horrid, horrid creature!

'I knew you would look at me like that,' said Kathleen, tears beginning to trickle down her cheeks. 'I expect I deserve it. But, before I go, I'd like to tell you something else. You're both pretty and jolly and clever, and everyone likes you. I'm plain and pale and spotty and dull, and I can't help it. But you don't know how I'd *like* to be like you! I envy you, and I can't help disliking you because you're all the things I'm not. You were very unkind once,

Jenny, when you imitated Mam'zelle and me having a quarrel, but . . .'

'I'm sorry about that,' said Jenny at once. 'I didn't know you'd come into the room. I don't wonder you wanted to pay me out for that, Kathleen. But you shouldn't have got Elizabeth into trouble too.'

'Well, I've paid myself out too!' said Kathleen. 'I don't like myself any more than *you* like me. I know I'm simply horrid, and that's why I'm going home. My mother loves me, even though I'm not as pretty and nice as other girls are. And she will perhaps understand and forgive me for running away.'

There was a silence. Elizabeth and Jenny simply did not know what to say. They were shocked at Kathleen's confession – and Elizabeth especially felt very angry because she had blamed Robert for things he hadn't done, and that was terrible.

'Well, Kathleen, all I can say is it's a jolly good thing you had the sense to own up,' said Jenny at last. 'I think more of you for that. But, my goodness, you're a spiteful, mean person, I must say! Don't you think so, Elizabeth?'

'Yes, I do,' said Elizabeth. 'And you've made me get Robert into trouble – and I'll have all that to put right. I wish to goodness you'd never come to Whyteleafe School, Kathleen!'

'I wish it too,' said Kathleen in a low voice. 'But I shan't be here much longer!'

She opened the door and slipped away down the passage. She went to the stairs and ran up, tears pouring down her face. She had owned up – and it had been even worse than she had expected! Now she would get her things and go.

Elizabeth stared at Jenny, and the two were just going to talk about Kathleen's confession when Joan came along. 'Hallo!' she said in surprise. 'What are you two doing here, looking so fierce? What's happened?'

Elizabeth poured everything out to Joan. 'Now don't you think Kathleen is a mean, deceitful, spiteful girl?' she cried. 'I'd never have thought anyone could be so horrid.'

Joan looked thoughtful. She remembered how unhappy and lonely she herself had once been in the summer term, when everything had gone wrong. She could guess how Kathleen felt. And how very miserable she must be to think of running away!

'Look here,' said Joan. 'Don't think of how mean and spiteful Kathleen's been. Think instead of how it must feel to be plain and jealous and dull, as Kathleen is, and to be unhappy and ashamed as well! Elizabeth, you were helped last term, and I was helped too. I'm going to help Kathleen! She hasn't been mean to me, so I don't feel angry about things as you do. I just feel sorry.'

She ran out of the room. Jenny looked at Elizabeth. They both knew at once that Joan was right. They had been thinking of themselves, and not of a miserable girl who needed comfort and help. 'We'd better go along too,' said Jenny.

'Wait till Joan's had time to say a few words,' said Elizabeth. 'She's awfully good at that sort of thing, you know. I sometimes think she's almost wise enough to be a monitor!'

'Well, we certainly are *not*,' said Jenny. 'I can't imagine how this can be put right, Elizabeth. I really can't.'

Meanwhile, Joan ran up the stairs to her dormitory. Kathleen was there, putting on her hat and coat, and packing a few things into a small case. Joan went straight up to her.

'Kathleen! I've heard all about it! You were brave to own up. Wait till Jenny and Elizabeth have had time to get over it, and they'll forgive you and be friends. They are kind and generous really, you know – just give them time.'

'I can't stop at Whyteleafe,' said Kathleen, putting on her scarf. 'It's not only that I've made enemies. I feel that everybody thinks I'm so awful. Look at your hair, all shiny and nice – mine's like rats' tails! Look at your bright eyes and red cheeks, and then look at me! I'm a sort of Cinderella!'

'Do you remember how Cinderella changed one night?' said Joan, taking Kathleen's hand. 'She sat in the cinders and moped, and maybe she looked just as plain and miserable as you do. But it wasn't just beautiful clothes and a coach that made her so different all of a sudden! Don't you think she smiled and looked happy? Don't you think she brushed her hair till it shone? What a silly girl you are, Kathleen! Do you know that you look sweet when you smile?'

'I don't,' said Kathleen obstinately.

'Well, you do,' said Joan. 'Your eyes light up then, your mouth turns up and you get a dimple in your left cheek. If you smiled a lot more, you wouldn't be plain long. Nobody's ugly when they smile. Haven't you noticed that, Kathleen?'

'Perhaps you are right about that,' said Kathleen, remembering how sweet her mother always looked when she smiled and was happy. 'But I never feel very much like smiling.'

Footsteps came up the passage and Elizabeth and Jenny came into the room. They went up to Kathleen.

'We weren't very nice to you just now,' said Jenny. 'We're sorry. Don't run away, Kathleen. We'll forgive you and forget all you did to us.'

'But Robert would have to be cleared from blame,' said Kathleen, 'and that means everything going before the School Meeting. I'm sorry, but I'm not brave enough for that!'

The girls looked at one another. Yes, of course the matter would have to be discussed there!

'So I'm going!' said Kathleen. 'I'm a coward, I know. But I can't help that. Where's my case? Goodbye, all of you – don't think too unkindly of me, *please*!'

CHAPTER SIXTEEN

KATHLEEN RUNS AWAY

KATHLEEN PICKED up her case and went out of the room. Joan ran after her and took hold of her arm.

'Kathleen! Don't be an idiot! You just can't run away from school! It's impossible!'

'It's not impossible,' said Kathleen. 'I'm doing it! Don't try to stop me, Joan. I'm going to walk down to the station to get the train.'

She shook off Joan's hand and ran down the passage. It wasn't a bit of good going after her. She had made up her mind, and nothing would stop her. The three girls stared after her.

'I feel simply awful about this,' said Jenny suddenly, in a trembling voice. 'I wish I hadn't imitated Mam'zelle and Kathleen that evening. That's what began all the trouble.'

'What are we going to do?' said Joan in a troubled

voice. 'We'll have to report that Kathleen has run away. But I can't help feeling that it's no good trying to stop her in any way, because honestly *I* wouldn't want to face the School Meeting as she would have to do when everything comes out. She'd probably run away after that, if she didn't now! She's not a brave person at all.'

Just then Nora came by. She was surprised to see the three girls standing at the door of their dormitory, looking so worried.

'What are you here for?' she asked. 'Didn't you know that the concert is beginning in a minute? You'd better hurry. *Why* are you all looking so solemn? Has anything happened?'

'Well, yes,' said Elizabeth. 'An awful lot has happened. We don't know what to do about it. It's dreadful, Nora.'

'Good gracious! You'd better tell me about it then, as I'm your monitor,' said Nora.

'I think we'd like to,' said Jenny. 'Don't let's go to the concert, Nora. Let's go to the common room. It will be empty now and we can tell you what's happened.'

Once a week a concert was given by those children who learnt the piano, the violin, singing or reciting, and usually most of the school attended, for it was fun to hear their own forms playing or singing. So the common room was empty when the four girls walked into it.

Jenny told the tale. She told it from the very beginning and, although she went red when she related how she had imitated Mam'zelle and Kathleen, she did not miss out anything. She was a truthful, honest girl, willing to take her fair share of any blame. Nora listened gravely.

'Poor old Kathleen!' she said. 'She *has* made a mess of things. Well, we've got to do something about it, but I daren't say what. We must find Rita and get her to come to Miss Belle and Miss Best with us.'

'Oh, goodness! Will they have to know?' asked Elizabeth in dismay.

'Of course, idiot! You don't suppose a girl can run away from Whyteleafe without the heads knowing, do you?' said Nora. 'Come on – there's no time to be lost.'

They found Rita in her study. 'Rita! Could you come with us to Miss Belle and Miss Best?' asked Nora. 'A girl in Elizabeth's form has run away, and we think we ought to tell the whole story to the heads.'

'Of course!' said Rita, looking startled. 'We'd better take William along too. It's a thing he probably ought to know about, and it will save time if he comes now.'

So in a few minutes six people were outside the drawing room where the two headmistresses were sitting writing letters. Rita knocked.

'Come in,' said a quiet voice, and in they all went.

Mr Johns was there too, and the three teachers looked surprised to see such a crowd of children appearing.

'Is anything the matter?' asked Miss Belle at once.

'There is rather,' said Rita. 'Elizabeth, tell the story quickly.'

So Elizabeth told it all, and when she came to where Kathleen had packed a small case and gone down to the station Mr Johns jumped up at once.

'I must go after her,' he said. 'I hope I shan't be too late.'

'But the train will have gone!' said Nora.

'They have been altered this month,' said Mr Johns. 'The one Kathleen went to catch doesn't run now – it's an hour later. If I go quickly, I can just get the child. Come with me, Rita.'

The two of them went out of the room, and in a moment or two the front door banged. They were gone. Elizabeth hoped and hoped that they would be able to catch poor Kathleen before she went home. Now that the heads knew everything she felt happier. Grown-ups always seemed to be able to put things right!

'Two things need to be put right, as far as I can see,' said Miss Best. 'The first thing is to put Kathleen right with herself, and make her see that running away never solves any difficulty at all, but only makes things worse. She thinks herself a failure, poor child, but no one need ever be that. If we can get that idea out of her head, things won't seem so bad to her.'

'And I know what the second thing is,' said Elizabeth in a low voice. 'It's to clear Robert of blame. I do hate to think I accused him unjustly – and he really has been decent about it. I feel terribly ashamed.'

'I am glad you feel ashamed, Elizabeth,' said Miss Best. 'We all know that you are just and honest by nature, but you will never do anything worthwhile if you rush at things impatiently and lose your temper.'

'No, I know. I'm doing my best to learn that,' said Elizabeth. 'But you've no idea how difficult it is, Miss Best.'

'Oh, yes, I have!' said Miss Best. 'I once had a hot temper too!'

She smiled her lovely smile, and the five children thought what a nice person she was. None of them could really believe that she had ever had a bad temper.

'Now what are we going to do with Kathleen if Mr Johns is able to bring her back?' said Miss Belle. 'I almost think that William and Rita would be the best people to deal with her. She would not be so much in awe of them as she would be of me or of Miss Best or Mr Johns.'

'She said she couldn't possibly face the School Meeting when they knew of her mean tricks,' said

Elizabeth. 'She isn't very brave – though sometimes she argues in class in a way I simply wouldn't dare to do.'

'That isn't bravery,' said Miss Belle. 'It's a thing that weak, obstinate people often do. They are always so afraid of being thought poor things that they like to draw attention to themselves in some way – by arguing or quarrelling or boasting – anything that will make people listen to them and take notice of them! You will never find strong, wise people quarrelling or boasting or trying to get attention – only the weak ones. It's a sign of weakness of some sort – and in Kathleen's case it meant that she thought herself a failure and was trying to hide it from herself and from the rest of you. Now she can't hide it any more and she has run away – just what you would expect a weak person to do.'

'Things seem sort of different when they are properly explained, don't they?' said Jenny. 'I'd never have mimicked Kathleen as I did if I'd known why she was behaving like that. Now I feel so sorry for her that I'd do anything to get things put right.'

'She's ashamed of her spots even,' said Elizabeth. 'She's only got them because she eats so many sweets! She eats more than the whole form put together!'

'She looks nice when she smiles,' said Joan. 'I told her so.'

'Good!' said Miss Best. 'It seems to me that if only

Kathleen would make herself neater and prettier, and get rid of her spots, poor child, that would be a good beginning. William, do you think you and Rita can manage to get some sense into her head? You have had some difficult problems this term, but I believe you will manage them all right!'

'And what about making her face the School Meeting?' asked William.

'You and Rita must decide that,' said Miss Belle. 'We leave that in your hands. If you think it best not to force her to be brave before she is ready, then you must just clear Robert of blame, and wait until Kathleen is brave enough to own up later on in the term. I am quite sure that if we handle her gently she will do the right thing in the future.'

It was surprising how much better everyone felt already, now that the matter had been plainly discussed and looked into. Kathleen's bad behaviour had grown from a very simple thing – the feeling that she was a failure. If that feeling could be put right, most of Kathleen's troubles would go. And that would be pleasant for everyone!

There came the sound of wheels in the school drive. Then the sound of a car door banging. Surely it must be a taxi! Everybody waited anxiously to see if Mr Johns and Rita had been able to bring back Kathleen

– and everyone hoped they had.

Footsteps came down the passage to the drawing room and the door opened. Only Mr Johns stood there! No Rita, no Kathleen!

'Didn't you find her?' asked Miss Best anxiously.

'Oh, yes!' said Mr Johns. 'She was in the waiting room, poor child, cold and miserable, wishing that she hadn't run away after all! When Rita went in and took her hand, she burst into tears, and came back with us quite willingly. Thank goodness the trains had been altered, and she had had time to think a little. If the train had come in as soon as she had arrived on the platform, she would certainly have gone.'

'Where is she?' asked William.

'Rita has taken her to her study,' said Mr Johns. 'You go too, William. I think you'll be able to help her – let her talk all she likes, and get everything off her chest.'

William went. The other four children got up to go too.

'I'm going to find Robert now,' said Elizabeth. 'That's something *I* must put right – but I'm not going to enjoy it one bit!'

CHAPTER SEVENTEEN

CLEARING UP A FEW TROUBLES

ELIZABETH WAS angry with herself as she went to find Robert. *I've done a really awful thing*, she thought. *I've accused somebody in public of doing a whole lot of mean things and he didn't do one of them. I got him punished – just at a time when he began to try and turn over a new leaf too! Everybody has helped him – and I was the only one who must have made him feel angry and unhappy. I do feel disgusted with myself.*

She couldn't find Robert anywhere. Then she met Leonard and he told her that the boy was out in the stables.

'Bess was limping a bit today,' said Leonard, 'and Robert is out there attending to her with the stableman. I saw him just now when I came in from the cowshed. You know, Elizabeth, Fanny and I see him every morning, and we think he's jolly nice. He's doing all he can to make up to the youngsters for ill-treating them – I can't help admiring him.'

'I admire him too,' said Elizabeth. 'But he won't admire *me* when he hears what I've got to tell him!'

'Why, what's that?' asked Leonard. But Elizabeth wouldn't tell him.

It was dark outside. Elizabeth got her coat and put it on. She slipped out into the garden and went across to the stables. She heard Robert talking to the stableman, and she put her head round the door.

'Robert,' she said, 'can I speak to you?'

'Who is it?' said Robert in surprise. 'Oh, you, Elizabeth. What do you want?'

He came over to her, smelling of horses. It was a nice smell. His hair was untidy and his face was flushed, for he had been rubbing the horse's leg with oil, and it was hard work.

'Robert,' said Elizabeth, 'I made a dreadful mistake about you. It was somebody else who played those tricks, not you.'

'Well, I told you that,' said Robert. 'That isn't any surprise to me.'

'Yes, but Robert, I told the whole school you'd done them,' said Elizabeth, her voice beginning to tremble, 'and I got you punished. I can't tell you how sorry I am. You've been mean to me, often, and I haven't liked you, but I've been much meaner to you. And I do think you're a brick, the way you came to watch the match and told me it was bad luck it rained. I – I – I think you've been big, and I've been very small.'

'Well, I think you have rather,' said Robert, taking her hand. 'But *I* haven't been very big, Elizabeth – it was only that I was so happy to think I've been able to change myself, and to have the horses I love, and I really felt I hardly cared about the match. So you see it wasn't very difficult to come and watch, and tell you it was bad luck it rained. But I'm glad you've found out it wasn't my fault that those tricks were played. Who did them?'

'I can't tell you just at present,' said Elizabeth. 'But, as soon as I knew, I came to find you to tell you I was dreadfully sorry for what I'd said about you. I'd like you to forgive me.'

'You needn't worry about that,' said Robert, with a laugh. 'People have had to forgive me a lot more than I shall ever have to forgive *you*. Don't let's be silly any more. It's fun being enemies at first, but it soon gets horrid. Let's be friends. Come and ride Captain tomorrow morning before breakfast. I'll ride Bess if her leg is better. And do cheer up – you look all funny!'

'I *feel* all funny,' said Elizabeth, swallowing a lump in her throat. 'I didn't think you'd be so awfully decent to me. I do get wrong ideas about people. Yes, Robert, I'd like to be friends. I'll be up early tomorrow morning.'

Robert smiled at her and went back to Bess. Elizabeth slipped away into the darkness. She stood in the cold wind and thought for a minute or two before she went in. How surprising people were! You thought some of them were so horrid, and believed all kinds of things about them – and then they turned out quite different and you wanted to be friends.

'Well, next time I'll give people a chance before I believe beastly things about them,' said Elizabeth to herself. 'I really must think twice, three times, *four* times before I lose my temper or accuse people of anything. It's so funny – I just hated Robert, and now I simply can't help liking him awfully – and yet he's the same person.'

But Robert wasn't quite the same person. He was different! He thought about Elizabeth too. It was brave of her to come and own up like that. She was a dreadful little spitfire, but he couldn't help liking her. It would be fun to ride with her and go galloping wildly over the hills in the early morning!

And meanwhile what about Kathleen? Things had not been going too badly for her, for William and Rita had been wise and gentle, though quite firm and resolute. They had let the girl tell them every single thing.

'I felt awful when the train didn't come in,' said Kathleen, crying into her handkerchief, which was already soaking wet. 'I felt as if that was one more thing against me! I couldn't even run away because there wasn't a train!'

'It's a good thing you *couldn't* run away,' said William. 'It's not a very brave thing to do, is it? You can't get rid of troubles by running away from them, Kathleen. They go with you.'

'Well, what else can you do with troubles?' asked Kathleen, wiping her eyes.

'You can look them in the face and find out the best way to beat them,' said Rita. 'You were funny, Kathleen – you were really trying to run away from yourself! Nobody can ever do that!'

'Well, you'd want to, if you were like *me*,' said Kathleen. 'I'm so unlucky. Nothing nice ever happens to me, as it does to other children.'

'And nothing ever will as long as you think and talk like that,' said William. 'It isn't our luck that makes good or bad things happen, Kathleen, it's just ourselves. For instance, you might say that Jenny has plenty of friends, so she is lucky. But she doesn't have friends because she is *lucky* – she has them because she is kind and generous and happy. It is her own self that brings her lots of friends, not her luck.'

'Yes, I see that,' said Kathleen. 'I hadn't thought of that before. But I'm not pretty and happy and generous like Jenny.'

'Well, why not make the best of yourself?' said Rita. 'You have a sweet smile, and you have a dimple that goes in and out, though we don't see it very often. If you brushed your hair one hundred times each night and morning as Jenny does, it would look silky and shiny. If you stopped eating so many sweets, your spots would go, and if only you'd go out for more walks and try to play games a bit harder, you would soon get rosy cheeks and happy eyes!'

'Should I?' said Kathleen, beginning to look more cheerful.

Rita fetched a mirror from the mantelpiece and put it in front of Kathleen's sad, tear-stained face. 'Smile!' she said. 'Go on, smile, you silly girl! Quick! Let me see that dimple!'

Kathleen couldn't help smiling, and she saw her miserable face change in an instant to a much nicer one – and the dimple came in her left cheek.

'Yes,' she said, 'I do look much nicer. But I'm so dull and slow too – and think of the mean, horrid things I've done!'

'You're dull and slow because you're not as healthy as you might be, and you're not happy,' said William.

'Give yourself a chance, do! As for the mean, horrid things you've done – well, you can always make up for those. We all do mean things at times.'

'I'm quite sure you and Rita don't,' said Kathleen. 'And anyway, William and Rita – please, please don't make me stay at Whyteleafe, because I simply *couldn't* get up in front of the whole school at the next weekly Meeting and say what I'd done, even to clear Robert. I'm a coward. I know I am, so it's no good pretending that I'm not. I shall leave tomorrow morning if you make me do that.'

'We shan't make you do anything,' said William. 'It's no good *making* people do things like that! They must want to do them themselves, if it's to be any good. Well, listen, Kathleen – we'll get Elizabeth to clear Robert of blame, but she shall not say who *is* to blame; but maybe later on you will feel differently about things, and then you can talk to us again.'

'I shall never be brave enough to own up in front of everyone,' said Kathleen. 'But I'll stay at Whyteleafe if I don't need to do that. I've told Elizabeth and Jenny and that was hard enough.'

'It was a good thing you did that,' said William. 'We will see that those children who know that it was you will not tell anyone else. So you need not be afraid that anyone is despising you. Do as Robert has done – turn over a new leaf – and smile as much as you can!'

'I'll try,' said Kathleen putting her wet hanky away. 'I don't *feel* like smiling. I don't even feel like turning over a new leaf. But you've both been so kind to me that I'll try, just to please you.'

'Good!' said Rita and William. Rita looked at her watch. 'It's almost your bedtime,' she said. 'Have you had any supper – or did you miss it?'

'I missed it,' said Kathleen. 'But I'm not hungry.'

'Well, William and I are going to make ourselves some cocoa,' said Rita. 'We are allowed to have our own gas ring, you know, as we are the head children of the school. Stay and have some cocoa with us – and we've got some good chocolate biscuits too. Even if you are not hungry you will like those!'

In ten minutes' time the three of them were drinking hot cocoa and nibbling chocolate biscuits. William was making jokes, and Kathleen was smiling, her dimple showing in her left cheek. When her bedtime bell went, she got up.

'You *are* kind,' she said, tears coming into her eyes again. 'I won't forget this evening. I'm glad you're the head boy and girl – I think you're fine!'

'Cheer up!' said William. 'You'll find things are never so bad as they seem. Goodnight!'

CHAPTER EIGHTEEN

THINGS ARE BETTER!

ELIZABETH WAS up early, and went out to the stables. Robert was there, saddling the horses, whistling softly to himself. He was completely happy. He was looking after something he loved, caring for the horses, and getting back from them the affection he gave them.

'It's a lovely warm feeling,' he told Elizabeth. 'I never had it before, because I never had a pet – and anyway I never much cared for any animal except horses. William and Rita couldn't possibly have thought of anything nicer! It seems strange, doesn't it, that instead of being punished for bullying, I get a marvellous treat like this! And yet it's stopped me from being beastly far more quickly than any punishment would. I just don't want to be horrid now.'

'You can't be horrid to anyone when you're feeling happy,' said Elizabeth wisely. 'I know I can't. I just want to be warm and generous then. Come on – let's go. Oh, Robert, isn't it strange to be friends after being such dreadful enemies!'

Robert laughed as he sprang on to Bess's back. The horse whinnied and tossed her head. She loved to know that Robert was riding her. The two children cantered down the grassy path and then galloped off over the hills. Elizabeth had ridden for years, and rode well. Robert rode well too, and the pair of them enjoyed their gallop tremendously.

They shouted to one another as they rode. Then Elizabeth had an idea.

'I say!' she yelled. 'Will you take Kathleen Peters with you sometimes? She might get red cheeks then!'

'Kathleen! I can't bear her!' shouted back Robert. 'She's an awful girl. Surely you aren't going to be friends with *her*!'

'Well, I am,' cried Elizabeth. 'I don't like her, Robert, any more than I liked you. But I've been so wrong about people lately that for all I know I may get to like her very much. Anyway, I'm going to give her a chance. So will you help?'

'All right,' said Robert. 'She doesn't ride badly. But come too. I really don't think I could bear to go galloping with her by myself. I should be bored stiff! There's one thing about *you* – nobody could ever be bored with you! You're either very, very nice, or very, very horrid!'

'Don't tease me about that,' said Elizabeth, slowing down her horse. 'I'm turning over a new leaf too! I want to be nice always. In fact, when I came back to Whyteleafe this term I had made up my mind to do my very, very best and be as nice as I could. And really, I've made the most awful muddles and mistakes! I know that I shall never be made a monitor!'

'You know, I'd rather like to be,' said Robert. 'It must be a lovely feeling to be trusted and looked up to, and to sit at the Jury's table. Still, we're neither of us ever likely to do that. I made a bad beginning this term – and you were the naughtiest girl in the school last term. My word, you *must* have been bad!'

Robert and Elizabeth were happy when they went in to breakfast that morning. Their cheeks were red with the cold wind, and their eyes sparkled. Elizabeth smiled at Kathleen, who was sitting in her usual place at the table, looking happier but rather nervous.

'Hallo, Kathleen!' said Elizabeth. 'Hallo, everybody! Gosh, I'm hungry! I could eat twenty sausages and twelve eggs!'

'Have you been riding?' asked Kathleen, pushing the toast towards Elizabeth. 'My goodness, you *are* red!'

Elizabeth laughed. 'It was fun,' she said. 'You should

get up early and come riding too.'

'Yes, do,' said Robert. 'You ride well, Kathleen. Why don't you come with Elizabeth and me sometimes? We could gallop for miles!'

Kathleen flushed with pleasure. She smiled warmly and everyone noticed at once how her dimple danced in and out. 'I'd love to,' she said. 'Thanks awfully. I like that horse called Bess best.'

'Do you really?' said Robert in surprise. 'How funny! So do I! She is a perfect darling, honestly she is. You know, she was limping yesterday and I was awfully worried.'

Soon he was telling Kathleen all about Bess and Captain, and Kathleen listened eagerly. She really knew quite a lot about horses, but for once she didn't boast, but listened humbly, glad that someone should speak to her in such a warm and friendly manner. She tried to remember not to let her mouth drop down at the corners in the way that made her so plain, but looked pleasant, and laughed at Robert's jokes.

She had been dreading that breakfast time. It wasn't going to be easy to face Elizabeth, Jenny, Joan and Nora, all of whom knew her poor, unhappy secrets. But after all it wasn't a bit difficult. Kathleen couldn't help feeling the warm generosity of the four girls near her, and it made her humble and happy instead of awkward and ashamed.

So breakfast was very pleasant, though some of the form were most astonished to see Robert and Elizabeth so friendly.

'You are a funny girl, Elizabeth,' said Kenneth. 'One day you are enemies and the next you are friends!'

'Last term Elizabeth was *my* bitterest enemy!' said Harry, with a laugh. 'I pinned a notice on her back, and on it was printed I'M THE BOLD BAD GIRL! I BARK! I BITE! BEWARE! My goodness, how furious you were, Elizabeth!'

'Yes, I was,' said Elizabeth, remembering. 'But it seems rather a funny joke to me now. Let's come and look at the noticeboard, Harry. I can see a new notice pinned up there.'

They went across to look at it. There *was* a new notice, rather an exciting one!

ELIZABETH ALLEN HAS BEEN CHOSEN TO PLAY IN THE MATCH AGAINST UPHILL SCHOOL, it said.

Elizabeth stared at the notice, her cheeks on fire.

'Goodness!' she cried. 'I've *really* been chosen this time! Last time Robert was chosen, and I was to take his place, but this time *I've* been chosen! I *am* pleased!'

'Yes, and this time it's an away match, not a home match,' said Harry. 'You'll have the fun of going off in the motorcoach to Uphill School. You *are* lucky!'

'Oh, it's marvellous!' cried Elizabeth, and she danced away to tell Joan and Jenny. Kathleen was with them, and the four were all smiles as they discussed the match.

'If only we could come and watch you shoot a goal!' said Joan, slipping her arm through her friend's. 'I do hope it won't rain this time, Elizabeth.'

'Oh, it couldn't be so unkind!' cried Elizabeth. 'Joan! Kathleen! Come and give me some practice at catching before dinner this morning, will you!'

Kathleen beamed. So few children ever asked her to do anything. It was lovely to be wanted.

'You really *have* got a nice smile!' said Joan, looking at her. 'Come on – there's the bell. For goodness' sake hurry. I was half a second late yesterday morning and Miss Ranger nearly went up in flames about it!'

Kathleen found herself humming a tune as she ran to get her books. How decent the girls were! It was easy to smile when you were happy. Kathleen had smiled at herself once or twice in the mirror that morning, and really it was simply astonishing what a difference it made to her plain face! She had spoken sternly to herself.

'No more sweets for you! No more greediness! No more silliness at all! Smile and be nice, for goodness' sake!'

And the face in the mirror had smiled back at her, its dimple showing well. Who would have thought that a smile could have made so much difference to anyone?

When school was over that morning, Elizabeth

rushed with Kathleen and Joan to get lacrosse sticks to practise catching and shooting. They bumped into Robert as they ran down the passage.

'Gracious! What hurricanes!' said Robert. 'Whatever are you in such a hurry for?'

'We're going to give Elizabeth some practice at catching,' cried Joan. 'Didn't you know she has been chosen to play in the match against Uphill School on Saturday?'

'No, I didn't know,' cried Robert, his face falling for a moment, for he was bitterly disappointed. He had very much hoped that he would be chosen himself – for after all he *had* been chosen before, and Elizabeth had taken his place, though the match hadn't been played, as it happened. Now Elizabeth was chosen.

Well, I mustn't be small about this, he thought. *I'll have plenty of chances to play in matches later on, I expect.*

He shouted after Elizabeth, 'Good for you, Elizabeth! Wish I could watch you shoot a goal!'

He went off. Elizabeth turned to Joan. 'That was nice of Robert, wasn't it?' she said.

Joan looked at her. 'Did you see his face when he heard that you had been chosen?' she said.

'No, why?' asked Elizabeth in surprise.

'He looked awfully disappointed, that's all,' said Joan, getting out her lacrosse stick. 'I expect he hoped that he might get the chance this time, as he was prevented last time by the School Meeting.'

'Oh,' said Elizabeth. She got her lacrosse stick too, and the three girls went out in the playing field. Soon they were throwing the ball to one another, and then Kathleen went into goal and let the other two shoot the ball at her.

But Elizabeth didn't enjoy the practice very much after all. She was thinking of Robert. She had prevented him from being able to play in the match last Saturday – and she couldn't help feeling that it wasn't very fair that she should be playing *this* Saturday. 'Though, of course, I didn't play last Saturday because of the rain,' she said to herself. She caught the ball and threw it to Joan.

'But I *would* have played if it hadn't rained, and then I would have played two Saturdays running, and Robert wouldn't have played once – though he really was chosen last week. I'm beginning to feel uncomfortable about it. I think I'll go and ask Nora what she thinks.'

So after dinner Elizabeth went to find Nora. The monitors were always ready to hear anyone's troubles, and the children went to them readily.

'Nora! Do you think I ought to let Robert play in the match on Saturday instead of me?' asked Elizabeth.

'You know it was because of me that he was told he mustn't play last Saturday. Well, I know he's disappointed about this. Shall I go to Eileen and tell her to let Robert play instead?'

'Yes,' said Nora at once. 'It's only fair, Elizabeth. Good for you! I'm glad you thought of that. There's one thing about you, you do like to be just, and that's a great thing!'

'I'll go and tell Eileen now,' said Elizabeth, and off she sped before she could change her mind. It was very disappointing for Elizabeth – but it would be a nice surprise for Robert!

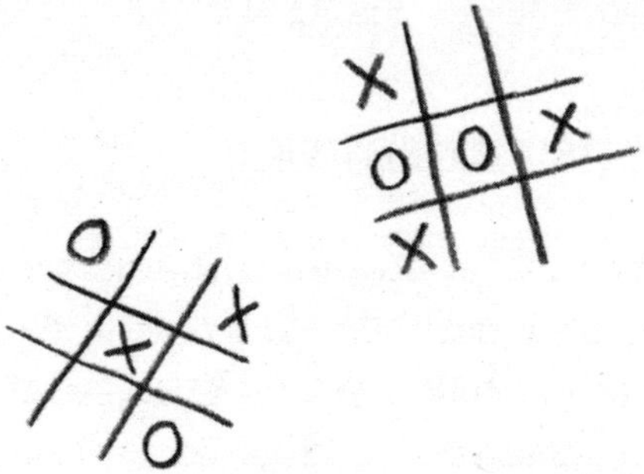

CHAPTER NINETEEN

A PEACEFUL WEEK

EILEEN WAS in the gym. She was very good at gym and games of all kinds. She was busy doing some exercises, but she stopped when she saw that Elizabeth wanted to speak to her.

'What do you want, Elizabeth?' she asked.

'Eileen, would it be all right if Robert played in the match on Saturday instead of me?' asked Elizabeth. 'You see, I've discovered that he didn't do the things I accused him of at the last Meeting – so I think it would be only fair if I let him have the chance of playing this time.'

'Right!' said Eileen, taking out a notebook and writing something down in it. 'I'll see to that. As you say it's only fair, Elizabeth. I'm sorry you can't play, but you've done the right thing!'

Elizabeth couldn't find Robert to tell him, and before

she could do so, Eileen had taken down the first notice from the board and put up another.

ROBERT JONES WILL PLAY IN THE MATCH AGAINST UPHILL SCHOOL ON SATURDAY, said the second notice.

Robert saw it as he came in to dinner. He stared at it in amazement. Surely Elizabeth had said *she* was playing! He stood frowning at the board, and Kenneth came up. 'Hallo!' said Kenneth, reading the notice. 'I wonder why that's altered. It said that Elizabeth was playing in the match when I read it before breakfast!'

'Yes, that's what I thought,' said Robert, puzzled. 'Why has it been altered? But I say – that's marvellous for me! I was jolly disappointed this morning!'

'I bet Elizabeth will be disappointed too,' said Kenneth. They went in to their dinner. Robert did not like to say anything to Elizabeth in front of the others, and she said nothing about the notice either.

It was Nora who told Robert about it. 'Did you see that you were playing in the match after all?' she asked.

'Yes, but why?' asked Robert. 'What made Eileen change?'

'It was because Elizabeth asked her to let you play instead,' said Nora. 'Elizabeth thought that would only be fair. And I must say I agreed with her.'

Robert went red. 'It's awfully sporting of her, but I can't let her do it,' he said. 'I know how badly she wants to play.' He went to find Elizabeth.

She was in the school garden, planting bulbs with John.

'Hie, Elizabeth!' called Robert. 'You're a sport, but I'd rather you played on Saturday, if you don't mind.'

'I shan't, Robert,' said Elizabeth. 'I've made up my mind. It's such a good way of trying to make up for the mistake I made. I should be ashamed of myself if I didn't do it.'

'But I don't mind whether you try to make up for your mistake or not,' said Robert.

'Yes, but *I* mind,' said Elizabeth. 'I shall think better of myself if I do this. Really I shall.'

'All right,' said Robert. 'Thanks. I only wish you were coming to watch, Elizabeth.'

'I hope you shoot lots of goals!' said Elizabeth, and went on with her planting. It was hard work. The crocus bulbs had come, and big patches of grass had to be lifted before the crocuses could be planted underneath. Then there were all the daffodil and tulip bulbs to plant too, though they were much easier to bury in the soil of the beds.

'There's so much to do and so little time to do it all!' sighed Elizabeth. 'I would like to ride oftener – and I would like to garden all day long – and I'd like to have more music lessons – and I'd like to spend more time with the rabbits – and I'd like to play games oftener. I wish I was like you, John, and only had one favourite thing to do, instead of about twenty!'

'Well, I dare say you have a more exciting time than I have,' said John seriously. 'Mr Johns is always saying I ought to do something else besides gardening in my spare time, because I shall become dull.'

'I don't think you're a bit dull!' cried Elizabeth. 'I love to hear you talk about gardening!'

'Yes, because you like gardening and understand it,' said John. 'But, to those who don't, I expect I do seem dull! You think of something else for me to do, Elizabeth.'

'Well, what about riding?' said Elizabeth. 'I never see you on horseback. Get Robert to take you out on Captain sometimes – he'd like that, and you'd enjoy it.'

The week went by, and Friday came. The School Meeting was to be held again that night. The children filed in as usual, not so grave as last time, for there were no serious matters to be discussed tonight. They always enjoyed the Meetings. They liked ruling themselves, making their own laws and seeing that they were kept.

The extra money was put into the box. Kenneth proudly put in a whole pound note from one of his uncles. Peter put in five shillings. Then the week's pocket-money was given out.

John Terry asked for money for the new crocus corms and it was given him. He also asked for money for a new garden fork, a smaller one than the one he used.

'Peter is going to help with the digging,' he said, 'and our fork is too big for him. We've never had one suitable for the younger ones.'

That money was given out also. Richard asked for money to buy a record of a violin performance. He was anxious to play the same piece himself, and Mr Lewis had said that if he could get the record and hear how a great master played the piece it would help him. William granted the money at once. The whole school was becoming very proud of Richard, for he played both the piano and the violin beautifully. He sat down, pleased.

'Any complaints or grumbles?' asked William.

Leonard got up. He looked rather apologetic. 'This is rather a silly grumble,' he said. 'It's about Fred. He does snore so at night – and, you see, I have to get up early in the morning to milk the cows, so if I am kept awake by the snoring, I can't seem to make myself get up in time. We've all told Fred about it, but he can't help it. So what can we do?'

Fred stood up. 'I've had a bad cold,' he said. 'I think I'll be all right when it's quite gone. Shall I go and sleep in the san by myself till Matron says I don't snore any more?'

'Yes, I should,' said William, smiling. 'It's about the funniest grumble we've ever had, I think. But Leonard *must* get his sleep or we shan't get our breakfast milk!'

Everyone laughed. William tapped on the table with his hammer.

'Before we dismiss,' he said, 'Elizabeth has something to say. Stand up, Elizabeth.'

Elizabeth stood up, red in the face. She had been thinking about what she had to say, and she said it straight out, without stammering or stopping.

'I want to say this,' she began. 'Last week I accused Robert of playing some mean tricks on me and on Jenny. You all believed me, and you said that Robert shouldn't play in the match as a punishment. Well, I was wrong. It wasn't Robert after all. It was somebody else.'

'Who was it? Tell us!' cried a dozen voices indignantly. William rapped on the table and everyone was quiet.

'Wait a minute, Elizabeth,' said William. '*I* want to say something. This is what I have to say: Rita and I, as Judges, have decided that for the present we shall not give you the name of the child who did the tricks. You know that in certain cases it is sometimes best not to refer the matter to the whole school. Well, this is one of them. I hope you will be satisfied that we are doing this for the best.'

'Of course!' cried half a dozen voices, for the head girl and boy were much liked and admired.

Poor Kathleen was sitting on her form with her knees shaking! She could not help thinking that the whole school must know it was she who had been so horrid. She looked down at the floor, and wished that a hole would come there so that she might go down into it and disappear! Jenny and Joan were sitting on each side of her, warm and comforting. They could feel Kathleen shaking and they were sorry. Well, it was a good thing that the Judges had decided to say no more about that!

Elizabeth was still standing up. She had a few more words to say. She waited for silence and then went on.

'I haven't got much more to say – except that I'm very sorry for what I said, and that in future I will always be careful to be quite sure before I accuse anybody. Robert was very nice about it indeed.'

She sat down. William was about to rap on the table to dismiss the Meeting, when Robert got up. He looked cheerful and bright, quite a different boy from the last Meeting!

'May I say something, William?' he asked. 'It's this. Elizabeth is letting me play in Saturday's match instead of her, to make up for saying wrong things about me. Well, I think that's very decent of her, and I want the school to know about it!'

'Good old Elizabeth!' cried somebody. Everyone thought that Elizabeth had behaved justly and rightly. The girl could feel this, and she was happy.

Then the Meeting was dismissed, and the children filed out to do what they liked for the half-hour before supper.

Joan sat down to write to her mother. Jenny put on the gramophone and made up a dance in the middle of the floor, much to the amusement of the others. Elizabeth went to practise in one of the music rooms. Robert began to read a book on horses.

Kathleen took up her sewing. She had spent all the money she had on two handkerchief cases to embroider. One was to be for Jenny, and the other for Elizabeth. Rita had said that it was possible to make up for nasty things by doing something nice – so she was doing it!

We learn a lot of things besides lessons at Whyteleafe School, thought Kathleen, as she sewed. And she was right!

CHAPTER TWENTY

THE GREAT LACROSSE MATCH

SATURDAY CAME, marvellously bright and sunny. There was a frost in the morning, and the grass glittered white. But it disappeared in the sun, and everyone agreed that it was a perfect day for the match.

Elizabeth tried her very hardest to be glad that it was such a fine day. It was lucky for Robert, but she couldn't help feeling disappointed that she wasn't playing. She had missed playing the Saturday before because it rained and now that it was so fine, she couldn't play!

'Well,' she said to herself, 'it's your own fault, Elizabeth Allen; you shouldn't have been so foolish – then you would have been playing today!'

She went up to Robert when she saw him. 'I'm glad it's fine for you, Robert,' she said. Robert looked at her and knew what she was feeling.

'I wish you were playing too,' he said. 'Never mind –

it will be your turn next time!'

The day kept fine. All the team who were going to play were in a great state of excitement. Nora was playing, and she told the others that Uphill School had never been beaten by Whyteleafe yet.

'If only we could beat them just this once!' she said. 'But I hear they've got an awfully good team. Eileen says they haven't lost a match yet this term. They really are frightfully good. All I hope is they let us get *one* goal!'

'Oh, Nora! We must get more than that!' cried Peter, a strong, wiry boy who was in the team. He was a marvellous runner and catcher. 'For goodness' sake let's put up a good show!'

'We'll do our best,' said Robert.

The morning went slowly by. Dinnertime came and the team could not eat very much, for they were all so excited. Elizabeth knew how she had felt the Saturday before. Oh, how she *did* wish she was going too! It was so terribly disappointing, but she was glad that she had been big enough to give up her place to Robert.

The sun shone in through the window. It was going to be a wonderful afternoon for a match. Elizabeth swallowed a lump in her throat. It was all very well to be big and brave and give up something because you thought it was right, but it didn't make the disappointment any less. Joan saw her face and squeezed her hand.

'Cheer up!' she said. So Elizabeth tried to cheer up and smile. And then she noticed something going on at the next table. People were getting up and talking – what was happening?

'It's Peter! He doesn't feel well,' said Joan. 'Isn't he pale? I believe he's going to be sick. I didn't think he looked very well at breakfast this morning.'

Peter went out of the room, with Harry helping him. He did look very green. Mr Johns went out too. Mr Warlow looked at his watch. He hoped Peter would soon recover, because the coach was coming to fetch the team in twenty minutes.

Mr Johns came back in five minutes' time. He spoke to Mr Warlow, who looked disappointed. 'What's happened to Peter?' asked John, who was at the same table. 'Is he better?'

'He's got one of his tummy upsets,' said Mr Johns. 'Very bad luck. Matron is putting him to bed in the san.'

'Golly!' said John. 'Won't he be able to play in the match then?'

'No,' said Mr Warlow. 'It's bad luck for our team. Peter was one of the best. We must choose someone else.'

The news spread round the tables, and everyone was sorry about Peter. He really was such a good player. And then one by one the children called out something, 'Let Elizabeth play!'

'What about Elizabeth?'

'Can't Elizabeth play? She gave up her place to Robert!'

'Well,' said Mr Warlow, looking at his notebook, 'I had planned to get someone else next time, but as Elizabeth really deserves a trial she shall play!'

Elizabeth's heart jumped for joy. She could hardly believe the good news. Her face went bright red and her eyes danced. She was sorry for Peter – but after all Peter had played in dozens of matches, and would again. Oh, she was really, really going to play after all!

'Good for you, Elizabeth!' called her friends, all pleased to see her shining face. The whole school knew, of course, that Elizabeth had given up her place in the match to Robert, and now they were really glad that she had her reward so unexpectedly.

Elizabeth sat happily in her place. Joan clapped her on the back, and Jenny grinned at her. 'Things always happen to you, don't they, Elizabeth?' said Jenny. 'Well, you deserve this piece of luck!'

'Elizabeth! I'm so glad!' called Robert from the end of the table. 'We shall be playing in our first match together! That'll be fun!'

Elizabeth couldn't eat anything more. She pushed her pudding plate away. 'I shall feel sick, like Peter, if I eat any more,' she said.

'Well, for goodness' sake don't then!' cried Nora. 'We

can't have another player going sick at the very last moment!'

Elizabeth rushed off to change with the others into her gym things. She found time to peep into the san with a book for Peter. 'I'm sorry, Peter, old thing,' she said. 'I hope you'll soon be all right. I'll come and tell you about the match when it's over.'

'Play up!' said Peter, who still looked rather green. 'Shoot a few goals! Goodbye and good luck!'

Elizabeth shot off, her heart singing. It was too marvellous for words. Everyone laughed at her face and everyone was glad for her. She found Robert and took his arm.

'Sit next to me in the coach,' she said. 'We are the only ones who have never played in a match before – and oh, Robert, though I'm awfully happy, I feel a bit nervous!'

'*You* nervous!' said Robert, with a laugh. 'I can't believe it. A fierce person like you can't be nervous!'

But Elizabeth was! She was very anxious to do her best in the match, to do her best for Whyteleafe School. Suppose she played badly! Suppose she didn't catch the ball but kept dropping it! It would be dreadful.

'Still, there won't be anyone from Whyteleafe watching to see if I play badly,' she comforted herself. She looked at Robert as he sat beside her in the coach, looking burly and stolid and not a bit nervous. It was nice to be playing with him after all.

I simply can't imagine how I hated him so much, thought Elizabeth. *It seems to me that if we dislike people, we see all the worst side of them because we make them show that to us – but if we like them, then they smile at us and show their best side. I really must try to give people a chance and begin by liking them, so that they show their best side at once.*

The coach soon arrived at Uphill School, which, as its name showed, was at the top of a steep hill. It was a much bigger school than Whyteleafe, and had the choice of far more children for its lacrosse team than Whyteleafe had. The Whyteleafe children looked at the opposing team and thought that they seemed very big and strong.

The teams lined up in their places. The whistle blew, and the game began. The Uphill team were certainly strong, but there were some fine runners in the Whyteleafe team. They missed Peter, who was the finest runner of all, but both Robert and Elizabeth seemed to have wings on their feet that afternoon. They had never run so fast in their lives before!

Both children felt honoured to play in the match, and were determined to do their very best. Elizabeth's nervousness went as soon as the game began. She forgot all about herself and thought only of the match.

She and Robert often threw the ball to one another. Both children had practised their catching every day for some weeks, and were very good at it. Neither of them dropped the ball, but passed it beautifully.

'Good, Robert! Good, Elizabeth!' cried Mr Warlow, who was with the team. 'Keep it up! Shoot, Elizabeth!'

Elizabeth saw the goal not far off. She shot the ball at it with all her might. It flew straight at the goal – but the goalkeeper was on guard and shot the ball out again at once.

'Well tried, Elizabeth!' cried Mr Warlow.

Then the Uphill team got the ball and sped off towards the other goal, passing gracefully to one another – and then the captain shot hard. The ball rolled right into the goal, though Eileen, who was goalkeeper, did her best to stop it.

'One goal to Uphill!' said the umpire, and the whistle blew. The game began again, and both Robert and Elizabeth were determined not to let the Uphill team get the ball if they could help it.

Elizabeth got the ball in her lacrosse net and sped away with it. She was about to pass it to Robert, who was keeping near her, when another player ran straight at her. Elizabeth tripped over and fell. She was up again in a trice, but the ball had been taken by the Uphill girl. Down to the goal sped the girl, and passed the ball to someone else.

'Shoot!' yelled all the watching Uphill girls, and the ball was shot towards the goal. It rolled inside before Eileen could throw it out.

'Two goals to Uphill!' called the umpire. He blew the whistle for half-time, and the girls and boys greedily sucked the half-lemons that were brought out to them. Oh, how lovely and sour they tasted!

'Now play up, Whyteleafe,' said Mr Warlow, coming out on to the field to talk to his team. 'Robert, keep near Elizabeth – and Elizabeth, pass more quickly to Robert when you are attacked. You two are running like the wind today. Shoot at goal whenever there's a chance. Nora, feed Elizabeth with the ball when you can – she may perhaps be quick enough to outpace the Uphill girl marking her.'

The children listened eagerly. The Whyteleafe team were feeling a little down-hearted. Two goals to none!

The whistle blew. The match began again. Nora got the ball and passed it at once to Elizabeth, remembering what Mr Warlow had said. Robert kept near to her and caught it when she passed it to him. He passed it back again, and the girl sped towards the goal.

She flung the ball with all her might. The goalkeeper put out her lacrosse net quickly, but the ball bounced off it and rolled into the goal.

'One goal to Whyteleafe!' said the umpire. 'Two to one.'

Elizabeth was thrilled. She couldn't keep still, but danced up and down even when the ball was nowhere near her. Nora got the ball. She passed to Robert, Robert passed back and Nora ran for goal. She shot – and once more the ball rolled right in! It was too good to be true!

'Two goals to Whyteleafe!' said the umpire. 'Two all, and ten minutes to play!'

The Uphill children, who were all watching the match eagerly, began to shout, 'Play up, Uphill! Shoot, Uphill! Go on, Uphill!'

And the Uphill team heard and played harder than ever. They got the ball – they raced for goal. They shot – and Eileen caught the ball neatly and threw it out again! Thank goodness for that!

Two goals all, and three minutes to play. Play up, Uphill! Play up, Whyteleafe! Three minutes left – only three minutes!

CHAPTER TWENTY-ONE

THE END OF THE MATCH

'THREE MINUTES, Robert!' panted Elizabeth. 'For goodness' sake let's play up. Oh, how I hope that Uphill School don't shoot another goal!'

The ball flew from one player to another. Elizabeth ran to tackle one of the Uphill girls, who was a very fast runner. She hit the girl's lacrosse stick and made the ball leap up into the air. Elizabeth tried to catch it, but the ball fell to the ground. She picked it up in her lacrosse net, and tore off with it.

But another girl tackled her and, although Elizabeth tried to dodge, it was no use at all. She fell over and the ball flew into the air. The Uphill girl caught it neatly and raced off with it. She passed it to another Uphill girl who threw it vigorously down the field to the girl by the goal.

The girl caught it, and shot straight for goal. It looked

as if the ball was flying straight for the goal net – but Eileen saved it by flinging herself right out of goal! She fell over as she caught the ball, but somehow she managed to fling it to a waiting Whyteleafe boy. He caught it and was off up the field like the wind.

'Pass the ball, pass it!' yelled Elizabeth, dancing about. 'Look out! There's a girl behind you! PASS!'

The boy passed the ball just as the Uphill girl behind him tried to strike at his stick to get the ball. It flew straight through the air to Elizabeth. She caught it, and sped off, followed by a swift-running Uphill girl.

Elizabeth passed to Robert who was nearby. An Uphill girl ran at him – and he passed the ball back to Elizabeth, who ran for goal. Should she shoot from where she was? She might get a goal – and she would win the match for Whyteleafe!

But Robert had run down the field and was nearer the goal now – she ought really to pass to him! Without another moment's delay Elizabeth threw the ball straight to Robert.

He caught it – and flung it at the goal. It was a beautiful shot. The girl in goal tried her best to save the goal, but the ball flew past her stick and landed right in the corner of the net. Goal to Whyteleafe!

And almost at once the whistle blew for Time! The match was over!

'Three goals to Whyteleafe!' shouted the umpire. 'Three goals to two! Whyteleafe wins! Well played!'

Then all the watching Uphill girls cheered too, and clapped their hardest. It had been an excellent match and everyone had played well.

'Another second and the whistle would have blown for Time!' panted Elizabeth. 'Oh, Robert! You were marvellous to shoot the winning goal just in time!'

'Well, I couldn't have if you hadn't passed me the ball exactly when you did,' said Robert, his breath coming fast as he leant on his lacrosse stick, his face flushed and wet. 'Well, Elizabeth – we've won! Think of that! We've never beaten Uphill before! Oh, I'm glad you shot a goal too!'

The two teams trooped off the field and went in to wash. It was nice to feel cold water, for they were all so hot! The two captains shook hands, and the Uphill girl clapped Eileen on the back.

'A jolly good match!' she said. 'It's the first we've lost this term. Good for you!'

Elizabeth hadn't been able to eat much dinner, but she made up for it at teatime. There was brown bread and butter and blackberry jam, currant buns and an enormous chocolate cake. The children ate hungrily, and the big plates of bread and butter and buns were soon emptied.

'I'm longing to get back to Whyteleafe to tell the good news,' said Robert to Elizabeth. 'Aren't you? Oh, Elizabeth, I *am* glad you played after all – and I can't tell you how glad I am that *I* was able to play! I hope we play in heaps more matches together. It was marvellous being able to pass the ball so well to one another!'

'You shot that winning goal well,' said Elizabeth happily. 'Oh, I'm so tired, but so happy. I feel as if I can't get up from this form! My legs won't work any more!'

All the children were tired, but their tongues still worked well. They chattered and laughed and joked together as they got ready to go back to the waiting motorcoach. Oh, what fun to tell the school that they had won!

They all got back into the coach. They waved goodbye to the cheering Uphill girls, and the coach rumbled off. The children sank back into their seats, their faces still red with all their running about, and their legs tired out.

But as soon as they got near Whyteleafe School they all sat up straight and looked eagerly to see the first glimpse of the Whyteleafe children, who would all be waiting to hear the result of the match.

Joan and Jenny and Kathleen had been looking out for the coach for the last half-hour. When they heard it coming they tore to the big school door. Dozens of other children ran with them. It was always the custom at Whyteleafe to welcome home the children who had been to an away match.

The lacrosse team waved their hands wildly as the coach rumbled up to the big school door.

'We won! We won! Three goals to two!'

'We've won the match. It was marvellous!'

'It's the first time Uphill have been beaten!'

'Three goals to two! Three goals to two!'

The Whyteleafe children cheered madly when they heard the news. They swarmed out round the coach and helped down the team, whose legs were still very wobbly from all the rushing about they had done.

'Jolly good! Oh, jolly good!' cried everyone. 'Come along in and tell us all about it!'

So into the gym went the team, and Miss Belle and Miss Best, and Mr Johns too, had to come along and hear all the excitements of the afternoon. Mr Warlow spoke for a while and told how well everyone had played.

Then John shouted out, 'Who shot the goals?'

'Elizabeth, Nora – and Robert,' said Mr Warlow. 'Good goals all three. Robert's was the most exciting because he shot his almost as the whistle went for Time. Another second and it would have been too late!'

'Three cheers for Nora, Elizabeth and Robert!' cried

everyone, and they clapped them on the back. How pleased and proud those three children were! Elizabeth almost cried for joy. To think she had actually shot a goal for Whyteleafe in her very first match. It was too good to be true.

Nora had played in many matches and shot many goals, so she just grinned and said nothing. But Robert was as pleased and proud as Elizabeth, though he did not show it quite so much.

Elizabeth slipped her arm in his. 'I'm *so* glad we both had the chance to play together,' she said. 'And oh, Robert, you don't know how pleased I am that I've done something for Whyteleafe, even if it's only to shoot a goal! I hated Whyteleafe when I first came here, but now I love it. Wait till you have been here a term or two and you'll love it too.'

'I love it already, thank you,' said Robert. 'And, what's more, I mean to do a whole lot more for it than just shoot a goal!'

There was a special supper that night for the winning team! Hot sausages appeared on the table, two for each one of the team. How delighted they were! And not only that, but anyone who had sweets or chocolates made a point of offering them to the team, so that by the time the bed bell went, both Robert and Elizabeth felt that they couldn't eat anything more at all!

Kathleen was as delighted as anyone. Her face was beaming as she brought a tin of sweets along. Elizabeth took a good look at her.

'Golly, you don't look the same girl!' she said. 'Your eyes are all smiling and your hair is shiny! You walk as if you wanted to run, and you've already got rid of your awful spots!'

Kathleen laughed. She had kept her word to herself and hadn't eaten a single sweet. She had begun to forget herself, and to join in the chatter and jokes of the form. She held her head up and smiled happily. Already when she thought of the horrid tricks she had played she could not imagine how she could have done them.

She had taken down Elizabeth's books from the top of the cupboard where she had put them, and had dusted them well. With scarlet cheeks she had given them back to Elizabeth, who had taken them with a word of thanks. A few scornful words had almost come to Elizabeth's tongue when she remembered how Miss Ranger had scolded her for losing her books, but she had bitten them back and said nothing.

Kathleen worked hard at the two handkerchief cases, and embroidered them carefully and well. Each had the word HANDKERCHIEF across it, and it was a long word to sew. There were blue forget-me-nots on Elizabeth's case and pink roses on Jenny's.

Just as Kathleen was finishing the very last stitch, Jenny came into the common room.

'My goodness, I wish I'd played in the match too,' she said, flinging herself into a chair. 'What wouldn't I do for hot sausages for supper! Hallo, Kath! What are you so busy about? Let's see.'

She bent over Kathleen's work. 'My goodness!' she said. 'What tiny stitches – and how nicely you've worked the roses! I wish I could sew like that. I want a handkerchief case.'

'Well, this is for you,' said Kathleen, delighted. 'I've done one for Elizabeth too.'

'But whatever for?' asked Jenny in surprise.

'To make up just a little bit for other things I did which weren't quite so nice,' said Kathleen. 'Here you are, Jenny – take yours and use it. I'm so glad to give it to you.'

Jenny was very pleased indeed. She took the handkerchief case at once. 'You *are* a brick!' she said. 'Thanks a lot. Here's Elizabeth! Look – hie, Elizabeth, come and see what you've got for an unbirthday present!'

Soon both girls were examining their new handkerchief cases in delight, and other children came round to see them. Kathleen felt proud when she heard their remarks.

It's much nicer to do something for *people instead of* against *them*, she thought. *But I'll never, never be brave enough to own up to the school that it was I who played those tricks! I* am *nicer – and kinder too – but I'm still just as much a coward!*

CHAPTER TWENTY-TWO

ELIZABETH IN TROUBLE AGAIN

THE TERM went on happily. Now that the quarrels between Robert and Elizabeth, and between Kathleen and the others, had been cleared up, things were much better.

Elizabeth worked well and shot to the top of her class. Robert was sometimes second and sometimes third, which pleased Miss Ranger very much, for it was by sheer hard work that the boy did so well. Kathleen too worked a great deal better, and had stopped arguing in the silly way she once had. Mam'zelle was pleased with her.

'The child in this class who has made the most improvement is the little Kathleen!' said Mam'zelle. 'Ah, how I thought she was stupid! How I scolded her! But now, see, her French essay is the best, and she rolls her r's in the right French way – not like you, R-r-r-r-robert, who will never, never get them right!'

Robert smiled – and Kathleen went red with pleasure. She had never been praised in class before, and it was very pleasant. She began to wonder if she was as stupid as she had always thought herself to be.

My memory does seem to be better, she thought, *and I like working at my lessons now. I was bored before. Maybe I shan't always be at the bottom of the class now! How marvellous! Wouldn't Mother be pleased if I came out top in something!*

She worked especially hard for Mam'zelle, and this was a great change for Kathleen, for ever since Mam'zelle had scolded her so badly she had disliked the French teacher and done her lessons carelessly. But now, somehow, things were different. For one thing the girl was healthier – she went out riding and walking with the others, and she even offered to help John, Elizabeth and Peter in the school garden.

'Good gracious!' said John. 'You're the last person I would have thought wanted to help! Are you any good at gardening?'

'Well, no, not much,' said Kathleen honestly. Three weeks before she would have boasted untruthfully that she knew everything about gardening. 'But John, I'd like to help a bit. Isn't there anything I can do?'

'You can wheel that rubbish over there to the rubbish heap,' said John. 'Then bring back the barrow and fork the next pile of rubbish in. It's really too heavy for Peter to wheel.'

Peter was very keen on gardening, and John was delighted to have him. Peter told John how Robert took him riding, and John grew quite interested in hearing about the horses.

'I'd really have to try riding myself,' he said. 'I've never much wanted to. I did when I first came to Whyteleafe, and then somehow I got so interested in gardening that I couldn't think of anything else. But perhaps I'll come tomorrow, Peter.'

Peter spoke to Robert, and it was arranged that John, Peter, Robert, Elizabeth and Kathleen should all go riding together the next morning – and off they all went, galloping over the hills in the pale winter sunlight. John loved it.

'I must come again,' he said, when he jumped down from the saddle. 'That was fine. Goodness, Kathleen, what red cheeks you've got! You always used to look so pale! Coming to help me garden this weekend?'

'Yes, please,' said Kathleen, overjoyed at being asked to help someone. She was beginning to find how lovely it was to make friends, and to *be* a friend. If you offered to help other people, they offered to help you in return, and that was how friendships began – and surely it was the nicest thing in the world to have good friends round you?

It was quite true what William and Rita said, thought Kathleen to herself. *I envied Jenny and said she was lucky because she had so many friends – and I thought that because I was an unlucky person none of those nice things happened to me. But now that I'm trying to be nicer, nice things happen to me too. It is our own selves that make us lucky or unlucky; it's our own selves that bring us friendship and kindness. I was always groaning and grumbling about everything and thinking I would always be unlucky and wouldn't be able to help it – but, as soon as I changed myself, I changed the things that happened too! What a pity that everyone doesn't know that!*

Elizabeth was working hard at her music, and Mr Lewis was very pleased with her. She and Richard were once again playing duets, and the big boy loved playing with the quick-fingered little girl. She looked up to Richard and thought he was wonderful.

'Can we play our duets at the school concert again?' asked Elizabeth. 'I do want to, Mr Lewis. Shall we be good enough?'

'Oh, yes,' said Mr Lewis. 'Richard is playing his violin too. Have you heard him play the same piece that is on the gramophone record he got, Elizabeth?'

'No,' said Elizabeth. 'I haven't. But I'd like to. Please play it to me, Richard.'

So Richard was sent to fetch his violin, and the big,

dreamy boy played a marvellous piece to his master and to Elizabeth. They both listened, enchanted.

'Oh, that's lovely,' sighed Elizabeth when it was finished. 'Oh, I wish I could play like that. Can't I learn to play the violin too, Mr Lewis?'

'My dear child, you already fill your days too full!' laughed the music master. 'No, stick to the piano.'

'But Richard plays the piano too,' said Elizabeth. '*And* the violin!'

'And he doesn't do anything else!' said Mr Lewis. 'But nobody can make him do anything else, so he might as well work hard at those. No one has ever made Richard pull a weed out of the garden, or ride a horse more than once, or keep even a harmless white mouse! He thinks of nothing but music.'

'I'll make him think of something else!' said Elizabeth. 'Come and practise with me at lacrosse tomorrow, Richard! You can't think how marvellous it feels to be good enough to play in a match!'

But Richard wouldn't come. He did play games sometimes, but so badly that he was worse than any child in the kindergarten. Not even determined little Elizabeth could make him leave his precious music, and she soon gave it up. Secretly she was very proud to play duets with him.

'One day Richard will be a famous musician and

composer,' she told Jenny and Joan. 'Then I shall be very proud to think that once I played duets with him.'

There was to be a play at the school concert. The children in Elizabeth's form were to write one themselves, and they spent a long time thinking it out. When at last they had worked out the plot, there came the labour of writing it.

Jenny and Kathleen proved to be unexpectedly good at this. Jenny could manage conversation very well, and Kathleen had a good imagination and thought of all kinds of things. Before the week was out, the two were writing out the play together, with helpful and unhelpful remarks from the other members of the class.

It amused Elizabeth to see the two heads bent over the paper. *It's just as funny to see Jenny and Kathleen like that as it was to see me and Robert*, she thought. *How silly we are when we quarrel! Well, I'll never quarrel again!*

It was a pity she said that, for she broke her word to herself the very next day! She quarrelled with John!

They had built a big rubbish heap, and John had said they would light it the next time they had an hour or two to spare. But when Elizabeth went to find John in the garden to light the fire he wasn't there.

Oh, bother! thought the little girl. *I did so want to see the bonfire burning! Well, if John doesn't come in the next few minutes, I'll light it myself. He won't mind.*

But she knew that he would mind really, for although he trusted Elizabeth in a great many ways, things such as lighting bonfires he always did himself.

Elizabeth fetched a box of matches. She struck one and held it to some paper she had pushed into the heart of the rubbish heap. It caught fire – and in a trice the bonfire was burning furiously! What a blaze it made! Blue smoke streamed out from it and flew over the shed nearby.

Elizabeth danced around happily. This was marvellous! How silly John was to be late!

And then she suddenly noticed something! The wind was blowing the flames of the bonfire near the shed!

'Oh! I hope the shed won't catch fire!' cried Elizabeth in alarm. 'Oh my goodness – I believe it will! John! John! Quick, where are you?'

John was coming down the path at that moment. He saw the flames of the bonfire at the bottom of the garden, and hurried to see what was happening. When he saw that the red tongues were actually licking the woodshed, he had a terrible fright.

'Elizabeth! Get the hose out with me!' he cried. Together the two children unrolled the hose and hastily fitted it to the garden tap. John turned on the tap and the water gushed out of the hose. The boy pointed it at the bonfire. In a few minutes the fire was out and only dense black smoke came from the very heart of it.

John threw down the hose and turned off the tap.

'What in the world did you light the bonfire for?' he said angrily. 'What an idiot you are! Don't you know by now that I'm head of the school garden? You might have burnt down the shed!'

'Don't talk to me like that!' cried Elizabeth, firing up at once. 'You said *you* were going to light it – and it would have happened just the same if you had, wouldn't it!'

'My dear Elizabeth, I'm not *quite* so foolish as to light a bonfire just there, with the wind blowing the flames straight towards the shed,' said John furiously. 'Have a little sense! I didn't *dream* of lighting it today! And you've no business to. Now we've ruined the bonfire and I meant it to be such a beauty. You're a real nuisance, and I don't want you in the garden any more!'

'*Oh!*' cried Elizabeth, with tears in her eyes. 'You hateful boy! After all I've done in the garden and all the help I've given you!'

'You shouldn't have done it for *me*,' said John. 'You should have done it for the garden and for the school. Go away, Elizabeth. I don't feel I want to talk to you any more.'

'Well, I'll certainly never come and help in the garden *again*!' shouted Elizabeth, and off she marched in a great rage.

But half an hour later a little voice spoke inside

her head. *You said you weren't going to quarrel with anyone any more. And you have already! After all, John was right to be cross. You might have burnt down the shed and all his precious tools and everything – and you've spoilt the lovely bonfire he wanted to light.*

And a voice was speaking inside John's head too. *Elizabeth didn't mean it. She was just silly, not bad. She's as disappointed as you are about the bonfire. And you know you* do *want her help in the garden. Suppose she takes you at your word and doesn't come any more? That wouldn't be very nice!*

I'll go and find her, thought John.

And the same thought came to Elizabeth. *I'll go and find John.*

So they met round the corner of the garden path, each looking rather ashamed. They held out their hands.

'Sorry I was piggy to you,' said John.

'And I'm sorry I was too,' said Elizabeth. 'Oh, John, I said to myself yesterday that I'd never quarrel with anyone any more – and I've gone and done it again!'

'You always will!' said John, with a laugh. 'But it won't matter if only you will make it up quickly. Come on and do some digging. It will do us both good.'

Off they went together, the best of friends. It takes more than a quarrel to break up a real friendship, doesn't it?

CHAPTER TWENTY-THREE

A THRILL FOR JOAN

TWO MONTHS of the Christmas term had already gone by. Seven School Meetings had been held, and the eighth was to be held on the next Friday night. A new monitor had to be chosen, because one of the old ones, a boy called George, had the flu and was in the san for a week or two.

'How are new monitors chosen?' asked Robert. 'Nobody new has been chosen since I came at the beginning of the term. I thought monitors were only chosen for a month, but we've had the same ones for two months.'

'Yes, because they're so good we don't want to change them,' said Joan. 'We *can* change them at the end of each month if we want to, but there's no point in changing them if we are satisfied. I think all our monitors are awfully good.'

'So do I,' said Elizabeth. 'I once thought it must be awful to be a monitor and have to keep all the rules and see that the others did too, but now I've changed my mind. I think it's rather nice to be trusted so much, and to have people coming to you for help and advice.'

'Well, the people who matter in this world are the ones who can be really trusted and who are willing to help anyone in trouble,' said Jenny. 'We get good training for that at Whyteleafe! One day *I'd* like to be a monitor, but like you, Elizabeth, I know I never shall be!'

'Well, nobody's answered my question yet,' said Robert patiently.

'What *was* it?' asked Elizabeth.

'I asked how new monitors are chosen,' said Robert. 'Do *we* choose them – or do the Jury, or the Judges, or who?'

'Well, the whole school chooses them first,' said John. 'We each write down the name of one we think we would like as monitor, and then the slips of paper are folded and passed up to the Jury.'

'What next?' asked Robert.

'The Jury undo them and see which three children have the most votes,' said John. 'They vote for whichever of those three they think would be best. Then their votes are passed up to William and Rita – and the two

Judges decide which child is to be made a new monitor.'

'I see,' said Robert. 'It seems very fair. Everyone has a say in the matter. That's what I like so much about Whyteleafe – we all have a say in things.'

'I can't quite think who to vote for,' said Jenny. 'I'll have to think hard.'

'So will I,' said Joan thoughtfully. 'It is such an honour to be chosen. The one we choose must really be worthy of it.'

'Can I walk with you when we go for our nature ramble this afternoon?' asked Kathleen. 'Elizabeth can't go – she's got an extra music practice with Richard.'

'All right,' said Joan. 'But don't be late. I'm leading the ramble, you know, and you must be on time if you want to start off with me.'

Kathleen was very punctual, and the two set off together with their notebooks, followed by the rest of the children who were interested in nature work. They were to find blossoming ivy, the last insect feast of the season, and to list and draw all the insects feasting on the nectar in the green blossoms.

It was fun to wander down the lanes together and over the fields. The pale winter sun shone down and the sky was the faint blue of a harebell. The trees were all bare except the firs and the pines, and the frost still glittered under the hedges.

Kathleen hummed a little song to herself as she looked about for the blossoms of the ivy. Joan looked at her.

'It's funny how people change,' she said. 'Last term I saw Elizabeth change from a horrid, naughty girl to a kind and good one. I felt myself change from somebody lonely and shy to somebody quite different. I've seen Robert change – and now you're changing too under my very eyes!'

'Yes, I know,' said Kathleen. 'But there's one way I haven't changed, Joan. I'm still a coward!'

'How do you mean?' asked Joan, surprised. 'Are you frightened of cows, or something?'

'No, of course not,' said Kathleen. 'I'm frightened of what people think! That's much worse than cows! Nobody but you and Jenny and Nora and Elizabeth know that it was I who played those horrid tricks – oh, and Rita and William, of course. And I know quite well that if it had been you or Jenny or Elizabeth you would all have been brave enough to get up in front of the whole school at a Meeting and say it was you!'

'Well, of course,' said Joan. 'Why not? You know quite well that the school would think well of you for owning up, and not so badly of you for doing the tricks. But if it leaks out that you *did* do them and didn't own up, why then, we should think much worse of you, and you'd think worse of yourself too! It's just a question of making up your mind to do it. Everybody has plenty of courage – only they don't always use it.'

'Have they really?' asked Kathleen. 'I mean, have *I* got plenty of courage if I like to use it? I don't *have* to be a coward then?'

'You *are* an idiot!' said Joan, taking Kathleen's arm. 'I mean what I say. No one has to be a coward – anyone can draw on their courage the moment they make up their mind to! Try it at the next Meeting, old thing – you'll see what I mean then.'

They found a great stretch of blossoming ivy just then, so they said no more, but busied themselves in writing down the large list of insects hovering over the nectar. But Kathleen was thinking over Joan's words. It would be too marvellous if they were true. If everybody had courage deep down inside them, why then, nobody *need* be a coward – they only had to take hold of their courage and use it!

I'll see if I can use mine at the next Meeting, thought Kathleen, though her heart sank at the thought. *It's tiresome to see all the other children standing up and saying things, and I hardly dare to open my mouth!*

So at the next Meeting, unknown to any of her friends, Kathleen sat with shaking knees, trying to take hold of her courage. The usual business was gone through – money put into the box, money given out, money granted or refused for several things. And then came the complaints and grumbles.

There was only one complaint and only one grumble, and they were quickly dealt with. Then, before the other business of choosing a monitor was put before the Meeting, William said a few words.

'I think the school would like to know that Fred is back in his dormitory, and doesn't snore any more.'

There was laughter at this, and a few cheers. Fred laughed too. William knocked on the table.

'I also want to say this – that the whole school has noticed and approved of the way that Robert has behaved for the last few weeks. Rita and I have had excellent reports from all the monitors. Also the stableman says that he really couldn't do without Robert now to help him with the horses.'

Robert flushed with pleasure. The school was pleased too – it was always good to hear that they had been right in their treatment of anyone.

And then Kathleen found her courage, took hold of it with two hands and stood up. Her knees no longer shook. Her voice was steady. She looked straight at the Judges and the Jury.

'I want to say something I should have said before,' she said. 'I want to say that I was the person who did all the things that Robert was accused of. I was afraid to own up before.'

There was complete silence. Everyone was most astonished. Those who hadn't known were surprised to hear the news – and those who *had* known were even more surprised to hear Kathleen owning up! Whatever had made her do it so suddenly?

Then Rita spoke. 'And what has made you able to own up now?' she asked.

'Well, it was really something Joan said,' explained Kathleen. 'She told me there was no need for *anyone* to be a coward. She said we all had courage in us, only we had to take hold of it. So I took hold of mine this evening – and Joan was right. I wasn't afraid any more.'

'Thank you, Kathleen,' said Rita.

Kathleen sat down. Her heart was light. She had got rid of a heavy load. She had found her courage – and she wasn't going to lose it again!

'We won't say any more about what Kathleen has confessed to us,' said Rita. 'We are all glad she has been brave enough to own up. William and I knew it was she, of course – and we hoped that one day she would be able to tell you herself. Now she has – and we are pleased.'

'We had better get on with the business of choosing a new monitor,' said William. 'Give out slips of paper, please, Eileen.'

The slips were given out. Everyone wrote down the name of a girl or boy they thought fit to be a monitor. The papers were given to the Jury and opened. The Jury then chose out the three names that had most votes and voted on them themselves. Their papers were given to the two Judges.

William and Rita opened the twelve slips of paper from the Jury. They talked to one another in low voices while everyone waited eagerly to know who had been chosen.

Then William knocked on the table with his hammer, and everyone was perfectly quiet. 'There isn't much doubt as to who you want for a new monitor,' he said. 'Her name appears on almost everyone's paper. It is Joan Townsend!'

There were cheers and clappings, and Joan went as red as a beetroot. She had had no idea at all that the school would choose her! But everyone had heard with interest what Kathleen had said about Joan's wise words on courage – and now Joan's reward had come! She was to be the new monitor.

'We have had excellent reports of you from all the other monitors,' said Rita. 'We know that you are to be trusted, that you are kind and wise for your age, and that you will do your best for the whole school. Please come up and sit at the monitors' table, Joan – we are glad to welcome you on our Jury!'

Joan went up to the platform, proud and happy. Elizabeth clapped madly – she was so proud of Joan, so pleased that she was honoured in this way.

Joan deserves it! she thought. *She really does! My goodness, if only I could be a monitor too! But I'm not the right sort of girl, and never will be!*

CHAPTER TWENTY-FOUR

A HORRID ADVENTURE

THE TERM slipped into December. The school was very busy planning and preparing plays and songs of all kinds. The weather was unkind, and many afternoons there were no games to be played out-of-doors.

'It's even too bad to garden,' groaned John, looking out of the window. 'The ground is so sticky that I can't dig.'

'Anyway, you'd get soaked through,' said Joan. 'It's a good chance for you to take an interest in something else! But I expect you'll get down one of your gardening books and pore over that!'

Joan was very happy to be a monitor. She took a great pride in her new honour, and did her duties well. She had to see that the children in her care did not break the rules of the school. She had to advise them when they came to her for help. She had to act wisely and kindly always – and this was not difficult for her because she was naturally a sensible and kindly child.

Elizabeth was very pleased that Joan was a monitor. She did not feel jealous, of course, but she longed to be one too. Still, Joan had been at Whyteleafe for far longer than Elizabeth – so she must wait her turn in patience. Though patience was not a thing that Elizabeth possessed very much of at present!

Elizabeth practised her music pieces hard and played the duets over and over again with Richard, for she was very anxious to do her best at the concert. Mr Lewis praised her.

'Elizabeth, you are working very hard. You are playing extremely well this term.'

Elizabeth felt proud. My goodness, she would show everyone at the concert how well she played! If her father and mother came to the concert, they would be surprised to see Elizabeth playing such difficult duets with a big boy like Richard!

'You're getting conceited about your playing, Elizabeth,' said Richard one afternoon. Richard never thought twice about what he said, and he could be very hurtful. 'It's a pity. I like your playing, but I shan't like *you* if you get conceited.'

'Don't be so horrid, Richard,' said Elizabeth indignantly. 'I don't tell you *you're* conceited, do I!'

'No, because I'm not,' said Richard. 'I know quite well that my gift for music is nothing to do with *me* really – it's something that has been given to me, a real gift. I'm thankful for it and grateful for it and I'm going to use it for all I'm worth, but I'm not conceited about it and never shall be.'

Elizabeth was annoyed with Richard – especially as she knew that what he said was just a little bit true. She *was* getting conceited about her playing!

But why shouldn't I be proud of it? she thought. *I haven't got a wonderful gift for it like Richard – so my playing is my own hard work, and I've every right to be proud of that!*

So she went on planning to show off at the school concert, and make everyone think what a wonderful pianist she was. But pride always comes before a fall – and poor Elizabeth was going to have a dreadful shock.

She and Robert, John and Kathleen had arranged to go out riding one afternoon before games. Peter came running up and begged Robert to let him go too.

'No, you can't, Peter,' said Robert. 'The horse you usually ride is limping – and I don't want you to have the other. It's a restive horse. Wait till your horse is all right.'

'Oh, please, do let me ride the other horse,' begged Peter. 'You know I'm a good rider!'

'Let him come, Robert,' said Elizabeth. 'You know he can ride Champ.'

'Well, but Champ really *is* a bit funny today,' said Robert. 'I'll see what he's like when two o'clock comes, Peter.'

When two o'clock came, Robert was not in the stables. The others were there. Elizabeth saddled the horses and looked for Robert. Still he didn't come.

'Oh, bother!' said Elizabeth. 'It's ten past two already. Wherever has Robert got to? We are wasting all our time.'

Peter sped off to look for Robert – but he came back in a few minutes to say that he couldn't find him.

'Well, if we're going for a ride we'd better go!' said Elizabeth. She called to the stableman.

'Hie, Tucker! Can I saddle Champ? Is he all right?'

'Well, he's a bit upset about something,' said Tucker. 'You have a look at him, miss.'

Elizabeth went to Champ's stall. The horse, which was a small one, nuzzled into her hand. She stroked his long nose. 'He seems all right,' she said. 'I'll saddle him for you, Peter. I'm sure Robert would say you could ride him.'

She saddled him quickly. Peter leapt up on to his back, and the four children cantered out into the paddock. Then away they went down the grassy field path, the girls' hair streaming out in the wind.

'We shan't have time to go very far,' shouted Elizabeth. 'We've only got about twenty minutes. We'll go as far as Windy Hill and back!'

They cantered out into a lane leading to the hill. And then something happened!

As they trotted round a corner, a steamroller started rumbling down the lane, which had just been mended. Champ reared up in fright, and Peter held on with all his might.

Elizabeth cantered up beside him and put out her hand to hold the reins tightly, but the horse tossed its head, gave a loud whinny and darted into an open gateway that led to a field.

And then it ran away! The three children stared in fright. Poor Peter! There he was on Champ, holding on for dear life, while the horse galloped like mad across the stony field towards Windy Hill.

'I'm going after him!' cried Elizabeth. She swung her horse round and galloped through the gateway. She shouted to him, and tapped him on his broad back. He set off swiftly, knowing that he had to overtake the runaway horse.

Over the stony field went Elizabeth, while John and Kathleen watched in fright. Far away galloped Champ, Peter still clinging fast.

Elizabeth's horse was bigger and faster than Peter's. He galloped eagerly, his heels kicking up the stones. Elizabeth urged him on, shouting loudly. It was a good thing that she was such a good rider and that she trusted her horse! On and on they went, gaining little by little on Champ.

Peter's horse was panting painfully. He began to climb the steep Windy Hill and dropped to a trot. Peter tugged at the reins and tried to bring him to a stop, but the horse was still terribly frightened.

Elizabeth galloped her horse up Windy Hill and at last overtook Champ. But Champ started in fright as soon as the other horse came up beside him. He stretched out his neck and began to gallop off again.

But Elizabeth had managed to get the reins, and when Champ felt her strong little hand on them he quietened down and listened to her voice. Elizabeth was good with horses and knew how to speak to them. After the first tug to get rid of Elizabeth's hand, Tapper slowed down and then, trembling from head to foot, stopped still.

Peter was trembling too. He climbed down at once. Elizabeth leapt down and went round to Champ's head. In a few minutes she had quieted the horse, but she did not dare to ride him.

'Peter, ride my horse and go back and join the others,'

she said. 'I shall have to walk Champ home. Tell the stableman what has happened, and take a message to Mr Warlow for me to tell him I shan't be back in time for games. Go on now!'

Peter rode back to the others on Elizabeth's horse. He soon recovered himself, and began to boast about the runaway horse. The three children rode home and gave Elizabeth's message – while poor Elizabeth had to walk Champ home for a very long way.

The little girl was tired and upset. Something dreadful might have happened – Peter might have fallen from the horse and been badly hurt! Why had she let him ride Champ without first getting Robert to say he could? Well, it was Robert's fault for being late for the gallop!

Her left hand hurt her. She had got hold of Champ's reins with it when she had tried to stop him, and somehow her wrist had been twisted. She tucked it into her coat, hoping it would soon be better. She was very miserable as she walked back over the fields and lanes, leading a tired and steaming horse.

The stableman was not pleased. Robert came running out when he saw Elizabeth coming back, and he was not pleased either.

'Elizabeth! I've heard all about it! How *could* you be so silly as to let Peter ride Champ! I couldn't help being late. Mr Johns kept me to do something for him. You might have waited! This wouldn't have happened then, for I would never have let Peter ride Champ in that state. You are always so impatient and cocksure of yourself!'

Elizabeth was tired and her hand was hurting her. She burst into tears.

'That's right! Be a baby now!' said Robert in disgust. 'I suppose you think that if you cry I'll be sorry for you and not say any more! That's just like a girl! It's a good thing for you that neither Champ nor Peter have come to any harm!'

'Oh, Robert, don't be so unkind to me,' sobbed Elizabeth. 'I've hurt my hand, and I can't tell you how badly I feel about letting Peter ride Champ.'

'Let's have a look at your hand,' said Robert, more kindly. He took a look at the swollen wrist. 'You'd better go right away to Matron. That looks pretty bad to me. Cheer up! It's no good crying over spilt milk!'

'I'm not!' said Elizabeth, wiping her eyes. 'I'm crying over a runaway horse and a hurt wrist!' And off she went to find Matron, nursing her hurt hand. Poor Elizabeth! Things always happened to her!

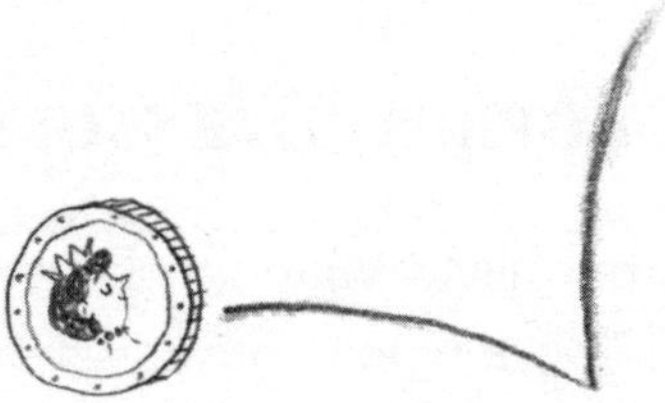

CHAPTER TWENTY-FIVE

ELIZABETH IS VERY TIRESOME

ELIZABETH WENT to find Matron. She was in the san with two ill children there. She came out when Elizabeth knocked at the door.

'What is it?' she asked. 'You can't go in!'

'I know,' said Elizabeth. 'I've twisted my wrist and I thought perhaps you could do something for it.'

Matron looked at the swollen wrist. 'That must hurt you quite a lot,' she said. 'How did you do it?'

Elizabeth told her. Matron soaked a bandage in cold water and wrapped it tightly round the hurt wrist.

'Will it soon be better?' asked Elizabeth. 'It's a good thing it's not my right hand.'

'It will take a little time to get right,' said Matron. 'Now, keep it as still as possible, please. And look, I will make you a sling out of this old hanky – like that – round your shoulder. That will help a bit.'

It was past teatime by now. Matron took Elizabeth into her own room and made some toast. Elizabeth was tired and pale and, although she said she didn't want anything to eat, she couldn't help thinking that the buttered toast looked rather nice. So she soon ate it up and drank the cocoa that Matron put before her.

Then she went off to the common room. Everyone was waiting to hear what had happened. Joan ran to her at once.

'Elizabeth! Is your hand badly hurt?'

'Well, it hurts a bit now,' said Elizabeth, 'but it's not nearly as bad as it was, since Matron bandaged it. It's all my own fault, as usual! I was impatient because Robert was late and I saddled Champ for Peter – and Champ ran away.'

'Poor old Elizabeth!' said Jenny.

Robert said nothing. He sat reading a book. He still looked cross.

There came a knock at the common-room door and small Peter poked his head in. 'Is Elizabeth here?' he asked. 'Oh, there you are, Elizabeth. I say – how's the wrist? I'm awfully sorry about it. I suppose you won't be able to play the piano for a little while now.'

Elizabeth hadn't thought of that for one moment. She stared in dismay at Peter. 'Oh my goodness!' she said. 'I had forgotten that. Oh, *dear* – and I so badly wanted to practise hard this week, and now I've only got one hand!'

Everyone was sorry for her. Robert raised his head and looked solemn. 'Bad luck, Elizabeth!' he said. 'I hope your hand will be well enough to play at the concert.'

Elizabeth was upset. She felt the tears coming into her eyes and she got up quickly. She hated people to see her crying. She went out of the room and went into one of the little music rooms. She sat down at the piano and leant her head against the music rack. She was angry with herself for doing something silly that had ended, as usual, in bringing trouble on herself.

Richard came along, humming. He didn't see Elizabeth at the piano, and switched on the light to practise. He was surprised to find her in the dark, all alone.

'What's the matter?' he asked. 'What are you crying for?'

'Because what you said has come true,' said Elizabeth sadly. 'You told me I was getting conceited about my playing – and that pride comes before a fall. Well, you were right. I did something silly, and now I've hurt my wrist and I can't play the piano, so I don't expect I'll be able to play duets with you at the concert.'

'Oh, I *am* sorry!' said Richard in dismay. 'Now I

suppose I'll have to play them with Harry, and he's not nearly so good as you. Oh, Elizabeth – what bad luck for you!'

'You shouldn't have said pride comes before a fall!' wept Elizabeth. 'I feel as if you made this happen!'

'Oh, don't be so silly,' said Richard. 'No, really, that *is* silly, Elizabeth. Anyway, cheer up – it may not be as bad as you think. I'll play to you, if you like. Get up and let me come on the stool.'

Elizabeth got up. She went to the chair in the corner and sat down, tired and cross. She didn't like Richard. She didn't like Robert. She didn't like Peter and his runaway horse. She didn't like herself. She didn't like anybody at all! She was a cross, unhappy, tired girl who didn't want to be pleased with anything or anybody!

But Richard's music made things much better. The little girl's frown went away and she leant back, feeling happier as the soft notes of the piano fell into the silence of the little room. Richard knew exactly what music to play to comfort her.

She stole away in the middle of his playing and went back to the common room. Perhaps her wrist would be better by the next day. Perhaps she was making a fuss after all. The others looked up as she came in.

'Come and do this puzzle with me,' said Kathleen. 'I can't find the bits that go just here.'

Everyone was kind to her, and Elizabeth was grateful. But she was glad when bedtime came, for her legs ached and her wrist still hurt her. Matron had a look at it and bound it up again.

'Keep it in the sling,' she said. 'It won't hurt so much then.'

Elizabeth hoped it would be better when she awoke in the morning. But it was still swollen and tender, though it did not hurt quite so much. She couldn't possibly play the piano with it! It was too bad!

And then Elizabeth found how difficult it is to do even the most ordinary things with one hand instead of two! She couldn't tie her hair ribbon! She couldn't tie her shoelaces! She couldn't wash herself properly. She couldn't do up a button. She couldn't even seem to blow her nose easily.

The others did what they could for her, but Elizabeth was not easy to do things for. She wouldn't stand still – she jerked her head about when Joan tried to do her hair. She stamped her foot when poor Kathleen tried her best to do up the buttons of her blouse and got them all wrong.

'Oh, dear – you've gone back to being the little girl who had a little curl right down the middle of her forehead!' sighed Joan. 'And you're being very, very horrid!'

'Well, so would you be if this had happened to you!' said Elizabeth in a rage. 'If it had been my right hand, I could at least have missed all the exams next week, but as it is I'll be able to do the exams, and have to miss the things I really love, like gym and riding and music! Oh, it's just too bad!'

In a few days' time Matron said Elizabeth could use her hand again, but, alas for Elizabeth, she seemed to have no strength in the hurt wrist, and did not dare to use it much. The doctor said she must do what she could with it, and that gradually it would be all right, but she must be patient.

Well, that was just the one thing that Elizabeth couldn't be. She was upset and she showed it. She was annoyed and everyone knew it. She was furious because Richard was now practising the duets with Harry. And when she found that she couldn't be in the play because her part, which was that of a soldier, meant doing some drilling and exercising with a wooden gun, which her wrist couldn't manage – well, that was just the last straw!

The form were worried about Elizabeth, and disappointed in her. They talked about it.

'She's just getting crosser and crosser,' said Jenny. 'Nobody can do anything with her. She can't help thinking about herself and the nice things she's missing all the time. It *is* bad luck that she can't even play games. She does love them so.'

'Let's think of some things for her to do,' said Joan sensibly. 'There's George in the san, getting better. Couldn't Elizabeth go and read to him? Then there's all the programmes to make out for our play. Elizabeth is awfully good at designing things like that. Let's ask her to help us. She can easily do it with her right hand. And there's those gold crowns we have got to make – Robert says he'll make them – and surely Elizabeth could paint them with gold paint?'

Everyone agreed that it would be a good thing to get Elizabeth to do a few things so that she might forget her crossness. So one by one they went to her and asked her for her help.

Now Elizabeth was sharp, and she soon guessed why the children were suddenly asking her to do things for them. At first she felt that she would refuse – why should she do things for them when she couldn't do anything nice for herself at all? Joan saw her face, and took hold of her arm.

'Come along with me,' she said. 'Let's have a talk, Elizabeth. I'm a monitor now and I have a right to tell you a few things and to help you.'

Elizabeth went with her into the garden. 'I know all you're going to say,' she said. 'I know I'm behaving badly. I'll never be a monitor like you. I'll never be able to forget myself and not mind when things go wrong.'

'You're a goose, Elizabeth,' said Joan patiently. 'You don't know what you can do till you try. There are only two weeks left of the term. Don't make them miserable for yourself. We all like you and admire you – don't let a little thing like a hurt wrist spoil our liking and admiration for you. You really are being rather trying. Everyone has been as kind and patient as possible. You make things very hard for your friends.'

Elizabeth kicked a stone along the path. After all, why should she make things horrid for her friends when her hurt wrist was her own fault and nobody else's? It *was* rather feeble of her. She took Joan's arm.

'All right, Monitor!' she said. 'I'll help you all I can. I'll do the programmes – and read to George – and paint the gold crowns. If I can't be a sport for two weeks, I'm not much good!'

'It's just because you're such a strong person really that we don't like to see you suddenly being awfully weak,' said Joan. 'All right – now do your best for us, Elizabeth!'

Once Elizabeth had really made up her mind to do something she could always do it. She could be just as patient as she could be impatient. She could be just as cheerful as she could be cross. And in the very next hour her friends saw the difference!

She set to work on the programmes. She could manage to hold the paper with her left hand, and it was quite easy then to draw and paint with her right. Soon she had done half a dozen excellent programmes and the whole form came to admire them. Elizabeth was pleased.

'Now I'm going to be a good girl and go and read to George,' she said, smiling cheerfully round. And off she went, leaving the others laughing.

'She can be a monkey, but you can't help liking her!' said Jenny. And everyone agreed!

CHAPTER TWENTY-SIX

A MARVELLOUS SURPRISE

THE LAST week of the term came. Exams were held every day, and the children worked hard. Elizabeth, Robert and Kathleen worked the hardest of all, for each of them wanted to do well. Elizabeth longed to be top of her form, and so did Robert. Kathleen wanted to be top in *something*, she didn't mind *what*!

It would be so lovely to tell Mother I was top in something, thought Kathleen. *I'm always so near the bottom – and Mother has been so perfectly sweet about it. It really would be a marvellous surprise for her if I could do well in something.*

Elizabeth's wrist was much better, but she still could not use it for playing the piano, and neither was she allowed to go riding, to play games, to dig in the garden or to do gym! It really was very hard luck indeed.

She was in the songs at the concert, but not in

anything else. She was not in the play and she was not playing with Richard. Harry was taking her place.

She tried to be cheerful, and she did not let anyone see how miserable she sometimes felt. She had pulled herself together, and was doing all she could to help the others in every way. She had painted the crowns marvellously for the play, and had even painted some trees for the scenery. Everyone thought they were wonderful.

She had done twelve programmes, the best that had been done in the school. Miss Belle was to have one and so were Miss Best and Mr Johns. Elizabeth was proud of that.

She had been to read to George and to play games with him every day till he had come out of the san. She had done lots of little jobs for Matron. She couldn't help John in the garden as she had been used to doing, but she wrote out lists of flower seeds for him, ready for the spring, and listened eagerly when he told her all he and Peter had been doing.

'She's really being a brick!' said Joan. 'There's good stuff in our Elizabeth! She can be the naughtiest girl in the school – but she can be the best girl too!'

Elizabeth went to watch the hockey and lacrosse matches, and cheered the players, though deep down in her heart she felt very sad because she too was not playing. It was awful not to be able to do any of the things she liked so much.

'You know how to grin and bear things, Elizabeth,' said Richard. 'I'll say that for you!'

Nothing that Elizabeth had ever done made the school admire her as much as they did the last weeks of the term. Everyone knew what a fiery, quick-tempered child she was, and they knew how hard it must be for her to be cheerful, patient and helpful. They were proud of her.

The school concert came. It was a most exciting afternoon. All the parents who could come, came to hear it. Mr and Mrs Allen were there, and were going to stay at a hotel the next day so that they might take Elizabeth back with them. Elizabeth flew to meet them, and they hugged her in delight. They were sad to hear that her hurt wrist prevented her from taking any real part in the concert, but they loved the programme she presented to them.

'I did it for you,' said Elizabeth proudly. 'Do you like it? The heads have my programmes too. And Mummy, please notice the gold crowns in the play, because I painted them – and the trees too.'

The concert was a great success. The play was funny and made the audience laugh loudly. Jenny and Kathleen were thrilled, because it was they who had written it out for their form. Richard played the violin most beautifully, and he and Harry played the duets that Elizabeth had been going to play.

She felt sad when she heard them, but she made her face smile all the time, and clapped hard at the end. She saw Jenny, Joan, Robert and Kathleen watching her, and she knew that they were proud of her for being able to smile and clap, when inside she was very disappointed.

At the end of the concert the results of the exams were given. Elizabeth listened with a beating heart. So did Robert and Kathleen. Jenny did not care much – so long as she was somewhere near the top, that was all she minded! Kathleen cared much more. She knew she had done her best, and she hoped she wouldn't be too near the bottom!

At last Miss Belle came to Elizabeth's form. 'Miss Ranger says that this form has done exceedingly good work,' she said. 'Some of the children have been surprisingly good. First come Elizabeth Allen and . . .'

But Miss Belle couldn't go on, because a storm of clapping interrupted her. Everyone seemed to be delighted that Elizabeth was top! Robert clapped hard too. How he hoped that he might be second! He had half hoped he might be top – but never mind, he might be second!

Miss Belle held up her hand for silence. 'Wait a moment,' she said. 'Let me finish what I had to say.

First come Elizabeth Allen *and* Robert Jones! They have tied for first place, so they are both top.'

Robert sat up straight, his face bright with surprise and delight. So he and Elizabeth were top together! That was almost better than being top by himself. Elizabeth was sitting just behind him and she bent forward and clapped him on the back.

'Robert,' she said, her face beaming, 'I'm *awfully* pleased! I'd rather be top with you than top by myself, honestly I would!'

Robert nodded and smiled. He couldn't speak because he was so pleased. He had not such good brains as Elizabeth, so he had had to work really hard to win his place – and how proud his father and mother looked!

Miss Belle read down the list. Jenny was fourth. Joan was fifth, and both girls were pleased. Kathleen was sixth, well away from the bottom – and she had top marks in history! Her cheeks glowed as she heard Miss Belle read that out. She was fairly near the top and she had the best marks in history. What would her mother say to that? Kathleen stole a look round the big gym, and saw her mother's face. One look at it satisfied Kathleen. Her mother was looking as happy as anyone in the room.

I can't think what Whyteleafe has done to my little Kathleen, her mother was thinking. *She looks quite different. She was always such a plain child, poor little thing, but now she's really pretty when she smiles – and how happy and bright she looks with all her friends!*

It was a splendid afternoon – and in the evening the last School Meeting was to be held. There was a surprise for the school then, which William did not announce until after the usual business had been dealt with.

All the money was emptied out of the box and evenly divided between each girl and boy. This was always done at the end of term, and the children were pleased, because it meant that they started their holidays with a little money in their pockets.

Then William made his announcement. 'I am sorry to say that we are going to lose Kenneth this term,' he said. 'Kenneth's father and mother are going abroad and he is to go with them. So we shall not see him again until they come back, which will not be for six months.'

The school listened in silence. 'I should like to say that we thank Kenneth very much for being a wise and good monitor for many terms,' said William. 'He has done many kind and generous things that most of us know nothing about, and we shall miss him very much. We shall be very glad when you come back, Kenneth.'

'Thank you,' said Kenneth, going scarlet. He was a quiet, shy boy, liked by everyone. The school was sorry to say goodbye.

'Well, as Kenneth will not be here to be a monitor next term, we have to choose another new one,' said William. 'You may like to have George back again, of course, or you may like to give someone else a chance if you think there is anyone worthy of being tried as a monitor. Nora, give out slips of paper, please.'

Nora rose, and gave out the slips of paper to each boy and girl. They took them and sat, thinking hard. It was unexpected to have to choose a monitor without talking about it between themselves first. Elizabeth chewed her pencil. Whom should she put? She decided on John – though she half felt that John wouldn't be a *very* good monitor, because he only understood one thing really well, and that was gardening! Still, it might be good to give him a chance. So she wrote down his name – John Terry.

Soon everyone had written down a name. The papers were given to the Jury, who unfolded them and counted them. Then the Jury too considered the matter and at last handed in their own papers.

William and Rita undid them, said a few words to one another, and then William knocked on the table with his hammer.

'Three names have been given the most votes,' he said. 'One is John Terry, the second is Robert Jones, whom the younger ones have voted for (you should be pleased about that, Robert!) – and the third is Elizabeth Allen.'

Elizabeth jumped. She had no idea at all that anyone would vote for her – or would even *think* her good enough to be a monitor. She had the surprise of her life!

'Now we have heard a great deal of Elizabeth this term,' said William. 'Some good, and some bad. But both Rita and I have noticed how well Elizabeth has tackled a big disappointment these last few weeks – and has tried to forget herself and to help her form in every way. So it is no wonder that so many people have voted for her.'

'We know that she brought disappointment on herself,' said Rita, 'but we mustn't forget that she hurt her wrist in trying to stop Peter's horse. It was a brave thing to do. Elizabeth, you are a real mixture! You can be foolish and you can be wise. You can be impatient and you can be patient. You can be unkind and you can be kind – and we all know that you try to be fair, just and loyal.'

Rita paused. Elizabeth listened, her heart thumping. Was Rita going to say that she must try again and perhaps be made a monitor next term, if she did well?

No, Rita was not going to say that. She smiled down at Elizabeth and went on. 'Well, Elizabeth, both William and I know you well by now, and we are quite sure that if we make you a monitor we shall not be disappointed in you. You will always treat other people better than you treat yourself – so we feel that it is quite safe to call you up to the monitors' table, and ask you to do your best for the school next term.'

With burning cheeks and shining eyes Elizabeth marched up to the Jury's table. She had never in her life felt so proud or so pleased. Oh, she didn't mind now not playing in the school concert – she didn't mind missing games and matches and gym! Her ill luck had turned into a piece of marvellous *good* luck – she was actually a monitor – yes, really and truly one.

She took her place beside Joan, who squeezed her hand in delight. 'Jolly good!' said Joan. 'I *am* glad!'

And there we will leave Elizabeth, sitting at the monitors' table, dreaming of all the marvellous things she would do next term. A monitor! Could it really be true that the naughtiest girl in the school had become a monitor?

I shall still do silly things, I expect, even now I'm a monitor, thought Elizabeth, *but never mind – I've got my chance! I'll show everybody something next term!*

And I expect she will!

BONUS BLYTON

Enid Blyton has been one of the world's best-loved storytellers for over seventy-five years. Her interest in writing began as a child, and before she loved receiving letters from the children who read her books, she enjoyed working with them as a teacher. *The Naughtiest Girl* stories are inspired by real schools and experiences. Turn the page to learn more about Enid as a child and as a teacher. Afterwards, you might like to write about your school and teachers and the people in *your* class!

THE LIFE AND TIMES OF ENID BLYTON

11 August 1897	Enid Blyton was born in East Dulwich, London. Two brothers are born after her – Hanly (b. 1899) and Carey (b. 1902).
1911	Enid enters a children's poetry competition and is praised for her writing. She's on the path to becoming a bestselling author . . .
1916	Enid begins to train as a teacher in Ipswich. By the time she is 21, she is a fully qualified Froebel teacher, and starts work at a school in Kent.
1917	Enid's first 'grown-up' publication – three poems in *Nash's Magazine*.
June 1922	Enid's first book is published. It's called *Child Whispers*.
1926	Enid begins editing – and writes – the phenomenal *Sunny Stories for Little Folks* magazine. (She continues in this role for 26 years!)

1927	So vast is Enid's output that she has to learn to type. (But she still writes to children by hand.)
1931	Having married Hugh Pollock in 1924, the couple's first child, Gillian, is born. Imogen, their second daughter, was born in 1935.
1942	The Famous Five is launched with *Five on a Treasure Island.*
1949	The first appearance of *The Secret Seven* and of *Noddy* mark this year as special.
1953	Enid moves away from *Sunny Stories* to launch *Enid Blyton's Magazine.* She is now renowned throughout the world – she even established her own company, called Darrell Waters Limited (the surname of her second husband).
1962	Enid Blyton becomes one of the first and most important children's authors to be published in paperback. Now, she reaches even more readers than ever before.
28 November 1968	Enid dies in her sleep, in a nursing home in Hampstead.

A NOTE FROM ENID BLYTON'S DAUGHTER

Enid had two daughters, Gillian and Imogen, both of whom read all her stories, often before they were sent to the publishers. Sadly, Gillian has died, but she wrote an introduction to *The Naughtiest Girl* which tells us something of her mother's life . . .

Enid Blyton was not only a writer for children, she was also involved in the editing and writing of books for teachers. She was a trained Froebel and Montessori teacher and had run her own school before she married.

She was very interested in the world of education and especially a mixed boarding school called Summerhill, which was opened by A. S. Neill in 1921. He believed that the school should be governed by the children themselves with the teachers only taking part if asked by the children.

In The Naughtiest Girl stories, Whyteleafe School was run in the same way with a Meeting held every week in the school hall. The head boy and girl presided over the meeting aided by twelve monitors chosen by the other children. It was a kind of school parliament where the children made their own rules, heard grumbles and complaints, judged one another and punished bad behaviour. All problems were discussed and decided by the children and only in very difficult situations were the head teachers asked for their advice.

Does your school have a student council? Do you know who its members are?

Summerhill, in Suffolk, is still a school today and, over its ninety-year history, has influenced many schools around the world. The school prides itself on children's 'right to play' and lessons are optional. Why not find out more about it by looking on the internet?

ENID AS A CHILD: ON THE PATH TO BECOMING A WRITER – PART TWO

When she was young, everyone thought Enid would follow a musical path. But when she was fourteen her life changed. She submitted work to a poetry competition in a magazine. It was run by Arthur Mee, whose encyclopaedia Enid loved! He liked her poem, and printed it and – best of all – said, 'Perhaps one day you will *really* write.'

But it took a long time – and many setbacks – before Enid regularly began to be published. Her first publication as an adult was in *Nash's Magazine* in 1917.

When Enid decided she wanted to be a children's writer, she decided to train to be a kindergarten teacher, so that she would be surrounded by children. She said, 'I would see naughty children and good children, and I would learn what the children wanted to read.'

Enid's father was amazed when she told him she wanted to train to be a teacher, instead of following her music studies. And he said, 'How like you, Enid, to tell me these things over the *telephone*! Why must you be so headstrong?' He said he'd have to think about giving Enid permission, but, in the end, said yes.

At the end of her teacher training, she was given a glowing report by the headmistress . . .

She has very good ability, is both musical and artistic and has shown teaching capacity of a high order. Enthusiasm and energy are marked characteristics. She had a real love of children and handles them well . . . As one of the best students we have had for some years, I can recommend her warmly for a responsible post.

In January 1919 Enid took on her first teaching job, at Bickley Park School for boys.

WHAT THEY DID AT MISS BROWN'S SCHOOL

In 1920 Enid Blyton became a governess to the four Thompson children, whose ages ranged from four to ten. The family lived in Surbiton, in Surrey, in a house called 'Southernhay'. Enid had a small room which overlooked the garden, and it was there that she wrote many of her stories. Enid's tiny class often had lessons outdoors in the summer months.

Enid was very popular with her students, because her lessons were both practical and creative. She worked with them to put on performances for which they made props, costumes and invitations – and even sold tickets.

In 1941 she published a long story called 'What They Did at Miss Brown's School', which was divided into monthly episodes. It's been hard to find for many years, but you can read extracts in these new editions of *The Naughtiest Girl* books. The character of Miss Brown and her tiny class is very much based on Enid Blyton and her school at the Thompsons' . . .

Here's the second episode . . .

2. February. Fun with the Seeds

THE MONTH of February was rather wet, for when the snow melted the ditches were full of water.

'February!' said Miss Brown. 'Look at the mud. I'm afraid we can't go for many nature walks until the fields are drier! We should sink up to our knees in Farmer Straws' field this week!'

'What a pity!' sighed Susan. 'I did want to do some more things in my nature book, Miss Brown. I've got lots of snow footprints there, and I've already printed the name FEBRUARY in big letters and coloured them blue and yellow.'

'Well, we'll certainly have some fun, even if we can't go out and find it,' said Miss Brown. 'We'll have some fun indoors. What about growing some seeds and seeing exactly how they send out their little roots and shoots? We have some acorns and chestnuts too that we gathered in the autumn. Shall we grow those, so that we get some tiny trees to plant out in the school garden?'

'Oh, yes, I'd like that!' said Mary.

'So would I,' said John, who loved growing anything. 'Miss Brown, can I grow a bean? Then when we have finished growing it I can plant it in the garden and it will flower and give me beans for my dinner!'

'So it will!' said Miss Brown. 'We'll grow beans *and* peas, and then maybe we'll have nice vegetables for our school dinner in the summer!'

'Please may I have a bean of my very own to grow?' said John. 'Not to share with the others, I mean. They could grow their own, couldn't they? It's more fun if we each have one to watch.'

'Very well,' said Miss Brown. 'And we will all grow them in a different way, shall we? This is called *germinating* seeds, and I will make *germinators* for you.'

It was fun making the germinators. Miss Brown made John's first. She took a small glass lamp chimney, and made John roll up a piece of clean blotting paper to fit the glass inside exactly. Then she told him to fetch a saucer of water and stand the lamp chimney in it.

She had some beans which had lain soaking in water, and she gave John four. He was very pleased. Miss Brown told him to put each one between the blotting paper and the glass of the lamp chimney, wherever he liked, so long as they were not below the middle.

John placed his beans all round the glass very

neatly. The blotting paper held them against the lamp chimney. The children could see them very easily through the glass.

'Miss Brown, the blotting paper is quite soaking wet now,' said John suddenly. 'Does it matter? It has soaked up the water from the saucer, you see.'

'That's why I wanted the water there,' said Miss Brown. 'The blotting paper becomes wet, the bean is kept moistened, the damp makes it swell and grow, just as it would in the damp earth and then you will see what happens!'

'What germinator am *I* going to have?' asked Mary impatiently. She always liked to get on with things.

'There's just time to make one more today,' said Miss Brown, looking at the clock. 'We'll make the others tomorrow.'

'I would rather like peas,' said Mary. 'How can we watch peas growing, Miss Brown?'

'Well, there is rather an amusing way,' said Miss Brown. 'We make them little cork boats and let them bob about on the water. I'll show you. Go to the cupboard, Mary, and get three small flat corks. Bring a glass jam jar back with you too. There are some old chalks inside, but you can empty them out and wash the jar. Then fill it half full of water.'

Mary did as she was told. Soon she was back with a

clean jar, half full of water, and three small corks.

'Peter, bore me a neat hole in each of the corks, please,' said Miss Brown, fetching some soaked peas from the windowsill. Peter bored the holes, and then Miss Brown told Mary to place a little pea carefully on to each cork, and to put the corks on the top of the water in the jam jar.

Mary did this, and the children looked at the three peas bobbing about on their cork boats.

'But how will they grow?' asked Mary in surprise. 'There is no earth to make them grow and they are not even touching the water.'

'They are already soaked and swollen,' said Miss Brown, 'and the water below the cork will attract the roots as you will soon see. Each little pea will send out a root through the hole in the cork, and this root will drink the water and keep the pea plant alive. It will send up its little green shoot soon after that.'

'How funny they look, bobbing about on cork boats!' said Mary, pleased. 'Thank you, Miss Brown. I'm so glad I've got my own germinator and my own peas.'

'Tomorrow we will think about Susan and Peter,' said Miss Brown.

Next day Miss Brown asked Peter what *he* would like to grow.

'I think I'd like a nice fat bean,' said Peter. 'But let me

grow it differently from John's bean, please, Miss Brown.'

'Very well,' said Miss Brown. 'Now let me see – we shall want another jam jar with only about two inches of water in it – and a small knitting needle and a cork to fit the jam jar. And the bean, of course. Get the things, Peter.'

Peter got the jar and a cork that fitted it. He put a little water inside. Mary found him a knitting needle in the cupboard, and he brought everything to Miss Brown.

Miss Brown drove the needle through the cork, and then put a soaked bean on to the end of the needle. The bean was balanced about halfway in the jar, a little way above the water.

'There, Peter!' said Miss Brown. 'There's your bean in its germinator!'

'But will it grow without touching the water?' asked Peter anxiously.

'You will see,' said Miss Brown, making sure that the cork was on firmly. The end of the knitting needle stuck up through the cork and looked funny. Miss Brown told Peter to put his jar on the windowsill, where the light could get at the bean.

'And now what about you, Susan?' she said.

'Miss Brown, could I have seeds that are *quick* to grow?' begged Susan. 'I don't think I can wait a long time to see them grow. I want quick ones!'

'Isn't she a baby?' laughed John. 'I always wanted *my* seeds to grow quickly when I was seven years old too!'

'I think we all wish that seeds grew more quickly,' said Miss Brown. 'Well, Susan, you shall germinate your seeds quite differently from the others. You shall grow mustard and cress on a piece of damp flannel!'

'Oh, I did that three years ago and it was such fun,' said Mary. 'Susan will like that.'

Susan was sent to get a piece of flannel out of the cupboard and an old painting saucer. She was told to soak the flannel under the tap and then to squeeze it out lightly. She did so and came back to Miss Brown.

'Now here is a packet of mustard and cress seeds,' said Miss Brown, giving her an envelope that rattled. 'Empty them carefully on to your damp flannel and then you may put your saucer on the sill with the others. You will find that damp flannel makes your little seeds grow – though some will grow more quickly than the others – and when they have grown enough we will cut the mustard and cress and have it with a bit of bread and butter at eleven o'clock one morning!'

'But what are *you* going to grow, Miss Brown?' asked Mary. 'You must grow something too.'

'I will grow a chestnut and an acorn in these little glasses,' said Miss Brown. She showed the children two small glasses, each of which had a place at the neck to support a chestnut or acorn. John filled the glasses with water to the neck, and then Miss Brown put a smooth acorn into the top of one glass, so that it touched the water, and she put a bright brown conker into the other glass.

'There!' she said, and put them on the windowsill. 'Now we shall have some fun!'

They certainly did! It wasn't long before John's four beans put out four little white roots that sucked up the dampness of the pink blotting paper. John had to put some more water in the saucer. One bean was very good – it grew and grew so that John felt he would really *see* it grow if only Miss Brown would let him sit for half an hour and watch it. But she wouldn't.

Then Mary's peas, bobbing on their little cork boats, gave her a great surprise by growing their tiny white roots right through the holes in the corks! Miss Brown hadn't let her take out the peas and corks to see if anything was happening, so Mary *suddenly* saw the roots one day sticking into the water from the underneath of the corks. She was very pleased. Out came her nature book, and she began to draw the peas and their little roots.

The next excitement wasn't Peter's bean but Susan's mustard and cress, which suddenly raised itself from the flannel because the roots grew and lifted up the seeds!

Then the seeds put out tiny green shoots as well, and the flannel didn't look like a flannel any more.

Peter was very impatient with his bean, but at last it put out its root, and then grew very quickly down to the water. It hung there on the needle, looking rather comical, and then put out a fat shoot.

'*All* our seeds are growing now,' said Peter, pleased, drawing a fat bean in his nature book, and then drawing another with a small root and yet another with a longer root, to show how his bean grew day by day.

'And have you noticed my little acorn and chestnut?' asked Miss Brown. She lifted the acorn up, and the children saw a strong white root poking out from the split shell of the acorn. The chestnut had a very fat root too, and the children could see where the shoot was going to force its way upwards.

'Your trees are growing!' cried Mary, pleased. 'What fun! We shall have mustard and cress to eat, beans and peas to plant and two little trees for the school garden!'

'Well, we've certainly had fun this February!' said Peter. 'What's for March, I wonder?'

'Just wait till February is over!' said Miss Brown. 'Why, we haven't finished our germinating yet!'

The seeds were a great success. All the peas and beans grew fine long roots, and sent up green shoots that opened out into green leaves. The mustard and cress grew well, and was cut and eaten with small squares of bread and butter at eleven o'clock. That really *was* a treat – and wasn't the mustard hot!

As for the little trees, they were lovely, and soon grew tall and strong. A day came when the pea and bean plants were carefully planted out in the garden, so that they might grow and give the children vegetables for dinner.

And Miss Brown's little oak and chestnut trees were carefully planted in two sunny corners to grow in strength and beauty.

'When I am grown-up and have children of my own they will come and pick up acorns and chestnuts from our trees, Miss Brown,' said Mary, 'and we can tell them how we grew them ourselves this February.'

'So we can!' said Miss Brown. 'Let us hope that nobody spoils our nice little trees, or your children won't get their acorns and chestnuts, Mary!'

Enid Blyton

THE FAMOUS FIVE

Join the Adventure!

Have you read them all?

ENIDBLYTON.CO.UK

IS FOR PARENTS, CHILDREN AND TEACHERS!

Sign up to the newsletter on the homepage for a monthly round-up of news from the world of

Enid Blyton®

Illustration by Laura Ellen Anderson.

JOIN US ON SOCIAL MEDIA

EnidBlytonOfficial BlytonOfficial

Enid Blyton®

is one of the most popular children's authors of all time. Her books have sold over 500 million copies and have been translated into other languages more often than any other children's author.

Enid Blyton adored writing for children. She wrote over 700 books and about 2,000 short stories. *The Famous Five* books, now 80 years old, are her most popular. She is also the author of other favourites including *The Secret Seven*, *The Magic Faraway Tree* and *Malory Towers*.

Born in London in 1897, Enid lived much of her life in Buckinghamshire and loved dogs, gardening and the countryside. She was very knowledgeable about trees, flowers, birds and animals. Dorset – where some of the Famous Five's adventures are set – was a favourite place of hers too.

Enid Blyton's stories are read and loved by millions of children (and grown-ups) all over the world. Visit enidblyton.co.uk to discover more.

Illustration by Laura Ellen Anderson.